CHANGE FOR THE RIGHT REASON

A BOLD NEW BEGINNING - A BUSINESS NOVEL

FOREWORD BY DR. JOANNE C. PRESTON
Ph.D., RODC – Registered Organizational Development Consultant

Honestly, I have not read either a business book or a consulting book that has been this refreshing for a long time. Being an international consultant and former Doctoral Dean of Management at Colorado Technological University requires a great deal of reading to stay current on large-scale organizational change and management development. So now, here I am with this book in front of me which will probably be a boring read, much like the others.

Boy, how wrong I was. After a short read, I found the author has a way with words, as well as a vast knowledge in the fields of business and change. Instead of making this into a textbook that drones on from one dry subject to the next, Wayne has turned the book into a refreshing fictional story that reveals the secrets of transforming a company through the use of new organizational architecture and business theory.

The story's novel begins with a Vietnamese immigrant, Thanh Nguyen, whose electrical engineering background has enabled him to build a flourishing mid-size high-tech business in Southern California. Well, that is until he begins having trouble with growth and a severe material shortage problem. Adding to his difficulty, the company is seeing little or no productivity gain that mirrors the critical epidemic that we have in our industry today and challenges the company to make changes or die. And then to make matters worse, Thanh has a personal tragedy that takes him out of the picture.

Faced with this dilemma, the board of directors hires the Jake Jensen Group that believes in making change for the right reason. The story of transformation now unfolds with Dakota Wells, Jake Jensen's partner, and interim acting CEO giving a presentation to Thanh's company employees. The idea is to explain the consulting firm's new approach to change, using system thinking in a newly designed organizational architecture, and to clarify how the employees and the company will both benefit.

During the meeting, two significant players are introduced who will be delivering the change process throughout the story in the company's training room, along with delightfully funny dialogue to lighten up the reading. Then we have the humorous vignettes of the characters personal lives weaving throughout the book to lessen the load of knowledge one is trying to digest.

From this point on after the employee meeting, the story continues to be fast-paced, as it expands and merges Wayne's four disciplines of theory: A new way to use System Thinking, new Throughput Theory, Product Throughput Pricing Program, and finally, using market-perceived value (MPV) to develop a new Horizontal Organizational Architecture.

Along with a transfer of knowledge, it will have you smiling and nodding your head affirmatively, for it makes an enormously entertaining read.

What is particularly exciting is that Wayne has provided thoughtful questions at the end of each scene to allow readers to reflect on the story and see how it applies to their own business situation or belief system. Also, the dialog in the novel is written in a way that explains these new concepts of business theory so that the reader can easily apply this new way of thinking about business and change.

As a business leader, consultant, educator, or student, you will find the story captivating and filled with knowledge that allows you to see business systems in a new light that solve the lack of productivity contagion that is prevalent in the today's business world. It's also a book capable of having a significant influence on our society and economy. So, I encourage you to turn the page and discover the secrets of making Change for the Right Reason!

    Joanne C. Preston, PhD, RODC
    Partner, Global Exchange Group

READER'S FAVORITE BOOK REVIEW
Congratulations on your 5-star review

CHANGE FOR
THE RIGHT REASON

READERS' FAVORITE REVIEW

Change for the Right Reason: A Bold New Beginning – A Business Novel by Wayne Coker offers one of the most powerful lessons I have had to learn in business and I must say that it came as a delightful surprise to me. First off, when I picked up this book, I didn't really think it would be in the form of a story, but it isn't just any kind of story. It's a quintessential tale that unveils the tips and strategies to implement the changes that will help an organization or business grow while getting employees actively involved and committed to the process.

The reader follows the story of an entrepreneur and the challenges he faces, both in business and in life, that bring his business to the brink of extinction. It is at this point that his company hires the Jake Jensen group. Follow the presentation as the company that specializes in change offers an entirely new approach to change. Can this consulting firm help the dying company and transform it into its new strategy for change? It's for the reader to find out.

Wayne Coker is a great writer and a serious educator, gifted with the rare ability to both educate and entertain readers. This is a well-crafted story, with a powerful conflict, well-developed characters, and a theme that has been discussed by many professionals: change.

Readers will love to follow these characters as they navigate a world of risk and challenges and how they build momentum and set on a path that catapults them to a satisfying finish. Change for the Right Reason: A Bold New Beginning – A Business Novel is laden with lessons in business and change, a book from a master in the field, crafted to delight readers and inform them. This book has a lot to offer to both independent entrepreneurs and leaders working with big teams.

CHANGE FOR THE RIGHT REASON

A BOLD NEW BEGINNING - A BUSINESS NOVEL

Our current organization architecture's productivity capability is on a **COLLISION** course with time, but to change it would be like changing spots on a leopard. Nevertheless, the case for making an effort to a newly designed horizontal systemic architecture is overwhelming—allowing us a unique opportunity to make...

CHANGE FOR THE RIGHT REASON

WAYNE COKER

AND FOREWORD WRITTEN BY

DR. JOANNE PRESTON, PhD

For Business Executives, Business and Engineering Students, and Educators

COPYRIGHT

CHANGE FOR
THE RIGHT REASON

COPYRIGHT © 2012 BY WAYNE COKER

All rights reserved. No part of this publication may be reproduced, stored in a retrieval system, or transmitted in any form or by and any means, electronic, mechanical, photocopy, or recording, and without permission in writing from the publisher, except in the case of brief quotations embodied in critical articles and reviews.

The Library of Congress Registration Number TXU 1-824-433

Written by Wayne Coker

Front and Rear Cover design and illustrations by the author

Cover title by Tom Carpenter

Page design, graphics, and illustrations are by Wayne Coker.

Products and company names mentioned are trademarks or registered trademarks of their respective companies

Quotations not attributed to anyone are by the author

ALSO BY WAYNE COKER

PRIDE AND DENIAL
The OSS and Viet Minh – Unforeseen
Allies in their Battle against Japan

A TONI NAKNI NOVEL
Action and thriller novel based on true events

ADVANCE PRAISE
by University Students and Graduates at the Time of their Review

Barrett Seller: As a current business student working towards my MBA, with a background in Political Science and Psychology, I have historically found that most business text to be dry and bland, missing a certain human touch as it were. What Mr. Coker has been able to do is take the important lessons that he is trying to impart and place them within a human context. This approach is unlike anything I had seen before in a business text and made it a much more approachable read.

In addition to his groundbreaking business storytelling approach, Mr. Coker has put to pen solutions to some of the most pressing issues of our day by taking a paradigm-shifting approach to the way western thinkers have attempted to solve world problems in the past. By shifting our mindset from a reductionist standpoint to a systemic approach, we begin to see the world as a much more entwined place. Political and Business Leaders of today and tomorrow would be remiss to leave Mr. Coker's book on the shelf. The thinking is dynamic, and the presentation is game-changing—well done, Sir!

Kyle Tippett: As a graduate of the Malcolm Baldridge award-winning Monfort College of Business at The University of Northern Colorado, I thought this book could have played a major role in the curriculum I was taught.

Through my studies, I read many business professional books that were designed to teach me the theories/concepts of the past. I read and interpreted many books but like many books I read on theories of the past I read the book, learned the information and un-learned it just as quickly.

I feel the reason for this quick turn-around on the knowledge I learned was the lack of connection to the information. I read the books, I understood the theories being taught, but I wouldn't necessarily apply the theory to any knowledge that I could connect with on a long-term basis.

Change for the Right Reasons allowed me and more importantly challenged me to understand the theories/concepts, but through the story-like approach, the author uses I connected the theory to real-life situations. These theories are presented and taught through real situations and use characters that the students would more than likely be able to connect with further than just reading dry, factual data. That is a facet I could have utilized to connect with the theories on a more long-term basis, had I been introduced to this book earlier in my education. I feel that Change for the Right Reasons would have allowed me to absorb and understand the information and quickly turn it into knowledge instead of learning only the theory, then quickly un-learning it as so many students do these days.

Clay Roscoe Claus: I'm nearly finished with my BS in Electrical Engineering, minor in Business Administration, and finishing with a certificate in entrepreneurship from the Keller Graduate School of Management. I'm proud to be part of this review process allowing me to inform others about this captivating book.

Wayne's engaging cast of characters takes you on a journey of business transformation and organizational architecture. The process of converting the lumbering corporate hierarchy of today to an agile business of the future that is only possible by implementing a new business system.

In this novel, the Jake Jensen Consulting Group guides Advance Tek Corporation (ATC) through the business transformation process. Wayne does an exceptional job imbuing character traits that enrich you with detail that allows you, the reader, to see business transformation through the eyes of each fascinating actor in this story

This didactic novel was not only entertaining; this business book is informative. Wayne's humorous approach to writing makes the story a fun and lighthearted read. Each vignette allows for a mental reprieve after each business topic. This sometimes makes dry and esoteric business concepts easily digestible using this concept of a novel makes for a real page-turner.

Wayne inspires the reader to become an agent of change. The business theory is a topic on which Wayne has undeniable experience due to his numerous years of research and immersion in the industry as a high-tech manufacturing professional, giving him perspective on the turbulent nature of change in business. "If you believe you have an opportunity for change, take it, and have no regrets," Wayne said. I would encourage you to read this book so you, too, become an agent of change.

Sridhar Prabhu: I completed my Bachelors in Electronics and Telecommunications from University of Mumbai, India, a Masters in Interdisciplinary Telecommunications from the University of Colorado, and my Entrepreneurship Certificate at CU.

The author's novel has succeeded in giving us a recipe that not only will help new ventures but also companies today struggling to find a foothold in the wavering economy. Wayne takes the problem companies, and the world economy as a whole is facing today and explains it in the simplest possible way. He then takes the example of a company in turmoil and shows with his concepts and ideas how, *change for the right reason,* can turn around the situation. The vignettes in the book almost take you to the world of the characters involved in this transformation. This book although having a heavy business and financial concepts keeps the reader entertained through the characters everybody could relate to – at times, I would laugh out loud at the entertaining dialog.

ABOUT

CHANGE FOR THE RIGHT REASON

To create a readable narrative with a daunting story of business transformation, the author has written the book as a novel. Through storytelling, Wayne is confident it will allow the reader to have a better understanding of the complex solutions involved in business transformation theory—and always seek the truth.

THE NOVEL

The fictitious ATC Company is a high-tech manufacturing firm that hired the Jake Jensen Consulting Group to transform ATC for growth, greater productivity, and help it out of its recent cash flow problems.

While Jake and Toni, his longtime friend sail across the Atlantic, his partner Dakota Wells and her crew, Jackie O' and Johnny Zapata, post-secondary professors at Pepperdine University, deliver the advanced business theory prescriptions developed by Jake Jenson.

The objective is to master these ideas and incorporate them into the businesses of the future. Learn them you will in this unique approach to knowledge.

The principles of explanation elaborated in this book came from four disciplines: *system theory, Wayne's throughput theory, horizontal processes*, and market-perceived value (MPV).

PROLOGUE

The narrative begins by introducing you to the owners of ATC, a high-tech firm, in a storytelling way—who they are, where they're from, and how they ran into trouble with their company.

ACT I - THE BEGINNING

Act I Scene I, begins by introducing Colonel Marty Westlake having dinner with Dakota Wells in Laguna Beach discussing a plan to transform the Nguyen's ATC firm with a sense of urgency.

Scene Two, the first step of the transformation process is an employee meeting at the Hilton Hotel, conducted by Dakota Wells. Her subject is global warming and energy as a vehicle to take THEM and US, *out of the equation for transforming a company*. This will be a real learning experience for the employees, and most likely, the reader.

Alternating with the Hilton employee meeting is several vignettes that keep the reader's riveted when Jake Jensen and his crew experienced a gale force storm somewhere on the high seas of the Atlantic.

During the second half of the employee meeting, Dakota discusses how our industry's *productivity* is now nothing more than smoke and mirrors in the way its performance levels are measured, creating a potential threat to our standard of living. The answer to the problem takes place in Acts II and III.

Act II – THE TRANSFORMATION PERIOD

Act II covers the major transformational theories. The main theorem relies on a freshly designed *horizontal, systemic organizational architecture*, and an advanced generation of Wayne's *throughput theory* that communicates with the markets purchasing criteria using *market-perceived value*.

Each theory is an existing one the author selected to work in harmony—allowing one to put the right pieces together in a way that will actively influence the market. This type of architecture allows the organization to make rapid changes to its internal system, gaining market leadership and deliver productivity levels not seen in decades.

A set of *measurement tools* is introduced that uses specific operational drivers in conjunction with the market and financial leading indicators. This unique system enables fast reaction time to keep or expand their market... Now, imagine having such a diagram on your monitor showing the attribute drivers blinking actual output results in real-time along with a separate month to date performance chart for each driver... This application allows management to make mid-course corrections to keep the system on track, rather than waiting a week or two or perhaps the month-end financial results...

The author's advanced application of *overhead to products* leapfrogs all cost systems including activity-based and standard cost systems. The simplicity is remarkable and supports Generally Accepted Accounting Principles (GAAP). Employing the product's *throughput* time enables the proper contribution of *total* overhead costs and measures individual product or service profitability. It's time in the overall system that counts, not specific product resources or labor.

There is a vignette at the beginning and the end of each scene, allowing the reader to take a break from the incredible store of knowledge, and have a few laughs. Most notably, LUNCHING WITH THE STARS where Jackie meets Quentin Tarantino in a wonderfully funny parody, of one of my favorite directors.

ACT III – THE RESOLUTION

Resolution brings to a close the new theories that will enhance the final stages of the transformational process. For businesses using *revenue recognition* accounting systems, which haven't changed since their inception,

Wayne has designed a revolutionary idea. The application clearly measures project *throughput* by applied standards resulting in percent complete by time, or steps in the project. This tool can also make intelligent decisions to improve quotations, on-time delivery, and profitability.

The unique organizational architecture also allows for advanced thinking, using *financial modeling*. The discussion centers on the underlying logic that moves from two-dimensional to three-dimensional financial modeling.

The resulting theories of the book allow for original thoughts for an *employee sharing of the wealth program*. An innovation that measures wealth using Economic Value Added financial performance to enable equitable worth to all employees that benefit both the company and shareholders—a vehicle that will help grow the economy.

Another remarkable new theory is ending the ever-increasing rise in the cost of *Hospital Care*. First, we would apply standardized software modules similar to those used in Enterprise Resource Planning to bring down the cost of electronic medical record software. Next, we'd employ the throughput time procedure to replace the dreaded lengthy, overpriced medical billing system. And, finally, cost reduction of medication for patients, by eliminating the overhead currently applied to medicine.

In summary, these new theories are revolutionary. They are not, however, abstract or far-reaching intellectual ideas—but logical thought-through innovative processes, with an added dose of system theory. They'll have a huge impact in reviving productivity and improved market share for businesses of the future and be one of the primary vehicles in *Evolution—Minimize the Risk by Design* that grows our economy unprecedentedly.

THE READER STUDY GUIDE TO ENHANCE THE LEARNING PROCESS

The idea behind *Change for the Right Reason* is to integrate intellectual knowledge with everyday life reflecting the struggle of schools and business. The story allows for an interaction of dialog of questions and answers between the consultant and the audience bringing to light questions one might ask if in the audience. And yet, sometimes we can be caught up in the story and gloss over the knowledge being discussed. To help with that idea, I have developed a set of high-level cognitive questions at the end of each scene. They encourage the reader to think creatively and openly express their ideas and thoughts.

In a classroom atmosphere, this process enables other students to hear a different set of explanations and allows a starting point for a discussion—thus, enhancing the learning process as you search for the truth…

SEE ENHANCING THE LEARNING PROCESS AT THE END OF EACH SCENE.

TO THE READER

As authors, we are the sum of the stories we tell enhanced by our experiences reflecting the way we wish to interpret them for others.

After several years into my retirement in the early 1990s, I planned for business acquisitions having decades of experience in executive management, but little or no background preparing me for this quest. So, I collected books related to my cause. They included leveraged buyouts and finance. The more I learned led me to the study of business theory...

I soon realized, we as students and professionals of the business world continued an education by antiquated ideas. The books had one thing in common: they focused on the knowledge that reflected the author's curriculum or consulting profession, with no solid, revolutionary ideas. Well... other than books such as *The Goal*, by Eliyahu M. Goldratt in 1984. *The Fifth Discipline* by Peter M. Senge in 1990 and systemic thinking books by Russell Ackoff who spent half-century as the premier evangelist of systemic thinking.

In 1995, I published the first edition of *Change for the Right Reason*, a book purchased by consulting and large manufacturing firms. My guess is that it was as boring to read as other business books.

By 2004, I had determined that there were no recent publications with enough advanced theory that could result in transforming our current business organizational architecture. Especially, one that was a page-turner—other than *The Goal* by Dr. Goldratt, written as a novel that sold over three million copies.

With that in mind, I decided that it was time for a business book written like a novel—one dedicated to business executives, business and engineering students, and educators. But it needed to be written in a way that would allow the reader to enjoy the learning process by reading fresh business ideas in a unique way.

By happenstance while reading for pleasure one evening, I read Thomas Russell's book, *Under Enemy Colors* and selected two paragraphs of great interest:

"I do not know why authors can but repeat what others have done before. Shall we forever make new books, as apothecaries make new mixtures, by pouring only out of one vessel and into another? Are we forever to be twisting and untwisting the same rope?"

"Perhaps, Doctor, you can invent a new species of a book," Hayden suggested. "The authors of this world would like a new pattern to copy, I should think."

After reading those words, I knew I was doing the right thing. So, I experimented with writing a business novel using a *plotline* and a *conspiracy* to destroy the business, then saved by the *hero*. The problem was it read like a thriller, distracting the reader from the knowledge for which the book was written. The idea for this *new species of a book* is to lighten the load of *learning advanced theories*, not weigh it down.

With that in mind, I settled on a book where the characters tell the story by their thoughts, their actions, and their dialogue. It's through their eyes and points of view we see a story of business transformation unfold. They presided over the training and transformational process of turning around a company in trouble. With brief moments in their personal lives, one can enjoy the short vignettes filled with light humor as they remove themselves from their consulting roles.

It's also a story of friendship, loyalty, and honor—without which, the transformational process will not take hold. There is no single main character. The transformational process is only possible with the help of *many players*. Therefore, each scene, except for the Prelude is played by one of the main characters written in the first person and present tense.

My overall purpose here is to present to you good storytelling, full of humor and knowledge to aid in building the businesses of the future—and grow our beleaguered economy to new heights. I'm hoping you'll find it so.

Any errors or views expressed in this book, are my own.

I would note that in Act III Scene Seven, Johnny is telling a story about an elderly lady who receives her college degree. And on graduation day, the faculty invited her to speak to the students and guests. The *idea* came from a similar story told in dissimilar ways on several websites with no author given, therefore, no way to give the proper credit. Nonetheless, I expanded on the idea and wrote it in a humorous and warm-hearted way so that perhaps, you'll not forget the message...

Wayne Coker
2017

"There are three rules for writing a novel—
Unfortunately, no one knows what they are."

W. Somerset Maugham

"Humor's the hardest thing to translate."
- Bharati Mukherjee

ORGANIZATIONAL ARCHITECTURE
A Legacy System

The *legacy system* is an old method that continues to be used because it still functions even though reaching its limitations and burdens new processes and technology. To change our organizational architecture, we must first have a change in our state of mind. Consider what Nelson Mandela once said...
I believe where you stand, depends upon where you sit.

Why won't you die? Legacy said.
"You can't kill an idea," Change *for* the Right Reason responded before the revolution began.

An idea from the movie, *V for Vendetta*

Gandhi once said: *At first they ignore you, then they laugh at you, then they fight you, then you win.*

The more you fight it, the more you fall behind to those who embrace it.

INTRODUCTION
The Cast of Characters

CONSULTING GROUP PARTNERS

JAKE JENSEN is the founder and partner of a transformation consulting and acquisition business - the *Jake Jensen Group*.

DAKOTA WELLS, Jake Jensen's partner was previously an executive working for Marty Westlake's acquisition group and a former navy commander.

CONSULTING GROUP CREW

JOHNNY ZAPATA has a post-secondary professorship at Pepperdine University and a Professor of Organizational Theory and Marketing. He also consults for the Jake Jensen Group: system processes and organizational architecture.

JACKIE O', consult with the Jake Jensen Group covering finance and information distribution and has a doctorate in finance and a post-secondary professorship at Pepperdine University.

DENNY CHANG works as a coordinator, with degrees in process engineering, computer science, and finance. He reports directly to Jackie O' and Johnny Zapata.

ADVANCE TEK CORPORATION—ATC OFFICERS

THANH NGUYEN: President of ATC

NINA NGUYEN: Vice President of Finance and Information Distribution. She is also the wife of Thanh Nguyen and plays a major role in the transformation process.

COLONEL MARTY WESTLAKE is retired from his acquisition firm and now helping out as temporary Chairman of the board of ATC—a former Green Beret officer who did four tours during the Vietnam War.

DAVID GLOSS, Vice President of Market Recognition
GARY EASTWOOD, Vice President of Product & Process Engineering
ED BLACKBURN, Vice President of Order Fulfillment—Operations.
BELINDA SHAKEELA, Vice President of Quality Assurance
MELINDA LOCKHART, Director of Human Resources

THE REST OF THE CAST

TONI NAKNI is a Six-foot-five, full-blooded, Creek Indian, retired naval intelligence officer, pilot, and longtime friend of Jake Jensen. He speaks volumes with only a few words, a twitch of the mouth, or a minuscule nod of the head.

SHERI is Johnny Zapata's girlfriend and full of surprises.
BROOKS is Jackie's best friend. The local surfers call her, Woodie.
ANTONIO is Jake's crew member aboard the ketch, Sophi.
LI'L MISS KITTY is Jake's twenty-year-old cat.

TABLE OF CONTENTS

Change for i
the Right Reason i
Foreword by Dr. Joanne C. Preston iii
Reader's Favorite Book Review v
Change for vi
the Right Reason vi
Copyright vii
Also by Wayne Coker viii
Advance Praise ix
About xi
To The Reader xiv
Organizational Architecture xvi
Introduction xvii
Table of Contents xix
ACT I 2
Prelude 3
Act I Scene 1 10
Act I Scene 2 18
Act I Scene 3 36
Act I Scene 4 42
Act I Scene 5 56
Act I Scene 6 70
ACT II 74
Act II Scene 1 75
Act II Scene 2 98
Act II Scene 3 134
Act II Scene 4 146
Act II Scene 5 159
Act II Scene 6 173
Act II Scene 7 197
Act II Scene 8 209
Act II Scene 9 220
Act II Scene 10 237
Act II Scene 11 244
Act II Scene 12 265
Act II Scene 13 298
Act II Scene 14 312
Act II Scene 15 329
ACT III 350
Act III Scene 1 351
Act III Scene 2 367

Act III Scene 3 380
Act III Scene 4 389
Act III Scene 5 399
Act III Scene 6 426
Act III - Scene 7 440
Appendix 455
Risk 456
The Teacher's Guide 458
Entrepreneurship 461
Acknowledgments 464
Latest Novel 466
About the Author 467

ACT I
The Beginning

PRELUDE
Welcome to America

THANH NGUYEN'S EARLY MORNING DRIVE TO WORK

Thanh Nguyen struggles out of bed for an early morning meeting with his company's officers. After stepping into the shower, he lets the hot water beat down on him as he lathers himself and then turns it to cold tolerating the punishing chill for a final cleansing.

After toweling off, Thanh looks into the mirror and sees a tall, sinewy Vietnamese man over a half-century old with threads of gray in close-cropped hair. He remains a ruggedly handsome man, but his face is somehow different now. The change is subtle, and yet the distinction is everything—having been strained by undue stress.

Right after shaving, his vision becomes blurred along with experiencing dizziness. Sitting down on the edge of his bed for a moment, Nina, his wife, looks at her husband with concern. His ill sensation soon passes allowing him to look up at her with a gentle smile and then dressed for work as Nina finishes her morning routine preparing herself for a day at the office. Together, they walk into the kitchen where Pham has prepared breakfast.

The Nguyen's housekeeper, Li Pham is a sweet little ancient-looking lady with silver hair twisted back in a severe bun. She's even short by Asian standards at four feet nothing, maybe eighty-five pounds with her purse in hand, even as a young woman. Now stooped with age, she must use a step stool to prepare their food. No way, would Thanh and Nina consider bringing in someone else to help Li, for it would only insult her.

Li, a longtime friend of Nina's mother, came to live with the Nguyen's and help care for her parents' because of their ill-health. Her father died in

1986 and her mother in 1991.

To shorten Li's bout in the kitchen, they both take their morning meal at the same time each day. For Nina this morning, Li has prepared a typical French-Indochinese breakfast dish of yogurt with sliced fresh strawberries, croissant, and coffee with cream and sugar. Thanh is having a traditional light breakfast of Mi Quang soup, a rice noodle dish with shrimp and a rice cake served with coffee, cream, and sugar.

Thanh peered down into his soup feeling a little unstable, light-headed and not very hungry. After taking a few sips, he stirs the rice and shrimp around in deep thought. With his fill of Mi Quang, he drinks coffee that's turned cold, setting it down he looks over at Nina reading the morning paper.

During breakfast, they had enjoyed pleasant conversations, but due to recent work-related problems, which they try not to discuss at home, Thanh and Nina have little to say to each other.

Without thinking, he takes another sip of cold coffee. With disgust, he puts it down, gets up from the table and leans over to kiss Nina goodbye. She looks up at him with worried eyes and tells him to drive carefully, and she'll be in the office at seven o'clock.

He smiles at her with a heavy heart and heads out the door and down the breezeway into the garage. Thanh gets into his Lexus and presses the start button bringing life to the engine. After slipping in his favorite CD, a song by Khanh Ly, he backs out of his tumbled-brick driveway, hits the gas, and is office-bound at five forty-five Friday morning.

It's a thirty-minute drive from his Newport Beach home to the Rancho Santa Margarita office park. This will allow him a little over an hour in his office to prepare for the meeting at seven-thirty. During the drive, Thanh remembers back to their arrival at the Orange County Airport in 1976.

A BETTER LIFE

With recent dark-laden clouds having passed over the airport, the Nguyen's deplaned on a glorious Sunday morning. The passing downpour left the area with the distinctive pleasant petrichor smell often accompanying the first rain, an earthy, pleasant sweet smell. In place of the storm came the brilliant rays of streaming sunshine bringing warmth and joy to the day. The lustrous sun lit up Nina's lovely face, even with tears of bliss running down her cheeks, making Thanh's heart skip a beat.

Nina spotted their new friend Marty Westlake in the crowd with a sign— *Nguyen Family Welcome to America.*

They arrived at the Orange County airport from Thailand during mid-August accompanied by Nina's mother and father. Her uncle was a former colonel in the Army of the Republic of Vietnam's Rangers, better known as ARVN Rangers. After the surrender, he found himself in a *re-education* camp. The Vietnam War had eventually killed the remaining members of their families.

By the mid-seventies, thousands of Vietnamese fled South Vietnam, escaping in unseaworthy boats while crossing the Gulf of Thailand. Almost one-third of the people perished at sea from starvation and drowning. Pirates robbed and killed these desperate people, while they raped and kidnaped many of the women.

The Nguyen's faced a bleak future under the new regime, so they pooled their resources with several friends and built a boat. To divert suspicion, they constructed their craft as a dragnet fishing vessel typical of the region, with one exception, they installed a more powerful engine.

After the families used their new boat fishing for a short period, making sure of its seaworthiness, they readied themselves to leave for a better life.

On a chilly moonless night shrouded in a low fog, the families struggled across the tidal mudflats and mosquito-infested mangroves—known locally as *bushes masquerading as trees*—to their waiting vessel.

The two families with children fed them a crushed sleeping pill with their dinner to quiet them during the crossing—not an uncommon occurrence when hiding and protecting the family during such arduous times.

With their powerful engine, they outpaced the pirates in the Gulf of Thailand—often referred to as the Gulf of Siam. They reached Thailand by navigating seven hundred miles in the open sea using Nina's Southeast Asia map from school, and a simple compass. A compass made from a magnetized sewing needle stuck through a piece of cork floating in a jar of water and a layer of light oil. The oil helped calm the water from the moving forces of the sea.

After spending months at the Nong Samet, Thailand refugee camp, Thanh sent a letter to Marty Westlake a former U.S. Army Green Beret officer. He served as a special advisor to the ARVN troops in the 1960s, and valued friend of Nina's uncle, the colonel in the ARVN Rangers. Thanh told Colonel Westlake of their plight and asked for his help in entering the United States. Marty responded with the answer to their prayers. Three months after Thanh's first letter from Thailand, retired Colonel Marty Westlake their new sponsor met them at the airport and later helped them settle into a cramped apartment in Westminster, California. He also wrote a letter of introduction to assist them in their search for employment.

Thanh and Nina were both well-educated. Thanh's father became a Western-oriented, urban Vietnamese landowner in Cochinchina. He possessed excess wealth as a result of the French development in vast new tracts of land.

Thanh abandoned the idea, knowing there would be no future being a landowner with a potential takeover by the North Vietnamese. Instead, he received an electrical engineering degree at Saigon University. Nina received her finance degree during the same period. They met, fell in love, and married a year after graduation.

With Marty's help, they both landed jobs and were soon bringing in enough money to support the family. Nina became the sole surviving child of her family, having lost her two brothers and a sister. Therefore, in Vietnamese tradition, she became responsible for her mother and father's well-being. Thanh felt that her mother, at times, an *une douleur dans le cul*—a pain in the butt—owing to her demanding ways. He loved her father, having been treated like a son.

Even with work and family responsibilities, they both went back to school to further their education. They spoke excellent English and French because of their mandatory Catholic education in Vietnam. Thanh finished with an MBA, and Nina received her master's degree in finance from the University of California, Irvine.

Later, after graduation, they both landed a good job at a power supply company in Santa Ana, California. Marty Westlake continued to help when possible and soon became part of their family and a lifelong friend.

Marty, the founder, and CEO of a successful business acquisition firm found himself in a constant search for good companies to acquire. In the process, he ran across an insignificant high-tech company manufacturing communication equipment with excellent growth potential, but too small for him to get involved. But then he thought of the Nguyen's. They were good at their respective professions and ambitious.

The following week, Marty asked the Nguyen's if they'd consider a partnership with him to develop real wealth. Excited with such an opportunity, they did a leveraged buyout agreement of fifty-fifty percent ownership with Marty. Several years later, with the stipulated agreement buyout of Marty's shares after repayment of the loan, they acquired Marty's share of the business.

Over the following years, the company grew to over three hundred million dollars in annual sales. The Nguyen's lived the American dream, until a few months ago, their company experienced a severe material flow slowdown.

Thanh's primary supplier in Jiangsu, China, shipped late for the first time in their relationship, and their quality dropped to a forty percent acceptance rate.

These purchased assemblies were labor-intensive, and with the company processes being final assembly and testing only, they were in no position to build them in time, leaving them in a difficult situation.

Thanh took a China Eastern Airlines flight out of LAX in the afternoon and arrived in Shanghai after a fourteen-hour flight—six-thirty in the afternoon Shanghai time. The expressways enforce a maximum speed limit of one hundred kilometers per hour. It's not unlike driving the freeways in the United States with good signs in both Chinese and English. The main exception, the light traffic—not because vehicles are rare luxuries for Chinese people, but due to the heavy and frequent toll charges which dampened widespread usage of these routes.

At the Four Seasons Hotel later in the evening, Thanh read travel literature about Jiangsu Province showing it to be one of the fastest developing provinces in China. The area has high-value biodiversity, and the coastline comprises vast wetlands, which are essential staging areas for migratory birds. Similar to travel brochures, you only read or see what they would like you to perceive to be true. Thanh heard the wetlands are threatened now, due to excessive growth, and reclaimed for agriculture and fisheries, creating an increase in water pollution.

The next morning, he eats an early breakfast, rented a car, and headed off for Jiangsu Province. Later, after a little over an hour into his drive, Thanh located his supplier's facility. His meeting with the owner became most unpleasant. Portions of his storeroom were set ablaze a few months ago, causing significant disruption to their workflow. If this wasn't serious enough, some of his most eminently trained employees left to start up their own business. He brought in additional labor, but their skill level, not as it should be, became a problem. He felt ashamed for the burden he placed on Thanh, his most valued customer.

Thanh became distraught over his supplier's position but understood his circumstances. With no alternative, he ended the contract owing to the poor quality. Thanh asked the supplier to contact him if things are improved to the point his quality was better or equal to his previous finished goods. He tried other manufacturers in the area, but none were able to respond in time or lacked the ability. With a heavy heart, Thanh left China and came home.

A local contractor to fill the orders never became an issue, other than a thirty to forty percent cost increase on each assembly, plus a premium for accelerated startup cost. Not having any choice in the matter, he placed an order with Howard Industries in San Diego. Later, he contacted a friend whose company searched out suppliers in Asia meeting Thanh's unique needs for high quality and labor-intensive assemblies. He assured Thanh it might take a few months, but doable.

Along with the late shipments and higher cost, their cash flow would go negative in six months. Nina, the company's CFO, believed if they stepped up their delivery, they should be okay. Thanh traveled to each customer to explain the current events. Every customer but one would be willing to work with him as long as the disruptions stopped and shipments brought back on schedule.

They Needed Marty Westlake's help, so Thanh met with him to lay out his problem. Marty is always busy but not so busy he couldn't help his old friend.

Marty sold his holding company to a British firm, and now with time on his hands, he began to build a solar and hydrogen-powered electric *boat*. However, Marty thought the word *boat*, being too disenchanting, used the more admired *kenning phrase* derived from the Viking myth for naming his innovating boat—*Wave Traveler, a* circumnavigate globe traveler over the *Whale-Road*...

Thanh and Marty discussed several ideas, but the most attractive was the Jake Jensen Consulting firm with its business transformation ability and acquisitions. Thanh met Jake several times at Westlake's home and found him to be a likable guy and respected by Marty. He'd read Jake's book *Change for a*

Better Reason several months ago and liked what he read.

Before their current problem, Thanh considered hiring Jake to help in transforming the business to increase market share—either this or look forward to shrinking business value. With their current problem demanding immediate action, he met with Jake's partner, Dakota Wells a few days later. She told him Jake and his friend were somewhere out in the Atlantic sailing his new refitted boat back from Barcelona, Spain. But she would be glad to help him. After an hour's consultation, Thanh signed an agreement.

ARRIVING AT THE CORPORATE OFFICE

When Thanh arrived at the Santa Margarita Parkway intersection, he took a right and continued down to Avenida Empresa Parkway. High technology companies populate the business park, both big and small.

He turned on his wipers for a moment to clear the windshield of drizzle from the low-hanging clouds. The wet pavement creates a subtle increase in tire noise from a thin layer of water forced through the grooves in the tires. The beautiful surrounding landscape glistened from the moisture and permeates the air with a crisp, pleasant fragrance evaporating as the day progressed.

Thanh made a left into ATC's parking lot, parks, and ponders for a moment before opening his door. Now standing next to his car, he takes a deep breath, locks his car, and makes the short walk to the front entrance.

While unlocking the front door, a doppelganger appears—an apparition reflection of him in the glass. Thanh shivers while wandering down the hallway along with an excruciating headache. Hearing the phone ring, he opens his door and shuffles toward it. With the room becoming blurred, Thanh answered with a whisper… "This is … this is… Thanh…"

With sweat streaming off him in torrents, the phone became unbearable to lift and falls from Thanh's grip. His condition is followed by a cluster headache bringing on the worst possible pain as his legs turn to rubber trying to take a few faltering steps. And like a discarded fast-melting ice cream cone on a hot summer walkway, he ends up in a heap on the floor. The room dims to darkness while a probing blackness wraps around Thanh like a soft blanket as he drifts off into a dark tunnel filled with a world of black dreams, and then…nothing.

PRELUDE
ENHANCING THE LEARNING PROCESS

The first question you're about to answer must come from what your personal thoughts are because you have not yet read the author's subject of outsourcing.

Thanh Nguyen headed to China to rectify a shipping and quality problem he had *outsourced* because of high labor content in a specific subassembly used in several of his products.

Question: 1

Consider the advantages and disadvantages of outsourcing for companies, and then consider how this may or may not improve a company's productivity. Depending, of course, if the outsourced assembly was part of an existing internal process, or never part of the company's capabilities.

What are your thoughts on outsourcing benefits and detriments?

ACT I SCENE 1
The Laguna Beach Dinner Meeting

WEEK 1 SATURDAY – DAKOTA'S ARRIVAL AT THE LAGUNA HOTEL

When nearing the small town of Laguna Beach during my Saturday evening drive, the sun hangs low over the ocean while bringing with it a wonderful aroma drifting over the shore and in through my open windows.

Laguna is a seaside artist and surfer haven that resides on a white sandy cove resting below the rising hills. You feel as though, the creation of these stucco buildings were constructed with no peripheral association with the surrounding world, it's more like an island off the coast of California. The locals say it's where God parked himself on the seventh day.

The name Laguna comes from Lagonas, named by the Ute-Azetcas, a coastal Indian tribe who first inhabited the canyons two thousand years ago. Even the Indians knew about location, location, location. A famous gate hung in 1935 best describes the community, it reads:

This gate hangs well and hinders none, refresh, and rest, then travel on.

Comparatively speaking, it still, a sleepy little town. So, the sign appears to have done its job. Jake once told me that Laguna is a quaint little village with a drinking problem.

Art galleries and an eclectic group of informal restaurants line the streets. The food served at these eateries varies from great tasting pineapple-and-ham pizza to every nationality of foods and elegant cuisine. You'll never go hungry in this beach town.

The place still has most of its original stucco construction with Spanish tile roofs, plate glass windows, and brass works. The buildings are highlighted by eucalyptus trees shimmering in the breeze, well-kept gardens, and colorful flowers growing out of pots that line the streets.

When entering the little village for a dinner meeting with my good friend Marty Westlake, I drive past the beach sandy volleyball court off to my right. I continue on for a block and find an open street berth to park at, and nosed my car in next to the curb and hoofed it back to the old historic Hotel Laguna. The place looks as though, at one time, it must have been a three-story California mission. It has white walls, Spanish arches in relief, and an eight-sided bell tower with a polygon roof covered in a red clay tile, except no ringing, having no bell. Hotel Laguna was the first in Laguna Beach and remains today, the most well-known structure. They built the town during a period before accountants ruled the world, and comes with a charming, romantic, and intriguing history.

After making my entrance, I hurry on past the hotel reception desk, down the hallway, make a left into the bar and survey the restaurant. No Marty. The hostess, a slender young lady sees me and walks in my direction.

"May I help you?" She said.

"Yes. Thank you, my name is Ms. Dakota Wells. Has Colonel Westlake arrived?"

"Yes. The Colonel reserved a table on the terrace, please follow me."

As we thread our way through the tables, I see an Asian couple. They take a brief look at me with a slight head bow, giving me the ultimate human gesture—a smile. I reciprocate with a polite nod while walking by their table.

Marty sees me coming and gets up from his chair. He's in his early seventies, but a handsome man still. His past military life has kept him ramrod straight as he juts out his hand. I grasped it feeling the warmth of his handshake flow through my body.

"Nice suit, Marty."

"Thanks, Dakota. My wife dresses me."

"Marty, you haven't been married for over thirty years."

"So... It's the same suit."

"Yeah, right, one of Forbes wealthiest men keeping a suit that long—even if it still looks great on you thirty years later ... I don't think so."

"Hey. It's the highest quality of worsted wool. Plus, I only wear it on special occasions."

"Christ, Marty, no wonder you have so much money—you seldom spend it—I don't get it."

The hostess waits good-naturedly for our chitchat and formalities to end. Marty looks her way...

"Sorry, we got carried away over a bloody suit. Please seat the lady."

The hostess responds with a pleasant nod...

"I'll have your waiter here in a moment."

"You're most kind, thank you," I said.

She smiles with a nod and heads back to her station.

"The seafood here is the freshest and best prepared in Laguna. What I like most is we can discuss business in the moderately quiet of the terrace and take in the fresh ocean air. The only sound we have to compete with is the surf as it pounds and crawls its way up the beach. Oh... Let me not forget the ponderous orange ball balancing on the edge of the horizon for our pleasure."

"That's what I love about you, Marty. You're such a romantic."

"I'm too old to be a romantic, Dakota," Marty said with chagrin.

Not wanting to verbally respond, I reach out and touch Marty's hand for a moment. With an elevated eyebrow, Marty looks down at my hand.

"Hey, it's a woman thing, we can't help ourselves."

Lightheartedly I pull my arm away and squared my table napkin.

Marty utters a grunt and nods politely. Quiet settles between us. Marty is preoccupied while gazing at the sunset.

I've known Marty for about ten years. We first met during my interview for a job with George Abbot, president of an automated guided vehicle company in Orange County.

MEETING MARTY

George was a Napoleon look-alike. His height was the same as Napoleon's at five-foot-six, but contrary to popular belief, Napoleon was taller than the average nineteenth-century Frenchmen.

With George's stocky build, gruff voice rolled-up sleeves on his Popeye-sized forearms, and a cigar wedged into the side of his mouth gave him the perception of a no-codswallop tough guy. But, underneath that bravado, he was foremost a real gentleman and smart as hell.

George's office was anything but tidy. I'm thinking he followed one of Napoleon's productivity secrets—not reading his incoming mail right away. Napoleon figured much of his mail brought overburden requests from others, and so he let it pile up, knowing the matter would pass by the time he opened them. Most of his mail included information with no value. He considered anything urgent would result in a messenger riding up on a sweating white horse, foaming at the mouth. Email and texting junkies may see the wisdom in Napoleon's logic and want to ponder on the idea.

George had no photographs of family or friends, keeping with his rough exterior. His outside office wall was glass, awarding us with a presentation of a heavy downpour.

During my interview, I could not help but notice seeing a man ambulating in the rain toward the building without an umbrella. He appeared impervious to the torrential rainstorm as though he was in his natural element, marching with a purpose and a strong military bearing.

It must be true, only sissies use umbrellas. And yet, I've been told, you absorb less rainfall when walking as opposed to running—beats the hell out of me? But, the truth of the matter, mathematically speaking, it's only true if you have a *tailwind* moving at the same speed you're moving toward shelter. If not, be a sissy and bring an umbrella.

A few minutes later, the man looked in on us with his soaking wet suit—no *tailwind*—immediately catching my attention. He mentions to George—sorry for interrupting, but will you be tied up for a while?

Since we were nearing the end of my interview, George got up from his seat and told him we shan't be long. He takes a moment to walk over to the impressive-looking gentleman with the short, gray, wet hair and strong, weathered face. After a handshake, George introduced us.

After the introduction, he asked Marty if he would like to chat with me about the position of Director of Operations. He nodded his head in agreement...

The rain soon turned to a sprinkle and the sun tried to peek in on planet earth. Marty took a seat on the sofa and gestured for me to take the nearby wing chair. We sat there for the longest time while he looked at me with his hazel-colored eyes that appeared to turn from green to blue. They were trying to decide what color to be while the sun slipped in and out behind the clouds. At this point, I got the indication he was waiting for me to say something.

With a blush, I told him of my life as a former navy commander with past responsibilities in executive-level duties of logistics such as inventory control, financial management, and physical distribution systems. As I rattled on, he seldom took his eyes off me. He patiently sat there listening with no gestures or facial expressions absorbing and recording everything I said. When I ran out of words, he stood, thanked me, and shook my hand. He told George he would be down the hall in engineering and please call him when he finished my interview. George nodded. Marty walked out the door.

Mr. Abbot called a few days later and told me I had the job if I still wanted it. He said it would be a good place for a person with my intelligence and background to grow into positions with greater responsibility.

With two years behind me, I was running one of Marty's latest acquisitions in partnership with Jake Jensen. We worked well together in the transformation process of our company. When Marty retired and sold his business, Jake and I became partners in doing business turnarounds and acquisitions.

My, how time flies with me middle-aged now, swimming a mile each day, five days a week to keep trim. My physical appearance looks the same as my days in high school and college, having been on the swim and diving team. Well... Close enough, my dark hair is shorter and wear glasses that cover my father's emerald green eyes, and yes, a few more facial lines—only a few I might add. My posture is still good because of my many nights at the family dinner table as a youngster and my years in the Navy.

GETTING DOWN TO BUSINESS

"So, Marty, what's our plan of attack?"

"Well, to begin with, I called Jake to update him last night using his SeaMobile satellite service aboard his ketch. I told him that Thanh had a stroke early yesterday morning. I further mentioned my meeting with you this evening to discuss, as you would say, a plan of attack. Jake said he wished he could be of help, but they will be out at sea for about a month. Their destination is Port Royal, Jamaica."

"Damn, Marty. We've had our share of difficult turnarounds, but this beats all. We're starting out this project with your best friend and the company CEO in a coma."

"Yeah, not a good way on the outset for making a business transformation..." Marty said, being silent for a moment. "It appears these tragedies have a tendency to follow me around from time to time, with most taking place back when..."

He paused with a longing look...

"So many young men killed who would have given the world a multitude of gifts." He said, in a whisper.

When seeing the thousand-yard stare, I reverentially kept quiet.

"This morning, I spoke with Nina, Thanh's wife, and the company's CFO. She told me she and her Board of Directors would like me to take on the responsibility of Chairman. I accepted, of course, and made a conference call to the board members to get confirmation on having you take over the CEO responsibilities during the transformation process." he said. "And if needed, you can take on any other tasks you or Jake consider necessary. Well, assuming you both agree."

"I'm sure Jake will have no problem. It should help move the process along a little faster," I said.

"That was my conclusion."

"How's Nina dealing with this horrible nightmare?"

"Well, I'm considered family, but Nina still won't show her grief. She will handle it in her own private way and bounce back. Nina's Vietnamese and made of bamboo—you can bend them, hit them, even kill them, but they'll not break. After spending many tours in Indochina, I know this to be true. Thanh isn't dead, but his prognosis is not good. He is my dear friend, and this grieves me."

"At least he's still alive, Marty..."

I stop in mid-sentence seeing the waiter nearing our table. Marty, with his back to him, looks at me with lowered eyebrows while pondering over a troubling thought.

I'm unable to respond due to the waiter arriving and standing there for a moment realizing he may have arrived at a bad time; nonetheless, he fills our water glasses in silence before speaking...

"Good evening. My name is Pablo," he said with a pleasant smile.

We both give Pablo a polite nod and a good evening.

"May I take a drink order?" Pablo said.

"Dakota?" Marty said in a firm voice.

"I'll make it simple ... a glass of a white, house wine please."

"It would be my pleasure," Pablo said. "And you sir?"

"I'll have a glass of Scotch. Thanks."

"Yes, sir. Would a Johnnie Walker meet with your approval?"

Marty looks up at the waiter and nods in a positive manner.

"Thank you, sir. I'll be right back with your order and menus."

Marty turns his water glass around in little circles while his eyes follow Pablo for a moment, and then hunched forward with his hands cupped and fingers interdigitated he looks straight at me.

"Thanh is at least still alive? What the hell kind of remark is that?"

The surf, the wind, and my surroundings freeze in place as I gaze into Marty's saddened hazel eyes and nervously try to respond...

"Oh my God, Marty... I'm so sorry it came out that way. I didn't continue with my thoughts because the waiter made a sudden appearance at our table."

"Please carry on," Marty said, with a measure of authority.

"Well, I was about to say at least he's still alive, which brings hope you can lean on. Please forgive my abrupt ending. It was inexcusable."

My eyes fill with tears, feeling the pain and knowing full well how he must have felt.

"I'm sorry, Dakota for overreacting."

"Thank you, Marty, but no apology necessary."

I turn to look obscurely away to rub my eyes in a moment of silence.

With a long pause, Marty changes the subject...

"I met with the Vice President of Marketing, David Gloss and Operations Vice President, Ed Blackburn at lunch today. We have agreed to meet early Monday morning and go through the client list and assign ourselves to a group of customers. The plan is to have a face-to-face with our contacts. We need to explain what happened and what we're doing about it. The order of our selection will be based on the importance to the welfare of the business."

"Way to go, Marty. Hit hard and hit fast. Customers get real jittery when they hear there is no captain running the ship."

With a sudden relief, the unpleasant moment passes.

"After settling in, you can take over the problem. I'll call David and Ed letting them know you accepted the temporary job of CEO."

"How and when do you want me to step into the position?"

"I'll meet you at eight Monday morning at the facility and introduce you around to the key people."

"Sounds good, Marty. I'm ready to eat. Are you?"

Marty replies with a sparkle back in his eyes...

"Absolutely, I'm starved. We won't need a menu having often dropped in for a meal. If I may, it would be my pleasure to order your dinner, assuming you like fish?"

"Please do Marty, and yes, I'd love a good fish dinner," I said with a thankful gesture.

The waiter arrives with the drinks and takes our order for dinner—grilled swordfish marinated with pesto over roasted potatoes and spinach with lemon rosemary vinaigrette.

"Would you care for wine with your dinner?" Pablo said with a noticeable but insignificant accent.

Marty gives it a thought...

"Please have the chef suggest wine best suited for our meal."

"It would be my pleasure, sir."

With a slight bow to each of us, he heads off to the kitchen with our order.

When looking toward the beach, I see a few people walking near the water as the ocean breakers crash onto the white sand and bring with it microforms of marine life. The evening has cooled with the sun dipping below the horizon leaving behind a sliver of orange glow settling low over the darkened Pacific thickening the night as darkness moves closer to shore.

Not taking long for our dinner to arrive, we sat on the dimly lighted terrace enjoying our meal with little to say. The chef selected a Chardonnay, which is noticeably oaken on its own but proves to be a splendid companion to the swordfish. Pablo happily informed us our wine comes from a remote valley in Peru where resident growers have their wine bottled by a local bottler. Our wine had the name of Talia...

Later, Pablo comes by and respectfully asks...

"May I add a refresher to your drinks?"

"Please," we both said.

He nods as he picks up the wine bottle and sparingly fills our glasses, and leaves in silence.

After dinner, a brisk sea breeze tousles my boyish-cut hair and tugs at my white silk blouse while I sip at my Banana Cow—a pink, creamy drink, with Creme De Banana Rum. I looked out over the patio railing while twirling my glass by the stem and notice that lack of light has stolen the coastline. The exception is the hotel lights reflecting off the endless silky surf pouring itself over the darkened beach.

While gazing at the glittering illumination dancing on the water, I ponder over the days ahead. I need to consider how to prepare the employees for the massive change in their work environment and making it my first priority.

With my elbows firmly resting on the table, I pick up my Banana Cow as light winks off the rim and then fix my eyes on Marty for a moment. When Marty realizes I'm gazing at him, he looks up to see me lifting my glass...

"To fair winds and following seas and to those adventurers that wish to make change for the right reason..."

"Đó là một bánh mì nướng tất cả chúng ta sẽ có biết, Tôi thích rằng, Dakota," Marty said in Vietnamese. "It's a toast we shall all come to know... I like it, Dakota."

ACT I – SCENE 1
ENHANCING THE LEARNING PROCESS

The following question is not technical, but important.

Question 1:
What is the ultimate human gesture, and why is it so essential we use it in our daily lives and in a business environment?

Question 2:
The next question is a subject often discussed throughout the book—email and cell phone texting.

What are your thoughts on Napoleon's productivity idea on excessive mail and those who receive gross amounts of email and texting every day?
How much time do you spend reading and sending them each day?
When regarding your future is this a good use of your time?

Question 3:
How would you prepare the employees for the massive change in their work environment during their forthcoming transformation?
With structural and people issues to deal with, describe how you would move forward with the process

ACT I SCENE 2
Employee meeting at the Hilton

TONIGHT'S INTRODUCTION

Before my engagement at the Hilton, I had received a cryptic and short phone call from Jake, my partner. The howling winds had masked his voice much of the time. He was trying to tell me good luck with the meeting and that conditions at sea were turning from bad to... Unexpectedly, his words crackled and then dropped off dead in mid-sentence.

I carried my concern for his safety with me while walking to the podium of the Hilton's largest conference room. At the lectern, I notice the main lighting is turned down several notches. In my new assignment as CEO, I am prepared to discuss major changes ATC is about to go through.

Standing at the lectern, the audience becomes quiet as I scan the seven-hundred-plus employees attending tonight's meeting while moistening my lips with the tip of my tongue...

"Good evening, everyone, I appreciate your attendance tonight. For some, I'm sure, it's been a great disruption for you and the family, so let's hope the fine dinner and your surrounding friends at your table help offset the inconvenience."

Applause sweeps over the audience...

After a long pause, I get everyone's attention...

"For those of you who don't know me, I'm Dakota Wells. Mr. Thanh Nguyen hired my firm, the Jake Jensen Group last week to improve the growth and financial stability of the company. Missus Nguyen and the Board of Directors have asked me to fill the position of CEO while Mr. Nguyen recuperates from his stroke. For those of you who are wondering about his condition, he is stable, but still in intensive care. I'm sure everyone wishes him a rapid recovery."

The audience stands in respect and applauds.

"Thank you. I'm sure Nina Nguyen and close friends appreciate your good thoughts and feelings."

With a noisy audience, I wait for it to settle down.

"Tonight, we will discuss our new future here at ATC... Now, with that said, we have a lot to cover, so I'll jump right in...

I'M OF THE OPINION THAT IDEAS ARE BORN TO FIT THEIR AGE, AND THIS IS THE AGE OF CHANGE FOR THE RIGHT REASON... Why change? Because we are not growing in our present economy, productivity is stagnating, and if we do not react, we will shrink in sales and size. When a company loses sales and has no recovery plan, it continues to decline.

There's a natural resistance to make a change, inevitably bringing with it fear of the unknown, self-interest and the need for security. Now, it is my pleasure to let you know everyone at ATC will contribute to the change and benefit from the change—these are not idle words; I mean everything I say...

To change businesses, governments, sports, science, or life, we must keep a broad outlook on our judgment level. Early judgment closes the mind to change... Ahh... This brings up a riddle I'd like to present to you...

What do our enemies in life, business competitors, or opposing teams in sports provide us?

...I ask you, the audience."

After a long moment, a young woman stands.

"Would that be a different perspective?" She said.

"Excellent, I'm impressed. These different views provide us with alternative images—but only if we have the vision and creativity to digest our surroundings and apply it to positive change...

We must blot out the use THEM and US in our conversations. The good guys versus the bad guys are a serious destructive force, making it an unhealthy way to look at the world. It speaks of a closed mind...

THEM and US come down to two things—are we going to live in this world together, or a world of THEM and US? More on this as it is our main subject matter for the first half of our meeting tonight...

We need mentors to keep out THEM and US from our thinking and conversations. The members of the Supreme Court, for example, each have their perception of how the outcome of a particular court case should be. They meet to discuss their views, with a few members, at times, trying to persuade others to think differently through a coalition or individual discussions. In the end, they vote on a decision.

They can agree to disagree, but seldom raise their voices in anger—albeit they can get passionate in their point of view. But, they do not call each other names or have a secret meeting to overcome the opposition. This is conduct every one of us could emulate, including, the Congress of the United States."

After receiving a pleasant response, I give the audience an appreciative nod and contemplate my next issue.

THE RIGHT VEHICLE FOR THE JOURNEY

"In tonight's journey, we will discuss the right vehicle for traveling into the future of business transformation. Our vehicle is a new *horizontal open-systemic architecture*, an architecture that will dramatically improve both *productivity* and *market growth*.

Without the right vehicle, we'll never get there. Unfortunately, with tonight's busy schedule leaves little time to explain the new architecture in depth. Nonetheless, I will try to describe the meaning of the keywords: *horizontal, open-systemic* and *architecture*.

I'll begin with the word *architecture*, which infers that the structure is of a specific nature. Jake Jensen being an architectural buff would say...

The architect designs a building by understanding the purpose and use of the building before planning the individual parts and their interaction with each other. After completing the drawings, the architect does not tell the contractors what to do but manages how they do things together...

This is a far cry from the formation and management of a vertical business organization... Architects would call our vertical business structures designed to serve utilitarian purposes, making them more banausic than inspirational.

Why do you suppose that is...?

Well, according to Dr. Russell Ackoff, an authority on system thinking who died at age 90, had thoughts about that. These are not his exact words, but his credence...

He believed business schools focus on the different functions within the organization such as finance, marketing, engineering, operations, and so on. How they should work as a system to improve customer perception and improve stockholder returns is not taught as the primary curriculum..."

I pause to browse the room seeing the audience taking an interest in this matter...

"*Horizontal* refers to a *process-driven architecture* that efficiently integrates with an open-systemic design. Essentially, everyone in the company works in subsystems, or as we call them, communities within the total system.

They also take responsibility for their processes and work at them in creative ways to improve both quantitatively and quality. This is accomplished without multiple layers of organization and being assigned specific tasks.

Open-Systemic is based on system thinking. We use the word *systemic* in place of the word *system* to put the emphasis on the idea that our actions can ripple through the system's organization by helping it or degrading it.

An open system, if you will, must survive within its environmental inputs. With a business organization, it takes in resources from its suppliers, banks, and investors...

To stay in business and grow, depends on excellent market perception compared to those of its competitors. To provide the level of perception required to its customers, the system depends on the system design and the interaction of its subsystems. It is the relationship and patterns of interaction of these subsystems that will reflect on them from outside their formal boundary, the customer. This is the employee reinforcement feedback loop that is received on a recurring basis that improves business-value.

This is unlike discrete departments being task-oriented in a vertical organization, even though, it can interact with external inputs and demands, but is unable to respond in kind.

The *open-systemic* part of the organization is the linchpin within the architecture. The normal organizational structure does not support this kind of behavior; as a result, we need to remove the old organization, it's the only recourse. Why is that…?

Because, the old organizations are task-oriented, and have hundred-fifty years of saying—this *is the way we have always done it*. If the organization is left intact, it becomes *them* and *us*, a fight that can have only one ending—the failure for the company to move in a positive direction.

It is *them* and *us*, which concerns me the most. I've given this topic serious consideration for discussion knowing this kind of conflict can have a devastating influence on our business environment and society.

The image of conflict that continues to trouble me time and again is the two different camps on global warming. With that in mind, I've prepared issues that created these two camps. By telling this story, which is rather lengthy, but critical, I'm confident we can leave behind the attitude relating to *them* and *us* during our business transformation…

By doing so, it will enable you to enrich your life and empower you to be the catalyst for a change of business as we know it today.

Before we get into global warming, I am going to make a quick comment on our last discussion for the evening—*Productivity*.

Software suppliers and consultants cover productivity improvement. They peddle every conceivable approach to improving productivity on the planet. Tonight, I will discuss impressive results in productivity gains over the last decade. With that said, I have serious issues with the reported productivity statistics, and with the effect information technology is contributing to productivity gains.

Why is productivity so critical? Well, it affects our individual *standard of living* and our overall economy. The ability of our current organizational structures to produce improved productivity is nearing the finish line.

The solution to the productivity problem is our new horizontal open-systemic architecture. Ah… Sorry. I'm getting ahead of myself. We'll discuss this in greater detail later in our second session on this subject."

After taking a glance at my notes, I continue…

GLOBAL WARMING, A BETTER THEORY

"Is there anyone in the audience who is not familiar with the *issues* of greenhouse gas global warming?"

After stepping away from the lectern, I wait for a response.

"Only the brain-dead wouldn't know about greenhouse gas causing global warming," yells out a guest bringing amusement from the audience.

"I didn't mean *heard* of global warming, but the *issues* that are at stake."

Numerous hands rise after I restate my question.

"As one can see, it's a complicated subject. The idea is to broaden your knowledge and make you aware of how our society polarizes the global warming weather system. Also, how it plays a role in how we respond to change in our own lives, and our own company.

One other thing I would like to emphasize... We're about to discuss a few dicey issues on global warming, and I'm not here to discourage anyone in his or her beliefs on the issue. It's about understanding *how to work together in solving system problems for the common good*. Okay, let's get started...

The Green movement emphasizes that energy waste in government, business, and our private lives can and should concern all, and I believe there is not a person here who would have an argument with that. It's how we deal with the main issues that become a problem which we will soon get into.

Polarization on any issue seldom moves you forward in solving the problem. IT IS NOW TIME FOR OUR NATION TO PROVE TO THE WORLD THAT A FLOURISHING ENVIRONMENT AND A STRONG ECONOMY CAN CO-EXIST. WHEN KNOWING THAT A GLOBAL WARMING GREENHOUSE ISSUE EXISTS, WE NEED NOT TREAT IT AS A BAD THING. IT SHOULD BE A CHALLENGING OPPORTUNITY FOR US TO USE AS A SPRINGBOARD TO ADVANCE OUR ECONOMIC POSITION IN THE WORLD. AT THE SAME TIME, WE CAN REDUCE OUR NEED FOR FOREIGN OIL AND THE WORLD'S CARBON EMISSION LEVELS...

With that said, there are long-standing policies by two camps: One is saying mankind is the cause of global warming and those who tell us it's a hoax...

Now, what I'm about to say will apply to every subject I'll be discussing tonight, remember it well...

WHEN ONE STANDS ON THEIR SOAPBOX WARNING THE WORLD OF OUR GLOBAL WARMING IS DUE TO GREENHOUSE GASSES CAUSED BY MAN, THEY SPEAK OF BUT ONE-FACTOR THEORIES IN A MULTI-FACTORED WORLD...

THEY OFTEN ENJOY GREAT POPULARITY, BUT LIKE MOST ONE FACTORED THEORIES, THEY EVENTUALLY TURN OUT TO BE WRONG...

THE REAL QUESTION IS NOT WHETHER THE EARTH IS WARMING, BUT WHICH OF THE MANY MULTI-FACTORS AND OR COMBINATION OF IT IS CAUSING ANY LONG-TERM RISE IN TEMPERATURE ON A GLOBAL SCALE AND HOW LONG WILL IT CONTINUE?

To carry forth this idea, these two extremes of THEM and US carry with it emotional positions that play no role in making good decisions. It amplifies why the terms THEM and US, negate the ability to make a change that will improve our environment. What's required of us is a common solution..."

I see a hand waving in the air...

"Please, let's hear your question..."

"Thank you, Miss Wells. This subject you're discussing tonight is most interesting. I've never understood why scientists make global warming so controversial..."

"There is one simple reason... Why is anything controversial? Well, people, but characteristically speaking, SCIENTISTS NEED SOMETHING TO ARGUE ABOUT..."

The audience has a good laugh.

"But then, the celebrities need to get their two cents in just making things worse. For instance, we have Leonardo DiCaprio explaining to us that there are more scientists who believe in global warming than those who disagree. That infers they must be right, and the others flat wrong. There are several problems with that statement.

Frederick Seitz, past President of the National Academy of Sciences, circulated a global warming petition among United States scientists. And his response was nineteen thousand two hundred signatures to debunk global warming. They included physicists, geophysicists, climatologists, meteorologists, and environmental scientists. The petition substance read:

There is no convincing scientific evidence that human release of carbon dioxide, methane, or other greenhouse gasses is causing or will, in the foreseeable future, cause catastrophic heating of the atmosphere and disruption of the Earth's climate.

And then, Dr. Arthur Robinson of the Oregon Institute of Science and Medicine announced: *More than 31,000 scientists had signed a petition rejecting the theory of human-caused global warming...*

There's more. But you get the gist."

In my discussion on this subject, KEEP IN MIND, THE QUESTION WE HAVE ABOUT GLOBAL WARMING... DO WE HAVE A SERIOUS *ABNORMAL* WARMING WEATHER CONDITION EMANATING A CONTINUED RISE IN OCEAN LEVELS THAT WILL CAUSE CATASTROPHIC CONDITIONS FOR OUR COASTAL REGIONS CAUSED BY GREEN HOUSE GAS?

To better understand the answer to that question, I'll refer to *The National Academy of Sciences, National Research Council, Board on Atmospheric Science and Climate* chart. I'll present it on the screen...

As you can see, it's illustrating lines of evidence of our global natural cycles over the last eight hundred thousand years...

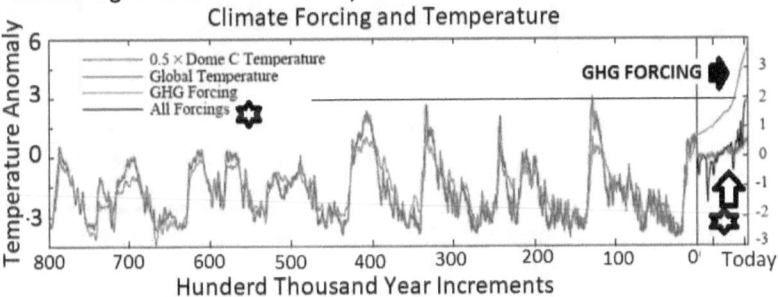

Notice the temperature peaks every hundred thousand years. And, please notice the current *ALL FORCING'S* noted with a star is evenly peaked with the previous one hundred thousand years—interesting point is it not...

Now, what in the world would cause such uniformity when it comes to measuring the weather? The answer is quite simple actually...

Every hundred thousand years the earth goes through an eccentricity, or a deviation of its circularity orbit causing the earth to become a more elliptical orbit. During the cycle, the greater the elliptic it becomes the less time during the period it spends near the sun. So, the planet receives less solar energy and cools down, and as it begins to warm again, it moves back closer to earth and ends after the hundred thousand year cycle.

We are now at the peak of one hundred thousand year cycle. Please notice how we have peaked during the current period when taking in the noted variables in the upper left corner of the chart. The biggest producer illustrates that Green House Gas has the biggest influence taking it a little off its norm...

Now, that sounds like pretty damning evidence GHG is the bad guy. But is it? Let's take a look at another chart by the U.S. Department of Energy and the summarization of the various concentrations of the atmospheric greenhouse gasses...

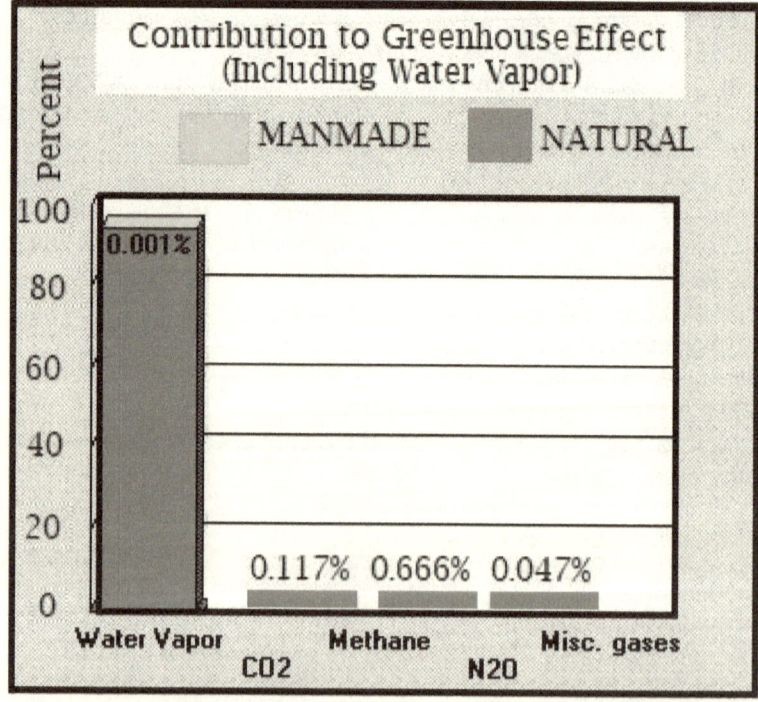

Just how much of the Greenhouse effect is caused by human activity...?

Well, please note the first bar in the chart shows water vapor alone contributes about ninety-five percent of the total, with manmade greenhouse gases noted at the top of each bar totaling zero point two seven eight percent."

I can see the audience is stunned by what I have just presented to them...

"I'll bet that got your attention, hey?

I would add, however, scientists are now battling out whether or not water vapor amplifies the CO_2 warming it produces. But let us not forget oversimplification can be very dangerous.

So, with this in mind, I'm going walk you through the various scenarios of THEM and US views of global warming to illustrate how such behavior is a lost cause by both sides.

GREENHOUSE GAS MODEL SIMULATION

"Greenhouse gas scientists say their models of global warming prove them right. Their one hundred year forecast spells out a global disaster. Now, ponder about this for a moment—system modeling science is only valid when you have inputs that are quantitative and measured for output.

Their hundred-year forecasts are using modeling global weather inputs with nonlinear activities that are chaotic, multi-factored, and dynamic. Let me mention an article from *Physics World* by physicist Bill Mitchell.

Global climate change has intrinsic difficulties in defining or measuring the mean global surface temperature.

How can you conceivably expect the outputs to be accurate? Especially, when the inputs cannot be measured with accuracy and the outputs cannot be verified."

No one spoke, coughed, or breathed. You could hear a pin drop as I break the silence...

"In principle, computer modeling is still in its infancy, a nightmare of complexity. Meaning, to model all the various notions causing the global warming issues requires a computer to measure the interaction at the molecular level of the chemistry going on over the entire globe. In other words, we'd need to know of the precise location of every air molecule at any given moment to simulate the primordial sea. Currently, an unheard-of capability requiring the ability to understand the laws of physics, motion thermodynamics, gravity, conservation of energy, and so on to re-create the bonds forming between every atom with a high degree of accuracy.

This kind of simulation would require a massive amount of processing capability way beyond any known computer we have today, or will have in the foreseeable future..."

I pause while looking at the audience with most looking slack-jawed...

"Not having ever heard what I just discussed with you, and when we find out a scientist makes a particular statement, we assume it must be true. It's difficult for us to grasp that science is subjective. When developing a study, the leeway is considerable, not to say scientists *stack the deck*, so to speak. But when they design a study that will in effect have a pre-determined outcome owing to one's need to have their findings published, are foremost in the scientist's mind when they should seek the truth, which is a far more difficult quest."

After taking a moment to let this sink in, I continued...

"Untested, unverifiable assumptions are not science, they're assumptions."

More silence, as the audience hunkers down.

"You won't buy a house without verifying that the house meets the levels of acceptance by a professional. You won't buy a business without the due diligence verification. Yet, many of us believe that a twenty or hundred-year forecast on global warming is accurate with no verification or hard science...

However, with you knowing the truth of our computer modeling capabilities in computing global warming issues, you'll think twice before accepting such forecast...

But when one does not have this understanding, and all they see and hear something long enough in great volume from the media, you soon become a believer. Each time you see anything that supports what you now consider is true reinforces your belief system.

Our news media often enlist themselves in moral crusades. By doing so, they create a good guy versus bad guy atmosphere that oversimplifies the problem at hand. However, it sells well.

When you have no alternative viewpoint on the global weather problem, how long can you *not* assume we have a catastrophic warming condition caused by *mankind*? Everything you read about global warming points to mankind being the cause.

The issue of mankind's global warming attracts people with agendas that produce slick documentaries. Al Gore's *Inconvenient Truth* tells of gloom and doom, and yet, he wins the *Nobel Peace Prize*...

Now, what do you think Mark Twain would have said about that?"

Moans followed by laughter circulate through the audience.

At this point, I offset the current disruption with a story...

"The Nobel Peace Prize reminds me of a story that Jake Jensen, my partner told me at dinner one night."

I pause as the audience settles down.

"Jake's father road fence as a cowboy in southern Texas when he was growing up, and there were two things a cowboy needed to survive the hardships of cow-punching. First, you required a good sense of humor. Second, be a great storyteller. Jake's father once told him about the story of a special chicken named Albert."

Taken' in the audience reaction, I notice the room is still as a caught breath with everyone anticipating the story...

"The story goes something like this...

Bo Diddley, a chicken rancher, had a couple hundred pullets (a young hen) and ten roosters... Any rooster not performing ended up in the soup pot. The rancher, being a little lazy comes up with the idea of putting different-sounding bells around the roosters' necks. This allowed him to sit on his porch, and from a distance, he could tell which rooster was performing, or not. Albert was his favorite rooster.

One day when testing the clanging of bells, he didn't hear Albert's bell. After investigating, he found all the other roosters with bells ringing chasing the chickens around the yard. To his surprise, Albert had his bell held in his beak to deaden the sound. He'd sneak up on a pullet to do his job and then amble on to the next one.

Bo Diddley was so proud of Albert; he entered him in the local County Fair. Overnight, Albert became a sensation. This resulted in the judges not only awarding Albert the 'No Bell Piece Prize,' but the 'Pullet Surprise' as well," I said with the beginning of a smile and my fingers in quotes."

A roar builds through the audience, along with a steady increase of cackles as I wait for them to settle down.

"Well, I thought you might enjoy that."

The audience responded with more applause.

"I'm hoping that makes up for any offense one may have taken about my Al Gore remark.

I'll say it again; our discussion is about polarized thinking in our society and, how we should solve a weather global system problem with creative thinking and a common goal.

Ah… So, where was I? Right… Why is it that the scientists who debunk greenhouse gas will never make a film? Well… The answer is they have no political agenda to satisfy or a leader who wishes to make headlines. Only the extreme side is at the forefront knowing that bad news sells…

With that in mind, raise your hand if you'd go to a movie with this title: *The Climate and nothing to worry about over the Next Hundred Years?"*

The audience has a good chuckle seeing no hands in the air.

THE EFFECTS THE OCEAN AND SUN HAVE ON THE WEATHER SYSTEM

"Well, strangely enough, there's little or no press coverage on the affect the oceans play in our earth's climate. The ocean system can jump from one stable mode to another within a decade. It has to do with the ocean currents, most often known as the *Ocean Conveyor*. Also, the level of salt content in any part of our oceans affects the system. The *La Nina* phenomenon is an example of how oceanic changes can affect the amount of precipitation that falls within a geographic region.

Australia, for instance, has experienced brutal drought conditions for years. The government blamed it on global warming—politics at its best…

And then in 2011, Australia had severe rainstorms, causing massive flooding. This is typical of the ocean doing its thing to the weather system that we refer to as La Nina—Southern Oscillation.

Then we had El Nino's effect on California going from drought to deluge. Global warming though got its share of blame during the long drought period.

The oceans and the atmosphere components intertwine in earth's climate system. Eighty-two hundred years ago, California's climate was similar to what it is today. And then with a sudden change, it took a steady course of intense winter storms and torrential rains for hundred fifty years.

Evidently, the massive glacial lakes in North-East America broke loose and poured enough freshwater into the Atlantic to cool and change the ocean's currents around the world...

Now, would you consider today's Greenhouse Gas scientist could have predicted such a change in their twenty through a one hundred year weather forecast in our multifaceted environment? Well, of course not. Now, you get my gist, hey?"

I watched the audience taking the seriousness of what I'm saying...

Our understanding of our ocean's dynamics is in its adolescence, relatively speaking. When we have a better understanding of this complex system, we can use the data in weather modeling, which will enhance the total weather system forecasting, well that is, someday, when we have the appropriate computing power.

If the ocean conveyor plays a major influence in the weather system and can jump from one mode to another within a decade; how would that affect global warming? Will it get colder, or maybe hotter? We flat don't know.

"Doctor Sami Solanki, director of the renowned Max Planck Institute for Solar System Research in Gottingen, Germany, thinks the sun is burning hotter over the last one thousand years. He also mentioned it has only been about hundred to hundred fifty years that the sun has increased in brightness...

Now, does that period sound familiar to you? It should. Greenhouse gas apparently contributed to global warming over the same period according to Greenhouse theorist. Now, could it be just a coincidence?"

Finishing with elevated eyebrows, I can see the audience reacting with intense interest as individuals re-adjust themselves in their seats...

"The increase in the sun's brightening theory measures the magnetic zones or sunspots on the sun's surface. A *beryllium 10* ice sample taken from Greenland goes back eleven hundred and fifty years that measures its activity over time. While the increase in magnetic energy from the sun increases, the beryllium 10 decreases.

Doctor Solanki's studies show *beryllium 10*, in effect, decreasing, which translates into the sun's increase in magnetic energy, along with hotter temperatures...

Let me count hands who didn't understand Doctor's Solanki's statement."

The audience seems complacent looking around seeing no hands and a few shrugs.

"Why is it then, the media doesn't discuss these matters? Do they regard this as much too complicated for us to understand? Evidently, they do, thinking it's not newsworthy?" I said.

The audience is silent.

Well, enough said on this topic."

With a breather, I glance at my notes before beginning the next topic...

THE UNSPOKEN ANOMALIES

"I thought you might enjoy hearing about the unspoke anomalies and their fascinating contribution to their share of greenhouse gas...

The U.N. Food and Agriculture Organization put out a report in April 2014 informing us that farming, forestry, and fisheries agriculture greenhouse emission have almost doubled over the last fifty years. Future estimates are indicating it may increase by another thirty percent by 2050.

To give you an idea of the noted greenhouse impact, I'd like to give you a sample of their report:

Per head, livestock can generate as much as twenty-five to thirty-five cubic feet of Methane emission every day...

Now, get this, it will blow you away, never hearing about this unspoken anomaly...

Its overall negative effect on the climate is twenty-three times higher than the greenhouse gas made up of carbon dioxide. They also say that the methane gas is responsible for eighteen percent of the total release of greenhouse gasses worldwide. This is more than the entire world's transportation, combined.

Synthetic fertilizers are the fastest-growing emissions sources of fertilizers having increased some thirty-seven percent since 2001.

Now, according to the Department of Energy chart you viewed, methane gas only represents zero-point six-six percent of the greenhouse total effect when including water vapor...

So, if the Department of Energy chart figures are correct, why not have the scientist from different camps come together and agree on how to collectively build on one opinion to approach the problem?

Well, PRIDE *and* DENIAL is your answer...

Now, one must find this fascinating why scientists with their intellectual opinion at stake, will respond with DENIAL of other studies that challenge their beloved views. Due to their PRIDE, they see nothing but flaws in these studies and ignore any fact if it doesn't fit their view...

There are global warming summits with well-intentioned bureaucrats and scientists from a hundred countries working themselves into a frenzy preparing papers warning the world of climatic disaster due to greenhouse gasses...

These climate change greenhouse gas theorist like to point to disastrous patterns such as Polar ice caps melting, the intensity of droughts and heatwaves, more hurricanes, the spread of disease, economic consequences, and the oceans become saturated with our emissions. But not mentioning these same cases are nothing new to planet Earth. The idea, of course, is to sell their side of the story with terrifying thoughts...

When indulging in your prejudice, it's not helpful when trying to understand how we get from A to Z. These summits are a waste of energy, no pun intended."

The audience shows their appreciation with gleeful chuckles.

"Meetings of this sort are nothing more than a *belief system* or CONSENSUS SCIENCE as opposed to rock-hard verified science—or to put in a more meaningful way, it's a bunch of diddly-squat science strengthening the idea of THEM and US..."

Again, a few more cheerful chortles roll over the audience.

"The term CONSENSUS SCIENCE comes from Michael Crichton who once said that global warming is nothing more than consensus science.

In other words, we have no debate—it's already established. These same scientists now say they are ninety percent sure global warming is caused by GHG emissions. Well, if the data were coming from consensus science, what would you expect...?

A few chuckles spring from the audience...

"This brings into question whether this is science or politics?

In prewar Germany, two hundred scientists said Einstein's theory of relativity was invalid. Hmm... One would have to say, based on consensus, Einstein must have been wrong..."

I pause for but a moment...

"This brings to mind what Jake told me about Kenneth Watt of UC Davis forecasting the coming of a new ice age, back in 1970. Glaciers had advanced and growing seasons had shortened around the world. He predicted that in the year 2000, the weather would be eleven degrees colder... By 1975, the scare was over.

Jake also mentioned Paul Ehrlich's 1968 book: *The Population Bomb*. Scientists were forecasting famine throughout the world. An opening quote out of Ehrlich's book: *The battle to feed humanity is over. In the 1970s, hundreds of millions of people, including Americans, will starve to death...*

Now, I don't know how many people read his book, but he got a great review from *Chicken Little*."

The audience was swept up in another joyful round of chortles...

"These two scares were nothing more than belief systems unchecked by verifiable science. Also, the news media added fuel to the stories, bad news sells... I believe it was Mark Twain who said...

Respect those who seek the truth, be wary of those who claim to have found it."

A lady yells out in her deep voice with a little gravel thrown in...

"Christ all mighty. This sounds like we're the mice, and the mad-scientist and news media are the Pied Piper."

The audience responds with applauding enthusiasm and gleeful laughter.

"What is your name?"

"Jenny."

"Well, Jenny, one can see you don't hold back on what you might be contemplating. I'm guessing if I want an honest opinion on how we're doing in the near future, you'd be my point person."

"Thanks, Ms. Wells. That would be me."

With a nod to Jenny, I continued...

"Getting back to our global warming conferences—why not have meetings that will provide both improved economics and environmental concerns...?

If they're done in a positive environment, they could be helpful by amplifying a message of awareness and give us a foothold, moving us in the right direction."

As they absorb that thought, I pause to assemble my next topic.

IS THE SKY REALLY FALLING?

I step back from the lectern, ponder a moment, do a two-step shuffle toward the lectern, click a computer image, and then with an animated adolescent voice...

"I've had my head stuck in the sand, so, is the sky really falling?"

My remark was followed by a hysterical boff from the audience.

I waited for a moment with a grin...

"To answer that question, I fossicked some interesting global weather information on the Arctic and Antarctica...

So, to bring us up to date in the South Pole region, a British Antarctic Survey research team focused on the Pine Island Glacier. It is one of the largest and most threatening in West Antarctica that appears to be retreating unrelentingly...

Apparently, this began with a large Pacific El Nino from 1939 to 1942, a precursor to the massive El Ninos seen in 1997 and 1998 and again in 2015 and 2016. These warmer events affected Antarctica's circumpolar deep water to move toward the glaciers responsible for West Antarctica by retreating glaciers.

With that said, let's take a look at NASA's 2015 studies showing that East Antarctica has been averaging zero point seven inches of ice thickening per year, enough to outweigh the losses from West Antarctica. Which means, the regions Antarctica climate conditions are not responsible for the change in warming, it's the Pacific El Nino warming the waters of West Antartica—an anomaly... Scientist still has the need to better understand regional declines in the Arctic as opposed those occurring in Antartica.

As you can see, we're still in our infancy in understanding climate change...

And yet, if one was to review the last Ice Age that hit Earth twenty thousand years ago, one might find a couple of interesting thoughts to consider. During this ice age that blanketed North America, glaciers had advanced and retreated over twenty times, and we have no understanding of the exact causes. But the likely results are the dynamic interaction of solar output, the distance between Earth and the sun, position, and height of the continents, ocean circulation, and the atmosphere composition...

In other words, one must keep an open mind and perhaps, consider these words of Robert B. Laughlin, co-winner of the 1998 Nobel Prize in Physics:

Six million years ago the Mediterranean dried up. Ninety million years ago, there were alligators in the Arctic. Three hundred million years ago Northern Europe was a desert, and coal formed in Antarctica. Climate change over geologic time is something the earth has done, without asking anyone's permission...

Who knows, but Laughlin's view on our current climate hysteria gives us something to consider when we ponder global warming.

It appears that when we feel passionate about a cause, we impose our belief on others such as Leonardo DiCaprio's climate change documentary, *Before the Flood.*

For you DiCaprio fans, I mean no disrespect... But he uses his star power to persuade others to believe that man is accountable for our current climate warming conditions. He doesn't discuss all the other possibilities that may induce any changes—that's Leonardo's pride and denial talking. Well, that and bad news sells...

Let's us not forget—THE CLIMATE IS NONLINEAR, DYNAMIC AND TURBULENT. To some, it seems to be random depending on how the course of events may develop. CLIMATE IS NOT MADE BY MATHEMATICALLY NEAT EQUATIONS PROJECTING IN A STEADY ENVIRONMENT OVER TIME and it's difficult to adequately understand what has happened in the past. IT IS SELF-ORGANIZED AND EVOLVING. THIS IS WHAT MAKES IT SO UNPREDICTABLE. MOREOVER; IT'S WHAT MAKES OUR WORLD SO BEAUTIFUL..."

IT MATTERS NOT

I take a deep breath and continue...

"I'm on my last leg of this discussion of THEM and US. This has been for some, I'm sure, a lot to take in for such a topic. But let me remind you, WITH THE EMPLOYEES HAVING AN ATTITUDE OF THEM AND US IN A COMPANY TRYING TO MAKE A CHANGE IN THE ORGANIZATIONAL STRUCTURE WOULD BE DISASTROUS. I can assure you; tonight's program will be with you for a long time for which your company transformation will benefit...

So, I'll finish up with *Cass Sunstein's* latest book that analyzes how polemical thinking or arguing for a particular position can feed on itself...

WHEN WE'RE WITH LIKE-MINDED PEOPLE, SOFT VIEWS HARDEN AND WE RESIST CHALLENGES TO OUR IDEAS AND BECOME DOGMATIC IN OUR VIEWS; HENCE, *GROUP POLARIZATION*: *THEM AND US.*

IT MATTERS NOT WHAT THE SCIENTISTS' SAY ABOUT COOLING OR WARMING OF OUR EARTH'S CLIMATE. THE REAL FACT IS WE HAVE NOT YET CRACKED THE CODE OF UNDERSTANDING HOW THE SUN, THE OCEANS, ANIMAL METHANE, AND MAN-MADE EMISSIONS AFFECT THE CLIMATE DURING THE EARTH'S HUNDRED THOUSAND YEARS ELLIPTICAL ORBIT.

If it were that simple, we wouldn't have so many scientists from so many fields of science standing on their soapboxes sounding off on their specific theories about climate change, or lack thereof.

So, let our scientific intellectuals strut their stuff like peacocks, and someday, in the far future, they will get it together, and for once, have a unified understanding of earth's climate...

UNTIL THEN, LET'S FOCUS OUR KNOWLEDGE AND ENERGY WHERE IT WILL DO THE BEST ON A QUEST FOR CLEAN ENERGY AND A ROBUST WORLD ECONOMY..."

I take a sip of water and step back out of the light with a bow. The audience responds with loud applause while I politely wait for them to settle in with a lazy smile.

Homing in on our final portion of the meeting, I stretch my back. Then resting my chin on the palm of my hand—not unlike Jack Benny, I ponder for a moment before stepping up to the lectern.

DISCUSSING THE BUSINESS CHANGE PROCESS

"Before we take our break and get into our next topic, we'll have a brief discussion on a macro view of the change or transformation process."

After taking a two-beat pause, I begin...

"You can throw the most advanced business practices and technology at our business structures and still only reap incremental changes. Why is that...?

That's because it lacks the creative part of the vision—the basic vertical organizational structure is still standing.

We haven't changed our command-and-control organization in over one and a half centenaries. When our cost is too high, we cut back a percentage of our *operating cost* developed by the financial people.

The exception to our current command-and-control would be the techie folks in a few of the more liberal, software companies. Sometimes, they have gone to the other extreme of little or no organization: Everyone is an associate. Engineers rule.

We spend billions of dollars on *manufacturing* tools, software for process analysis, system analysis, and product processing. We use these tools to make micro improved performance in the manufacturing area that only represents five to twenty percent of our total operating cost...

Nothing wrong with this investment, except the business office personnel function as they did in 1950, except for computers that brought us up to the 1980s. The only thing different in new software applications has been minor bells and whistles, giving us little if any productivity increases.

Improving manufacturing operations has been with us since the Industrial Revolution. During that period, overhead functions were a minor part of the total cost. By the 1960s, that trend reversed. We haven't yet recognized the business as a total system, and the whole system must be evaluated for system process improvement."

While looking around the room, I see ants in everybody's pants.

"Now that we've finished with this part of our discussion, calls for a brain-teaser..."

This caught their attention...

"When nearing the Ranch after returning from a horseback ride, the horse goes faster and faster until it becomes difficult to control. Why is that...?

Well, it's because the horse knows it's at the end of the ride and it will soon drink water and enjoy its oats, so, let's take a fifteen-minute break..."

They responded with rousting gleeful chuckles from the audience.

"Please be back at half past the hour."

Still standing at the lectern with my laptop in front of me, I'm distracted for a moment as the room plunges into an invisible wall of noise. It permeates the air with seven hundred people getting up, stretching, and then moving toward the restrooms and lobby.

A shiver goes up my spine while opening my laptop. With fearlessness, I click on the Internet and then check the Atlantic Ocean weather off the coast of West Africa.

A moment later, I gasp ... and then with but a whisper...

"Oh my God... Gale force winds up to eighty knots."

Feeling a hot flash flow over my body, I contemplate the extreme danger that Jake and Toni are in.

ACT I – SCENE 2
ENHANCING THE LEARNING PROCESS

This scene covers a lot of territory; therefore, let's narrow it down.

Question 1
How would you best describe the new organizational architecture and its advantage over the vertical organization?

Question 2
The author uses global warming as a method to illustrate the destructive power of *them* and *us*.

Was the author's example a good one, if so, why? What are a few other thoughts that might be used to convey this idea of *them* and *us?*
Why is this topic so central to the storytelling of transforming a company?

ACT I SCENE 3
Meeting Davy Jones

WEEK 2 – DURING DAKOTA'S SPEECH AT THE HILTON, JAKE JENSEN, AND HIS CREW ARE EXPERIENCING A GALE FORCE STORM SOMEWHERE IN THE ATLANTIC.

    A gray sky bleached by sunlight spotted the horizon with flashes of blue. Sailing in fair winds and a following sea, *Sophi,* a fifty-two-foot ketch would lift her stern running up a swell and then plunge into a deep valley. She cut a white foamy path through the trough before cresting the peak of the next wave.

    In this seemingly infinite ocean, her assembly of wood and fiberglass looked like a spot of micro-marine-life floating several miles above the ocean floor.

    At the helm during an early morning watch stood Antonio Garcia. He signed on with Jake Jensen in Barcelona, Spain to crew on Jake's freshly acquired boat to Jamaica. For the last five years, Antonio occasionally sailed on this boat for the previous owner. So, when Jake asked him if he wanted to tag along and crew for him, he accepted. The offer was a good one, monetarily, and he had a senorita friend who lives outside of Kingston Harbor, their destination.

    The ship's bow cut a path through the deep blue ocean swells showing caps of white foam on their shoulders as walls of water lifted her hull letting her dance to a buoyant tune with such a breeze.

    With Sophi's deck rolling from the undulating seas Antonio is checking her sails and scanning for a rogue wave as would an Indy 500 driver checks his surroundings. The warm breeze felt good on his bare sun-browned skin as he breathed in the scent of salt spray tasting the damp saltiness of it on his tongue. At times, with the wind being right, he could smell the nauseating trace of coiled hemp rope offset with the aroma of fresh-brewed coffee coming from below deck. Their time at sea up to this point had been fair winds following the direction of the sea. Since yesterday, they had been receiving storm weather reports with whole gale winds of up to eighty knots heading their way.

Until about an hour ago, they were still sailing high-wide-and-handsome on the open sea. Sophi's crew is trying to out-run the storm at less than ten knots, even with a stiff wind, but a hopeless endeavor indeed.

As Antonio swept the horizon as the sun came up, bringing with it a red sky, warning them of the leading edge of a frontal system soon to be on them. When out at sea like this, he finds it difficult to believe anything else covered the earth's surface other than the never-ending sea. It's in this environment that has taught him the insignificance of humans on the planet Earth.

Gradually, off in the distance, the red sky good to it word brings a mass of dark clouds forming on the horizon like the head of a black viper. Its impartial threat just as deadly was preparing to strike with its venom, creating death and destruction sending them to Davy Jones' Locker.

Davy Jones, according to seagoing sailors presided as the overseer of evil spirits of the deep. You would find him spasmodically perched among the rigging on the eve of gales, hurricanes, and other disasters. When sea-faring men eyed his presence, it became a warning of death and disaster.

As kids, Antonio and friends used to tie bandanas around their heads, wear their mothers' hoop earrings, carry wooden swords and walk the plank over a wading pool. During such times, they would sing Captain Hook's song about walking the plank...

The crew knew where the storm was coming from, how fast, and a description of its behavior. With that in mind, the men gave the boat the once-over, including the engine, pumps, sails, and rigging. Accomplishing that, they sealed and double-checked their hatches again.

Antonio met with Jake and his long-time friend Toni to discuss how they should best engage the storm. Based on wind and sailing conditions, their strategy was to begin by reefing—pulling in—the mainsail or dropping it altogether and then sailing under their jib and mizzen. If things got worse, even after a double reefing, they would go bare poles before the wind and sea, using only their diesel engine. They knew controlling their speed would be critical and figured that a three to the five-knot range would help them keep good steerage. But at some point, they expected to accelerate down the face of a huge wave at fifteen plus knots. If they attacked the wave at the correct angle, they should be able to keep the craft under control.

When driving a boat down a giant wave, it can be like riding a surfboard, with one little exception, it's a hell of a lot more dangerous. Taken' it straight down would bury the board or boat in the trough of the wave. The surfer can end up being sent head-over-heels and then laugh it off to try again. The boat is another matter. There's a good chance it would pitch-pole, somersaulting it into the wave, fill with water, and then sink like a sea anchor—and you along with it.

When you drove the boat at too great an angle across and down the wave, the boat could roll over on its side and be ripped apart by tons of water. Then the obvious happens—you'll die.

So, to hopefully survive such a maneuver, one needed the skill to surf down the face of each wave at the correct and precise angle. Only serving time at sea in gale conditions can one learn the skill to navigate such a maneuver. If not, but having spent enough time at the helm and understood the execution, you might get the hang of it—if you survive long enough. They were fortunate the entire crew had the appropriate experience to carry out this subtle tactic in helmsmenship.

They discussed keeping the breaking crest of the wave on their windward quarter. Should a crest rise over the ketch, the helmsman can head the ship straight down the wave toward the bottom of the trough. But the crew needs to keep their fingers crossed trusting the wave would decline to shit on or pitch-pole them.

How long they could continue to steer before the wind depends on upon their seamanship and knowledge of the sea. Owing to the exhausting demand at the helm, they changed watch every thirty minutes and kept a dry cabin with prepared hot thermoses of soup and coffee. This was a necessity during the upcoming conditions.

With the wind running at twenty-five knots, they suited up in their foul weather gear, life vests, and safety harnesses. They are now prepared for what Mother Nature had in store for them and pulled in the main and double-reefed the jib and mizzen sails. The seasoned crew gives it their best and dig deep into their reservoir of strength to see them through. But, they need a certain amount of luck to play a major role in the outcome.

Later, the sky turned dark as though a large shade had been pulled to cover the sunlight. The temperature took a drastic drop bringing with it icy rain lashing the deck as lightning penetrates the blackness with its jagged brilliant light. Now that the storm is showing its muscle, Jake and Toni came out on deck again. Jake yells at Antonio to fire up the diesel engine while they pull in both the jib and mizzen sails to run under bare poles.

It wasn't long when Antonio senses the extreme pressure exerted on his palms from the helm, and the increased angle of the deck beneath his feet. He can hear the rush of water sliding along the hull creating a vibration in the rigging. The stress continues to ratchet up. The forces of the storm intensify the trimming of the boat. He is now an integral part of the vessel, bodily grappling with its demands and the limits to which he can push her.

The fury of the storm engulfs them as rain falls from pitch-black clouds so close you can touch them. Then, a sudden force of the wind sends the rain in like a thousand horizontal fire hoses. Antonio feels the cold water driving into his nose, ears, and eyes trying to physically send him off into the foaming sea.

In these conditions, Jake demands that the crew wear the orange survival suit anytime they were out on deck. Even so, Antonio felt chilled to the bone, believing the whole world was now a churning sea of water.

With the storm reaching gale force-velocity and winds of sixty-five and eighty plus knots, the high winds created long waves spanning four-to-five hundred feet between peaks. Spindrift froth is running along the surface of the waves in a churning angry way. They're surfing at much greater speeds than expected, up to twenty knots in the sixty-five foot plus high waves if measured from trough to peak. Not bad, considering they had a maximum hull speed of twelve knots—Sir Isaac Newton at work.

Owing to Sophi's excessive speed, her masts became just about horizontal as she raced with her bow angled toward the bottom. Only a skilled crewmember at the helm can keep them from ramming her nose under the water and pitch-poling em'.

Toni comes out on deck to tell Antonio he's going to rig a dragline to slow the boat using a double anchor line and a lunch-hook, and reminds him to keep an eye on it. It may not work and fly back on board the boat.

With a half-dozen waves behind them, Antonio turned in time to see the lunch-hook clawing at the air coming back at *Sophi*. It scarcely missed him and landed in the cockpit. Not long after the incident, having heard the anchor landing on the deck, Toni came out of the cabin, looked at the anchor, then Antonio.

Antonio gave him a fearless smile and yelled...

"I believe the *little bugger* got scared out there."

Toni made a slight nod then goes below. A short time later, he comes out on deck with a one-inch nylon anchor rope. Weighted at one end is a spare sea anchor with a heavy plow. He secured the loose end then threw the hefty anchor into the sea. It created a sheet of spray as though it were a distressed water-spirit. Toni watched it for a moment as it trailed behind the stern. Now that it reached its depth, the heavy weighted taut line seemed to register a one-knot decrease in their speed.

Shortly after Toni's rig slows the surfing speed, Antonio looks down at the helm's glowing digital clock telling him it's almost time for Jake to relieve him from his watch. The waves are rising, and the wind velocity is getting unbearable in the open cockpit of the helm. The rain and wind ripped at his eyes as though needles were being driven into his face.

In the last two hours, the waves have turned from black to black with white streaks capped with white tiger teeth as spindrift blew off the waves. It didn't take long when the sea turned frothing white, creating a startling contrast to the blackened sky. The strain on his hands, arms, and legs become unbearable due to the extreme pressure at the helm trying to keep the boat out of danger. He had read historical novels about the huge ships of the line during a storm taking eight helmsmen at the double wheel of such vessels as *HMS Victory* to keep it under proper steerage.

He now found himself at the crest of a *monster* wave, then looks down and sees they must be at least seventy-five to eighty feet above the trough of the wave. It has the appearance of looking down from an eight-story-building.

"Oh Mother, Mary of God," he said morosely to himself—being the good

Catholic. He can't even cross himself, even if he wanted to. To do so, he'd need to pry his frozen hands from the helm which would be a fatal error. Such a move would cause the wheel to spin violently out of control and their rudder to lose steerage.

As they slide down the wave, Antonio loses control of the helm due to the high velocity of the fast-moving wave. The cabin door struggles open, and a flash of light briefly douses his night vision.

With partial vision restored after the cabin door closes, he sees Jake yelling something. But he can't hear him due to the scary, screaming wind, and the enormous roar of the waves. Again, Jake screams as Antonio focuses on his mouth and the look on his face when he points over Antonio's head at the wave. Antonio turns his head to see the crest of the wave rising over them. He knew it would finish them, pitch-poling the boat over and slamming her down on her mast. Even with the heavy nylon line streaming taut from her stern as though tied to the pier, it was not enough to stop her acceleration.

Looking back at Jake, he sees him attaching his six-foot-long web strap from his body harness to one of the numerous large metal rings located at strategic places around the boat. The clip is a sturdy spring-loaded hook called a carabiner most often used by mountain climbers.

Antonio is finding it difficult to breathe in the water-laden air as he gulps and gasps for oxygen, feeling stunned by the sheer volume and frigid temperature of the water cascading over them.

With the rain turning to hail in the high-velocity wind, it gouges at his eyes and rips at his flesh until blood washes down his face.

He sees Jake moving his hand straight down, emulating a German Stuka dive-bomber screaming to earth. He was yelling something, as Antonio watched his mouth form the words, "Straight down." He nodded his head acknowledging Jake's order while shouting... "Si si, *Capitán*," then fearlessly fights to reposition the rudder.

Jake struggles to get to him.

Ultimately, Antonio positions their rudder into neutral knowing this will take them into a straight descent into the depth of the valley of death to meet Davy Jones.

ACT I – SCENE 3
ENHANCING THE LEARNING PROCESS

If you didn't get seasick after reading this scene, consider yourself a seasoned sailor.

Question 1
When the storm intensified why did they run with bare poles?

Question 2
Why did Jake order Antonio to steer the boat *straight down* into the valley of death, to meet Davy Jones?
Why would this concept be essential in business strategy?

Question 3
What would you do if given such an order?
Be specific in your answer of either why you would or would not have executed the order.

ACT I SCENE 4
Meeting at the Hilton

WEEK 2 – LATER, FRIDAY NIGHT AFTER THE BREAK, DAKOTA'S SUBJECT IS PRODUCTIVITY

My watch says it's half past the hour. I sweep a gaze across the audience to see everyone is back and settled, so taking a deep breath...

"Thanks for being so prompt. I was reflecting on what a great audience you've been tonight, realizing what a pleasure it will be to work with you over the upcoming months..."

Finishing with an incandescent smile, I receive a nice response...

"With that said, let's get into our next topic for tonight ... productivity."

THE PRODUCTIVITY DISCUSSION

"Now... I know that *productivity* may not have the same emotional impact on you as our previous topic, but it should keep you riveted, nonetheless."

I hesitate with a subtle smile...

"I know what you're thinking...

Oh please, PRODUCTIVITY a riveting subject?"

I waited for the laughter to settle down.

"We all know what the word productivity means, but other than that, it has little relevance to most of us. But when you leave tonight, you'll understand the implication it is having on you and our nation, and the significant role it plays in our growth and profitability for your company.

Now, to get you in the right frame of mind, I'm going, to begin with, quotes from Princeton economists William J. Baumol and Paul R. Krugman. William J. Baumol, co-authored *Productivity and American Leadership,* and here is what he had to say about productivity...

It can be said without exaggeration that in the long run probably nothing is as important for economic welfare as the rate of productivity growth.

To further, emphasize my point, Paul R. Krugman in *The Age of Diminished Expectations* wrote...

COMPARED TO THE PROBLEM OF SLOW PRODUCTIVITY GROWTH, ALL OUR OTHER LONG-TERM ECONOMIC CONCERNS—FOREIGN COMPETITION, THE INDUSTRIAL BASE, LAGGING TECHNOLOGY, DETERIORATING INFRASTRUCTURE, AND SO ON—ARE MINOR ISSUES...

As you can see, this discussion is a vital topic, and yet, there is little mention of the seriousness of the productivity problem in either the business world or the news media. However, I'm here tonight to tell you, we as a nation are moving at a declining rate of productivity, now and in the future. Why is that? Well, let's begin with the standard of living.

THE STANDARD OF LIVING

To define the standard of living, you'd say it's one's wealth, comfort, material goods and necessities available within a geographic area and influenced by inflation.

Now, to broaden that picture a little let me address the positive influence on our standard of living. I'll begin with illegal and then legal immigrants... I know, for some, illegal immigrants are fighting words."

I finish with a passing smile.

"From the standpoint of anyone's belief system, I'm not here to change those thoughts—the subject is too full of landmines...

But, what I'd like to point out is the influence these workers have had on improving the overall standard of living for most Americans. You may then compare this positive information to that of what you consider being negative and form your own opinion.

ILLEGAL IMMIGRATION

When removing the illegal immigrants working at tasks most Americans would rather leave to someone else, could leave a vacuum of labor to contend with. These tasks include restaurant dishwashers, cleaning houses and high-rise buildings, and labor-intensive agricultural work.

They do not compete in the higher-skilled types of jobs with United State citizens. To replace these workers would be a daunting task, therefore, causing chaos in services and agricultural output.

For instance, in Brewster, Washington, farmers will tell you that Americans picking apples are so rare that asking them to replace the Mexican labors is a fantasy.

The trained apple picker can work at a rate earning them about a hundred and twenty dollars a day, and yet, Americans will not apply for these jobs. It's hard work and long hours to earn the pay, but for the Mexicans, it's a fortune.

One would say why not pay more and hire Americans? Well, like most businesses, we must work in a competitive world. Apples from Chile and China keep prices down. To keep prices competitive, apple farms must survive on small to medium margins. This is but an example of how people coming from south of the border help in keeping down the cost of living in the United States.

I'm sure there are those who worry about illegal immigrants flooding our country. However, I would ask you to imagine that our country as a large *buffer* zone that expands and contracts for these illegal immigrants.

Our country's ties with Mexico are an integral part of our economy. When our economy expands, there is a demand for low-wage Mexican immigrants...

When the economy shrinks, illegal border crossings decrease, and at some point, there is an exodus until the *system* balances again... We'll see a chart showing a drastic reduction in border crossing in a moment...

To help explain the reduction in border crossings, the Mexican government undertook an aggressive contraception campaign by setting up family-planning centers across Mexico during the 1970s. According to World Bank figures, the fertility rate in Mexico has declined from six-point seven children per woman, down to two point one. This is near a nation's replacement level—or a static position. Mexico expects to continue at a declining birth rate while their economy makes gradual improvements.

From 1995 to 2007, GDP grew by three point seven percent per year. Then from 2007 to 2009, Mexico did not fare well during the Great Recession, but some economic growth resumed in 2010.

I'm now going to show you a chart illustrating how Mexico's declining birth rate and their GDP growth has made a huge influence on Mexican citizen's no longer having the need to cross our borders as they once did. Here's another bit of an amazing story I'm sure none of had heard anything about...

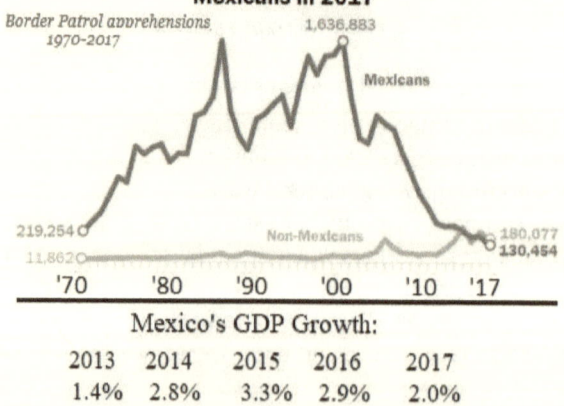

More U.S. border apprehensions of non-Mexicans than Mexicans in 2017

Mexico's GDP Growth:

2013	2014	2015	2016	2017
1.4%	2.8%	3.3%	2.9%	2.0%

The audience let out a big gasp when seeing the chart...

As you can see, Mexico's illegal aliens crossing the border will become a mere trickle compared to the past. However, non-Mexicans are now becoming a major story in the headlines with people leaving Central and South American countries like Venezuela coming to us needing asylum. But they are a very small percentage when compared to previous crossings, and those who are refugees seeking asylum should be processed according to U.S. immigration law, a legal obligation to provide protection who qualify as refugees.

Eventually, if we stop and kind of legal or ill legal crossing to a point of almost no crossings, over time, it will leave us with a severe vacuum of people willing to take the unwanted jobs we citizens refuse to take, increasing our cost of living. Immigration needs reforming; THEM and US will not solve the problem.

John Steinbeck once said... *We had come to fear a man with a hole in his shoe.* How true that is...

LEGAL IMMIGRATION

Now, for legal immigrants... The United States attracts fifty-plus percent of the world's educated immigrants, compared to Europe's five percent, with both Japan and China at zero percent. In January 2004, our Congress capped the number of annual visas to sixty-five thousand, with the idea, their legislation would save jobs for U.S. citizens.

With that in mind, let's review the following evidence showing educating and hiring foreigners can contribute to domestic job creation...

UNESCO reports that students born outside the United States continue to account for a substantial portion of U.S. science and engineering degrees. Of all the PhDs in engineering, mathematics and computer sciences, foreign students account for about fifty-five percent of doctoral degrees...

Now ... how can Congress overlook these incredible results when comparing American student body to the small band of those born outside the US?

Another amazing case in point is that forty percent of the Fortune five hundred companies were founded by immigrants or their children. Regrettably, when foreign students graduate and become ready to work in a business environment, our government denies their visas, prohibiting employment, and needlessly constraining our economy.

One would think our bicameral Congress with the upper and lower house falls into the category of *Dumb and Dumber—"*

Hearing the name of that crazy movie brings out cheerful chuckles.

"Susan Hockfield President of the Massachusetts Institute of Technology points out... *Eight of the nine winners who shared in the Nobel Prizes for chemistry, physics, and medicine are American citizens... Of the eight, four of the Americans came from outside of the United States.*

Hmm... Maybe I'm too kind to Congress. So, let me bring to light that we've been a democracy for over two centuries, and in all that time, the lunatics are still running the asylum...

These words brought out a loud burst of applauding and laughter.

I wait a moment with a mischievous smile...

"Ah, back to Susan. She further notes...

That of the thirty-five young innovators recognized in the 2009 Technology

Review magazine for their exceptional new ideas, only six had a high school education in the United States... Moreover, MIT foreign-born graduates alone have founded an estimated two thousand three hundred and forty active U.S. companies employing over one hundred thousand people.

And nationwide, she has this to say...

Immigrant-founded companies produced fifty-two billion dollars in sales, with a workforce of four hundred and fifty thousand.

So, with these pettifoggin' Congressmen *who don't get it, the others are missing the point* that a small group of immigrants is producing hundreds of thousands of jobs—"

I'm interrupted again by applauding and laughter...

"And yet, they continue to muddle on speculating they're saving jobs—"

Again, applauding and laughter come from the audience...

I pause for the moment before moving on...

"Our nation rides on the shoulders of businesses—nevertheless, almost half of Congress consists of lawyers who disproportionately apply unneeded regulatory compliances on small business.

These *nothingburger legal eagles* in Congress, I'm sure, could stand up and first-degree me to death, and convince a jury I'm out of my mind and should be put away. But much of what I say forms on the side of the truth."

I pull away from the lectern with conviction in my smile.

The enthusiastic smiling audience stands and applauds, bringing everyone to their feet as I wait them out before continuing...

"Another point on immigration is our need for new blood. Our ratio of birth to death rates will decline to a point where we would have fewer workers to offset the growing population of the retired. Our birth rate was one percent higher in 2007 when compared to 1975, with a death rate improvement of seven percent. Apparently, this trend will continue...

Let's look at a chart showing the world population declining growth rate in millions going into 2100. In other words, the world population continues to grow, but then the rate of growth moves downward at a fast clip.

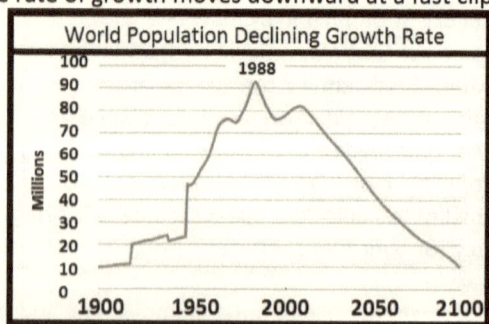

In 2016, the US population increased by only point seven three percent, representing two-point four-five million people, with the help of about one point five million legal immigrants—which will continue to shrink at a faster rate. The population will eventually decrease to the point that certain asset values will decline, particularly, housing prices as demand shrinks. But by then, most of us will have moved on to *Marble Town*."

My colorful remark brings chuckles and smiling faces...

LET'S KEEP OUR HEAD ABOVE WATER

"Now, let's move on to our box retail stores that help improve living conditions for many. These stores import inexpensive items for the average income worker and the less financially fortunate. Some would say Walmart is ruthless, but it supplies one point five million jobs, which pump additional money into the economy. It also accounts for about two percent of America's GDP. Costco has a different business model than Walmart. Costco pays higher wages owing to a wealthier customer base that buys higher-margin goods and in bulk, translating into a higher point of sale per square foot. A demographics showing up as one-tenth the size of Walmart...

Today, we depend on two-income families to prop up the income levels for increased spending, with the added benefit of helping our economy... I would add, if the new President in 2017 adds a big tariff on incoming goods from Asian countries, Wal-Mart and Costco would have to raise prices, resulting in a heavy burden for U.S. buyers, especially, those who can least afford it, therefore, dealing out a lower standard of living...

The biggest improvement in the US living standard had to do with the climbing valuation of our homes. Our property value is like a stunt plane climbing and grasping at the thinning air with its propeller to pull it higher. When the stunt plane reaches its limitations, there is a sudden reversal, and it plunges back down toward earth. With a stunt plane, however, it can pull itself out of the dive. It's under control, as opposed to the housing market that can get out of control and then make a monstrous *kaboom* delivering a heavy blow to the rest of the economy.

The last time the housing market crashed, the Federal Reserve stepped in and recapitalized the banks through quantitative easing, shoveling in almost five trillion dollars by the end of October 2014. Being banks, they used this leveraged money to drive up the stock market two hundred percent from 2009 to 2014, as opposed to lending the money back into the system...

Now, getting back to our subject, I would say these and other such contributors in the past gave us a breather. But we can't continue on this path, for it won't be long, and we'll have reached our limitation of treading water trying to keep our standard of living from taking us to a place we don't want to go. Why is that...?

Well, to raise our standard of living, we must, I repeat, we must revive our level of productivity. A topic we will discuss next."

I take a sip of water, the wonder drug while studying the audience.

PRODUCTIVITY BASICS

"In economics 101, we were taught that whatever enables a person to produce more in a given time can boost productivity. When measured as an individual task, this is true.

But measuring productivity in a business system is a different story. When the system output changes due to a delay in throughput, the productivity goes down. And yet, individual productivity can show improvement.

Meaning, no matter how well individual productivity shows big gains, it plays no part in a company's overall productivity output. When the employees are working at high efficiency and then have a constraint in the system output, the system will not produce improved productivity gains...

Productivity is enhanced by good system design that removes as many system delays or constraints as possible to improve throughput.

With that said, we in the United States have heard about a continuing rise in productivity. The government measures the gain in hours worked to the value gained for goods output. Therefore, if the hours worked gained were two percent and the output of goods was three percent, the gain in productivity would be one percent...

When measuring your business, you'll need to use earned hours measured against the goods shipped from a previous period. To broaden the picture, let's review a company with a fixed service cost contract. When developing the system processes, the number of employees is established. For a fixed cost service company, the productivity readings and profit will be flat. That's because, no matter the output, the income stays the same. Now, with our current understanding of productivity as many economists would have us believe, why have we continued to see productivity continue to rise?

As a hand rises, I nod toward the employee.

"That would have to be due to Information Technology."

"Thank you; I appreciate your fine response."

With a moment of pause, I scanned the audience...

"With that productivity topic in mind, we'll cover IT next."

INFORMATION TECHNOLOGY

"We have been using sophisticated computers and IT software for over a decade. But to the best of my knowledge, there is nothing new in technology that allows us to decrease our workforce and keep the same output. Worst yet, profits cannot find any wiggle room to grow. The high cost of IT sucks out any profits with its depreciation, updating hardware and software, IT employee payroll and benefits, office space, and annual support cost at twenty-two percent of the purchase price...

To best describe business productivity problems, let me quote from memory Paul A. Strassmann's book, *Information Productivity*...

When one examines the vast disproportion between the top-ranking U.S. industrial firms, in terms of Information Productivity and the bottom foot-draggers, one finds that a large percentage of organizations are not productive.

Furthermore, Strassmann said: *Corporations' information technology costs have been rising faster than wages and salaries. The ratios of information management costs to profits and assets under management have continued to show a remarkable decline...*

In other words, for over a decade, IT has delivered little productivity to the major firms around the world.

This is what Jake Jensen has this to say concerning this subject...

The truth is... Advanced software systems replaced manual systems over the last four decades... At this point in their evolution, these technologies are now, a substitute or duplicate of the same technology with applications enhancements, refinements, and bells and whistles...

Meaning these killer apps have run out of steam."

After the audience has digested Jake's thoughts, I continued...

"As Jake alluded to, these IT refinements do not make for greater productivity improvements. For instance, Enterprise Resource Planning software, the main engine that drives most manufacturing firms hasn't changed its MRP I inventory and scheduling engine system since its inception in the late 1960s. Well, other than upgrading and renaming it MRP II.

Then we have a new fax and copy office machine with the new touchpad screen requiring eleven steps to send a fax document with confirmation. Now, compared to the ten-year-old version with the same capability, but without a touchscreen, took three steps. Now, that's progress in the wrong direction... But, I must admit, the tech look reminds me of my beloved touchpad phone."

I sweep the audience seeing shaking heads with understanding smiles...

"Now, let's move along to logistics technology software. This application of software has been one of the key drivers of productivity for retail and manufacturing. Its design enhances the throughput of goods and services with faster response to customer demands and improves the ratio of labor to sales.

Today's logistics software, more or less, has now reached its limitations. In the future, computers will become faster, but not significantly any friendlier.

This wonderment in IT is no longer helping the employee or business to achieve improved throughput... In high-value companies, engineers have now identified, designed, manufactured, and installed most of the tools that work with and enhance the IT systems.

Now, the only advancements available are little more than a repackaged new look and perhaps a bit faster—but much like the annual design changes for the automobile industry. The car will still only drive you from point A to point B. So, without a change in the systems organizational architecture, you cannot continue to overcome the lack of good system processes by just refining the system with information technology. Now, aside from our IT discussion, does anyone have additional thoughts on why productivity continues to *theoretically* rise?"

DOWNSIZING

After a long moment, an employee yelled, "Downsizing."

"Thank you, sir," I said, acknowledging the man in the front row. "You're right, downsizing will change the ratio of employee to sales...

The word *downsizing* is an overused buzzword spin for layoffs that seldom bring a positive response to the profit ratio...

But it will bring an adverse effect on the business and employees caught in the cutback. But consider this..."

I pause for but a moment.

"How can a company stabilize the current system by removing a portion of the employees to improve cash flow, and yet, keep the business performance at the same level of output and quality?

To best answer that dilemma, let's use the internal combustion engine as a system illustration for improving the fuel economy...

We'll begin by removing a spark plug wire... Having done that, I ask you... Will it improve the mileage?"

When browsing the audience, I only see shrugs.

"The answer, of course, is no. Your fuel economy will get worse because the other cylinders are doing *extra duty*...

On the other hand, if the engine is designed to improve gas mileage when one or more cylinders are not participating, the gas mileage will improve...

Okay, let's be moving on to our next subject."

HAS PRODUCTIVITY BEEN IMPROVING?

I pause a moment to moisten my lips while glancing at my notes...

"We now need to ask the question... Will our productivity, unquestionably, be improved if we contract out certain manufacturing tasks and cut back on personnel?

To answer that question, let's walk through a hypothetical gain...

The first step is to measure the hours worked. In this case, previous period hours worked compared to the current period hours worked showed a *two percent gain*...

For step two we compare the difference for earned shipment hours measured against the previous period hours that result in a net gain of two point five percent...

The last step is to subtract hours worked from earned shipment hours, resulting in a point five percent gain...

Well, so far, it looks good. Mathematically, the results show productivity gain by subcontracting the assembly work. But is the end result correct?

I see shrugs and a few shaking furrowed brows.

"Let's walk through the event....

When contracting out the labor, and then laying off personnel, does not make for a productivity gain. It's a theoretical cost reduction—and that's a maybe... How can this be?

Well, to realize a cost reduction, you'd have to compare what you'll be paying for contract prices to the standard cost buildup, WITHOUT OVERHEAD COST.

Does anyone have the answer why we wouldn't include the *overhead cost*...? Come now, don't you folks in accounting be bashful. Ah... I see a hand. Please tell us your name and why we shouldn't add in the *overhead cost*."

"Thanks, Ms. Wells. I'm Chuck McAllen, hoping the audience doesn't think us accounting types don't know what we are doing most of the time—"

Chuck is interrupted with chuckles from the audience.

"I believe it has to do with standard cost accounting requiring us to change the overhead ratio due to the direct manufacturing labor being reduced... So, with the likelihood of any overhead reduction during the outsourcing, the result will be less labor to absorb the overhead cost, therefore, increasing the overhead rate. This could end up costing more to outsource the labor. Well, that's it, Ms. Wells."

"Thanks, Chuck very impressive response to the question. I would note, however, the overhead cost adjustment wouldn't happen until year-end, but it must be included when making an outsourcing comparison..."

I waited for a moment before continuing...

"Now, let's discuss how governments measure their nation's productivity output using two different measurements... Multifactor and the traditional standard labor productivity process, I have touched on...

But, before we get into that subject, I need to explain what multifactor productivity consists of and how it is computed."

MULTIFACTOR PRODUCTIVITY

"Multifactor productivity is a Worldwide European designed measuring system that theoretically addresses labor productivity shortcomings...

Multifactor *output* measures the goods and services produced utilizing the combined *inputs* from the *cost* of labor, capital, materials, energy and purchased services... The key word here is COST, NOT OUTPUT SUCH AS HOURS. The program itself has its own problems when collecting the noted specific data from about fifty-four industries in the U.S. then manipulating, weighting, and summarizing... Multifactor has additional shortcomings being akin to the Standard Cost Accounting's wannabe replacement—ACTIVITY BASED COSTING—adding more gobbledygook when seeking the truth...

I say this because the more complex it is, the longer it takes. Multifactor uses more people, each with their own *perception of variables and assumptions* that skew the data resulting in a greater risk of error.

One last important thought on the subject...

How can one mention the word productivity and multifactor productivity in the same breath, when multifactor measures *cost efficiency, not productivity*?

Okay, enough of my thoughts on the shortcomings of multifactor, and on to measuring productivity gain."

PRODUCTIVITY GAIN MEASUREMENTS

"Financially speaking, how does outsourcing improve productivity, other than financial wizardry...? Well, it can be improved when outsourcing product assembly, reducing non-exempt labor payroll expense and keeping the same output. Later, the product returns as a material asset and added to inventory.

A study from the Upjohn Institute for Employment Research by Susan Houseman said this about productivity growth... *The federal government's measure of productivity growth of the U.S. manufacturing sector during the past fifteen years may be widely overstated due to outsourcing and the shift to offshore production of goods. My findings provide a direct link between productivity measurement, offshoring, and inequality.*

Let's not forget our standard of living is defined by productivity, employment, higher wages, and economic growth—and outsourcing has a negative influence on our standard of living.

Let me summarize quotes from Houseman's thoughts...

While economic theory holds that improvement in a population's standard of living is directly tied to its productivity growth, one of the great puzzles of the American economy in recent years has been that large productivity gains have not broadly benefited workers in the form of higher wages.

I have three charts from the Bureau of Labor Statistics that illustrates Susan Houseman's thoughts.

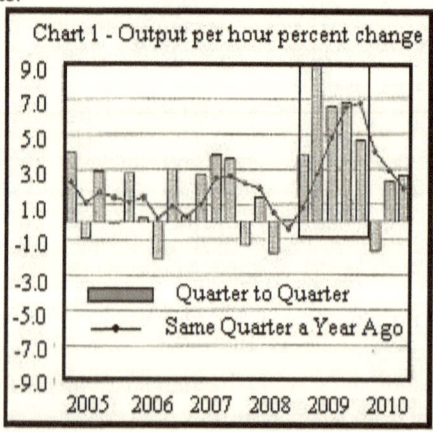

CHART 1 shows the high increase in productivity reported during a five-quarter period that's illustrated within the *rectangle*, during the four quarters from 2009 and the first quarter of 2010.

Productivity In the fourth quarter of 2008 is less than zero percent, followed by a period of unprecedented layoffs. This drastic variation resulted in exceptionally high productivity gains. How could this be possible...?

The answer lies with temporary services helping squeeze out additional sales. The service cost is expensed rather than showing up as a labor contribution to the cost of goods sold, resulting in a positive benefit that increases productivity.... Here, let me bring up a chart showing you the drastic change as full-time employees are traded for part-time employees..."

The audience reacted with shaking and understanding heads and moans...

"At a Senate hearing soon after the results, *Fed Chairman Ben Bernanke* referred to these gains in productivity during the four quarters of 2009 and the first quarter of 2010 *AS EXTRAORDINARY AND UNFORESEEN.*

Now, how can a man in his position be so inept as to make such a statement, when it is so obvious to anyone what took place? Well, you be the judge. Enough said—you get my point. Now, let's look at CHART 2.

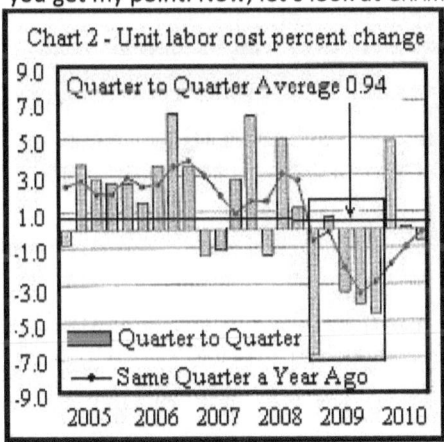

When viewing CHART 2, what happened to wages during that same period?

To best answer that question, I've enclosed the same five-month period noted in CHART 1 with a rectangle. As you can see, the wages traveled south. They are like the reflection of high-rise buildings on a lake. If this was a true gain in productivity, there should be no reflection in the negative lake, but an increase in wages... Let me repeat what Susan Houseman said:

Economic theory holds that improvement in a population's standard of living is directly tied to its productivity growth. It's one of the great puzzles of the American economy in recent years that large productivity gains have not broadly benefited workers in the form of higher wages.

These two charts reflect her thoughts...

Now, let us move on to CHART 3. Since the five quarters captured in the previous rectangle are an anomaly, I have left them out in doing an average.

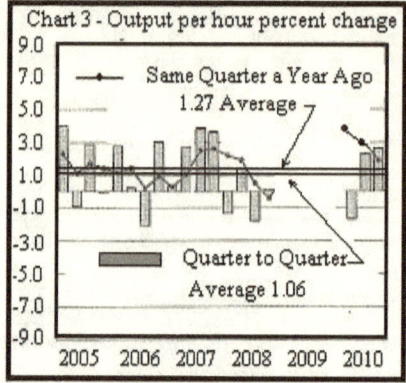

Please note that the new average is now one point zero six, compared to one point two seven.

From 2005 through 2010 our productivity has, for all intents and purposes, flatlined at one percent. Now, let's take a look at the overall productivity trend since 1950 by reviewing the Five-Year Rolling Average chart developed by the government's Labor Department.

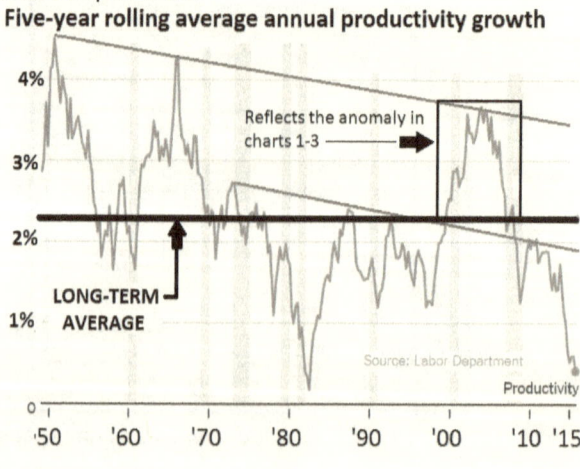

As one can see, productivity has gravitated downward for about sixty-six years. This trend indicates there is nothing in the cards that will influence an increase in productivity. Well, other than our new architectural model.

I would add, without productivity growth, there can be no wage growth. Without wage growth, other than the cost of living increases for some, there can be no long-term recovery. And when interest rates rise, it will only get worse."

The audience absorbs these thoughts with concern.

"Outsourcing will continue to play a part, but for how long is hard to say. During the late nineties, Susan Houseman noted we added an average half-percentage point each year to the productivity gain which correlates with the five-year rolling average productivity chart...

It would seem our businesses are running on fumes trying to produce productivity. Mergers and acquisitions often show an improvement in productivity, but they have a terrible effect on society.

Well, that gives you an idea of the narrowing scope in which productivity has been operating...

Give me a moment, and I'll interject an additional quote from my partner, Jake Jensen."

I sipped my water while reviewing my notes, then continued...

"Um…. This is what Jake had to say...

System processes that improve workflow through an organizational design and new technology advances should be the only true means of measuring productivity—it's the process efficiency that matters.

When we clutter up the true meaning of productivity by measuring with multifactor productivity, outsourcing, consolidation of companies, and downsizing for short-term profit, we do all of us a disservice by inhibiting our future standard of living… And these actions will have a long-term negative influence on our economy."

I wait a moment seeing the importance of Jake's stance on productivity roll through the audience...

"We still have more to cover, but let's take a fifteen-minute break..."

ACT I SCENE 5
Meeting at the Hilton

WHAT DOES THE FUTURE BRING US, ECONOMICALLY SPEAKING?

I gazed out over the audience as they return from a quick break and settle in. A moment later, I continue...

"Thank you, everyone, for being so prompt...

My next topic is short but enlightening. We'll review various sources of economists and their perspective on productivities declining trend. What's interesting is their assumption alluding to the cause of productivity's downturn.

I'll begin with Moody's Analytics. They have once said the long-term downturn in productivity will be due to the lack of investment in machinery and technology, which suggests an average one point five percent projection through 2035...

My second group of economists has expressed the idea that education, experience, and information technology's contribution would unlikely continue to help in any significant advances in productivity. Their consensus forecast shows a declining growth rate in productivity that would influence a decline in real GDP growth rates.

In 2017, James Picerno, a veteran financial journalist said... *'There are several theories about why US productivity has fallen recently. Although no one's really sure about the cause, there appears to be a smoking gun in the sluggish rate of growth in capital spending by businesses.'*

I agree with their conclusions driving a bleak productivity future, but the real force in productivity decline lies with the vertical organizational architecture. This type of architecture and its inability to create improved productivity through controlled throughput is running a collision course with time.

Let's finish this subject with a quote from *The Economist* magazine...

Companies have been benefiting from the productivity gains of their investment in technology and from outsourcing to Asian economies. However, those gains may start to run out: profit growth as a share of American GDP has peaked...

What makes this potential future decline in productivity so devastating is what I said earlier...

Productivity growth is the dynamic force in a market-driven society. With productivity slowing at an ever-increasing rate, so goes our standard of living. Our country's decline in productivity will also have a negative influence on the world economy."

I pressed on that thought with my microphone in hand while stepping away from the lectern, and then asked the audience for dialog on the subject...

"Would anyone like to comment or ask questions before moving on?"

It didn't take long. Ed Blackburn stands up with genuine concern on his face.

"My God, Ms. Wells, you've painted a damn ugly picture for us tonight, specifically, when speaking about our future standard of living due to declining productivity...

Why is it, we've not heard more about this problem before?"

Finished with his statement, Ed takes his seat.

I gave Ed a winsome smile—but there was nothing in my smile suggesting a tall story...

"It is ugly, Ed. And we've not heard much about the problem for many reasons. First, I would say, software suppliers would not want to be broadcasting this—unless they can bring a real solution to the table, which they can't.

Second, business consultants don't want to acknowledge this subject when they don't have the answers to the solution.

Last, on the list are the economists who don't look at productivity solutions systemically, but rather look for the common traditional solution—and this is *not* where the answer lies...

Does that answer your question, Ed?"

I asked, removing my eyeglasses for a moment.

"It did until you mentioned the economists look for common traditional solutions. What the heck does that mean?"

Ed asked with a creased brow.

THE ECONOMISTS AND THE TRADITIONAL SOLUTION

"Ed, I have no short answer to that question, but I'll give it a try...

We have had productivity increases ever since man chipped out arrowheads. But as things go, everything has its limitations, and productivity is currently bumping its head against the upper limit line of the growth curve, called the stationary phase.

Now, if the economists were thinking systemically, they would have seen the limitations of the discrete functions of our current organizational structures negating the ability to improve productivity.

Unfortunately, the community of economists has a tendency to look at the world differently. They look at historical trends. With productivity, this is now a dangerous pattern to follow...

The common traditional solution, I speak of, is made up of historical trend indicators such as *lagging investments.* Why lagging investments? Because... How much a country invest matters. It would seem apparent, the more capital per worker invested, the greater the output per worker. However, we know systems have their limitations. Meaning you cannot expect worker output to continue at an ever-increasing level by pouring money into the system. Well, unless you redesign the system to be expandable—but ultimately, even that will have its limitation...

Another common prescription for productivity improvement might be *tax cuts on capital gains* to provide investments. But this too is another way of pouring money into a limited system as we just discussed.

Additional *government backing for promising technologies* might be another. A new company will improve its productivity, but it too will bump its head against its growth trend at some point.

Hmm... And yet, perhaps, another idea would be a decline in the rate of *capital accumulation.* That's when capital accumulates, producing more wealth than consumed...

Mr. Blackburn, I see you squirming in your seat," I said. "Am I missing the point of your question?"

"Oh no, you're doing fine, I'm now beginning to understand," Ed said. "It's just... Well, I'm sorry, but do you have any well-known economist that's been off the mark about productivity growth?"

Reviewing the audience for a moment, I consider the question.

"Ed just asked me if I could conjure up a real-life economist—one that hasn't yet captured that we may have a productivity nightmare coming down the pike...

The answer is yes. Give me a second, and I'll pull up a file. I like Ed's idea—it brings a face to those who deny we have a productivity problem. Here we go...

Ahh... When going back to a *Charlie Rose Show,* I took notes of Rose interviewing economist Martin Feldstein, President of the National Bureau of Economic Research, Harvard University.

They covered a broad range of economic issues, and productivity was one of them. From my notes, I'll quote what they had to say about productivity.

Feldstein began by saying...

Our productivity is strong, and we are setting standards which other countries aspire to.

Charlie Rose then asked Feldstein, *Are there things in place to maintain that productivity growth?* Charlie's no lightweight either, he asked a great question."

I glanced at the audience for a moment seeing their interest peak...

"There is a long pause by Mister Feldstein, and then he begins by saying...

We have an incentive structure here in the United States. There is a lack of regulation and a lack of a government role in our business enterprise, and all that helps. I'm optimistic about our future.

His response was nothing more than saying he's optimistic, and in essence, we don't have the same problems that the European Union does—which has no relevance today regarding the improvement of any gain in productivity.

I'm sure Feldstein is brilliant when discussing the monetary issues of our global economy. But when it comes to understanding productivity issues, he falls in with the rest of his breed, showing little understanding of the underlying systemic principles.

I have one more example you might be interested in...

Give me a moment...

Ah... Here we go; I have some quotes from our one time Chairman Ben S. Bernanke...

These quotes took place during a discussion he had on productivity on August 31, 2006. Bernanke had this to say when referring to sustaining an economic growth rate without causing inflationary pressure...

The consensus among leading researchers estimates the expected longer-term rate of productivity growth to be at about two and a half percent per year...

Now, here is the interesting part as he continues with information that makes his past statement, useless...

Moreover, until we have a complete understanding of the factors behind productivity growth in the past five years, we should be cautious in drawing any strong conclusions about the future...

With the Chairman being new on the job, he had yet to learn the essential aspects of political-speak—"

The audience has a gleeful response...

"This reminds me of the onetime presidential candidate, ol' whoosis name who hadn't yet grasped the importance of political speak—you remember him? He was the Massachusetts Senator who responded to a question about his vote against an eighty-seven billion dollar supplemental appropriation for military operations in Iraq and Afghanistan by saying...

I actually did vote for the eighty-seven billion before I voted against it."

The audience has another joyful round of chuckles...

"Well, since we're on the subject, Mark Twain had this to say about our politicians...

Politicians and diapers must be changed often, and for the same reason—"

The audience goes into a slaphappy response along with applauding...

After the conference room quieted, I continue with a fast-disappearing smile...

"With Congress's approval rating running between eight and eighteen percent, we have long memories when they say something unattended or stupid.

During Bernanke' tenure, the Gallup poll showed that Americans thought he was doing a poor job with a twenty-two percent rating. So, with long memories, we hear him saying...

"New technologies will translate into higher productivity only to the extent that workers have the skills needed to apply them effectively. If the recent gains in productivity growth are to be sustained, ensuring that we have a workforce that is comfortable with and adaptable to new technologies will be essential.

His statement is true up to a point. Employee skills will play a major role, but not at the essential defining level that would continue with good productivity gains. That is not possible in our current organizational structures.

Brett Arends, an award-winning financial columnist, had this to say about Ben Bernanke...

When the time comes to write Ben Bernanke's biography, I already have a great title: How about, 'Behind the Curve'?"

His remark gets an understanding chuckle from the audience.

"Well, you get my point. On a more positive note, I would say, if we do our job well in transforming your organizational architecture while improving productivity, others will follow. This could turn the tide on moving us back to a world of growing productivity. But, is the world business community ready to listen? For this, I have no answer."

Spinning my water glass a half turn, I look out at an attentive audience...

"Tonight, I have outlined our problems with THEM and US, climate change, little or no productivity gains, and productivity through the eyes of our economist... Why is this so important?

Well, it's because we need to start somewhere in designing our way back to prosperity. And these issues are the cornerstones to turning our company and economy around."

After a deep breath, I continue...

"Therefore, here and now, seems like the right time and right place to start. This change in performance will also be the lynchpin that puts us back into a world leadership position."

When looking over the top of my eyeglasses with an engaging smile, the audience responds with joyful cheering and applauding.

Not waiting for any degree of silence, I speak louder while standing on my toes and flush out a few emotional tears...

"All of us here tonight can play our part by showing the business world how to design and build the company of the future—"

The audience raises applauding and cheering as I take several steps back staying out of the limelight to collect my composure.

Back at the lectern with the room becoming quiet again, I continue...

"The future declining productivity level of our economy is not speculation— it will have a negative impact on our standard of living and GDP. Well, that is if an improved level of productivity is not forthcoming...

Now, I know this sounds depressing, except, this company is going to be the light at the end of the tunnel."

With more applauding, I respond with a smile and a nod, even though, my feet are killing me, giving me a lower back pain. I should have realized my first choice of shoes for tonight would have served me better. While stretching my back, I let the audience anticipate where we're going next.

VIRGIN TERRITORY FOR PRODUCTIVITY

"Aside from future expansion in innovation within specific areas of technology, there is virgin territory for massive productivity improvement—our business architecture...

It is essential—we waste little time positioning ourselves to tap into this new structural design. Our future standard of living could depend on it.

I might add that Western European businesses will have the most difficult time due to their heavy regulatory burden that inhibits flexibility to change their business structure.

As your surrogate *leader,* I'm inviting you to take part in our new *horizontal open-systemic architecture*, and coupled with information technology, we will continue to make strong advances in productivity. The potential gains in growth are huge..."

The room fills with applauding.

DAKOTA FINISHES HER PRESENTATION

I take a few steps back and inhale a deep breath. Exhaling, I advance toward the lectern.

"Well, we've covered a lot of different territories tonight that must have your minds spinning about now, wondering where in the heck is she taking us, right?"

I press, while taking off my eyeglasses waiting on a response...

It didn't take long as I slip my eyeglasses back on...

My new friend Jenny yelled...

"We're not up to speed yet, Ms. Wells, but we're betting you'll get us there soon enough."

"Jenny, you're the best. Can we meet after class? I'd love to meet you and shake your hand."

Then someone from the audience hollers...

"Who would have thunk, Jenny, the teacher's pet?"

This brought about joyful laughter from everybody.

Jenny sits there with complete composure. If you looked close, however, you might see her sparkling eyes and a tugging at the corners of her mouth, displaying what some of us might call the beginning of a smile.

"We need to continue on, folks. Open-systemic architecture and system thinking would have been far too complicated an issue to get into tonight. However, on Tuesday morning next week in your training room, we will have a rollout of the new architecture...

In a moment, you'll meet our two crew members that will train you on the steps of the transformational process. Afterward, we'll have a Q and A, then call it a night.

Before we continue, though, I would like to mention that Denny Chang, also part of the crew isn't here tonight. That's because he's still on his honeymoon in Hawaii and won't be back until Sunday. Denny has wonderful credentials. He has a degree in process engineering, computer science, with a recent MBA in finance. He will take his direction from our two key members that will be representing the Jake Jensen Group during the transformation process.

Denny's training sessions for groups and individuals will also include training your process engineering people, who in turn, will head up the transformational process...

It's time now to introduce Johnny Zapata and Jackie O'. Both are distinguished university professors with post-secondary teaching jobs, allowing them flexible schedules...

They will give a brief bio of themselves and a quick outline of their specific roles in the transformation process...

Johnny Zapata will cover system and process development, and Jackie O' will cover financial and information distribution... Now, please let me introduce, Johnny Zapata."

As Johnny walks to the lectern, there is a nice round of applause from the audience, along with swooning and giggling. Johnny has movie-star looks and the charisma to match. My friend, Chuck, tells me, Johnny gets the same look on his face that Robert Downey, Jr. gets. You know the one—it's when he looks like he knows something amusing and won't share it with you. Nevertheless, he has the attention of every woman in the room, particularly when his eyebrows wiggle and he flashes his nuclear smile.

After finishing with his bio and upcoming agenda, Johnny speaks about a key matter concerning the transformation process.

"I'd like to speak for a moment on *business culture*. Change must take place within the context of conversations and actions that exist in your company. We often refer to this as the *business culture*.

During the transformation process, we will make mistakes. When growing up and making a mistake, most thought of it as a bad thing and reinforced when we entered the workforce. People seldom make mistakes deliberately. Fortunately, we learn from our mistakes. Well, most of the time...

If you measured scientists by their mistakes in developing new technology, lots of firing would take place. It's through their mistakes they can advance the learning process. When you work for a business that wants you to avoid mistakes in judgment, you suppress learning. And then, regrettably, much of the time in business, we look for whom to blame when we make mistakes, and doing so, will undermine the collaborative efforts in the transformation process.

In part, your response to mistakes will determine the future course of the *business culture*. What do we learn when doing something right? Well, nothing that I know of. Mistakes, however, are positive when we learn from them. Einstein said...

Anyone who has never made a mistake has never tried anything new...

But, when we continue to make the same mistake over and over again, well that may have an unfavorable consequence."

With Johnny's smirk, the audience responds with an appreciative chortle.

"To develop the proper culture, we need to ask how the mistake happened to avoid its repetition...

Tonight, it's my pleasure to leave you with two quotes—one from Benjamin Franklin, and a credo by Jake Jensen. What I'm about to read is on the last page of tonight's agenda...

We often think a notable change in our society or business as a new phenomenon of the last century. But I would have you consider the enormous change our nation went through after the Revolutionary War with England.

Benjamin Franklin did a fine job expounding on that subject with this quote...

To get the bad customs of a country changed and new ones, though better, introduced, it is necessary first to remove the prejudices of the people, enlighten their ignorance, and convince them that their interest will be promoted by the proposed changes, and this is not the work of a day...

Jake Jensen has this to say... *People in a process-driven, horizontal open-systemic organization share in the responsibility for, and contribute to, a successful future for both themselves and their company.*

With that said, I leave you with a few words from Jackie O'."

The audience applauds along with more swooning and giggling.

As Jackie moves toward the lectern, the audience becomes abnormally quiet, as though sealed in hermetic silence. Her resemblance to Halle Barry is astonishing, especially, in her black silk dress worn for the occasion. She's noticeably taller and carries more lean muscle, but is no less beautiful. Jackie' elegant look is clarified by her fluid, graceful movements that strike everyone in the room, both men and women. After coming out of their trance, they give her a warm, hearty welcome.

Finished with her bio and upcoming agenda, Jackie speaks of other matters about the transformation process.

"Tonight, I would like to leave with you a subject that begins where Johnny left off. The subject is the method of our transformation process. Not the schedule or sequence, but the framework involved in the change process.

When changing the balance of power, the rhythm of daily activity and physical relocations of employees is commonplace in the business transformation process.

What's important in this process is how the handling of the transactions will influence near-term performance. With that in mind, there are a few basic principles that should facilitate the transition."

Jackie takes a moment of silence to show the seriousness of her subject.

"The CEO communicates a need of change to the employees and how the employees will take part in the change. As you have surmised, that's the reason for tonight's meeting...

There will be a selected group of employees who will work with your system and project engineers in elevating the performance level of the system processes. This will result in identifying the new benchmarks for a given process design.

Each and every one of you will benefit from the change through personal growth, knowledge, and a global sharing of the wealth, unlike anything you have ever experienced."

Jackie's caught everybody's attention.

"That's it for tonight, but we have a lot more coming at you during the upcoming months. Thank you for your time."

Jackie received a nice round of applause and whistles. When leaving the podium, she exits the stage sailing as sleek as a four-masted schooner on the open sea.

With her exit, I inform the audience that we'll now have a fifteen-minute Q and A.

Later, after finishing the Q and A, I stand at the lectern for a quiet moment...

"Before we end our conference tonight, I'd like to comment on a few things, and then address my closing remarks.

I think you ought to know that our transformation process will *not* include, kick-off meetings with win-win, hit the ground running, and team building...

Nor, will we be using any intellectual or slick buzzwords like a paradigm shift, mission-critical, empowerment, and re-engineering during the coming sessions... We're here to help, not make it a pep rally or intellectual conference.

Most importantly, you need to know that there will be no layoffs due to improving the processes. If we have any fluctuation in employment, it will only increase as a result of increased sales, or attrition."

With the audience responding to an appreciative applause, I wait until there is complete silence, and then take a deep breath before continuing...

"They say England was a master of the nineteenth century, the United States dominated the twentieth century, and that China and India will be the powerhouses of the twenty-first century... I say, hold on there...

With our population of three hundred million plus, we still have tens of thousands of us filled with creativity and the pioneering spirit...

But what we need are places to let them germinate, and your company will become fertile ground to plant the seeds. Seeds that will grow and create the competitive environment needed to expand our economy and drive it into the forefront of nations in economic growth and a green society."

The audience explodes with applause.

"One more thing before closing... I would like to mention how we teach for a better learning experience. We want you to be involved as much as possible. So, ask a lot of questions no matter how trivial you might consider them because there are others with the same question, but only too timid to ask.

The learning sessions are, essentially, a way to introduce you to the coming changes. Then you'll be working together while learning on the job—making it the most powerful way to learn.

A select group of your leaders will have special training by Denny Chang. These folks will work alongside everyone in the learning process, which, over the long term, will be a continuation of knowledge-building.

If time were not an issue, we would have some of you teaching part of the class, not unlike Johnny and Jackie's way of allowing their students to teach portions of particular subjects at the University. Why is that? Because it's those who learn the most—are those who do the teaching.

After we leave, each one of you will be encouraged to be an instructor as part of the ongoing training...

Well, that covers it. Except, perhaps, for an image I'd like you to remember..."

I take a fast moment and click on my last illustration.

"The picture, of course, is telling us don't look back. Keep looking ahead."

With a gleeful smile, I hear the audience let out a roar of laughter and applause.

With a quiet house, I continued...

"What I'm saying is it's too late to change the past, but not too late to change the future... Winston Churchill had a simple mantra...

Never give in— never, never, never, never.

With Churchill's mantra in mind, I would ask you to think of it when building a great company—remember, failure *is less of a physical state* and *more of a* state of mind..."

I take a long pause while scanning the audience...

"I would like to close out the evening with one last important little story, one you may want to share with those of you who have children...

Back in the Middle Ages, a king had a large boulder placed in the middle of a well-traveled road. And then hid in a comfortable villa next to the road to see who might remove the obstacle and free up the roadway. He watched as many wealthy merchants and landowners rode around the boulder. None of his loyal, wealthy subjects took the time to remove it.

Later, a peasant pulling a large load of goods down the road to the marketplace stopped and pondered while looking at the boulder placed in the middle of the road. After considering the problem, he removed his staff from the cart, brought over a smaller stone and leveraged the boulder off the road.

While cleaning up and removing the smaller leverage boulder from the road, he noticed a purse covered in the dust where the large boulder had rested. Puzzled over the find, he opened the purse and found that it contained many gold coins and a note from the king. The note read...

To my loyal subject who removed the boulder from the king's roadway, I leave you with my thanks and a trivial sum of wealth.

What the peasant learned was what many of us seldom understand—for each obstacle in life, there is an opportunity to improve your well-being. Therefore, let this transformational process for this company be the purse of gold that will enhance your future.

Well, that's it...

Thanks for coming and enduring our long presentation. I'm hoping you have enjoyed the stories and the new knowledge you have immersed yourself in tonight helping everyone in their endeavor to build a new company..."

With an appreciative smile, I watch the audience explode into standing ovation...

As the audience makes a slow exit, many of them drift up to the front of the conference room to meet the three of us before heading home.

I'm having a nice chat with Jenny and others from the audience, while the women all giddy-eyed circle Johnny like Indians around a wagon train. I'm sure he felt comfortable being the center of attention while radiating his boyish mannerism and charming ways.

Jackie did not go unattended. The men strut around Jackie like fighting roosters. She handled herself with style, even though she felt overwhelmed with the attention.

Thirty minutes later, the room clears out. Johnny, Jackie, and I gather up our things and walk out together—happy, but exhausted from a long day.

Before leaving the Hilton parking lot, I try to call Jake. Again, I'm frustrated with my inability to contact him and continue to worry about my friends while pulling away from the Hilton.

DAKOTA HEADS HOME

While driving south on the Pacific Coast Highway, I stop for a late-night snack and cocktail. After finding a small booth near the front window and placing my order, I unwound by watching the traffic go whizzing by. With my food and drink having arrived, I contemplate on the enormity of the project while sampling one of my Greek egg rolls with a garlic dipping sauce and Bloody Mary.

The most threatening thing endangering our progress is the time constraint. An admiral once told me I had the intelligence, but not the time, regarding a logistical problem that lay ahead of us. This made him mindful of Napoleon Bonaparte. He said Napoleon used to tell his generals, *I will give you anything but time.*

Later, I felt a little more relaxed while heading down the highway. It didn't take long to reach my turn off onto Emerald Bay and then into my oversized three-car garage. After shutting off the engine, I disembark, close the garage door, walk into the house, and head toward my patio.

One would say I live in what you might call an elegant green home. It has geothermal cooling and heating, and rainwater reuse. Jake did the rough architecture and specifications. The home sits in the middle of a tropical garden on the edge of a cliff overlooking Laguna Beach bay. It has three guest bedrooms, each with its own bath. The rest of the house includes an office, eat-in kitchen, a central garden atrium, and a master bedroom suite. The suite has ten-foot-high windows overlooking the bay and an adjacent fifty-foot lap pool. It's furnished with a simple, clean look that's elegant and comfortable. The white walls are alive with beautiful bright-colored paintings, benefiting from sun ray's bouncing off the angled walls.

I leaned against my patio railing and gazed across the black ocean running out as far as the eye can see, then ending with a break of a lighter shade of black sky running along the horizon.

While pondering over Jake and Toni out in the Atlantic somewhere, I feel an uneasiness knowing they're fighting gale-storm conditions which can be a serious threat to any vessel, particularly, one of its size. But with Jake and Toni being seasoned sailors, they should come through the ordeal okay.

Watching the reflection of the moon ripple across the bay, I feel a whimsical smile forming, knowing how these two guys are most likely making fun of it all. And here I stand, worrying and stewing over their safety like a mother hen—while they have a kick in the ass time. *Men*... With that thought, much of my tension diminishes while stretching my arms high in the air, yawn, turn and walk back into the house toward my big, beautiful bed.

After crawling in between my freshly laundered sheets, I reach up and turn out the light. While my eyes become accustomed to the dark, the pale blue moonlight shines its glow across my bed as my heavy-laden eyelids close and my mind wanders. It didn't take long when my awareness of the outside world fades, and I fall into a deep sleep.

ACT I - SCENE 5
ENHANCING THE LEARNING PROCESS

Question 1
Why is it, we no longer have the ability to produce productivity levels capable of producing an increase in our standard of living? Moreover, why is it so important?

Question 2
Why do economists have trouble understanding multifactor productivity is doing us a disfavor when broadcasting their results? Can you give any examples?

ACT I SCENE 6
It Was a Crapshoot

WEEK 2 – THE CREW'S FLIRTATION WITH DEATH—THE AFTERMATH

With their rudder now positioned in straight alignment with the hull, they surfed straight down into the trough of the wave. It gave them their best chance of survival, which remained slim and none at this point. Nevertheless, if they made it out of the trough safely, a straight rudder would help them rise to the top of the next wave.

Unfortunately, the high velocity of the fast-moving wave carried the ketch and crew down into its gauntlet, replete with death-dealing unimaginable ferocity.

The wave fell on them as though a toilet *flushed a turd down a drainpipe, but it didn't pitchpole them—it was a crap*shoot. Nonetheless, flushed down the drain by an eighty-foot-high wave is not what you would want to win at the craps table, especially, when pushed down into a swirling black watery grave.

How long the crew stayed submerged, they did not know. But when the ketch headed to the surface, it popped up like a nuclear-powered submarine with tons of water rolling off Sophi's deck. If not for the harnesses they were wearing and their web belts attached to the deck, they would have been swimming with the fishes, literally, drifting downward to visit Davy Jones' locker.

Antonio felt as though he went the full ten rounds with George Foreman. He endured the beating, but with bruises and sucking in water-laden air.

When Jake looked at Antonio, they laughed with relief, shrugged, and changed the watch—that is after Jake pried Antonio's hands loose from the helm.

When going below deck, Antonio could see Toni strapped into his bunk with safety belts and blood running down his forehead.

"Evening, mate," Antonio said, trying to acknowledge Toni with a strained asymmetrical smile on his frozen, bloody face.

"What kind of shave-tail driving be that? Christ, how's a sailor to get any friggin' sleep before his watch?"

Wearing a cantankerous face, Toni's eyes closed on a blank face.

Antonio continued with a lopsided smile, knowing full well that Toni gave him a compliment. The compliment, of course, Toni talked to him.

SATURDAY, THE FOLLOWING MORNING

Antonio downs a large bowl of hot oatmeal and a cup of good Navy coffee then struggles out of the cabin to relieve Toni's watch.

Toni's standing there with one of his rum-soaked stogies wedged into the corner of his mouth as if he were waiting for a trolley car to come by. Antonio thrashes about making his way to the wheel as Toni makes an effortless move to the side while gazing down at him with his dark, intimidating look.

With great effort, Antonio grabs hold of the helm, looks at Toni and nods. He's acknowledged with a reassuring Creek Indian response—a stone-faced nod so minuscule, if you would've blinked, you'd have missed it.

After stepping around Antonio, he glides over the deck resembling a black Jaguar heading off into the night, then morphs into a stream of blackened crude oil as he flows down into the cabin—spooky.

While on the morning watch, Antonio notices the sun making a slow rise above the horizon playing peek-a-boo through the clouds. The flashes of sunlight highlighted the menacing size and power of the waves, not a comforting sight.

While moving along at the bottom of a sixty-foot deep trough, he sees nothing but a massive wall of water surrounding their microscopic sanctuary. Today, he's not so cocky. He feels his insignificance in the water world of giants and senses an increase in apprehension and fear.

When exchanging their watch, Jake tells Antonio the storm will soon pass and the worst is over, but it will continue to be an unrelenting game of seamanship for at least twenty-four hours.

SUNDAY MORNING

Twenty-four hours later, Antonio is on watch again. The winds were dropping and showing thirty-knots, a nice fresh breeze compared to their gale-force winds of eighty knots. The waves no longer had their tiger teeth showing at the crest of each wave, they were more like large swells, rather than waves, making steerage much improved.

Jake and Toni come out on deck to deploy the jib and mizzen sail. With the wind not quite due aft of *Sophi*, the jib unfurled, stabilizing the bow. Antonio feels an instant rudder response at the helm. *Sophi* lifts herself out of the water and picks up speed. It's akin to the feeling you get lifting off in the elevator—noticeable, but not obvious. This feeling is the reason he goes to sea—assuring and comforting when the boat is behaving as it should.

Toni sheets the mizzen as the sail fluttered and snapped searching for the wind. When finding it, it bellows out in the manner of a beautiful white cloud.

After shutting down the diesel engine, Jake gives him a new heading—south by southwest that will slip them into the Atlantic trade winds and head them toward the northern coast of South America.

As the sound of the wind whips through the rigging, Antonio looks at Toni and sees a seventeenth-century pirate with a black and white bandana tied around his long black, windblown hair. Right then, Toni, unexpectedly, shouts...

"I'd say Antonio can take the gaff. Let's say we make the boy flapjacks with ham and eggs for breakfast this morning."

Toni has now recognized Antonio as part of the crew. With Antonio hearing Toni's remark, he gives off a huge gratifying smile, then begins to laugh giddy-like, as the stress of the storm wears off.

Later that night during the dogwatch, *Sophi* ran under full sails with Antonio steering by a star. It didn't take long though, and the star disappeared behind the cloud cover. He responded by turning his attention toward the waves and the wind as his guide. With the cloud cover still misbehaving, he checks his compass heading using the binnacle that produces a dim red light at the helm.

Eventually, his star became visible again, peeking out on the starboard side of the mainmast, right where it belonged. Toni taught Antonio that it is much easier to steer by a star than following the compass needle. But with the stars moving across the arching sky east to west from their rising and then drop off the horizon, you need to find a new star about every twenty minutes, or you will head to someplace you weren't planning to sail.

With a stiff twenty-plus knot wind creating a chop on the fledgling Atlantic rollers, *Sophi* skimmed along with little effort during her voyage to Jamaica.

ACT I - SCENE 6
ENHANCING THE LEARNING PROCESS

There's a meaning behind this story of three men at sea faced with a death-dealing storm.

Question 1
What is this meaning to you? How does this match up with your philosophy of how to do business in your field?

ACT II
Transformation Period

Our universe is a system designed with a singular directive - spread energy

THE LAW OF PHYSICS THEORY GOVERNS ALL SYSTEMS

Molecules organize themselves into structures in a way that enhances the system to disperse energy...

When considering the law of physics, one must say, our business *vertical organizational systems* are destined to die as in Darwin's survival of the fittest—like the horse and buggy, hardline telephone, typewriters, Mimeograph, and fax machines...

In its place comes a new *open systemic architecture* with self-organizing capability to transform and enhance the way its energy is best used to disperse this energy in the form of products or service. It's a system that will survive and multiply as it reorganizes its structure.

To make this sweeping change to a *horizontal open-systemic architecture* brings uncertainty, upheaval, and fear, but this is nothing more than the precursor to change and transformation.

We need only to place our faith in the human capacity for creativity and fortitude that possess the energy to illuminate the darkness.

WAYNE WOULD ASK YOU THE READER, TO ABSORB THE KNOWLEDGE PRESENTED TO YOU IN THIS BOOK, AND MAKE IT SO.

ACT II SCENE 1
Organizational Architecture

WEEK 3, TUESDAY – JOHNNY ZAPATA EXPLAINS *THE NEW ARCHITECTURE*

INTRODUCING JONNY ZAPATA

Hi, I'm Johnny Zapata, a professor of Organizational Theory and Marketing at Pepperdine University. If you'll remember, I'm the newbie Jake Jensen Group consultant who's getting a bit nervous about my first big gig.

Like much of life, some things fall into place for a reason. Jackie O' loaned me her book, *Change for a Good Reason,* by Jake Jensen. After reading Jake's book, I told Jackie about my interest in his work. Two weeks later during a meeting with Jake, he invited me to join the group. After accepting his offer, I did an in-depth study of his theories and soon became a crew member.

JOHNNY BEGINS HIS NEW GIG

My day starts out with dark clouds and rain as I look out my condo window overlooking Santa Monica's Bay with its choppy slate-gray and white froth surface. Not wanting to be late on my first big gig, I pulled out of the condo's garage at six twenty-six in the morning and headed south toward Orange County on the San Diego freeway, about an hour commute.

As I drive toward the sky with its growing darkness promising a continuation of my windshield wipers to struggle against the violent rain raging out of the dark, low-hanging clouds. I love the rain, except when cars spray dirty water over my washed and waxed car—just then I'm hit with a fifteen-foot-high rooster tail of dirty water. But, being the good-natured guy that I am, I yelled, "SHIT..." WHAT? Try it sometime, it helps...

I wanted to make a good impression when driving into the client's parking lot. But now, my car resembles a race car coming in last after a muddy day of road racing during the Baja 500—while I'm dressed to the nines—a bad combination. When taking the 405 off-ramp in Orange County, it's another ten-minute drive until I pull into the ATC facility parking lot at half-past seven. Climbing out of my mud heap, I'm greeted by the morning sun peeping out between the clouds with its smiling face for but a moment.

In the reception area, I'm welcomed by Nina Nguyen, Thanh's wife and Vice President of Finance, where we take the time to chinwag for several minutes, then head toward the training room.

THE TRAINING ROOM

I offer my hand as Nina introduces me around to a few of the key people and continue to mingle until eight o'clock. At the lectern, Nina officially introduces me and then tells us to enjoy the morning session. She doesn't dillydally around.

After Nina takes her seat, I thank her for the nice introduction and then thank the audience for coming this morning. When observing the room, I'm impressed with what looks like full attendance. Seated in the first seven rows are seventy smiling faces looking up at me waiting to hear what I have to say.

The room is large with floor to ceiling windows looking out on a patio with landscaped grounds. The shade trees would block any glare of direct sunlight on our sunny California days. Today, it rains on my parade, but everybody seems to be in good spirits and ready for the task at hand.

"For those of you who may surmise my name Zapata rings a bell, it's because, apparently, you remember a Mexican revolutionary by that name, or perhaps, the movie, *Viva Zapata!* Who is, by the way, a distant relative."

While removing my jacket, I continue speaking...

"However, one must remember, in Mexico, most Mestizos are often thought as being related in one way or another."

With Johnny's wide smile, the audience burst out with gleeful chortles, seeing a man who cuts a dashing figure, tall and athletic-looking, perhaps in his late thirties—obviously, not your stereotype college professor.

"I'll be around ATC during our scheduled training sessions for the next few months, so please, call me Johnny. Our discussion this morning is going to be an introduction to your new system's organizational architecture..."

I glance at my notes before continuing...

"To understand the transformation process, we're going to travel from a state of not-knowing into what the Buddhist's call enlightenment... Change cannot take place without the likes of you. As Ms. Wells pointed out, we cannot have a, THEM and US, and expect to make this work. You will need to throw yourself into the unassuming nature of not knowing, letting go, and *dance* with the system."

Clicking on my *Mexican hat dance* recording—I go into dance mode.

With a few screams from the ladies, the others begin clapping and laughing. After I finished my short exhibition, I turned off the recording.

"You see, this transformation process isn't as tough as you expected."
Ed Blackburn shouts...
"Well, that depends on who's doing the dancing."
His response brings out joyful chortles from the audience.
"That's true, I see your point," I said with a grin. "I've found that by doing the dance, it gets your attention while bringing you into the learning process...

Now, I say these things, knowing full well, each of you has your own cultural patterns, needs, emotions, strengths, and weakness. We cannot wave a wand about trying to change your views.

We've planned the sessions to allow one to be involved in the process, and as you participate in this wonderful opportunity to learn, you'll be contributing to the design of building a self-organization within your company.

We are not designing a mechanical system here. It's made up of the human mind, heart, and soul—this is not a technology thing, it's a human thing. *Real systems* cannot be controlled to change their behavior, no matter how hard you try, but they can be redesigned to change their behavior as we TANGO with it to the benefit of the total system, and those to whom it is entrusted."

I look about and see a gentleman with his hand about to rise and focus on his name card placed on the table...

"Yes, Steven, it looks like you may have something to ask or say."

"Thank you, I do, Johnny. It has to do with your comment on the idea you can't control a system. You mind elaborating on that?"

"I can, but let me ponder on that for but a moment."

I shuffle back a few steps with my chin resting on my palm. A moment later I'm at the lectern with an answer...

"Steven, would you call a country's government a system?"

"Why yes, of course."

"Good. Remember now, we are talking about real systems. Our subject could be such things as the Democratic or Republican Party. These are whole systems with relationships to innumerable other entities...

With that in mind, what country would you say has the most control over their economy and their people?"

"Oh ... it would have to be China."

"Correct. China is able to execute a plan without any opposition or chaotic debate. A few years ago, the government instructed the country's local governments to cut their carbon dioxide emissions by twenty percent.

Now, here's the rub—the local governments had no problem with the guidelines, they just turned off the power for twenty percent of the time causing rolling blackouts. To offset the power outage, the factories continued to operate with their diesel fuel generators spewing out over a million tons of fuel monthly contributing black soot particles known as aromatic hydrocarbons into the atmosphere—and at times, making things worse."

I gave the audience a look around with a glance and focused on Steven.

"Say no more," He said, cheerfully, "I get your point."

The understanding audience responds with nods and smiles.

ORGANIZATIONAL ARCHITECTURE: A STATE OF MIND

With a silent audience, I continue...

"Jake Jensen once told me...

Good design takes complexity and makes it a crystal-clear, linear, minimal experience.

Now, this is what we're going to discuss today... The process of changing from our existing organization to a new organizational architecture...

The human body and a business organization are similar in system performance—product comes in, and the product goes out, but in a different form than when it came in—if either one of them stops, they will perish...

Hmm, sounds like *system performance* is a topic we should talk about. Let me put an image on the screen, the same one you have lying in front of you."

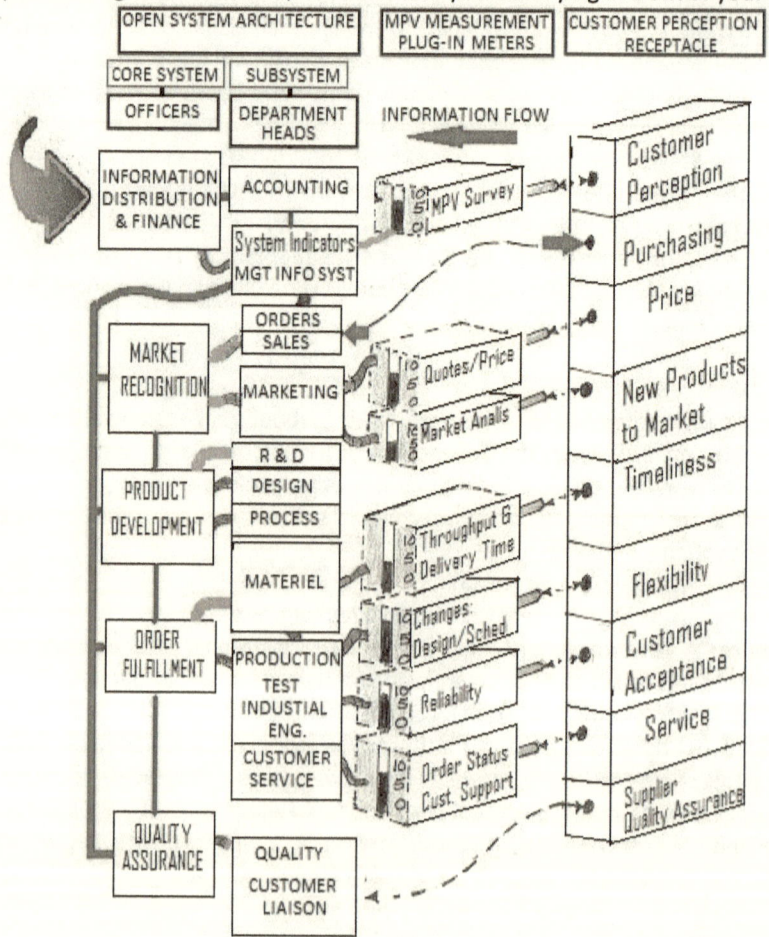

"Let me begin by explaining the basic differences between the new organizational diagram to that of other organizations. Then we'll move on to how the system communicates with the outside world that we call a STATE OF MIND...

I'll start off by saying this manufacturing diagram is not a *cookie-cutter* for every industry. For other industries such as trucking or utilities, you would expect a few changes in organizational titles and different purchasing criteria from their customers.

As you can see, the diagram illustrates the core system related to their subsystems and the subsystem's connections to the customer perception criteria in the fourth column connect by the plugin meters. The obvious, of course, is your current organizational chart has no relationship to this diagram. More on this in the next diagram...

I would also point out that this new organization is not a *cross-functional organization* or rigorously horizontal. It is now referred to as a *horizontal open-systemic process-orientated organization*. Open systems have communicating ports that exchange useful information between internal processes and external sources.

Let me tell you what Jake Jensen beat into my head:

In a vertical or horizontal organization, you work in isolation from the outside world—your customers. In a systemic environment, you communicate through feedback and response—which then makes the process personal."

THE NEW OPEN-SYSTEMIC DIAGRAM—A STATE OF MIND

"Let's analyze the diagram; I call the *STATE OF MIND*...

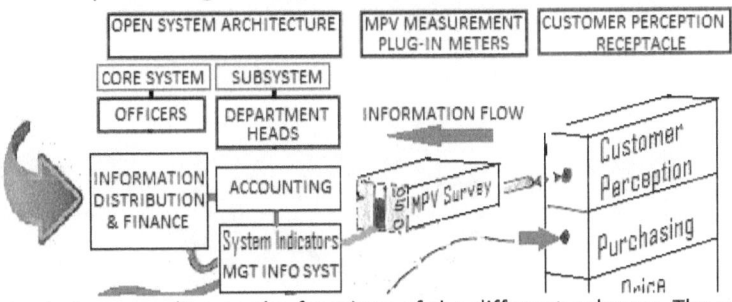

I'll begin by expanding on the functions of the different columns. The FIRST COLUMN in the diagram is the CORE SYSTEM AND OFFICERS, with FINANCE showing its relationship to the SECOND COLUMN SUBSYSTEM, Department ACCOUNTING, and MANAGEMENT INFORMATION...

THE third column is the PLUG-IN METER sending feedback from COLUMN FOUR, the RECEPTACLE, using our company's *Market-Perceived-Value* survey to the appropriate Subsystems. Please notice the large arrow showing information flow. We will be using the acronym MPV when discussing market-perceived value. Much of the MPV intellectual content comes from Bradley T. Gale's book

Managing Customer Value, and *The Basics of a Market-Perceived Quality Profile.*

THE FOURTH COLUMN, shown as the receptacle, represents the customer perception of its buying criteria, or MPV..."

I'm about to move on to the next subject when a lady in the front row raises her hand. With a smile, I admired the classy lady who was born to wear sweaters just long enough to give her perky chest the attention it deserved.

"You have a question, I bet."

She responded with the educated robustness that went with the sweater...

"Thanks, Johnny, my name is Belinda. And I do have a question. What do you mean when you say the STATE OF MIND?"

"Hmm... The best way to answer that is with a *Shakespearean* quote...
There is nothing either good or bad, but thinking makes it so.
Our state of mind is the one thing that will separate us from the competition, and that's knowing how to use the information to better organize and deliver—*thinking makes it so.* Does that answer your question, Belinda?"

"Wow... does it ever. Thanks, Johnny that was beautiful."

I respond with a nod and smile.

"Okay, our next subject is the subsystem."

SUBSYSTEM AND ITS FLOW OF INFORMATION

"To best illustrate how the organizational system interacts with the customer, let's take a look at ORDER FULFILLMENT, a CORE SYSTEM...

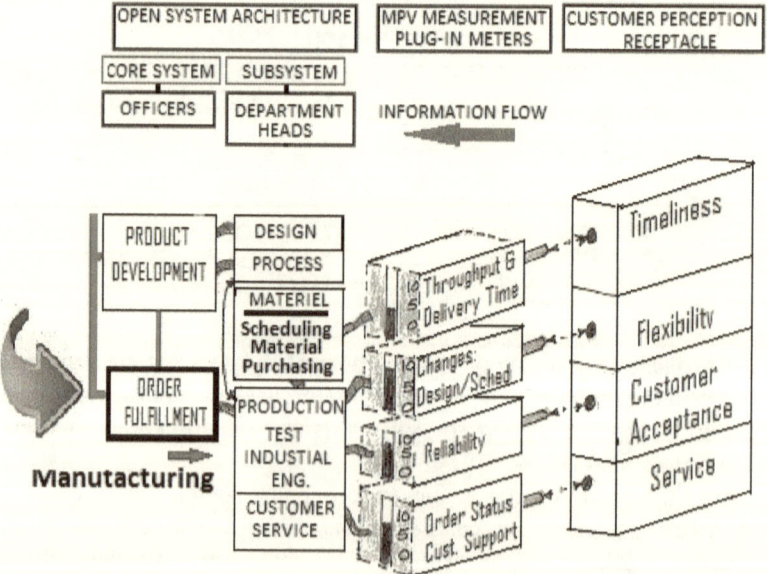

As you can see in the first column—*ORDER FULFILLMENT,* a CORE SYSTEM of manufacturing connects to its subsystems—*Production, Test, and Industrial Engineering* that connects to *Materiel,* and *Customer Service."*

All of a sudden a hand begins waving in the air.

"I see an urgent signal coming my way."

I offer a nod...

"Yes, Diane?"

"Thanks, Johnny. I see you have either misspelled *material* with an 'E,' or I don't understand what *materiel* means."

"I've been known to make an error or two in my presentations," I said politely... "But *Materiel* spelled with an 'E' is correct...

The word materiel refers to logistics, or the movement and planning of labor and material, often used in military jargon. Those employees responsible for *Materiel* in a business environment, purchase the material, control the inventory, and plan the production schedules, permitting high-performance throughput delivery time."

I glance over to Diane as she gives me an understanding nod.

"Before moving on in our discussion, do we have any questions about materiel?

I see no response, shrug, and move on...

"Manufacturing is measured by its ability to be *flexible* in customer *design changes and scheduling*. The deliverable product must also be *reliable* to meet the customer's high acceptance rate.

And last, the CUSTOMER SERVICE must provide *order status* and *customer support* to meet the customer's expected high standards.

And as a reminder, let's not forget engineering, a CORE SYSTEM called PRODUCT DEVELOPMENT is now systemically tied into the processes that influence both *Materiel* and *Manufacturing*. Meaning that the *Engineering* group must always be heads-up and sensitive to the company's and customer's feedback on *throughput time, design changes, and product reliability*...

STRUCTURE DETERMINES BEHAVIOR.

"Our next discussion is ORGANIZATIONAL STRUCTURE, a term we'll be using over the course of our various discussions. The term implies there is an interaction between the different disciplines within the architecture. In other words, its form will determine the way it interacts, thus, its behavior.

My mother once explained to me about behavior modification. She told me...

Stop acting like your father."

With my dippy grin, I get a cheerful response.

"The employees, however, will determine the eventual effectiveness of the performance demands to influence customer perception and stockholder value... I'm going to put up an image that will help illustrate what I mean...

It is called a *causal loop* diagram and shows you how feedback loops illustrate cause and effect between the customer and their *order status* system, centered between the two loops...

Ahh... Here it is... In this illustration, the company is receiving negative feedback due to delays, telling them to review the appropriate constraint's design and perhaps up the benchmark.

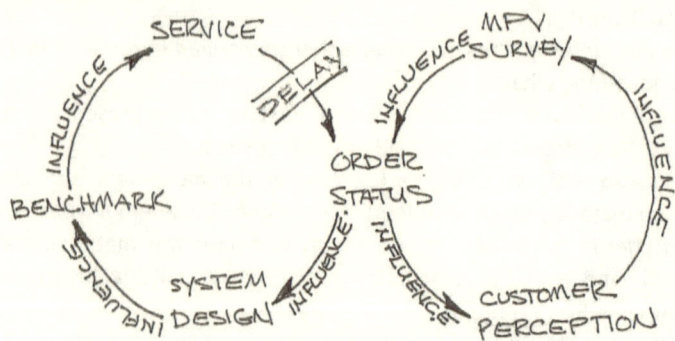

Any delays in the order status system can cause deterioration in salesforce effectiveness—thus reducing orders booked, which limits the growth of the business. Without this kind of causal loop feedback and a system designed for a fast response, your company will be a business of the past...

Do we have questions or comments at this point?" I said, seeing a rising hand. "Yes, Ms...?"

I hesitate when seeing the lady seated in the back of the room.

"I'm sorry; I can't see your name card."

A petite young beauty stands up.

"Hi, Johnny, my name is Jennifer, and I work in marketing...

I would like to comment on this diagram. When first looking at it, I became a little confused. But when considering the two previous diagrams and your additional explanation, I now find it fascinating...

My interpretation at this point would be when organized in a new architecture, you begin to conceive and visualize in system and process terms, as opposed to tasks being delivered from above."

Finished, she took her seat.

"You're right on the mark, Jennifer. My students took a bit longer to come around with that thought."

But in reality, my student's grasp these ideas rather well, but she's cute—too bad mixing business with pleasure is taboo...

"Is there anybody else with a question or comment?"

After a long moment, I see a hand floating above the surface ready to go airborne...

"Is that hand indicating a question?" I said, "It's Joyce, right?"

"Yes, sir."

"Please don't call me sir until I reach my eightieth birthday."

I face her with a stern face that morphs into a wide grin.

"Yes, sir, I mean no sir... I mean ... okay, Johnny."

Joyce is a young, shy little thing who tries to stay in the background, and only brought out a few chuckles from the respectful audience. Back when, during a dance social, the other ladies would have referred to her as a sweet little wallflower.

We wait as Joyce blushes...

"I'm a material planner. So, I guess I'm now part of the materiel subsystem, right?"

"That's correct, or soon will be. That's a crucial position, I might add."

"Thank you. I'm wondering why we are no longer a separate department and now joined at the hip, so to speak, with the other noted departments?"

"That's not only a legitimate question but also a great one. However, I'm going to hold off for a bit, because I will be covering that subject in a few minutes," I said apologetically.

MY FIRST GIG REQUIRES AN APOLOGY

"Before we go on to the three steps of change, I should tell you that Dakota has asked me to deliver this session in two stages instead of one in our initial schedule. That's due to the length of the subject matter.

She thought there is too much to assimilate, thinking two sessions would enhance the learning process, and so, the second session is scheduled for Friday at the same time.

Some of you may know that this is my first big consulting gig. I must tell you, the process of teaching university students as compared to consulting business professionals is vast. The knowledge I pass on to you takes place in a short time period, influencing the economic outcome of your business and hundreds of employees—a huge responsibility.

My technical knowledge is good, but I'm still learning about timing and delivery. I'm a fast learner, so please be patient with me. My friend Toni would call me a shavetail or maybe a little wet behind the ears," I said with a titter.

"We're with you, Johnny," Jennifer yells, followed with additional acknowledgments from the audience.

"That's kind of you, much appreciated."

THE THREE STEPS OF CHANGE AT ATC

"Let's move on now to the three steps necessary for change:

STEP ONE—why make the change?
STEP TWO—problems with top-down organizations, and...
STEP THREE—how the new system works, Step 3 A, B, and C."

I need a booster shot of caffeine throughout the day, so not being sure about coffee availability in the training room, I was pleased to see that they had a nice spread of pastries and coffee. Regrettably, it would be impolite at this point to fetch some of the wonderment. So, trying to be prepared, I brought along my backup forty weight varnish remover.

"Excuse me, I need a shot of my Starbucks iced coffee."

Ahh... The joy of sipping caffeine and feeling it kick in...

STEP ONE THROUGH THREE

"S<small>TEP ONE—WHY MAKE THE CHANGE</small>? Well, let's begin with the formation of our current business organizational structure. It's derived from centuries of top-down organizations such as tribes, armies, and governments, in a natural progression...

Nevertheless, business system architecture should be organic due to external system inputs such as investors and customers, then satisfy them with the appropriate outputs, or die.

When trying to run a business system through a bureaucratic organization, it can enslave the system's ability to be the best it can be... Now, what I'm about to say is said in jest, for the sake of visualizing corporate America during everyday management routines, but with a bit of humor thrown in to highlight the truth of the matter, so please don't be offended...

A non-organic organization depends too much on various levels of management, each manager thinking the employees must keep busy by assigning day-to-day tasks, with the idea it makes a difference in improving performance. Then with busy-work assignments, emails and text messages flowing like the great Mississippi River, the employee presumes they need an assistant—"

The audience interrupts with laughter.

"Then of course, if you're lucky enough to be a Vice President of a Fortune Five Hundred company and one of the CEO's *team* members, you'll attend his or her meeting for planning meetings in an exclusive resort somewhere in the Caribbean, grazing on any additional wages for employees or profits...

However, for those lower in the food chain, not unlike plant-life—"

Laughter springs from the audience again...

"Their meeting can be found in a drab, windowless room. This is where the team leader is sitting at the head of the table, arms folded and hoping he's out of arm's reach so no one can strangle him."

The class brings about more cheerful chortles...

"When the meeting is over, making matters worse, everyone goes back to work forgetting everything discussed, except the leader, who believes he or she is making things happen for another step up the ladder."

This thought has everyone nodding with chuckles.

"Now, what I'm about to say will cover most companies, but not all. If it covers you folks at ATC, I must say again, please don't be offended...

It has to do with learned culture from the different companies you've previously worked for. The idea is to give you an awareness of something I'm sure you haven't thought about. If you are honest with yourself, you will know in your own mind, I speak the truth. In your new organization, you don't want to bring your old habits and baggage formed from the past...

What the heck am I talking about, right? ...Well, this brings up...

STEP TWO—PROBLEMS WITH TOP-DOWN ORGANIZATIONS...

First, I'd say, we'll begin with people and their *self-importance*, which includes most of us, getting in the way. We deserve success because we are so brilliant, creative, and talented..."

I harrumphed good-naturedly while taking a bow that lightens up the mood with laughter.

"This perception of ourselves carries with it blinders, not allowing one to see our poor image, driving one to overreach and become complacent, or resistant to change.

And lastly, managers within bureaucratic organizations have a tendency of finding a way you *can't* do something as opposed to *how* you can, or when saying *yes, it* may require approval from a higher authority.

A manager's self-importance is directly proportional to the frequency of saying *no*. Saying *yes* can lead to a possible mistake, something most managers try to avoid. The same holds true with mitigation, a state of mind in which a person of lower authority is trying to deliver a message of utmost importance to one of higher authority. In doing so, the messenger will try to placate or soothe these thoughts because of our culture in big business, or, perhaps, our cultural heritage...

In your new organization, we must be assertive and clear how we communicate. In this type of environment, there should be no offense taken, when a decisive matter needs to be addressed with urgency. We must separate ourselves from our past cultures. To ignore it impedes our ability to transform the business...

Then, of course, being *assertive* doesn't mean saying to your boss, how about getting that damn thing fixed, not tomorrow, not today, now."

With a smirk, laughter permeates the air.

"Ah... It's good to see you still have your sense of humor, I was afraid to see a few of you might take up the idea of sticking pins in a voodoo doll, either that or throwing a rotten tomato at me."

This encouraged a few more chortles.

"Not to worry, Johnny, we get the jest. As you said, if we're going to be making changes we appreciate the way you're going about it," Ed Blackburn said.

"Thanks, Ed, much appreciated."

After a nod toward Ed, I gaze out toward the courtyard for a moment to clear my mind.

"On the lighter side of making a *change*, Jake told me something, I had never given much thought...

We often talk about re-engineering the business, even though; it's never been engineered in the first place.

This brought out chuckles from the audience.

"Moreover, with the word *change* on my mind, I was viewing a Tommy Lee Jones interview one time, and he said...

You can't change your mind if you don't have it made up."

Tommy Lee's remark strikes close to home, sending delightful bubbling laughter through the audience.

"With that said, I can now say, we have an opportunity to engineer a new system of organizational architecture as we move on to STEP 3 A, B, AND C."

STEP 3A - THINKING IN LOGICAL, MINIMAL, AND SYSTEMIC TERMS

"Only in the new organizational architecture can you grasp logical, minimal thinking, and in system terms, put it to work...

The vertical organization is a place where the incubation of *linear nano-thinking* takes place, crushing creativity and prevails in the governing of the company.

Our new architecture is the home where *creative* and *logical thinking* is nourished and plants the seeds of system thinking—a discussion we will have in a later session...

Yes, Derrick, do you have a question...?"

"I do, thank you...

How would you best describe logical thinking?"

"Well, there is no fast or easy answer to that question, Derrick. Today, I still have a lot to cover... However, in our next session, I will cover both creative and logical thinking, which is an interesting subject...

But, on the lighter side of logical thinking, my mother was at her best. She taught me more about logic than I might have learned in a lifetime...

She told me, *if you fall out of that swing and break your neck, you're not going to the store with me...and if you ask why it's because I said so."*

Followed by chuckles, Ed said... "You just have to love your mom."

His remark brought about nodding and smiling from the audience...

"I do, Ed...

Okay, moving on to *minimal thinking*...

But wait, hold on there, I know what you're thinking," I said. "Minimal thinking does not mean you are stupid or a low IQ."

The audience reacts with understanding joyful smiles.

To clear things up I would like to quote Fritz Schumacher who was an international economic thinker, statistician, and an economist that published a book in 1973, titled, *Small is Beautiful*...

I bring this up because what this new organization is going to do is make a change from big to small—*SMALL IN TERMS OF DOING BIG THINGS WITH LESS.*

Thinking in minimal terms is but one of many steps that will build the new organization...

With that in mind, I'll try to give you samples of thinking minimal...

Richard Serra is one of America's best contemporary artists, and his understanding of creativity, processes and minimal thinking is absolute...

If you have the opportunity to see Serra's work, you will understand the term, minimal thinking while admiring his gigantic creative plates of towering steel. They bend and curve, leaning in and out, carving out private spaces in large public areas.

Then we have, Steven Wozniak, a founder of Apple Computer that is a master at engineering in the minimal sense, which included creative and artful electrical circuits, components, and exterior design—total simplicity was his aim.

Einstein looked for the one formula that would explain the universe and known matter. He didn't find it, but we're still looking...

He's also been credited with having said...

Any intelligent fool can make things bigger and more complex. It takes a touch of genius and a lot of courage to move in the opposite direction.

Even Einstein's quote is simple and to the point....

And I would add, this is something Elon Musk CEO of Tesla could have benefited from rather than building his monster cash eating machine..."

This perked up the audience with nodding understanding heads.

It's quiet for a moment when I notice a hand waving...

"Yes, Jennifer?"

"Excuse me; I believe the quote you spoke of was by Woody Guthrie."

The audience looks up at me for a response.

"Ahh... You are correct, Jennifer, sorry about that...

Like I said, any fool can say something wrong—it takes a genius to get it right."

I finished with a shameful look.

The audience applauded gleefully.

I waited for a humble moment, and then continued...

"What I'm about to say is one of the most paramount things you can take with you when you leave this session today...

Your designers of business systems and those employees that work within these systems must deliberate with uncluttered and creative minds such as Serra, Wozniak, and Einstein...

Their responsibility is to engineer simplified business processes reflecting an image of beauty that improves performance within the systems of the new architecture. Anything less, won't allow the business systems to grow into the future."

I wait for a moment allowing this idea to be absorbed.

"Moving on now, I'd like to express a few ideas about thinking in *systemic terms*. My Creek Indian friend Toni Nakni tells me everything's interconnected—the wings of an eagle affect the breeze. The crow warns warriors of danger. A dark cloud covers the sun and changes our mood, and then the rain comes delivering us life...

Little systemic alterations in our system influence our ability to survive. For instance, when the body gets hot or cold, the system reacts by sweating or vital organs constricting. Your finger pulls back when near extreme heat or cold."

At that point, Ed Blackburn, the good-natured elderly Irishman, opened up with a joyful remark...

"You know, I have that problem, but it's not my finger."

Everybody in the room goes into a range of embarrassing titters.

"I'll leave that one alone, Ed. But thanks for that information."

After taking a long breath, I continue...

"One should envision the investors, suppliers, your business, and the customers as one organic system. The nerve endings of your processes must be sensitive to internal and external feedback loops. At first, when you visualize it as an employee, you can see how each subsystem community influences the performance level of the business—a subject we will cover today."

I take a moment to assemble my thoughts on the next subject...

STEP 3B - SUBSYSTEM-COMMUNITIES AND THE WORD TEAM VERSUS GROUP

"Now, we're going to cover STEP 3B, subsystem-communities associated with the *Open–System architecture* diagram we've been discussing, but with the emphasis on the words communities and group as opposed to the word team.

The business system receives customer performance level perception through the feedback loop, noted as a plugin-meter in the diagram. Before the Market Perceived Value report is fed to the subsystem-communities the information is weighted and rated...

Subsystems are like the drivetrain or steering assembly within a vehicle's total system which is straightforward, but why associate the word community and the word group as opposed to the word team with subsystem?

Hmm... Let me first simplify the meaning of the word Groups and Teams...

The word *Group* identifies with individuals who bring together independent thinking along with new creative ideas to enhance their subsystem quality perception and throughput knowing it will improve the overall system.

Ah... the word *Team* identifies with those who coordinate work activities defined by their leader or manager. To be more exact, let me say...

We use the word team throughout our industries to show how to collectively work together to improve and be measured for overall team performance. However, team members lose sight of the total business system when focused only on their own output responsibility and under command and control environments that deliver tasks and busywork...

Let us not forget, managers and economists alike place no value on work they cannot measure. They assume that if one is not busy, the company is losing money on their investment.

The word Team also conjures up competitiveness, not a good attribute in a total open-systemic organization. We're Americans, and at heart, we're still cowboys. Train us, give us responsibility and a goal, and then let us get with it. We don't perform well treated as a utility—we like the idea that we count for something.

The word Team is a misunderstood and overused word. It lost any real meaning in the corporate world. But the word seems to have a nice ring to it. Today, the word *team* is nothing but a label. Hell, even the US President has a team...

Its worth is nonexistent when trying to make changes in the process, or an organization. It's but another way for managers to feel good when saying our team is the best. Our team will perform for you. Be part of our team. CEO's have even hired consultants to give them team-building organizations knowing everybody seems to be doing it, or it's the political thing to do. These organizations talk team, but only reward individuals.

Now, let us speak about the word *community*. I use the word community as opposed to the word team because it is associated with groups, not teams of people in an environment with shared interests such as a belief, resources, same needs, a collective outcome, unity of will, and kinship...

Now, one would have to say it sounds a lot like a description of the word, *team*, right? However, two essential things differentiate the two...

First, I'd say that community encourages independent creative thinking—not found in team theory. Independent thinking is only for management because they know better, right—?

A gleeful laugh springs from the audience...

I wait a moment with a smile...

SECOND, a community requires group leadership. The **group** leader is an integral part of the subsystem who contributes to the process and watches over throughput while training and keeping his or her *group* in the community focused on their responsibilities... Meaning, there can be multiple **groups** in the community such as Materiel, with Material Planning, Production Planning, and Purchasing.

The **group** leader does not get distracted by ideas such as keeping track of tasks and individual productivity. Subsystem community group leaders, at some point, will grow to become the CEO's of the future."

With a short pause, I continue.

"Well, I hope I articulated that well enough—do you have any questions or comments?"

Ed Blackburn raises his hand.

"Yes, Ed."

"Holy crap, Johnny, that bit of articulation, as you put it, is fascinating. Although the term *team*, as opposed to using the word group is subtle, the real differences lie below the surface, and yet, rather important...

It sounds as though what you're saying is—the term *team* is at odds with system thinking, and, not helpful in an open-systemic or system environment."

"That's right, Ed. You boiled it down as well as one can. Thank you for that idea.

Is there anyone else with their thoughts on this subject?"

Seeing no hands, we move on.

STEP 3C - IDENTIFY AND TRANSFORM A SUBSYSTEM

I found Joyce in the audience and nod to her...

"Joyce, this is where I answer your question. It's in my discussion I pointed out for STEP 3C."

Shy Joyce returns a nod and whispers a thank you.

"As you may remember, Joyce had asked me the reasoning behind the consolidation of her department within the new materiel subsystem...

The answer lies with the idea that departments under the same roof, so to speak, would better be served as a single collective subsystem, in this case, Purchasing, Material Planning, Production Scheduling, and Stockroom. They are discrete entities within the total organization, and yet, they have a common link—they provide the material and labor loading from the same master schedule, but never synchronized with the same work schedules.

Now, imagine a vehicle's engine trying to go forward while the rest of the drivetrain isn't ready yet. That's what takes place when you have different departments having separate schedules and priorities.

During the process of mapping areas in the subsystem by the employees, simulated modeling software will show up the constraints, and redundancies. With your instruction in system thinking and modeling, you will see leveraging points that can enhance the behavior of a subsystem to improve the total system performance.

This knowledge will guide you when the re-mapping process begins, allowing you to verify that the changes have, in fact, produced a higher performance for the entire system. The added benefit should allow order volume to increase without adding additional employees, a nice side benefit—and that's real productivity at work...

Now, remember this, there are no layoffs due to improved productivity. Slack time is okay as long as system performance is not disrupted. Layoffs kill further productivity and creativity. I've already talked to Ed about this change, and he's gnawing at the bit to get into the mapping process...

Ed, is there anything you'd like to comment on?"

"Well, what you covered today feels right. I look forward to contributing what I can to our new business architecture."

"That's insightful, Ed. Thank you, Sir. Okay, I'm ready to move on to our next subject—how *subsystem integration flattens out the new system architecture*...

Well, maybe not, the clock shows we're halfway through our discussion—meaning this is a good place to begin our next subject tomorrow...

I'd like to thank you again for your support and for helping me make this deliverable another successful step in forming your new company. I'll see you tomorrow morning at eight o'clock."

The audience delivers a nice response as they rise and leave.

With me being last out the door, I take a brisk walk down the hallway when I hear Dakota yell my name...

Startled, I turn around and see her waving her arms and walking with urgency toward me. Oh, crap, I'm in trouble on my first gig.

JOHNNY MEETS TOM AND A NEW FRIEND

While heading toward the restaurant to meet my friend, Tom, I'm reflecting on Dakota's interception of my great escape in the hallway this morning. Most notably, the part when I heard her say how proud she was of my performance today. Apparently, she ran into someone telling her about my apology and being wet behind the ears. Her two-minute talk elevated my spirit, and I'm ready for a little fun tonight.

I've not seen my friend Tom in over three years. Last I heard he was a general manager for a high tech firm down in Brazil. At the time, he told me he lived in a beautiful compound with his wife and a personal bodyguard. It would seem kidnapping was a lucrative business in the city where he worked, and security was mandatory. He also told me the other reason for a bodyguard was if they saw a foreigner driving a vehicle, they'd drive their car into you creating an accident, and then sue you. It was a scam with the government. If you wanted to leave the country, you had to pay a bribe to settle the case. Even today, corruption exists at all levels of society from the top of political power to small municipalities.

We both thought sushi should be on the fare tonight, so I gave him directions for Roku's in Santa Monica on Ocean Avenue. Since I had an early rise the next day, I told him we should meet at six o'clock.

Having arrived early with a reserved table, I'm considering a drink might be in order. When in Rome, order a Sake Martini made from Junmai Ginjo Sake, shaken with fresh cucumber—you don't want to overwhelm the taste of sake.

"Ah," I expel after taking a sip. It had a biting dulcet taste of a subtle fruity like sweetness—but then combustion takes over as the sake delivers its true self, the inferno goes down the trachea and into what is now the lava bin. We know alcohol solves none of your problems, but neither does milk.

It's my first time here, so, looking around at my surroundings, I'm provided with a pleasant surprise. Toni told me he enjoyed the food, and the interior looks like Zen had a chance meeting with Frank Lloyd Wright.

I'm about to finish my drink and in walks Tom. Christ, his hair hasn't changed since I first met him ten years ago—it's one of those pompous hairstyles where the hair length doesn't appear to change. It's as though, each hair is in the same place as it was the day, the week, or the year before and lacquered in place with a can of satin clear lacquer aerosol. We used to razz him about his hair looking like a helmet, it could stop a bullet fired at close range, and then at night, he would remove it before going to bed.

Tom's a good-looking guy, about six-foot-two-inches, one hundred seventy pounds with little muscle accounted for. He said due to playing football at Colorado State University required him to work out with weights so much; he no longer has the desire to step into a gym. That's nuts, I told him. If he didn't add muscle soon, he would be shuffling along with a walker in ten years with two air horns attached.

At one time, he used to wear eyeglasses that looked like a 1954 Buick windshield—that is, until I introduced him to something a little more fashionable. He's old school—his clothes, politics, food, and business. You'd assume he was in his late eighties. Nevertheless, his endless love affair with young women puts him somewhere around eighteen.

When looking at the puddle of Sake in my glass, I kill it. Tom ambles over with his shit-eating grin, arms spread wide for a hug—what a guy.

We hug and slap each other's backs for a while, and then I nod to the maître d' to take us to a nearby table. A waiter soon arrives and takes our drink order for two Red Sun's—being it's a Roku homebrew. During our catch-up period, we order our entrees, Tom, with grilled Kobe filet mignon—we go out for seafood, and he orders a side of beef. For me, I have the Chilean Sea Bass with spicy lobster sauce—a man of the twenty-first century.

As we drink our homebrew, Tom grabs a handful of almonds like a ditch digger excavating the almond dish. He then shakes them in his hand like a pair of dice before shuttling them to his mouth, dropping them in one by one crushing them with his back molars.

During his eradication of the almonds, he stops for a moment and grins from ear to ear.

"I had a blowout with my wife before leaving on this trip," He said. "She told me I was a little baby."

I looked surprised...

"A little baby?"

"That's what she called me during her tirade, screaming that she had to take care of my sexual needs, my social life, and my laundry. Oh yeah, the wife also mentioned that she has to instigate any conversation we have and that I needed a lot of attaboys, like a little baby. Now, is that a joke or what?"

I accepted his story with a thin smile, knowing full well she's right, and yet, he has impeccable timing. With the last almond disappearing from the dish, he turns his beer bottle in slow motion on the tabletop, lifts it to his mouth and drains it as the waiter brings us our dinner.

During dinner, Tom tells me of his business conference in Paris next month.

"*Ooh, la, la, France magnifique*," I said. "It has a great climate, great food, wine, and *beau femme*."

Tom looks up from his plate after spearing a chunk of Kobe beef.

"Everything you say is true, except for one problem."

"What's that?"

"They're French...

When I'm proving my point in a discussion showing why they should consider looking at the problem differently, they shrug, puff out their cheeks, and change the subject."

"I guess they can be a little unreasonable. The French do, however, love their politics, art, wine, food, and clothes," I said.

"You left off a few of their most important loves...

They love to make people unhappy by demonstrating in the streets. They love change, as long as no one knows they love it. They love to change things that don't exist. They love the idea of being negative such as when offered an opportunity, they will say, it won't work. They love seeing a conspiracy and a plot in everything, and never believe what they have been told. Hell, they even reason their cats are smarter than us Yanks—"

"Okay, I get your point. But Tom, let us not forget the millions in loans and military assistance they gave us in the Revolutionary War, and without it, it's unlikely we would have this conversation."

Tom ignores me for a moment while chewing his Kobe...

"Johnny, I don't get along with the French, and they don't appear to like me."

"Why is that?"

"Essentially, it's because I'm not French."

"Well, you can't argue with them on that point."

With dinner behind us, we continue to work on more Japanese brewskies.

Then my world as I knew it, changed. In walk two beautiful ladies—one is a brunette and the other with a beautiful golden head of hair.

Tom's somewhat married when he's at home, but not on the road—hard to believe, I know. Me, however, I'm a little bashful on making contact for the first time. But Tom has no understanding of the word, *bashful*.

Tom looks at me with a childish grin...

"Would you like a couple of guests?"

Before I can muster up an answer, he had them in tow.

I rise from the table to watch Golden-Hair walk toward me with her head held high, shoulders squared and perfect posture while looking into my eyes. Stopping but a few feet in front of me, she offers her hand...

"I'm Sheri," She said.

I tried to ratchet up my voltage for my already electrifying smile, but she somehow survived it. So, having failed at that point, I lost it, thinking, I must have looked and acted like Jackie Gleason in the Honeymooners when he goes, *bah, bah, bah.*

I was dumbstruck with her beauty, elegant dress, soft voice, and most of all, her presence when she entered the restaurant and stood there for a moment, dominating the room. And the room is better for it as though she owned it. Hell, what do I know, maybe she did...

Time stood still while babbling a string of incoherent words. Subsequently, having come around enough, I'm able to tell her my name and then asked her if she and her friend would like to sit and have a drink with us. They seemed to like the idea and accepted my invitation. After taking a seat at our table, Tom ordered a round of brews. While nursing our home brewskies, we discussed our favorite movies and pets.

"Would you ladies like to hear my adventures with the pet devil?"

They laugh with a favorable nod.

"The She Devil's name was Seri and was no ordinary cat. My friend Marsha was moving into a new apartment that didn't take pets and pleaded with me to take care of her cat. Marsha planned to go back to Texas in less than a year, and then she'd take the cat with her...

I had no other choice in the matter, owing to my one and only flaw—I can't tell a beautiful woman no."

The ladies take one look at each other, then giggle.

"One day after arriving home from the university, I picked up the oversized fur ball and sat down on my sofa."

I finished with a whisper-like voice...

"If only, I had known the consequences of doing so."

Abruptly, I have their attention.

"I had Seri on my lap and petting her, when unexpectedly—she turned her head hundred and eighty degrees and sank her fangs into my wrist, then takes off like a bolt of lightning to parts unknown."

The ladies, gasp.

"After washing my wound and applying several bandages, I'm on the hunt. When I found the little devil, I was taking no chances, having slipped into two hot oven mitts—"

A few giggles from the ladies interrupted me for a moment.

"When grabbing hold, she hissed and clawed back while shrieking something only the devil could scream as I pulled her out from under the bed."

After hearing this, the ladies respiration and heart rate made a noticeable jump of a few notches.

"I held her tight while searching her head for the three sixes—and sure enough, there they were tattooed into her skull."

Talking with a hushed voice helped in my delivery seeing them with goosebumps showing on their arms trying to shrug off the thought with a few weak chuckles.

"No way," Sheri said nervously.

With lifted brow, I look about the table...

"No way, you say? Well, just wait until you hear what happens next..."

I paused for effect, then lean forward at our candlelit table to gaze into the eyes of our guests and see their interest heightened...

"One of my previous girlfriends had a birthday party for me at my place and gave me a beautiful little bamboo Chinese pagoda birdcage."

I take a swig of beer wetting my lips. To heighten my story, I looked around at the other tables with darting eyes to see if anyone else is listing.

Satisfied, I began with a whisper...

"Inside the pagoda, a cute little finch began to sing its tiny pulsating heart out. At first glance, I felt love for the sweet thing. So, after the party, I temporarily, hung the birdcage above the dining room table with string for safety sake, knowing the little roaming devil would stalk her."

Sheri's friend has her hand over her mouth and wide-eyed. Sheri has her hands in white-knuckled fists, both girls expecting the worst.

Not wanting to disappoint...

"The next day between early classes, I looked in on little Tweety bird... Yep, you guessed it...

The devil had jumped up and hung onto the birdcage until the string broke, which brought it down in pieces."

There is more gasping as the ladies wait to hear the *coup de grace*...

"Now, I have a beautiful thick white rug in the living room where I found a speck of blood and a single little black and yellow feather. The evil deed must have happened a moment before I arrived home when seeing the cat lying on the couch licking its chops. To make matters worse, I found out later that this furry devil told little Tweety bird's parents about it."

"Oh, my God."

The girls shout out with tears in their eyes as they nod their head up and down, chanting...

"She is the devil. She is the devil."

We were in the presence of multitasking girls.

As the evening wore on, I would glance over at Tom. He was showing off for Sheri's friend like a Bantam rooster—swirling a toothpick around in his mouth, and through body language, strutted about—all the while still sitting down.

Please... I'm not making this up, but I guess you would have to had been there.

This just shows Tom's insecurity by trying to show how tough he is.

Before you know it, ten o'clock rolls around. So, being the responsible guy that I am, I inform the ladies of my early morn rise and ask if we can escort them out to their car.

As we near Sheri's Mustang convertible, she looked at me...

"I'll be gone for a week starting this coming Friday. So, how about having dinner with me Thursday night?"

With my atomic smile and blazing white teeth shimmering off her beautiful blue eyes, I show my acceptance.

Sheri's eyes sparkle as she hands me her phone number written on a parking ticket.

For you guys out there, I sure hope you've been paying attention and taking notes.

Watching the girl's head off down the road, we can see a bank of coastal fog creeping toward us in the night.

Standing there in the cool ocean breeze, Tom gives me his sad bloodshot eye look.

"I'm sure that woman fell in love with me."

After having said that, he removes the toothpick from his clenched teeth.

"Did she have any other choice?" I said.

Tom is only staying over for the night, then off to a business meeting in Orange County the next morning, and then, later that night, he's off to Chicago—ah, the life of a businessman. We shake hands, hug, and pound on each other's backs and say our good buys.

It isn't long before I'm crawling in between my bedsheets with a shit-eating grin and butterflies in my stomach. After turning out the light, I look at the clock...

"DAMN, IT'S ELEVEN-FIFTEEN," I scream.

ACT II - SCENE 1
ENHANCING THE LEARNING PROCESS

The following questions will allow you to see how your thoughts might change as you gain additional knowledge in this new organizational architecture when reading further into the book.

Question 1
Why would changing to a horizontal open-systemic organization allow for greater productivity, inspire employees to be the best they can be, and flexibility to respond to the customer?

Question 2
Why is creative thinking such a significant ingredient in organizational architecture? Moreover, why does it not flourish in a vertical organization?

Question 3
What are your thoughts on *team* versus *community?* Do you agree or disagree and why?

Do you see the author's point of view to move away from the term, team?

Why does this make sense for a horizontal organization, but fundamentally, not a vertical organization?

Question 4
What are your thoughts on Johnny's friend, Tom? Do you know anyone like him?

ACT II SCENE 2
Organization Architecture

WEEK 3, FRIDAY MORNING –OPEN-SYSTEM ARCHITECTURE (OSA)

JOHNNY'S DAYDREAM

Having arrived early at ATC Friday morning, I find myself sitting in the lunchroom sipping a hot cup of coffee. Feeling relaxed, I let my daydreaming wander while thinking about last night...

You remember Sheri, the golden hair lady at Roku's restaurant. Well, last night, I had dinner with her at the Wildfish Grill. We arrived in the evening not long after the sun had settled in for the night. The sky had a purplish look to it with a fresh brush stroke of painted fuchsia running along the horizon.

While waiting for our table, we sat at the bar sipping our drinks doing the dating game while getting to know one another. Outside the window, we can see the last of nature's neon light show being flattened into the black of the night and replaced with the soft lights of the bar reflecting off the window.

I can't help but enjoy watching Sheri perched on the barstool, her torso erect and proper, but not without a subtle hint of sensuality flowing through her tall, slender body.

Sheri carries herself as though she were royalty herself from the Land of the Fjords, Trolls, and Vikings. She is the perfect image for Frank Sinatra's song HAIR OF GOLD, EYES OF BLUE...

With his words floating through my mind I see her bright-blue eyes frame her Roman nose—a nose that displays her strength of character, and beautiful lips that speak with a voice polished by old money.

She's wearing a head-turning, ankle-length, gray shoulder-exposed dress with flared sleeves and an empire waist, which made apparent her long slender figure. The dress looked as though it cost more than Estonia's GDP and accented her tanned shoulders. Around her neck was a beautiful gold necklace that matched the color of her hair.

She took my breath away when I looked into her back-lit blue eyes—the kind you look into and feel you've gone astray and lost somewhere in a fog. She is the most pleasing put-together woman I've ever seen. Had I taken my pulse, it would have jumped to a hundred-yard sprint rate.

Sheri told me she was from Oklahoma and that her dad was in gas. "How nice for him," I said, concluding that the poor girl from Oklahoma had a dad that owned a few gas stations somewhere out on Highway 40.

She is well-educated, worldly, and connected with celebrities and politicians. Hmm... One would have thought this should've been a clue she didn't come from a middle-class family, but it didn't register at the moment.

Later, sitting at a cozy table, we heard someone call out my new friend's name using a phony French accent, "La Sheri."

When approaching our table, Sheri looks into his eyes without looking up, along with an outgoing smile. He looks Eurasian with a Kim Jong-il bouffant hairstyle. You know the one, where the hair adds three inches to his height. He wore a black collarless shirt buttoned at the top with extra-long black pants to cover his black shoe lifts. His most outstanding characteristic was his height— he was no bigger than Pokémon standing on J. Lo's booty.

Then with a funny thought, I wondered if the grass tickled his balls when he ran across the lawn.

WHAT? He has really short legs.

During our introduction, I found out he's Sheri's hairdresser. He sat with us for a short while waiting on his table. Finding it difficult to hold any kind of conversational chit-chat with Kim Jong, I decided to liven up the conversation...

"How would the two of you like to hear my creepy story about a new Chinese restaurant that I ate at the other night?"

With both giving me a smiling nod, I begin my story...

"Well, with the idea I should try out this nearby restaurant, I find myself sitting at a table taking in the menu while drinking a beer. Eventually, I ordered the Chicken Surprise.

Not long afterward, they bring my meal consisting of a large pot with a lid and a side of rice with vegetables. Diving into the rice, I notice the pot lid rise. With a double-take at my beer and shake of my head, I continue to eat my excellent rice.

A moment later, I'm distracted again as two beady eyes look at me from the under the rising lid. Wasting little time in calling the waiter over, I tell him of the rising pot lid with the two beady eyes looking at me.

The waiter responded by asking me, what you order?

I told him the Chicken Surprise..."

Seeing they were both hooked, line and sinker, waiting for the outcome, and being a natural linguist, I used my best Mandarin Chinese accent...

"Ahhh... So sorry, I bring you Peeking Duck."

There is a nanosecond of silence thinking Peeking—Ah... Peking— and then Sheri lets out a loud giggle. Kim Jong, however, goes into a hysterical fit of laughter, falls off his seat, and rolled up like a Chinese spring roll. We wait a short moment while as he gets his composure back. However, by then, he's told that his table is ready.

As he scooted off to his table with the stride of a shackled convict, I asked Sheri if she thought he used a booster chair. She said nothing, only looked at me. Damn, not everyone appreciates my Don Rickles kind of wit. Regrettably, it's my childlike compulsion to say what's on my mind...

Anyhow, she broke into an amused grin and then giggled. She probably shouldn't have encouraged me...

"How would you best describe your hairdresser?"

"Gee, I don't know? Well, sweet, and as you noticed, short," Sheri said.

"How about sweet and sour *shrimp*?"

"You're such a nut," she said with a giggle.

Our waiter soon joined us and took our orders. Sheri ordered peppery ahi tuna tartare. However, my stomach was growling, so I ordered a man-sized, aged steak and a bottle of red wine—mister sophisticated.

During dinner, we did not lack for conversation. The only exception was when Sheri prepared her bite of exotic tuna, did our table become quiet—and then more time elapsed chewing it into a semi-solid liquid before swallowing it. She says she likes to enjoy every little flavor. Me, I take in food like a wood-chipping machine takes in tree limbs.

After finishing our meal, we ordered after-dinner drinks. Now, I'll be the first to admit, dating isn't my game, but I make do.

Later, the waiter noticed my empty glass and came over to ask me if he could bring me another.

"That would be great, thank you."

The waiter glances down at Sheri's wine glass, then heads toward the bar, having seen little change, perhaps, less one sip or a little evaporation.

We were having such a good time; neither of us had realized how late it was. With both having to work the next day, I paid the bill along with a nice tip. Before leaving, I thanked our waiter for making it such a pleasurable evening. On the way out, we stopped at Kim Jong's table. Sheri leaned over and whispered in his ear. They both giggled.

As we walk out the front door, Sheri expresses her friendship with Jong...

"One has to love the image he tries to keep up. He's so cute."

"Image? He's too tiny to have an image."

She giggles, then grabs my arm, and we walk out into the dark of the night...

Parked in front of Sheri's Newport Beach home with a beautiful view of the ocean, we sit for a moment undecided what to do next. So, as things go, I escort her to her front door.

She looked up at me...

"It's late, we have had way too much to drink, and with you having a long drive ahead of you, why not spend the night at my place?"

I stuttered for a long moment rattling off a stream of incoherent words, but, ultimately, I came to my senses.

"Gee, how could anyone refuse such a kind offer from such a beautiful woman?"

Then, of course, any other answer would've been un-Latin of me. Un-Latin, hell... I'd been a damn fool.

We were up early, played around, showered, and dressed for work. With me being the master chef that I am, I fixed a dynamite breakfast of high-protein pancakes. You begin by blending in four egg whites, two whole eggs, two tablespoons of flaxseed, two cups of whole-wheat flour, two tablespoons of Canola oil and two tablespoons of baking powder.

Ahh... Pour en faire une pièce maîtresse (Ahh... to make it a masterpiece). One must soak a cup of raisins in hot water and then add enough of its liquid to give the pancakes the right consistency for pouring into the frying pan. To get a nice crispy crunch around the edges, pour about an eighth of an inch of Canola oil in the pan and place over medium heat.

The result will be lip-smacking pancakes, good enough for four people—making it about right, given that Sheri was a light eater.

After finishing her pancake and poached egg, Sheri looks at me with a broad smile...

"Well, Johnny, I might consider the idea of you spending more time with me, if you'd promise to make breakfast every morning..."

Her head is cocked waiting for my response...

Ahh... This sounds more like a commitment to me—scary stuff. So, I dodged her question by giving her a direct answer...

"I wasn't sure if you had approved of my overnight test in the sack. So, thinking of a way for my point-standing to go up, I fixed my special pancakes."

This seemed to work as we laugh, kiss, and run out the door...

It was a half-hour drive to Advance Tek from Sheri's place allowing me to drive onto the parking lot at seven-fifteen on a beautiful sunny morning.

THE LUNCHROOM

While drinking coffee in the lunchroom with last night's images still on my mind, I glance up to see Dakota with three production employees walking to the coffee machine. I tried waving as they head toward a table at the other end of the lunchroom. Hmm... Apparently, they didn't see me.

With the four of them seated and chin-wagging away, I sauntered over for more coffee, then head toward their table.

I stood there looking down at the ladies with my good-humored smile.

"Good morning ladies. Do you mind if I sit with you?"

The three production lady's looked at me with the giggles. Dakota gawks at me above her eyeglasses with hoisted eyebrows, then nods to a vacant chair.

"Is this a great morning, or what?"

I look at Dakota with trepidation while taking my appointed seat.

Then everyone looks at me in unison with a gleeful smile as Dakota grabs a napkin and hands it to me.

I give Dakota a puzzled glance.

"What?"

The three ladies have joyful titter as Dakota wipes her hand across her mouth and then whispers...

"Lipstick."

It's seven forty-two, so I excuse myself and head toward the training room with my tail between my legs. Well, it could have been worse—lecturing in front of the employees with lipstick plastered over my face. Well, so much for my great morning.

THE TRAINING ROOM

After saying my good mornings, I'm ready for my delivery, but for whatever reason, the audience wasn't. They insisted on quizzing me about my quirky behavior. Oh well, not wanting to ignore a good opening for self-deprecating humor, I liven up the audience with my humiliating experience in the lunchroom.

When hearing the story, the audience responds with a cheerful guffaw.

With a bit of self-satisfaction, I take a moment to inhale my cup of coffee's wonderful aroma of old-fashioned Navy, black coffee.

Jake told me there's no better way to begin your day aboard ship, then to have a cup of Joe.

I scanned the audience wondering who made the coffee...

"Who made this excellent navy brew?"

"Why that be me, Cap'n," Ed Blackburn said.

"Arr... You be a good deckhand. I put my spoon in the center of the cup, and she holds true. I'm thinking you can sip this brew with a fork."

This brought out chuckles as I lift my cup for a toast...

"Here's to swearing, lying, stealing and drinking, mate..."

The audience has a gleeful time with my toast as I show my delight and take a sip of the hot brew...

"If I'm not mistaken, our next subject is how to flatten the organization. We'll begin by discussing the role of managers and Leaders in a Horizontal Open-System. This discussion will help us understand the first major step to flatten our organization, STEP ONE, A, B, C, D, E, AND F ."

STEP ONE - A - MANAGERS AND LEADERS

I take a moment for another sip of coffee...

"What I'm about to say will shock many of you. So, if you would, please hold your questions until I'm finished getting across an import change in management.

For those involved, they were informed at a meeting with Denny Chang and

Ms. Wells yesterday afternoon...

The various levels of *managers* as we know them below department heads are no longer necessary in the new horizontal, flattened organization."

When hearing this news, there is a momentary gasp from the audience.

"Not to worry...

The *managers* aren't going anywhere, but their responsibilities will change along with the new title of *Group Leader* - a leadership role. We don't take this move lightly. Let me bring up a section of the new organizational chart to help illustrate what I'm about to explain how this will work, and why...

Group Leader - a leadership role

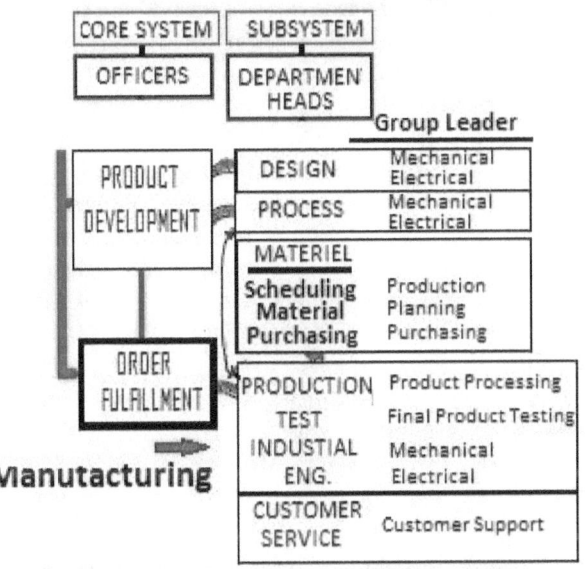

The Department Head will determine the number of Group Leaders by specific responsibility or perhaps the workload.

The term manager, as we know it, no longer fits in an open-systemic environment at this level. The current level of manager titles will no longer exist when the new organizational architecture is integrated. This is more than a title change. The Group Leaders will take on new responsibilities in their new subsystem communities as Denny Chang conducts their unique training over a three-month period.

These new assignments become far more rewarding and educational in running a business, along with advances in promotions and pay grade."

I glance at the faces around the room waiting for a response and see several hands waving...

"Yes, Ms...?"

"Sharon Ehmke. Thanks, Johnny. With this announcement behind us, may we ask questions now?

"You may, and thank you for asking."

"Thanks, Johnny. What is the difference between a manager and a leader?"

I waited a moment for Sharon to take her seat...

"Well, first off, our new business will need three levels, Officers or Directors at the upper level and a CEO at the head of the organization. At the lower level, we need leaders, not more managers."

I continue to see puzzled faces...

"Leaders and managers are two different distinct positions. Leaders will complement the new architectural organizational system. However, give me a moment while I explain a few things before discussing the major differences between the two...

In the new organization, the leader is at a level where the *action* takes place in making a change, and above all in a transformation of the system process like the one you are about to be involved in. At the upper level, management will help keep order and consistency in a system forever in a creative mode.

It's not unlike the architect who manages how contractors do things together, as Ms. Wells pointed out in her meeting at the Hilton..."

In a classic article in the 1977 *Harvard Business Review*, Abraham Zaleznik had this to say...

Managers embrace the process, seek stability and control, and instinctively try to resolve problems quickly—sometimes before they fully understand a problem's significance...

Leaders, in contrast, are willing to delay closure to understand the issues more fully. In this way, Zaleznik argued, business leaders have much more in common with artists, scientists, and other creative thinkers than they do with managers...

Organizations need both managers and leaders to succeed, but developing both requires a reduced focus on logic and strategic exercises in favor of an environment WHERE CREATIVITY AND IMAGINATION ARE PERMITTED TO FLOURISH.

Jake Jensen told me, Abraham's words would be difficult for him to express in a more simplified and articulate manner. Abraham's only problem was the vertical organization. This type of organization continues to be a roadblock negating this kind of thinking—CREATIVE SYSTEM THINKING, to be exact.

"With Jake Jensen's thoughts on changes about to take place in the new organizational architecture, we have a formula for a successful new organizational business model...

Ah... Speaking of great creative thinkers makes me conjure up Truman Capote...

Supposedly, he said that he could only think horizontally, incredible right? But in his case, it was lying down with a cigarette in one hand and sipping a martini with the other—what a guy."

The audience loved it by showing a gleeful chuckle along with their applauding—knowing that Truman's books and stories would be missed.

"Okay, let's move on...

Now, with everyone having a better understanding of why your company managers are changing their responsibilities to subsystem group leaders, I believe this would be a good break to answer Sharon's question...

Specifically, what is the difference between a MANAGER and a LEADER?

Well, a MANAGER in a vertical structure directs employees to work on predetermined goals or projects by assigning tasks while measuring their efficiency. As managers, their cost-effectiveness is measured by their results, sucking the creativity out of everyone while placing them in lockstep with the demands put upon them.

In a few cases, unapproachable demands on a consistent basis, especially, in areas where there are many variables involved in the process. Often resulting in employee warnings or firings, making for high turnover, therefore, affecting both throughput and quality.

Then we have those managers in vertical organizations who will talk until blue in the face about the importance of positive team play at each level of the organization. However, during the performance review, it's one-sided as the reviewer asks how are you performing for me? And what they should be asking is how can we work together to produce quality processes and a throughput of goods or services.

They look at teams being a critical part of the organization, and yet, they only grade one's individual performance as opposed to the whole team's performance. What's with that?" I ask.

I hear a chuckle...

"Good point," Ed said.

"Now, on the other hand, our GROUP LEADERS in their new leadership roles will focus on training, innovation, creativity, and adaptability that will help develop the true entrepreneurial spirit...

They will measure their own progress regarding throughput and SPC quality. The ultimate measurement is the customers MPV feedback, and EVA valuation compared to their benchmarks."

Before continuing, I study the audience reaction to my thoughts...

"I'm sure a few of you are still wondering why a manager can't fill the bill. Well, maybe, the best way to describe why a manager is becoming obsolete is to read out of the manager's playbook. In business school or management classes, most of us will have read the qualities of a good manager.

Now, having prepared a list of seven qualities that explain why they don't fit in the subsystem community group leaders should be more than enough to get my point across. In the discussion, feel free at any point to ask questions..."

I take a moment to clear the air while taking a sip of cold coffee.

"I'll begin with the MANAGER...

As a MANAGER, you make organizational decisions and identify problems and courses of action.

LEADERS, along with the employees, focus on improving their community processes and use minimal and system thinking to identify ways to improve the performance of the system.

As a MANAGER, you plan strategies to improve quality and cost savings.

LEADERS focus on improving the system throughput processes for improved customer perception using SPC process control charts to verify that their quality and performance are on track with the MPV benchmarks.

As a MANAGER, you bank on control and identify the team goals, assign work schedules and tasks with a short-range view often assigning busywork.

LEADERS have no need to assign tasks because keeping busy is not a priority. The idea of busy work has no relationship with improving performance, no matter one's responsibility. One way or another, everyone influences the system throughput and quality.

Using a variation of the phrase, "It's the economy, stupid" coined by James Carville, Bill Clinton's strategist... I would say, IT'S THE THROUGHPUT AND QUALITY THAT COUNTS, STUPID."

The remark generated joyful laughter from the audience.

As a MANAGER, you *empower* the *team* to improve themselves and their quality of work. Doing so will enhance their self-esteem, and in return, they'll offer you their cooperation...

The problem with this thought is it's contrary to their conditioning of receiving day-to-day tasks. This conditioning idea has the workers lose their initiative and self-confidence to decide on their own—albeit, even managers with the best of intentions are often complicit in an employee's lack of success.

LEADERS and their employees, on the other hand, will be encouraged to use their knowledge and creativity to improve the business performance. Their self-esteem doesn't need developing—other than, encouraging words that can move them in the right direction, as opposed to criticism."

I see a hand beckoning my attention...

"Yes, Marty?"

"Thanks, Johnny. I just wanted to make a comment...

As you know, I'm a mid-level manager of mechanical engineering. At first glance during yesterday's meeting made me a little hot under the collar. However, when Denny and Ms. Wells finished with their discussion at our meeting yesterday, I pondered about it overnight, I now feel elated...

Oh, and, my wife thinks it's a great move."

His comment raises a few chuckles from his friends. Marty gives them a piercing glance and then lets loose with a grin.

"Why do I feel elated? Because at heart, I'm an engineer trapped in a taskmaster's body—confined to meetings and relaying messages. It's both a burden on me and the business system. This new opportunity will allow me to use my creativity and engineering skills; therefore, permitting me to improve the system and our products by better utilizing my time and passing on my knowledge to my employees...

I'm sure that most of us feel the same way."

His engineering friends and others applaud him.

"That's it. Thanks, Johnny for these new opportunities."

"That's kind of you Marty, but the thanks should go to the Nguyen's for their vision and confidence in the transformational process…

Are there other questions before I carry on…?

No? Last chance…"

I take a deep breath before I continue…

"As a MANAGER, you are between top management and your team. You ensure that communication is smooth and articulated.

LEADERS receive communication inputs through their key indicators delivered in real-time or everyday updates. For other matters, they communicate with the core officers or directors on an exception basis—a go-between only burdens the system as Marty so eloquently pointed out.

The core officers don't need numerous feedback meetings from those below them. There is no substitute for getting out among the community of employees every day and asking their advice and opinion benefits both the employee and management, well, that and a smile go a long way with an employee. It makes them feel they are as one, as opposed to THEM and US… Well, you get my point.

As a MANAGER, you evaluate and examine processes and procedures, and then decide on the best choice to produce an improved outcome.

Jake Jensen knows from experience, this approach can cause serious problems owing to the manager's inability to understand the impact that his or her decision might have on other departments. This is a common occurrence that creates time-consuming meeting trying to get at the source of a problem set in motion, unknowingly, by another department.

LEADERS and their subsystem community of employees become the experts in their environment as they work together to improve their processes and procedures. If they decide to make any changes that may influence another part of the system, it's flagged. A system process engineer will be contacted to review the changes. Once the changes have been reviewed and accepted, then and only then can the change be implemented.

As a MANAGER, you sit in your office tracking the progress of each individual's activities and effectiveness by measuring the productivity of each employee, then offer feedback and counseling.

LEADERS don't measure individual productivity knowing it has no bearing on the total throughput, unless, the worker *creates* a *bottleneck*. In that case, the leader will evaluate the proper response that could involve additional training…

Well, that's enough examples. I'm sure you get the idea. For those managers in the transition process, it sounds daunting after a visual track up the management ladder, so to speak. It's a state of mind, and one would expect this when faced with change. However, with Marty's input today, the company managers have already moved into a new state of mind. I'm impressed…

Remember, anytime your emotion gets in the way, Shakespeare will pull you through. What was that quote, Belinda?"

"Oh, boy, let's see… Ahh…

There is nothing either good or bad, but thinking makes it so."

We applaud her while watching her blush a deep red from her neck up not unlike a rising thermometer.

"Superb, Belinda...

When one gets to see the beneficial results for the company, the employees, and your family, the change will be a good move.

As I mentioned in our previous sessions, these new Group leaders will be the CEO's of the future, and that's because they are performing an internship, not unlike a doctor of medicine. When the time comes, they will be well-grounded to run our future corporations."

Hoots and high-fives, coming from our new group leaders, triggers cheerful chuckles from the audience.

Then after a quiet moment, I continue...

"This change will create a flattened, streamlined, two-level, fast-moving system of management...

I'm now going to switch gears for the moment and discuss the current *command and control* of the army. It has always been designed as a top-down hierarchy. Our Special Forces and SEALs, however, were designed as a bottom-up organization, one that can react to inputs in a fast and efficient way. They've been organized into groups of ten to twenty men and given considerable discretion and responsibility for planning their assigned mission.

Units like Special Forces have been off and on since the Revolutionary War. General Washington's Rangers, under the command of Colonel Thomas Knowlton, were organized as American's first elite troops. The Rangers were fast-moving hard-hitting professional soldiers doing reconnaissance while gathering intelligence. George Washington had a fine sense of a fast response knowing the strong relationship between power and information.

And yet, here we are today, with the world's business communities still built on the shoulders of a top-down hierarchy, an organization that goes back to ancient army warfare.

We know the command and control structure is inefficient in today's business environment due to its excessive burden trying to improve business value. Nevertheless, we hold on to it like a newborn with a security blanket."

I take a moment to see what response I may have brought about. It didn't take long...

Ed Blackburn stands up to say a few words...

"You do indeed believe in what you're delivering. It's great to see the pleasure and passion you bring to our sessions. These are huge changes you're asking of us, and most reassuring."

"Thanks, Ed. And yes, I do believe in what I'm teaching. And, I feel honored being part of this new organizational change. Like I said, this is my first time being involved in a business atmosphere charged with such a huge responsibility. One that will allow you to succeed and become a new breed of a world-class organization..."

Seeing that I had finished my response, all was quiet for a moment, when a sudden response of applauding rolls through the room, and then silence...

"Thank you, for being so kind to such a long dissertation for saying thank you..."

Laughter...

"Okay, it's time we move on... And now, we're going to switch over to a new subject, levels of competency within our subsystem communities..."

STEP ONE B - A SHORT DISCUSSION ON LEVELS OF COMPETENCY

"The competency level within a job description will now define the employee's pay grade. There will be cost-of-living increases, but no personal review pay adjustments as you have had in the past."

The audience shows unrest, having said that...

"Please, let me explain...

Human Resources will remove the current policy for individual reviews after Ms. Wells, officers, department heads, and human resources meet during an upcoming weekend. Their agenda is to discuss a policy for competency and pay grades—allowing employees to make advancements through training and test.

The results will be a new employee policy program which will include a global sharing of the wealth system."

I take a moment before continuing...

"Whoops, I see hands in the air. "Yes, Janet."

"Thanks, Johnny, I have two questions: What the heck is a global sharing of the wealth, it sounds interesting. The other question is related to competency and pay grade information is forthcoming, but would you mind giving us an idea what the heck *competency level* means in relation to our responsibilities?"

"I'd be glad to...

Let me begin by trying to answer your question or interest in sharing the wealth. At this point, I have little information because nothing has been settled until the meeting takes place...

But in short, employees will for the first time be sharing in the wealth generated by the company. To my knowledge, this will be unlike any wealth-sharing program ever offered to all employees of existing companies.

The idea is to create a tool that can have a positive economic impact on the employees, the company, and the economy if other companies can see the huge advantages.

This message is nothing but a precursor, so with that in mind, I'll have to leave this subject until the company policy is finished and ready for all of you to be brought up to speed.

Does that help, Janet?"

"Wow, I'll settle for that until the company is ready to educate us on this new change," Janet said.

The audience followed by a happy applauding.

"Good to hear...

Okay, on to the next question, competency level. The short answer to a person's competency level is nothing more than one's ability to fulfill a specific role or function. So, when measuring an employee's understanding of the workplace in such things as creativity, communication, innovation, systems, and minimal thinking, and so on will result in the level of competency—that's it.

Does that answer your question, Janet?"

"I get your drift. And it works for now, but I'm sure we'll all get a better understanding when we meet for the policy change. Thanks, Johnny."

"Thanks, Janet, for being so understanding. It's much appreciated.

Ah... Another question... Yes, Derrick."

"Thanks, Johnny. I've noticed that you use the word creativity and logic in your sessions numerous times. If I'm not mistaken, you mentioned in our first meeting you would cover these subjects during this session. Would this be an appropriate time for that discussion? And lastly, I was wondering if most of us were born with the ability to be creative?"

STEP ONE C - CREATIVITY

"You are correct, Derrick. And yes, I'd be glad to cover those two subjects. There is no quick answer to your last question being born with creativity. Nonetheless, I'll try to cover this interesting topic in our discussion...

Not unlike much of science, there may be multiple answers or degrees of what is true. However, let's not forget the interworking of the brain is a work in progress...

Now, let's begin with the word *creativity* and then I'll bring to light its many *roadblocks*...

Creativity is producing something original and useful, and without it, we would see a sweeping negative influence on business and our society. IBM took a poll of one thousand five hundred CEO's that identified creativity as the number one leadership competency.

Professor Paul E. Torrance's study on creativity shows that the correlation to lifetime creative accomplishment was more than three times stronger for children than was having a high IQ.

The Greeks and Romans believed creativity was an act of divine inspiration. It wasn't long when they began to realize it may be hereditary or a special talent. Still not satisfied with a believable answer, they had to assume creativity came from the gods through meditation...

From a historical, point of view, it's no wonder we believed creativity was magical, sibylline, and linked to madness.

Then in the eighteenth century, they began to ponder over that it may be a human characteristic. Today, there are those who try to nurture and develop the creative talents within us on a day-to-day basis...

Now, to give you a more direct answer to your question is everyone capable of being creative?

...Well, Professor James C. Kaufman of California State University, San Bernardino tells us that *creativity is teachable...*

Ahh... Well, maybe, but I believe everyone is blessed with creativity when we enter this world. But, unfortunately, our education and business world stigmatize those who make mistakes or those who ask what's perceived to be a stupid question...

Ahh... This is what my mother once told me...

Some mistakes are too much fun to only make one..."

This brought back my cheerful audience with good ol' laughter...

"I'd say you might find the truth somewhere in that thought...

Well, as children, we don't hold back from being embarrassed by saying or doing something that may sound stupid. And yet, schools today and in the past haven't understood the importance of allowing kids to be wrong or be who they are. As we grow into adults, we become self-conscious about saying or doing something out of the norm, not wanting to look stupid in the eyes of others...

Why is it that we have so many creativity roadblocks in our business culture? To give you an idea, I'm going to hit on structured vertical organization roadblocks..."

STEP ONE D - CREATIVITY AND ITS ROADBLOCKS

"Much of the time growing up in our educational environment during grades one through twelve, and our time spent at the workplace, we have had teachers or managers who have destroyed our ability to be creative—and were unaware of what they were doing.

They continue on this course by discouraging us from asking lots of *why* questions. And then with too many *why* questions, they feel you are disruptive.

Then we have the word *no* that they respond to when the student or employee asks or present an idea. And when the teacher or manager answers with a *no or not now,* establishes their authority over you—and don't forget it...

The word *no* can have many connotations, none of them are good. I say this with the idea the Holy Jewish Chutzpah has the audacity when it comes to spirituality to never take no for an answer..."

I wait a moment seeing the audience contemplating my words...

"It's no coincidence we stop asking questions when hearing the word *no* thrown back at us. Then, of course, we lose our motivation and stop any engagement in school or in the business world, resulting in a lack of creativity.

Now, let's move on to the desolate suggestion box, with most hanging on the wall of companies worldwide. These boxes have been around for decades, and at best, they only collect dust. The problem is employees seldom use them because they know from experience their suggestions will fall into a shredder or black hole. Seldom are they even acknowledged, much less any action taken on their submissions.

Then, we have companies pushing and encouraging employees to enter a contest waving the creativity flag for the best money-saving idea, with the winner receiving a wonderful cash prize. Unfortunately, you'll seldom hear the results. Creativity, once again, crushed...

Why is that?

Well, the corporate vertical organization is but a species with most having unintentional creativity roadblocks embedded in the system. The biggest roadblock is the need to *control*...

With that in mind, let's take a walk through the common characteristics such as doing song and dance routines to get your attention while letting you know how wonderful they treat you. And, of course, they control you from the top down to the lowest level.

These organizations can't help themselves from feeling superior to their subordinates, and that brings about an atmosphere of THEM and US.

Then we have freshly minted managers in vertical organizations enveloped in meetings, statistical reports, and everyday tasks.

Overwhelmed, the manager has no time to be creative in the confines of his or her office. Stress often builds resulting in negative thoughts and influencing one's personality.

This kind of atmosphere can lead to a self-fulfilling process that we would call *The Set-Up-To-Fail Syndrome*...

The stressful pressure put on a manager can result in poor relationships with their employees...

For instance, it can begin with a strong relationship between the manager and a key employee.

Then at some point, an employee full of creative ideas fails, perhaps, in a minor assignment.

With many middle managers too concerned about protecting their career, they become paranoid thinking this employee incident could have repercussions from upper management. This leaves the manager with no other choice but to give out a few harsh words with the employee.

Not liking such a response over such a trivial thing, the employee distances himself from the manager, defeating any more creative ideas.

Seeing such a response in their relationship, the manager begins to tighten the controls over the employee.

The employee feels the aggressive action and begins to withdraw further from any kind of association.

The manager retaliates by showing his lack of confidence and increases his supervision.

The employee now withdrawals and may even ignore instructions.

The manager is now convinced the employee cannot perform his duties without extreme supervision.

The employee gives up, and now with the idea of leaving owing to frustration or anger.

As you can see, this kind of behavior on the manager's part has an unintentional ending that could have brought about an acceptable relationship, therefore, forcing the employee to leave...

The real loser in all this is the company due to its structural behavior and control, destroying self-worth and creativity in the workplace...

Is the manager to blame, or is the vertical organization at fault?"

I look around the audience for a response.

"Yes, Ed."

"I'm at a loss for words...

But the correct answer would have to be the organization...

Well, other than that, I have to say this has been a real eye-opener of a session. I'm hoping all our new leaders see the wisdom of what you have enlightened us with today. Ahh... That's it."

Ed then continued to stand and began to applaud while bringing in a supporting applauding audience.

I wait until quiet has returned, then continue.

"Jake once told me a delightful little story that pretty well sums up what happens to managers in a vertical organization put into that position—his story goes something like this...

When he was a kid in high school, he had to take driving lessons. One day, the teacher showed the class a cartoon to illustrate a subject matter he wanted to discuss...

It begins with the father all dressed for work sitting at the table with his family enjoying his morning breakfast.

After breakfast, he gets up and hugs the kids, and kisses his wife goodbye at the door. The family watches him from the doorstep as he almost steps on a butterfly. He almost falls over so as not to step on the sweet little bug. And then, after climbing into his car, a transformation takes place. He gets this psychotic look on his face as his hood ornament turns into a gun sight."

The visualization struck close to home as the audience has a gleeful chuckle.

"Well, you get my drift. We may be one of those who transforms ourselves when sitting behind the wheel of our vehicle, doing and saying things we would never do at home or while walking down a crowded street.

Jake feels that many managers fall into the same syndrome when they walk into their office. They're essentially nice people caught up in a bad organizational environment entrenched in our business world. There are, however, a few companies that understand this problem. Toyota is one of them.

One reason that Toyota's manufacturing plant in Georgetown, Kentucky is so successful is that it implements ninety-plus percent of its employees' ideas. This soon becomes a breeding ground for creativity—but it takes good training.

That's my long version of creativity and their roadblocks...

Before we get into creative thinking as opposed to logical thinking, I have a few thoughts that will influence creativity within individuals...

It involves eating good calories and performing lots of exercises—in other words, keeping physically fit."

STEP ONE E - SMARTER, STRONGER, AND FASTER THROUGH EXERCISE

"One should perform a minimum of a half-hour of daily exercise four to five days a week. It can be aerobic or weight lifting. If done properly, it will improve, in effect, every part of the body, including cognition—resulting in re-energizing our creativity.

Hey, I know what you're thinking—as if long hours at the gym could somehow improve our minds you say. Well, let me share with you fascinating findings by scientists who study these things...

Not too long ago, researchers had sweet-talked, if you will, the human brain into growing new nerve cells by having a few selected folks do a three-month aerobic workout routine. The exercise causes older nerve cells to form dense, interconnected webs, allowing the brain to run faster and more efficiently. They also sprouted new neurons, and the higher the individual was in cardiovascular fitness, the more nerve cells they grew. Age is not a constraint in building a strong, active mind. Good to know, as one gets older..."

I take a moment to look down at Ed, causing a joyful outburst, including Ed.

"Apparently, this begins with the muscles. Let's take the bicep or quad as a thought, contracting and freeing the weight. Doing so sends a chemical and a protein called IGT-1 into the bloodstream and on its way into the brain.

Mister IGT-1 then takes on the responsibility as the leader of the neurotrophic factory. In his new position, IGT-1 begins to send out instructions to increase the level of production of certain chemicals, including a key product called a brain-derived neurotrophic factor. These instructions will not only result in slowing down the aging process but could reverse it.

Science has shown that the frontal lobe, a platform of executive functioning allows the brain to improve decision-making and long-term planning.

What's that I heard you mumble, Ed?"

"Where do I sign up? I'm slipping in both those areas."

This brings out a few more chuckles.

"For us mortals, aging is not kind to us."

When scanning the audience, I see nods from those with more mileage than others.

"Okay, back to our subject...

There are other side benefits that improve blood volume and brain volume while building new capillaries resulting in less inflammation in the brain. As many of you may know, capillaries are the smallest blood vessels. These guys transport the nutrients and waste forth and back through your body's tissues.

I should also mention another benefit from exercise is having fewer mini-strokes that can impair cognition without you even knowing about it...

However, not unlike building up muscles, you lose these beautiful little neurons and their connections when you no longer have a lifelong built-in routine of exercise.

For you younger folks in the audience who might consider hitting the gym for a few months to eliminate any old timers' problems or Alzheimer's disease, forget it, that won't work—it's a lifetime commitment.

Now, we know it's easy for me to stand up here and preach the gospel on fitness training and its benefits. However, each one of you needs to consider where you want to be in life when you get older. We know we live in a fast world getting what we want a lot quicker than we did back when. You're deliberating, you don't have time—you want results, now...

Now, I'm not here to change your way of life, but inform you of the benefits of physical fitness...

Enough said, but are there questions before moving on to the really tricky, sticky stuff, like creativity as opposed to logical thinking?"

When skimming over the audience, I see no hands...

CREATIVE AS OPPOSED TO LOGICAL THINKING

"Creativity versus logical thinking, hmm ... there is no easy answer to this subject. Nevertheless, I'll give it a try...

Many consider the human brain is but two halves, with the left cerebral hemisphere being logical and the right creative. In other words, there is a contrast between creative thinking and logical thinking. However, creativity only resides on the right side of the brain is a myth. Without the use of the left side of the brain, it'd be like going to another room for something, and then forget what you were looking for... Well, that's a bad example, but you get the drift...

The reason it's a bad example is that something entirely mystical happens when you forget what it was you were going to do or look for. Our scientist has been working for decades on solving this problem but failed in the process, until now. There have been new breakthrough papers shedding light on the problem. I won't go into it, but it has to do with walking through a doorway causing the brain to tuck the reason away because it was generated in another room...

Hey, it beats the hell out of me?"

I crack up along with the rest of the audience...

While still laughing, I finished the subject with...

"Some research scientist made the remark...

Doorways are bad, avoid them at all cost..."

"No, shit," Ed remarked.

We all go slaphappy for a moment more...

"With the room settled down and quiet, I continue...

The real reason the two sides aren't isolated is that each side communicates with the other at around billion signals per second utilizing two hundred and fifty million nerve fibers in the corpus colosseum. Well, that gives one the idea, isolation of the two halves is a myth...

Logical thinking is analytical or reductionist, whereas, creativity is imaginative, intuitive and more in line with system thinking.

So, if you're concerned with innovation being the only focus, one would expect that creative thinking would be the choice...

But, if one became preoccupied with the idea of correctness or coming to a conclusion the validity of a process will be reliable, we would use logical thinking...

On the other hand, what if you're concerned about innovation for an improved process as well as the validity of the process? That means you'd need to deal with both logic and creativity...

Now, it's unlikely that the two rationalities would contradict one another if it came from the same person...

To continue with this line of logic, I leave you with a quote of a more *whimsical* description of logical and creative thinking from a mathematics professor...

Logical and creative thinking allows the brain to take off in all different directions, spinning in place and bouncing here to there.

It brings forth a catalyst from your billions of random synapses dancing to electrical impulses allowing your cogitation to take off in unexpected directions, often leading to solutions that linear thinking would shudder at the conjecture...

One other thing I would add ... this comes about not unlike a mail delivery system—but at the speed of light...

The letter sent to the brain comes to life delivered by two chemical components arcing across the synapses and reacting like a hydrogen fuel cell producing electricity to a motor...

Ah... With an exception, it sends an electrical signal to the brain that systemically influences our body with what I call little nuclear explosions generating ideas and movements that can be creative, logical, uneventful, or even stupid."

I waited for a moment for that to sink in...

"Now, much of my reasoning on this subject has been developed from logical thinking ... hmm... Or ... or was it my creative thinking...?

Ahh... Then, of course, most would say it must have been my stupid thinking."

I gander around with a playful look seeing the audience responding gleefully...

"Well, as you can tell from my smart mouth, the subject beats the hell out of me. Sorry folks, but that's the best I can do."

The audience responds with joyful applauding.

"I'm sorry it took so long getting there but did it answer your question, Derrick...?"

"Absolutely, that was a serious thought-provoking answer. Not only was it a brilliant answer but an informative one, I can't thank you enough."

I'm about to thank him, but he stands and applauds, bringing the rest of the audience in with him...

"Well, one can only hope it has been as informative to the rest of you like it has for Derrick."

There is another outburst of applauding.

"That's good to know people—because creative thinking will be the lifeblood of your new organization."

I take a moment to consider a few thoughts on my next subject.

STEP ONE F - CEO ROLE IN AN OPEN-SYSTEM ORGANIZATION

"Let's move on to a new subject, the role of CEO in the architecture..."

The organic business system can function without a leader telling it how to respond to certain conditions—

Ah... We have a question right off the bat that's great. Yes, Dolores?"

"Johnny, might you explain what you mean when you say a system can operate without a leader?"

"A system you say. Hmm... Give me a moment to put together an answer....

Ahh... Okay, you'll love this..."

Let's discuss an ant colony as a system. An ant brain has two-hundred-fifty thousand brain cells—and yes, an ant has a brain. A human brain has ten thousand million. Therefore, it takes a colony of forty thousand ants to have a brain the size of a human...

This is good to know, giving one hope, when you're down and out on any given day."

After the giddy cheerful outburst, I continued...

"A single neuron In the human brain can only respond to what the neurons connected to it are doing, but string them together, they can do the job..."

I then gaze down at Ed.

"Well, for most of us, anyhow."

This created a few more chuckles along with Ed's chortle.

"The ants, being a communal group of folks are similar to a human brain when comparing the number of neurons, but each ant can only do one thing relatively simple...

But as a community of ants, they can respond collectively to a given event such as defining how they will move in a pattern allowing them to forage more efficiently in a new area.

There are no leaders in ant colonies. Each ant decides what to do next. They can switch from doing general housekeeping to foraging. These little buggers, if you will, are great homesteaders and food finders...

Now, this illustrates how a system can operate without a leader, but luckily, we have a few more brain cells. With that in mind, we require a leader to set the system in a direction that will best benefit the collective group of employees, customers, and stockholders. We call that leader, the CEO... Well, I trust you get my point."

The story seemed to generate a nice response from the audience.

"I thought you might enjoy a little narrative on ants, thanks to Dolores...

The open-system is systemic and responds well to specific levels of input, and the CEO is one of those inputs. He or she isn't just a figurehead addressing financial matters or being the sacrificial lamb when things go wrong.

Not everyone feels the thrill of change; therefore, we need a leader capable of giving us the inspiration to carry his or her vision into the future.

Jake Jensen has strong feelings about the responsibilities of a CEO or president passed on to him by his friend Wayne Coker...

The qualities for a nation or Company's CEO must have a creative mind, leadership skills, curiosity, and most importantly, know what questions to ask.

The CEO must continue to excel in knowledge, listen well and pay attention to the concerns of the people, other nations, or their customers.

Ultimately, the CEO must be capable of learning the basics of system thinking, be flexible, and have a reasonable understanding of economics and finance—leaving no excuse for not understanding the financial position of the company.

One other thing, *don't get too full of yourself; you might not be as good as you think you are...*

Wayne surmises when a business fails, the chances are good, the failure occurred due to the CEO not understanding one or more of the noted requirements. Furthermore, the CEO may have no clue she or he created the systemic effect of the business failure.

These qualities should also apply to those who have aspirations for growing a business, no matter their current level of responsibilities..."

Before heading into the question and answering period, I take a moment to breathe in much-needed stimulating oxygen.

QUESTIONS AND ANSWERS

"I'm ready to go to Step Two, but first, let's cover any questions you may have..."

With a scan of the audience, I see a hand rise and glance at the employee's name card...

"Yes, Judy."

A tall, athletic woman, not beautiful, but a handsome-looking lady not unlike Meryl Streep stands up.

"Thank you, Johnny. I'm an electrical engineer with a comment and a question...

My comment is much like Jennifer's. When seeing the system processes run through the organization, and the concept of having a seamless system connected to supplier and customer is brilliant. The visualization of the idea alone makes you want to be part of such a change...

But what's puzzling is why this organizational model is not in the mainstream of today's businesses."

With Judy taking her seat, I gave her my only answer...

"Thank you, Judy, for that nice comment. Now, for your insightful question...

Regrettably, I have no smattering of an answer for you. Nonetheless, let me elaborate on your comment if I may, while I consider your question...

Our particular unique *Open-Systemic Architecture* or *OSA* theory as we call it can improve process performance by connecting the open system's distinct subsystems to their respective Market Perceived Value categories.

Measuring Market Perceived Value, or MPV as it is often called has been around for years. However, its primary use has been a tool for marketing, not for the business architecture.

Then In 1995, Jake Jensen's book articulated the need for MPV in a detailed layout of how a systemic and horizontal organization should plug into the customer receptacle and measure the purchasing criteria response...

How many of you know the name, Mary Parker Follett?"

I ask, but see no response, except for a few shrugs, and then a hand rises.

"Yes, Nancy, I take it you have an answer."

"Isn't that the author who wrote *Eye of the Needle* and *The Pillars of Earth*?"

"Ah, no. I would have to credit those novels to Ken Follett, close, but no cigar."

"Right," Nancy said with a blush.

"That's okay; I get them mixed up myself...

Mary Parker was, among many things, an American social worker, consultant, and author of books on management, and a political theorist. She was far ahead of her time. Today, she would have been a force to reckon with. In 1933, she said this about the horizontal organization...

Cross functioning, in which a horizontal rather than a vertical authority would foster a freer exchange of knowledge within organizations...

Now, let me say a few words about the idea of *system thinking...*

The theory or concept has been around for decades, but it too, has been an uphill battle for functional organizations to buy in on the concept, but not for lack of trying owing to Peter Senge, the Senior Lecturer at the Massachusetts Institute of Technology.

Peter is the author of several books, including the universally acclaimed *The Fifth Discipline*, and for decades, he has been trying to incorporate system thinking into our business organizations..."

While gazing into my cold coffee cup, I'm considering where I should go from here, when I hear a voice and look up to see a rising hand...

"Yes, Max?"

"We've heard what you've had to say, but I'm sure you had a point after veering off from MPV."

"You're right Max," I said cheerfully, "I've just been pondering on that very thing while gawking down at my cold coffee."

The audience has a good-natured laugh. A moment later I see a young lady running down the aisle spilling steaming coffee.

"Wait, I have hot coffee for you."

The coffee runner caught everybody's attention.

The audience turns their heads like a school of fish swiveling on a dime to see who's causing the excitement.

She is Asian, five foot ten—and the word *delicious* comes to mind, but she's acting like one of those ridiculous prize girls on the *Price Is Right*. My alimentary canal tightens, and then my larynx shuts down while gasping for oxygen. Ronald Reagan once said: *The alimentary canal is where there is a big appetite at one end and no sense of responsibility at the other.*

The five foot ten Asian beauty stands before me with coffee in her upheld arm. I reach for the coffee with a tilted head and a lopsided grin...

"Why thank you... Ahh?"

"Lora. The name is Lora."

I respond with my best impression of Hugh Gant's self-deprecating smile...

"Thank you, Lora."

She replies with a tantalizing look.

Hastily, I take a sip of coffee.

Lora looks up at me...

"I didn't know you were so tall."

Again, I borrow from those in the know and take a line from The *Big Sleep*, by Raymond Chandler...

"I'm sorry, I didn't mean to be."

"But thanks for the coffee."

"You're welcome, Johnny."

After a giggle, she returns to her seat.

The audience chuckles over the little sideshow.

"I apologize for our little interruption folks. But, it would seem Lora gets a little hysterical under pressure."

With the audience looking back a Lora, they have a cheerful laugh as she facepalms herself.

"Oh look, now she's talking to her hand, poor thing."

Lora and everyone else has a good laugh with her head still buried in her palm as she wags her finger at me with the other hand.

With a short nanosecond wait of my ten heartbeats, I get back on track...

"Well, Max, back to your question of what my point was in changing direction when I was discussing MPV, and then for whatever reason, I begin talking about Mary Parker and Peter Senge...

I know it was a radical jump, but the idea was to bring your attention to the missing *link* when developing the concept of horizontal organizational architecture and MPV...

What everyone needs to understand is that THE MISSING *LINK*, BEING MPV, brings together SYSTEM THINKING, HORIZONTAL ORGANIZATIONS, AND THEIR SUBSYSTEMS GIVING THEM THE ABILITY TO HAVE INTERACTION WITH THE CUSTOMER'S PURCHASING CRITERIA...

It's the combination that provides the knockout punch. Without it, the theory of system thinking is a difficult sell for any organization.

The Jake Jensen Group is counting on this combination to catch hold and make *change for the right reason* the platform of our businesses of the future...

IT'S PUTTING ALL THE RIGHT PIECES TOGETHER IN A WAY THAT WILL INFLUENCE THE MARKET. AND TO DO THAT, ONE MUST THROW OUT ALL THE RULES, AND THAT'S THE BEAUTY OF IT. CAN YOU DIG IT?"

"We can dig it!" Lora shouted.

Her response has a joyful audience applauding, although, she can no longer see them with another facepalm, trying to cover her embarrassment.

What a gal. I waited for the class to settle down...

"Judy, I guess I've had enough time to ponder over your question. Why is this model not in today's business organizational mainstream?

It isn't a short answer due to the many variables in one's comfort zone. To begin with, the CEO must know of the new organizational theory. However, if one is aware of the theory, the easiest answer would be organizations don't like change, especially, when CEO's don't like personal risk.

Then we have those leaders of business organizations who don't believe change is possible or consider the personal risk is too great, as I mentioned before.

Then we have the CEO who advances up the management ladder where *cover your ass* syndrome was business as usual—a principle of management that tries to minimize their personal responsibility and accountability. As one can image, this condition often ends up paralyzing the organizational behavior. Meaning, change of any kind will never take place.

You may find the CEO is under great time pressure, which does not allow for clear consideration of the subject. While others are so rigid, structured, and inflexible that making a change is philosophically difficult for them...

Is everyone following my meaning, so far?"

Seeing a few smiles and numerous nods, I continued...

"Good...

Alright then, a CEO may not want to disturb their current comfortable position, that or become complacent and underestimate one's capabilities.

As you can see, there are a lot of reasons we have had little or no change in our structured organizations, but perhaps, one of the most powerful is the lack of visionaries...

But once the few visionaries see your company's model performance in the business world, they too will move into horizontal open-systemic organizations.

Then following the visionary leader takes over by those who fall into the herd mentality. Some CEOs may not understand the change, but survival has its own influence, and they too will make the change. A change that will help their business and the nation's economy…

The other possibility is a new generation of leaders who don't carry any old baggage, allowing them to challenge the old ways, then move their companies into our innovative architecture."

Ed stands up… "Without question, I'm not a new generation guy, but with this new knowledge, I'm ready to shed my old baggage."

This brought about a joyful response of applause that radiates throughout the room.

"It's great to see such enthusiasm. Sometimes you wonder what has happened to our leaders in producing our future business organizations. It looks like if we can get the word out, folks like yourself and your new company will plant the seed."

Hmm… I need to get us back on track. It's getting late in the morning…

"Before moving on, let's cover any more questions."

Another hand rises… "Rick," I said with a nod toward a young, short, wiry guy with corkscrew brown hair about to stand up, wearing what the Navy called *birth control glasses*.

"Thank you. I'm our resident computer scientist. When looking at my organizational diagram you passed out, my question would be, how do we measure our performance with that of our competitors?"

"That's a good question, Rick. If you don't mind, I'm going to hold off for the moment, because I will cover that detail in Step Three of our discussion."

Rick nods with a respectful thank you.

"Okay. I'm moving on to STEP TWO…"

STEP TWO A - PERSONNEL REPORTING CHANGES

After getting my mind around my next subject, I take a quick sip of Lora's coffee.

In our new subject, personnel reporting changes … there'll be shifts in your employee reporting structure, but most are not difficult to overcome…

However, the most notable are three departments, process and product engineering, and quality assurance. These three will be going through major changes. The managers involved in this change have met with Dakota Wells, and everybody seems comfortable with the adjustment."

STEP TWO B - PROCESS AND PRODUCT ENGINEERING AND INDUSTRIAL ENGINEERING

"To give you an idea of the changes, I'll begin with process engineering…

I'm sure most of you know *process engineering* reports to manufacturing.

But with our new organizational arrangement, this creates three major problems...

The FIRST PROBLEM lies with process engineers using engineering drawings to develop visual aids, a practice prone to errors and a redundant process. But with no alternative, you did what was necessary.

The SECOND PROBLEM is far worse with the process engineers having little or no influence on product design. The new change in the reporting structure, however, process engineers will work alongside product engineers to develop finished engineering drawings, streamlining the production process.

This change will shorten the throughput time and lower inventory levels, relieving millions of dollars for better investment, and faster customer response time elevating their perception.

The last and FINAL PROBLEM is engineering changes have been difficult to control, making delays in the system...

With the reorganization, no change orders will be issued without a process engineer sign off, then the process engineer will hand-carry a new engineered visual aid signed off by the appropriate engineer, and if necessary, to the production floor and instruct the appropriate supervisor of the change.

With the process and product engineer's working together, they will become seamless in their ability to expedite new products into order fulfillment workflow.

Now, on the other hand, Industrial Engineering will continue to report to manufacturing but maintain a close relationship with process engineering in new tool design and capital expenditures for new equipment.

Let's take a moment for questions. When finished, we'll take a fifteen-minute break. Do I see any hands? Yes, Robert?"

"Thanks, Johnny...

I'm not an engineer, but I see your reasoning for moving the process engineering group to product engineering, but I'm curious, why does industrial engineering stay with the manufacturing folks?"

"Good point, Robert...

Well, Robert, industrial engineering, and manufacturing have a long history together—and for a good reason. They make things happen in the manufacturing area such as supporting them in plant layouts, tool design, review new automated equipment, justify manufacturing's capital expenditures, and, production line set-ups and so on...

Does that answer your question, Robert?"

"It does, thanks, Johnny."

"Are there any more questions? ...No. Alright, please be back and in your seat at twenty past the hour."

As the room clears, I head out along with everyone else."

STEP TWO, C - QUALITY ASSURANCE

"At twenty past the hour, everyone has returned from the break.

"Thank you for being so prompt...

Let's move on to our next subject: *Quality Assurance*...

When the new testing procedures are in place and producing quality subassemblies, the quality control people on the production floor will transfer to an area of their choice giving them the best opportunity for growth.

I should also mention, quality assurance will continue to inspect your incoming supplier's goods, and final product assembly and test acceptance.

Their current position in customer liaison, however, will be to a large extent, different—a discussion we'll have during another session...

The management of Market Perceived Value will be an added responsibility for quality assurance, a process quality program... By that, I mean the data is well-timed and accurate...

I'm now ready for more questions."

I notice Sandy with a raised hand and give her a nod.

"Johnny, won't we be making a dangerous move by removing the quality assurance inspectors from inspecting the in-process subassembly product?"

"That's an excellent question. Let me answer that by giving everyone an interesting background on Jake Jensen's friend, Wayne Coker. He did an amazing thing back in 1969 by removing the production line's quality assurance. But first, let me give you a little history on the subject...

During this period, Wayne was the director of manufacturing at Dataproducts Corporation, and one of the youngest in the high-tech industry. Wayne's responsibility was producing the company's high-speed line printers and disk drive machines.

In this new position, Wayne wasted little time with their batch controlled manufacturing processes, and within six months, they were producing products in an innovative system they called, *progressive assembly*, but in fact, it was the first *just-in-time manufacturing operations in the high-tech industry... And years before the Japanese took credit for it in the 1970s...*

One must remember, in the late 1960s, the line printer wasn't much smaller than a Baby Grand Piano producing 600 lines per minute.

The disk drive machines were about the size of two large refrigerators with two upright three-inch diameter shafts, each holding twenty-five, twenty-four-inch diameter discs with a total storage of five megabytes of data." I said with a gleeful grin. "They were, truly, the prehistoric dinosaurs of our high-tech industry. But at the time, these products were a huge step in technical advances in printing capability and computer storage..."

I waited for the audience to finish mumbling with one another, shaking their heads, and sending off chuckles.

"Well, as you can see, we have come a long way since then, except, for our organizations...

Okay, back to Wayne. He knew there must be a better way to process these new high technology products. So, with the idea of televisions being high volume, he contacted the nearby Packard Bell television manufacturing plant. Ken Brown, their senior manufacturing engineer gave Wayne and a few of his engineers a tour of the long central line of chassis with feeder lines of subassemblies and parts.

At the time, Dataproducts, like all high tech manufacturers had a batch control planning system that defined specific kits for assembly. When assembled, they were put back into the stock room where they waited their turn to be pulled to the next higher assembly—a process that produced low inventory turns and tying up millions in cash.

Liking what he saw at Packard Bell, Wayne hired Ken Brown away from the television manufacturer to work with his process and industrial engineering staff. They designed and revamped the manufacturing processes to increase throughput and reduce the inventory levels.

When finished, they soon had line-printer chassis moving down a track on a cart, not unlike the automated-guided vehicles of today. Feeder lines of complex high-tech subassemblies fed into this moving line of chassis.

A new software planning tool made this possible; *Material Requirements Planning*. MRP-I used a setback time for scheduling subassemblies. Each subassembly, or goes into, if you will, in their case, was set for a one-day setback, leaving a one-day buffer in final assembly.

Work-in-process went from batch control processing of three turns per annum to almost twelve turns, within fourteen to eighteen months, freeing up millions of dollars for better use—an amazing transformation for the period. Even today, the average company in the information technology world had an inventory turnover of nine...

With final assembly's one-day inventory buffer, subassembly throughput time and quality became a serious issue...

To assure high-quality subassemblies, they had built-in test points at selected workstations. In essence, the workload for the assembler at a test station was balanced, allowing for both testing and assembly, with the testing process being of a very short duration.

The results were so impressive, the quality assurance director agreed to remove the additional burden of quality line inspectors.

It didn't take long for the word to spread of this new way to build computers and their peripheral products. High technology companies from around the globe (including Japan who introduced it to the world in the 1970s) began to visit the plant to see this new development in manufacturing that in today's world calls JUST-IN-TIME MANUFACTURING...

Now, I would add that your business lends itself to designing out the quality assurance inspector during the manufacturing process...

Well, Sandy, do you feel a little more comfortable with the change?"

"You bet I feel a lot better, thank you."

Now, on to the last step, STEP THREE A, AND B.

STEP THREE A - HOW THE NEW SYSTEM WORKS

"In explaining the architectural side of the *plug-in* measuring system, I'll not go into much detail...

But I'll need to use our open-system diagram, which I'll have on the screen momentarily...

I should also mention, two weeks from now, we'll be covering this diagram once again with an in-depth discussion during our meeting about *Having a Fresh Perspective*..."

While scanning the audience, I find Rick...

"Rick, this is where I answer your question on measuring our performance with the competitors."

Rick responds with a nod and whispers a thank you.

"In a few cases, I'll be repeating myself from our previous Tuesday meeting while covering the *plug-in* measuring system diagram—so as to refresh the basic concept..."

I clicked to open the diagram file...

OPEN SYSTEM ARCHITECTURE		MPV MEASUREMENT PLUG-IN METERS	CUSTOMER PERCEPTION RECEPTACLE
CORE SYSTEM	SUBSYSTEM		
OFFICERS	DEPARTMENT HEADS	INFORMATION FLOW	
INFORMATION DISTRIBUTION & FINANCE	ACCOUNTING	MPV Survey	Customer Perception
	System Indicators MGT INFO SYST		Purchasing
	ORDERS SALES		Price
MARKET RECOGNITION	MARKETING	Quotes/Price Market Analis	New Products to Market
PRODUCT DEVELOPMENT	R & D DESIGN PROCESS		Timeliness
	MATERIEL	Throughput & Delivery Time	Flexibility
ORDER FULFILLMENT	PRODUCTION TEST INDUSTRIAL ENG.	Changes: Design/Sched Reliability	Customer Acceptance Service
	CUSTOMER SERVICE	Order Status Cust. Support	Supplier Quality Assurance
QUALITY ASSURANCE	QUALITY CUSTOMER LIAISON		

"Okay, let's begin with the *Information Distribution* box adjacent to the curved big arrow. As you may remember, this data facilitates the information needed to process products and service to the customer—along with MPV feedback for each of the subsystem indicators.

STEP 3 B - MARKET PERCEPTION

"In this discussion, will focus only on your customer's marketing perception that drives your s*ubsystem indicators*, and your *leading indicator*, we call *Market Perception Value*.

In the near future, a survey group will provide you with a compiled potential and current customer database of information about your company's perception in the marketplace.

The data includes criteria in the various purchasing categories for each of your customer's three highest-rated suppliers measured on a scale of one through ten. They define the customer's procurement decisions in the diagram's *Customer Perception Receptacle*.

The feedback gives the level of performance needed to make design changes that can influence the customer's purchasing decisions toward your company as opposed to your competitors.

For instance, using the one to ten scale, and the customer's noted highest rating is a nine for product *timeliness* by one of the three top competitors—"

I stopped mid-point in what I was saying and pointed to the TIMELINESS PLUG-IN RECEPTACLE shown midway down on the diagram and then continued...

"For those who may want to make notes on your diagram, I'll repeat that again...

If the highest rating is a nine for *Product Timeliness* by one of the three top competitors, and your rating is four, indicating you have a serious problem to overcome. They would see you as performing at less than half of the top performer. Your poor performance may be due to such things as poor material planning, bad shop scheduling, shop-floor process problems, or system constraints.

Now, let's say *Service* represents order status and customer support and has a service rating of nine, which is two points higher than your competitors'. That means few resources are required to streamline the service process near term. Your company resources are valuable and should be managed as if you were looking for the best return on your investment.

But, I'm not suggesting the *Service* Employees must not assume they don't have to worry about improving. They must continue looking for improvements. Then if a few resources are required, I would encourage you to allow the changes. If major resources are required, and resources are available in the future, you will have a jump on incorporating the ideas.

Any questions so far?"

I take a moment to roam over the audience.

"Yes, Richard."

"Thank you, Johnny. Using a survey of our customer perception brings up the question of who will take our surveys."

"Good question, Richard. Your answer lies with quality assurance who will select the appropriate market survey consultant and the questionnaire they will use.

We'll cover more of this in greater detail in a later session, but does that answer your particular question, for now, Richard?"

Richard nods with a smile.

FINISHING UP THE DISCUSSION

"I'm sure that you're wondering how you'll make all this happen...

Well, we'll soon have sessions addressing Market Perceived Value architectural changes, System and Policy Improvement with Systemic Thinking in mind, and Systems performance modeling..."

When looking at the clock, I see it's time to end the session.

"It looks like we have run out of time. However, we covered the fundamentals of the new architecture...

But, before we finish the day's session, I'd like to make one last comment on this new organizational architecture...

Your new organizational structure and its behavior will someday make a profound change in how you conduct business while influencing others. These new architectures will become highlighted or more visible in our future slow-moving economy, changing it in a positive way, unseen in decades.

Okay, we are now, according to the clock, closed... Well, maybe not, Ed seems to have a question."

I glance down at Ed.

"Johnny, I'm curious about how long it will take the transformation period to run its course?"

"Well, you won't be able to measure it with an egg-timer," I said with a chuckle. "However, my best guess would be around three months."

"Oh? That's faster than I thought it would take. Thanks."

That's it until Friday. You have been most gracious. Thank you."

I've noticed Nina has been watching me with great amusement as the ladies went out of their way to walk in my direction while leaving their best smile behind.

And then, Lora stops by to apologize for her action.

"I am so sorry if I brought any shame to you, Johnny. If my father had seen me, he would have disowned me. Please forgive me."

"Trust me, your father will never know."

"Oh, Mister Johnny, you are most kind."

She gives a subtle bow, and then turns and runs out the door.

"What can I say?"

A GOOD LAUGH

While grabbing my coat and briefcase, Nina strolled toward me...

"Do you have time for lunch?"

I never turn down lunch, particularly, when the client asks me.

"I'd love to, Nina. My system is always on full alert to satisfy my vivacious appetite."

"Vivacious?" Nina said cheerfully. "That's great. Would you mind waiting in the lobby? I need to get my purse."

I give Nina a slight bow...

"*Il me fera plaisir Madame, Nguyen.* (It would be my pleasure Madame, Nguyen.)"

"*Je ne savais pas que vous parlait français, Johnny*, (I didn't know you spoke French, Johnny.) Did you take it in school?"

"No, I picked it up from a Parisian girl I used to hang around with."

With a shake of her head, Nina forms a grin as her eyes light up and then heads down the hallway to her office.

Several minutes later in the parking lot with Nina and her purse in hand, I see to it she's buckled in before closing her door. A moment later, I'm sitting behind the wheel.

"Well, Nina, do you have any special place in mind for lunch?"

"I do, and you will love this place. It serves Indian food."

"Sounds good, just point me in the general direction."

"Well, your first step is to leave the parking lot," she said with a titter.

"Hmm... It appears my wisenheimer ways are rubbing off on you."

"Wisenheimer?"

She responds with a blush and high-arching brows.

"That would be a wiseass, a smarty-pants, or big mouth."

"Oh."

She puts her hand over her mouth holding back a giggle...

"Ah... I guess you would call Jake Jensen a wisenheimer too."

"Yeah, apparently, that's why he hired me," I said. "And you should laugh more often—it's contagious."

"As strange as this may sound, laughter is what I wanted to talk to you about during lunch."

"Laughter?"

I cut my eyes toward her with a cocked right eyebrow.

"Yes. Laughter, I'll explain after we order our lunch."

Having arrived at the restaurant and ordered Vegetable Samosas and Chicken Tikka Masala, Nina sends me a smile...

"You have a great sense of humor that you bring to our discussions, keeping people alert and engaged. Is this by happenstance or by training?"

"For me, I've always been a wiseacre."

"Wiseacre," Nina said, with eyebrows levitating above normal. "That's a funny word. Oh, that must mean you're a wisenheimer."

"Yeah, I plead guilty."

"I bet you have your classes at Pepperdine in stitches."

"Perhaps, but I know students and business folks alike are under stress much of the time, at least those who care about their future.

Conceivably, one who engages in humor can perceive situations from... Ahh, perhaps, an interesting vantage point, knowing there is little else in the world that makes one feel better than a good laugh...

It stimulates while engaging us in the learning process. They say it liberates our creativity and provokes a higher level of thinking skills and visual imagery. Life itself is neutral. We can make it positive or negative. Laughter helps us keep it on the positive side...

"What an insightful thought. But I must ask, why don't more people laugh?" Nina said somberly.

"I'm no expert here, but on the negative side, we have those who are a step away from being narcissistic. Meaning, any person who never laughs shows a sign of profound insecurity. They feel vulnerable to risk one's self to appreciate the humor of others and have a tendency not to tell the truth for the same reasons.

But then we have those who just take themselves too seriously and are unable to laugh at one's self, like those who have the ability to use self-deprecating humor, which is the uppermost form of humor. If you can't laugh at yourself, one has a good chance to end up in therapy."

"Johnny, would you mind expanding your thoughts about laughing at yourself."

"Well... Much of what we do during the day is off-the-wall or even bizarre sometimes. Then we'll find ourselves in a whimsical frame of mind, thriving on silliness, piercing wit, and the ability to laugh at ourselves.

To give you an idea of what I mean, I was running late for a class during a workout at Gold's gym one morning. So, rather than be late, I take a quick shower and show up in my workout pants and sweatshirt.

I'm standing there in front of the class during my lecture with my right leg over my left leg trying to look sophisticated. The only thing missing was a vintage tobacco pipe sticking out of my mouth. So, wanting to add to the cool look, I try to slip my hands into my pants pocket, putting me into a panic..."

And then with an alarmed look of raised eyebrows and open mouth I realize, I can't find my pockets."

Nina's now waiting in anticipation...

"My fingers are flapping around searching for my side seam pockets like the wings of a squawking chicken looking for her baby chicks."

Nina giggles.

"The students seeing my dilemma began to chuckle—that turned into loud laughter. So, putting my hands backward into my pockets, I glance about while whistling the theme song to *SpongeBob Square Pants*... Then the class jumps in singing the lyrics...

Now, this gets me in the mood as I do a SpongeBob dance routine.

Bad move on my part, because that's when the whole class gets out of control singing the song, dancing, and laughing hysterically."

We chuckle at the thought.

"That's a funny picture you painted, I get your point about being able to laugh at yourself."

There was a moment of silence...

"But why are some people afraid to laugh?"

"I'd have to say one is taking a risk if you laugh when people around you don't. In doing so, you'd be exposing yourself in front of these people bringing more pressure than you would want to deal with."

"When is laughter not appropriate?"

"I'm not sure...

Perhaps at a funeral, and yet, when taking that into account, I've seen funeral ceremonies where the speaker had the audience in stitches. This releases a lot of tension, making for a wonderful memory of the deceased...

I'm not sure there's a problem within the total context of a discussion or speech for inserting laughter... For instance, Woody Allen said...

His grandfather was a very insignificant man, actually. At his funeral, his hearse followed the other cars."

We both crack up...

"Now, it can't get any more insignificant than that now can it," Nina said.

"Hell, if you can laugh at a funeral, you should be able to laugh anywhere, well, maybe not. The *appropriate time* is key. I'm sure that during a heavy discussion in the President's War Room would not be the appropriate place."

"I see your point, Johnny."

We become silent for a moment as Nina takes a sip of water.

"Can laughing help in our day-to-day muddling through life?"

While swirling the ice around in my water glass, I considered her question...

"Well, laughter helps you take your day and put it in perspective. It also allows you to take a step back from any particular situation and see it for what it is. When we laugh, we're communicating good-natured intent. So laughter has a bonding function with individuals or a group—in other words, most laughter is not about humor—it's about *relationships between people*...

And for the most part, it's positive, but it can also have its negative side. There's a difference between laughing with and laughing at. People who laugh at their fellow employees for making a mistake or saying something wrong with the idea of having them kowtow, relegating them out of the group....

This kind of action shows poor self-worth. It's an inability to laugh at oneself. However, I don't mean for this to be confused with jokes from comedians like Jay Leno or insults from the late Don Rickles, or wisenheimers like myself...

Laughter can produce endorphins and enkephalins which are natural painkillers more powerful than morphine. However, you don't want to tell your friend a joke when he cuts a finger off using the power saw, because it won't in all likelihood, help the situation...

But when the initial shock wears off, you could say not to worry Bud, well, unless they get it stitched on backward," I said. "Now, with such a ridiculous statement, you have to laugh."

"That is ridiculous, especially, when you visualize the finger stitched on backward and wiggling," Nina said, with a guffaw.

"Essentially, you need only to remember the definition of something funny is what makes *you* laugh. Our sense of humor differs from one person to another, and it won't cure our anxieties or ills. Nevertheless, the positive effects of laughter on psychological functions include a drop in the pulse rate, the secretion of endorphins, and increased oxygen in the blood. If you're deathly sick though, you don't want to stay at home watching the Three Stooges, rather than going to the doctor or hospital...

Ronald Reagan said...

W*hen the American people are happy, good things happen: they invest, they save, and they have children.*

He thought to put the nation back on the road of cheerfulness was a most practical endeavor..."

We both sat there for a moment bathed in stillness.

I soon broke the silence...

"What in the world brought about this discussion, Nina?"

Nina takes a moment to collect her thoughts while from the periphery of her eye, she sees the waiter coming out of the kitchen heading our way.

"Well... You're seldom away from one's responsibilities. Our belief system tells us that technology will make our lives easier—when in fact, it can make it more complicated if you let it, as you so vividly pointed out.

When I see you bringing laughter to our meetings, it helps us engage in our time with you. We are so stressed out with our instant needs—we forget how to laugh at ourselves when getting into predicaments we find ourselves in as you have so colorfully pointed out. It took you, an outsider, for me to see that."

I look at Nina with a relaxed smile...

"People are creatures of routine, liking to do the same thing, the same way, every day. I've noticed that humor has a tendency to expand our comfort zones helping us adapt to change with a lot less anxiety."

"Why is that?"

"Because most of our anxieties are predictable—therefore, we can prepare ourselves with the weapon of humor. You cannot laugh and be apprehensive at the same time..."

ACT II - SCENE 2
ENHANCING THE LEARNING PROCESS

Question 1
Just to have a little fun dialog, what did you ladies and gentlemen learn from Johnny's dating game?

Question 2
What would happen if a vertical task-oriented organization tried removing their huge overhead burden called, managers?

As one can see, creativity is an essential topic of this book, and most likely, everyone has a better idea of what creativity means, more or less.

Question 3
With this thought, how can you help enlighten others to consider these terms, allowing our schools, businesses, and governments to begin a redesign of their organization to one that allows creativity to flourish? Doing this could play a part in growing our economy again?

It looked as though the author believes that a smile and laughter is another subtle, but a vital factor in leadership and building relationships.

Question 4
What are your thoughts? With negativity being such a killer in relationships and in business, do you have experience how a smile and laughter has helped you in keeping a positive outlook on life or improved a relationship? Give an example.

ACT II SCENE 3
Business Lunch

WEEK 3, SATURDAY MID-DAY - JACKIE MEETS NINA FOR LUNCH IN LITTLE SAIGON

At seven thirty-eight Saturday morning, Nina's phone rings in her beautiful French Indochinese style home nestled in a park-like atmosphere of tropical plants. It sits back off Brighton Road overlooking Little Treasure Cove and the Pacific Ocean, Newport Beach.

"Giữ lấy ... Tôi chỉ là một người giúp việc ít tuổi, (Hold on... I'm but a little old housekeeper)," Li said in her sing-song scratchy Vietnamese voice.

Li stopped her cleaning and toddles over to the telephone on her short rickety legs. "Nguyen residence," Li Pham said in her broken English.

With the call on hold, Li heads toward the kitchen's expansive bi-fold French doors leading out to the flagstone patio with unsteady steps.

Nina Nguyen is finishing a light breakfast under the shade of a large table umbrella. She's having her second cup of coffee while envisioning how Thanh would be out working in his beloved flower gardens.

His pride and joy are the deep red flowers of the Hoa Dao or Peach Flower. It's a native flower of Vietnam and rare to see them elsewhere in the world. He grows them in clay pots on the patio with their branches draping lazy-like over the side dazzling you with their beauty and wonderful aroma.

During the early morning hours, the sun is trying to penetrate the fog bank that wraps a silver blanket along the coast as it rises above the surf and drifts along the beachfront. From their home perched high above the diminishing heavy mist, Nina is now lost in thought as she gazes out over the dark blue Pacific ocean. A moment later, she realizes Li Pham is standing next to her.

"*Bà Nguyễn*... You have a telephone call from a Jackie O."

"Thank you, Li."

Nina walked across the patio with her cup of coffee and then through the double French doors of her office to take the call.

"Hello, this is Nina."

"Hi Missus Nguyen, this is Jackie O'. We met last week at the Hilton."

"Yes, Ms. O', I read your impressive bio before the meeting."

"That's very kind of you."

"How may I help you, Ms. O'?"

"Well, first things first—is your husband's condition improving and is he still in a coma?" Jackie said, with apprehension in her voice.

"Thank you for asking. Thanh's condition is steady, but he is still in a coma."

"I'm so sorry, Missus Nguyen."

"Thank you. There seems to be urgency in your voice … what's on your mind Ms. O'?"

It would seem Nina has little tolerance of conversation for its own sake on the telephone.

"Please, if you don't mind, my friends call me, Jackie. I'm sorry for such an early call, but we have a tendency to start out in a hundred-meter dash and then shift into the five-thousand-meter run. So, please excuse my sense of urgency, I need to see you as soon as possible."

"Ms. O' …Ah, I mean, Jackie. I'm meeting with Marty Westlake this morning. Would a lunch date work for you?

"Yes."

"Are you familiar with Little Saigon?"

"Yes."

"There is a wonderful little restaurant on Bolsa Avenue between Brookhurst and Magnolia Street. It's called Pho Ho. A childhood friend; Kim Phan owns it. Have you had Pho before, Jackie?"

"No… I don't believe so."

"Oh good, you will love it. It's the perfect meal. While we enjoy our lunch, we can talk business and have our privacy. Ah… Is there anything I need to bring?"

"Not a thing. We need to go over our *Performance Driver* recommendations planned for you."

"Why Yes, I understand. Would eleven-thirty be okay?"

"Thank you, that would be great. See you then."

After getting off the phone with Nina, I drive over to Johnny's place in Santa Monica. We planned to discuss our ATC transformational timeline.

After finishing my business with Johnny, I'm headed south down the 101. After a little over an hour drive, I turn onto Magnolia and motor along toward Little Saigon. When stopping behind several cars at a stoplight, I see Bolsa Avenue up ahead. So, with a green light, I take a right turn on the main artery running through Little Saigon. The area has a considerable variety of shops, cafes, markets, herbalists, bakeries, delis, and many types of Vietnamese restaurants. Tucked away somewhere in these shops is the Pho Ho.

The passing addresses tell me I'm close, so I look for the restaurant belonging to Nina's friend. Off to my left is the name Pho Ho up on a plaza sign, so I pull into the left-hand turn lane. I waited for the traffic to clear, and then turned into the plaza. Sandwiched in between a fabric shop and a video store is my destination. After finding a place to park, I head toward the restaurant.

Entering, I notice a beautiful Vietnamese woman emerge from behind the counter who greets me with a bow.

"Are you Kim Phan?" I asked with a polite nod.

"Yes. You must be Ms. O'. Nina called and told me to expect you."

"It's a pleasure to meet Nina's longtime friend."

"That's very kind. May I seat you?" Kim said, with a slight bow.

"Please. A quiet location—we have business to discuss."

Kim seats me at a booth in the rear corner of the restaurant.

"Nina says I'm being treated to Pho. If I may ask, what is Pho?"

"Pho is a favorite Vietnamese meal. It is rice noodle soup made with a savory beef broth. It's served with thin slices of lean flank, accompanied by a plate of limes, nutty bean sprouts, and a fresh bouquet of spicy greens," Kim said proudly.

"You said that with such elegance. My mouth is watering already."

"You may substitute the thin beef slices with bull cock. It is a favorite Vietnamese delicacy," Kim Said.

"I'll consider that when we are ready to order," thinking, I can't let this pass... "Does size matter?"

Kim gives me a hesitant look, blushes, smiles, puts her hand over her mouth, turns, and shuffles away in quick, short little steps giggling.

A few minutes later, Nina enters the restaurant. She's backlit by the bright sunlight that presents a woman who knows how to make her presence known. She's tall for a Vietnamese woman and slender like a fashion model with stylish short hair. Nina may be in her fifties but looks like she's at a photoshoot while strolling in her elegant way between the tables. She is wearing a long gray-silk-tunic slit from the waist down worn over wide charcoal pants and dark gray sandals.

I waved at Kim with a pleasant smile as she heads toward our table.

"Hi Nina, you look exquisite."

"Jackie, you are much too kind, especially, coming from such a beautiful woman."

Nina seats herself across from me at our table.

"Tell me about the outfit you're wearing. I've never seen anything quite like it."

"Thank you. It's an Ao Dai, by Ralph Lauren."

Nina takes a pen and small sticky notepad from her purse...

"It's pronounced spelling is *oh yai*, but the Vietnamese spelling is *AO DAI*."

After writing it out on the pad, she handed me the single sheet.

"*Oh yai?*" I said, with a tilted head and spiking eyebrows.

"That's right, Jackie. The design dates back to the mid-1700s when Lord Vu Vuong of the Nguyen Dynasty decreed that both men and woman should wear an ensemble of trousers and a gown that buttoned down the front. In the 1930s, Cat Tuong brought us the modern version of the Ao Dai. In 1950, two prominent Saigon tailors changed it again, similar to what we wear today.

However, nothing stays the same. Ralph Lauren added a little western touch to the design, and I fell under his spell."

"Now, I remember the ensemble. But I'm more familiar with the colorful display of silk patterns and didn't know it by name."

"Yes, that's understandable, but by using darker colors, Ralph Lauren has moved the design into a resurgence of cultural ties between East and West.

Well, enough about fashion. Let's take a moment so I can get to know you better. According to your bio, it would seem you are very athletic having received a scholarship in track and field. If I may ask, what type of events did you participate in?"

"The Heptathlon, meaning you competed in seven different events."

"That's amazing. You must have been very fast."

"That's true. Jake tells me I'm still fast on my feet."

"That Jake, he's a real wisenheimer," Nina said with a giggle.

"Did you by chance pick that word up from Johnny Zapata?"

"I did, he seems to be a natural wisenheimer."

"Yeah, that he is."

"Being the athlete you are, you must have been a real tomboy learning to compete in track and field, and as you mentioned in your bio something about kickboxing, driving race cars and such."

"That's true... My dad told my mom, he wished that I had had a Serengeti migration of stuffed animals instead of dozens of toy cars, trucks and speed tracks everywhere in the house. He said that after finding a cache of my broken race cars and trucks under his pillow one night."

Nina has a gleeful chuckle with understandable nods.

"Please continue, I'm sure you've had an interesting childhood."

"True... Well, even as a young child, I started out lecturing. While sitting next to the Chinese Ambassador one evening during dinner, I informed everyone at the table that the Chinese don't use the alphabet. They draw pictures.

The ambassador told me I was a smart little girl. He then took out a notepad and a pen from his jacket and began to draw a character on the paper. He then asked me what I thought his symbol meant.

After considering his question for a moment, I told him it was a soldier holding a rifle. The ambassador laughed and then told me, *that's your name, young lady.*

That picture, means Jackie? I asked him.

He told me it did, then asked me if I wanted to keep it to practice writing my name.

Without question, I shall always treasure it, I told him."

"Please, let me give it a try, Jackie?"

"Why, of course, I'll know it when I see it again."

So, Nina brought out her notepad and pen, and without hesitation, she puts pen to paper...

"Is that your soldier holding a rile a parade rest?"

With a few joyful tears, I cast my eyes on Nina... "Oh Nina, you are amazing. I've not seen my little character in years having practiced it as a child, then set it aside for other interests.

See. Is that not a soldier holding a rifle?" I said with joyful memories.

Nina responds with a subtle smile, then after a long moment, she leans closer and is about to say something, and then lingers for an instant...

"When I see you up close, I can't get over the resemblance between you and... Ah, the actress...."

"Halle Berry?" I said.

"Yes ... that's the one."

"Well... Interestingly enough, I met Halle at my parent's home a few years ago. When she walked into the living room, we both did a double-take feeling as though we had found our long lost twin sister. My mother did charity work with her and wanted me to meet her. When we stood side-by-side, my folks shook their heads in amazement...

Halle, of course, is flat out one-of-a-kind beautiful. I'm a little more boyish, athletic-looking, and maybe five or six inches taller."

"My, what a nice experience it must have been to meet her."

"Yes, I felt very fortunate... Halle's a wonderful lady and lots of fun."

After some silence, Nina said, "Is it true, you were a kickboxer champion at one time?"

"Yes."

"Do you still participate?"

"No," I said with a weak smile. "In my last fight, I hit my opponent's right fist so many times with my head, I broke her hand. At that point, I figured I was getting too old for this sport and called it a day."

Nina looks at me for a short moment, then her eyes light up as we both burst into a gleeful chuckle.

While relaxing for a moment, we sip our water.

"Is your last name your family name?" Nina said.

"No. My father comes from a Zulu heritage. His name is Nonkululeko. My father was Consul General of the South African consulate in Los Angeles where he met my mother. She worked for the U.S. State Department. Her family is from Austria...

He understands the business world; therefore, he encouraged me to change my last name. Nonkululeko is a name much too difficult to pronounce, much less spell correctly in a business environment.

With my father being a long-time friend and admirer of Jackie Kennedy Onassis, I was blessed by her first name. So, I thought it only appropriate to take an abbreviation of her last name—it's short and easy to remember... O', not a name you easily forget. There are few students at Pepperdine University that don't greet me by Ms. O' on campus."

"Well, Jackie, I believe it's more than your last name. You have the stature, charisma, and warmth demanding respect for that of a strong leader."

"You are most kind."

"If I remember correctly, you're also a professor of Organizational Theory, and Finance, is that right?"

"Yes."

"We feel fortunate that Jake and Dakota have people like you helping us in our hour of need..."

"Thank you, Nina."

Well, we should order now, enjoy our meal, and then discuss business."

"Perfect," I said.

Kim heads toward our table then looks down at me with her pencil and pad ready to take my order, when her hand made a sudden move to cover her mouth suppressing a giggle...

"Did you still want the sliced beef or the ... or the bull cock with your Pho?"

Now, she's beyond help and begins to giggle and stomp her little feet on the floor in silence.

Nina looks over at me with embarrassment...

"Please forgive my friend," as she turns to give Kim a strange look.

"I believe I'll stick with the sliced beef, thanks," I said with a wink.

"Nina. Will you have the same?" Kim said, with a more somber tone.

"Yes. Thanks, Kim."

"May I order you a drink?" Kim asked me.

I hesitate...

"Jackie, I'm having Vietnamese iced coffee. If you've not had one, you have missed a treat. May I order you one?"

"By all means, please."

Kim then leaves them to discuss their business.

BACK TO BUSINESS

Nina sat up straighter at the table and then focused her attention on me...

"Now seems like a good time to talk about what's on your mind, Jackie."

"Well, as I mentioned on the phone, it's important we discuss our *Performance Driver system*...

But first, let me apologize beforehand on how I'll present my discussion knowing your wonderful education and a background in finance. You may know much about what I'm about to say, but as a teacher—we need to tell our story in logical steps. So please, don't take offense, I'm not talking down to you."

"Well, Jackie, there is an old Chinese proverb...

The old horse in the stable still yearns to run five hundred meters."

"I wouldn't consider you anywhere near the stable for a long time to come, Nina," I said cheerfully.

"Well, maybe not, but it would seem, everybody, no matter age or experience yearns to achieve great deeds."

"That is so sweet and so true."

After repeating the proverb, I said, "I'm sure I can put that to good use someday in my class. Thank you, Nina."

Nina responds with a delicate smile.

"Well, back to business...

Traditionally, the finance profession has focused on historical financial information when controlling cost...

Finance also champions such calculations as units produced per hour, hourly rates, set-up costs, standard hours, re-work costs, task duration, and labor variance reports...

Unfortunately, these measurements promote individual activity or tasks and ignore system performance..."

I pause for a moment to consider how I'll broach my main subject...

"Most of this task-orientated effort is for not, having little to do with improving business value or the system processes," I said with a little noticeable apprehension.

"You're doing fine, Jackie, and I agree with you, please go on."

Feeling more comfortable, I get into my pitch...

"When making operational improvements, it's neither operational nor financial indicators that are sufficient on their own for guiding your business...

To offset this miss guided financial approach, we are suggesting the use of a well-balanced *Performance Driver* and *Leading Indicator System* that can provide perspective and evaluate progress toward improving the value of the business system...

Ahh... I should perhaps, leave the rest until after we eat seeing that Kim is headed our way with a tray of food."

"I agree, it's time to enjoy our Pho."

Kim places our meals on the table along with our iced coffee.

"Please enjoy the meal," Kim said, making a gracious bow.

We acknowledge her with a thank-you. But before she leaves, I'm already sampling my Pho.

"Not wanting to be impolite, but yummy, this is so good."

"I'm pleased you like it."

I respond with a smile, wasting little time taking a sip of my iced drink.

"Nina, this is wonderful, how do they make this glorious iced coffee?"

"It's appealing and strong taste comes from the French dark-roast coffee beans and chicory. However, what makes it unique is the rich blend of sweetened condensed milk and crushed ice.

And as one might have guessed, you have to be careful not to drink it too often... It isn't what I'd call calorie-free," Nina said, with a sublime smile.

"Well, I'm now hooked on Pho and iced coffee—thanks to you Nina."
After eating and a little chin fest, we talk business again.

THE PERFORMANCE DRIVER DISCUSSION

"If I'm not mistaken, we left off in our discussion about a well-balanced *Performance Driver* and *Leading Indicator System*...

With that in mind, I'll begin by saying when managing your business using only the leading indicators; it will seldom produce the desired results.

I gave Nina the diagram to study for a moment.

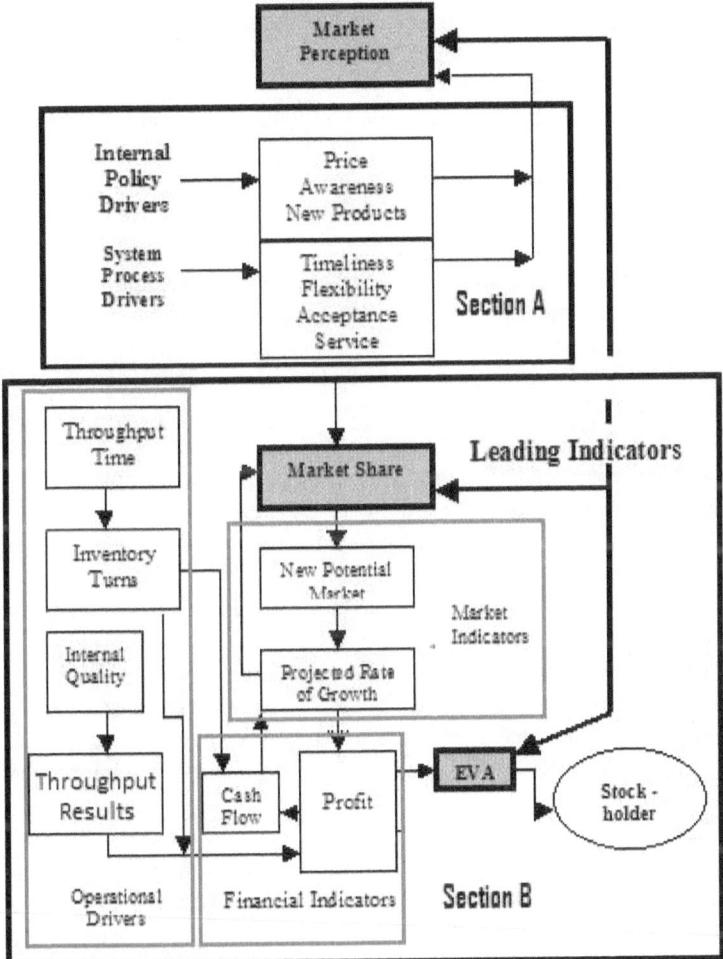

Meaning, you'll need performance drivers that drive the system which drives the leading indicators.

We don't have time to go through the performance drivers in any detail, so I have brought along this flowchart for you to evaluate. If you approve, I will use it for our scheduled meeting next Tuesday."

"As you can see, there is the upper section noted as *Section A* and the lower one is *Section B*. The upper section of the diagram refers to the customers' purchasing criteria data that drive your company's system, which influences market perception...

We won't be discussing Section A in our upcoming session because we've already discussed it during our *Organizational Architecture* meeting...

However, in several weeks, we'll be covering it in detail during a session we call *Having a Fresh Perspective*...

For today's discussion, I've included it in the diagram so you can see its relationship with the other drivers and indicators as a total system...

In Section A, we have the *System Process* and *Policy Drivers* that drive the *Market Indicators* in the lower section...

On the left side of Section B, you'll see the *Operational Drivers* that drive the *Financial Indicators*..."

While sipping what's left of my iced coffee, I wait for a reaction from Nina as she nods her head while studying the diagram.

"You've put a lot of thought into this, Jackie, and I can see at a glance the systemic relationship between the market and the stockholder. It reveals how both the drivers and indicators influence the *Leading Indicators*...

It's refreshing to see the thought process that allowed you to bring this together. Like most of us financial people, we get caught up in the day-to-day activities of the business while forgetting how to reason in creative ways...

I'm often guilty of using indicators based on standard cost accounting and using only the leading indicators to drive the projected numbers...

Nice job, Jackie, you have my support for Tuesday's meeting."

"You don't know how much I appreciate those words—it means a lot."

"Thank you, Jackie, I seldom hear that."

"Are you going to attend each of the three sessions on Tuesday morning through Thursday?"

"Do you need me?"

"Oh yes, unquestionably, the people have great respect for you and any positive comments made during the discussion would be most helpful. As you know, we have little use for hype. So, what's needed is reinforcement from time to time by the leaders."

"In that case, you can count on me."

"Thanks, Nina. We covered a lot, but it was essential for me to get your blessing on this new system, having only through Monday to make sure the presentation is ready. Well, that and wanting to know you a little better, I hope you don't mind."

"Jackie, it was my pleasure to get out and share my favorite meal with such a nice, talented person. Well, I guess we should go now, knowing you have a lot to do. The meal, of course, is on me—I insist."

"Thanks, Nina. Now that you have me hooked on Vietnamese iced coffee, would it be possible for Kim to make me one for the road?"

"Yes, of course, give me a moment."

JACKIE'S INTRODUCTION TO LIGHTNING

After Kim hands me a disposable cup of iced coffee, we thank her for the nice meal, walk out toward our cars and say our goodbyes.

After slipping into in my restored 72' Porsche 911, I crank it up and rev the RPMs. I will miss the little bugger. I'm replacing it with a Shelby GT-500 rocket sled in a few weeks, having a need for speed—no chick car for me.

After slipping it into gear, I head toward I-405 northbound and fight the traffic for about two hours. When motoring off the I-10 freeway, I head north on the Pacific Coast Highway taking me to Malibu where a take left into my garage.

It's late afternoon, and I'm a too frazzled to do any prep work for Tuesday morning, so a little surfing would clear my mind. After changing into a pair of faded red boardshorts and a tattered old tee-shirt, I grab my shortboard, walk out my back door, and hit the sand running toward the big-daddy waves.

I should mention that I've removed the lining from my special tight-fitting boardshorts because they can be a problem. I've often seen lifeguards pulling guys out of the surf when tangled up in their huge baggy shorts.

I surfed until the sun darted behind dark storm clouds coming in off the Pacific like a freight train, bringing with it a layer of darkness. It didn't take long for the surf to become rowdy as the rain and temperature began to fall.

The darkness was soon lit up like a Roman candle when bolts of lightning struck nearby. With my board over my head, I run toward the house like a scared little kitty.

Nearing my tetherball pole, I see it emit a soft blue-white glow called St. Elmo's fire and came to an abrupt halt—knowing it could be a precursor of a lightning strike. Just then, the lightning hit the pole creating super-heated expanding air and then collapses—creating a shockwave equal to eleven pounds of TNT if you're within thirty feet of the strike that sent me flying along with an enormous bang.

While lying on the sand and dazed from the lightning pressure wave, I twitch and move a few muscles about after several seconds or perhaps a few minutes, I'm not sure. Still feeling a little disorientated, but with a little effort, I struggle to a sitting position, but I'm feeling lucky not having had a direct hit by the lightning.

My ears are ringing too, or to be more precise, they're buzzing as I gaze down at my tee-shirt… Yikes, no tee-shirt resulting from the steam explosion created by the rapidly vaporizing rainwater on my body. While staggering to my feet, I touch my hair and realize it was standing straight up, "Holy shit."

I seem okay after checking myself out. So with a shrug, I look around, take a deep breath and drop my shorts—not to worry, no one is on the dark beach in this heavy rainfall and lightning striking all about us. Ahh... Well, other than Ms. Stupidio.

With shorts, a ragged torn tee-shirt and board in hand, I lift my head, thrust out my chin, and breathe in the water-laden air. The air smells like the electric bumper cars that we used to drive at the amusement park as kids. With my lungs full of burned-air molecules, I do my slow and deliberate stripper walk into the house singing an *Adam and the Ants song*, STRIP...

When entering the bathroom, my mirror grabs my attention. "Yikes." My hair looks like a blackbird blasted with buckshot.

After a quick jump into a hot shower, I dry off and slip into a Hilton white terrycloth robe as the rain spatters on my windows and pounds on my roof like a cattle stampede. This gets me thinking. Ah... What a wonderful night for *trail-drive chili*, an American national treasure.

When Jake Jensen's dad was a young cowpuncher down in Texas, he said the cooks planted oregano, chilies, and onions among the patches of mesquite to protect them from foraging cattle. These trail gardens supplied the spices they combined with beef to make trail-drive chili using a chili piquin' (chili puh-keen), a chili pepper that grows wild in much of Texas. To make trail food, they pounded dried beef and beef fat with their spices, mixed in with salt—yummy.

After turning the lights down, I load a few CD's by Sting, put my burner on medium, place a previous batch of frozen chili in a five-quart pot, and add hot tap water. While the chili is heating, I make a quick batch of cornbread and a hot cup of mulled wine.

I'm now staring out the living room window over the rim of my hot cup of wine and listening to the storm, all curled up in my comfy chair waiting for my dinner.

A short time later, I'm awakened from my mellow thoughts as a sharp smack of the wind hits the window trying to force its way in into my home. All the while, the surf rips up the beach as the wind and the rain are at each other's throat due to the torrential downpour trying its best to beat down the wind, while rainwater gurgles down my gutter's drainpipe.

If I'm not mistaken, I remember reading about a lad in England who was walking in the park and got struck by lightning. He said he felt a little tingly and shaken, but *not stirred*... then I laugh at my 007 addition.

Apparently, less than three weeks later, he won over one million pounds playing the Lotto. Hey, you got to be positive when blown away by lightning.

ACT II - SCENE 3
ENHANCING THE LEARNING PROCESS

Question 1

Do you know anyone that you can relate to that lives up to the Chinese proverb: *The old horse in the stable still yearns to run 500 meters*? If so, share your thoughts.

If you are at the age where you feel the same urge and have taken steps to run the 500 meters, share your thoughts.

Most, will throw up their hands, and say it's hopeless. Those who don't are rare indeed; therefore, when possible, support them in their quest, for we need every 500-meter runner we can find.

Question 2

In the diagram why does it show *inventory* influencing both cash flow and profit?

ACT II SCENE 4
A New Set of Measurement Tools

WEEK 4 – TUESDAY MORNING – A BRUTAL LEG WORKOUT BEFORE BREAKFAST AND THEN A DISCUSSION WITH JACKIE ON THE OPERATIONAL DRIVERS

Johnny and I are ready for serious eating after torching a thousand calories during our morning workout at Gold's Gym.

While strolling down the street to the Rose Cafe for a killer breakfast, Johnny glances at me...

"Jackie, I may need to cut back on my workouts."

"Why would you want to do that?"

"Well, if I continue to improve my body at this rate, I'll be attracting too many groupies... And this, of course, will bring in the paparazzi."

After giving him my gimlet-eye, I ignored him for the rest of the short walk. The place is close enough to the beach you can smell and breathe in the sharp taste of the salt-laden air. Entering the restaurant, I can see the familiar crowd. The place seems to draw a mix of lifters from Gold's, beach locals, and yuppies that bring a large crowd today.

After the manager had escorted us to a nice table on the canopy-covered patio, he left us with a coffee decanter, our menus, and told us the waitress will be with us shortly.

It's still a primal morning, but you know it will be another hot day. With a grumbling stomach, my system is demanding immediate calorie replacement. Ah, at last, the waitress heads toward our table as I take notice and see she's new here. The waitress stood at our table looking down at me with an eagerness to take my order.

"I'll have ten egg whites with diced chili peppers, two large whole-wheat buttermilk pancakes, a side of cottage cheese with sliced tomatoes, and large orange juice ... oh yeah, and a lot more coffee."

"Shall I bring two plates?"

"Huh?"

Johnny takes a deliberate easy-going glance at our waitress, dazzling her with his boyish smile and pearly whites...

"To simplify things, I'll have the same."

With her head shaking, she heads back toward the kitchen.

"I've heard that smile of yours attracts women like cats lured to catnip and gets a woman to show you their intimate clothing."

"True, but how come it doesn't affect you?"

I smile.

"Our waitress won't fall for it either," Johnny said.

"Why's that?"

"Because she has the semblance of Daisy Duck—"

"Daisy Duck?"

"Yeah, fresh and innocent, right off the farm."

"No matter, she's more than a decade younger than you."

"You know everyone tells me I look ten years younger."

"What they mean is your infantile behavior."

"Oh yeah, well growing old is mandatory, growing up is optional," Johnny said, with his Stan Laurel routine.

It isn't long, and our waitress is back again with our breakfast. No sooner had she set my orange juice down, I had it in my hand ready to chug it back. She pours more coffee from the decanter, then looks over at Johnny and giggles.

When she leaves, I ask Johnny, what's with the giggle.

"Giggle?" He said, "I didn't notice."

"Yeah, right."

I'm always a little unsettled on my first assignment with a new client and eating and talking helps me take my mind off the upcoming event. So, while taking a bite of pancakes, I'm considering something fun to discuss when our waitress comes by to refill Johnny's water glass and then walks off.

"What's with that?" I said, pointing my finger at his water glass.

"That, my dear is a water glass."

"Oh never mind."

While pouring another cup of hot bean juice, I bring up the subject of coffee mugs...

"I was reading Lee Child's new book, *Nothing to Lose*, and Reacher, his main character, describes the best shape of a coffee cup. In case you didn't know, he's a habitual coffee drinker," I said. "So, what would you consider is the best shape, short and wide, tall and thin, curved, and so on?"

"Are you sure now ... that you're talking about coffee cups?" Johnny asks with a grin forming.

I'm puzzled for a moment, then turn beet red.

"You are such a bad boy."

We make quick work of our breakfast and then chin fest a while longer drinking our coffee when the waitress drops off our check...

"You reckon you'll be able to make it until to lunch? Good lord, you eat enough to feed a family for a month in Somalia."

She looks at us with contempt, then moseyed back to the kitchen.

I'm startled by such a comment...

"Fresh and innocent you say, smart mouth maybe, just your kind of girl."

"Well, I sure misread the Daisy Duck look. But at times, it's difficult to distinguish between Daisy Duck's appearance and Magica De Spell Duck."

"Who's Magica?"

"She's an insane and cruel duck antagonist in the TV show, *Duck Tales*."

"Ah... I see your point, Magica sounds like our waitress."

We both pull out of Gold's Gym Parking lot at six forty. Johnny motors up to university for his morning class, and I head toward ATC. By seven forty, I pull into the ATC parking lot, meet Nina in her office, and then we walk to the training room together.

THE TRAINING ROOM - A DISCUSSION ON MARKET PERCEPTION

Before the session started, Nina introduces me to a few employees who I have cordial conversations with, and then excuse myself and head toward the lectern. After opening my laptop, I connect it to the video cable then select the appropriate folder for today's discussion...

I still have a few minutes to kill, so I grab a cup of coffee while noticing the room is half full. At eight o'clock sharp, Nina gives me a formal introduction. I thanked Nina and those attending my presentation...

After taking a sip of coffee, I begin today's discussion.

"Our session this morning is market perception. The booklet I've passed out to you has a few diagrams, computations, and benchmark information that I'll be displaying on the screen behind me."

I then raise my booklet for everyone to see.

"Is there anyone without a booklet?"

Seeing no hands showing, I continue...

"We're now all set for our measurement tools discussion...

The session is quite lengthy, requiring three separate engagements starting at ten o'clock here tomorrow and eight o'clock the following day.

In today's session, operational drivers are our topic of conversation. Tomorrow, we'll be discussing the market and financial indicators. Then on Thursday, our last day on this topic, we will cover the market and financial leading indicators.

Now, let's get on with today's subject—operational drivers...

The operational performance drivers influence the leading indicators. Drivers and indicators are like financial ratios, except they carry more punch..."

PERFORMANCE DRIVERS AND THE LEADING INDICATOR SYSTEM

"Before we continue on our main subject, I would like to give you a little insight into the use of financial ratios...

When using financial information to make strategic decisions based on historical information is one-dimensional and linear in thinking. For instance, previous training taught us to measure our financial ratios to see if the business is operating properly. We also used it in making bad decisions, but with good intentions.

Financial, operational performance ratios use calculations that measure units produced per hour, hourly rates, and task duration. This data may be useful, but it measures tasks and ignores system performance...

When one is trying to understand why a specific ratio had gone bad, it is more like chasing your tail trying to grasp what had happened...

It's now time I get into the meat of today's subject. So, let's take a look at the first image: *Performance Drivers and Leading Indicators...*"

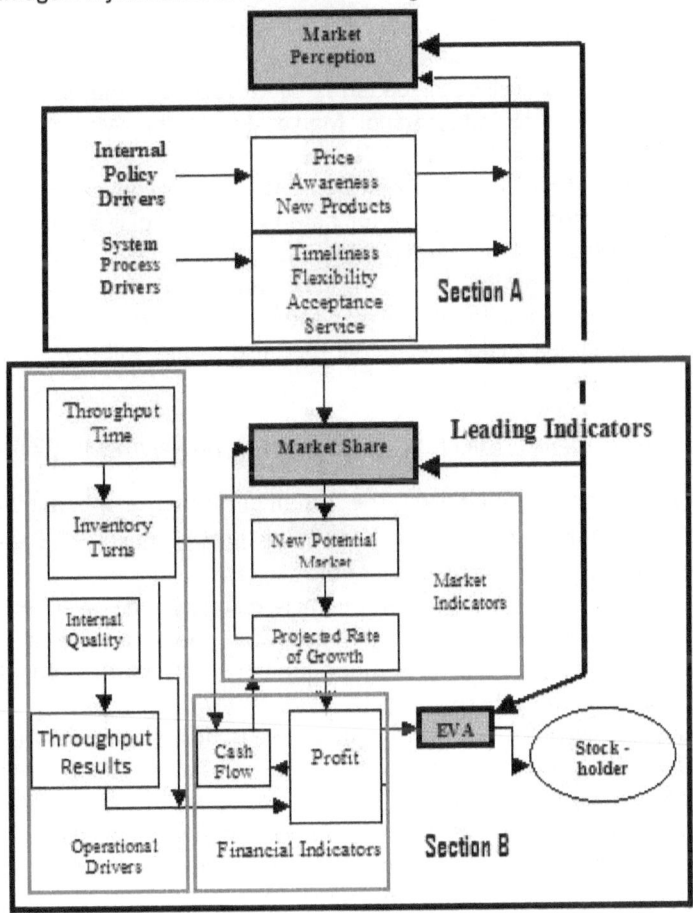

"However, before I get started, are there any questions? Yes, Dolores?"

"Thanks, Jackie. Will we at some point discard the financial ratios?"

"The short answer is no, Dolores. Financial ratios have their place, but we need indicators that will help in making good strategic decisions when trying to create value for both the customer and stockholder. The finance profession should be one of the driving forces supplying the new organization information that can guide the company to higher performance levels.

We find performance *drivers* in three categories: *internal policy* and *system process*, shown in Section A of the diagram, along with *operational performance drivers*, shown in the lower section, Section B in the first column.

These *performance drivers* are the attributes in a system environment that enable the business to *perform* at *designed outputs*, the outputs that will influence the market and stockholder...

For instance, the attribute, *throughput time* measures products going through the system that influences inventory turns, cash flow, and market perception...

In a discussion we'll have later, I'll talk about how design plays a role in improving business profitability, and growth.

When using a well-balanced array of drivers and indicators, you can influence the leading indicators of Market Perception, Market Share, and Stockholder Value, measured by EVA.

If you would please, open your booklets and you'll notice the large white area at the bottom of each page for note-taking. The diagram illustrates the different drivers and indicators that influence the results of the leading indicators. As you'll notice, the leading indicators are the shaded boxes.

We'll not spend any time discussing the internal policy and system process drivers in the upper section, Section A—because Johnny will cover it during his session *Having a Fresh Perspective*."

OPERATIONAL DRIVERS AND THROUGHPUT TIME

"First on the list for review is the system performance operational drivers, which include THROUGHPUT TIME, INVENTORY TURNS, INTERNAL QUALITY and THROUGHPUT RESULTS displayed in the first column of the diagram.

THROUGHPUT TIME is measured in the market survey and *operational drivers*. The market survey reflects TIMELINES in the customers' perception of buying criteria. Johnny, as you may remember during his *Organizational Architecture* class touched on this subject.

A business system product throughput time is most often measured in days, but will now be converted to hours for precise measurement. LITTLE'S LAW states that the average throughput time is in direct proportion to the average work-in-process inventory. Let's say we have a thousand-gallon tank of work-in-process, and the throughput is ten gallons *IN*, representing one order, and ten gallons *OUT*, indicating the finished product.

To empty the *thousand*-gallon tank takes one *hundred minutes* to produce ten units—*thousand* divided by hundred. Or, if you will, ten new products delivered.

Now, if we decrease the work-in-process level of water to one hundred gallons with the same volume of throughput capability—what would be the results?"

The audience responds with a loud, "Ten minutes for one unit."

"Excellent," I said, "Three fundamental processes control the inventory level...

First is the time it takes to process the assembly...

Next, we have queue time that represents the scheduled setback time from the next event, or better said, between events.

Finally, there is the possibility of constraint time. When knowing each of these limitations, it will give you a benchmark to achieve when designing your throughput time.

Delivery performance or customer *timeliness* relates to speed and dependable delivery dates. Fast deliveries are always more reliable in a properly designed system. High inventory has a tendency to create variations in workflow, because of routing, quality, and batching of jobs, which have a negative effect on delivery time...

A just-in-time process keeps inventory moving, making delivery schedules timelier. During our three sessions of measurement tools, we'll discuss a variety of formulas. When explaining a formula, I will write the formula for you on the whiteboard behind me.

To evaluate the throughput or flow time—you'll need to divide work-in-process value by the product's unit cost value of goods sold, which I'll write for you on the board as a formula."

$$12 = THROUGHPUT\ DAYS = \$1,000,000/\$85,000$$

"So, with twelve days of throughput time at the current rate and your benchmark being six days, you'd have your homework cut out for you. Does anyone have a question?"

Good, I see someone in the back row.

"I can't see your name card. Sorry."

"Thanks, Jackie. It's Chuck. I'm wondering if the computation is factored by each product or the average of all products."

"Thanks for your question, Chuck...

If the different products were close to identical in their cost of goods sold and processed similarly, then one should consider combining work-in-process and use an average cost of goods. With that said, I doubt that's the case with your company's large variety of products. Are there any questions...?

No... Okay, let's move on to our next subject."

I stand there for a moment mulling over my next topic...

INVENTORY TURNS

"The term *Inventory Turns* is basic knowledge for most seasoned employees. For those not familiar with the term, I'll take a moment to explain. But let's not forget, throughput time is linked with inventory turns through work-in-process.

The turns of inventory are the number of cycles the inventory turns over in a year. Inventory turns have a huge influence on total system performance, making it a subject of serious concern...

Inventory, as one might image can include both material and labor. The purchased material is a non-value-added portion of the inventory when not part of in work-in-process. Therefore, any material sitting in the stockroom is a liability to cash flow and the use of funds for a higher return on investment. So, when inventory turns increase, the *burden* on cash flow and investment decreases.

Let's not forget, the inventory shows as an asset on the balance sheet, but it is a liability to the operations of the business until it ships...

Roughly, twenty percent of the inventory line items influence eighty percent of the *purchased material* value. To minimize the liability, these items require a close watch.

Now, let's cover the *labor content* value in work-in-process again. Remember, it's the actual *process time*, *queue time*, and the *system constraint*...

Raw process time will have little need for improvement once it has been engineered and stabilized—only new engineered products with reduced labor content, workflow, real-time scheduling, and machine capabilities can improve throughput time.

Queue time is nothing more than a buffer between assemblies. An excessive buffer takes the place of bad processes or scheduling problems, and can only shrink after clearing up these difficulties. If there are particular products with identifiable *constraints*, they need addressing. Another constraint is the total system constraint—the transformation process addresses this problem. The inventory turn computation can be addressed by the a*nnual cost of goods sold divided by* either one or a combination of *WIP, finished goods, raw material...*"

INVENTORY TURNS = ANNUAL COST OF GOODS SOLD
WIP OR FINISHED GOODS AND RAW MATERIAL

"*The benchmark* for inventory turns, defined by throughput time, must meet or exceed the MPV survey report set by the three top competitors. If necessary, inventory levels need to be lowered until reaching their benchmark with acceptable process time, queue time, and constraint time...

If time in a constraint is limiting the throughput for a product, it needs a fast response for correction. The engineering people must continue to keep any part of the product's throughput moving without hiccups through their process... Does anyone have questions...?

I see no hands so we can move on..."

MANUFACTURING - EMPLOYEES INTERNAL QUALITY

"Internal Quality, our new subject measures how well the manufacturing processes are performing. Measuring internal labor quality is not a straightforward issue. For instance, you have a cash flow drain when employees do nothing but rework. Rework is a red flag. It means there is a process problem engineering needs to address by evaluating the real-time control charts for stability and capability of the process. Rework should *not* be an issue when reworking a human error—it has no influence on cash flow when it is within the fluctuations of the process stability level.

One other thing... Manufacturing quality inspection should confine its time to their assigned processes, not specific products—these inspections are to improve process improvement and stabilization" I said. "On the whiteboard is the computations for labor rework and material scrap..."

$$\text{LABOR REWORK \%} = \frac{\underline{\text{LABOR REWORK DOLLARS}}}{\text{WORK-IN-PROCESS DOLLARS}}$$

$$\text{SCRAP MATERIAL \%} = \frac{\underline{\text{SCRAP MATERIAL DOLLARS}}}{\text{WORK-IN-PROCESS DOLLARS}}$$

Finished with the formulas, I take a few chugs of water before our benchmark discussion.

"The BENCHMARK should be ZERO for both labor and material measurements—whether it is achievable depends on the stability of the processes... Are there questions?"

I wait for a moment when I spot Frank in the first row raising his hand.

"Yes, Frank."

"Thanks, Jackie. Would you mind giving us a recap on that again?"

"I'd be glad to, Frank; I may not have articulated that well enough...

When rework impedes throughput or causes instability during processing, it is reason enough for rework charges...

But, as I mentioned, the process needs to be resolved before continuing the production. The resolution needs to be an all-out assault using the necessary resources available. If there is no resolution of the problem causing the rework in the manufacturing process within the hour—then rework needs to continue until engineering corrects the problem. Does that help, Frank?"

"Absolutely, thanks."

"Now, let's discuss Employee productivity..."

INFORMATION TECHNOLOGY PRODUCTIVITY

"Employee Productivity has been the darling of business ratio improvements for decades, but time is running out on the ability to continue with any noticeable improvements. The exception might be new companies with innovative products giving them a leg up for a while. Then we have our new approach to the business architecture.

The most crucial attribute to influence productivity is the *design* of the organizational architecture and its use of new or existing information technology for the indirect G and A. However, for the direct employees' PRODUCT THROUGHPUT TIME is what produces effective productivity growth, and is the cornerstone of our new organizational architecture.

To measure information technology's contribution to the company's organization, we're to use a formula developed by *Professor Shlomo Maital from MIT*. It falls under the category of TOTAL FACTOR PRODUCTIVITY. As you may remember, Ms. Wells mentioned this to you at your Hilton meeting and has little use in computing employee productivity...

However, to use the professor's we're going to diverge a little from the original equation. The formula stays the same, except where the professor uses *total assets* to measure workflow; we're going to replace it with the *total cost of information technology*. Why is that...?

Well, *Paul Strassmann*, the author of *Information Productivity*, notes that only about eight percent of the major corporations had capital asset costs greater than their costs of information management. Knowing that information technology cost outweighs all other assets, it only makes sense to use it to replace total assets. It also covers the wide range of almost all industries; except, perhaps, heavy industry such as metal fabrication, ironworks, and mining."

MEASURING IT AND WORKFLOW USING TOTAL FACTOR PRODUCTIVITY

"Well, theoretically, the total value of IT money spent is to improve productivity, knowledge, and enhance customer perception. We will use TOTAL FACTOR PRODUCTIVITY to measure two events, workflow productivity, and IT productivity. The information can provide us with workflow and IT expenditure contribution value added by an employee. This method permits one to see if IT expenditures are providing the required return on investment," I said. "The computation, however, is a little more complex, compared to the standard formula for the productivity ratio.

Let me begin the computation process by saying the total month scheduled IT expense has two major ingredients...

The FIRST is the IT INDIRECT TOTAL COST (row 3 in TABLE ONE) of procurement and service cost associated with software expense, computer hardware carried as an asset and depreciated, consulting cost, and outside support cost.

SECONDLY is the IT DIRECT COST (in row 4 of TABLE ONE) resulting from the employee operating cost that we'll subtract from the value-added cost.

TABLE 1 - IT AND WORKFLOW FACTOR PRODUCTIVITY

	Year	2008	2007	Aver.	% Change Yr. to Yr.
1	Sales	110,000,00	100,000,000		10.0%
2	Material cost	29,000,000	24,000,000		20.0%
3	IT indirect cost	1,000,000	1,000,000		
4	Value Added: Sales less material and IT direct cost = value added	80,000,000	75,000,000		6.7%
5	Total employees Less IT employees	250	251		-0.4%
6	Value added row 4/ Total employees row 5 = Productivity per Employee	320,000	298,805	309,403	7.1%
7	IT "Total Asset Value"	15,000,000	14,700,000		2.0%
8	IT Assets row 7 / employees row 5	60,000	58,566	59,283	2.4%

Okay, now with both TABLE ONE and TABLE TWO up on the screen, I can go through the process..."

TABLE 2 - COMPUTATION TABLE

Example: Table 1 row 6 shows 309,403 and row 8 shows 59,283 — displayed in Table 2 row 9 show the computations

	Productivity Change	
9	Labor Contribution ratio – Rows 6&8: 309,403 / (309,403 + 59,283) =	0.84
10	IT Contribution to productivity – Rows 9&8: 0.84 x 2.4% =	2.1%
11	Productivity change: Row 6	7.1%
12	Productivity change less IT contribution – Rows 11&10: 7.1% - 2.1% =	5.0%
	Contribution to Productivity Summary	
13	IT contribution – Rows 10&11: 2.1% / 7.1% =	29.1%
14	Work flow contribution - Rows 12& 11: 5.0% / 7.1% =	70.9%
15	Sum	100%

"TABLE TWO's COMPUTATION TABLE illustration shows the shaded areas of the formulas for the *Productivity Change* column that match the numbers to the shaded areas in TABLE ONE and TABLE TWO. When using this method, you will see how the two tables develop the final numbers to the equation.

I'm sure many of you would consider a spreadsheet to be more desirable, and you'd be correct, but far more difficult to display to an audience.

Please, note that *Value added,* within TABLE ONE, row four shows *sales less material* in the computations. Why is that?" I asked looking around the room.

It takes a moment, and then a few hands rise into the atmosphere like balloons rising in the hot air.

"Yes, Blake."

"Thanks, Jackie, I didn't notice that was the case until you pointed it out.

But my guess would be if included, the value would influence getting an accurate productivity reading."

"Why is that, Blake?"

"Hmm... Well, the best way to express it would be to say that changing the material cost ratio of labor from one year to another owing to material cost fluctuations would affect the resulting productivity measurement with either a negative or positive influence."

"Would anyone disagree?" I asked. "No one is jumping out of their seat to disagree with you Blake, so I would have to say you did an excellent job."

"Thank you, Jackie."

With an acknowledgment, I take a short moment...

"While we're at it, let's take the time to answer any more questions you may have... Yes, Teresa."

"Jackie, I know we discussed leaving out material cost due to the material and labor ratio problem. But, can you elaborate more on the value-added side?"

"Thanks, Teresa. These questions show your interest so keep them coming. Sometimes I find myself moving a little too fast on these complex subjects." I said with an apologetic smile.

"Well, in simple terms, the difference between raw material cost and what the customer will pay for a product is the value-added. The value-added could be a specific technology, skill level, specialized knowledge, or workflow of an organization. In the industry, one might say value-added is the contribution suppliers add to material for which customers are willing to pay—as opposed to producing it on their own. For manufacturing companies, this is a normal ongoing event. For the general public, it boils down to their perception of value. Does that get us back on track?"

Teresa nods a thank you.

"Paul, I believe you have a question."

Paul sends an affirmative nod.

"Thanks, Jackie... Would you mind summarizing why it is so important we need to know the difference between IT contribution and workflow?"

"I'd be happy too, Paul...

Our upcoming efforts will focus on improving workflow and system processes with the idea of improving productivity. Therefore, we need to understand the contributing factors such as IT or workflow in the resulting changes. Only with accurate information can we make intelligent decisions when designing a new organizational architecture—you dig?"

"I dig," Paul said, with a smile.

"When making a heavy capital investment in IT, you would hope to see a significant improvement in your investment."

I subconsciously rub my legs owing to the heavy lifting this morning.

"Let's finish this operational driver dialogue with the final step...

Financial modeling can illustrate the relationship of profitability and the

EVA benchmark, so, once you achieve an EVA benchmark, you'll need to have frequent performance level reviews that will allow you to elevate the system benchmark."

I take a moment to finish my second bottle of water before continuing.

"Are there are any more questions...? No? Perhaps this is a good place to end today's discussion. Tomorrow, we will begin with the *Market* and *financial indicator*...

However, I would like to add a thought...

Imagine having a *Performance Driver and Leading Indicator* diagram on your monitor blinking actual daily output results, along with a separate month to date performance chart for each driver. Such a tool would allow management to make mid-course corrections to keep the system on track, rather than waiting a week or two or perhaps the month-end financial results...

That's it, folks. Thanks for your time and contributions to our discussion. See you tomorrow at ten o'clock sharp."

While watching these nice people leave the room, I'm thinking, why is it I get so uptight before a presentation, but with the session behind me, I find myself ready for the job at hand.

ACT II - SCENE 4
ENHANCING THE LEARNING PROCESS

Question 1
What is *LITTLE'S LAW*?
Get creative and define a simple example of how it works? Also, what are the three processes that control the inventory level?
Moreover, why is it essential you understand these processes?

Question 2
Why does the author teach us to measure the processes and not the specific products? Why can't you use this new process as the only measurement process in a standard cost accounting system?

Question 3
How does the author's new productivity measurement relate to added value?
Also, why is it imperative to leave out material cost in the equation?

ACT II SCENE 5
A New Set of Measurement Tools

WEEK 4 – WEDNESDAY – MARKET AND FINANCIAL INDICATOR SESSION AT ATC

JACKIE O'S MORNING CLASS AT PEPPERDINE – SUBJECT, INFOMANIA

After having had a six-mile run and my normal high energy carb and protein breakfast this morning, I'm on my way to the Pepperdine campus. During the drive, I consider my options on how to handle a problem brought up at our last faculty meeting—the problem of cell phones and the Internet disrupting and corrupting participation in the classroom.

A few of the professors have already taken various forms of action out of desperation. They've chosen to switch off the classroom Internet access when appropriate, along with prohibiting cell phones. Professor Erskine told her students if she caught anyone on their cell phone, she would reduce their total grade point average by two percent for each occurrence.

One professor even banned laptops from her classroom. She said she was sick and tired of staring at the backs of laptops as opposed to looking at her students' faces. It was a rather radical move, but she's only five-foot-two in heels.

We decided that we would each try our own way and then share our experiences, successful or not.

While standing in front of my class this morning, I address the students in my usual manner, "Good morning ladies and gentlemen."

"Good morning, Ms. O'," The class sings out.

I looked around the classroom for a long moment, causing the students a little uneasiness.

"Let's see the hands of those who do not plan to graduate or become part of the business community."

Everyone freaks out at the question as the students gazed around at each other with a curious look, but no one raised their hands.

"Good, it looks as though everyone wants a career in the business world. Now, is there anyone who would not like to be a chief executive officer one day running a successful business?"

A few raise their hands.

"Is there anyone who does *not* want to know where I'm going with this?"

I see the class clown raise his hand and nod my head.

"Well, Mister Mallon, no surprise there."

A gentle laughter rolls throughout the class.

"Let me continue, and you'll get my drift. Let's say you're a CEO and have a keen interest in improving employee productivity—not system productivity, but employee productivity.

So you hire a management consultant. Not long after the request, you receive a letter with statistical information to consider."

I clicked on a computer file to display a business letter on the screen.

"Now, please read the letter, and then I will begin looking for a response."

DEAR MISTER CEO:

IN RESPONSE TO YOUR REQUEST FOR A FAST AND LOW-COST BOOST IN PRODUCTIVITY, WE HAVE DEVELOPED AN INTERESTING APPROACH.

AS AN ESSENTIAL PART OF IMPROVING YOUR OVERALL PRODUCTIVITY LEVEL, I AM PRESENTING A TOPIC THAT CAN HAVE A DRAMATIC IMPACT ON IMPROVED PRODUCTIVITY. IT HAS TO DO WITH THE CONSTANT INTERRUPTION THROUGHOUT THE DAY FROM TECHNOLOGY DEVICES.

NUMEROUS STUDIES SHOW THAT ANYWHERE FROM NINE TO FIFTEEN HOURS PER WEEK ARE DEVOTED TO READING, ANSWERING, OR CREATING EMAIL MESSAGES ON A COMPUTER OR HAND-HELD DEVICE. THAT IS TWENTY PERCENT LESS TIME THAN THE AVERAGE EMPLOYEE HAD AVAILABLE TO PERFORM THEIR JOB TWENTY YEARS AGO—THAT'S EQUIVALENT TO LOSING ONE DAY OUT OF THE WORKWEEK.

MICROSOFT AND THE UNIVERSITY OF ILLINOIS FOUND THAT IT TAKES, ON AVERAGE, 16.5 MINUTES FOR AN EMPLOYEE TO GET BACK TO WHAT HE OR SHE WAS DOING AFTER RECEIVING AN EMAIL. WHEN CONSIDERING THE NUMBER OF EMAILS AN EMPLOYEE RECEIVES, ONE CAN SEE THE SERIOUS BURDEN IT CAN PUT ON SYSTEM PROCESSES.

IF I HAVE YOUR INTEREST, PLEASE CONTACT ME AT...

While waiting for the class to read and digest the letter, I see from their faces they're shocked at what they have read.

"Now that you have read this interesting letter ... my question to you is simple and straightforward. If you were the CEO, would the letter surprise you? And if so, what kind of action would you take to solve the problem?"

Hands popped up everywhere from students wanting to get their opinion presented.

"Way to go ladies and gentlemen. Seeing I have your attention, I'd like to hear what Ms. Bloomberg has to say about my questions?"

"Well, first off, like ... is this like true?"

"Regrettably, it is."

"Wow... It's like totally a shock when thinking these devices were helping our productivity. Well, having the responsibility of CEO, I would want more valid information, but I would totally need to discuss this with my executive staff on ways to solve the problem."

"Good, but what steps are needed to solve the problem?"

"I'm not sure."

"Well then, let me get you kicked-started. Class, why do we use email? Remember now, you're in a business environment...

Yes, Ms. Abbott?"

"Well, like... You know, meaning to communicate with another employee, customers, or suppliers," Ms. Abbott said.

"Yes," I said. "Give me an idea of what you might ask someone in your company."

"Okay, how about this? Hey Cathy, should I be taking my laptop to the meeting later today?"

"Thanks, Ms. Abbott. Now, who'd like to comment on her need to email?...

Yes, Mister Will."

"Logically, I would say due to the excessive emails causing a loss of productivity, I would question the level of importance for justifying the use of Ms. Abbott's email."

"That's perceptive Mister Will. You hit a bulls-eye. But, please expand on that answer."

"Awesome point, Ms. O'... It sounds like the meeting is not a pressing issue at the time of the email. So, rather than an email, I'd hold off until I see my friend later at the next break or lunchtime. If the meeting were imminent, I'd call her on the phone."

"Excellent, you tagged a level of importance to the subject."

I take a moment to moisten my lips with a subtle swipe of my tongue.

"Class, could Mister Will, have taken it a step further...?

Yes, Mister Yao."

"We see where you're going, Ms. O'. And I would have to say neither email nor a phone call could justify bothering someone for an answer to that kind of question. If you see someone who may know the answer in passing, ask, if not, take the laptop to the meeting."

While listening with pursed lips, I nod with approval.

"That was excellent, Mister Yao. Okay, class, now, tell me what approach the CEO might choose to improve his productivity problem...?

That's great, lots of volunteers. Okay, how about Ms. Clarkson?"

"Thanks to Mister Will and Mister Yao, the answer pops right to the surface. Take your time and consider the level of importance of your phone call or email before responding. You don't want to stand out as a muttonhead among your associates when knowing the disruption is costing the company lost productivity or creating a system bottleneck."

"That was excellent, Ms. Clarkson. Who'd like to respond where this is going? Ah... Mister Lee looks as if he may have the answer. He always has that little grin he gets when he feels he hit the jackpot."

Joyful chuckles bounce around the class.

"Mister Lee?"

"Thank you, Ms. O', I believe you're about to discuss our use of laptops and hand-held devices in the classroom," he said, with a toothy grin.

"You get an attaboy, Mister Lee. Now, I have a foundation to build on."

Apprehensive titters and moans roam about the class.

"Now, who does not see the parallel between the CEO in our discussion and the classroom teacher?"

No response, but a nervous tension is building.

"My understanding is you've heard the options tried out in other classes. Not to worry, we will work together to solve the problem knowing it must be in the best interest of the students and the professor."

This seemed to work as the hands rose. I nod to our senior member of the class, at sixty-eight years old.

"Yes, Missus Stringfellow."

"Well now, I've become pretty well attached to my techie stuff. But yes, there are parallels. There are even parallels with me and my twenty-year-old cat such as the students' browsing the Internet or scanning a cell phone text and me trying to get my primeval cat's attention when pooping on my carpet. Not, unlike the teacher's response, I get zilch."

A gleeful chortle burst throughout the class.

"Thanks, Missus Stringfellow that was an interesting and illustrative response, but it doesn't quite answer the question of the parallel between CEO and teacher...

Like a growing number of students in our universities, you bring your laptops to most of your classes instead of a notebook to take notes, and then make use of the wireless Internet...

So, how does disruption or lack of participation compare to the business workplace when using your laptop in class to communicate with the outside world or another student in class?"

Hands made a rapid fluttering in the air.

"Ms. Erskine?"

"Like, if we don't know the answer, we shouldn't be here. There must be a return on investment. In the workplace, low productivity in the system processes will influence the throughput with delays, resulting in a lower return on investment. In the classroom, a lack of participation or disrupting the class will lower the students' or parents' return on investment."

"Very good, Ms. Erskine, cell phones and the computers working the Internet are two devices we must contend with to improve classroom participation and reduce classroom disruption.

I see the laptop as an excellent tool for note-taking as long as the screens are not hiding your beautiful faces."

This brings out hoots, whistles, and one loud hee-haw, which brought scattered laughter from the class.

"Is there anyone in the class that thinks he or she cannot function in a classroom environment without the use of a cell phone or Internet access?"

I step back from the lectern a few steps, hearing only silence. Then a few hands rise.

"Yes, Ms. Woods?"

"It's not like I can't survive. It's that there are a few of us who are great at multitasking and can handle both classroom activities and the Internet—and oh, yeah, the cell phone, too," she said.

"Multitasking on the phone or computer while eating yogurt and doing your nails, are one thing," I said receiving gleeful chuckles from the class. "However, would you say you can drive and safely talk on the cell phone?"

"But, of course."

"Well, did you know multitasking forces the brain to share processing resources, even if they don't use the same regions? The shared brain infrastructure produces an overload; thus, slowing down the process time...

These cell phone distractions cause twenty-six hundred deaths each year..."

I pause for a moment...

"Now, I see no one blinked or gasped at what I just told you. But, had I just mentioned that from 2001 through 2016, there were twenty-three hundred soldiers killed in Afghanistan, most of you would feel the loss, as you should, while others speak out against the war to bring home our troops... Now, why is it we don't react or show concern when hearing about traffic fatality?

The class became stone-cold quiet.

"It would seem that cell phones have become an extension of our young men and women triggered by a blast of dopamine released in the brain, and on average, it uses one point nine of your daily hours or five years of your lifetime. People are in constant contact with them checking their phones for updates and alerts in social situations. You're glued to your phone when walking your dog, walking down a busy sidewalk, between each set working out at the gym, and on and on it goes. It's like we're a monkey conditioned to press a button for food. Take it away from us, and we go into serious withdrawal and the five stages of grief..."

I wait for this to sink in as the class looks at me in awe.

"I'm not trying to preach to everyone about what you should or shouldn't do with your cell phone while driving your car... Well, maybe I am, but my point is when you're using your cell phone in class, it will have a distraction for both you and others around you...

With that in mind Ms. Woods, do you still consider being what you refer to as a multitasker as one able to take part and not cause disruptions to the class?"

There is total silence and no response from Ms. Woods, and then, she looks up with an embarrassing grin.

"Ah ... on second thought, your point is well taken."

"As you will hear your waiters tell you... Excellent choice. There are a couple of options for dealing with cell phones, and the Internet. However, I'd rather that you, the bright students of the class give me additional options."

Hands shoot into the air...

"Mister Waldman."

"Well, being adults at this point in our lives, and since we are referred to as Mister or Ms. in class," Waldman said with a grin as the class kicks in with chuckles. "Oops, sorry, Missus Stringfellow, no disrespect intended."

"None taken, young man," she said in a warm response.

"We would prefer you ask us not to use the Internet as opposed to shutting the Internet off creating a dead zone using a portable cell-jamming device—"

"Wow, is that possible, Waldman?" Ms. Woods yelled out.

"Yes, I just read several Harvard professors are using them. And knowing this an option for Ms. O', I say we keep our cell phones off during class."

"Does everybody agree with that?"

All the students raise their hands along with a few hoots.

"Okay, you have voted a classroom ruling that there'll be no use of your cell phones and laptops to communicate, or using the Internet. Those who break the rule will be settled by voting on the degree of punishment or warning...

Now, before we get into the fun stuff, let's see who can answer this simple question... Which of the following sentences is correct?

I would *like* to go home now. Or, I want to go home, *like* now."

"Ah... Miss Cline, please enlighten our class."

"*Like*, it's the first one," She said getting a roar of joyful chortles.

"That's right Miss Cline. Why is that so?"

"Because in the second sentence, the word *like* was used as an interjection."

"Very good Miss Cline... Is this clear to anyone?"

Mr. Mallon stands up... "Would you mind writing that down for me on the whiteboard, so I can better understand what that means?"

His response brings about amusement from the class.

"Well, Mr. Mallon, I would, if I thought you could read."

My response ignited the class into a boff of gleefulness as they look over at Mr. Mallon.

"Okay, *like* let's get back to the fun stuff ... finance."

"Missus Stringfellow, I believe it's your turn at the lectern today to instruct the class on forms of equity in different organizations."

"Oh, dear..." Mrs. Stringfellow said.

With most having gone through the pressure to teach the class, her fellow students let out a respectful chuckle.

"It's okay, Missus Stringfellow, you'll find that when teaching the subject—

you, most of all—will absorb the knowledge far better than sitting in the class and listening," I said.

After my class, I head south for my day at ATC.

THE TRAINING ROOM

After stepping up to the lectern and saying my good mornings, I take a moment to scan the audience...

"Well, in John Steinbeck's, *The Grapes of Wrath,* Grandpa alluded to *I'm full of piss and vinegar this morning."*

This instigated cheerful chuckles from the audience including Nina's giggle before she spoke up...

"What brought that on, Jackie?"

"Well, I had a great session with my university students this morning, and now a great audience to share knowledge with."

I received a nice response from the employees.

MARKET INDICATORS

"As you may remember, our subjects for this morning are the *Market and Financial Indicators,* and for tomorrow, the *Leading Indicators.*

Today, we'll begin with the market indicators: *New Potential Market,* and *Projected Growth Rate.* The figures used do not represent your company, but I'll be describing a fictitious company you own.

To refresh you with the market indicators, I'm going to bring up section B of the *Leading Indicator* diagram on the screen.

There we go, this should be helpful...

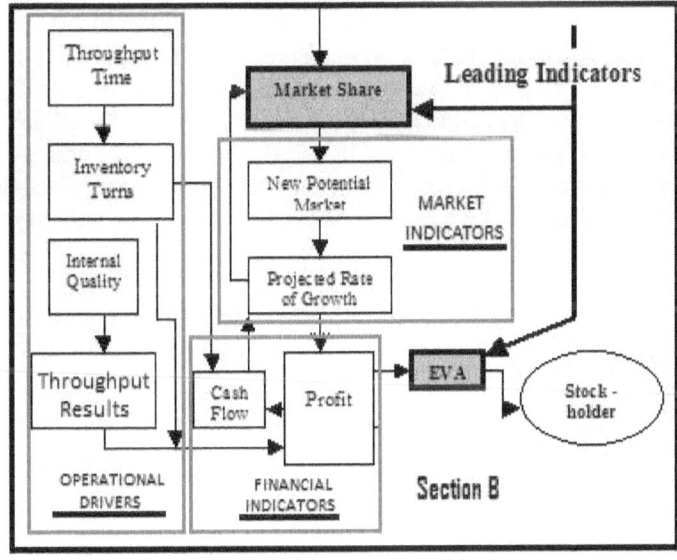

Now, with Section B as a reference, let's start out with the NEW POTENTIAL MARKET INDICATOR example of the computation illustrated in the image I'm about to display...

The Computation

New Potential Market Example: noted in millions

Total Market Value:	100.0
Minus Company's Current Market Share	-5.0
	95.0
Minus Market Share of Competitors w/ Higher MPV Ratings	-30.0
Available Market	65.0
Company's Awareness Level 50%	x 50.0%
Company's Potential Market	**32.5**

We'll begin at the top with the noted TOTAL MARKET VALUE: The *hundred million* dollar value is the *total market value* available to the business, less the *five million* dollars of your current market share, and the *competitor's* share seen with a greater market-perceived value rating than your own at *thirty million* dollars...

To find the *company's potential market* share, multiply the *New Potential Market* value (available market) at *sixty-five* million dollars times your market awareness at *fifty percent*, resulting in *thirty-two point five* million dollars.

The Benchmark for the *Potential Market* is a key part of the process. Previous new orders and sales success rate define the relative size of market growth needed to hit a targeted benchmark. If For instance, the company had a projected growth rate of three million per year with a sales success rate of one out of three, you would need a potential available market of nine million for each year. By increasing the sales success rate, you can leverage the potential market size, but you'll need to have the market's highest MPV ranking.

Your company's expense budget for developing the awareness level will be a growth rate factor. If the cost associated with developing an awareness level with a nine million market is not possible, then reduce the growth rate to an affordable level."

PROJECTED GROWTH INDICATOR

"Projected *Growth Rate Indicator* is our next subject—"

A hand rises in the back row.

"Yes, Jimmy. Do you have a question?"

"Sorry, I have poor hearing and forgot my hearing aid. I'll need to come and sit in the front row if that's okay?"

"Of course it is. Come on down Jimmy...

Speaking of hearing, I have an interesting sidebar while Jimmy makes it down in front. It's a story I read about a Mr. Shapiro, a rising economist... He said...

"*People are better at predicting the winner of American gubernatorial elections when they watch the candidates on television with the sound turned off...*"

There is a moment of silence, and then everybody lets out a gleeful chuckle.

"Laughter was a good choice."

The audience responds with more chuckles as I wait for Jimmy to take a seat...

"Now, back to work...

When *measuring* projected growth rate, you're comparing the company's *actual* growth rate with the *planned* growth rate. The two factors that control a company's growth rate are the business system constraints and market constraints.

Aside from a good marketable product, throughput capability, market perception, and cash flow influence the business constraints. Cash flow is critical, meaning, there must be enough cash to support and exploit any additional capacity, process improvement, and market awareness necessary to grow the company.

To accomplish accurate *Benchmarking* for projected growth, you'll need to use computer model simulations that we'll be discussing in a future session called *System Modeling*.

Why simulations? Because only through simulations can you handle the variables within the business system. You can, of course, develop, excel spreadsheets that can give you a fair picture of *what-if's*, but it's time-consuming with potential errors. Once you have the benchmarks set, you can compare the actual numbers over a fixed period."

FINANCIAL INDICATORS

"Let us finish this session by discussing the last two financial indicators— *Cash Flow* and *Profit*...

Cash Flow is often analyzed when suppliers demand money or the business needs new equipment or additional people. Without these demands, scant attention focuses on cash flow.

However, when cash is tight, management requires volumes of cash flow data—normally, when it is too late to fix the underlying problem.

When your company is investing in new processes, technologies, equipment, research, growth, and customer awareness, you should measure cash flow performance. The cash flow indicator measures the success of your business and growth strategy against a benchmark.

Four components influence cash generation—*PROFITABILITY, INVENTORY TURNS, ACCOUNTS PAYABLE* and *ACCOUNTS RECEIVABLE*. When you're not meeting the company's cash flow requirements, you'll find that the root cause is in one or more of these four components.

Cash flow's *computation* is a dynamic process with projections in increments of perhaps six-month periods or less, and using financial computer modeling is recommended. Here's the formula using the financial statement..."

$$\text{CASH FLOW} = \text{INCOME} - (\text{ACCOUNTS PAYABLE, DEBT PAYMENTS, TAXES}) + \text{DEPRECIATION}$$

"Ah... I see hand. Tony, is it?"

"Yes... Thanks, Jackie. Why do you add back in depreciation?"

"Good question. Well, depreciation is added back in the cash flow statement because it is a non-cash item, which reduced the net income, therefore, you need to add it back in," I said with a nod and a smile and nod from Toni.

"Okay, moving on... When *benchmarking* cash projections, one should use financial model simulations over time that project values resulting in benchmarks. That is, of course, if the cash flow supports the growth and profitability strategy. If not, the PROFITABILITY, INVENTORY TURNS AND ACCOUNTS PAYABLE and RECEIVABLE need review. This would include possible adjustments in redesigning throughput and a system architectural review to improve productivity—or perhaps a new strategy.

In these smaller increments of measurement, trends are more relevant than individual peaks and valleys..."

After taking a deep breath, I continue...

"Our last financial indicator is PROFITABILITY. When investigating the correlation between profits with productivity, it's best to use pre-tax profit. The components that have the most influence on this indicator are productivity, capital investment, and growth, straightforward computation as you'll see in this formula..."

$$\text{PRE-TAX PROFIT} = \text{NET SALES} - (\text{DIRECT COST} + \text{OPERATING EXPENSE})$$

$$\text{AFTER TAX PROFIT} = \text{PRETAX PROFIT} - \text{TAXES}$$

The economic value-added, or EVA as we like to call it benchmark defines the profitability *Benchmark* through the dynamics of the system drivers—INTERNAL POLICY, SYSTEM PROCESS, and OPERATIONAL DRIVERS...

A spreadsheet might help in a system design to support an EVA benchmark level, but a financial modeling program would save a lot of time."

I take a moment to glance at the wall clock confirming my built-in timemarker.

"If you've been following the booklet, you can see we have finished Part Two of our three-part session. This session moved along relatively fast. Tomorrow's session, however, gets more complicated.

That's it, folks, have a good day. I'll see you in the morning."

As the audience shuffles out of the room, they gesture their thanks and goodbyes. A few minutes later, I gather up my stuff and head out to the parking lot.

JACKIE'S HOUSE-SITTING WHILE PLAYING WITH THE TOYS

After climbing into my little 911, I power her up. She creates a unique sound as it sings when giving her the juice as we motor north to Malibu near my home. I'm staying over at Jake's place off and on during his voyage across the Atlantic.

Jake designed this wonderful home doing both the architecture and contracting over a three-year period. It's unlike any home you will ever see. To do it justice, it would take me a while to describe it, so I'll leave my comments to his car collection lined up in his eight-car garage. In position one is his pristine 37' Chevy pickup with a Corvette engine. Next to it is a restored black 57' fuel-injected Chevy Bel Air. And still in restoration is a 1966 Shelby 427 Cobra. In the last two positions are the Bonneville Salt Flats Streamliner, and a restored black 1980 450 SEL Mercedes he bought off the showroom floor in late 1979. He calls it his little "Merk-a-dee-deez," named by Cathy, a favorite girlfriend long ago.

The reserved stall next to the 450 SEL is for a new car he bought, but no one has any idea what it is.

For me, I raced at the drag strip during my high school days and continued racing until a few years after finishing college. The smell and sound of high-performance engines are in my blood. And, of course, that's the real reason for agreeing to stay at Jake's place—I get to drive each of the cars except for one, the Streamliner, and that one I play with.

The Streamliner is a mind-blower, made from a beautiful Art Deco sculptured carbon-fiber body. He calls it "Brute Force Incorporated—a name he came up with during his time in the service. Jake designed the engine when he was in high school, but never built it.

However, he raced his B-gas 1933 Ford coupe and B-altered 32' Ford coupe that held the NHRA record for several years. The chopped and channeled 1932 Ford B-altered had a 1950 Oldsmobile engine with an original design of forty-two hundred RPM. Jake told me when he crossed the finish line with the modified engine—it was pushing eighty-six hundred RPM. The racing fans would stand up to listen to the harmonic sounds produced by the high-revving engine screaming to the finish line. I know well the sound—nothing in the world like it.

His most nagging problem after each run was replacing the special lightweight push-rods on his hot dog budget. From the 1950s through the 1970s, drag racers, for the most part, financed their racing from out of pocket, and innovation was foremost. For instance, Jake and his friend designed a variable camshaft timing gear for their 1950 high RPM Oldsmobile engine. It could advance or retard the camshaft timing, producing improved horsepower and torque performance throughout the engine's effective RPM range. It amazes me how two high school kids did this back in 1958.

He told me his biggest thrill was when he raced Poncho Gonzalez, the number one international tennis star back in the 50s. Jake raced his 1933 Ford B-gas flathead engine coupe against Gonzalez's 1955 Chevy with a 57' Corvette engine sporting a 471 GMC blower. They raced down the Imperial Highway on a Tuesday night, race night. This was where racing fans would line up and down the raised embankment running along the new highway to watch the fastest modified street machines in Southern California. It was known as the Imperial Highway with four lanes running a straight mile that carried little or no traffic late at night, well back then that was true.

He told me he had Gonzalez by three or four car lengths for most of the race, but at the finish line, he'd only beaten him by several feet. And then Gonzalez screamed on passed him as if he was sitting still owing it to his superior horsepower and high-end gearing. At sixteen years old, he now had bragging rights to say he had beaten Poncho Gonzalez, the number one tennis star in the world.

While Jake was in Japan during the early 60s, he had his drawing of the reverse-blown flathead-engine he designed painted on a white coffee mug. He kept it with him until he took it down to a high-performance flathead-engine builder not long ago and had his dream engine built. Now that Jake finished installing the engine in his Bonneville Streamliner, it rests in his garage waiting for its day on the salt flats.

Well, I can't drive the Streamliner anywhere, but I can fire it up and listen to the sounds. The engine tested out at over seven-hundred-horse power on fuel and six -hundred-horse power on gas—all from three hundred and four cubic inches. This makes it the most powerful Ford flathead engine ever built. Ford manufactured flathead V8 engines from 1932 to 1953. Using fuel, he expects it to exceed three hundred miles per hour on the salt flats of Bonneville.

What makes his engine unique is the exhaust, and the intake valves have switched places.

When using a Roots-type blower, it forces the fuel up into the enlarged and polished previous exhaust ports. Both the intake and exhaust have lightened extra-large stainless steel valves. Two spark plugs per cylinder ignite the forced air and fuel mixture.

The new exhaust routing has only about four inches to travel when exiting out the top of the engine into tuned exhaust stacks. A special Isky-designed roller cam takes care of the change in position of the intake and exhaust valves.

The original Ford flathead design lost a great deal of horsepower pushing out the exhaust through the convoluted chambers cast within the engine block. This new design removes that problem and allows for exceptional breathing.

TIME TO PLAY

When reaching Jake's place, I park in front of garage door number six and hit my special remote. Garage door numbered five and six rises as it puts chills up my spine when eyeing that beautiful streamliner floating there like a rocket in flight.

I went into the house and changed into my blue jeans and a white tee-shirt for my afternoon of thrills, then headed to the garage. After removing the wheel chocks from the streamliner's rear wheels, I roll the car out to the huge circular drive, then replace the chocks. Going back into the garage, I roll out the two-wheel cart with three batteries mounted in series leading to two six-foot cables hooked up to an Indy 500 special designed electric motor. The motor is mounted on a small stand that has a long extension allowing it to slide into a tube that connects to the engine's special crank.

I stand there for a moment daydreaming about driving over three hundred miles per hour on the salt flats. Jake said I could drive it when he takes it to Bonneville—I can't wait and become a member of the Bonneville 300 MPH Club.

My senses heighten smelling the nearby vegetation as the late afternoon sun settles behind the hill casting long shadows over the car and me. It brought with it a silence that creeps down the hillside waiting on the ear-splitting roar of the engine.

After pushing the appropriate instrument panel toggle switches to the on position, I walk to the front of the streamliner and insert the electric motor extension ready to fire up this fire-breathing monster. Gasping for oxygen, I ready myself for the fury of the sound as I lean on the starter motor's two handles with my finger hovering over the red start button. It's the same feeling of anticipation you get sitting down for a great meal when half-starved and saliva forms in your mouth.

I push the starter button, the engine spins over, coughs, shakes and sputters. Then like magic, the eight internal combustion chambers synchronize bringing life to the engine with a roar as it comes out of a deep sleep.

Looking at the Streamliner, I'm ready to rumble as I climb into the cockpit that felt like squeezing into a pair of tight jeans. I let it idle for a moment while listening to its captivating sound as the chassis rocks and rolls. The ground shakes as if it were an eight-point-six on the Richter scale making a sound no other engine in the world can make.

The house is isolated from the neighbors. So, with that thought, I increase the RPM sending me into ecstasy when the engine screams like a banshee shooting three-foot-long flames out of the exhaust stacks. The sound reverberates throughout the Malibu Hills as critters from far and near dive for cover.

ACT II - SCENE 5
ENHANCING THE LEARNING PROCESS

Question 1
What did you learn from Jackie O's morning class at Pepperdine University?
Also, do you have other ideas on how and when you should use your email to make better use of the day at work or at home?

Question 2
How do you leverage your sales success rate to increase market share? Moreover, what are the two factors that control growth rate?

Question 3
Other than it's nice to have lots of cash on hand, why is it an essential indicator to keep your eyes on?

Question 4
What are your thoughts on any desire to drive a streamliner powered by Jake's reverse blown flathead engine at speeds exceeding 300 mph?

ACT II SCENE 6
A New Set of Measurement Tools

WEEK 4 – THURSDAY MORNING – JACKIE DISCUSSES THE LEADING INDICATORS

MEETING LI'L MISS KITTY

It's getting dark out when I back my 911 into the garage next to the one and only *Brute Force Bonneville Streamliner*. After disembarking, I give the 911 a pat on the roof and then the streamliner's nose cowling wishing them a good night, then close the garage door.

Who needs pets?

I exited the garage through the back door and ignored the elevator in favor of climbing the sandstone steps leading to the rear house entry.

When nearing the entrance, I see an orange glow filtering through the glass walls and roofline. It's the sun's last spark of radiance as it forms a halo around the mountain's black silhouette behind the house before sliding into obscurity—making for a beautiful ending to a great day.

When entering the kitchen, the occupancy switch lights come on, and music from the *Deadwood* HBO series permeates the air. The hidden entry facial recognition camera informed the house communication system that Jackie is in the house.

Dancing through the kitchen toward the refrigerator I sing out...

"Jackie has arrived."

This isn't your ordinary kitchen. Jake loves to experiment with fun recipes for his guests and needs a large area for friends to come and help or stand around and shoot the breeze.

There are two commercial stoves, and a four-bay glass door refrigerator positioned to augment the workflow for the stainless steel and wood-chopping-block counters. Supporting the counters are the refurbished blood-red ancient Chinese kitchen cabinets pulled out of an old Chinatown hotel in San Francisco still showing they are worn-out, nicked door panels.

The upper cabinets are stainless steel with glass doors set at an angle. The glass reflects the old Chinatown hotel's darkened, polished wood floor and its richly-colored throw rugs.

With its efficient layout and designer art, the indirect lighting added subtle warmth to the atmosphere making for a fun place to cook—even Julia Child would have felt right at home here.

The place won't let you boil an egg and toast bread because you'd feel guilty not using your creative juices in fixing something fun to eat. While envisioning my dinner, I feel a warm, soft rub against my leg. Ahh… Little Miss Kitty—Jake calls her "Li'l Kitty."

"Meow, meow, meow…"

She's a twenty-year-old cat beginning her nagging meow routine for something to eat. Poor little thing belongs in a nursing home. Much of the time, she has a problem controlling herself where she poops, finding it difficult to climb into or out of her sandbox. The way she walks, it won't be long until she needs a walker with wheels.

Nonetheless, Jake told me the damn cat will probably outlast him having clocked her at three hundred sixty MPH. I told him that's not possible.

It's not impossible when measured in meows per hour, he responded.

A winsome smile forms as I head toward the pantry to get her favorite meal—sliced chicken in gravy. Yummy.

"Meow," said Li'l Kitty several times, confirming my yummy sound.

Jake needs to cut back a little on Miss Kitty's gravy. From the rear, she looks like she swallowed a bowling ball that's hanging by a chain, swinging from side to side when she waddles across the floor on her little old rickety legs.

With Li'l Kitty's nose down in her bowl of favorite yummy, I express in a soft voice…

"You need to watch your waist, Miss Kitty."

I'm sure it was sheer coincidence, but she looked up from her bowl licking gravy from her lips and then gives me her squinty-eyed look of disapproval.

I'm planning to do a bit of serious swimming in the pool tomorrow morning, so I'll need a few additional calories. With that in mind, I look in the refrigerator and then the freezer for chicken—spying a package of ground chicken breast, I placed it in the microwave for defrosting.

With chicken on the menu, I open the refrigerator and pull out stuffed green olives, onion, pitted dried plums, and Monterey Jack shredded cheese. From the walk-in pantry, I select a large can of diced tomatoes with jalapenos, ground coriander, cumin, a sweet potato, and a package of seven-inch multigrain tortillas.

Later, after cooking the chicken in a large skillet until it's no longer pink, I added spices and the other chopped ingredients, then covered and placed on a medium burner. After fifteen minutes, it was time to turn down the burner to low and wait until the liquid evaporates. After scooping out my makins and placing them on three tortillas, I added a handful of cheese on each to make them a double yummy.

If you're still reading this and haven't fled to the kitchen to prepare a double yummy, I'll continue. The others will have to catch up.

While working on my last tortilla, Little Miss Kitty manages her way up onto the table then wanders over near my plate to spend the necessary time to investigate her private parts. After a few licks and satisfied everything was okay and in the right place, she brought her nose up near my dish.

When yelling at her to get away, she withdrew a fraction of an inch. Then while trying to push her away; it was like pushing on a heavy iron anvil. Gads, for a cat close to needing a walker, I'm getting my ass kicked—survival of the fittest. My father always told me never to trust a cat to watch over your food.

The next morning after finishing my four-mile swim, I watch the morning sky turn from black to a light purple. My endorphins are zooming along at supersonic speed after two hundred thirty laps in a little under an hour, allowing almost seven hundred calories to go up in flame.

Getting out of the pool, I use my hands to squeegee off the water from my birthday suit. Now, now—I know what you're thinking... I was only skinny-dipping. Gee, even John Quincy Adams, and Theodore Roosevelt were skinny-dippers—not a pretty sight I am sure.

I grabbed my towel, finished drying off, then shimmy into the house singing Little Anthony and the Imperials', *"Shimmy, Shimmy Coco Pop."*

After a shower and togged out in my new outfit, I zip into the kitchen. Gads, I'm so hungry, I'm drooling like a Saint Bernard while fitting myself into an apron. I'm going to scramble up a half-dozen egg whites and add in my leftover makins from last night.

Forty-five minutes later, I'm out the back door, down the steps, and into the garage. After climbing into my 911, I crank it up...

Clank, buzz. Clank, buzz. Clank, buzz... Sheeeit...

I just sat there gawking out my bug-splattered windshield in disgust, and then a grin forms. I didn't hesitate to scurry out of my dead on arrival Porsche and double-timed it to garage door number two. Opening the door, I mumble...

"Gee, I guess, I have no other choice."

With a spring in my step, I slide my hand over the restored 1957 fuel-injected, high-gloss-black Chevy Bel Air...

"Bummer... Well, if you insist."

After firing it up, you can't help but hear a rumbling coming from the twin exhaust. "Hoo*rah*," I shout, sounding off like a recruit to a drill sergeant.

I slipped out of the garage with a happy-face as the car rumbles down the hill to the Pacific Coast Highway. Not wanting to leave a vapor trail behind me, I settle into cruise control, then select a CD from Jake's new GPS and CD player.

With the windows rolled down, the cool, moist morning air flowed through the car whipping my hair into a tangled mess. "Hoor*ah*!"

Toni tells me it's pronounced, *oohrah*.

THE TRAINING ROOM

After stopping off for a pit stop to... Ah, among other things, I fiddle with my hair, then head toward the training room, grab a hot brew, and then jaw with the folks as I down my cup of coffee. A short time later, I'm standing at the lectern with my endorphins still in high gear as I sing out to an unsuspecting audience in a singsong Nina Simone voice...

It's a new life for me. And I'm feeling good ... how about you folks?"

Everybody cracks up and chants: "Sing it, Simone."

"Okay, only if you sing along with me."

The audience stands and claps their hands jamming in a sing-along...

In the end, they clap and whistle.

With everyone settled down, I look around at eager faces...

"That was great fun, but, we need to move on to our studies this morning."

THE LEADING INDICATORS: MARKET AND FINANCIAL

"We are on the last leg of our discussion about a new set of measurement tools. Let's begin by looking at Section B diagram in your booklet for the leading indicator system where we'll be covering Market Share and EVA...

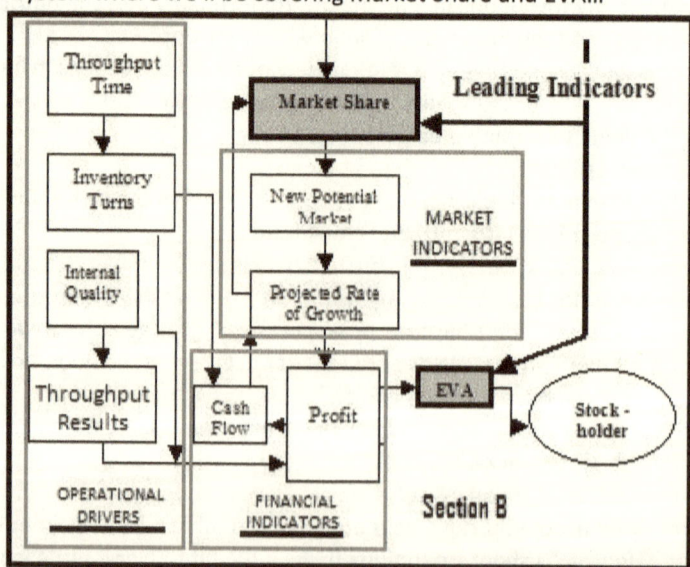

The *Market Share* indicator measures whether the strategy defined by the system benchmarks set for *Market Perception* is working. For instance, when the actual market growth rate exceeds the company's benchmark growth rate, the *Projected Growth Rate* indicator needs re-defined...

The growth of the business does not necessarily mean additional market share acquisition, even though—actual growth may exceed expectations...

It's possible the business could be losing market share when the market expands at a faster rate than the company...

Computation for market growth equals the change in sales for a current period compared to the previous year as a percentage...

This is an example of the formula...

> CURRENT PERIOD 150M (MINS) PREVIOUS PERIOD 125M = CHANGE 25M
> PREVIOUS PERIOD 125M / CHANGE 25M = CHANGE 20%

Next, is *benchmarking projections*. For setting benchmarks to acquire a greater market share, three events must take place...

FIRST, you must bring innovative products to the market.

SECOND, acquire an MPV perception lead over competitors.

AND LAST, increase market awareness within the market segment.

Benchmark projections must result from financial computer simulations...

Are there any questions?

Seeing content in the class, I gave us a little breather while checking my notes and toss back a slug of water.

"Now, we get into the fun stuff. Well, only if you're an accountant."

The room goes into applause, booing, and then laughter.

And then fumbling with a make-believe necktie, I present my best Rodney Dangerfield impression...

"Well, it's obvious; we accounting types get no respect."

The audience responds with gleeful chuckles...

"As you may guess, our next subject is EVA—and a lengthy session it is..."

ECONOMIC VALUE ADDED

"Now, before jumping into the specifics of economic value added, I would have to say for you non-financial folks, EVA can be difficult. It's not unlike asking financial people trying to follow a discussion of a microchip design...

However, it's important to get the gist of the idea how EVA financial information works, especially, for decision-makers within the company. Many of you folks sitting here today are in positions of great responsibility that will be instrumental in future profits and growth...

Let me give you an idea what happens when leaders of a company don't understand the financials. For instance, as in many past cases of huge bankruptcies such as Enron, THE CEO CLAIMED HE DIDN'T KNOW OR UNDERSTAND THE FINANCIAL DEALINGS GOING ON IN HIS COMPANY. THAT'S NO EXCUSE IN MY BOOK—BECAUSE HE SHOULD HAVE.

Had he understood the company's financials, and was an honest person, thousands of people would still be at work and investors would not have lost millions of dollars—well, you get my drift... In 1896, Alfred Marshall said...

There is no profit unless you earn the cost of capital.

Simply put, EVA allows shareholders to see a gain or lack of gain when their allocation of after-tax profit is greater than or equal to the expected return on the original capital invested.

EVA enables a company to find its true value resulting from the *Performance Drivers* output. As you may remember from our first session of *measurement tools*, we discussed these performance drivers...

To iterate the discussion, they are the *internal policies, system processes,* and *operational drivers*. These guys drive the results of the leading indicators, which we call *market share, market perception*, and *EVA*. There needs to be clarification, however...

Theoretically, according to the original authors of EVA, accuracy requires specific accounting adjustments. Some examples might be amortization of goodwill, R&D expenditures, interest payments, and non-interest bearing current liabilities...

R&D costs, for instance, are spread over their expected economic useful life; therefore, making these adjustments an integral part of the EVA process. IN OTHER WORDS, *EVA* HAS STANDARDIZED THE FINANCIAL ACCOUNTING PROCESS INDEPENDENTLY OF THE BALANCE SHEET APPROACH—MAKING IT UNACCEPTABLE TO US...

However, Anderson, Bey, and Weaver of *Lehigh University* have published a White Paper, *Economic Value Added Adjustments: Much to-do about nothing*. In their paper, *they note:*

The author of the EVA process, Stern Stewart in 1991, O'Hanlon and Peasnell in 1996, and Young and O'Bryne in 2001 converted the economic value accounting numbers into correct estimates of value for the use in the EVA process.

But the folks at Lehigh University called it *wrong* or *unnecessary* accounting numbers. Anderson, Bey, and Weaver had this to say about the evidence needed to make adjustments to EVA:

UNFORTUNATELY, THE CITED EXAMPLES OF *EVA* DO NOT PROVIDE ANY INFORMATION ON THE ABSOLUTE OR RELATIVE IMPACT THE INDIVIDUAL ADJUSTMENTS HAVE ON COMPUTING *EVA*... ALSO, THERE IS NO THEORETICAL OR EMPIRICAL EVIDENCE THAT THE *EVA* ADJUSTMENTS CONVERT 'WRONG' ACCOUNTING NUMBERS INTO CORRECT ESTIMATES OF ECONOMIC VALUE.

THE JAKE JENSEN GROUP THINKS THE IDEA THAT THE *EVA* PROCESS REQUIRES AMORTIZATION OF *R&D*, GOODWILL, INTEREST PAYMENTS, AND NON-INTEREST BEARING CURRENT LIABILITIES SHOULD SPREAD OUT OVER THEIR EXPECTED ECONOMIC USEFUL LIFE IS NOTHING MORE THAN ACCOUNTING GOBBLEDYGOOK...

Jake would say...

Much of our accounting rules need a final resting place on Boot Hill...

We'll be discussing more on current accounting rules in an upcoming session.

Back on our Subject, I must say, these amortization costs are part of the total system throughput cost of doing business. R&D, for instance, is an integral part of the total operating system. One must ask to what end will this finite financial engineering amortization help us to better understand the company's

EVA performance...

Well, as Anderson, Bey, and Weaver pointed out from their viewpoint, IT HAS NO RELEVANCE."

I take a moment while looking around for a response.

"Gobbledygook?" Ed said, with raised eyebrows...

"For a finance person, you are a whole new breed."

"Well, Ed... I enjoy finance, but like many professions, we get caught up with ourselves and want to control the way the world works. The more complicated we can make it, the more demand there is for us.

We play an essential role in the world of business, but we need to reevaluate our GAAP rules and simplify the accounting process. Sorry, I get sidetracked discussing this subject. Let me get back to our EVA adjustments.

One could say, without using the EVA accounting adjustments we've been discussing—it no longer meets EVA standards. Nevertheless, it mirrors RIM, the *Residual Income Model* indicator. Therefore, if you'd like, we can call it whatever you want, but for training, we will continue to call it EVA. Not to worry, though—there are companies out there using EVA without using the accounting adjustments. So, don't feel lonely...

EVA is also an exceptional vehicle for a global sharing of the wealth system. Your CEO, Ms. Wells, is designing a new system that she'll soon present to the officers of the company, and together, they will develop the new global sharing of the wealth system..."

I take a moment to change gears while removing my bottle cap and take a swig of good old tap water.

"Okay. I'm now ready to get into the EVA process. Let's make sure you are using the booklet in front of you to follow along in the multiple steps. If you don't, you may get lost in the process."

THE EVA PROCESS

While fidgeting with my marker, I take a moment for everybody to open the booklet and find the EVA section.

"The EVA formula for computing is straightforward when seeing it displayed on the screen...

$$EVA = \text{NET OPERATING PROFIT AFTER TAX (NOPAT) MINUS THE COST OF CAPITAL}$$

The *net operating profit after tax* is the easy part; it's the *cost-of-capital* which becomes esoteric... ALL THE UPCOMING TABLES ARE IN YOUR NOTEBOOK...

Therefore, we need to do a step-by-step process to uncover the nuances in arriving at an accurate EVA. Not to be disheartened—I've seen a thirty-eight-page paper written by a colleague of mine on the subject.

To keep things relative, I'm using the necessary data from a previous privately-owned company where needed. The process will take six steps to compute the EVA result, and we'll begin with the COST OF CAPITAL.

THE COST OF CAPITAL – STEP ONE THROUGH STEP FIVE

Okay, let's jump into the process of building an EVA, beginning with...

STEP ONE, THE RELATIVE COMPARISON PERCENT OF EQUITY AND DEBT FROM THE FINANCIAL INFORMATION...

The value data shown is the actual results from another company I was working with, and giving the weighted relationship between both equity and debt. There will also be additional financial values needed in the upcoming steps coming from the same source."

STEP 1	THE RELATIVE COMPARISON PERCENT OF EQUITY AND DEBT		
Description	Weighted Value	Formula	Weighted Percent
Equity	$4,115,692	Equity/(debt + equity)	48%
Debt	$4,454,908	Debt/(debt + equity)	52%
Total	$8,570,600		100%

After waiting for a moment, I asked the audience if they had any questions about STEP ONE. The only notable response was a few shaking heads.

"Okay, let's move on to...

STEP TWO, the COST OF CAPITAL... The mission here is to find the relationship between the expected rate of return and the stockholder's investment risk—unfortunately, the answer only comes after a long, but rewarding journey...

Professors of finance have written numerous papers on the subject, but like most things intellectual, they needlessly take their writing to the nth degree...

I would recommend going to a minimal logical approach for the calculation, the CAPITAL ASSET PRICING MODEL, or CAPM. It seems to fit the bill when used to determine an appropriate rate of return of an asset.

The **CAPM** has *three components plus the equation being* THE FOURTH...

THE FIRST COMPONENT is a *risk-free return rate.*

THE SECOND COMPONENT is the *beta factor* number and...

THE THIRD COMPONENT is the *market risk premium return-rate*—CAPM Equation.

And the FOURTH COMPONENT is the *cost of equity equation*...

Now, Let's begin with the...

THE FIRST COMPONENT, A RISK-FREE RETURN RATE...

STEP TWO	FIRST COMPONENT - RISK-FREE RETURN RATE	
RATE OF RETURN (INTEREST RATE) FOR 3-MONTH U.S. TREASURY BILL		**2.00%**

Its rate of return is the interest rate offered in a three-month U.S. Treasury bill. During unsettled economic times, the rate can fluctuate considerably...

THE U.S. TREASURY BILL ACTS AS A PROXY FOR THE RISK-FREE RATE because of short-term government-issued securities, historically speaking, have zero risks of default. This rate implies that any additional risk taken by investors results in a higher rate of return.

For this exercise, however, I'm using a ***two percent rate of return***.

As I mentioned early, these figures for the EVA come from a previous

PRIVATELY-OWNED COMPANY. Therefore, I didn't want to change the computations for the benefit of keeping the data current. Up next we have the...

SECOND COMPONENT OF STEP TWO WITH TWO TYPES OF BETA FACTOR CALCULATIONS: PART A AND PART B...

It measures the stock price volatility in relation to the rest of the market. When one is only interested in a publicly owned company, it's not difficult, but the privately held company will require some explanation shown as a table.

PART A IS A PUBLICALLY OWNED COMPANY BETA CALCULATION... And one need only go to the YAHOO WEBSITE and make two clicks...

FIRST, CLICK on the Finance tab, and then type in the company symbol for a quote, such as TSLA for TESLA, Inc.

SECOND, CLICK the STATISTICS designation that you'll find in the header running across the top... On this page, you'll find the word **BETA** with its assigned calculation found under TRADING INFORMATION FROM STOCK PRICE HISTORY..."

I pause for a moment while contemplating my next subject...

THE SECOND COMPONENT, PART B OUR NEXT BETA SOURCE, WE'LL BE FORMULATING A PRIVATELY OWNED COMPANY...

There is no specific single index needed to calculate beta for our privately held company, although the S&P 500 is perhaps the most common proxy for the market...

As a privately-owned company, you could select from available indices best associated with your type of company, such as Technology, the Internet, Utilities, Oil and Gas, and so on...

But, let's move on now and assign out private company beta...

To help in digesting this next step, I'm going to show you an illustration of how to arrive at the proper *beta* figure...

STEP TWO	SECOND COMPONENT, PART B			BETA FACTOR TABLE FOR PRIVATELY OWNED BUSINESS			
SOURCE	NO. OF YEARS	YEAR FOUR ROI	YEAR THREE ROI	YEAR TWO ROI	YEAR 1 ROI	Average
S&P 500	2			1.38%	11.96%	6.67%
PRIVATE CO.	2			3.40%	5.47%	4.44%
	(THE NOTED ROI = (NET INCOME/TOTAL ASSETS)			Column 1	Column 2	
	MARKET RATE OF RETURN = The S&P 500 is used for the company			Private Co. Avg - Risk Free Rate	Market Rate Avg - Risk Free Rate	
	Row 1	Risk Free Rate of Return		2.00%	2.00%	
	Row 2	Co. Stock Average ROI		4.44%		
	Row 3	Market Rate of Return			6.67%	
	Row 4	Average Return (minus) Risk Free		2.44%	4.67%	
	Row 5	Column 1/Column 2 = BETA		0.52		

There it is in all its glory, so let me help you through the process...

PART B - THE UPPER PORTION is showing the comparison of the results for the private and public company shown as the S&P 500... But, before I continue, I should mention my preference would have been able to use all four years of data as opposed to my two years shown in the table. However, at the time, I was unable to retrieve the additional necessary private business financial information...

With that said, I'll begin to take you through the rest of the table necessary to formulate the beta number...

IN PART B'S LOWER PORTION we'll start with the Risk-Free Rate of Return in row one, which in our case; I used a three-month U.S. Treasury bill often used as risk-free of two percent...

Its purpose is to subtract the risk-free return rate, at two percent, from both the private company average return and the S&P 500 average return, with the results shown in row four.

With this known, we can now calculate the beta by dividing the results shown in row 4, column one, by row four, column two, giving us the beta number of **zero-point five-two.**

GREAT, NOW WE KNOW HOW TO CREATE A PRIVATELY HELD COMPANY BETA FACTOR NUMBER, BUT WHAT DOES IT MEAN?

WELL, THE BETA INDICATES, first off, the volatility or risk of a particular stock relative to the volatility of a select market index...

To be more specific, a beta of one indicates the figure moves with the market, in our case, the S&P 500 index...

If our beta is less than one, as shown for our private company, the value is theoretically less volatile than our market index. To open up the horizon, let's say our beta is one point two, illustrating twenty percent more volatility than the S&P 500 at one...

Or, conversely, if an Exchange Traded Fund beta is zero point six-five, illustrates thirty-five percent less volatility than the S&P 500.

For our private company in the table with a beta of zero point five two means, we'll have forty-eight percent less volatility than the S&P 500. This indicates the asset return is expected to underperform against the benchmark of one, by forty-eight percent. Well, that is if the company doesn't improve its performance for a better return on assets.

That covers STEP TWO, COMPONENT TWO, PART A AND B, leaving us...

...COMPONENT THREE OF STEP TWO. It's the MARKET RISK PREMIUM RETURN-RATE— CAPM CAPITAL ASSET PRICING MODEL EQUATION... And, and as a reminder... The FIRST COMPONENT had a *risk-free return* of TWO PERCENT, and... Our SECOND COMPONENT, the PRIVATE COMPANY had a 0.52 BETA FACTOR *result used* in the next step...

This gets more complicated, but I'll make it as simple as possible....

IT'S MADE FROM TWO PARTS... THE **S&P 500** and the THIRTY-DAY TREASURY BILL...

PART ONE **S&P 500** EXCEL SPREADSHEET FOR THE COMPOUND ANNUAL GROWTH RATE (CAGR) and how it's formulated.

After you've built the simple diagram in a spreadsheet I have just illustrated, you'll enter the year and the ending historical value for the ten year period shown in column B.

The values in column F are the results. The ENDING/PRESENT VALUE NOTED IN E-TWO REPRESENTS, cell F-Two that reflects the figure in cell D-Three.

The eight sixty-six shown in F-Three reflects cell D-Twelve. The F-four is nine reflecting B-12 minus one. The CAGR percent formula is: ((F2/F3)^(1/F4)-1) resulting in **13.89 percent.**

	A	B	C	D	E	F
1		S&P 500 compound annual growth rate (CAGR)				
2		Years	Year	Value	Ending/Present Value:	2,790
3		1	1-Jan-18	2,790	Beginning Value:	866
4		2	1-Jan-17	2,275	(Number of Years) - 1	9
5		3	1-Jan-16	1,919	CAGR as percent	13.89%
6		4	1-Jan-15	2,028	Excel Macro	13.89%
7		5	1-Jan-14	1,822		
8		6	1-Jan-13	1,480	STEP 2 COMPONENT 3	
9		7	1-Jan-12	1,301		
10		8	1-Jan-11	1,283	S&P 500	
11		9	1-Jan-10	1,124		
12		10	1-Jan-09	866		

PART TWO-COMPONENT THREE OF STEP TWO, THE THIRTY-DAY TREASURY BILL... IT'S THE COMPOUND ANNUAL GROWTH RATE FOR THE TEN-YEAR NOMINAL THIRTY-DAY TREASURY BILL JUNE 2017 through May 2018.

As in the previous diagram, the values in column F are the formulas. The present value cell F-Two reflects cell-D at Two Point Five-zero. The beginning value of Cell-F reflects One point Two Five in cell D-Fourteen. F-Four is the number of years cell in B-fourteen minus 1. The CAGR percent formula is: ((F2/F3)^(1/F4)-1) resulting in **6.50 percent**.

	A	B	C	D	E	F
1		30-day treasury bill compound annual growth rate (CAGR) - Ten Year Nominal				
2		Years	Month	Value	Ending/Present Value:	2.50
3		1	May	2.50	Beginning Value:	1.25
4		2	April	2.25	(Number of Years) - 1	11
5		3	March	2.25	CAGR as percent	6.50%
6		4	February	2.15		
7		5	January	1.99	STEP 2 COMPONENT 3	
8		6	December	1.60		
9		7	November	1.60	30 DAY TREASURY BILL	
10		8	October	1.50		
11		9	September	1.30		
12		10	August	1.40		
13		11	July	1.45		
14		12	June	1.25		

FINALIZING COMPONENT THREE OF STEP TWO, THE RISK PREMIUM RATE... Subtract the **6.50 percent** CAGR TEN-YEAR NOMINAL THIRTY-DAY TREASURY BILL from the S&P 500 CAGR **13.89 PERCENT**, resulting in a **7.38 PERCENT RISK PREMIUM RATE** used in the next step... OKAY, WE'RE NOW READY TO COMPUTE THE **CAPM** CAPITAL ASSET PRICING MODEL EQUATION in **STEP TWO, COMPONENT FOUR...**

STEP TWO (COMPONENT FOUR) CAPITAL ASSET PRICING MODEL EQUATION (CAPM)	
Component One: Risk free rate =	2.00%
Component two Part A or B: Company Beta factor =	0.52
Component Three: Risk Premium Rate =	7.38%
(CAPM) = risk-free rate + (company's beta x risk premium).	5.8%

It's been a long road, but this table summarizes the results from component one, two and three making the process reasonably self-explanatory by showing the previous results building up to Component Four...

Well, I don't see any frowns, but I have to ask, do you have questions for the CAPM equation...? No? Okay, let's be moving on to...

STEP THREE. *It computes the after-tax cost of debt...*

The after-tax formulation is preferred due to the deductible interest expense from the tax. However, we need to know the pre-tax result before we can compute after-tax. The pre-tax profit includes the debt interest paid computed as an expense. The computation is the annual amount of interest paid on the total amount borrowed or annual interest expense divided by the total amount borrowed. Let's look at how we would calculate the after-tax cost of debt in my illustration table."

STEP THREE - AFTER-TAX COST OF DEBT CALCULATION	
Cost of Debt - Pre-Tax and After Tax	
Annual Interest Expense	$29,828
Total Amount Borrowed	$300,526
Pre-Tax cost of Debt = Annual Interest/Total Amount Borrowed	9.93%
After Tax Cost of Debt = Pre-Tax Cost of Dept x (1-32%) a tax rate sheild	6.75%
When using a 32% as the tax rate, the tax rate sheild is 68% or (1-32%)	

"The calculation is straightforward, showing the first two rows as the actual results from the financial information available to me. The next three rows are nothing more than performing the formulas as noted... So, do we have questions...? ...No...? Okay then, it's time to move on to my next table..."

STEP FOUR *IS THE COST OF EQUITY AND AFTER-TAX DEBT. THE ILLUSTRATION SHOWS THE TOTAL WEIGHTED AVERAGE FOR THE COST OF EQUITY SHOWN IN STEP TWO, COMPONENT FOUR, AND THE COST OF AFTER-TAX DEBT REFLECTED IN STEP THREE.*

Step Four Return on wt. average: cost of equity and after-tax debt		
Step 1 x Step 2 = Average		
Step 1 Wt. Equity	Step 2 CAPM	= Average
48%	5.8%	2.81%
Step 1 Wt. Debt	After Tax cost of Debt Step 3	
52%	6.75%	3.51%
Total Weighted Average		6.32%

As you'll notice, it would seem there is nothing complicated here illustrating step one times step two resulting in the average weighted cost of equity and after-tax cost of debt...

But again, I must ask, do we have questions...?

Well, seeing no one squirming in their seat and no hands flapping in the breeze, I'll close in on the last two calculations...

STEP FIVE *COMPUTES THE COST OF CAPITAL, WHICH SUBTRACTS FROM NET PROFIT IN STEP*

SIX...

From a strategic point of view, the cost of capital is the minimum return required by capital investors, which one can compare to the actual net operating profit after-tax from the business... With the idea, it will persuade the investor to make a given investment... But, I'll expand more on this in STEP SIX...

So, we'll close in on the final steps by taking a look at our new Step Five image for calculating Cost of Capital requiring the previous four steps to calculate the necessary data...

The total equity and debt in STEP ONE times STEP FOUR the cost of equity and after-tax debt, equals the total cost of capital...

You'll also notice the calculation in STEP FIVE shows the cost of capital at a little over half a million dollars..."

STEP FIVE - COST OF CAPITAL		
Step One Equity & Debt	Step Four - Cost of Equity & AfterTax debt	Step One x Step Four = Cost of Capital
$8,570,600	6.32%	$541,418

I take a moment before I continue so as to consider my approach to the last two calculations in step six...

"**STEP SIX,** our EVA formula is shown in two tables, *Figure A and Figure B*...

Now, with the new EVA calculation, **FIGURE A** image on the screen let me explain the necessary steps in the formula to achieve *NET OPERATING PROFIT AFTER-TAX*...

STEP SIX - FIGURE-A EVA CALCULATION				
Column 1	+ (Column 2	X	Column 3) =	Column 4
Net Profit (After Tax)	Annual Interest Expense		(1 - Tax Rate)	NOPAT
$973,924	$29,828		0.68	$994,207

Yes, Susan, do you have a question?"

"I do, thank you. What is operating profit?"

"The simplest way to convey it is to say it's equal to earnings before interest and tax payments..."

"Thanks, Jackie, I understand..."

But to compute NOPAT in figure A, you need to add back in the interest expense times the shielded tax rate. Remember, the shield is one, minus the tax rate, and in this case, it's sixty-eight percent of the total interest expense...

With this class full of highly intelligent folks, I know someone sitting out there has already calculated the shielded tax rate results..."

I wait a moment looking around the class when I see Gary Eastwood with his great outsmile...

"Okay, Gary, let's not make a mistake here, or you'll never live it down..."

The class swivels their heads toward Gary with smiling faces and a few chuckles'.

"Well now, Jackie, if I make a mistake and everyone laughs, I'll feel great. But if we don't hear any laughs, it will be humiliating knowing that no one noticed it because I'm so unimportant..."

The class let out a hysterical boff of laughter...

It took a while for the class to settle down having no clue Gary had a humor streak going through him. But humor is not uncommon when coming from highly intelligent people...

"That was a wonderfully funny remark Gary, sounds like something Woody Allen might have said...

So, what's the answer to the shielded tax rate result?"

"Give me a moment, my answer left me with all the goings-on..."

A moment later, Gary speaks up...

"The shielded tax rate would be twenty thousand two hundred eighty-three added to the net profit after tax.."

"That's correct, Gary. Thank you, much appreciated...

I wait a moment before I continue...

"Okay, moving on now, I'd like to point out that companies with no debt have no interest expense; therefore, the *net operating profit after tax* is equal to net profit...

It's time to finish our EVA calculation journey with our last step...

STEP SIX *CALCULATION* **FIGURE B...**

Give me a moment and I'll have the table ready to comment on...

Okay, now with our NET OPERATING PROFIT AFTER-TAX FROM our previous **STEP 6 FIGURE A**, and **STEP FIVE'S COST OF CAPITAL** we can finish the last of our calculation for EVA...

Subtract **STEP FIVE'S COST OF CAPITAL** noted in *column two* figure B from **STEP SIX FIGURE A'S** NOPAT shown in *column one figure B. Column three* shows the EVA result...

In this scenario, we have a positive increase in the investors' expected minimum return of nearly half-million dollars...

STEP SIX - FIGURE-B EVA CALCULATION		
Column 1	Column 2	**Column 3 = (EVA)**
NOPAT	Cost of Capital	Column 1 - Column 2
$994,207	$541,418	**$452,789**

Firms that earn higher returns than the cost of capital benefit shareholders and account for increased shareholder value. You might say if the net profit is less than that of the cost of capital than it's a poor investment...

Okay, that's the last step...

Oh, and I should mention, after today's session, I'll leave a CD copy with Ed Blackburn of all the tables in an Excel format. The file is set up for you to enter the nine necessary entries of financial information of any company allowing you to instantly compute the EVA results. I'm sure Ed has your company email address, and he can send a file to each of you...

"Are there any questions?"

"No takers?

"Ah... I see bashful hand about to surface...

Yes, Gloria, what's on your mind?"

"Thanks, Jackie... My husband dillydallies around the stock market, so I'm wondering if one knew the EVA results, if it would be helpful?"

"That's a reasonable question, but in the stock market and using the EVA as a guide to buy or sell alone is not advisable, because it gets more complicated when you throw in all sorts of other variables. Meaning, even with a good EVA, the market may react poorly because of some bad news on one of their product returns...

Playing the stock market and buying into a private company are two entirely different processes of due diligence..."

I give Gloria a shrug...

"Thanks, Jackie. Your answer really helped me better understand the basic idea..."

...Okay then, we'll move on to our next subject: *Benchmarking* the *EVA*..."

Before moving on, I grab my bottle of water and have a knockback...

"BENCHMARKING THE EVA establishes a target for future stockholder value, but there is no known rule-of-thumb for setting the best performance level. But, we'll establish a benchmark to use in your projected employee global sharing of the wealth, which I'm sure you will be interested to hear more about that from Ms. Wells...

Now, I would say when the EVA output level does not meet the planned projections; review the performance drivers and indicators to redefine the strategy and the resources necessary to put the plan on course...

We're about there, with only a need to cover the SUMMARY OF EXTERNAL AND INTERNAL DEMANDS."

SUMMARY: EXTERNAL AND INTERNAL DEMANDS

"It would seem as though you can't wait for the next diagram."

The audience has a good laugh.

"Not to worry, this is the one you have been waiting for—the last one."

A sigh of relief and joyful chuckles rolls across the audience, while I bring up the last diagram.

"As you'll notice, the diagram illustrates the influence from both external and internal. With that in mind for our summarization, the main purpose is to illustrate all the different indicators that influence the outcome of growth.

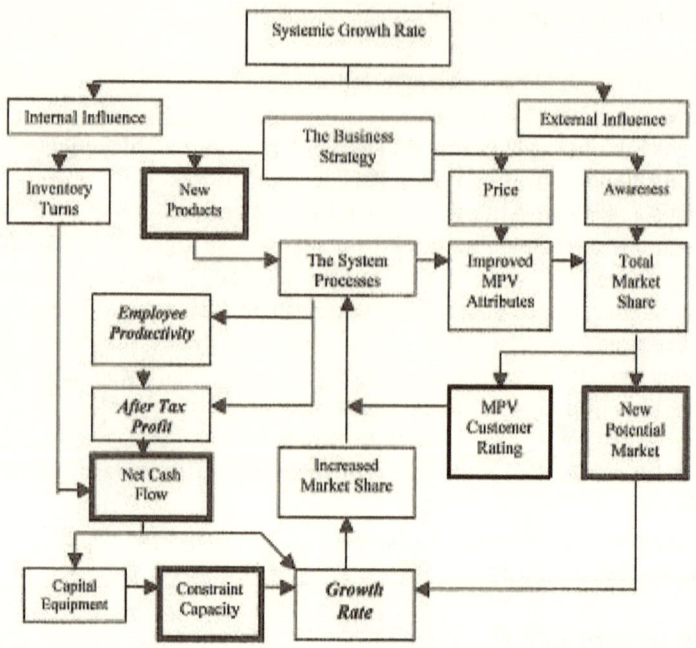

Please note the heavy lines around the boxes in the diagram showing the potential constraints in both the external and internal growth rate. At the bottom of the diagram, you'll see arrows pointing to Growth Rate...

This flow of influence gives you an idea of the system dynamics and how important it is to have the proper organizational structure to execute quality growth and profitability.

Well, I believe we've done it. That was the last of my general discussion notes and our last image diagram. This session was lengthy—however, it's a crucial step in developing your new business architecture. Are there questions before we call it a day?"

The room becomes quiet as Nina stands.

"Thank you, Jackie," she said with a slight bow and a touch of urgency in her voice to close out the session... "That was a great presentation."

She's quick to make known her need to get people back to work, then takes her seat.

"Thanks, Nina," I said, reading Nina's message, "And thank you all for being an appreciative and involved audience."

The audience applauds, then files out of the training room. A moment later, Nina is standing next to me.

"You have now confirmed my feelings about you, Jackie."

"How's that, Nina?" I said with apprehension, thinking today's subject may have taken too long.

"I just want to let you know, I loved your little sing-along skit. It shows you have incredible leadership capability, and I notice the audience seldom takes their eyes off you. I would also mention, Dakota and Jake are well aware of your leadership ability, and someday, you will run one of their companies."

"Wow... I'm dumbfounded receiving such a wonderful compliment."

We chitchat a moment longer, and then Nina heads back to her office.

I stand there still a little paranoid when I'm around Nina, not wanting to disappoint her, but after what she said, I need to lighten up. With that thought, I gather up my stuff and turn out the lights.

Getting the hungries while driving home, the idea to grab a ripsnorter hamburger and chocolate malt comes to mind; you know—a little something to take the edge off the hunger pangs. A moment later, Ernie's Beach Burgers flashes before me.

A LAZY AFTERNOON AT ERNIE'S BEACH BURGERS

When nearing Malibu, Ernie's Beach Burgers comes into view. Ernie has great burgers and malts—the old-fashioned kind, thick on both counts. The 1920's building looks over the highway that runs along the coastline and incoming surf. Ernie's been a place I've been hanging out ever since surfing Malibu beach as a kid—still, do at times. Thankfully, there are things that never change, it still brings in many of the same crusty critters I used to see back when.

When pulling into the parking lot, the car draws a crowd while trying to park next to the walkway. After shifting into park, I glance up and see my old surfing buddies eating munchies out on the deck and drinking beer.

While scooting out of the car, the crowd closes in...

"PLEASE ... don't touch the car," I shouted.

"Hey, what's cooking, babe?" Jerry barks.

I look up to see Jerry with the ocean breeze tousling his extra-long, salt-encrusted sun-bleached hair.

I give him my naughty up-to-no-good smile.

He reminds me a lot of Mickey Rourke when he played in *The Wrestler*. I mentioned that one day, and now his buddies call him Ram to irritate him.

"So, what's with you and the groovy *Black Widow*?" He yells.

"Just joyriding," I holler.

I'm excited to see my ol' buddies. These roughnecks have become inseparable brothers-in-arms ever since they joined the Marines and became a four-man recon team—during the Panama flare-up and the Gulf War. In this dangerous environment, they learned to live through it with mockery, wit, and snappy retorts. As far as I can tell, these guys haven't changed since joining the Malibu fire department after mustering out of the service eighteen years ago.

When heading up the stairway, I'm thinking back to when I first met them on the beach while surfing and they were still going through their firemen training. And now that I've surfed with them off and on over the years, I have to keep on my toes and ready to step into *their* world.

When approaching the table, Randy gives me the eye...

"Hey babe, how's the wife and kids?"

Do you see what I mean? Fortunately, having been around Johnny and Jake enough, I've gotten quicker on my feet. When looking down at the table, I see four weather-beaten happy faces looking up at me, waiting for a retort.

"Well," I said standing there at the table. "The kids did multiple piercing of every open hole on their bodies and decorated themselves with silver gewgaws and outlandish tattoos, and then ran off with a rock band. To top it off, my wife hooked up with a crew cut bull dyke that looked like a young Marlon Brando in drag, and spits tobacco," I said with a hangdog look.

Ah... It appears I passed muster because the guys came unglued with a guffaw while high-fiving me.

"Have a seat, babe," Doug said.

"Thanks, guys," I said with a smirk.

Before taking a seat, I leaned over Randy, pushed his hand aside and grabbed myself a handful of fries.

"So, what are you ol' timers doing today, besides surfing?"

After taking a seat, I dip my fries into a bowl of ketchup.

"Same old shit we've been doing for almost two decades—surfing, hanging, and looking at the babes," Doug said.

Doug has a grin that rides above his gray, whisker-laden square jaw forming deep lines creasing his well-tanned face like dry riverbeds. He has those underwater coral blue eyes that make the ladies weak in their knees when he lays his eyes on them.

"Nothing new there," I said gleefully.

All at once I take notice of a pretty lady waiting to take my order.

"Hi. Sorry, I didn't see you."

"Hi. I'm Janice. What can I get you?"

"Janice," I said, "I'll have your half-pounder with wheat bun, shrooms, tomatoes, lettuce, and triple cheese. Oh yeah ... and a side of cottage cheese in place of fries, these guys will clean me out of fries."

"Yeah, giving away *any* portion of *her* food would be like a major humanitarian gesture," Randy said, causing a round of amusement.

Just then, I'm distracted when seeing a guy sitting on the Bel Air's front fender having his picture taken.

Kong, the quiet giant, gives the guy a hard stare, then blares out with his foghorn voice...

"Move your butt off those wheels, dude."

Kong's real name is Danny. Back in the day as a teenager, I was a real surfing dude and befriended most of the Malibu local surfers. When sitting on the beach one day with Doug, Jerry, and Randy, we watched Danny walk out of the surf. This was back when they adopted me as one of the dudes, or perhaps, more accurately, their mascot.

Danny stopped on dry sand and then shook his body like a Labrador retriever. Kong is one extra-large, hairy dude with a shaggy uni-eyebrow that stretched across his low forehead; thus, the name, Kong.

While Danny was spraying saltwater around the beach, Doug told me Kong had a new girlfriend who liked to comb *all* of his hair. I remembered that moment well when wrinkling up my nose and sang out...

Extra, extra, read all about surfing gorilla...

Kong snatched up his surfboard with one hand as though he were picking up the morning paper and headed toward us. Still dripping profusely, Kong left a trail of water in the sand when he heard the guys laughing, and then grumbled, what's so funny?

The kid looks up at the sound of the incoming foghorn, then took off like a fly about to be swatted by a cow's tail.

"Thanks, Danny."

"Nice wheels, babe," Kong said.

"Mine or the car."

"Both, babe."

"Thanks, Danny."

Janice is standing next to me patiently waiting for me...

"Anything you'd care to drink with that burger?"

"Double chocolate malt would be great."

"One double chocolate malted coming up," she said.

"Did you say malted?" I said. "Are you from New York?"

"Oh no, but I picked it up from a song by Jonathan Richman."

"A song about chocolate malts, that's great, how does it go?"

With a pause, she looks skyward reckoning about the words...

When finished with her song, she giggles, then blushes...

"That's all I can remember."

The guys rolled their eyes.

"I love it," I said, "I shall make it my theme song when drinking a chocolate malted. Thanks."

"You aren't going to share the malted with these guys are you?" Janice said with a titter.

"Of course, she won't share it. And please hurry with the order before she eats our entire goddamn plate of French fries," Randy growled.

His loud gravel-like voice traveled across the deck sounding like a rock crushing machine as ketchup dripped from his twenty-past-eight handlebar mustache.

Janice giggles and starts to walk away when Randy stands and leans over to whisper something into her ear. She nods, giggles again, and sashays her way toward the kitchen as Randy watches her before taking his seat at the table.

"What were you looking at Randy?" Jerry said.

"Hmm... Well, I like her better when she walks away," Randy said.

This brought about a round of guffaw from his buddies.

I was just about to say something when Ernie, the owner, steps out on his deck. He soon spots me and waves hello. With a social smile, I wave back. Ernie has no neck, a pursed mouth, a snub nose with the heavy-lidded eyes of a manatee that leaves the impression of disappearing in his large, fleshy face. His quivering jowls settle his sternomastoid muscle and his multiple chins rest on his white dress shirt, which sports a narrow orange tie. He then turns and disappears into the restaurant.

"With that narrow orange tie, Ernie looks like Porky Pig sucking on a carrot dangling under his chins," Randy said.

The guys crack up and give him a high-five.

Instead of giving Randy a high-five, I give him a slap on the back of his head. "Not nice."

Everybody cracks up, especially, Randy, while rubbing his head.

With a quiet moment hanging about, I take the opportunity to jump in and grab more fries smothered in ketchup.

Randy gives me a hard look with his shaggy sun-bleached, half-cocked scarred eyebrows. At an early age, he surfed at the Rockpile in Laguna Beach and took a head-pile-driver into the rocks.

"Damn, girl. How is it you still eat like a half-starved Godzilla grazing away in downtown Tokyo? And yet, you look like a triathlete in training."

"Why little ol' Randy ... you knows I nibble at my food, darlin', and then getting hotter than a welding torch during my nightly sex burns a lot of calories."

My response to Randy is in a singsong Southern accent, eyelashes fluttering with spread fingers held to my chest causing an outburst of a loud roaring cachinnate.

"You laugh, but if I remained any more sexed-up, I'd spontaneously combust."

This brought about another roar of laughter as everyone, but Randy gave me a high-five.

Randy looks befuddled, and yells out," You? ...Sex? Yeah right, little miss goodie two shoes."

Randy's retort held little water.

"Admit it, Randy, she bested you," Kong said.

Oh shit, Randy was now going to be gunning for me, so I made a quick change of our subject...

"So, Randy, what did you say to Janice before she walked away?"

"Nothing... Janice has the hots for me after I saved her one night."

"You saved her?"

Ah... Shit—here it comes.

"Yeah... She coughed and started to turn purple after taking a sample bite of my fish dinner."

Gee, maybe not.

"Oh my God, what did you do?"

"Well, I turned her over my knee, lifted her skirt and licked her rear end. She liked it so much; she coughed up the fishbone."

"Get serious, that's so stupid."

Jerry's bushy eyebrows began to twitch in delight...

"Tell us, Randy, what's that maneuver called?"

"The Hind-Lick," Randy said.

Then, of course, the guys go into hysterical laughter...

"You know, Randy, I seldom know when you're funning me or if you're gunning for me."

"Not to worry. We're never sure about that ourselves."

A short while later, Doug eyed me...

"Jackie, did you hear that Randy's dad died last week?"

I just knew he wouldn't be funning me on such a serious subject.

"Oh, Randy, I'm so sorry."

Randy shrugged with a sad expression...

"Well, he was pushing his late seventies, and I told him that his fast food would kill him someday."

"A heart attack?"

"Oh, nothing like that," Randy said, "A pizza delivery car ran over him."

I'm puzzled for a short moment.

The guys can't hold back any longer and go into another round of hysterical boffola.

"You morons are a bunch of sicko's," I said with a giggle.

They're a tough group even though they love me, but, as you know, I have to be constantly on the alert for a good-natured joke. About then, Janice leans over to slide a giant platter in front of me.

Oh my, God, a monster burger covers most of the plate. It should have its own zip code. Behind the waitress is the busboy. He has a sixty-ounce water pitcher filled to the brim with chocolate malt.

With an open smile, I grab hold of the giant pitcher with both hands and then give the guys my squinty eye look as I down my malt. After placing my half-empty drink down and wearing a chocolate mustache, I scanned the table with one corner of my lip tightened and raised with contempt. The guys, of course, shake their heads and roll their eyes around.

Later, after putting away a chunk of my burger, Randy gives me a hard look.

"You know, watching her eat is like watching a lioness with her head inside the caverns of a zebra somewhere out there on the African savannah."

"Dude, she'll eat every last scrap to shut you down, Randy," Kong said.

That was enough to trigger the guys to place bets on my gastronomic abilities. Me, I suck up the extra thick malt through two straws sounding like the suction of a Hoover vacuum cleaner.

Forty-five minutes later after cleaning up my plate and sucking the last drop of chocolate malt out of my pitcher, which, of course, is driving the guys' nuts, I call the waitress over.

Seeing my order for a piece of rhubarb pie and a cup of coffee heading to the kitchen, I look around the table...

"Rhubarb is one of my many favorite pies."

"Yeah, and how many other favorites do you have?" Randy said.

While looking up at the cloudless blue sky, I contemplate...

"Well..." I drawled out, "I like chocolate ... banana-cream ... apricot ... strawberry ... boysenberry ... peach ... cherry ... blackberry ... pecan—"

Randy lost it as his eyes rolled back into his head shouting...

"Enough, enough... Good God, I'm sorry I asked."

Thinking this scene is way too funny; his buds let out a great outburst of slaphappy laughter and high-five me.

Later, finishing my rhubarb pie, I dab my lips with a napkin and eye my friends with a piercing glance.

All of a sudden, they looked at each other with a nod, give me a shrug, stood up, and bow toward me as though I were the Queen of Sheba.

"We submit to your glorious ability to be a *big oink*," Randy said.

Then all of us have a loud, hearty laugh.

While passing a moment of time, I reach for more leftover fries.

"So tell me, Doug, how does your new bride like you working as a fireman, and then on your off days you're out with the guys surfing and drinking. You're rarely home."

"Good observation," Randy said.

"Why's that?"

I'm staring at Doug with a frown waiting for his response.

"Tell her, Doug," Randy said.

"Well, I'm having breakfast the other morning, and Lori says... 'You're hardly ever home. So I want a divorce.'"

This gets my attention.

"What's the problem? I told her. You agreed to the vows for better or worse.

She told me... 'The problem is I'm not happy anymore.'

I told her... Anymore? Hell, you've never been happy as long as I've known you.

She tells me... 'Well, why in the world did you marry me?'

I'm thinking, good point then told her... Please, would you mind asking me an easier question?

Lori then gave me a dirty look, grabbed her glass of orange juice and threw it in my face, snatches her purse and heads off to work.

Yesterday, I received divorce papers from her attorney."

"I'm so sorry, Doug."

"Don't be," Randy said, "Doug called last night, and the four of us headed out and partied into the morning hours."

"Oh," I mumbled, "How is it the rest of you guys have stayed married so long?"

"It's not been easy for our wife that's for sure," Randy said.

A few minutes later, Jerry puts on a serious face, stands up and looks out over the highway. And then he did a funny thing, he puts his hand over his heart. We turn in that direction to see a funeral procession drive by as it snakes its way down the Pacific Coast Highway. A couple of minutes later, Jerry sat down after the last of the cars go by heading south.

I'm astonished...

"Damn, Jerry that sure was a respectful thing to do."

With his lower lip quivering and with an ever so slight upward turn of the mouth, he glances over at me.

"It would seem the least I could do since I've been married to the woman for over twenty years..."

I'm slack-jawed.

"And as Randy said, it has not been easy on our wife's."

I'm now flabbergasted as I cut my eyes at Jerry.

Then I let loose with a scream, "YOUR WIFE!"

At that point, I'm gawking at the silent table to see what his friends have to say.

They can't hold it any longer as they lean back and let out a cachinnated roar.

"You... You bastards."

I couldn't help but join in with the joyful merriment... They once again got me. But as usual, fun with these guys is at my expense.

ACT II - SCENE 6
ENHANCING THE LEARNING PROCESS

Question: 1
Why is it imperative for those in a company's responsible position to ask questions when not understanding something in the financial statements?
Can you name examples?

Question: 2
When you're a shareholder or investor, why is it vital to have the financial report illustrate a gain or lack of for their expected return when compared to the after-tax profit? What is this process called to calculate the results?

Question: 3
What is the difference between what the author is suggesting as a guide to EVA that conflicts with the original measuring of amortization?
Do you agree, if so, why?
Do you disagree, if so, why?

Question: 4
When the EVA level of output does not meet planned projection, what is the plan of strategy to bring it back on course?

Question: 5
There is a lot of interaction going on between Jackie and her surfing buddies during her lunch at Ernie's Burgers.
So, was the author preparing you for the next step in the learning process? I'm not sure there is a right or wrong answer, but use creative juices and have fun with it.

ACT II SCENE 7
Streamlining Material Flow

WEEK 4 – FRIDAY MORNING – JOHNNY'S CLASS C MATERIAL FLOW STRATEGY

JOHNNY'S CAUGHT EATING OUT OF THE PEANUT BUTTER JAR

I'm having dinner with Sheri again at a new restaurant, Loews, in the Santa Monica Beach Hotel. It's a real hotspot with a beachfront setting.

For our main course, Sheri has wild, striped sea bass with fiddlehead fern, green leek couscous, fresh pine nuts, and smoked tomato cream. For me, I'm a steak-and-potatoes kind of guy, so I ordered a Black Angus filet with German potatoes and asparagus—and being the sophisticated sort, I held off on the ketchup.

After dinner, I ordered Sheri a Yellow Parrot. For me, I had a Black Russian—tough guy. Well, maybe not. It used to be that ironworkers would say…

You ain't an ironworker unless you get killed.

Now, that's a tough guy.

While waiting for our drinks, I study Sheri for a moment…

"How's Pokémon doing?"

She gives me a strange look.

"You know ... Mister Booster chair, Kim Jong II, Little Boll Weevil."

"Little boll *weevil*?"

"You know, he's the one known as the lesser of two weevils."

She giggles.

"Two weevils," then more giggles. "Oh, you must mean my hairdresser. Isn't he a sweetheart? I'll let him know you asked about him."

"That's not necessary, just tell Kim, he should work less on hair and more on tall."

With a giggle, she excuses herself and heads to the powder room. Ten minutes later, we have our drinks sitting on the table. As the waiter scampers off, Sheri heads toward our table.

With just enough of her drink to moisten her upper lip, Sheri puts it down and pulls out a cigarette. After seeing I had a look of disapproval, she nervously tugs at her napkin under her drink and then looks up at me with a pouty look.

"Not to worry, smoking is a part-time satisfaction—mostly after a dinner or with a drink."

Smartly swirling my Black Russian around, I take a sip and enjoy the warm feeling as it snakes a hot path into my stomach while surmising that smoking seems rare today. It's most often done by a loner standing and shivering outside an office building or apartment. With that thought, I look into her eyes...

"You didn't have one on our last date?"

"Sorry, seeing that it bothers you, I'll put it back."

"No, that's not necessary. Sorry. Light up, I'm just surprised is all?"

Always being the gentleman sort, I take her matches and light her up. She takes a puff, inhales, and coughs. On the second try and wanting to look more sophisticated, she takes in a long draw like Ingrid Bergman would have in Casablanca, then tips her head back and blows the smoke straight up looking more like a twelve-year-old with her first cigarette standing outside the schoolyard.

She gives me a sheepish look...

"It has this way of relaxing me," She said, flipping her hair to the side.

My only response is a devilish grin.

"You aren't impressed one bit, are you?" she said.

"You impress me, but not your smoking."

We have a great laugh.

She took one more hit from her cigarette, then tries to put it out, but with little success. So, she ignored it and allowed it to lay there smoldering and smelling up the dinner table—part-time smokers.

While looking at the cigarette ash in the ashtray reminded me of an old trick that Tom showed me back when. With that idea in mind, I gazed over at Sheri through the rising remaining cigarette smoke.

"Sheri..."

"Yes."

"Ah... I have this feeling we are coming together as one person this evening, spiritually speaking, of course. "

"Oh, Johnny, that's such a sweet thing to say."

Women are such romantics. This should be easy.

"To prove my strong feelings, I would like for you to raise your hands a few inches above the table, palms down, and close your eyes."

Now that I have her in a romantic mood, she responds well as I put my thumb in the ashtray for a liberal coating of ash.

"Keep your eyes closed while I hold your hands, then I'll put your hands together as though you were about to make a prayer," I said.

I took hold of her hands and then transferred the ash from my ash-laden thumb to her palm while putting her hands together.

After pulling my hands away, I clean the ash from my thumb...

"Now, put your mind in a glorious place and meditate beautiful thoughts. I'll do the same."

"When I say open your eyes, keep your hands together."

I waited for a moment—not too long, not too short...

"Okay, my sweet. Keep your hands together and open your eyes. Watch now while I dip my finger into the ash provided by your cigarette," I said. "And then I'll smear it onto my palm."

She's getting misty-eyed already. What a babe.

"Now, close your eyes again and put your mind back into those wonderful thoughts you were having, and I'll put my hands together, close my eyes, and allow myself transported into your beautiful little world.

When, and if, I arrive, we shall hold hands, and by doing so, I'll have transferred the ash from my hand to yours. And then after a moment of silence, I'll have you open your eyes, and you will feel relaxed."

"Oh, Johnny, I feel tingles running up and down my body."

Woman.

I waited an appropriate amount of time...

"Keep your eyes closed now as I speak of my journey. I felt as though I was in a misty state, but I'm sure I held your hand. So, my sweet, open your eyes now and see the wonderment of feeling as one with the ash transferred to your palm."

She does so, and her eyes widen. Then fill with tears.

"Oh, Johnny, I don't know what to say."

"Say nothing, my dear...

I think this is the beginning of a beautiful friendship."

Damn, I was trying for a Casablanca, Humphrey Bogart impression, but it sounded more like WC Fields.

I leaned over to take hold of her hands, and then told her of our growing closeness and other wonderful things that women like to hear...

What? I'm trying to improve on my dating game.

Guys don't forget to keep taking notes.

Our love-in session soon passed when Sheri changed our discussion from romance to baseball.

"Yesterday, you mentioned as soon as you were off the phone; you'd be heading out to play baseball in some league... Ahh... What did you say your team name was? *I Got a Woody?* Or something like that. Did you win?"

With her eyebrows at half-mast looking puzzled and waiting for an answer, she picks up her drink.

"*I Got a Woody...?* I said with my mouth agape. "Please... The team name is *We Got Wood* ... and I was a brute force at the plate and a flying gazelle around the bases."

"Wow! What was the score?"

"We lost ... thirty to zip."

"I'm impressed," Sheri said with laughter bubbling in her voice.

After finishing another drink, we leave the restaurant, walk to my car, and drive to my place.

The next morning I'm up at five-thirty—and no workout this morning. I'd promised Sheri a great breakfast, so I showered and dressed in good time for not being an early bird and all.

I walked over to the bed and gave Sheri a light kiss on the cheek. No doubt about it this is one beautiful babe. She opens one eye, mumbles something, frankly speaking, not very nice, then turns over while wiping saliva drool off her cheek.

In an appropriate response, I head toward the bathroom…

"I'm flushing your cigarettes down the toilet."

When hitting the toilet lever, the sound of flushing water travels into the bedroom getting Sheri out of bed in a flash and into the bathroom.

"Just kidding," I said.

She slugs me in the arm.

"A little cranky in the morning are you?"

She did an about-face and marched back into the bedroom.

With that behind me, I head toward the kitchen. "I'll have great omelets ready in fifteen minutes."

Unfortunately, minutes later, she hears me rattling a spoon around against a glass peanut butter jar.

"What are you doing in there?" She shouts.

"Oh, nothing," I said with a whimper.

A moment later, she walks in on me eating peanut butter out of a jar and looks at me as though this was the most disgusting thing she had ever seen…

"Well, I suppose that's going in the omelet isn't it?" Shari snarled.

Then doing an about-face, she marched double-time back into the bedroom.

The only thing missing was her swagger stick and hobnailed boots. You'd assume by now I'd have a handle on this dating thing, but women have no rules and move in unpredictable ways. You know, if I ever figure out a woman, I'll be the smartest man on earth.

THE TRAINING ROOM

Due to my morning breakfast fiasco, I arrived at ATC earlier than expected. Sheri was acting like a brat, so I put the peanut butter in the omelet… WHAT? I thought it tasted pretty good. Obviously, Sheri had other thoughts.

While conversing with the folks in the training room, I notice it's nearing eight o'clock, and having mingled and hobnobbed with about everyone in the class, I grab myself a coffee and head back to the podium.

I sip my brew waiting for everybody to take a seat…

"Good morning."

A responsive, good morning rolled through the audience.

"As you may know, this session was not scheduled on our agenda. Jake gave me the idea several weeks ago, thinking it would make a good addition to our manufacturing consulting...

The idea of the presentation is to streamline material flow. The topics have been split into two groups: Class C, and Class A and B parts. I realize it has little to do with overall organizational theory in business transformation. It does, however, make a huge difference in improving productivity, throughput, and cost reduction for manufacturing...

Our session today is to take the first step to improve your inventory system without getting into the various aspects of supply chain management, a topic we'll cover in four to six months."

THE NEGATIVES OF MICRO MANAGING CLASS C PARTS

I pause for a moment trying to get my arms around my next starting point while uptaking more caffeine into my system. It's a great kick-start for an added buzz setting me off in the right direction...

"It's my understanding you have four thousand Class C parts, give or take a few," I said with a smile, "Representing about seventy percent of your inventory line items. Does that sound right?"

Jethro, the purchasing manager, raises his hand and nods an affirmative.

"Thanks, Jethro. Let me take a moment and try to identify the micro-managing tasks involved in processing Class C parts...

Each time a part is issued, it relieves a quantity from the stockroom inventory. That same part number can be amplified with different orders and different assemblies. A single part number, at times, can account for hundreds of transactions a month. This multiplied times the full array of parts in the inventory system equals a tremendous burden on available time and contributes to errors.

For many Class C parts, you have a backup reorder bag that you update purchasing with for a new order after breaking the seal. Then you have the added man-hours to cycle-count four thousand part numbers.

The material planner or buyer uses the material explosion to determine what parts to purchase, the quantity, and when to purchase. But it's a difficult undertaking when planning or buying Class C items because of the total volume and errors in the system—making the results prone to bad decision-making.

For any purchased part, speaking in general terms, an inventory update happens during receiving, inspection, and stocking...

The digital invoice moves from receiving to accounting for a transaction and payment based on your *current* forty-five-day terms. If a part from a particular supplier made four deliveries in a month, theoretically speaking, there would be four payments every forty-five days from the delivery date—in this case, four payments within a month. This overall process of Class C parts takes the largest chunk out of the money allocated to manage the material flow. Now, does that sound familiar?"

I sweep the class as I straighten my tie.

The audience is in awe when hearing what Johnny had to say.

Then laughter springs from Belinda Shakeela.

"You bet it does. It sounds like my multiple ongoing trips to the grocery store."

The audience responds with understanding joyful nods.

"Well, I can't fancy any answer more appropriate. Thanks, Belinda."

After a short pause, I continue.

"The number of transactions and orders placed can only lead to a degree of error. Now, let me identify the impact of this process on the system. It can create line shortages, higher shipping costs due to expedited orders, slower product throughput, and poor perception by the customer with late deliveries. These Class C parts delaying the system are less than a dollar. Does this sound about right?"

I see understanding nods while scanning the audience...

"Nina tells me your Class C parts represent fifteen percent of overall inventory value, which falls in the mid-range of most companies. But, what makes this interesting is you're spending the lions' share of processing inventory parts on Class C parts. That's a serious problem.

With that in mind, we need to streamline the material flow and improve product throughput by eliminating Class C line shortages...

And as you might guess, I have a solution to the problem..."

STREAMLINING THE CLASS C PROCESS

"The following is a starting point or outline for Class C. The process may need modification, depending on circumstances, and improved over time...

The first thing we'll need to do is break down the Class C into two parts: Class C and Class D. We do this by exploding a bill of material made up of the combined products and sorted by the different class of parts. Next, sort the Class C parts by each of their total annual value. There will be an obvious differentiation of value defining Class C from Class D parts. The next step, of course, is to update the appropriate line items to the Class D inventory listing.

The next major activity is to remove the long stockroom fence running along the wall facing the production area. In its place, install three-foot-wide shelving, open on both sides. Designate areas of the shelving as 'Class C and D Electronic' and 'Class C and D Mechanical. Fill the shelves with containers in part-number order for each designated area...

The idea is to have six months of inventory on the production floor for Class C and twelve months of Class D parts. An exception could be for parts that take up an inappropriate amount of space due to quantity or size...

Your new inventory levels should include active inventory only, with a mix that will change over time, but the value is so low it will have little influence on the total inventory value.

Your stockroom will carry a mirror image of the inventory designated for the production floor adjacent to and behind the Class C and D boxes facing the production area. Anything less than a mirror image in inventory complicates the process and adds a lot of additional steps and labor plus the added possibility of line shortages. This set-up is critical for the batch control to work...

When manufacturing has a shortage, a production employee takes the empty container to the stockroom. The stockroom clerk moves the backup container into position on the self to replace the previous outage. Afterward, the clerk makes a withdrawal entry into the system triggering the buyer to batch the part outage by the supplier, requiring but one purchase of Class C and D parts a month.

Class C and D items on the production floor bill of material will show no extensions for quantity or value, it isn't needed. Once the product ships, the full extended bill of material will reduce the inventory value. This is for inventory valuation and profitability reasons only. As far as Class C and D inventory turns are concerned, the difference in value is insignificant when compared to the huge benefits.

The net results in making these changes will reduce the number of stockroom transactions, fewer orders placed, no expedited orders, no line shortages, faster throughput time, and better customer perception...

There'll also be a large decline in transactions for the Stockroom, Receiving Inspection and Accounting. Overall, this translates into a huge increase in system productivity and requiring few, if any, new employees during growth periods...

Are there any comments or questions before we go on to our next subject?"

Ed Blackburn raises his hand. As the Vice President of Order Fulfillment, Ed carries a great deal of responsibility. He is, however, a free spirited Irishman with a permanent subtle smile who finds life a bit absurd much of the time. He speaks fluent Spanish and has an MBA degree from Stanford. Ed is bald, sports a gray, well-trimmed beard, Ben Franklin glasses, and in most cases, well-worn suits, but well-liked and respected.

"Yes, Ed?"

"My God, Johnny, the process is so simple, why hasn't it been common practice for the last twenty to forty years?"

"Let me try and answer that by asking you a few questions, and then your answer will become clear...

But, first, let me preface that with a few notations: There are, I'm sure, manufacturing companies not constrained with an overburdened organization and doing something similar...

I would also add that a few companies use lean accounting rules and set up their assembly areas by product and move their designated material to that area. And at times, production employees take on the responsibility of placing the orders.

As you might imagine, using a lean accounting process represents another set of problems. However, it seems to work for certain types of small manufacturers.

Your question, though, sounds as if you're wondering why we haven't made this common practice for the last several decades. Well... Part of the answer is found in several places...

First is our self-reliance on the ERP system. The next one is the vertical organization—with its inherent inability to see the world as a system of processes...

Now, with that in mind, let me ask you a few questions so you may form an answer to your own question.

Ed, how long has ERP or MRP been controlling the way we order and how to inventory our material?"

"If I'm not mistaken, I believe you mentioned it was being used in the late sixties," Ed said.

"That's right, who taught you how to tie your shoes, and do you still do it the same way?"

"Ahh... It was but a few years ago, but I'm pretty sure it was my mom, and yes, I do it the same way each time."

Ed has the audience in gleeful chuckles.

"The MRP system hasn't changed in over four decades, and yet, we continue to use it in its original design. Why change something that theoretically works, right? We're not contemplating of a way *not* to use it to make our life a little easier, it's the other way around—it's how *can* we use it to make life a little easier."

"Okay, I get your drift on the ERP, but what about the other point you mentioned, the vertical organization?" Ed asked.

"What is accounting's main concern for inventory value?"

"One would assume it must be inventory turns."

"That's right," I said. "Does Accounting ever focus on the problems that Class C parts cause in the process of manufacturing the products?"

"I wouldn't think so," Ed said with a grin.

"How many people take the time to understand the cost involved in managing Class C parts? And how many will buck the system and convince finance we should slow our inventory turns down to a half or one per year for these Class C and D parts?"

Light bulbs come on as everyone begins to titter and Ed is grinning from ear to ear...

"Okay, it would now seem obvious we get it."

"Good," I said. "When completing the new Class C system, you will love it. But it will take a focused effort, Ed. So, you may want to consider making this a high priority program and move it in the right direction as fast as possible."

"I'm on it," Ed said.

CLASS A AND B PARTS

"Okay, let's move on to Class A and B parts. You have a great deal on your plate right now, but I'd like to see you do a few things to help your cash flow as soon as time permits. You might begin by source-inspecting the local fabricators and subcontractors producing Class A and B parts. Parts manufactured out of state, or the country is a separate matter you will need to address. Select the vendors with a high probability of on-time delivery and acceptance and set up a five-day inventory buffer, as opposed to your current four to twelve weeks.

After the high-end suppliers are up to speed, go back to the problem suppliers and work with them to improve delivery and acceptance—or move on to another supplier. Afterward, you should put a plan together to narrow down the supplier base, if possible.

Four to six months out, you should be ready for a session in *supply chain management*. We'll be discussing real-time sharing of purchase orders, inventory, and shipping information of your Class A and B parts. The aim is to move inventory in and out fast ... not unlike the Italian government changes its Prime Ministers."

Cheerful chuckles spring from the audience.

"Well, we've completed our session, unless you have questions."

My eyes swept the room seeing content faces, so I thanked them for their attendance and told them to have a nice weekend.

JOHNNY'S EVENING AT THE BEACH

While driving home, I ponder on how nice it is to have nothing to do tonight, but first, I'll have lunch, then head up to the University and take care of a few things. After that, I'll call Jake on his satellite phone service and let him know the outcome of today's session—it should please him. In the afternoon, I'll take a run on the beach.

Late into my run, the sun is setting low in the sky but still radiating warm rays, and if not for the cool ocean breeze playing across my face, it would feel a lot hotter.

Halfway through the run, my sneaker lace trips me up causing an ungainly fall onto the concrete path running along the beach. I must have looked like a goony bird on Midway Island coming in for a landing. If you're familiar with these wonderful birds, you'll know they make but one kind of landing—a crash landing—or in their case, it's more like a head-over-tail-feathers landing.

Well, anyhow, my fall only shook up my pride when landing in front of a group of inline skaters who chuckled as they flew by. Hmm... It appears I have a real problem with my laces coming undone, but there is just one person to blame for that—my mother, of course.

After my run, I began walking along the beachfront walkway and bumped into the owner of a men's shop I frequent.

He recognized me right away and acknowledged me with a nod...

"Hey, howzit Johnny."

"Doing well, thank you... Howzit yourself?"

"I've never felt better."

"Good to hear."

But, I'm thinking, one wouldn't want to see him if he was ill. The guy is about fifty and looks like the Mummy in an old Boris Karloff movie.

"It looks like you're still carrying a full bag of poop for your dog. Haven't you trained that dog to carry its own poop bag yet?"

He looks at me with a whimsical smile...

"Train, you say? Hell, if I don't pick it up, he'll eat it."

I gave him an understanding smile, then mosey on down the walkway.

Later, I'm finding myself kicking a beer can toward a trash container. With a jump shot in mind, I picked up the dented can and make a standing one-foot jump shot off the deck shooting it like a basketball toward the trashcan. I nailed it—resulting in a personal awesomeness. Your whole day can be a disaster, but nail a swish in the trashcan, and for a moment, you have risen to a status higher than Michael Jordan.

All right, I know what you women are thinking, but it's a guy thing. For instance, when a guy finishes with an old shampoo bottle, he'll conjure up the need to dunk it in the wastebasket. At that point, he'll open the shower door as his brain computes the trajectory and velocity necessary to drop it in. He can almost feel the pebbly surface of the basketball before the bottle leaves his grip for its final swish into the trash. Then, of course, if he misses the shot, it may lay on the floor for a while...

Later in the day, he may get another urge to dunk something while sitting at his desk. By wadding up a piece of paper into a miniature basketball, he sinks it into a trash can across the room. For a few guys, it can be the sole purpose of rising in the morning...

Oh, wait a minute now, I said for a few guys.

Right after my beer can dunk into the trashcan; I look up the walkway and see a little kid rolling toward me on his skateboard pulled by a little pink rat. The Kid's wearing a white tee shirt about five sizes too large for him. As he approaches, he looks up at me through his light blue eyes set above a pudgy little nose surrounded by freckles on a well-tanned face. Then shaking his shaggy dirty blonde hair, he smiles showing off his missing teeth and then springs into the air for a high-five. "Yo dude... Awesome shot."

I respond with a low-five. The little pink rat then comes over and yaps at me. With me being an animal lover, I squat down and try to calm the little rodent, but almost bitten several times, I look up the kid.

"What kind of rat do you have here?"

He responds with the giggles...

"Aw, dude, it's not a rat, it's a Taco Bell dog, and I gets five bucks an hour for walking it."

"You deserve ten bucks for hazardous duty pay."

Liking the kid, I pulled out a fiver and handed it to him.

His eyes pop out with his good fortune as he grins from ear to ear...

"Gee... Thanks, mister."

We had a good laugh, then the kid skateboards his way on down the beach, as a nice sunny day ends with a beautiful and exceptional sunset—too bad, there's just one a day. The clouds are all puffy and white with brilliant gold reflecting off the bottom as the sun starts its disappearing act while sinking into the horizon engilding everything it shines upon. Off in the distance, a silent orchestra plays, *Nearer My God Thee*—so goes the myth of the last song played as the *Titanic* sank below its floating ice grave.

A little further down the beach, the Santa Monica oceanfront pier began to brighten up with little lights twinkling in the dusk, making like a trail of pixie dust along the pier. The new roller coaster is missing the thousands of interconnecting supports that held the old wooden coasters together. It now looks like a winding road floating in the sky.

As I near the Santa Monica pier, the sun has reached a point where long shadows are being cast, and black silhouettes are prominent along the beachfront. As the evening closed out, I stop and gaze at the Ferris wheel and roller coaster silhouetted against the sky bordered by two tall palm trees—and thinking what a great photo it would make.

When hanging out at the beach at night as a kid in high school, we used to feel safe when smoking and watching the submarine races while having a beer under cover of darkness. The sound of the surf provided an additional blanket of privacy.

A short time later, I'm home and jump into the shower. The sand and grit collected from my run along the beach pools near the drain. With a towel wrapped around me, I pick up the phone and order in Chinese food, having left my kitchen in a real mess this morning—I didn't cozy up to cleaning it now.

With a high dose of sodium and starch from the plague-ridden noodles in me, I brush my teeth and hit the sack. When lying down, I could smell Sheri's fragrance radiating off the pillow and let out a sigh as I conjure up my childish behavior this morning.

ACT II - SCENE 7
ENHANCING THE LEARNING PROCESS

Question 1

This story is a discussion on how to improve throughput and decrease overhead through a simple new idea of dealing with class C parts.

With that in mind, tell us how vertical organizations cripple the ability to make this kind of change.

ACT II SCENE 8
Having a Fresh Perspective

WEEK 5 – TUESDAY MORNING. JOHNNY'S TOPIC: MARKET PERCEPTION

AN EVENING WITH SHERI

I'm heading toward my condominium's elevator for a ride down to the underground parking on my way to pick up Sheri. She's arriving at LAX at six twenty-two this evening from her San Francisco flight. It won't be a pleasant drive owing to the evening traffic and weather.

When I pulled out of the underground garage, I set the wipers on slow resulting in streaks on the windshield, and just enough to make the highway look like an impressionist painting.

Jake told me that his dad used to smear tobacco from several crushed cigarettes on the windshield back in the day to avoid a collection of little rain droplets. With today's price of cigarettes, it's a good thing we have windshield treatment and cleaner—science at work.

I drove south on Lincoln Boulevard until it intersected with Sepulveda Boulevard near the multiple LAX entries. While waiting for a stoplight, I scanned the airport roadmap system resembling the arteries leading to the bowels of the human body. After turning into the appropriate artery, I found my way to parking lot P-seven in the lower intestines.

In the terminal, I hoofed it down concourse seven to find that her flight arrived a few minutes early, and yet, one could have stopped over for a beer and still had time to greet the first arrival.

Sashaying her way out of the departing gate, Sheri scans the area with anticipation as she throws her head back and tucks her golden hair under her visor cap.

I'm leaning against a column across the concourse aisleway, my legs crossed and arms folded with my Captain Jack Sparrow grin—you know the one but without the gold teeth. She sees me, gives me a smile, then waves. We walk toward each other with anticipation, meet, touch, and then Sheri gives me a wet kiss. It must have been my killer grin—with me needing a strong distraction to remove the image of the peanut butter jar incident.

She looks ultra-sexy in her white floral cuffed tunic that's only buttoned halfway down, so her flat little tummy shows above her mid-rise curvy skinny jeans. The slim shape of denim gives the illusion to her incredible elongated legs, and adding to her sporty appearance are white sling-back heels and the dark blue visor cap. Slung over her shoulder is a leather bag that was either a *giant* purse or a carryall for *Imelda Marcos's* shoe collection. You couldn't miss her in a crowd. Any man being in his right mind within eyesight would have her on his radar—unless, of course, he was a eunuch, or as they say in doggie world, neutered—Arf Arf...

I grabbed her carry-on, then we headed toward my car. With me having business at ATC in the morning, we drove to her place in Newport Beach.

The commute down the 405 was miserable, but having arrived in one piece gave reason to grab a beer from her *icebox*—well, that's what my mom still calls it. With a Corona in hand, I stroll out on her deck to take in the sights.

Sheri touches my arm.

"I'm going to *refresh* myself for dinner. I'll only be a few minutes."

After walking the planks of her deck for over an hour, I find myself leaning on the patio railing watching a sailboat edging in toward the docks under power with an all-girl crew. While drifting off into other thoughts, I deliberate why the word *refreshes*—would seem to have a different meaning for a woman than a man. For a man, *refreshes* can mean but one thing, taking a pee and washing our hands. Dumbfounded by the idea, I moved on to other unsolved mysteries of the universe.

As time wore on, I come out of my stupor when Sheri in all her stealth walks up behind me and kisses the back of my neck. When I turned around, she had little smile lines at the corner of her sensuous mouth under a new hairstyle. And then danced back, showing off her new stunning, black silky dress that clung to her curves like oil flowing over her voluptuous body. Wow! It was worth the wait.

Pleased to see my expression, she responded with...

"Good boy. I see you're still drinking a beer, I'll be right back."

A moment later, Sheri's back from the kitchen with a glass of white wine and takes a seat on a deck chair near me. As Sheri lounges in her chair and sipping her wine, we remain quiet. The sky darkens, and the harbor boats illuminate their surroundings reflecting liquid images off the glossy, inky black water.

"This is nice and domestic," Sheri cooed.

I mumbled...

"Domestic? Woe... Yeah, all we need is a porch swing, a braided cotton rug, and me wearing a cardigan sweater with a pipe stuck in my mouth. And you with a shawl draped over your shoulders, your hair up in curlers stroking a cat, and Lawrence Welk playing in the background."

She giggles as I take a seat on the deck chair next to her and place my feet up on the railing. A moment later, Sheri has her shoes off and her bare feet up next to mine. Then with a slow, but deliberate move, she rubs my leg with her foot. Sir Isaac Newton, to prove his point of gravity, was pulling Sheri's silky black dress down her legs while I leered at them with a longing.

"You're making eyes at my legs," she said playfully.

"I was wondering if you'd mind holding off on dinner a short while."

"What did you have in mind?"

"Follow the Pied Piper."

I stood up mimicking the playing of a flute then sauntered my way toward the bedroom.

Attracted by the idea of playing the game, she followed zombie-like behind me.

"Are you luring me into a devious event?"

"No. More like an uplifting event."

It was a late dinner.

After we showered and dressed the next morning, I'm in the kitchen fixing my French toast specialty, professor, consultant, humorist, lover, and chef.

The previous day, I had stopped and picked up a loaf of French bread and real maple syrup.

This morning, I cut the loaf into two-inch sections and then let them soak in a bath of beaten orange juice, milk, and eggs. After heating them in a hot oven for ten minutes, I broiled them until they turned a light brown while setting the table with a jar of peanut butter and maple syrup.

After Sheri takes a seat at the table, I serve her a plate full of French toast covered with melted butter and then ask if she wants peanut butter or real maple syrup. With a cute little snicker and without hesitation, she grabs the syrup. I tried both but gave syrup the edge.

THE TRAINING ROOM

I arrived at ATC early in the morning giving me enough time to chat with most everyone in attendance. The room is made up of corporate staff, department heads, sales and marketing people, and several key employees.

At the lectern, I look around the room and say my good morning.

With a nice response from the audience, I pause for a moment before conveying my opening remark…

"Today's topic is market perception, and as a reminder, the final session will resume here tomorrow at eight o'clock. And as one might guess, I'm now catching on to these consulting gigs."

"You get an attaboy, Johnny," Ed said.

"Thanks, Ed...

Okay, everybody has a busy schedule, so let's dig in. The folder in front of you is a composite of the images I'll display today and tomorrow."

TOTAL QUALITY MANAGEMENT AND ITS FAILURE TO GAIN MARKET SHARE

"Your MPV learning experience might be comparable to what some businesses are using known as *Total Quality Management* (TQM). The idea is to improve the performance of the whole delivery system that'll differentiate their business from the competition. TQM is a management strategy aimed at embedding quality processes to support their internal and external customer. It also relates to shareholders and employee's quality of life, but for comparison, we need to stick to *customer* quality only.

One might say, a good description of TQM is when the departments and employees work together to assist one another to achieve a common objective. Now, that sounds respectable, but nothing changes, it's still the same old organization after integrating TQM.

Conceptually, it's a great idea for these companies. It can result in a limited improvement in overall performance. But in reality, it's nothing more than a good tune-up job...

It requires lots of meetings and frequent new posters to keep the image in place—if not, everything falls back into the same old mold. When one thinks about it, this is how propaganda works...

Now, propaganda may be a harsh word, but for TQM to function, it must tap into the emotions through images, slogans and selective use of information...

Unfortunately, investing in a total customer quality approach may fail because of either or all of the following events...

FIRST, management deploys resources for improving business activities based on what *they think* will increase market share, and may focus on issues that have little impact on the market's purchasing criteria.

SECONDLY, management completes a customer survey of their product and services without comparing them to their competitors using ratings like *poor, fair, good, or excellent*... Then the management team develops ambiguous or *World-Class Benchmarks* for improving service. The lack of specificity disperses efforts among the business activities instead of those deemed most significant by the market.

LASTLY, management uses surveys for their current customers, and leaves out major potential customers in the market."

A hand rises in the audience.

"I see a question coming—yes, Robert?"

"Thanks, Johnny. My question is why don't they include potential customers?'

"As I mentioned earlier, TQM sees itself as a quality provider for the internal and external customer, shareholder, and employees only. Measuring potential customers is not part of TQM's scope."

With a glance at the audience, I turn my attention toward Robert.

"Thanks, Johnny," he said with a nod.

"Are there any other questions?"

With little movement from the class, they seem ready to move on.

INTRODUCTION TO MARKET PERCEIVED VALUE

"In our discussion today, we'll cover how customers determine their product purchasing decisions that will quantify the level of performance a supplier must achieve to gain market share... Ah... Simply put, the method consists of Market Perceived Value results that drive the system processes and internal market policies such as *price, market awareness*, and *new products*.

To what method do we begin to understand how the market perceives your company's MPV?

FIRST, we must discover how the customer purchasing criteria and relative importance or its weight relates to your system processes and market policy...

While the customer determines the criteria and their weight, they *are* measurable. The markets weight or relative importance of the criteria will determine how best to use your resources.

As part of the methodology, use the same attributes for market perception and your *top three competitors who are usually in control of the market.*

The competitors' data differentiates you from them and becomes the target benchmarks for improving your system processes and policies.

The process of measuring these attributes further reinforces efforts to create customer value. Data from the market-perceived value survey *defines* the design for the processes that influence the purchasing attributes...

When I say *define*, it's not unlike designing an aircraft for takeoff *defined* by air temperature and density, the wind, runway conditions, and flap setting. In other words, they are your parameters for your design.

When selecting processes for improvement depends on which ones are most central to customer perceived value. The level of importance may be determined based on the value rating and weighting of each attribute...

The attribute with the highest weight is the first to receive allocated resources. This attribute will have the greatest impact on improving customer value and market share. This method organizes data in a way that assists in establishing the strategy for increasing market share and profitability."

A hand rises like old glory flying in a breeze.

"Yes, Melvin. It's Melvin, right?" I ask with a cocked eyebrow.

"Yes, but I prefer Mel. So, what you're saying is it's like a selection of opportunities that identifies the best return on your investment."

"Give that man a cigar. You're right on target."

"Thanks, Johnny ... by the way, nice suit."

"Thank you—Mark Twain would have told you...
Clothes make the man, naked people have little or no influence on society."
With a chuckling audience, Ed shouts, "I think he meant that for guys like me."

His remark raised the level of gleeful chuckles.

I wait until everybody settles down...

"Let's move on now to our next subject—market share..."

USING MARKET SHARE IN THE MPV METHODOLOGY

"Market share has a distinct role in the MPV methodology. There are several ways to measure the company's market share; the two most common are ABSOLUTE MARKET SHARE and RELATIVE MARKET SHARE. My notes on this subject tell me Jake refers to author Bradley Gale's position in his 1988 book, *The PIMS*...

It's vital to note that the target market measurement is also a market segment. Mercedes-Benz is a market leader in their segment of the market, but not when compared to the entire car industry.

ABSOLUTE MARKET SHARE compares the company's sales to the sales of its competitors within the same market segment and is a reference point for the company's market share. Absolute market share is not the preferred choice, as it is difficult to get accurate information in many industries, and it provides no frame of reference.

RELATIVE MARKET SHARE is your company's competitive position within the product market segment. Market share is easier to determine than absolute share and provides useful information for decision-making...

You'll find that the three top competitors in your market segment will control the market. Each of the three competitor's percent share of the market should *define* your performance benchmarks... Let's look at TABLE ONE now..."

TABLE ONE

Competitor	Est. Sales ($MM)	Market Share %
Competitor A	25	28%
Competitor B	20	22%
Competitor C	15	17%
"The Business"	10	11%
(5)Minor Competitors	20	22%
Total Market	90	100%

The table shows us an example of *The Business* in bold and quotation marks, along with the three top competitors, and the combined total of *five other minor players*...

When using the sales figures of the competitors, the calculations position each company's relative market share. These three top competitors own two-thirds of the market. As you can see, this is all straightforward—but before moving on, do we have questions?"

With a content audience, I'm primed and ready for my next topic.

"Good. Our next subject is purchasing criteria and system drivers?"

THE MARKETS PURCHASING CRITERIA AND SYSTEM PROCESS DRIVERS

"Within any market segment, there is differentiation—some attributes are valued or weighted differently by people within market segments. An attribute's weight is dynamic; it changes with a customer's expectations and intentions...

For instance, performance attributes such as speed, size, and price of high technology products change more often than attributes like awareness and service.

These weighted attributes help allocate resources when designing the business processes. In other words, the weighted criteria of each attribute will define the degree of importance of that attribute in the overall design process...

Or as Melvin, I mean, Mel, so vividly pointed out; getting the best return on your investment is the objective.

As a rule of thumb, MPV needs reviewing at a minimum of twice a year—the more frequent, the better. It should measure current customers, potential customers, and an aggregate of the two...

Momentarily, we're moving on to internal policy drivers. But, first, I have a proposition to make. If you let me slip to the back of the room to fetch a cup of coffee, I'll tell you a quick marketing joke... Do we have a deal?"

With nodding heads and chuckles, I retrieve a coffee.

"Thanks, folks, I needed this. You know how I go into fits without my caffeine. And it's not a pretty sight...

Okay... Here's my side of the bargain.

The king of mattress retailing in his part of town became troubled when a competitor selling a different brand of mattress opens next door. His new adversary soon displays a large sign, *Best Deals, and Quality Ever*. It wasn't long until another player leased the vacant building on the King's opposite side with a sign that read *the Lowest Prices in Town*.

With panic and concern for his business, he knew time was running out, but after pondering over the problem, a solution comes to mind. Several days later, he unveils a sign twice the size of his competitors over his front door. It read *Main Entrance*."

I waited for but a nanosecond in the silent room when a slaphappy response rolls over the audience. Then Vinnie raises his hand.

"I don't get it."

"Sorry, Vinnie, I guess you won't see me on *The Tonight Show* with that joke, hey?" I said with a lopsided smile to a joyful audience.

"Well, that concludes our deal and now back to business."

INTERNAL POLICY DRIVERS: PRICE SENSITIVITY AND MARKET AWARENESS

"**M**arket *price sensitivity* is not a component of market perception surveys. Nonetheless, pricing is of great importance in defining the overall business strategy since every one percent change in price can have a significant impact on profit and market perception...

To develop answers to our price sensitivity analysis, we'll compare the weights of the customer's purchase criteria to price. When the customer-weighted price is equal to or greater than purchase criteria, the market is price-sensitive. However, the influence of price on purchase decisions may be different between market segments...

Here, let me put up the next image."

Just then, the power goes out. Nina jumps up with concern...

"Let me find out what the trouble is and the severity of the problem."

Just as Nina was about to exit the room, the power came back on. She stood there momentarily, then turned back toward Johnny...

"Sorry, Johnny, it's important I find out what happened. I'll be right back."

In a flash, she's through the doorway.

"Well, Johnny... Since we need to kill a few minutes, how about you give it another try-out for *The Tonight Show*?" Vinnie said.

With a joyful audience, they chant...

"One for *The Tonight Show*..."

"Okay. Okay. Let me ponder for a second... All right, the power outage brings to mind a sweet story... It reminds me of a little ol' retired couple who lived back in Saint Cloud, Minnesota during last year's winter...

One morning, they were eating breakfast and listening to the radio when a news bulletin came on announcing there would be over twelve inches of snow that day. And then the commentator asked the residents to park their car on the odd-numbered side of the street because the snowplows needed the room to navigate down the side streets. Hearing this, the little ol' lady was out the door to move her car.

Several days later during breakfast, they receive another request over the radio for the residents to move their cars to the even side of the street because of the heavy snowfall. Respectfully, the little ol' lady moves her car to the even side.

A few weeks later during breakfast, the radio announcer tells the residents to move their cars to the—

Then all of a sudden, the radio goes dead due to a power failure. Ma looked at Pa with panic on her face and asked him what side of the street do I park the car?

With love in his heart, Pa looked at Ma..."

I finish up with my Jay Leno impression and shrug with outstretched arms...

"Why not just leave the car in the garage, this time, Ma?"

An immediate cachinnate came from the audience. Even Vinnie laughed.

Just then, Nina walks back into the room and looks at me with her arms spread apart...

"What did I miss?"

"Nothing at all, just entertaining the troops in your absence...

So, where the heck were we?"

"Price sensitivity," Nina said.

"Right. Oh, by the way, what happened to the power?"

"It seems it was a transformer here in the business park, but our backup generator came on and took care of the problem."

"Thanks, Nina. With power restored, let me put TABLE TWO our PRICE SENSITIVITY image up on the screen...

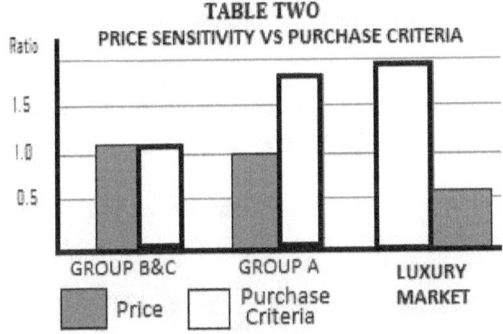

Now, let me *recap* where we left off a few minutes ago...

To develop answers to our PRICE SENSITIVITY analysis, we'll compare the weights of the customer's purchase criteria to price. When the customer-weighted price is equal to or greater than purchase criteria, the market is price-sensitive. However, the influence of price on purchase decisions may be different between market segments...

The PRICE SENSITIVITY image shows how this may be the case. A business survey measured customers in four of its market segments. They showed a significant difference in how Group A segment weights price as very sensitive, compared to segments of Group B and C. And then we have what you'd expect in the luxury market, most notably in the car market.

In our PRICE SENSITIVITY image, price sensitivity in Group A comes in considerably lower than purchase criteria, making it a favorable market for wider margins, therefore, the business strategy would be to pursue Group A's purchase criteria.

All right, we're closing the gap on finishing this session. Let's move on to MARKET AWARENESS...

MARKET AWARENESS is another key component in internal policy drivers. If someone in your market is unaware of your products or services, they will remain your prospect—that or your competitor's customer.

This segment of the session is not how to market your products through awareness, but how to measure the effectiveness of your targeted efforts.

When awareness is low, you'll need the appropriate resources to increase the awareness within market segments that'll produce the highest return...

Now, let's look at TABLE THREE, our MARKET AWARENESS image.

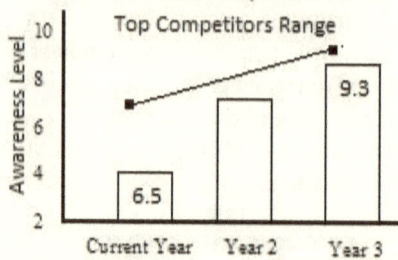

We can see that GROUP A in the projected market awareness chart shows a nine target rating in year three. The idea would be to develop a product that could expand their market while generating the highest return owing to low price sensitivity.

In return, even with no additional resources dedicated to GROUPS B AND C'S market segments, their awareness will increase as a by-product of efforts in GROUP A."

After a quick scan of the room, I decide this is a good place to end the session...

"Don't forget, this session is part one of part two. So, do we have questions before we call it a day?"

With no responses, I continue...

"Well, that's it, folks. Be here for our part two discussion on ESTABLISHING A MARKET SURVEY."

As the employees exit the room, I finish packing my few belongings, slip on my coat, and then see Vinnie leaning against the wall near the doorway.

"What's up Vinnie?"

"Well, I joined the Orange County Athletic Club last month and soon realized that the weightlifting equipment was intimidating. It's obvious you work out a lot, so I thought maybe—"

"Whaddya need, Vinnie?"

"Well, I was wondering if someday, you'd mind meeting me at the club and show me the ropes, so to speak."

"Sure, I do my workouts in the morning. If you want to meet me at six tomorrow morning at your gym, I'll see if I can be of any help."

"That's swell, Johnny... Do you know where it is?"

"I believe I know the place, but the address might be helpful."

"Here, I have one of their cards. Thanks again. See you in the morning."

"You may not thank me by the time I get through with you," I said with a semi-sadistic smile.

ACT II - SCENE 8
ENHANCING THE LEARNING PROCESS

Question 1

I'm sure Total Quality Management (TQM) expressed by the author must have differed from what you perceived it to be. Can you describe three points of view that make the process a poor choice to use in improving market perception?

Question 2

How does the MPV process help a company set its benchmarks for improving the business processes and then enhance their competitiveness with its three top competitors?

Question 3

How does a company know it's in a price-sensitive market? What options does the company have if they overpriced selected products, other than marking down the price and shrinking profit margin?

ACT II SCENE 9
Having a Fresh Perspective

WEEK 5 - WEDNESDAY MORNING –JOHNNY'S TOPIC, THE MARKET SURVEY

JOHNNY AT THE ATHLETIC CLUB

I arrived before six o'clock at the Orange County Athletic Club, so I decide to indulge in a chocolate protein shake and a toasted Rye bagel. While sitting at a table in the health bar, I notice a guy drinking what could be a lime smoothie, the healthy bugger.

Later while draining the last of my protein shake, I glance over the rim and see Vinnie stampcrab his way into the gym. He stands out like a *Twinkie* in a health food store. Vinnie is about five-foot-eleven and perhaps a hundred fifty pounds soaking wet. He's what the gym rats would call a skinny fat guy: Skinny arms and legs, with a chubby midsection—not unlike a potato with arms and legs made of toothpicks.

Vinnie waves at me with a beaming smile and then stops to select his choice of coffee from a dispenser at the coffee station. With coffee in hand, he walks toward my table near the window slapping his feet up and down as if he were wearing water fins on his feet. He pulls out a chair and has a seat.

I was about to ask him about not paying for the coffee when I get a whiff of his aftershave... "Good God, Vinnie, you smell like you dropped by Kmart and tried every fragrance of cologne they had on the shelf."

"Oh... Well, I knew I'd be sweating a lot, and didn't want to offend you."

"Never mind Vinnie, but I have to ask, is the coffee free here?"

He shook his head forth and back as if he had a fly buzzing around in his ear.

"Oh goodness no, it's because I befriended the manager and now he gives me free coffee for being a good customer."

"What? I thought you haven't worked out much because of the intimidation factor."

"True, but I'm here seven days a week on the elliptical trainer only."

"Seven days a week?" I said. "You want to be careful in that area of hyperactivity. It's known to generate an intensified electromagnetic field that'll sterilize you in no time at all."

Vinnie has panic written all over his face.

"As in neutered?"

"So, tell me something about your health history before we get started."

"Well, a little over four years ago I weighed two-hundred-seventy pounds."

"Not good Vinnie. Someone of your height and weight would have to be careful not to pull small moons out of orbit."

Vinnie gave me a strange look, then broke out with a gleeful chuckle.

That's a healthy gesture, Vinnie, when you can laugh at yourself...

So, tell me, was your weight gain over a long period?"

"More or less, I've weighed that much since I was a teenager."

"Was your drop in weight over a four-year period?"

"It was."

A silent moment goes by as I finish off my beagle.

"Persistence shows fortitude. You'll need that same drive to continue your quest for a healthy body. I'm assuming you've had little physical training over your... How many years is it now?"

"I've had no physical activity, and I'm fifty-five."

"What's your current calorie intake?'

"It's about eight hundred calories," Vinnie said with pride.

"Christ, Vinnie. That sounds like the calorie count for a forced laborer in the Gulag. Keep that up, and you'll die a slow death."

"But I eat the right stuff, lots of vegetables and one egg white for breakfast."

"Gee, a whole egg white. That's about twenty calories. Shit, Vinnie, you can't eat like Tweety bird if you're serious about building muscle—you have to feed those babies properly. A good starting point for you would be twelve hundred calories with a macronutrient ratio of thirty-five percent protein, forty percent carbohydrates, and twenty-five percent fat which should give you good muscle gain while keeping lean. At your age and nutritional intake history with no physical training, you'll need to build up your testosterone levels by making sure your fat intake is made up of saturated and monounsaturated fatty acids. Stay away from polyunsaturated fatty-acids because they'll suppress your testosterone production...

Oh, and stay away from the starchy carbs and focus on fresh vegetables. As your muscles grow, over time, you will need to increase your calorie intake."

"Gee, that's a lot to remember. And I'm not sure I can eat that much."

I feel a smile form, but not much of one.

"I need to tell you, Vinnie, whether it's me or someone else who trains you, you'll be wasting our time and your time if you don't eat enough of the right calories."

"Wow... And I thought the weight lifting part would be tough."

He looks up as a poor example of a healthy young man walks past our table...

"You mean I'll be like that super skinny guy?"

"Hell no... That boy is so skinny; he needs but one back pocket. Remember this—sixty to seventy percent of bodybuilding is the proper diet. Are you up to it?"

"I'm going to give it a try, and I won't let you down."

"You won't let me down. That's not the point. This is a way of life. If you stop the training process and proper nutrition, you'll go back to where you started, and damned fast."

"I've lost over a hundred pounds and want to live a long life. I'm ready for whatever it takes."

"All right, Vinnie, let's get you started."

With Vinnie's knowledge of physical fitness and nutrition, you would have assumed he just arrived from the planet Ork. His history with the lack of understanding anything about health and fitness will take months, if not years, to change a lot of bad habits. For some, it won't ever happen.

I'm distracted for a moment as a well-put-together babe walks by. Even Vinnie perks up...

"Please tell me what machine I should use to attract a babe like her."

"You mean, today?"

"Yeah."

"Hmmm... You should begin by cozying up to the ATM in the lobby."

Vinnie gave me a weird gawp.

"So, not wanting to waste your day of training, you're going to need follow-up training. And with me living too far away to help in your day-to-day workouts, I'm going to recommend a friend who is a professional trainer and lives nearby. He has a degree in nutrition from U.C.L.A. and is a graduate of Muscle Beach in Venice," I said. "His name is Craig. Would it be okay to give him a call? He won't be free, and he won't be cheap."

Vinnie contemplates this opportunity for a moment...

"That would be great, Johnny. Thanks."

"Okay, I'll need to run you through the body parts this morning so you can get an idea of what to expect from Craig's training. Craig's a stickler on form as I am—form is everything. We'll start you out with light weights until you know the proper form for each body part. Did you bring water?

"Water?"

With that response, he gave me the befuddled eye of a gerbil spotting a nearby cat.

"Yes, water. You need to drink a minimum of sixty to ninety ounces of liquid a day. However, the true test of proper hydration is your pee needs to be a light lemon yellow. If it's darker, drink more water. If it's clear, drink less. So get a bottle from your friend behind the counter and let's get started."

As we walk out onto the exercise floor, I'm blinded from the glittering chrome and mirrors while taking note that there are more women than men. In fact, it bears the resemblance of a ladies battalion storming the beach and crashing through the doors wearing their shimmering spandex tights and leotard tops sporting every color in the rainbow. Many had matching sweatbands that served no purpose other than trying to appear as though they might break a sweat. They patrolled their captured beachhead drinking Gatorade while doing chatty-Cathy with others. The rest of the battalion had most of the glittering chrome weight machines surrounded and had taken control of the aerobic area. Whatever happened to rusty barbells, heavy plates, and tough, sweaty guys?

With a longing memory of tough-guy gyms, I gave Vinnie a onceover...

"We have less than an hour to train you through all your body parts—you do know them, right?"

"Body parts?"

Vinnie's appearance morphed into a caveman seeing fire for the first time.

"Yes, your body parts."

Vinnie then transformed from a caveman to a transfixed deer with its eyes caught in the headlights.

He had no clue, so I take the time to point out the main body parts and then have Vinnie repeat them back.

"Shoulders, arms, back, chest, and legs," he said.

"Great. When Craig trains you, he'll train one of the five body parts each day of the five-day week, so avoid the gym on the weekend. You must leave time for the muscles to heal themselves after breaking them down.

Before we get into any lifting, let's do push-ups. This will give me an idea of your strength level, so I know where to begin when you're lifting weights, assuming you know what a push-up is?"

Vinnie all wide-eyed now nods his head.

"Get yourself in position."

He reluctantly gets down on a rubber mat.

"Back straight, toes on the floor, hands about shoulder-width. Okay, give me ten...

Vinnie, you resemble a sway-backed horse. Straighten out your back before you begin."

With Vinnie finishing his ten pushups, he collapses.

"That was great, Vinnie, but next time, you'll need to move more than your head up and down. Well, we have to start somewhere. You'll be doing them as one should in no time. Next, we're going to do leg raises on the bench."

After he received multiple instructions and four sets later...

"That's not bad, Vinnie, you'll have good form with more training."

Vinnie appears bewildered and flat on his back as I wait him out...

"Vinnie, you can get up now."

Vinnie tries to get up while comically bicycling his legs while his hands claw harmlessly at the air, and yet, Vinnie continues to stay flat on his back.

"Vinnie, you remind me of a pet turtle I used to have as a kid. His name was Wally. I'd put him on his back, and he'd flop his extremities around like you do."

"Crap. How do I get up?"

"Put your feet firmly on the floor and grab hold of the bench with both hands and lift your upper body forward."

Ultimately, Vinnie struggles to an upright position.

"Gosh, I suppose, *Wally* is my nickname now," Vinnie said with pride.

Let's go over to the Smith Machine and do bench presses. Grab the bench next to you and roll it under the horizontal bar."

Wally struggles to pick up one end of the bench, and then in agony, he wanders aimlessly trying numerous times to position the bench under the bar. Unable to move it into position, he gives up and sets the bench down.

"Come now, Vinnie, just cause you have a crack in your ass don't make you a cripple."

Vinnie looks at me with a perplexed look and multiple expressions. His face resembles that of a virtual cartoon character displayed on a PowerPoint animation slide show.

"Wally, it's good that your weight training, because your motor skills are like a newborn giraffe," I said with a compassionate smile. "Here, let's try dumbbell squats instead, we're running out of time."

After showing him the movements, he finishes his first set of three reps with his twig-like legs while draining all the color from his face using five-pound weights. The lifter next to us finished with his free-weight three-hundred fifteen-pound squats, then checks out Vinnie as he begins to cry like a little girl.

"Vinnie, are you okay?"

Vinnie nods, and grab's his water bottle then leans against the dumbbell rack as I wait him out. It wasn't long when Vinnie comes around...

"Johnny, why do those two guys have a different form when squatting?"

"Oh, you're referring to one of them with his quads parallel to the mat, while the other guy kisses the flooring with his ass before rising."

"Kissing the floor?"

"Well, speaking as a gym rat, they call kissing the floor with your ass a brown star."

"A brown star?

Vinnie wrinkled his nose.

"Vinnie, it's seven o'clock, I need to run. Oh, one other thing, when Craig works your legs—no complaining. If you do, he'll be calling you flatty flat pants—that, or tell you to paint your nails pink with nail polish before showing up. Oh, yeah... Grab a box full of tissues to take with you on your training day."

"Why's that?" Vinnie said giving me a puzzled glance.

"To wipe away your tears."

THE TRAINING ROOM

After saying my good mornings at the lectern and a little dehydrated, I take in a guzzle of water while taking a slow scan of the room.

"Did you know for the price of one bottle of Evian, you could receive one thousand gallons of tap water?"

This gets the audience attention.

"Interestingly enough during a *CBS News* show, they informed their audience that forty percent of bottled water comes from the tap. When *Good Morning America* conducted a water taste test of its studio audience, unknowingly, they chose New York City tap water as the heavy favorite over the oxygenated water 02, Poland Spring, and Evian."

The audience was awestruck as they shook their heads in disbelief.

"The bottled water industry is an environmental menace with bottles cluttering landfills. The Container Recycling Institute says nine out of ten plastic water bottles end up as garbage or litter at a rate of thirty million per day."

Jaws drop as heads shake hearing this unbelievable figure.

"Most of all, it's shameful the amount of energy that's used in producing and transporting something you can get out of your faucet. The industry racked up seventeen billion dollars last year...

But more importantly, I have a news bulletin for you. Yesterday, when thumbing through a magazine, I noticed an ad... Now, get this, an ad for diet water, and another for Skinny Water at more than two dollars a bottle...

Thank God, my weight was getting out of control drinking the regular stuff..."

The entire room goes into hysterical laughter...

"Okay, one more bulletin on water. Did you know too much of a good thing can kill you—?"

There was no hesitation from Ed as he barks out...

"That's what my wife tells me when she has a headache."

The men in the audience have slaphappy response while the ladies seem shocked, but then the giggling takes over.

"That's not what I had in mind, Ed...

Most people know dehydration can cause serious health consequences. What they don't realize is too much water can also be dangerous, they call it water intoxication. It affects the production of nerve impulses impairing the mental processes as cells take on extra water and expand.

It's stressful on the body's organs, particularly, when it enlarges the brain, which has little room within the skull. This is brought about by diluting your ratio of salt to water intake...

Well, that's my morning medical bulletin. For those who need to partake in high levels of activity, drink enough water to stay hydrated and increase your salt intake."

"Does that mean when my wife doesn't have a headache, and I'd like to take on a high-level activity, so to speak, I should have her drink lots of water and slip her salt tablets?" Ed said.

I shout a response as the audience came unglued with a thunderous howl of laughter.

"Ed, I believe the image you left us with is more than we asked for."

Ed waited a moment as the laughter subsided...

"Sorry. It was my private thought, and it just slipped out."

"I'm surprised to hear you say anything—shall we say objectionable about your wife? My understanding is you take her almost everywhere you go."

"That's true, but I do it, so I don't have to kiss her goodbye," Ed said.

Everyone lets out a burst of laughter.

Now, all of a sudden, Ed's embarrassed...

"I'm just kidding, of course."

ESTABLISHING MARKET SURVEY CRITERIA

"Let's be moving on now. We will begin with establishing a market survey using a new image I'm about to project... You'll find a copy of in your folder showing the attributes noted as Section A."

I wait until everybody has a chance to digest the contents.

Attributes in Section A

<u>Internal Policy Drivers</u>

- *Awareness:* The degree of potential customer awareness of your company and products.

- *New Products to Market:* The speed and frequency of new products to market is essential in going after greater market share.

<u>System Process Drivers</u>

- *Timeliness:* Throughput time and on-time delivery.
- *Flexibility:* Business responds well to design changes and schedules.
- *Customer Acceptance*: Product meets specification and functional requirements. Product is durable and easy to operate.
- *Service*: Order status is easy and fast. Post-sales support and timely maintenance.

"In our discussion today, these noted attributes may be helpful as we walk through the process of establishing the market survey criteria...

Are there questions before continuing?"

A woman in the back of the room raises her hand.

"Sorry, I can't see your name."

"It's Lori. How did you arrive at these specific attributes?"

"Well, if you remember back to the PERFORMANCE DRIVER AND LEADING INDICATOR SYSTEM, the attributes are identified in Section A of the chart. These attributes *represent* deliverables from a supplier to the customer. For instance, the attribute, NEW PRODUCTS TO MARKET falls into a supplier Internal Policy Driver and a deliverable in SYSTEM PROCESS DRIVERS.

Does that answer your question, Lori?'

"Yes, I think so," Lori said with a nervous laugh.

"You think so?"

She's now discussing this with her friend sitting next to her.

"Okay, I get it," Lori said with a giggle.

"It would seem I need frequent back-up when good articulation is needed." Everyone shows gleeful amusement.

THE SURVEY

"The purpose of a consulting survey is to track customer perception of the client and their three top competitors, but why use a consulting firm for the survey and not your company?

Well, when conducting a survey for data about your company, it's imperative that an independent group perform the survey to prevent bias by using a random listing along with your company name to collect the data.

With the survey completed, you'll need to enter the data into a spreadsheet or database designed for survey information...

Now let's take a looksee at a new image of the survey, TABLE 1 and 2."

TABLE 1 – LEAST IMPORTANT OF THE PURCHASING CRITERIA

Column 1	Column 2	Column 3	Column 4	Column 5	Column 6
Purchase Criteria	Relative Importance Weighted	Competitor #1	The Business	Competitor #2	Competitor #3
New Products	10%	9 = 0.9	7 = 0.7	8 = 0.8	6 = 0.6
Service	10%	8 = 0.8	7 = 0.7	7 = 0.7	6 = 0.6
Least Important Total	20%	1.7	1.4	1.5	1.2

TABLE TWO - TIMELINESS, FLEXIBILITY, AND ACCEPTANCE

Column 1	Column 2	Column 3	Column 4	Column 5	Column 6
Purchase Criteria	Relative Weight	Competitor #1	The Business	Competitor #2	Competitor #3
Timeliness	35%	8 = 2.8	6 = 2.1	7 = 2.45	6 = 2.1
Flexibility	20%	8 = 1.6	7 = 1.4	7 = 1.4	7 = 1.4
Acceptance	25%	7 = 1.75	6 = 1.5	7 = 1.75	5 = 1.25
Least important	20%	1.7	1.4	1.5	1.2
Grand Total Table 1 & 2	100%	7.85	6.4	7.1	5.95

"The two new tables display the calculated weighted averages for a simulated survey based on customer criteria. The *least* important purchasing criteria and the *most important* differentiate the tables. Column two through six, rank and weight the value.

For instance, in SURVEY TABLE 1, note the dark-shaded areas in row two, *New Products*, column one through three. The first column displays *New Products*; Column two *ten percent*. You'll notice the figure in column three, the number one competitor, has a *relative ranking of nine* among the competitors, with a *weighted value* of zero point nine on the level of importance.

Column Two shows the relative importance of the purchase criteria of ten percent that's used to compute the zero point nine.

In SURVEY TABLE TWO, you'll notice, the *most* important purchasing criteria are in *bold* typeface.

TABLE 2, column four, *The Business,* shows the weighted grand total of six point four. The total includes both TABLE ONE and TABLE TWO. This ranking makes it the second-lowest when compared to five-point nine-five in column six, which influences the markets decision to buy.

The survey emphasizes and illustrates the improvements that need implementing in *Timeliness, Flexibility,* and *Acceptance* to capture greater market share. Without the survey, a business may improve processes of the market's least importance, or not understand the degree of change required.

To make serious headway, the three noted areas of improvement must leapfrog the highest competitor to get the market's attention. With the most essential issues accomplished, then begin the process of improving the remaining purchasing criteria in order of importance. You'll notice that both *New Products* and *Service* are weighted at ten percent...

Let's complete the survey with two new tables, TABLE A with Price coming in less important than Purchase Criteria, and TABLE B - AWARENESS...

TABLE A - PRICE VERSUS PURCHASE CRITERIA

	Example: Enter Percent
Price	40%
Purchase Criteria	60%
Total	100%

TABLE B - AWARENESS: GRADED ON A SCALE OF 1 TO 10

		Competitor #1	The Business	Competitor #2	Competitor #3
Awareness Level	1=low 10=high	9	7	8	7

The AWARENESS level is straightforward using a one to ten when measuring your business awareness level with those of the three top suppliers. Yesterday, we discussed these two attributes, so I'll close with a general summary...

But, first, I would like to know if there are questions...?

...No? Okay, let's move on and summarize today's benchmark discussions...

To give you an idea of the complexity involved in obtaining data for benchmarking, I have compiled a typical benchmarking method example...

BENCHMARKING SUMMARY

"Robert C. Camp's 1989 Book, *Benchmarking*, helped raise the level of benchmarking knowledge in the business community for developing business strategy. Jake's idea of benchmarking used Bradley Gale's purchasing criteria and coupled them with specific business processes, producing a fundamentally different result. Well, other than they both require benchmarking when establishing a business strategy."

Then with a sudden burst of energy, a hand rises from the audience.

"Did I spark some interest, Jennifer?"

"Yes. Thank you, Johnny. Okay, I understand MPV, but how does Robert Camp approach the subject?"

"Well, you might say Camp's benchmarking is a self-improvement process. It measures the different processes that produce products and services against world-class companies," I said.

"So, in other words," Jennifer said, "you're setting the benchmark higher than your competitors to influence the customer's perception. So, how is that different from the Jake Jensen approach?"

"That's a most insightful question, Jennifer. The answer lies in the benchmark process itself and how it's measured. As we know, the Jake Jensen approach pulls the benchmarking data from a customer perception survey that ties the data into specific processes within the organization.

Robert Camp's benchmark results come from *best-in-class* data in all industries, not within a selected industry. This process exhibits excellent best practices in the organization, referred to as THE BALANCED SCORECARD. It assesses the organization from four different categories: the customer, employee, process, and finance. Theoretically, employees learn how they contribute to the organization's success, allied to that of *Total Quality Management*.

There is no customer perception survey, but, you'll need to hire a consulting firm that can access the necessary information, and as far as I know, there is no single source to retrieve the material...

It has complex issues and can be time-consuming to data-mine. Give me a moment, and I'll show you an example of the complexity of the process needed to gather the information to assemble a best-in-class program—"

I'm interrupted with an urgent hand flagging me down.

"Yes, Melinda, do you have a question?"

"Thanks, Johnny, I do. I'll begin by mentioning the last company I worked for where the management tried to perceive what the market thought of them and their competitors for their marketing strategy. Could that process or a similar one be of use for our purpose?"

"Probably not... The problem lies with our egos because they'll not allow us to perceive how others may perceive our company or us."

"How so?" Melinda said.

"Well, I'd have to say, we want things to be like the world as we perceive it—and how we perceive something, channels through our system's five senses, sending messages for our brain to interpret. Now, this is where we satisfy the ego—and guess what? Our choice will be the one that best supports our vision of the world...

Meaning, it's rare we know the truth. Closing in on the truth is what we're after. To make my point, let me tell you what ROBERT MCNAMARA told us a decade after the VIETNAM WAR...

WE THOUGHT THE COMMUNISTS WERE TRYING TO TAKE OVER INDOCHINA WHEN IN FACT, THE NORTH VIETNAMESE COMMUNISTS THOUGHT THEY WERE IN A CIVIL WAR...

Do you get my point?"

"Wow, your McNamara comment nailed it," Melinda said.

"I'm glad you asked. Thanks, Melinda.

"Now, I'll click on Camp's best-in-class program process...

You'll need to read it, so take your time to digest the process steps while I grab a coffee..."

Best in Class Benchmarking Process

Identify your problem areas – This may include informal conversations with customers, employees, or suppliers, research techniques such as focus groups or in-depth market research surveys; questionnaires, re-engineering analysis, process mapping, quality control variance reports, or financial ratio analysis.

Identify other industries that have similar processes - For instance, if one were interested in improving a hand-off system, one might try to include air traffic control, cell phone switching between towers, and transfer of patients from surgery to recovery rooms.

Identify organizations that are leaders in these areas - Look for the very best in any industry and in any country. Then consult customers, suppliers, financial analysts, trade associations, and magazines to determine which companies are worthy of study.

Survey companies for measures and practices - Companies target specific business processes using detailed surveys of measures and practices used to identify business process alternatives and leading companies. Surveys are typically masked to protect confidential data by neutral associations and consultants.

Visit the "best practice" companies to identify leading-edge practices - Companies typically agree to mutually exchange information beneficial to all parties in a benchmarking group and share the results within the group.

Implement new and improved business practices - Take the leading edge practices and develop implementation plans that include identification of specific opportunities, funding the project and selling the ideas to the organization for the purpose of gaining demonstrated value from the process.

Seeing everyone was waiting on me, I continued...

"As you can see, it's time-consuming and expensive. Well, that and it's based on the internal organizational perception of hundreds of pieces of input that needs compiling. After a year or less, the data could be obsolete."

I notice Ed wanting my attention.

"Yes, Ed?"

"Wow. That's a real eye-opener of a to-do list. It would seem as though the MPV survey measured against our respective processes is a no-brainer when compared to the best-in-class benchmarking process."

"That's true, Ed. But it's only the tip of the iceberg. Go on the Internet and check out all the consulting websites offering best in class programs with reams of charts and document files requiring long-term expensive programs.

There are two other best-in-class benchmarks that have no relevance in your new organization such as cost accounting measuring output per hour, cost, quality, and set-up time. And then their quality approach using Six Sigma quality management aimed at achieving zero errors by removing process defects from existing processes...

Are there any comments or questions before I continue? ...Yes, Melinda?"

"Holy crap, everything you've mentioned is contrary to a Jake Jensen transformation process, sounding just like the thing a vertical organization would want to play with," Melinda said with a titter.

"What you say is true, Melinda. This is *old school* stuff from the cost accounting world. They would say, WHAT YOU MEASURE CAN BE IMPROVED UPON.

However, if your customer doesn't perceive those improvements in purchasing criteria to be better than your competitors', you're spinning your wheels... Now, let's discuss MPV market awareness level and customer price expectations...

When measuring your MPV, it's like grading your company's performance by a review board made up of customers entering numbers that show up on your company's performance appraisal. It sounds like Camp's BALANCED SCORECARD, except, we're focused only on our customers and potential customers as opposed to world industry best practice. By using the information, you can improve on those critical areas that need improvement and help in identifying current trends that could affect you and your competition. A trend showing an overall lower performance for you and your competitors can be significant. Why did it happen, and what does it mean?

Jake had this to say about MPV influencing this new architecture...

It's not unlike a digital nervous system, where the appropriate part responds to an input from a demanding output."

Watching the class for a reaction, I see heads turn to one another and chatter for a moment.

"Network television often faces the dilemma of a rating decline. Why did the ratings of a particular program make a dramatic drop from last year's record high? Is it because another network has a stronger program drawing from that network time slot? Is it a change in the viewing time, the director, or a storyline that's responsible? And as you may have noticed, MPV is equivalent to the network Nielsen ratings.

If there is significant volatility in the industry ratings, there may be an element of concern. Perhaps it's a bad year, or your whole industry suffered slow economic growth. And then, again, certain materials could cause delays in shipping, or new regulations increased expenses for businesses in your market. Or, perhaps, it's due to a rise in customer expectations? Is it a buyer's market?

Whatever the cause of these anomalies, it will be the well-informed business that identifies these trends that can set a strategic plan in motion to increase market share.

Market measurements will establish whether changes made to your procedures, products, and processes are effective by showing an increased value to your customers and market share. It highlights where you're successful and not so successful, and where you should and should not make improvements, making it the cornerstone of information guiding your transformation process.

When you share the results with a new potential customer, it shows them your commitment and adds to the goodwill and corporate image of the business...

I have two more final noteworthy comments about the relationships between your employees and their customers, and the OEM market...

You do not want to establish and maintain *personal* relationships with your prospective customers. Relationships and market perception are not, either-or issues—they're both needed to build market share. The idea is to identify those qualities and issues the customer cares about the most in creating a business relationship.

The purchasing criteria used in my examples are for original equipment manufacturers, businesses like yours.

Okay, last chance. Are there questions?"

Nina raised her hand...

"Yes, Nina."

"Johnny, I have but one comment...

Before the meeting, I became apprehensive about how this benchmarking perception session would work when conceiving it to be a complex issue. But as it turned out, I found that the presentation made the process both simple and refreshing, especially, when comparing to Camp's Best Practice."

Nina and the audience respond by applauding.

"You're most kind. Thank you," I said, nodding with appreciation.

"That's it. Our session has ended. Thanks for your comments and contributions."

As they drifted out of the training room, I chatted with folks until the last one cleared out then turned out the lights before heading out.

JOHNNY'S RELAXING TIME IN PARADISE COVE—WELL, MAYBE

I'm looking forward to some relaxing time in the sun and great seafood as I head north on the 405, then over to the coast highway to Malibu—destination, Paradise Cove Beach Café. When nearing the cove, I turn off the coast highway and head down a beach road ending at the Paradise Cove Pier that juts out into the surf and but a stone's throw from the restaurant.

The Café opens out onto a sand patio with plastic chairs and tables offering umbrellas made of dried palm leaves. There is a palm tree at each end of the building planted for effect—as palm trees are not native to the coast, except, for the Fan Palm growing in California's desert region.

Today, the Cove's expansive parking lot is about empty leaving good parking spots next to the beach. When getting out of my car, I take in a fresh whiff of salty air while stretching my back to get the kinks out.

I stood there absorbing my wonderful surroundings and decided to take a stroll along the beach. After removing my shoes and socks, I rolled up my shirt sleeves and pant legs, put my stuff in the car, locked it, and then walked out on the sand.

I'm cruising for a suitable piece of real estate to settle my weary butt on such as a large rock or washed up driftwood. I found a well-traveled tree-trunk near the cliffs accompanied by trees and shrubs, so I settled in, fortunate the beach has few visitors today.

The warm sun rays relax me as my eyes close. I'm only hearing and smelling the cool, green air. Yes, green. The woodsy scent of eucalyptus trees mixes with the fresh, pleasant odor of the sea after it has rained. Then with the sound of the surf pounding the beach and the birds squawking at each other, I fall into a mellow state of mind.

With a short snooze behind me, my attention is drawn toward the pier where I notice the great swells pushing the waves high along the pilings. There are a few surfers taking advantage of the high rollers coming in as they apply their skills, then wipe out—being part of the thrill, I guess—me, I'm land-based.

In front of me, just beyond the surf is a pelican soaring up and down riding the flow of the complex wind currents. And then making a sudden move, it tucks its wings in and dives like an Olympic diver hitting the water with little or no splash. It wasn't down long when the large bird shot up to the surface and threw its head back as though it were chugging down a shot glass of gin.

And then its head turns just enough to see a fishtail appear before disappearing down its huge beak—pelican, one, fish, zero.

Having rested my little brain, I decided to head toward the surf and feel the cool, damp sand between my toes. Throughout different geographical regions of the world, you will find lots of sand. It blows in your face; it gets in your eyes, in your hair, and in your food—but not between your toes—where it belongs.

Along the way, the warm sun penetrates my body when eyeing a weathered, well-tumbled branch near the surf. Feeling the wet sand and frothy sea lap at my feet, I watch the seawater chase sandpipers up the slope of the beach. Standing among the long strands of kelp, I select my stick as I inhale the salty essence of the damp sand. My newfound stick is about the right size to use in the primeval skill of poking things with sticks. It must be a guy thing, and yet, I'm sure Sigmund Freud would have had something to say about that.

I soon became weary of poking various batches of seaweed, feathers, crab bits, and a dead seagull as the sandflies get the best of me, so I looked around for better poking opportunities. Ahh... I see the shimmering reflection of tide pools where one can poke starfish, anemones, urchins, and barnacles.

Well, it didn't take long, and I became tired of poking at the little devils, so I head back toward the Cafe. It used to be, I could poke things for hours, but, that goes for most anything I poke now.

While walking on the warm sand headed back for a late lunch, I feel a little prick on the underside of my foot. I glance down and see a river of blood running its way through the miniature hills and valleys of sand. Damn, sticking out of my foot is a piece of brown glass, perhaps from a beer bottle. So, I grit my teeth and pull it out, then remove my necktie to clean the wound.

Ah... Clean may not be the appropriate word here. Maybe, dusting off the sand would be more relevant. Anyhow, after doing what I could, I use my tie to wrap my foot and hobble back to the Café. Well, so much for my new silk tie and my mellow state of mind.

When entering the restaurant, I notice the lunch crowd has cleared out. It's a homey fun place, and it has what they call their Mojito Hut cloaked in a tropical facade where they sell the Cuban drink, Mojito. Black and white photos of celebrities and various shots of the beach and folks sitting at the bar cover the walls.

With a stiff upper lip, I head toward the restroom showing little concern for my wounded foot as the sounds of the Beach Boys filter through the air from their classic, colorful jukebox.

While in the restroom, I wait for a customer to leave, then put my foot up on the edge of the sink and cleaned the cut and tie with soap and water. After squeezing out the water from my necktie, I dried my wound with a paper towel, then held a clean, dry piece of folded towel to the cut and wrapped it in my damp tie.

While finishing up, a guy who could be an extra from a low-budget gangster movie walks in heeling to one side in a perverse troubling way and sees me with my foot on the sink. He's wearing a *dreadful* appearing tattersall fabric sports coat lifted from a *wannabe congressman* and doused with *Pay 'n Save* Cologne hanging around him and permeating the air.

His dyed black untrimmed slicked-back hair looks like it was marinated with a whole jar of *pomade*. His cigarette butt has an inch-long smoldering ash dangling below his mustache—one that looks like two old worn-out toothbrush bristles blackened with eyebrow pomade riding above his lip—and enhancing his look is the stench of dried vomit. And with his hair-cream shimmering in the fluorescent light, *Pomade* gives me a quick onceover from his gray, gaunt face while leaning at an unnatural angle. Then in his gravel-toned voice—textured by too many years of booze asked me...

"Do you always wear a tie on your foot?"

"Only when I'm unable to find my shoe," I said.

He sputtered and wheezed in amusement as he shuffled off to the urinal. Still, at his precarious angle, he pees on the wall.

After wiping the blood off the sink, I wash up and comb my hair. When leaving the men's room, I notice *Pomade* hanging on to the urinal.

With a growling stomach, and satisfied I would be okay for several hours, I decided to stay and enjoy a bountiful meal at a table outside under the shade of an umbrella.

After hobbling to a table, I settled in and placed my injured foot on a chair, suffering only minor throbbing. I relax for a moment and enjoy the sea breeze and the pounding surf.

With nothing better to do waiting for my waitress, I notice two seagulls fighting over something disgusting in mid-flight. Fortunately, I'm distracted by the waitress standing at the table ready to take my order.

While finishing the last of my soup, a seagull flew toward me with what looked to be the original nauseating prize hanging from its beak. It came in low, but at a high velocity, not unlike its big brother, the inverted gull wing World War Two Corsair fighter plane. As it approaches me, it screamed *eeeeeeeeeeeek,* making the hairs on the back of my neck stand at attention causing me to throw up my hands in defense. Then at the appropriate moment, Corsair's little brother releases the revolting *bat glide bomb* that glides through the air with amazing accuracy, landing in my soup.

Then at the last nanosecond, Corsair's bantam sibling pulls up missing the umbrella by fractions of an inch as though powered by a twenty-five hundred horsepower Pratt and Whitney engine. Pappy Boyington, the World War II Corsair ace couldn't have done better.

Christ, the goddamn seagull kills my appetite and now lands on a nearby table to stamp its *little* twig-like legs as though it was a sumo wrestler. Then the little shit cocks its head to give me his beady evil eye wanting to battle with me over his friggin prize.

So, I do the adult thing and flip the nasty little bird, the bird, hoping that would help. Well, that and it was the only retort that came to mind at that moment, being a little slow on my feet—so to speak.

I decided to just write off the afternoon to bad karma, so I flagged down my waitress to pay my bill, and then head off toward the emergency room for a shot and stitches.

Whoopee. Gee, another fun and relaxing day on the beach, under the California sun.

ACT II – SCENE 9
ENHANCING THE LEARNING PROCESS

Question 1
The author brings to light the chief aspects of working out at the gym. Why does he consider that so central in your life?
Is the author right?
If not, why?
If so, why?

Question 2
The author has a thing against bottled water flooding the market. Does he have a good reason?
If not, why?
If so, why?

Question 3
Why is it vital to do the market survey as illustrated?
How does it help in the decision-making process for improving market perception in those areas most needed?

Question 4
Why is it that the managers of a company shouldn't be second-guessing what their customer perception is of their company?
And, what does the truth have to do with it?

Question 5
What are your thoughts on the Best-in-Class programs the way the author has presented them?
Does it make sense to you?
If not, why?
If so, why?

Question 6
Does anyone have a sad, but a funny story not unlike Johnny's day at the beach you'd like to share?

ACT II SCENE 10
Meeting Jake and Toni in the Caribbean

WEEK 6 - MONDAY – PORT ROYAL, JAMAICA

DAKOTA FLIES TO JAMAICA

Late Friday evening, I'm at the Sherwood Gallery in Laguna Beach to view Michael Kalish's new paintings and party with the owners. One has to love Kalish's work, it's so unique. As the night rolled on, I had a tendency to make a periodic visit to a particular painting. Later in the evening, after one too many glasses of wine, I gave in to temptation and bought the thirty-eight by thirty-six Einstein portrait.

Later, after pulling into the driveway, I saunter down my walkway abubble with excitement. I open my front door and bounce into the living room looking for the right place to hang my new art acquisition when I'm distracted by my ringing phone.

"Hello," I said with a warble.

"Come and get me, Dakota," Jake said, with a laughing whimper.

"Hello? Jake? I can't hear you… You're breaking up."

"You're a real comedian… You've been hanging around some wisenheimer too long."

"That's true… I don't know why I put up with that guy."

"Okay smarty pants, you need to take a few days off. I need to spend time with you getting up to speed on ATC. I'll be on the run when I arrive home with our next project. As you know, it starts late next week. So, can you mosey on down to Jamaica and pick me up?"

"I'll be there. When do you get to Port Royal?'

"My best guess is Monday afternoon."

"I'll make flight arrangements with American Airlines to fly out of John Wayne Airport to Miami Sunday in the morning twilight. My next call will be to our friend Charlie at On-Demand Charters and have him get a jet ready for a flight out of Miami to Port Royal early Monday with a return flight to John Wayne Airport on Tuesday."

"You're the best, Dakota. Say hi to Marty for me. See you later."

"Will do... See you Monday."

After hanging up the phone, I make a mental note to give Marty, Nina, Jackie, and Johnny a call tomorrow morning. They'll need to know about my plans to meet with Jake and that I'll be back to work on Wednesday...

Later, Monday morning Dakota's charter jet takes off from Miami Airport headed toward Port Royal, Jamaica.

On that same morning in the growing light of first dawn off the Jamaica coast, a tired old tramp steamer with rusty bleeding scuppers carves its way through the waves. The ship created white foam bursting off the bow forming a silver stream of water along the ship's hull.

With a sudden shift of the wind, wisps of dark smoke billowed and swirled from the ship's single exhaust stack toward the starboard lookout on the bridge. The churning black exhaust was bad enough to make the sailor's eyes water and put a foul taste in his mouth while bringing on a hacking cough. Later, as the ship changed course a few degrees, the lookout reports a sail on the horizon, one point off the starboard bow.

From out of the south like a butterfly dancing over a green meadow, a deepwater ketch slices her way over the Caribbean swells headed toward Port Royal, Jamaica on the southeast end of the Island. As the two vessels pass each other in the first morning misty light, the lookout scans the vessel with his binoculars and sees the name, *Sophi,* painted on the ketch's stern.

Later in the afternoon, a few miles from shore my high-speed boat bounces over the rolling sea with her bow pointed toward the oncoming ketch. In the aloof, I see my big Creek Indian friend drop a couple of canvas bumpers, a boarding ladder and then removes a section of the lifeline aft amidships. When approaching the craft, I can see the long, slender hull of a deep-keel ketch cleaving the water, making mirror images of waves at her bow. When closing the gap, the dark green paint on the hull displays a dull silver frosted look created by an angry ocean salt spray.

Jake purchased the ten-year-old ketch in the port of Barcelona, Spain. He sailed her out of the Mediterranean Sea into the Atlantic and down the west coast of North Africa to Casablanca.

After stocking up on fresh water and food, they sailed south along the African coast. As the ketch approached the equatorial current, Sophi sailed the Atlantic trade winds south by southwest where the lethal storm almost took them to Davy Jones locker. But later, good weather befriended them as they sail on and reach a new compass bearing near the northern coast of South America. They are now driven in a northwestwardly direction toward the old pirate waters of the Caribbean created by a high-pressure area off the South Atlantic—and the indispensable Guiana current. Sophi is in high spirits as she navigates her way in the fresh breeze.

I gunned the boat beyond the ketch and came about to motor along the starboard side of *Sophi* until I reached the boarding ladder and throttle her down enough to keep pace. When looking up to throw a line, I'm greeted with a hint of a smile from Toni Nakni. He's got to be the best-looking, biggest and baddest Indian you'll ever see—a former Navy SEAL and Naval Intelligence officer.

Toni pads his way along the deck as though he were a cheetah on the hunt and caught both my fore and aft lines, then secured them. With taut lines, and the engine off, the powerboat snuggles up to the canvas bumpers for a slow free ride into port.

"Permission to come aboard, Sir."

"Permission granted, Commander Wells."

With little or no expression, Toni reaches down for my hand and pulls me on board the ketch as though I were a sea bass.

"Jake's down below. Antonio brewed up a pot of coffee in the galley—care for a cup?"

"Thanks, Toni, a cup of brew would hit the spot. Who's Antonio?"

"He's a friend of the previous owner and crewed several years on this boat."

"Why is he with you guys?"

"The owner suggested that Antonio could be helpful for such a long voyage having crewed for him on many occasions. So, after Jake talked with the kid about what he expected from a crewmember, he hired him. For Antonio, it was a chance to earn his passage and be with his girlfriend in Jamaica, and a wallet full of cash."

Toni yelled down to Antonio...

"Hey, Antonio, topside with two cups of coffee, mucho pronto. There's a bonita senorita on board."

A moment later, I get my first glimpse of Antonio bounding up the ladder and landing on deck without spilling the coffee.

Antonio eyes me with the look of a young Antonio Banderas...

"It is a pleasure to meet such a beautiful, senorita."

"Antonio."

After a short moment of jawing, Toni barked...

"Don't stand there like a fence post, get a move on son while you're still young—we got work that needs doing."

There was no hesitation from Antonio running below deck to ready the boat for debarkation. Toni heads toward the stern like a silent fish gliding through the water. Jake tells me, according to his brother's in arms, he's a legend and feared by his enemies.

A little later, glancing above the rim of my coffee cup, I watch Toni behind the helm for a moment as he moves with an economy of motion for a man so big. His face has that neutral, relaxed look. No, it's more of a blank, expressionless face. One that sends a strong emotional message—do not disturb. Neither his face nor his body language will give away what he is thinking. He's not a hugging and kissing sort of guy—having devoted his career to hunting down and killing bad guys. He says more with his eyes and gestures than with words and can intimidate you at times, but knowing him as I do, I'm glad he's my friend. Toni and Jake are both loners. Their friendship is more like family. There is nothing they wouldn't do for each other. Jake is ten years older and treats Toni like a younger brother.

Jake told me he plucked Toni out of the South Pacific Ocean one day when he was sailing among the French Polynesian Islands. Toni's single-engine plane had lost power and then attempted to glide toward him crash-landing but fifty yards from his boat. He threw out his sea anchor, grabbed his life vest, and jumped over the side with a hatchet in hand. With the plane sinking, he smashed in the windshield enough to climb in and pull Toni out of the cockpit. A moment later, the plane sank almost seven miles below the surface finding its way down into the deeper waters of the open ocean.

Toni was in a bad way, with profuse bleeding from a head wound. Having no major medical supplies, unforgiving on his part, he remembered seeing a tampon box in a cupboard above his bunk. It was, however, a good alternative. He knew that the cellucotton in the tampon was first used as a battlefield dressing in WWI. After pouring Irish whiskey on the wound, he applied several tampons and secured them with several yards of rigging line. Wasting no time, Jake sent out a mayday picked up by a passing cruise ship. Within a few hours, Toni's headed toward Papeete.

Three days later, Jake visited Toni at the Mamao General Hospital in Papeete. The doctor told him he had understood that someone tied tampons to his wound and wondered if that was him. Jake nodded and apologized for doing such a stupid thing, but that's all he had to work with. The doctor told him it was one of the most bizarre and brilliant ideas he had ever seen when coming to saving someone's life on the get-go. It's a good thing the tampons worked, he told the doctor, because his first thought was to take the rigging line and tie it around Toni's neck to cut off the blood supply. Jake told me he thought the doctor wouldn't ever stop laughing.

Feeling good about his unorthodox dressing of Toni's wound, Jake headed down the hall to visit with Toni who took a liking to Jake. Later into his visit, Toni got around to telling him he's Creek Indian, born and raised on an Oklahoma ranch that his dad still worked and owned.

Jake told him his great-grandmother was full-blooded Creek Indian. His dad was a deep-fried Southern Okie who grew up on an Oklahoma ranch where he rode fence. He played the Jew's harp and shot rats as large as cats in the bunkhouse—I'm sure there was a little exaggeration involved there, but as kids, we like to believe what our dads tell us.

This little discussion along with having saved Toni's life had bonded them as blood brothers from then on.

Looking out across the bay, I squint when a splash of sunshine reflects off the sea. A fresh wind soon arrived raising a chop in the bay along with snapping halyards making a musical theme against their aluminum mast.

After finishing my coffee, I put my cup down and waited for Jake to come up on deck. It didn't take long when I heard my name—I turned to see a facsimile of Jake Jensen. He still looks like a middle-aged athlete as opposed to someone his age ready to settle into a senior care center. But now, with his time at sea, he looks more as if he were a seafaring Viking with his long golden hair blowing in the breeze, short-cropped beard, and well-tanned lean, muscular body. Well, that should be no surprise, given that his mom's ancestors were Vikings...

"Captain Jake, I assume."

He has a half-smile that frames a soaked rum stogie clamped between his teeth and then removes it.

"Would you be the boarding party, Antonio was babbling about?"

"Arr, Cap'n. Well, I see you survived the storm. I'll bet that had to be a rousing experience."

"That we did mate. Old *Sophi* spits in her eye and sailed along as though it were a good day off Laguna Beach."

"That's what you say, Ittimàaska—*that's Kemosabe in Creek for you Lone Ranger fans*—we were shitting in our flat hats as we dropped in on Davy Jones's locker, but fortunately, he wasn't in."

Jake and I crack up.

"I had no idea Toni had a sense of humor," I said.

"Hell, I didn't know he could string that many words together."

We have a good laugh at Toni's expense as he goes back to his blank, expressionless face again.

"What happens to *Sophi* after we leave?"

"I made arrangements to take her into dry dock and refitted under Antonio's supervision. We'll anchor here in Kingston Harbor."

An hour later, things are shipshape as we climb aboard the powerboat and motor to the boat rental dock. While I take care of the rental, Jake calls Spectre taxi. Fifteen minutes later, Jake pulls off another wow when a uniformed driver in a pristine 1957 Black Bel Air convertible with red interior and the top down shows up.

From the dock, we head to Bull Bay where we drop Antonio off at his friend's house. This is where Antonio gets misty-eyed as Jake says his thanks and goodbyes and tells him he'll stay in touch, while Toni stands there like a cigar store Indian. Before leaving, however, Toni nods to Antonio, and said

"Taska."

When hearing the word *taska*, tears run down Antonio's cheeks and continued to tear as his crewmates, and I drove down the road toward the Hilton Hotel where we're staying for the night. When blowing him a kiss, I'm rewarded with a wave and a smile. He's a sweetie.

That night, I asked Toni what taska meant. He told me it's the Tuskegee word for warrior. When hearing that, I told him he must have thought a lot of Antonio to consider him a Taska, but he flat ignored me, no surprise there.

Tuesday, the next morning, we're driven to Norman Manley International Airport. Forty minutes later, in the Embraer 650 charter jet's cabin, Captain Julien set the brakes and slides the throttles forward until they clicked putting them into takeoff position. With the engines roaring and shuddering, the captain released the brakes while glancing at the colorful display of the instrument panel to see that the engines had synchronized. The plane accelerated as the airspeed indicator showed 105 knots. At 117 knots, the copilot yelled, "Rotate." "Roger that," Captain Julien said as he pulls back on the yoke giving them a canting of the wings for liftoff. With its wheels up at 400 feet and a climb rate of 2,500 fpm, they're soon cruising at 41,000 feet over Caribbean waters.

ACT II - SCENE 10
ENHANCING THE LEARNING PROCESS

Question 1

Can one create world-class businesses by themselves? What did the story illustrate on behalf of that thought?

ACT II SCENE 11
Introduction to Systems Thinking - The First Step, removing Non-System Thinking

WEEK 6 – TUESDAY MORNING – ANOTHER DAY WITH JOHNNY – HIS TOPIC: SYSTEM THINKING

JOHNNY PONDERS OVER SHARP-TONGUED WOMAN

Outside the window on the sixteenth floor of my condo, the never-ending waves roll in and tug at the sand along the beachfront under the watchful eye of a graphite black sky.

It's four-thirty on a Tuesday morning when my radio alarm comes to life with NPR discussing the music of a new South African band. I begin my day by rolling out of bed at the speed of a crustacean. I'm not a morning person, but workout days call for fortitude while rousting myself toward the shower guided by the little LED glow lights plugged into the wall sockets—not unlike landing lights for aircraft.

The hot shower warms up my body as I come out of my coma. Sorry, but my body needs to shut down near flat-line, not unlike a hummingbird's heart rate dropping down from twelve hundred heartbeats per minute during its flight and down to near zero when snoozing on a branch.

When finishing with my twenty-minute shower, I dried off and head into my bedroom. WHAT? A twenty-minute shower before a workout you say…

I left the bathroom door open for light as I slip into a pair of black workout shorts, black tee shirt, and my new *Chuck Taylor's All Stars* low-cut workout shoes for my morning at the gym. The Chuck Taylor's are a flat, thin-soled shoe, great for deadlifts.

After fetching my black gym bag from the closet, I place it on the bed being careful not to wake up Sheri. She pilots those Gigantes 747's for United and now has a few days off.

I pulled my dark blue pinstriped three-button suit from the closet and lay it next to my gym bag packed with a pair of gray socks, a Zegna gray tie, clean black boxer briefs, and a white shirt.

Ready for my morning workout booster, I find myself checking out what little there is left in my refrigerator.

As I contemplate over my meager selection, I guzzle down a few chugs of a half-empty container of milk. Now, who in the world ever had the canniness of an idea to yank on a cow's tit and then drink whatever the hell comes out of it...

Oh, it now dawns on me why that might be. Sorry. Stupid thought. Well, there's that, and cows share many human genes.

With a need for protein this morning, I pour sixteen ounces of milk into the blender. Low on ingredients, I add a cup of yogurt with traces of mold, but with a hardy immune system in it goes. Next is an overripe banana turning black, and then one tablespoon of flaxseed, two tablespoons of peanut butter and a tablespoon of honey. Ah... What the hell, being out of protein powder, I toss in a can of tuna. WHAT...? Don't knock tuna until you try it.

While it blends, I grab the last piece of dried Rye bread and put it in my countertop broiler with olive oil sprinkled on top.

While I'm shoveling everything down, I fancied how nice it is to be a guy that lives alone. You can stand and stare at an open refrigerator as long as you want and drink out of milk containers without getting *sharp-tongued* from a woman. For instance, Shari noticed I had leftover dirty dishes in the sink, and told me they looked ready for carbon dating.

After brushing, flossing, and sloshing mouthwash around, I stroll into my bedroom. My teeth are so glistening white, it would make Erik Estrada's smile look like a *before* picture of a toothpaste whitening commercial.

I glance at Sheri lying there half-covered, looking beautiful and indecent in a good way. Hmm... Now, I'm considering the idea of jumping back in the sack or head to the gym. While rationalizing that idea, she farts in her sleep...

Well, justification fell through the crack, so to speak, hence my fast exit, as I grab my gym bag, my suit, and hightail it to the elevator taking it down to underground parking. WHAT?

I tossed my bag into the back seat, hung up my suit and slipped in behind the wheel of my black Audi V-10. With the clock illuminating five-twelve, I fire up the ten-cylinder beast and drive out of the well-lit garage. As I nose out into the darkness, I'm confronted with low visibility owing to the sea fog—the breaking waves create minute particles of salt allowing the water vapor to condense, thus the morning fog—meteorologist.

I took a left out of the driveway just as light started to steal the morning darkness. After a short drive, it's time to make a left and head south on Ocean Avenue. Well, it was Ocean Avenue until it turned into Palisades Beach Road, and then into Neilson Way, and then into Main Street—all within three and a half miles. It's not unlike many European cities that rename their avenues every few blocks, but you still have to wonder.

After turning left on Rose Avenue and right on Hampton Drive, I soon arrived at the famous Gold's Gym in Venice at five twenty-one. The low hanging morning fog is now dispersing at rooftop level. With a chirp of my Audi locks, I head to the gym.

I had a wicked, but rushed intense workout of deadlifts and lunges, then ready myself for a morning at ATC with a quick shower and primping.

Finished, I gaze into the mirror for a spitting image of me to admire my immaculate togged out tailor-made suit and glowing white shirt while giving myself a shameless smile. With such a glowing portrait, I'm rewarded with a flash of light reflecting off my polished white teeth.

With a glance at my watch and seeing its six twenty-five, it's time to hit the road, Jack. So, I head south on the 405 with the rest of the morning commuters and see the fog give way to the rising sun.

SYSTEM THINKING - THE TRAINING ROOM

I cut it close this morning, walking in at seven fifty-five—not good form on my part. With a few minutes to spare, I grab a coffee from the back of the room and then saunter up to the podium while saying hello to familiar faces.

I stood at the lectern for a moment sipping my coffee, said my good mornings—and then jumped into my scheduled discussion…

"Our topic this morning is *System Thinking*. System thinking can be difficult to grasp or digest at times so my dialog may be redundant or too far-reaching for some—and not enough for others…

Some would say a system structure is the behavioral output of the structure—change the structure and the system behavior changes. Up to some point, that's true…

However, for an organizational structure to behave systemically, the vertical structure must be eliminated and replaced with a horizontal architecture. This will allow the employees to be creative as they engage in system thinking and see the interrelationship among the key components of the system.

System thinking theory considers the system as a whole, therefore, allowing a behavioral change that's under control. I'll not travel too deep into the subject but bring to light its intrinsic value as one of our building blocks in the transformation process. For the process to work in our new environment, it's critical that the employees have a reasonable understanding of system thinking.

Why is that…? Well, it's because it's at the heart of the new horizontal organization that interacts with the new MPV portion of the system, which would help ground the new group leaders in this new process. Also, there'll be several of your process engineers assigned with the responsibility of system modeling, requiring a more in-depth understanding of system thinking…

Are there questions before moving on to our next subject?"

The room seems content, so I continue…

NON-SYSTEM THINKING

"Non-system thinking, our next subject, has the tendency to push hard during a system's interruption looking for common solutions. For instance, when things go amiss in an organization, most people analyze the various parts by seeking the source of the obstacle. When finding it they tear it down into smaller pieces... But, when the situation continues to worsen, we're now in the non-system thinking mode—only searching for the problem.

So, the answer must be, the need for bigger guns, or the government solution, throw more money at it. Over time, the more you use non-systemic solutions, the need for resolution amplifies, and so we continue to set out to find the common solution.... What do we call that condition...?"

Waiting for an answer, I remove my water bottle cap...

"Yes, Belinda?"

"Sounds like an addiction," Belinda said.

"That's true, Belinda... But, it's also the way we have been taught to solve difficult situations, which is the ANALYTICAL OR REDUCTIONISTIC approach.

In situations of complex structural quandaries, we try to solve the dilemma by looking for a different solution using the reductionist-thinking methods from the get-go. Almost every academic discipline has led us down the path of reductionist thinking. This does not allow us to deal with the complexity of the interaction going on between components in a system.

We also *intuitively* examine things in a reductionist way. When I was a kid, I would tear down my bicycle to little components to see what made it work. What I didn't study was the interaction of the parts, so when I had a gear-selecting dilemma with my bike, I considered the derailleur as the source of trouble. But, after replacing different parts long enough and getting no results, I did, however, by pure happenstance, find the hitch. It was in a sticky rusted cable that *controlled* the derailleur—an external system from the derailleur, but a component of the total system.

By using the system approach, I would have had a better understanding of how things work together—even as unassuming as a bicycle.

By disconnecting the other components to make it easier to isolate and resolve the situation, we, in fact, make it more difficult. When trying to understand the complex issues in our business organization, this process does not take into consideration the *whole*.

System thinking allows us to tackle obstacles at a higher elevation, which helps narrow the search, but at some point, the origin of the problem might use reductionist thinking to get at the local source of trouble...

Now, let's switch gears, so to speak..."

SYSTEM THINKING

"From this point on in our discussion, I'll try to stay focused on system thinking as it applies to business organizations. Otherwise, the subject can dive too deep into the theory for an introduction to system thinking. However, I'll use other types of systems other than organizations up to a point, to simplify the learning process...

By definition, a *system* is an assembly of parts interacting with one another functioning as a whole that provides a purpose. When you're taking or adding parts to the system, it'll no longer function as it once did—good or bad. The position and arrangement of the connecting parts are crucial. Change the structure, and behavior changes. Natural system parts are open to their environment and can organize their internal structure with surprising and amazing results.

System thinking allows you to put things together the right way—"

A hand goes aloft.

"Yes, Virginia, I see you have a question."

"Thank you, I do. How do you identify a system by looking at its parts? It could be a bunch of objects strung together."

"You'll know by asking yourself four questions. Let's try it, okay, Virginia?"

"I'll give it a go."

"Let's use the stock market as an example of a trading system. Okay, first question... Can the parts be identified?"

"I'm not too familiar with the stock market."

"Is there anybody that can help Virginia with this question...?"

"Yes, Margaret."

"I'd be happy to, being I dabble in the market. There are three parts—a buyer, facilitator, and seller."

"Excellent. Okay, Virginia, you should be okay for the next three questions... Do these three parts influence each other?"

"Why yes, they do," she said with a titter.

"Good. Do these parts when working together produce an output?"

"Yes."

"Lastly, I would ask, does the interaction behavior of these part's, over time, result in a verity of circumstances?"

"Yes, they cause the market to have fluctuations."

"Thanks, Virginia, being correct on all counts and for giving our audience such an insightful question."

Virginia's ordinary look with no distinguishing features made a sudden change as she gave Johnny a wide smile, showing off her beautiful white teeth.

"Okay, let's be moving on...

When faced with the idea you need to improve system performance, it's essential, you know what purpose the system serves—such as vehicles, trains, and airplanes serve as transportation.

When using *System thinking*, the idea of a system needn't be in isolation but can have connections to other systems. This means that you can't solve a system's component part affliction, without understanding or observing the connections and interactions encircled by its boundaries—"

Another hand begins to surface.

"Do you have a question, Patricia?"

"Yes, thank you, I do. What are the boundaries of a system?"

"Excellent question...

Systems need to distinguish themselves from their environment by establishing a boundary...

For instance, the systems of mining, transportation, and many service industries, do not depend on a host of suppliers to be inside their boundaries...

There are, however, manufacturers who must include suppliers in their boundaries that produce major components that make up their products, especially, in the automotive and computer industry, therefore, making suppliers part of a bigger system.

Surprisingly, your new horizontal open-systemic architecture is the only one *designed* to have ports in its innermost boundaries that interconnect with the market—accomplished through the MPV interaction system...

Am I getting close, Patricia?"

"Yes. I'm getting the hang of it now. But how do you analyze a system when it interacts with another system making it larger in scale?" Patricia asks.

"Oh, you are good, Patricia, great question."

I pause contemplating the issues of the question...

"Hmm... When we raise our elevation observing systems at work, we can see how they nest well together in other systems. Let's take, for instance, the impact of oil on manufacturing companies that use oil as a primary composition for plastic parts used somewhere in most products, shipping materials, or oil for transportation.

We began nesting systems when the oil exploration companies began selling its service to the oil-producing companies, who in turn, sell their product to the oil refiners. And they sell their products to services who sell to fuel stations, and the chemical companies that sell products to plastic companies. Plastic producers sell their products to manufacturers that sell to the end-user such as service companies, retail outlets, or perhaps to other manufacturers. The buying public, the engine that fuels the economy, in turn fuels all the world's industries.

Outside the boundary of this huge system are the power and transportation systems that interact with the other systems. The balancing of the system or possible constraint is the available ore or various fuels in old Mother Earth. When viewing the total system, delays can be brought on by almost any constraint owing to various forms of shut down...

I'm afraid to ask, but does that cover it well enough, Patricia?"

I eagerly await her out.

"It does, Johnny. So, after hearing what you and Ms. Wells said about national security and oil, it's best we engage ourselves in system thinking. Most notably, we need to have a better understanding of our economy, our company, our standard of living, and our well-being."

After scanning the audience, I pause to summon the proper words...

"Sometimes, I'm humbled by your questions and answers. You have taken upon yourselves to turn it into a real learning session to enhance the transformation process for a bold new beginning...

I'd say you deserve a round of applause."

So, I applaud the audience as they too jump in.

I wait for the room to quiet down, and then continue...

"Okay... Let's be moving on... In an organization, most notably, the vertical organization—it is the interplay of relationships between the different parts that create a behavior pattern of its own. Each organizational output is unique to any one company. Therefore, when looking at the behavior of each part, their individual actions are not predictable.

If you ask an employee about their perspective of the whole organization, they'll more than likely have a different view from that of another employee elsewhere in the organization. Why is that...?"

"Yes, Daniel?"

"Well, based on what we've learned in our sessions, it sounds like a social issue in the different parts of the vertical organizational system, each one presuming their view is correct. It's the idea of belonging to a group or a team.

An example of that during the late eighteenth century, the Corsicans were tribal. So, when trying to form a single entity to confront the French and drive them out, it failed. Being tribal, their first loyalty was the tribe, and then the country—not unlike the dilemma in Iraq and Afghanistan. So, in 1794, they had to convince the British to help rid them of the French. And that, of course, was short-lived, since Corsica is still French territory.

It would appear that changing one's functional biased perspective is vital in the process of the social interaction of the components in solving complex system organizational situations," Daniel said.

"I'm at a loss for words as impossible as that may sound. That was an excellent reply." I said. "And, if that answer doesn't drive it home, I have nothing else to add...

Let's be moving on to system thinking. Our first concern for applying system thinking is with your new architectural organization, but the application of system thinking can be put to use with most anything with a system such as a human, or scientific and engineering endeavors. And as Daniel so vividly pointed out, system thinking can even be put to use in governments and countries.

The military, however, has been using system thinking since the 1990s for use in warfare. But, with conflicts in Afghanistan and post-war Iraq with no standing armies to confront, flaws raise their attention to reveal serious limitations in the application of a useful system in this type of warfare. It became obvious, however, after the nine-eleven attack, when sending in the first American forces into Afghanistan. They were a small band of elite troops sent there to help fight and coordinate the Northern-Alliance efforts of the three tribes who hated the Taliban, and not realizing they also hated each other. The U.S. mission was successful but only due to their training and leadership.

It's interesting that Daniel's observations of the Corsican's tribal devotion is something our military should have realized before considering their approach to using system thinking when confronted with any kind of tribal behavior..."

Wanting to move ahead, an amusing idea of system thinking comes to mind. I scan the audience and then focus on David, a mechanical engineer...

"David, what would happen if you installed an eight hundred horsepower Chrysler engine in a Volkswagen Beetle without changing the component part infrastructure?

He laughed... "Are you asking me for the answer?"

"You bet. I'm told you paid your way through college working as a mechanic."

"That's true. Well, the answer is obvious, but it's a fun concept," David said, with a chuckle. "For starters, the huge engine would overwhelm the car's infrastructure. The car brakes wouldn't hold up for long due to the added weight. The car's suspension system would handle like a fifty-year-old dump truck with the front tires levitating above the road, the drivetrain would soon fall apart, and that's just the beginning of your misfortune. One would have to call it a systemic nightmare."

I looked around in amazement as I review the audience...

"Like I said, it's obvious you folks are here to learn, and it shows with your interaction—and that David, was another brilliant response."

David laughed... "Anytime."

"Are there questions...? no? Okay, moving on..."

David's Volkswagen's system problems are similar to natural systems, they reach equilibrium—a state of balance due to the equal action of opposing forces. There is a positive and negative *feedback* that encourages or discourages a change in the system that regulates it; therefore, keeping it in a steady state.

The Volkswagen system was sent out of balance—requiring it to fight back against the opposing forces. Over time, though, one of two things had to happen, replace the existing running gear with the appropriate one, or replace the engine with a smaller one to bring it back to a steady-state.

The state of natural systems oscillates along a mean condition, known as a *dynamic equilibrium*. When a steady state of input and output is no longer in balance, the system is going to fluctuate out of its normal upper and lower limits of the mean. If the system continues to have energy, it'll seek to establish a new mean when reaching its limitation. Let's cast an eye at a diagram that'll give you a more graphic idea of what I'm talking about...

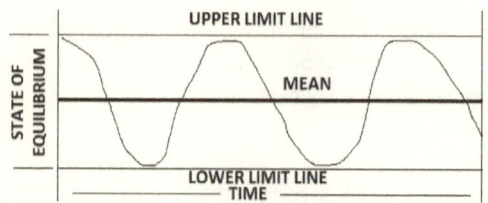

From a geographical point of view, the earth temperature moves up and down the mean temperature. Any of the controlling variables such as the climate, the oceans, the sun, the vegetation, and perhaps even human activity can move the temperature either above or below the mean. If stressed, the system will establish a new state of equilibrium or self-destruct...

Let's use the ice age as an example. We do not know precisely what caused either of the two known ice ages, other than one of the many variables I mentioned—less us humans, of course. But, perhaps, changes in the atmosphere caused by the earth's orbit, or the sun's orbit around the galaxy.

The diagram does a splendid job of illustrating the state of natural systems and how they oscillate along a mean condition known as a *dynamic equilibrium*... Before moving on, do you have questions?"

Seeing content faces and a few shaking heads, I continue...

THE CIRCLE OF INFLUENCE

"Now, let's get acquainted with an interesting subject called the circle of influence using links and loops. It's an introduction only, but it'll be enough, so you don't wrinkle up your nose when Denny begins lessons on how to use it in your business, along with system thinking.

We are looking to see things systemically, or in circles of influence, rather than in the straight lines of a specific segment. A circle, as opposed to a straight line, can tell a story as Peter Senge might say, being the author of the *Fifth Discipline*—a must-read...

Within any element, you can draw arrows called links that affect another element, while repeating themselves and influencing in degrees of good and bad. *Links* do not exist in isolation; they live in a circle of causality or a *feedback loop* where each element is both *cause* and *effect*. Its influence can be broad, but sooner or later, it returns home...

Let's bring up an illustration of what I'm talking about...

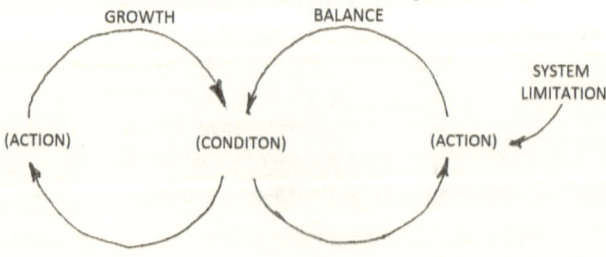

Let's take a moment to study how the arrows represent the influence of direction during the changes in a system's growth while trying to keep it in balance..."

I kept silent while they absorbed the intent of the illustration...

"Keep this image in mind as I continue...

The *Reinforcing* and *Balancing Loops* are the two building blocks for a system illustration. These Reinforcing loops generate both exponential growth and the collapse of a system. Each continues at an ever-increasing rate. The housing market is an example of exponential growth and exponential collapse.

During the boom, it was *spend, baby, spend. We're on a roll.* You can be assured there was a reinforcing loop moving along with you in your pursuit of happiness...

However, with the market collapse, it was, *oh baby, we're spiraling into a black hole*—not a kind reinforcing loop when taking you to unexpected lows. During the life of a reinforcing loop, good or bad, it must eventually meet head-on with a *balancing* mechanism that limits its direction...

For instance, the bad or negative loops do not always produce unfavorable results. More often than not, they are stabilizing. They counteract a balancing power to the system—much like we discussed earlier on Earth's climate. Also, depending on the subject, these cycles can be in any time increment, including geological time."

Ed's gleeful smile showed his need to interject a comment.

"Okay, Ed, What's on your mind?"

"How'd you know?"

"What can I say, other than I'd like to play poker with you. Your face is an open book."

"That's what my wife tells me..." Ed muttered with a grin. "Well, speaking of geological time that's what the bottom of the housing market felt like."

Knowing well the anguish, we joined in for a few chortles...

"I'm sure we all felt the same, Ed...

Us folks here on planet earth depend on many balancing processes which regulate our earth, our climate, our environment, our bodies, and even our economy. As citizens, it would be helpful to have a better understanding of our economy, and its balancing points, a benefit from system thinking...

By this, I mean, we often hear politicians giving us outrageous promises of bringing back manufacturing jobs, increasing our wages, and growing the economy, and a chicken in every pot as they used to say. They tell us this, without a clue that it isn't going to happen. Only our businesses can perform this deed, but it can't happen until we can show them the way.

Our citizens get hoodwinked by these fraudulent snake oil salesmen, calling themselves, politicians. This pains me seeing these dishonorable people take office. Well, you get my drift, enough said...

You'll find that when balancing processes, the constraints will raise their heads showing a delay. The system is narrow-minded on how things ought to be. So, without making the appropriate correction to your customer's satisfaction, the system would eventually drive the customer away. Let me give you an example of an athletic club predicament..."

THE BEAR CREEK ATHLETIC CLUB

"The Bear Creek Athletic Club, a pseudonym, opened a facility at the first of the year. Management did a market-perceived value study of the three top competitors in the metropolitan area enabling them to design their facility to leapfrog their competitors in the marketplace.

First, they included a fast turnaround workout designed for those with the limited time that included a variety of workout machines and free-weight for a novice or bodybuilder. To keep the fixed cost down, they only offered a few showers and lockers and two staff members on eight-hour shifts during their twenty-four-seven availability. There were no trainers, other than if you brought one with you. Their membership fee was only twelve dollars a month, much lower than their competitors—with no cancellation fee contracts.

A Membership contract was available online or at the facility. Your photo is taken allowing admittance owing to the facial recognition software instead of carrying a card around. The club's website allowed the members to grade the facility by weight and rate perception using seven categories.

They expected to reach full capacity in nine months—their *perceived* constraint being the locker room and showers. Their break-even capacity was sixty percent... Four months later, they were at seventy percent capacity—the owners were ecstatic. But during the fifth month, the *parking* attribute dropped from nine down to a five. In the sixth month, membership and attendance dropped. In the seventh month, the membership and attendance fluctuated between sixty-five and seventy-five percent capacity... We call this teeter-tottering. It's the systems target level until it comes to rest.

The club owners had not considered the severe impact of *parking capacity* on membership satisfaction—it was not in their circle of influence. When a member became delayed getting into the health club due to no close-in parking, it became a welcome excuse to skip exercising or go elsewhere. The owners dedicated to their workouts did not consider their gym to be like other services or stores that serve the public...

In reality, most people won't circle the parking lot. They'll try to find something nearby, but give up if nothing is found in the first past, feeling they're wasting time.

The system ultimately stabilized at a seventy percent capacity—its natural target, or constraint level. This is a good example of how a parking constraint in the system limited the growth rate of a company and then settled into a natural operating range...

Let me bring up another causal loop diagram of the athletic club's condition causing the constraint.

The athletic facility needs a new target goal such as a new balancing target or alternative for the parking area...

Some alternatives might be renting spaces from the supermarket across the street or validated parking tickets from a nearby parking lot. If this fails, their facility has reached its limitation...

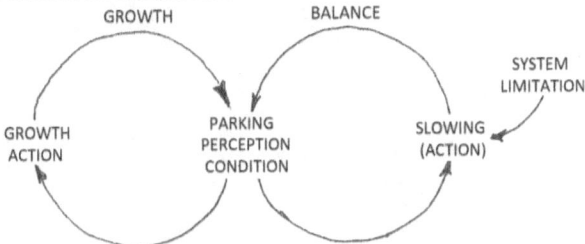

Okay, let's move on to having delays in the system...
Ahh... Well, unless you have questions. Yes? No?"
Seeing a content audience, I take us to our next subject...

EXCESSIVE GROWTH WITH DELAYS

"Delays will create an unwelcome disruption in the system. They may be subtle enough to ignore them at first, but don't underestimate the damage they can do to the system. An example might be ordering more material than necessary to offset delays—or having excessive growth amidst a business system..."

I see Victoria has a question and acknowledge her with a nod.

Victoria swishes her long, dark hair back from her face...

"I'm not sure what you mean by a company would be in trouble if it grew too fast. Sounds like a good thing."

"Good timing, I was about ready to convey a story Jake Jensen told me..."

Back in the mid-seventies, his manufacturing company produced products for one of the world's first mass-market desktop computers. To be more specific, it was shipped as a kit to be assembled...

The founders, a university professor of electrical engineering, and a former electronics marketing manager developed an advanced designed computer product at the right time, but it ran out of control...

The computer company had a compounded growth of seventy-one percent per month. Thirty percent is excessive even over a year. It wasn't long when one of Jake's machinists took a high-paying position as a stockroom manager. He was smart and loaded with enthusiasm—so they hired him. The poor judgment didn't end there in their anguish to fill positions. So, a few months later, Jake's previous machinist became head of the purchasing department.

As the growth pressure increased on this new management lacking the proper knowledge and skills, they continued to fill important positions with good people but lacked the proper experience. Eighteen months after their splash into the computer world, and overwhelmed with undeliverable orders, they imploded.

With that in mind, I have Jake's illustrations showing two charts of the company's growth rate...

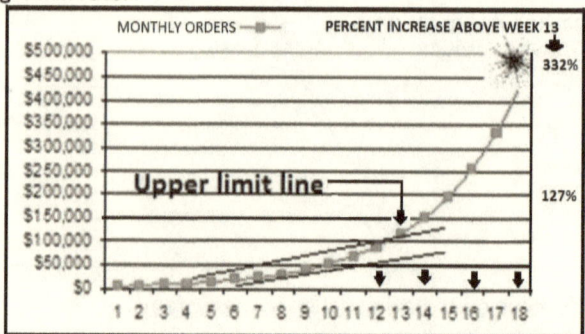

Okay... In the first chart, we have monthly orders... You'll notice in month thirteen, they move above the sustainable growth rate upper limit line. Now, take in the incredible growth rate from month thirteen to month eighteen. Their order increased three hundred thirty-two percent in six-months, ending with the company implosion, drawn in by Jake.

The second chart illustrates the employee-hiring rate... As you can see, the organization lost its way early on, but totally went off the rails as the operation crossed over the upper limit line...

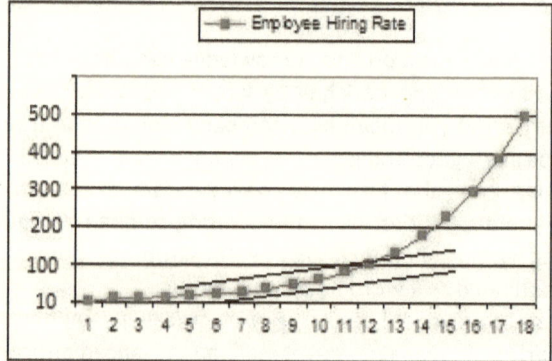

"Holy crap," Ed said, "As they say, a picture is worth a thousand words showing its exponential growth. Without a doubt, it explains the implosion on the eighteenth month—it's amazing they lasted that long. My guess is momentum kept them going for a few months."

"Please say no more," Victoria said, "I'm sorry I asked ... that's a sad story."

"It is a sad story indeed, and it didn't need to turn out that way. In a moment, I'll have a causal loop diagram of our imploded computer company on the screen. This'll allow you to get a better understanding of these diagrams.

The major reason for showing a system diagram is to help identify these bad guys, known as delays, running amuck in the system. One of the best ways to improve cycle time or throughput time is to rid your system of delays. Let me bring up the new diagram that illustrates the problem... "

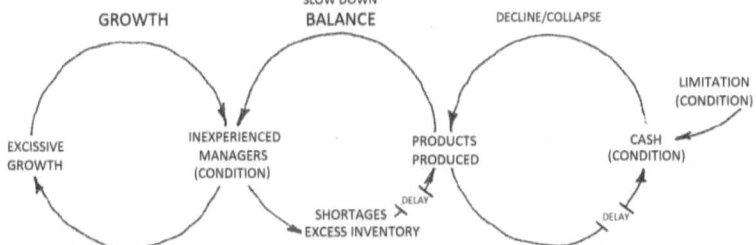

I wait a moment for the audience to absorb the illustration...

"First, however, I'd like to say owing to the company's exponential growth, the system begins to feed on itself trying to support the current quandary. By that, I mean, it's promoting inexperienced employees to fill key decision-making positions allowing the system to balance itself due to its limitations—as natural systems do... In this case, delayed shipments and excess inventory ate up cash—pushing out their accounts payable beyond ninety days—cutting off needed materials to produce products for their customers.

Now, with the system still trying to exceed its ability to balance itself on negative cash flow, it reaches its limitations—causing the company to implode...

Even if the founders lacked the management skills, but had a basic understanding of system thinking and able to develop circles of influence, they would have had an early warning of their problem. With this knowledge, they may not have collapsed—and become one of today's computer giants...

An interesting assumption is it not?"

Before continuing, I whisk over the audience seeing compassionate faces considering such a thought.

"The idea of the underlying dynamics of a system is to illustrate these circles of influence, if not understood and utilized, it can drive customers away and leave a negative perception of the business. Or as the example would indicate, the exponential growing computer company imploding in on itself...

Yes, Jamie. Do you have a question?"

"Can a fast-growing system be a good thing, if constrained by either an internal or external input?"

"Another excellent question ... the answer, of course, is yes. Let's use vegetation For instance...

It has two major elements of positive and negative feedback loops that control its growth amidst its circle of influence—nutrients and sunlight. The greater the exposure to sunlight and rich, moist soil, the higher the influence of positive feedback loops...

Take, For instance, the vegetables grown in Matanuska Valley, Alaska, where vegetables grow in a rich, glacier-ground volcanic soil on long summer days. The Matanuska farms are capable of growing three-foot corn, a nineteen-pound carrot, a thousand-pound pumpkin, a seventeen-pound zucchini, and a hundred-pound cabbage to be shown at the state fair looking for first prize...

But, even these fast-growing large vegetables soon reach their limitations in their unique environment when negative feedback loops influence their growth. Does that answer your question, Jamie?

"It does. Thank you, Johnny."

With a nod to Jamie, I continue... "Next, we'll check out how the circle of influence functions in your business."

THE CIRCLE OF INFLUENCE AND ATC'S INDICATOR SYSTEM

"Let me put up Jackie's diagram she used in her *A New Set of Measurement Tools* session. It allows the viewer to stay out of the details and see those areas of importance needing improvement. When using actual values, we would have seen segments of the results which would be a linear interpretation of the total output. We are now seeing how each segment or part affects other segments somewhere in the system that may alter the total system.

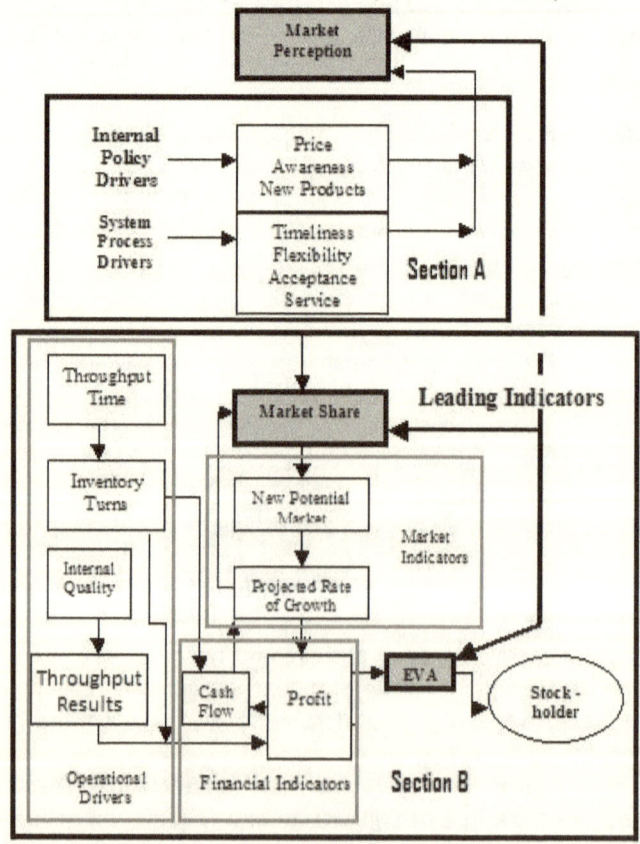

Give me a moment, and I'll have a new diagram showing the system's circle of influence indicator...

There we go. Now you can compare the two and see it has much of the same nomenclature as in Jackie's diagram. The circle of influence, however, illustrates the various indicators and their affect on the system...

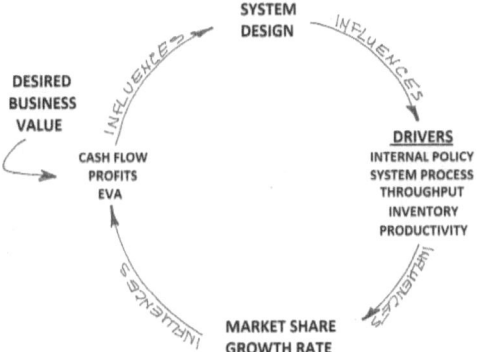

Please take a moment to view the diagram, and then I'll continue...

"As you can see, these segments of dynamic flow influence one another while they ceaselessly come full circle. As the circle of influence pattern develops, they'll display situations that show various degrees of fluctuation, or oscillation along the mean of those things measured—for better or worse.

Let's not forget, every system will reach their limitations or balance at a given point in time. When possible, design a new system. If not, they'll eventually die...

Each segment of a system has ties to its relationship with the whole. By looking at just one segment of a system in isolation, we have no understanding of its importance to the output of the system—negative or positive...

To end this topic, I would add if there ever was a forever-perfect design that lives on in perpetuity; it would be the *immortal* Hydra, a microscopic animal that lives in pools, lakes, and rivers in warm climate regions.

For those curious about what the little creature looks like, I have a nice image for you. Here we go, meet Mister Hydra..."

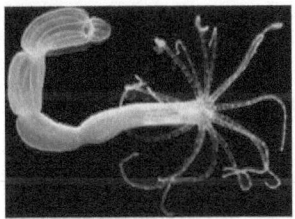

The audience shows their appreciation with wows and interaction with one another.

With the need to finish our discussion, I decided to discuss a vehicle example and finalize the session.

"Next, before ending our session today, we're going to have a discussion about a vehicle system that should enhance your understanding of systemic thinking."

A VEHICLE EXAMPLE

"A vehicle is a collaboration of subsystems that make a total system. External inputs to the system such as changing the type of fuel, the tire pressure, brake pads, or the suspension, and you'll have a different driving result. Outlying event inputs can also change the results such as oil or water on the street, a pothole or weather...

Yesterday's vehicles had minimal interactions between subsystems, other than the engine itself and drivetrain. But, today's vehicles are far more complex with their internal networks, sensors, and electronic control units allowing the subsystems to work together. These smart subsystems might include automated skid recovery, smart-independent wheel action, electronic steering, or sensors sending data to a chip controlling the automatic transmission.

This internal network interaction of today's automobile is what functional organizations have tried to do to enhance their flexibility and processing with various software applications, but with limited results...

That's why it is imperative that the design of the business architecture needs to be a horizontal process-driven system. Well, that and the employees trained in system thinking to enhance the system's component parts and their relationship with the market."

FINALIZING THE SESSION

I paused for a moment to gather the right words...

"I suppose one could go on forever with various scenarios of why system thinking plays such an import role in your new business architecture, but by now, I'm sure you're getting the idea...

Are there questions...?

Yes, Dietrich?"

"Thanks, Johnny. With a fair understanding of organizational architecture and today's session, I'm beginning to grasp the fundamentals of system thinking—well, from a limited point of view..."

Dietrich hesitates...

"But I'm unsure how problem-solving is done. Is this something you'll be discussing?"

"You're right on target, Dietrich. I'll be covering that topic on Friday...

It's an important subject, and I would recommend that the officers, department heads, and community group leaders attend this session. The department heads should consider the idea of inviting other key personnel.

The key subject matter is *Systems Modeling*. The idea is to give you a better understanding of simulations and how they help improve your system performance. Not to worry, it's not too technical.

Process engineering ordered two programs of *isee Systems* software, with *isee* spelled with a little '*i*.' The two programs are differentiated, by design, *Stella* will be used for educational and research with an introduction to Systems Thinking. The other program is *iThink* designed for system modeling operations, research, resource planning, projects, and financial analysis. These new products should be here today.

The *isee* software offers a practical way to visualize and communicate how complex systems and ideas work while communicating the mental process involved in shaping the new business environment... I might add, I have four books for those of you who would like to understand the science of system thinking. I'll give the title of the books so you can write them down...

Limits to Growth, by Donella H. Meadows, Jorgen Randers, and Dennis Meadows...

Introduction to General Systems Thinking, by Gerald M. Weinberg...

And *The Fifth Discipline*, by Peter Senge...

As far as *Russell Ackoff* goes, there is a large selection to choose from. Each one is full of great information on the subject..."

Finished, and out of desperation, I sip the last of my cold coffee.

"I'm going to take a moment to address how we evaluate our surroundings or encounters based on our previous knowledge—an interesting subject...

Unfortunately, most of us have been schooled knowing that reductionistic thinking is how problem-solving is best accomplished. Needless to say, we must move beyond this kind of reasoning and see things as a whole with interconnecting parts.

This idea of using only our previous knowledge of problem-solving was not unlike our understanding before circumnavigation of the globe when we assumed the Earth to be flat...

Speaking of Earth, I thought you might be interested in my dad's view of living on Earth...

He said... *Living on Earth is expensive, but it does include a free voyage around the Sun every year...*"

They loved it by showing a joyful chuckle throughout the audience...

"Still under the assumption the Earth is flat, the Europeans discovered the Americas. It was then that the invading Spanish conquistadors came upon the Inca Indians. The native people were in awe of the new creatures that had four legs, shiny armor, and could spit fire that killed. Those of you familiar with classical mythology would call them a centaur...

And what made it more unbelievable, the rider dismounted and then walked on two legs—the fact they could separate at will."

The audience responded lightheartedly...

"That may sound ridiculous to us, but put ourselves in their sandals—

without our understanding of the world as it is today, we too would reason things in the same way. When we are unaware of our surroundings enclosed within a system, we operate like bats hanging from the cave, making nothing but bat guano."

The audience has a gleeful chuckle with that visual deduction in mind...

"I'm sure you have a meaning behind that statement, Johnny."

"I do, Ed... If we can leave the cave long enough, we can see an interconnected system. With that idea in mind, we can see the unseen forces at work—allowing us to work with and change them. For instance, our managers of today isolate themselves in their caves, if you will, and read static reports, have meetings, and send emails... So, I ask you, why then is system thinking so important?"

While overlooking the audience, I see a hand rise...

"Yes, Richard?"

"It sounds to me, like the employees with an understanding of how their systemic business system operates; they no longer need to be task-driven. The workforce can now rationalize things for themselves, ask questions and gain knowledge on improving their system. With customer feedback on performance, the staff can establish new benchmarks and enhance the company's performance and perception."

"That was excellent, Richard. If I may, I'll elaborate on your thought. The new system allows people to view the organization from a broad perspective seeing the system process interaction, patterns, and contemplating new ideas with creative thinking. This type of reasoning allows the employees to improve the overall system's performance and its connections to the outside world...

Now, how is that possible in a hundred and fifty-year-old vertical organization using reductionistic thinking?

Those of us using system-thinking are *The Darwin's of evolution* that helps evolve their business into a horizontal-systemic organization structure that would allow others to study the system and perhaps make changes."

I see smiling nodding faces.

"Wow, *The Darwin's of evolution*... I like the sound of that. I can use that in our new marketing rollout when Nina gives the okay to deliver our message to the world," David said—*Vice President of Market Recognition*

"You're right, David, it does have a nice ring to it for your purpose...

Well, to continue with my train of thought, I would say when you're in a functional organization, and the customer complains about the throughput time of your products, it's doubtful that the head of engineering would know anything about it. Even if he did, he'd shrug— thinking this is not his Gordian knot—then continue to contemplate his task at hand...

Well, we have covered a lot of ground this morning, and it's time we end this session. However, I have a final word for you—our transformation sessions are to instruct you, the employees, to do the actual changes. Our time here is short, so you must be able to understand the basics of system thinking and reasoning behind the transformation process. Dependency on the Jake Jensen group for future growth can only weaken the long-term value of the business.

However, I don't see this as an issue with this group. So, let's give us a nice round of applause for being a bright and interacting group of folks."

The audience responds with smiling faces, a few whistles, and applauding.

"Now... I would like to leave with you two quotes, one from Peter Senge's book, *The Fifth Discipline*, the other from Jake Jensen...

Peter Senge had this to say...

Organizations learn only through individuals who learn. Individual learning does not guarantee organizational learning. But without it, no organizational learning occurs."

I pause to gaze into the eyes of the attentive audience.

"By the same token, Jake Jensen likes to say...

Not everything an organization learns counts and not everything that counts does an organization learn. But, without learning, nothing counts."

This has the audience nodding and chuckling.

"Well, having said that, we've had a good day, thanks to everyone here. One other thing, let's not forget our next session on the *Introduction to Systems Modeling—the Next Level of System Thinking*, Friday morning at eight o'clock."

A few minutes later, having wrapped it up, I head toward the parking lot.

DINNER AT AGO'S

I'm sitting in my idling car and decide to be prudent and give Sheri a call now rather than on the 405, knowing it will be close, as it is to make my class at Pepperdine in time.

"Hi, Sweetie," Sheri said.

With high expectations, I ask her...

"How would you like to have dinner at Ago's in West Hollywood tonight?"

"Gee, that sounds wonderful. Isn't that the one owned by DeNiro and another guy?"

"That's the one. I'll try to get us an outdoor table. It's Italian cuisine cooked the way I like it—in wood-burning ovens."

I'm visualizing Sheri over our candlelit table, sipping wine—ah, *life* is the cat's pajamas.

"Sounds divine, baby. I hope you don't mind, but I went to the grocery store today and stocked you up. You're such a bachelor—it would be nice to have someone look after you." Sheri said sweetly.

Gulp the dreaded words all bachelors' fear—SOMEONE TO LOOK AFTER YOU. Then a *sharp-tongued* woman comes to mind. Gee, I can scarcely get the words out...

"How nice."

Ah, how *life* can take a turn.

ACT II - SCENE 11
ENHANCING THE LEARNING PROCESS

Question 1
What did you have to say about Johnny's protein drink made with a can of tuna? Moreover, have you ever tried it?

Question 2
Can you give an example of how system behavioral output differentiates one company's system from another?

Question 3
Can you identify the four main questions enabling you to identify a system? How can that be helpful in the decision-making process?

Question 4
Can you solve a systems component part problem without understanding the interconnections within its boundaries?
Explain.

Question 5
Can you draw a simple circle of influence of growth and its balancing point of limitations?

Question 6
What are your thoughts on Johnny's fear about—SOMEONE TO LOOK AFTER YOU?
Act II Scene 12, Systems Modeling the Next Level of system Thinking

ACT II SCENE 12
Systems Modeling the Next Level of system Thinking

WEEK 6 – FRIDAY MORNING, A DAY WITH JOHNNY – HIS TOPIC: SYSTEMS MODELING

JOHNNY AND THE SHARKS

Sheri greets me with a towel as I step out of the shower.

"You sure spend a long time in the shower." She said with a snub.

Damn, attacked at stupid o'clock in the morning.

I thanked Sheri for the towel, wrapped it around me, and headed toward my closet.

"Johnny."

"Yes?"

"Would you fix a *large* breakfast this morning? I have a busy day ahead of me."

Large? Be nice, I'm thinking. But damn it all, she eats like a sparrow. So, I add twenty percent of an egg to her one egg, and then she'll leave having eaten half her meal. Oh well, I'll finish off the rest.

"Why, of course, dear."

During Sheri's five-minute shower, I finish dressing, slip into my shoes, comb my hair, and head toward the kitchen. After getting the coffee maker percolating, my refrigerator grabs my attention for a long moment, as always.

As a kid, I'd stare for the longest time checking out the refrigerator for something to eat, and then I'd call my mom and ask her where she hid the jelly. She'd reach in and pull out the jelly right in front of me, then wave her hand over my eyes to see if I was blind, then walk off—this, of course, was an everyday occurrence.

Today, I find the refrigerator loaded to the hilt, but disorganized. Then, of course, I guess that depends on one's perspective. While I'm putting a menu together, I'm drinking out of an orange juice container.

"WHAT ARE YOU DOING?" Sheri screams.

At that moment, with my head tipped back sucking in the juice, I snap my head around in panic. Orange juice pours down my laundered shirt.

"Oh my God, Johnny... You're such a child," she said.

With a disgruntled look, she turns and walks out of the kitchen.

"Sharp-tongued," I mumble, right in front of *my* refrigerator.

The sharks are circling, and the theme music to Jaws is going through my head. After cleaning up the mess on the floor, I head to the bathroom to clean myself up. Having just changed into a new shirt, Sheri looks at me and giggles.

"What's with the giggle?"

"Your spilled orange juice reminds me of a joke my daddy told me when I was a little kid."

I stood there with my hands on my hips losing most of my bad thoughts waiting for her to tell Daddy's joke.

"What did the little chick say when its mother laid an orange?"

She eyed me with her cute little grin.

I gaze at her in bewilderment and shrug.

"Look at the orange marmalade," she said.

Turning on her heel, she giggles her way into the kitchen.

It was so stupid I had to chuckle, especially, at myself for getting so upset. Maybe we can make this work. Dressed in a new shirt and tie, and finding humor in my shark attack, I fix a great breakfast, well, at least for me.

THE TRAINING ROOM

Arriving at ATC sooner than expected, I cruise the production area and watch free enterprise at work. Spotting Jenny, I stop to chitchat for a while. A short time later, she nods toward the production clock showing seven forty-five. I thank Jenny for a nice conversation, then head toward the training room in high spirits—she's always good for a laugh.

Grabbing a cup of coffee, Ed approaches me with something on his mind...

"So, Johnny, how's the life of a bachelor?"

"Well," I said, "I met a new girl, her name is Sheri. She's gorgeous, intelligent, and most of all—she's hot for me."

"Well, that pretty well covers any further questions I may have."

I take a moment to mingle with the folks but cut it short; it's about time to begin the class.

While standing at the lectern collecting my thoughts, I surveyed the room. It was a full house: the company executives, department heads, process and industrial engineers, and a few senior employees.

At eight o'clock sharp, I said my good mornings...

THE NEXT LEVEL OF SYSTEM THINKING

"**W**ell, that was a pleasant good morning response, and much appreciated...

As you know, *Systems Modeling* is our topic this morning and one of the most essential sessions you'll attend. Our discussion is an overview in layman's terms of systems modeling and how it helps put systems thinking into practice, and provides a structure of how to approach changes in the system processes.

Generally speaking, system modeling combines process mapping and simulation that enhances your ability to understand the world of system thinking.

The simulation takes into consideration both space and time—or, if you will, a three-dimensional world spread out over time.

A *PROCESS MAPPING FLOWCHART* should be the first thing undertaken when doing a layout of the business system processes because they define the workflow. You'll need to collect detailed data while analyzing and recording the activity. More on that in a moment...

To give you an idea what a process map looks like, and to lighten up the idea of process mapping, I have prepared an oversimplified flowchart of my special French toast breakfast for my good friend Sheri...

First, though, drum roll, please..."

Chuckles sprout throughout the audience...

"Here it is on the screen for all to salivate owning to my delicious recipe ...

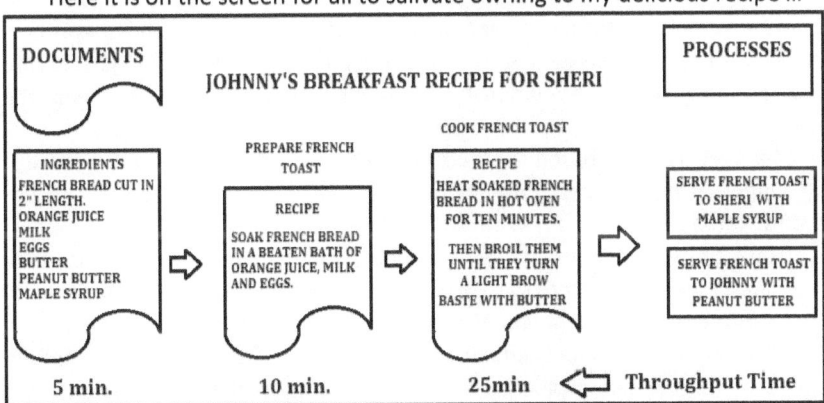

For those of you that have a hankering to try out my one of a kind delicious French toast recipe, I'd be happy to print out a copy for you after class..."

The audience reacted by smiling nodding heads and applauding.

Salley in the first row speaks up...

"Peanut butter on your French toast?

"As you might guess, there is a funny story attached to the peanut butter part of the recipe..."

"Let's hear it," Ed called out.

"Some other time, Ed. We have a lot to cover today..."

I pause to collect my thoughts, then continue...

"Process mapping is the first step in building the simulation model, so, as one may presume, it's critical that the mapping process represents an accurate depiction...

I've drawn the symbols for the recipe document and process with just two of a dozen or more of the different type of signs used for this purpose.

There is a large assortment of workflow software apps available, but when you're on the floor analyzing and mapping, it's best to sketch out the process first. More on that later during our discussion about redesigning and designing the system.

Oh, don't forget to add in the throughput time, similar to my illustration, it's an important element and can be rendered vertically or horizontally.

The simulation modeling program takes the workflow program results a step further by validating the mapping process. Whether you're designing a new process or revising a current one, your key concern should be an accurate interpretation of the process. This subject is also expanded on when covering the redesigning or designing a new system.

Simulation software with proper inputs is a sound way to model complex processes and predict performance...

Sophisticated simulation tools are now available in packaged software— Discrete, Monte Carlo, and Dynamic-based.

I'm recommending you use the Dynamic-based software due to its ability to support systems thinking theory, and capable of defining the operational behavior of systems processes. The new *language* of system thinking software allows you to model the relationships that cause delays and constraints in the system...

The best Dynamic-based software on the market is *isee's* software package by *iThink®*. It has a short learning curve of a day or so. However, to execute sophisticated processes, it may take awhile longer...

While the software is capable of modeling almost any process relationship, the user must understand the software's assumptions. This enables you to compare the results of simulations to the actual business performance.

Your system modeling will take a great deal of up-front time to go through your processes, but when completed, it should level off allowing moderate use.

I would add, you should consider assigning two engineers as your new project managers and *modelers*. This job is not only for the transformation process, but it's also full-time for a company of this size and growth potential— an indispensable task. During the transformation process, your decision-making is going to revolve around this information made available to you—making it a serious undertaking."

I notice Gary Eastwood gazing at me with his steel-blue eyes and lopsided smile. With a nod, Gary stands up, walks to the podium, hands me a slip of paper and then takes his seat.

After a quick read, a nod with a smile, I observe the audience...

"It looks like Mr. Eastwood wasted no time knowing our need to fill these positions... Will Randy and Lora, our ATC newbies, please stand up."

As they stand, you see that they were sitting together in the back of the room with their young, fresh faces looking like two little kids caught skipping their English class, and I take a moment to acknowledge them...

"Randy... Lora... I understand you two are fresh off the farm having graduated as systems engineering grads from Stanford. I'm under the impression you both wish to be the system process modeling program managers."

With the audience gazing at them, Randy and Lora blush while giving a positive head nod.

"Well, Mister Eastwood, your leader, handed me a note. It says you two have been chosen to be the new project managers for the system modeling program."

We applaud them as the newbies turn a brilliant red with happy grins, then high five each other.

"Well, congratulations Randy and Lora. It's always nice to have a face you can associate with when starting a new program...

Denny Chang is going to have Tony Gray, the Managing Director of Dynamic Systems come in and help us in our consultation with system thinking, and the *isee* modeling workshops...

He'll also be around during the early stages as you develop your simulation engine. Greg will report to Denny until Randy and Lora are up to speed.

Systems' thinking helps in our view of the world. Whenever you're mystified by the disconnected events of business dynamics, friends, world events, or even yourself, these actions make sense when viewed as patterns over time.

As humans, we're good at recognizing patterns. However, there are, at times, when no patterns materialize. This is when, for whatever reason, randomness comes into play—not often, but one needs to be aware of it. When understanding a pattern behavior and then seeing it misbehave, you can intervene and positively influence the events...

Before jumping into our next subject, do you have questions?

Ah... Nothing but happy faces and a few shrugs..."

SYSTEMS MODELING

"It's time we discuss the modeling process, except, we'll take baby steps as we learn about the modeling diagrams. Then, we'll cover the connection between system thinking and system modeling...

Noticing parts of a system is easy...

For instance, parts of a tree would be the roots, trunk, branches, and leaves. For the parts of a manufacturing system, or as system thinking folks would call them, *tangible things*, are what you'd see during a facility walk-through such as fixed assets that you'd find in the production area with a variety of machines and conveyors. Well, you get the concept.

Systems must have a flow of information through a form of *interconnections* for them to function...

Trees, For instance, have *chemical flows* that send signals to the *intangibles* from one part to another. For instance, with water retained in the tree, it sends a signal from the roots to the leaves to close their pores. Then on a hot day, leaves lose some of their water content and signal the twigs to contact the roots and have them send up more water. But when there has been very little rain and a long hot summer, the root water source is dehydrated leaving the tree deprived of its needs. The twigs soon break down and send high pitched sounds of thirst turning into a crescendo of distress as the day wears on—and here you thought trees were dumber than a stump..."

With a goofy grin, the audience releases joyful chuckles.

"For the manufacturing company, intangibles are non-physical like patents, goodwill, and so on. But beyond the non-physical, it's not that straightforward due to the human element—with the brain being an *intangible*. We may know the human brain is capable of sending the appropriate signal to execute an event, the problem, however, is how someone might *interpret* the signal. If taken wrongfully, this is where things can go amuck, causing uncertainty in the system's behavior.

So, if you're looking for a system intangible with reliability, HIRE A TREE..."

Then with my Jack Benny stance, I acknowledge the silliness or absurdity of such a remark, while watching the audience crack up. I pause just long enough for the audience to hear me speak when I see a hand rise...

"Yes, Norma."

"Thanks, Johnny. But first, I must say, you sure know how to keep our interest—"

The audience cuts in with applause...

I smile with a nod...

"My question is ... are system's *intangible* assets more important than *tangible* assets?"

"Good question. As you begin to understand relationships in the system world, you would soon learn the answer is no. They both interact, and each has their own role within the system... Thanks for asking, Norma."

Norma gestures with a nod.

"Sometimes the best way to understand how a system behaves is to watch it at work...

For instance, a manufacturing plant's inventory control sends out a signal that a part is needed to fill demand on the production floor. This action triggers the material planner or purchasing agent to respond with urgency. It may also require the production scheduler to consider rescheduling specific products.

The missing part may have been due to a one-time problem, a constraint in the system, an ill-trained employee, inventory error, overloaded production schedule, or perhaps a late shipment from a supplier.

The result of the missing part is no longer just an inventory problem—it affects the entire system behavior, and perchance their customers' system's behavior... Are there questions or comments?"

With a content audience, I continue...

STOCK

"Let's be moving on to the component parts of our system modeling program. We have what's called the *stock,* the foundation for systems. It's one of the tangible parts of the system. It contains things that you can count or measure.

Vinnie, what have we discussed that should match up to this description?" I said. "And Vinnie, if you get this wrong, you're going to wear the dunce cap for the rest of the day."

All eyes are on Vinnie.

"You're right, Johnny. If I'm wrong, I'll be happy to wear the dunce cap, but that won't happen. That's an easy question. The answer is the trunk of the tree holding the water. The trunk is the stock of the tree."

With my arms outstretched and upturned palms angled toward Vinnie, I applaud along with the rest of the audience and a mix of laughter.

"Goodman, Vinnie. He's correct—the trunk acts as a linear spring for the leaves... Let's move on to *Flow,* our next subject on our list of system parts."

FLOW

"Flows influence the rate of change in stock over time. Give me a moment, and I'll have an illustration of stock and flow on the screen that you'll find in the system modeling program...

As you can see, the valves represent the rate of flow coming in—ah, I see Lewis has a question," I said with a nod.

"Thanks, Johnny. Is that supposed to be a cloud, exhaust, or perhaps a cotton ball, and what does it mean?"

"You got it right the first time; it's a representation of a cloud. It may contain whatever the flow might be illustrating. It's also is a symbol of a starting point or ending—a to and fro so to speak."

I pause with my focus on Lewis...

"There is much more to the cloud, but I'll discuss that later in the session."

Lewis nods.

"Let's use our manufacturing company as a continuing example of inventory fluctuations such as inventory coming in and going out... In this case, the modeling *stock* would be where the inventory status is kept, and the stock levels can change due to the decrease or increase in flow rate...

As a rule, we monitor stocks to make decisions and to take appropriate action that raises or lowers the levels of stock to acceptable ranges. When grasping the dynamics of stocks and flows, you begin to understand the behavior of complex systems.

If I may use the term, *system thinkers* again, they use systems behavior graphs to understand trends over time. For instance, if you wanted to know the manufacturing system's limitation, we would measure the systems constraints over time. By using stock and flow as a representative of our system, it would allow our model to calculate the flow through the systems constraints...

Our theoretical company's main constraint is the test area of high-tech products. The mix of products can influence the rate of flow. However, if you had a real-time scheduling system such as *nMetric*, which many do not and should, would allow better use of the constraint...

Ed, we need to visit nMetric sometime next week. Okay?"

"I'm there for you, Johnny."

With a nod and a smile, I contemplate my next subject.

FEEDBACK LOOPS

"*F*eedback loops are the next subject in our system modeling discussion...

Not every system has a control unit, but for most, it's relatively common, with a few having a rather elegant design.

I'm going to start by discussing vertical organizational structures. They, too, are systems, albeit, not good ones. Nonetheless, they, too, have corrective feedback loops that show up when a problem appears. And when it does a well-meaning person removes what seems to be the obvious trouble, temporarily solving the interruption while allowing a steady-state of its environment to exist. Doing so, may give this person high praise and become an employee of the month."

A smiling and nodding response ripples through the class.

"However, later on, the problem reappears, calling for the same solution. Is there anyone who could give us a good example we might benefit from?"

I do an eye tour of the audience seeking an answer.

"Yes, Rita."

"Well, in a vertical organization, we are not in a system-thinking mode. So, I would imagine it would be like the brave little Dutch boy who stuck his thumb in the dike to save the country from destruction. He is then proclaimed a hero, and everybody relaxes with the assumption everything is under control. Except, in real life as well as in the author's fable, the dike continued to spring leaks throughout the dike. I believe we would call this a systemic event, and sooner or later destroy itself and the town..."

Finished, Rita relaxes back into her seat.

"Well done, Rita. I must say that was a creative and visual explanation of what happens when intervention takes place in a system environment. But, for vertical organizations, it's an accepted addiction...

What's even worse, if I may use a portion of an overused cliché—?

They keep doing the same thing over and over and expecting a different result."

Guffaw finds its way through the audience.

"Now that we understand why vertical organizations have trouble with the idea of feedback loops let's get on with the fundamentals of how they work. At one time, I had read a story about grain beetle's behavior. Hell, it could have been a fairytale for all I know, but it makes for an interesting story to help you digest the idea of how feedback loops work...

So, lady's and gent's, I give you the grain beetle...

A grain beetle will always migrate to the center of a silo's stored grain. Why is that...?

Well, the answer lies within Mister Grain Beetle's *heat-sensing* feedback loop. Consider it as a military heat-seeking missile navigating to its target.

It lets the beetle know in what direction to move when hunting down those yummy eggs, larvae, and pupae of the many species of grain insects...

These little fellows need the higher temperature to grow or incubate such as the Indian meal moth and yellow mealworm. One might say the grain beetle is the farmer's best friend, well, maybe not...

In case you were wondering how I picked grain beetles, I knew Vinnie would perk up and absorb this with great interest—right, Vinnie?"

"Yes, I now have it in-*grain*-ed into my little head," he said with a titter.

The audience responds with a cheerful chortle.

"So tell me Vinnie, is it as deeply *rooted* in you as your tree information?"

Vinnie and the audience crack up.

With a muted room, I continued...

"Feedback loops are able to control the stock to stay at specific levels by adjusting the flow both in and out as shown in my next illustration...

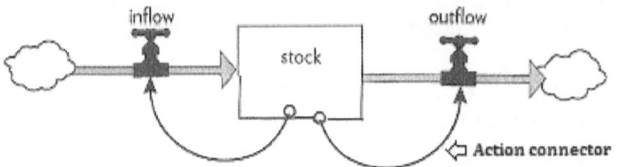

This is how a dam is designed by setting spillway crest heights that adjust flow rates in sluices and canals.

The stopcock is activated by the curved arrow shown as the ACTION CONNECTOR signaling either the inflow or outflow. Notice, I emphasized ACTION CONNECTOR. That term becomes essential as we get into an actual example of a model diagram...

You should consider this a quick introduction session, and not intended to make a model builder or system thinker out of you—well, at least not yet. With your introduction to subjects like economics, you can put what you've learned today to work.

For instance, contemplating the Fed's actions using one of its many tools to *theoretically* correct an economic problem—speculating that the economy we will call A must have influenced the Fed, we'll call B...

So, can A influence B, and can B influence A? ...Well yes, we know the *flow* of events goes forth and back between the Federal Reserve and the economy such as a rise in interest rates...

In your day-to-day job during the company's transformation, your new knowledge is going to give you a better understanding of how individuals within communities can be feedback loops...

For instance, when an engineer sees a design going in the wrong direction, he or she can illustrate the problem and put it back on track. Try to visualize the engineering community as the stock and the engineer as a feedback loop acting as the *action connector* within engineering correcting the design...

Who'd like to draw a diagram on the whiteboard showing this relationship of engineering and design?"

All at once the audience chants... "Vinnie... Vinnie..."

Vinnie stands, walks up to the whiteboard, bows, then drew a diagram.

"Damn, let me try that again."

A couple of minutes later, he stands back to admire his work...

"How's this one look?"

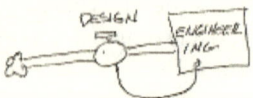

"Well folks, if that's correct, please applaud."

The audience greets Vinnie with mixed applause and joyful chuckles. With a puzzled look, Vinnie takes his seat.

"It looks like something isn't quite right. Anybody else, see the problem?"

"Yes, Ed."

"Vinnie forgot to put in the arrowhead leading into the stock, and he has a puny cloud," he said grinning at his friend Vinnie.

"The missing arrowhead is correct...

Let's thank Vinnie, for being a good sport."

Applause builds with smiling faces and then back into the quiet zone as I added the arrowhead and stock connection...

"Vinnie, your rendering wasn't perfect, but close enough."

SYSTEM MODELING

"Let's move on to system modeling...

But first, I need to show you a simplified model of a foundry system that Jake Jensen assembled as an illustration of the customer's software manual while developing the constraint scheduling software architecture used to control the throughput in an Oklahoma foundry...

It shows four process symbols using an old version of *iThink®* modeling software back in the mid-90s, and the descriptions I added in for clarification."

With my laptop, I selected the appropriate image and clicked.

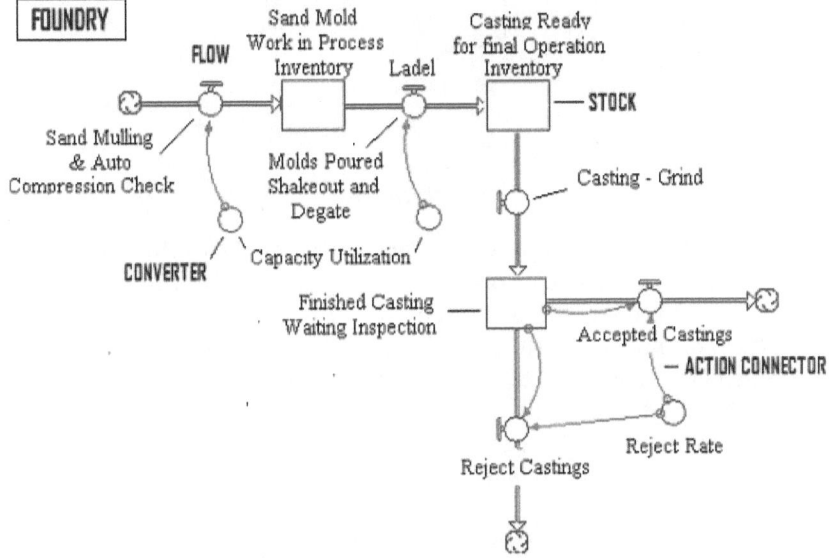

"Ah... An interesting diagram is it not? My first impression is what looked to be something out of LEONARDO DA VINCI'S sketchbook...."

Giddy cheerful laughter rolled through the audience.

"The intended mapping is not how to use the *isee* software, but to give you an idea of what the symbols and mapping look like, plus insight into the building block interactions of each.

Our illustration is a manufacturing process, but you can use the software for anything where there is a need to monitor flow...

For a manufacturing firm, business processes center on the flow of ORDERS, MATERIAL, SKILLED LABOR, MACHINERY, INFORMATION, AND MONEY.

The simulation and modeling process includes inputting the required data into a table to get output results displayed in graphs, tables, animation, Quick Time movies, and files..."

THE MODEL BUILDING BLOCKS

"To step through the four different building blocks, we're going to use the foundry image model of which we have already discussed three components to a degree—Stock, Inflow, and Outflow. But to refresh your mind, I will simplify their part in the process of model building...

We'll begin with the next illustration, the SAND MOLD FLOW diagram, a partial view of our previous foundry diagram..."

I clicked on the appropriate image, the SAND MOLD FLOW DIAGRAM...

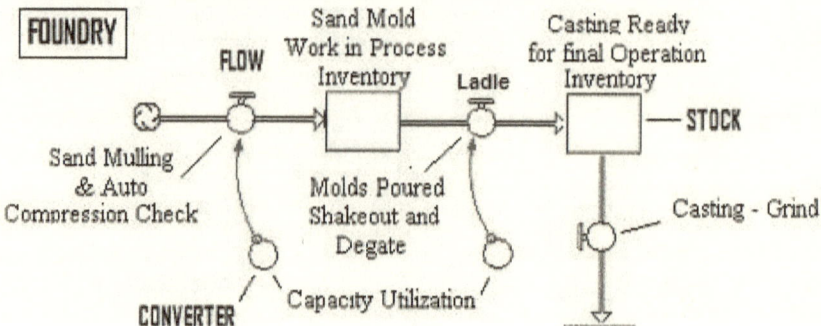

"There it is. Flow is shown with its label above the first valve. Its notation shows the sand mulling casting process—

Yes, Jimmy? You seem to be puzzled."

"Well, not exactly... Well, sort of, I was wondering what the heck sand mulling is that you just mentioned noted under the first flow cloud. Sorry to interrupt."

"That's okay, Jimmy. In my training, I flew with Jake to Oklahoma to see the operation first hand, along with a laptop to compare the actual event with model process...

Sand Mulling is not unlike preparing a pancake recipe. It's a machine where you pour special casting sand into a mixing machine. Then you add water as it mixes into a fluffy consistency. Then when it's under pressure, it feeds the molds with the mixture. ...That's it, Jimmy."

"Cool... Thanks, Johnny."

"You bet. Now on to the STOCK. It's the accumulator shown as a SQUARE, upper right in the diagram. It determines at any point in time, the available source of sand molds ready for the next step—pouring the mold. This action takes place at the valve showing LADLE—with the ACTION CONNECTOR communicating the number of ladles poured into the mold...

STOCKS and FLOWS are interdependent—OUTFLOWS *deplete* the STOCK while INFLOWS *replenish* it. When used together, STOCKS and FLOWS become the dynamic model building blocks.

The STOCKS INFLOW and OUTFLOW CONVERTERS are the two independent circles shown in the sand mold diagram as *capacity utilization*. Their relationship to FLOWS functions like a potentiometer—as it controls, changes, and regulates the FLOW volume—not unlike controlling the volume on your radio.

The CONVERTERS control capacity utilization. Their relationship to STOCKS acts as calculators, keeping track of the various STOCK'S capacity within the system—or the proportion of one STOCK relative to another—an important relationship controlling constraints and throughput. This is accomplished by accumulating the assorted OUTFLOWS over a period...

UP NEXT ON THE SCREEN IS A REJECT AND ACCEPTED RATE OF THE PRODUCT...

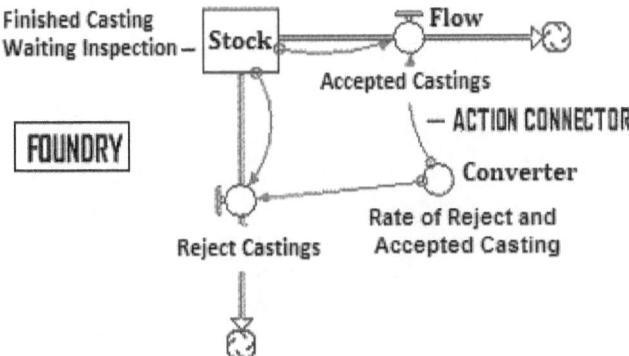

It has the CONVERTER, the noted circle calculating and communicating through the ACTION CONNECTORS the number of *accepted* and *rejected* casting.

ACTION CONNECTORS in the *Reject Rate Example* show lines of communication among STOCKS FLOWS, with the previously noted CONVERTERS illustrated in the SAND MOLD FLOW DIAGRAM...

So, when sensitive to your surroundings regarding STOCKS and FLOWS, you may ask yourself, why is the INFLOW accumulating? Where is it coming from? Moreover, where is it going...? Are there questions...?

No? Hmm... My enlightenment must be operating on all eight cylinders—that or I'm putting you to sleep..."

"Sleep, no way. You've turned a complex discussion into simple steps making it effortlessly digestible," Ed spoke out.

The class confirms this with smiling and applauding.

"That's good to hear. Thank you... Now, it's time to switch gears..."

SYSTEM THINKING'S RELATIONSHIP WITH SYSTEM MODELING

"In this part of our discussion, we will study system thinking's relationship to snapshots of the modeling program results...

When working with modeling programs, you'll need insight into how they relate to the real world. So, let's begin by discussing delays in a system—and why they are crucial to recognize, correct and simulate, before redesigning the system."

DELAYS

"We know about delays in our personal world such as expecting a movie from Netflix the next day. You can't wait—it played in the theaters but a few months ago, and you missed it. You rush to your mailbox expecting to find the little red envelope and discover it's not there—it's been delayed somewhere in the system. Delays are everywhere in all systems—each step is a potential delay. When modeling and the previous STOCK has a delay, it will create a delay for the next STOCK and the entire system.

Before there was just-in-time-manufacturing, Jake tells me they knew about delays, but they accepted it as a norm in the process of producing goods; therefore, they manufactured high-tech products in what they called *batch inventory*...

Production scheduling used what they called set-back times for each assembly starting from ship date. For instance, when using a goes into setback chart using a one-week setback for each subassembly, and with the last setback at eight weeks, you can see how the inventory grows exponentially. The result in this kind of scheduling produced an inventory turnover of something less than twice a year. That's a heavy burden to pay for delays. It also illustrates the system's *rigidity*.

Each assembly setback, *a* STOCK *for our purpose,* had its own FLOWS going in and going out. Now, they didn't deliberate in these terms but understood how it worked...

I'm now going to *expand* on a portion of a subject matter I had three weeks ago on OPEN-SYSTEM ARCHITECTURE...

Jake's friend, Wayne Coker, understood the burden this batch control process was having on his company and other high-tech companies' cash flows and reliable ship dates—all in the name of DELAYS...

Wayne was young enough that he carried no baggage from the old system. This left him with fresh ideas he shared with his young crew and his senior process engineer Ken Brown. Together, they developed the first JUST-IN-TIME MANUFACTURING for high-tech companies in the 1960s. With fast throughput and high inventory turnover, they were able to ship with precise delivery dates. Remember, the faster the throughput, the fewer delays, and that equals reliable ship dates.

However, new DELAYS surfaced, but they learned to deal with them as they came up. They knew intuitively, they had created a new system that was producing other potential DELAYS—but not as significant as before.

Remember, this period happened before the industry knew anything about system thinking and constraint theory that was still in the development stages in the 1950s and 70s. And Goldratt's theory of constraints wasn't known to us until the 1984 publication of the *Goal*... Had the engineers understood the concepts, their system would have had greater flexibility in the design— according to Jake Jensen.

Goldratt's theory stated that there is only one constraint in a system at any given time restricting the output of the entire system—with the remaining links becoming non-constraints.

When the main constraint no longer restraining throughput, the system runs better but not *substantially* stronger—because a new constraint just migrates to a different part of the system becoming the next weakest link..."

You might want to call CONSTRAINT THEORY a SYSTEM LAW—if there were no constraints, *systems could produce and grow with an infinite output...* Use your imagination for a moment, and contemplate what the world have looked like at the beginning of plant and animal life..."

The audience gets all giddy like shaking their head and chuckling.

I wait for a long moment before asking if they had questions before moving on.

"Yes, Danny."

"Not a question, but a comment...

It would seem Goldratt was a man ahead of his time with his ideas being similar to *system thinking* applied to production processes and flow through manufacturing systems, using *Constraint Theory*. I've read his publications, but never exposed to system thinking until now, therefore, I've not associated constraint theory with system thinking."

"You are right, Danny," I said. "I too felt the same way having read Goldratt's publications. Then later, learning about system thinking, I found the subject so fascinating, I absorbed everything I could get my hands on until I became comfortable with the topic. However, I'm still not qualified as one would call a *system thinker*...

Nevertheless, I know enough to teach those with little or no understanding and introduce them to the world of system thinking such as today with you folks. However, Denny Chang, our colleague will take over where I leave off..."

Okay, let's move on...

When discussing the amount of delay time, the subject needs to be relative to the elapsed time of a system. For instance, if you're discussing throughput of a product that takes several months, you needn't worry about delays measured in minutes. But if it's anything like the manufacturing throughput time of a cell phone, then a few minutes delay will get your attention.

As you may remember in a previous discussion, we had a problem crop up when moving an assembler from one assembly line to another causing a delay—that resulted in a behavioral problem and a delay for the whole system..."

I paused to take a quick glance around the room.

"So, what have we learned about delays?

David raises his hand.

"David, let's hear what's on your mind."

"Thanks, Johnny. Well, we know delays can cause a change in system behavior, and they must be relative to the stock and flow throughput time of the system. Well, that and there can only be one constraint at any given time limiting the system output, so, we should check for the next one when the original constraint is resolved."

"Excellent answer David. And, here Ed was telling me you slept through most of my discussions."

Ed sits there with a foolish grin on his face as he turns to toward David, then laughs along with the rest of the audience.

VISUAL DELAYS IN DIAGRAMS

"I'm now about to show you an example of a customer perception causal loop diagram that reflects the *iThink* stock and flow structure we'll soon be covering...

The causal loop and stock and flow discussion will center on poor customer perception due to delays in the system.

The causal loop illustration should be familiar to most of you. It's similar to the one displayed last Tuesday during our *System Thinking* session."

I clicked on the CUSTOMER PERCEPTION CAUSAL LOOP DIAGRAM

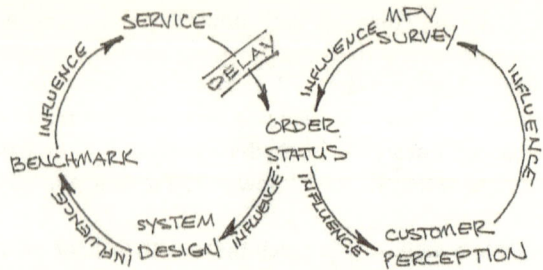

"I will give you a moment to review the causal loop diagram and consider how you would present it to the rest of us here today..."

The audience became uneasy with a few biting their nails.

Not to worry, it will be a random selection. The lucky one will get to take over for the moment and explain what the diagram is telling us..."

With moans coming from the audience, I wait for them to digest what the illustration is disclosing to us.

"Well now, I see a lot of moving lips, shrugs, and nervous twitching in your seats...

I'm ready if you're ready. With this wadded up piece of paper, I'm going to turn around and throw it over my shoulder. Whoever it hits first, wins the prize."

I turned and threw my random candidate selector high and hard over my shoulder. When turning around, we all chuckle seeing it land on Ed's head.

"Why is it always me? Now if that were a thousand dollars riding on that throw, it would be in the back row somewhere," Ed said shaking his head.

His moaning, of course, brought about joyful chuckles while David, his good friend, leans over to Ed...

"It couldn't happen to a nicer guy."

"That's okay everybody, I'll nail this one."

With Ed now standing behind the lectern, he narrows his eyes at me...

"I've got control of the class now, right?"

"You got it."

"Can I get others involved in the discussion?"

"Of course, you can."

"Okay... But before I get started," Ed said with an eye toward David. "Tell me, David, did Lea, your wife, deliver her baby yet?"

"She did, several days ago."

Applause comes from the audience.

David stands and takes a bow, but doesn't take his seat yet as Ed barks another quick question.

"Boy or girl?"

"I have no idea... I didn't check it out that close."

Everyone cracks up.

"WHAT?" David said. "I wanted a Great Dane, not a kid. But then, Lea told me I'd need to take care of the dog. But having found a middle ground, I told her she could have her kid, but she had to take care of it," David said with a straight face.

The slaphappy response came from the guys while the ladies shrieked. "Just kidding," David said with a giddy grin.

The audience had a good time hearing David's ridiculous story.

"Well, after acting as your straight guy, I'm going to ask you to be my answer guy...

First question... What's causing the customer's bad perception of the company's service, and what kind of feedback loop is the company receiving to acknowledge the problem. Oh, I would add, what tools are available to correct the customer's poor perception...?

We're waiting, David."

Now everybody has their eyes back on David as he looks at me...

"What the heck just happened here? My assumption was Ed had to explain this."

"In truth, David, his questions gets at the heart of how to explain what the causal loop diagram is displaying. Knowing the right question gets at the truth. And at times, the questions can be more intriguing than the answers... Try it..."

"See David, I'm not as dumb as I look."

"True," David said with a grin. "When I first laid eyes on you, I'd wondered if you could feed yourself."

The audience, of course, cracks up along with Ed.

"Okay, okay," David said holding up his arms to quiet the laughter.

"All right, Ed, please repeat those questions again?"

After Ed had finished, David continued...

"Well, first, I would say the MPV feedback loop of the company's service shows signs of poor performance. With our knowledge of system thinking and new system architecture, we can redesign the service area while testing it with our *isee* modeling program. The new design corrects the delay problem, so we raise the benchmark signifying the proper grade level necessary to climb above the three top competitors. The cycle continues until the feedback loop reaches a balancing point with their customer's high expectations.

Now, with that said, as I check out the diagram—what's the big deal? A child could've told us that."

"That's why I choose you, David," Ed said.

This set off another round of chortles as Ed continued to speak...

"Let's applaud David's great answer and being a good sport."

While the audience settles down, Ed takes his seat next to David and pats him on the back.

David smiles...

"With our causal loop diagram behind us, I bring up our next illustration...

"If you would, let's turn our attention to the *iThink*-modeling *diagram* STOCK AND FLOW STRUCTURE in the ORDER STATUS SYSTEM...

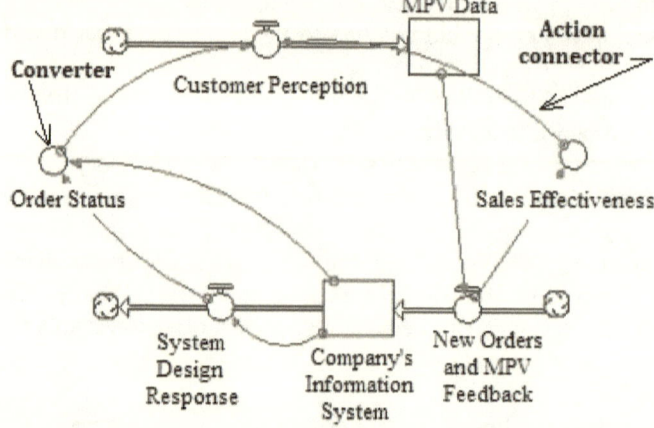

To simplify the diagram, the message concentrates on the customer's perception when initiating new orders, and their influence on the company's internal systems design...

If this were a full-blown diagram, the cloud to the left of the system design response flow might have been removed and replaced with a subsystem requiring a design change.

We know what STOCK and FLOW symbols are, but as a reminder, the little circles, the CONVERTERS, represent *Order Status* and *Sales Effectiveness*. They capture decision rules or perform the intermediate computation. The feedback loop ACTION CONNECTORS, represent information FLOWS connecting CONVERTERS with STOCKS.

As one can see after analyzing the diagram for a moment, the system is measuring the new orders and the effectiveness of the system design through the MPV feedback. If for instance, the customer criteria feedback loop registered a five, they would need a quick response to find and correct the DELAY coming from a constraint in the SERVICE SUBSYSTEM. The other possibility is a constraint in another subsystem supplying information to the service area causing the DELAY...

If slow in response or no action taken, it could cause deterioration in the sales force effectiveness and reduced orders booked—which would limit the growth of the business...

What I'm about to review is model simulation at a very high altitude, so you can get a whiff of an idea of the engine's capabilities, and nothing more.

To find the source of the problem and measure the effectiveness of a proposed change, we'd want to use model simulation. When simulating the system equations over time using assumed initial values for the system variables generates a dynamic behavior...

A validated model is to perform different analyses such as sensitivity analysis and what-if analysis to support decision-making for a course of action. In our case, this means designing a new system of flow through the service subsystem.

Well, we've covered the chief aspects of system dynamics, so let's move on to other forms of knowledge needed to better understand system thinking and the use of system modeling. We'll begin with *resilience* and its importance in system design..."

RESILIENCE

"When designing your new business system, you'll need to keep in mind what the system thinking folks call *resilience*...

There is a fine balance when designing fast throughput—with system resilience...

I see Sharon has a question."

"What do you mean by resilience in system design?"

"Resilience is the system's ability for a fast recovery in case of a mishap. For instance, the engineering crew has designed a new product with tight throughput requirements. After a final review, everything looked good in the model simulation—except; they overlooked a purchase part presenting them with demand and on-time delivery dependability...

So, I ask you, the audience, what other considerations were available to make the throughput design more efficient without adding another possible breakdown of the system?"

I study the audience for a moment...

"Yes, David?"

"Thanks, Johnny. The first thing, of course, would be a component review of the possible candidates that could cause a delivery problem...

Hmm... And after identifying the problem components, you'll need to keep additional stock on hand and remove it as a just-in-time item...

Next, I would find a substitute part, if possible, or a backup design that represented no delivery problems. I'm sure there are others, but that should do for a starter."

"Excellent, David. This is the perspective one should keep in mind when working at a fast pace while designing a new resilient system.

But wait, I believe Ed would like to squeeze a word in. Yes, Ed?"

"I'm wondering if wearing both suspenders and a belt could be considered a simple analogy of something resilient?" Ed said, arousing laughter.

"An interesting rationalization, Ed, but no, that would be redundancy...

Let's dig into system resilience a little deeper such as a real-life scenario of a system without the proper resilience in its design—the *Titanic*..."

I could see that the name *Titanic* had caught their attention. Everyone sat upright and still ready to absorb what I had to say...

"We know the spark that caused a fatal chain of events began when the ship hit the iceberg. It created numerous opening along a three hundred-foot span down its hull when the iceberg buckled the plates and popped the rivets—a collision of pure happenstance...

The big question, of course, what caused the collision, and why did it sink..."

I take a moment to heighten their interest...

I'll begin by saying the ship was on a course to avoid a large ice field with icebergs floating among them...

The collision was another matter...

Two ill-fated occurrences were the dominant unforgiving forces behind the chain events sinking the ship...

The first incident came about due to the unusual weather masking the tip of the berg from the experienced watchful eye of the look-out—until it became too late to stop the eventual string of events...

To avoid hitting the berg at their current speed and heading, they had less than five minutes to decelerate and change the course of a fifty-three thousand ton ship as they reversed its engines and turned the rudder.

The second mishap came about owing to the period technology of the sluggish rudder control. It took thirty slow agonizing seconds adding to their response time—when every punishing second added failure to the ship's ability to slide by the berg without grueling damage..."

Seeing the audience hanging onto every syllable of my story, I take a moment to handpick the appropriate words for such a heartbreaking ending...

"Think about this for a moment...

When you consider the *unsinkable Titanic* had mere seconds preventing the ship from slipping harmlessly by the iceberg, one would have to say *fate* had booked passage—taking fifteen hundred souls with it to Davey Jones locker..."

The audience gasped and shuddered, thinking of such a horrible tragedy.

I wait a few moments before going to our next event...

"Now, here is where resilience comes into play...

As for the Titanic's theoretical design being unsinkable, with watertight transverse bulkheads, it sadly received substantial holes running along the hull pouring water into the foremost forward six watertight compartments of the ship's sixteen compartments.

Adding to the problem, the bulkhead design was but two feet above the waterline and not connected to the upper deck allowing water to pour over the bulkhead of the remaining compartments causing the domino effect. Knowing the consequences of such a design, what was their motivation not to seal off each compartment baffles me...

A reasonable solution to the ships bulkhead resiliency would've have been watertight bulkheads connected to the main deck at various bouncy points along the length of the hull. This type of design would have kept the ship afloat long enough for a tow into a harbor.

The final design flaw came about when the hull could no longer keep the necessary integrity to hold together—and broke apart. As far as we know, this problem was not the designer's fault, considering they were at the edge of technology of steel shipbuilding. However, with today's shipbuilding knowledge, in all aspect of the Titanic's failed resilience design, the ship would have continued to sail to its nearest port...

Interestingly enough, most ships seldom sink from a single catastrophic incident. Like the Titanic, it's most often played out when one event leads to successions of similar events—until the infrastructure reaches its balancing point and collapses...

Are there questions before we start our next subject, *self-organization*?

Yes, Ed."

"Wow, your story took my breath away...

It was not only interesting, but it drives home the need for resilience in the design process. You can visualize the sequence of events and begin to understand the interconnection of the system design or lack of in the ship's demise." Ed said.

The class acknowledged Ed's words with nodding and applauding.

With an appreciative smile, I nod several times to the audience and Ed.

"Thank you. I must say that was my notion when Jake told me the story during my introduction to system thinking...

Well, it's time to move on to our next subject..."

SELF-ORGANIZATION AND SYSTEM MODELING

"System thinkers would say your company's transformation process is moving into what they would call self-organization. The idea encourages creativity and the freedom to experiment with new ideas while using system modeling. Modeling ensures that any new change enhances the total system consistently over time before altering the organizational processes or structure.

Without modeling capability, we could design a subsystem that looks great—and then after it runs for a while; a systemic failure may raise its unpleasant head, and perhaps, result in unfavorable consequences.

Natural systems, of course, don't need modeling capability; they must move through the evolutionary process as they go through the natural selection.

Along the way, they take on subtle changes—that may improve or over the course of time, they may disappear—

Whoops... It looks like Vinnie needs to sprint to the men's room, either that or has an urgent question—I'm not sure which..."

Vinnie and the audience let loose a cheerful laugh.

"Thank you, Johnny, for your consideration. My hotfooting to the John can wait, but not my question..."

I give Vinnie a nod and smile...

"What if the dinosaurs had known how to use dynamic system modeling programs, would they still be with us today?"

Guffaw fills the audience.

"Well, I must admit, that type of question never crossed my mind. I'm not sure why—it's such an academic stimulating question. Well, we should let you ponder on that one by yourself."

I wait for the silliness to filter out of the room...

"It's time we get back to system modeling...

Today, we can use the *isee* system modeling program and build a future horizontal organizational architecture. An organizational structure that allows employees to *orchestrate* their communities in subsystems while enhancing the total system, as opposed to *command and control* from the different parts of a vertical organization.

System modeling, however, is not the real world, but it is as close to it as we can be under our current understanding of system behavior.

The vertical organization is static, regimented, and too binding in design to take advantage of today's technology that leaves us with zero system resilience.

The horizontal systemic organization, on the contrary, has the creative ability to produce new processes and take on a certain amount of risk, while using technology to its advantage.

When using model simulation and a creative workforce in the new organization, it allows you to DESIGN in resilience, and REDESIGN on the fly while improving performance and perception in the market.

For some, the idea of self-organizational architecture can be damned scary stuff that threatens the power structure of the vertical organizational businesses of the world. However, they better get used to it, because it won't be long—and it will be knocking on their front door," I said with a grin.

The audience explodes with applauding smiling faces.

With a hushful audience, I continue...

"Our next subject is events and historical trends. We'll use the stock market owing to its many chart examples capable of showing trends over long periods...

Ed tells me his friend Gary loves the stock market. Is that right, Gary?"

"Love? I wouldn't say that's a word I would use," Gary said gleefully.

"Johnny, I don't believe *love* was the word I used in my conversion with you on the stock market the other day," Ed said with a chuckle.

I respond with my Rodney Dangerfield impression.

"Love. Hate. What do I know? I get no respect, just because I get the two words mixed up at times."

The audience cracks up with giddy laughter. And then with a settled audience, I continue...

"Let's move on now to our next subject..."

EVENTS AND HISTORICAL TRENDS

"A system structure defines system behavior which is a range of events and mannerisms created within the system...

Let's take a look at my next chart of a system and its mannerisms, the Dow Jones in all its glory...

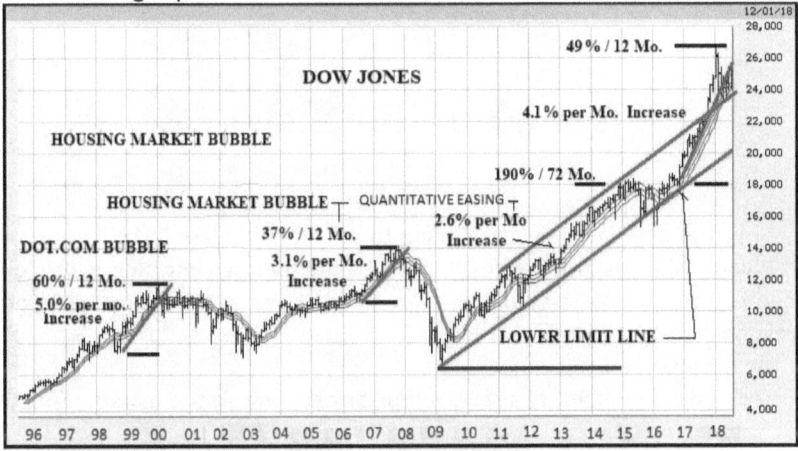

Complements of Big Charts of MarketWatch

When we review the historical trend of the Dow Jones Index, say from 2009 through 2018, this type of growth is an anomaly of events that has the public hyped up with great expectations of going on forever. This happened with the stock market during the twenties, which as you know, crashed and created the Great Depression...

The first two anomalies tried their best to keep going up, with the Internet Dot-com bubble crash ending 2001. The obvious indicator being the **five percent** monthly rally raise over the last **12 months**...

And then we had the housing market bubble crash ending in October 2007 with a **three-point-one percent** monthly rally increase over the last **12 months**. Both bubbles are at about a sixty-five-degree angle.

Now, we have had seventy-two months at **two-point-six** percent monthly rise owed to a Quantitative easing of four point five *trillion* dollars up through *October* of 2014. And then the Index continued to rise at **Four-point one percent** per month as the stock moved above the upper limit line in late 2017 with a **forty-nine percent** increase over the twelve-month period at about a seventy-degree angle... At this point, sometime within six to twelve months, the chances are good, it will begin to appear it's falling off the cliff, and eventually settle or have a dead cat bounce at or near the lower limit line... And then, if it falls further, we're looking at eighteen-thousand to sixteen-thousand before it begins to recover. In plain English, the system is running out of gas...

And now, we have the National Home Index showing we've been in Bubble number two for five years.

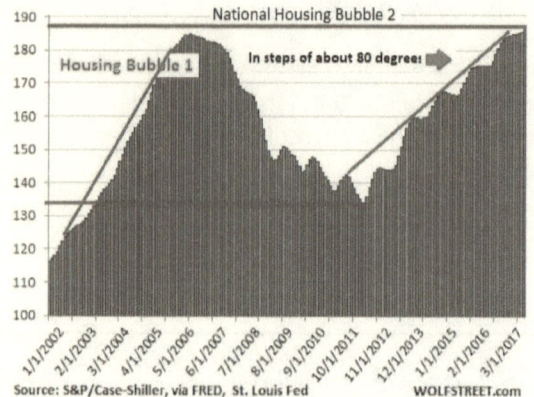

With the housing market beginning to take a fall in late 2018 and on into 2019 along with a slowing of GDP going below two percent, and with global economic headwinds raising their ugly head, I see a good possibility of a recession coming our way."

The audience lets out a moan...

"Let's take a moment to see how Wall Street controls the market using the next simple illustration....

With Wall Street's money, tools, knowledge, and the ability to sway the media of the stocks perceived behavior of current or future events—they can build mountains, valleys, or the lowlands to satisfy their insatiable driven avarice... With the new Dot.Com introduction, they shamefully created the ridicules Internet bubble using *any stock* ending with Dot Com and *negative* profits—the stock of the future where the sky was the limit. Well, that is until the crash in 2001. During the housing hype, ending in 2007, they had developed a new form of financial engineering that crippled the economy.

The stock market is but a system that Wall Street influences with one thing in mind—the well-being of Wall Street, whether it goes up or down while the small investors line Wall Street's pockets...

Our economy has benefited little from this last rise in the market, but Wall Street traders pulled in a record number of bonuses measurable in the tens of billions of dollars..."

"Well, it's time we leave our friends at Wall Street and back to something closer to home—the production line...

Let's say an assembly line is moving along well within its upper and lower control limits. Then along comes a do-gooder with the idea of removing one assembler from the production line to help in another area—thinking the others should be able to pick up the slack. Now, I ask you, with the assembly line short a person, what would the near term result be?"

I waited for an answer...

"It looks like Patty may have the answer... Patty," I said with a nod.

"Well, Johnny," she said rising from her seat, "I would assume that person changed the sequence of events of what was a smooth running line and changed the structural behavior, therefore, the results. Well, that and perhaps altering the systems scheduled output due to poor quality or quantity. And possibly, end up causing a poor performance perception by customers...

Hm... Now, if that person had understood what we are learning in these sessions, chances are this would never have happened...

Sorry, I don't often have much to say. However, we find these sessions so interesting that you and Jackie present us, we want to learn more and more—that's it," Patty said taking her seat.

We applaud her for an excellent answer...

"Thanks, Patty; I'd be unable to add to your well-spoken answer, well, other than to ask another question...

What happened to the assembly line as a subsystem, other than slowing down and creating quality problems? You may want to try and visualize back earlier in this session about the stock, flow, and feedback loops. Ed, I see you fidgeting in your seat, does that mean you have an answer?"

"Well, one thing is clear, I'm not playing poker with you, the way you can read people, mainly me," Ed said, bringing a few chuckles. "Well, Johnny, to answer your question, the production line sooner or later yields to the *balancing loop*... Right?"

While nodding, I gesture for him to continue.

"When using SPC charts, the assembly line over a given period would again operate at a level of consistency of acceptable quality, but at a lower output, therefore, becoming a constraint in the system."

"Excellent Ed, however, we would want to add that system thinking is more than events influencing behavior. Systems can surprise us when we get too fascinated with the events they generate. We must keep our minds open while digging for historical clues within the system's behavior from which events flow...

Hmm... I have one another question...

What have we left out of our discussion about the system modeling diagrams we've been studying? Come on now, think about it...

Is that Lewis chuckling?"

"Yeah, it's me. The answer has to be the *clouds*," Lewis said with a titter.

His remark brought about smiling faces and nods from the audience.

"That's right, *clouds* and *boundaries*..."

CLOUDS AND BOUNDARIES

"As you may remember, clouds represent the beginning and the end of flows. They are, for the moment, to simplify a subsystem under discussion that identifies the boundary for the system diagram. Rarely, though, do they mark a real boundary. Why is that...?

Nina, you appear ready to jump in with an answer."

"Thanks, Johnny. Well, having absorbed most everything you've covered so far, I would say there are no *true* boundaries. Systems are influenced by other systems, elements, or events," Nina voiced with finality.

"Nina is correct, of course. Our boundaries are knowledge or perception of the world around us. For most of us, when we take out the trash, our one perception is it will drop out of sight—someone else's problem—or in our case, hidden in a cloud...

The boundaries of business are straightforward. Where it gets complicated is when we're developing a modeling program of an entire system and its outer boundaries, no matter the software design...

And when it gets out of hand is when we're trying to perform accurate output of complex systems like our environment. These boundaries are so huge and requiring innumerable kinds of stocks and flows; they obscure the answers to the questions at hand. This makes it difficult to know the truth... And it's the *truth* we seek...

Okay, I see it's time for a break. We still have a few things to cover, so please be prompt, and we'll begin in fifteen minutes with the subject of limitations."

After taking a head break, I review my notes on limitations.

LIMITATIONS

"Thank you, it looks like everybody is refreshed and back in their seats."

I pause for a sip of water...

"Limitations of a system should be no surprise having often discussed this subject, but I'm going to put a little different spin on it this time around...

The most noteworthy input of a system's growth is the one with the greatest *limiting* ability to perform—that's the guy you need to keep your eye on...

In most of our discussions, we have referred to limitations as constraints within the system, which, of course, are feedback loops limiting the system capability. Constraints or limits can move from one location to another depending on events taking place within the system...

For instance, sales increase at a rate the system isn't geared for—a limiting factor. The major limiting factor might boil down to one critical machine holding up the flow of goods. Quality can be the limiting factor owing to unqualified or ill-trained employees in a fast-growth condition—not unlike the computer kit company we discussed in our previous session that imploded in on itself...

It's these layers of limitation that can sneak up on you and bite you in the ass, so to speak," I said playfully.

"It's important to understand no system is capable of perpetual growth—it's flat impossible...

Even if we're able to convince the businesses world how to extend productivity's life into the future, in the end, the lack of productivity growth hammers a death warrant on the door of economic expansion.

We must understand this and live within the limits we have surrounding us. If we choose not to accept this as truth, then, of course, the system will impose the truth upon us—and it'll not be a nice outcome...

Eventually, the working-class incomes will continue to shrink while driving down their buying power and bringing with it a decline in our standard of living. And this event will influence our companies' growth, forcing layoffs and further shrinking demand, and in the end causing the collapse of our economic system.

Ed, it looks as though you have something to say..."

"I do, thank you. Excuse my French, but that's scary shit you're talking about. Let's hope our company model will highlight our success and show other companies how it's done."

The audience responds with sober applause.

"I might note the Fed has now come around and sees productivity growth has slowed—with no sign that it will recover... Moreover, the FED has acknowledged that globally speaking—they see no possibility to reverse the trend, with it being beyond the FED's capability... For us, it's great news, the truth is out of the bag. "

I look over the audience with outstretched arms and a smile...

The audience begins to applaud with great enthusiasm and smiling faces...

REDESIGNING OR DESIGNING A NEW SYSTEM

"When considering a redesign or designing a new system, you need not build models with their equations to express your ideas or make circles of influence...

Ah... With most of you being of the computer age, I have to ask, is there anyone not familiar with the pencil and a sheet of blank paper?" I said gleefully.

Adding to my silliness, I hold up the two examples. The class has a good chortle as Vinnie, and a few others raise their hands.

"Hmm... Well, for some, this may be a little cumbersome, but you'll get the hang of it...

Please write or draw pictures, diagrams, and arrows showing connecting points using symbols that we discussed earlier in the meeting when we went over my recipe for pancakes... This will allow you to focus on the task and strikeout mistakes and uncertainties while giving you the flexibility needed to redesign or design a new system.

After feeling comfortable in your assumptions, share your thoughts and diagram with others urging them to develop their own perception of how it might work. Before long, with open minds, you'll see the truth—and when you do, you're ready to model your hypothesis.

However, keep in mind, if things are not what you theorize when seeing the computer model results, be flexible and ready to scrub these ideas and move on...

Unfortunately, due to PRIDE AND DENIAL, brushing aside ideas is seldom done in the scientific community, economists, business management, or with those who govern our society.

There are three things you need to keep in mind when designing a new system—we'll call them the rule of law...

AN *ACCURATE* FLOW OF GOODS, SERVICES, AND INFORMATION...

NO SYSTEM *DELAYS*...

AND FAST THROUGHPUT...

The result of how well these rules perform in the system can influence the reaction time of the feedback loops...

Are there questions, before moving on...?

Ah... No questions I see. Our next subject is language, a powerful tool for change..."

LANGUAGE IS THE POWER OF CHANGE

"We each perceive our own world through filters in our nervous system and our language...

Language is far more powerful if articulated well, rather than strategy, structure, or culture...

Hitler and FDR knew that to be true and could move a nation to mobilize itself—regrettably, one for the wrong reason, and the other for the good of mankind.

For those knowledgeable in the science of system thinking, one must remember that knowing something is half the equation in moving your thoughts into change. The other half verbalizes it in a way that people understand and respond to while keeping the language firm, meaningful, and truthful. If you need to invent a word to heighten your point of view or enrich your meaning, do so—the world of hip-hop does it," I said, arousing laughter.

"Well now, there are a few of us who are not so removed from what's happening."

Hmm... The audience could use a quick break, so I ramped myself up and sang a rap rhyme while making up the words and the right moves...

"Senor Spaghetti rides across the Serengeti chasing the Ninja Turtles wearing girdles..."

This, of course, brings the audience in clapping as I continue with...

"While Batman turned cheap and fat wearing flip flops looking for Cyclops on a magical mystery tour yelling okey dokey don't choke me..."

I have no idea, what I'm saying," I said laughingly.

However, the out-of-control audience drowned out my voice.

"You folks are too much," I yell.

"We're too much?" Ed said, bringing on more laughter...

"Sorry, I got carried away. But, it's your fault, you folks encouraged me..."

Along with the laughing, there were those few in the audience yelling out variations of, "Yeah, right, Johnny."

With a peaceful class, I continued...

"Well, it seems we've covered our subjects for today."

And then drawing out the word so, "So, with that, I'll finalize our thoughts on system thinking..."

SOME FINAL THOUGHTS

"One should always remember being *surprised* is part of our complex world demonstrating how little we know. This is true because we like to believe we're knowledgeable on many levels, and yet, much of the time, we come up with lame answers to a question...

For instance... It would seem, for whatever reason, it's difficult for most to say, I have no idea, but if you would like, let me check it out for you...

But, when you're unable to respond in this manner, it's apparently due to a lack of self-confidence or insecurity...

When one passes out the wrong answers, it only serves to push the effort of design in the wrong direction, complicating the struggle to keep things on track, either that or making the person appear foolish.

And now, you need to understand that system thinking by itself cannot bridge the gap of correcting the inadequacies of a vertical business organization...

Businesses need a design that can utilize and enhance the organizational architecture using system thinking—and that, of course, is why we are integrating system thinking into your new system architecture.

For us to go further into the modeling process now, would serve no purpose. This session's primary purpose is to show you the benefits and the basic process of model mapping and simulation...

And let's not forget, simulation-model forecasting depends on the quality of the data used during simulation, a subject Dakota Wells drove home during greenhouse-gas simulation problems. So keep in mind the implication of bad output when entering *accuracy* and *reasonableness*—and *never* use *linear assumptions* to prove a theory, when knowledgeable of the power of feedback loops...

That's it, everyone, our session is complete. Ah... However, I do have one other thing for Randy and Lora...

As soon as Denny is on board, work with him to purchase the *iThink®* simulation software along with the *iThink process improvement guide*, which includes a CD with process improvement *iThink* models...

After you both grasp the knowledge of mapping and simulation, you need to plan on having classes on the macro view of the modeling process. The classes should include officers, department heads, and the key people in the system processes. When the MPV survey results come in, you'll be ready to go.

You should expect the MPV results within several months. By then, you'll be knowledgeable about process performance in those areas deemed most critical...

That covers it, session over... But for you lucky ones wishing to have my French toast recipe, line up at the copy machine, and I'll hand out a copy..."

With an empty room, I gather my belongings, turn off the lights and amble out to my car.

JOHNNY AND TONI'S NIGHT OUT

On the way home, my excitement to see Sheri wanes with no idea what to do, knowing she has matrimony on her mind, even though, we've never talked about it. Instinctively, an old saying comes to mind...

I guess I could get married—happiness is not the only thing in life...

Well, on the other hand... *Everyone should get married at least once...*

Sheri is on another flight over the Pacific, so I'm going to take advantage of my free time. At home, I'll change into my workout clothes, drive over to Gold's Gym for a workout, and give Toni a call. Toni doesn't talk much, but when he does, you want to listen up.

Toni likened to the idea, so at seven o'clock sharp, I head south for a one-minute down the street to Toni's condo and pull up to the curb.

Ah... There he is talking to some guy in front of his residence. They both cast an eye over as Toni acknowledges me with a gesture and then refocused his attention back to the guy in a wheelchair. They seemed to have a strong common bond as they nod with little or no words done in whispers. A moment later, the man in the wheelchair gives him what looks to be a crisp salute. With a nod, Toni turns and walks toward the car...

As we head toward Wilshire Blvd, I asked Toni if that gentleman was a long-time friend.

"Yes, an honorable man."

With one short on words, I left it at that. Toni has eighteen years on me and has become my mentor and a good friend, having met him a few years ago through Jackie.

Toni wanted to try out a new restaurant he'd read about located upon twenty-fourth and Wilshire—they serve a great southwest cuisine. After dinner, we're planning on heading up to Hollywood to play pool and chew on some rum-soaked cigars at Hollywood Billiards.

Toni is comfortable with this wedge of silence sitting between us like an invisible shroud as we drive down Wilshire Boulevard. Pedestrians fill the sidewalks and crosswalks. The gas-guzzlers are like a never-ending stream of robots, taillights twinkling, and turn signals and brake lights flashing. It's the human race moving to the rhythm of the night.

It isn't long until we're having drinks at the bar waiting for our table. When observing the row of men sitting down from me, their silhouettes remind me of my mom's clothespins lined up on the clothesline.

With a need to break the silence, I ask Toni how he would deal with my current situation with Sheri.

Toni has no reaction other than continuing to gaze at the colorful array of booze bottles. After chugging his beer, he wiped his mouth with the back of his hand, then probed me with his steel blue glittered darkened eyes...

"Do I look like freakin' Doctor Phil McGraw?"

Then unconsciously, his lower lip has a sudden twitch as his eyes softened to a good-humored sparkle—meaning a possible grin.

I respond with a simper knowing he's more comfortable with silence.

After dinner and some coffee in hand, and knowing Toni was a graduate of the US Naval War College, I asked him...

"Tell me... What is it they teach at the Naval War College?"

Toni was silent for a long moment as he selected a few choice words...

"It's comparable to political science, except with a few Tomahawk missiles thrown in."

Johnny, *AKA* Sigmund Freud gets Toni to open up. Knowing not to push it, I told Toni I'd get the car. He nodded and headed toward the men's room.

Pulling up near the restaurant's front entrance, I see Toni heading my way on the run when I'm startled by the passenger right rear door opening, and an Asian thug points a gun at me. Then magically, he disappeared. Next, I hear a scream and a cracking bone, and then the gun hitting the sidewalk.

"Daddy's home, little boy."

Toni didn't mess around as he delivered a blow to the mastoid process behind the left ear, immobilizing him. Being unconscious, he laid him out on the concrete walk.

Having alighted him from my car, I watch Toni remove the thug's gang jacket and then his shoelaces to tie his wrists together behind his back. With the guy out cold, Toni slipped the jacket over his shoulders and zipped the jacket up a few inches from his neck with his arms tucked inside—it was then the carjacker lost control of his bladder.

Toni looks at me and asks if I'd give him a hand. He tells me we'll lift this mug up high enough to slide the top of the *No Parking sign* under the inside of his jacket, and then lower him down.

After finishing up, we stand back and appraise our work. The thug looks like he's hanging from a coat hanger with his feet dangling above the sidewalk.

Toni removes the attempted carjacker's belt and wraps it around the sign pole and the thug's torso and arms, cinching it up extra tight. After snatching the gun, he disassembled it and puts it in the thug's jacket pocket—it was safe there; now that he's in a straitjacket dangling in the air with a broken arm.

By this time, a small gathering forms—so, feeling inspired, I open my trunk and remove a black marker, tape, and a sheet of paper from my stationery supplies. With a marker in hand, I wrote...

I'M A CARJACKER CAUGHT BY SURPRISE, PLEASE DON'T CALL THE COPS, AND I'LL GIVE YOU A PRIZE... IF NOT, I'LL HANG HERE WANTING TO HOLLER WAITING FOR THE POLICE TO MAKE THEIR COLLAR...

DON'T TELL MY MOMMY I WET MY PANTS AND CALL TONI WHEN YOU GET A CHANCE...

CARJACKING THUG

I attached the message to the thug's chest with tape. Toni reads the message and nods his approval. We hear sirens as we pull out from the curb. A moment later and a block away, the black and white pulled into our previous spot.

Jerry Watkins steps out of his patrol car with a half-eaten cold burrito in his hand. He's a small compact man with thinning, dark hair, gleaming green, close-set eyes and a typical regulation mustache perched above his mouth—a fifteen-year veteran of the Santa Monica Police Department.

His overweight, forty-something partner is close behind him, trying to cram a double cheeseburger into his mouth.

With Jerry's perpetual puppet grin, not unlike Phil Mickelson's, he looks up at the thug hanging from the sign to read the message left on his chest. His perpetual grin turns into a joyful smile.

With a half-eaten burrito still in his right hand, he waves toward the crowd...

"Did you observe a big bad-ass Indian guy hang this perpetrator?"

They responded with nodding and laughter.

Jerry takes a bite out of the cold burrito while maintaining a perpetual grin, knowing it had to be their part-time defense instructor, Toni Nakni.

The news media soon arrived taking lots of pictures, video coverage, and notes. The next day, the *Santa Monica Daily Press* headline reads: *CARJACKER HUNG OUT TO DRY*... While mentioning the note attached to his jacket...

It was so popular, it became national news in the papers, the Internet and YouTube with the audience wondering who the big mystery bad-ass Indian was named Toni...

ACT II - SCENE 12
ENHANCING THE LEARNING PROCESS

Question: 1
How does mapping processes help when preparing a new system design in organizational architecture?

Question: 2
How does simulation help in the finalization of the mapping process?
And, what is the best software for simulation when designing with system thinking in mind?

Question: 3
What is the relationship between *stock* and *flow*?

Question: 4
Give an example of how feedback loops influence system performance?

Question: 5
What are the four different building blocks used in system modeling?
And, what are their relationships with each other?

Question: 6
How do *delays* influence the system?
And why is *resilience* relevant to system design?

Question: 7
What do *clouds* and *boundaries* have in common?

Question: 8
What do *limitations* and *constraints* have in common?
And, how do they influence the system?

ACT II SCENE 13
The Application of Product Overhead

WEEK 7 – WEDNESDAY MORNING ALTERNATIVES OF PRODUCT COSTING

JACKIE'S MORNING ROUTINE

When opening my eyes at five o'clock sharp in the morning, I am unlike most men and women keeping track of time using clocks and calendars. I've never used an alarm clock to wake up. I do, however, depend on a clock or watch for the exact time. My father taught me early in life that humans have many capabilities locked up in us we don't use today—the built-in clock is one of them.

I lay there for a moment listening to the sound of the surf coming in through the open window. My home is sandwiched between two narrow households on a strip of sand between the Pacific Coast Highway and the incoming surf. When I'm away while house-sitting for Jake, I miss the sanctuary of my home, but today is one of my off days from Jake's place.

My home's location is perfect for me, being born and raised in Santa Monica and not liking to be too far from my nest, and I'm close to Pepperdine University where I teach. When traveling, its location isn't far from the Los Angeles or Santa Monica airports. Regrettably, the Santa Monica Airport is being shut down in 2028. Its prewar history is where Douglas Aircraft produced all of its internal combustion piston-powered aircraft.

My father is wealthy and plugged in with the right people in government and business. Me, I'm an easygoing, laid-back person. Nevertheless, I have the same determination and drive that took my father out of poverty in South Africa.

After popping out of bed, I wash my face, dress in running shorts, tee-shirt, and raggedy ol' baseball cap, then head toward the kitchen—my favorite room in the house. I'm having Toni, Jake's good friend over for dinner tomorrow night. Toni lives down the road in Santa Monica and is your every-day bachelor. Being ex-military, he never had to fix a meal, so he eats out or orders it in. This morning, with a need for energy before my run, and knowing full well the theories whether you should eat before or after a long hard run, I do what my body tells me to do. With an early dinner last night, there was no way I'd run without replenishing my depleted energy source.

Someday, when taking my last dying breath, I hope to have a chocolate-malt mustache with my face falling into a large juicy burger. However, I'm not sure I want to go to heaven, because Friedrich Nietzsche said... *In heaven, all the interest people are missing.*

After a great breakfast, I'm on my way down to the compact sand near the waterline while smelling rain in the air. It's here where the sand is hard and damp with a flat surface that I begin my six-mile run, interlaced with six, sixty-meter sprints...

Being as one with nature, I purr along ten minutes into my run feeling the overburden moist breeze as I make tracks through the low-hanging clouds and ocean mist spray. My body seems to glide above the sand swimming in the water-laden air next to the roaring surf, putting me in a zone where one could go on forever and fly to the heavens. Jake calls runners like us, *zombie runners.*

Forty minutes after the start of my run, I jump into the shower—damn, no hot water. After leaving a message for my plumber, I slide into my new, cute little Shelby Cobra GT-500 Super Snake at six thirty-five. I wasted little time and woke up eight hundred fifty of her corralled ponies making them chomp at the bit and whinny—ready to stretch their legs. When the pure horsepower awakens, the sound sends a chill down my spine, and the adrenaline starts pumping—pure American brute force. This car leaves a poor carbon footprint, so to compensate, I promised not to cut my strip of grass running along the side of the house.

While pushing down on the heavy-duty clutch knowing this car leaves hard, I tried to be careful and not leave something behind—such as my differential. With a giggle, I shift into low and pull out onto the highway swiveling my head scanning for the California Highway Patrol and drop the hammer. As I speed-shift through six gears with my pony express, she leaves a contrail down the Pacific Coast Highway heading south while cutting a hole through the wind.

JACKIE'S MORNING AT ATC

An hour into my ride, my rumbling and thundering ponies gallop into the ATC parking lot. After dismounting my loyal Mustang, I head to the office and sign in with the receptionist. A moment later, I find Nina in her office where we have a pleasant coze for a few minutes, then head toward the training room.

It's nearing eight o'clock when I evaluate my health risk of having a third cup of coffee this morning. And yet, while pondering on that for a moment, I grab and fill up a large cup, and walk to the podium. When scanning the room, I see company officers, department heads, senior employees, and accounting types—having just met a few this morning. With an abundant amount of caffeine in my system, I said my good mornings.

"As you know, our topic this morning is about applying overhead in our business system. We'll be hearing a lot of accounting and financial jargon, therefore, demanding plain talk to keep the level of understanding at a place of digestibility. Anytime we get into the esoteric and mystical world of accounting, we try not to have a long session. If we do, it will require a two-part discussion, not wanting to repeat the long discussion we had on system modeling."

OVERHEAD AND ITS INFLUENCE ON BUSINESS PROFITABILITY

I take a moment to renew my thoughts while savoring another sip of my splendid Java.

"Historically speaking, by the 1920s business organizations began to use the standard cost system... And this led to standardization and a universally applicable system of accounting ensuring that the inventory accounts came from the general ledger. This change in accounting led to a simple method of pricing products, using direct labor standards and material standard cost along with an allocated ratio of manufacturing overhead times standard hours.

During the early twentieth-century, overhead was seldom over twenty percent of the overall cost. Companies at that time also had limited product lines which found the new cost accounting standardization an acceptable method of establishing product cost.

For those not familiar with the process, I will give you a simple example for a monthly period...

If the *manufacturing overhead* equaled two-hundred thousand dollars, and the direct expense was one-hundred thousand dollars, the ratio would be two to one. This ratio equates to an overhead rate of two hundred percent.

In other words, if an assembly put into inventory with a direct labor content of ten dollars, the overhead add-on would now bring the total value to thirty dollars, less material cost.

Questions...?"

The audience radiates contented faces.

"Okie-dokie, no takers, I see... With an exploding consumer demand after World War II, product unit cost lowered through process innovation and companies diversifying their product lines—shrinking the ratio of direct labor compared to indirect. Further shrinking labor contributions were labor-intensive products—that became fodder for outsourcing. The exception is discrete contract-manufacturers the recipient of those outsourced products.

Over the years, the ratio of manufacturing overhead to labor became a distorted way to price products. Today, the *Standard Cost* system used in accounting is no longer the *solution* as it was early in the twentieth century.

What I've said is old hat—nothing new here. However, there is more to the story, so we'll need to discuss alternatives. But first, I have a question for you...

Why is it essential to add overhead to products?"

I scan the room seeing hands in the air.

"Yes, Kathy?"

"Thank you, Jackie. Well, I'm aware of one reason—manufacturing overhead is a value-added process in producing the product; therefore, considered an asset in the inventory value."

"That's an excellent, answer, Kathy. It's the manufacturing system processes that add value to the product. That's why a business will elect to buy products priced less than they can produce them or have the technology they do not possess. In short, value-added processes differentiate one business from another...

Speaking of inventory value, overhead added to inventory value is on the positive side in a sense it meets GAAP rules. What is the negative side?"

I'm scanning for answers when a few hands surfaced.

"Yes, Fred?"

"When adding value to the inventory, profits are affected."

"That's right, Fred ... how so?"

"I was hoping you wouldn't ask me that, having read that somewhere."

Fred had a flush face as he let loose with a titter.

"That's okay, Fred. Can someone else answer the question of how inventory affects profit? Yes, Neil?"

"Well, I believe when the burdened labor overhead portion of the inventory increases, the income statement reflects the same amount."

With a long second of silence, he continues...

"So, when an inventory inflates above the previous standard inventory level, the expenses are reduced by the same amount creating a higher profit—does that sound right, Jackie?"

"You're right on, Neil. For those of you who don't speak with the evil mysterious tongue of accounting that Neil spoke," I said, "I will translate the evil into plain English..."

"First off, let's simplify debits and credits by saying *debits are negative* and *credits are positive*. If you add them together, they will *total zero*. One cancels out the other—it's that simple.

Namely, the indirect cost becomes a burdened ratio added to the cost buildup for costing and pricing purposes that follow the completed assembly or product into inventory. At that point, we've created an increase in inventory value—a positive theoretical asset.

The accounting system subtracts the burdened ratio amount allocated to inventory from the income statement, which is a *negative*. This lowers the expenses and influences a positive profit margin. When the inventory inflates with no increase in sales, profit margins can increase.

Conversely speaking, with the throughput improving, the inventory decreases, showing less profit during this period due to lower inventory levels adding the cost back in the financial statement.

However, the process will improve the cash flow and continue at this rate until the throughput and inventory match up. Do you dig?"

After seeing nodding cheerful folks, I continued...

"Okay... What have we learned from this discussion...?

Well... We know the inventory level increases due to the overhead added-value for products. We also recognize that inventory levels can manipulate the profit margin and that the Standard Cost system distorts the pricing process.

By knowing these essential accounting practices, how does that help us? Well, I can think of two things...

FIRST, knowing these practices tells us to reduce the excess work-in-process and finished goods inventory by streamlining and reducing the *throughput* time of products... And LASTLY, and most paramount, we must change the way we add overhead to product pricing...

Improving *throughput-time* not only solves the profit manipulation but also improves customer perception by faster response time, and on-time delivery. To help in that area, Johnny had a recent discussion for our need to acquire real-time software with Ed. How did that go, Ed?"

"Great. Johnny picked me up, and we went to visit an old friend of his, Chris Koski, president of *nMetric* that produces a real-time software application. She understands our need and has offered to come out here early next week to give a presentation to the process and industrial engineering folks...

The idea is to have process engineering deliver products into the workflow with fast throughput built into the design process as soon as possible."

"Sounds Great Ed... That leaves us with one more subject I'd like to discuss using the standard cost accounting method for *Make or Buy Decisions*.

MAKE-OR-BUY DECISIONS

"To begin our make or buy example, let's say you get a good quote from a power supply source in China—an assembly that you build in-house...

Now, give me a moment while I write the information the purchasing manager has given me on the whiteboard..."

Cost		
Labor	15.00	*Note: See below*
Material	15.00	
Mfg Overhead	40.00	
In-house cost	70.00	
Outsource cost	31.00	
Savings	39.0	

Includes payroll tatxes, unemployment insurance, social security and medical

"Please digest what I've written while I give you a long moment before asking my first question..."

My posture is poor as I stand with my chin resting on my upturned palm and gaze out at the audience—not unlike Johnny Carson. Seeing they are ready, I make a gesture and ask my first question...

"All those for outsourcing the power supply please raise your hands...

Well now, that's the lion's share of the audience. Okay, those who would not outsource the power supply please raise your hands...

For those of you that voted against outsourcing, who would like to tell me why you objected to the idea? Yes, Daniel."

"Ah... No answer yet, but a question. With that answered, I can give you my reason for the objection. Will manufacturing overhead have a reduction due to the outsourcing to show a net positive result for outsourcing?"

"Let's give Daniel a gold star. Great question... And the answer is no... In most cases, manufacturing-related overhead is a fixed cost. So, what's your reason for objection?"

"Well, if there is no cut back on any of the manufacturing overhead, how does that help the company cut expenses? It's just moving jobs to another state or country that ends up costing you an extra dollar, 31 versus 30."

"Daniel's right. Does everybody see his reasoning?" I said, encouraging applause for Daniel.

But first, let me explain... The financial statement will show a direct labor-saving until the next time you compute overhead at the fiscal year-end. At that point, the overhead ratio goes up due to less direct labor to absorb the overhead cost—increasing the overall product cost and inventory value offsetting any gains...

Not very attractive is it?"

The audience is stunned as they look around with sagging jaws.

"When you know what questions to ask, the answer will soon surface. However, there has been, and are now, many companies using the Standard Cost system in the decision process to outsource their labor. One would also see a *false reading* of improvement in their productivity due to the change in the labor to revenue ratio, therefore, encouraging a decision to purchase...

With that said, I trust we have eliminated standard cost as a way to price products and make-or-buy decisions...

So now what...?

Well, we'll want to check out the current alternatives. But first, I should mention we'll be discussing one in our next session developed by the Jake Jenson Group that we must cover before making any decisions.

Today's topic is a precursor giving you a leg up in the next session...

I'll begin with the idea that we add overhead to inventory because it's an added-value process, however, does it matter what vehicle or costing alternative we use? Well, of course not.

For instance, *Activity Based Costing* has been replacing the Standard Cost system in companies for some time. And there are other companies with a different approach as we walk through them..."

THE ACID TEST

"Before we start with alternatives for a costing application to overhead, I would like for you to consider my *acid test* question that narrows down the accounting alternative that best describes the *acid test*...

DOES THE OVERHEAD COSTING ALTERNATIVE ENABLE THE THROUGHPUT TIME TO INFLUENCE THE OVERHEAD CONTRIBUTION, THUS AFFECTING PRODUCT COSTING AND PROFIT MARGIN?"

Silence...

"Is there anyone the audience who has a better understanding of what I described as the acid test? If so, please take a stab at describing it in a way that might be a more digestible language or explanation of the acid test...

Hm... I see no stirring in the audience...

"Was my explanation that bad, or does the cat have everyone's tongue this morning, as my mom used to say?"

At last, a few of hands surface.

"Ah-ha, I see candidates emerge into the spotlight. How about you, Nancy, you've been quiet this morning?"

"Thanks, Jackie. I'll take the bait. Throughput time could be a consideration for an alternative measurement of the overhead application to inventory. If so... Ah... If so, it would influence the product cost and profit margin by product when dividing the total throughput time by the run quantity...

Am I close?" She said with a titter.

"That was brilliant, Nancy."

We reward her with applause. When the audience settles down, I continue...

"As I mentioned, this subject will give you a snapshot of our next session this coming Thursday—PRODUCT THROUGHPUT COSTING. I believe you'll find it an interesting and rewarding discussion.

Now, back to the costing alternatives..."

PRODUCT COSTING ALTERNATIVES

"When talking with Nina," I said gesturing toward her, "she showed great interest in this session. Evidently, you're using the Standard Cost system, and she understands the problem when using it, but until now, she has found no acceptable alternatives. I hope this session will help everyone with a better understanding of the various types of software to choose from—but there is only one that meets the acid test. I'll explain them in enough detail so that you can develop an image of the process and decide whether this meets your expectations...

We'll begin by addressing ACTIVITY-BASED COSTING or ABC as it called and promoted as a solution to the problems of labor-based allocation...

FIRST ALTERNATIVE - ACTIVITY-BASED COSTING

"ABC applies overhead by measuring the total time spent or the use of a resource activity for each of the various ones used when producing the product...

Each resource has a weighted standard cost. Add up all the standard cost resources for that product gives you the total cost...

For instance, if on average, a product uses thirty percent of an expensive resource available time—the time spent at that resource becomes the unit overhead cost when developing the cost build-up for that product...

As a case in point, one product might use more time at a big-ticket machine than other products—but assuming all products labor and material cost is similar, the expensive time at the machine would be the same for all products if not for the use of ACTIVITY-BASED COSTING.

From an accounting point of view, because of their training, the logic makes good sense. It's also a rather expensive accounting method because of its complex measurement system, and in a few cases, relative to one's perception of time spent in any given resource.

It's an improvement, but not the answer...

Why is that?

Let me begin by defining resources as people, machines, etcetera...

Now, much of the time there will be products burdened with a heavy overhead allocation because of their time spent at certain resources is greater than other products...

But why penalize a particular product routed to a high capital asset piece of machinery which sits idle for most of the month because of poor judgment in the acquisition...?

With this in mind, it brings up a key question for you to consider...

If the resource is not a constraint, what difference does it make?

I noticed this perked up the audience ears.

"Let's not forget, IT'S THE TOTAL SYSTEM THAT PRODUCES PRODUCTS, NOT SPECIFIC RESOURCES. THIS MEANS WE SHOULD FOCUS ON THE ELAPSED TIME IN THE TOTAL SYSTEM FOR MEASUREMENT—but more on that later...

There are three ways for ABC to define the time spent at a resource...

FIRST, one may make use of employee surveys and interviews that determine the result.

NEXT, would be the process engineer applying a standard runtime which would include setup time.

LASTLY and most often used are software-related using estimates or calculations how much time is spent on an activity or a resource.

Now, to me, this smells of the cost-accounting syndrome. Even with my doctorate in finance, I must say, only an accountant could dream up a solution like this—a detailed, complicated account of cost..."

I take out a moment to watch the audience have a few chortles at the expense of us accounting types.

"Now, for the ABC *acid test*—does the costing alternative enable the idea that throughput time influences the overhead contribution, thereby, affecting product costing, and profit margin?"

The audience responds in good humor, "Nooo..."

"Why is that not so? Ah... I see Nancy may have an answer."

"Well, when adding up all the necessary resources, you do achieve a presumed or calculated total throughput time. The problem is it's not an actual elapsed time of throughput."

"Great answer, Nancy...

I should mention, I believe General Motors uses ABC cost accounting methods to determine the overhead cost of giving them *what they think* is the true cost of their products. Good for them, but maybe, when they learn of our new PRODUCT THROUGHPUT COSTING = VALUE program, they'll reconsider...

Enough on ABC, so, let's move on to THROUGHPUT ACCOUNTING..."

SECOND ALTERNATIVE - THROUGHPUT ACCOUNTING

"THROUGHPUT ACCOUNTING was developed by Eliyahu Goldratt. It does, however, have a serious flaw for our use—it does not recognize cost."

Seeing a hand going ballistic in its attempt for recognition, I nod...

The young man that stood up looked as though he just graduated...

"Yes, Bill?"

"Who is this dude, Eli ... Goldratt?"

"Well, first, I have to say, we shouldn't be calling him dude."

The audience thought this was a delightful response displayed with a few chuckles.

"Doctor Goldratt was an Israeli physicist turned business consultant. He developed the science of throughput technology and wrote numerous books on the subject. Even today, there are many companies using his theory.

Jake Jensen is also a great admirer of his work. By the way, I should mention that Doctor Goldratt died in 2011. I'm sure the business community will miss his brilliant contribution to enriching our lives."

Bill responds with an apology... "Sorry about the *dude* part, Jackie."

With an acknowledged nod, I continue...

"We're going to discuss throughput accounting, known as TA, owing to its basic principles for consideration and the many companies that take this practice seriously. It's an alternative to cost accounting for measuring the system output, which is a relevant point...

Simply said, TA measures the relationship between three system-level dimensions: THROUGHPUT, INVESTMENT, and OPERATING EXPENSES. Let me give you an example of each of the three critical monetary variables:

THROUGHPUT measures net sales less total variable cost seen as raw material.

Namely, TA measures how effectively the system moves the investment value through the system and converts the results to a throughput value or revenue for the total system...

The INVESTMENT covers money invested in the system such as inventory, machinery, buildings and other assets and liabilities. Inventory does not include the allocated overhead cost. The process does not associate with inventory values, other than to lower work-in-process value through faster throughput...

OPERATING EXPENSES include all expenses except for the cost of raw materials. TA reasons that employees and equipment are fixed cost, not a variable—an important ingredient of TA theory. Therefore, the cost is an expression regarding value delivered, not efficiency...

With no overhead allocation to a specific product, it's not relative to individual product profitability but does a good job of focusing on production priority going through the system's constraints.

Most importantly, TA is an internal reporting tool, meaning the business still relies on the use of cost accounting application that passes GENERALLY ACCEPTED ACCOUNTING PRINCIPLES of applying overhead to products and inventory.

So, as an alternative, there is no value owing to its disassociation with cost and incapable of recognizing separate product profitability. TA is good for certain companies, but it won't work for us."

THIRD AND LAST ALTERNATIVE - LEAN ACCOUNTING

"Let's move on to LEAN ACCOUNTING, our last candidate for the acid test...

This process looks at manufacturing operations through the eyes of value streams, rather than by product. The value stream is the expenses a company incurs to design, engineer, sell, market, and ship a product—thus, disassociating itself from cost...

However, the value stream process has a serious problem when measuring individual product profitability, and doesn't recognize that the business system processes are value-added.

The basic process is much like Activity-Based Cost Accounting—being resource-based in measuring activity, and is akin to throughput accounting as it measures throughput, but through different value streams. Both disassociate cost as an attribute. This alternative does not meet the acid test, but not a bad thing, it's just not our cup of tea...

I'm now going to change direction ending our acid test subject for today and finish up with a preamble discussion on TARGET COSTING AND PRICING."

TARGET COSTING AND PRICING

"The development for NON-TARGET PRICING is where *cost results* come from *the actual design process*, rather than using the cost to *influencing the design*.

For instance, NON-TARGET PRICING begins by designing the product and then work up a price by allocating labor, material, total overhead, and profit—which will define the selling price.

Factors that influence TARGET PRICING include current market share, market awareness, and the competitive price response.

To calculate TARGET COST, subtract the standard profit margin and total overhead contribution, based on the TARGET MPV throughput time, from the TARGET PRICE. What's left is the total value of direct costs, for which the design group can assign both direct labor and material. The three values must total the new target price.

But not to fret, the TARGET PRICE is a separate discussion we'll cover in our next session.

If the company is unable or cannot conform to TARGET COSTING, it will not pass the acid test. The TARGET PRICE is the correct process because it's market-driven.

Well, it would seem that closes out our session for today. Questions before we call it a day...?

What, no questions...?

Okay, let's meet tomorrow at one-fifteen, and we'll finish up with PRODUCT THROUGHPUT COSTING. Thanks for the great interaction, see you tomorrow."

After chitchatting with Nina for a short moment, I head out to my car. I'm having lunch with my friend Brooks at one o'clock at Gladstone's—where Sunset Boulevard dead-ends into the Pacific Coast Highway...

LUNCHING WITH THE STARS

I arrived twenty minutes early, so I take a refreshing break in the ladies room. When walking back to the reception area, I'm met by an attentive young lady with a pleasant smile. With a menu in hand, she escorts me to a booth overlooking the surf. While waiting for Brooks to arrive, I order a Corona beer and nurse the brewski along—Toni tells me pacing is everything.

The next thing I know, a tall stranger sits down across from me with a whale of a smile while slapping down a binder full of paper labeled with *Kill Bill Three*—this gets my attention.

Wasting little time he looks me in the eyes and launched into his quick way of speaking...

"Hi, Halle, nice to meet you..."

Unexpectedly, his hand shoots across the table to shake *Halle Berry's* hand.

I make an automatic handshake response.

"I'm—" I said unable to continue.

Like a machinegun, the stranger sprays me with bullets of words as I try my best to slip a single syllable in sideways. About ready to try again, he fires back up with his arms moving non-stop gesticulating with a pleasing, but elegant coordination emphasizing his speech.

We know that sign language is beneficial for the deaf—but evidently critical for Quentin—owing to his Italian side of creative juices trying to help paint what he's conveying to you.

Having realized what's going on—and with whom I'm speaking, Quentin Tarantino continues to rattle on as I reach for what must be a movie script and go through it.

While Quentin sucks in additional oxygen, I spend a moment glancing through a few pages and then gauging from his writing, I observe him with a frown...

"Is this a novel? It's written with such detail in what is going through a character's mind like in a novel, as opposed to a screenplay letting the visual screen and dialogue take its place."

"Yeah, I get that a lot," he said. "Somehow while writing a script; my hand guides me and ends up in a novel format. I'm not for the most part fond of movie script-style writing. When I'm finished, and it's ready for production, I adapt my writing to a manner more suitable for shooting a movie—sometimes on the same day."

"That's fascinating—"

Cut off again, having narrowly escaped a release of the giggles, I am now under the assumption one needs to be more assertive here.

"I've written in a great villainous action part that you will love. You become Uma Thurman's nemesis—and, if I may say, you're looking very fit. You'll be great."

With that said Quentin grabs the binder from me, looks for and finds a specific page, turns the binder around and shoves it back...

"Here," he points. "Read this to me. It's one of my favorite lines. I'd love to hear someone else say the line, especially, you."

My giggle almost surfaced, but what the heck—I'm a showgirl at heart. After reading the character's part a few times to myself, and with my best intentions, I read the dialogue back to him...

"That's it. That's it. I knew you'd be perfect for this part. Intellectually, you and Uma will get along well..."

As Quentin continues to shift his arms about, I look up to see Halle Berry approach our table with a wide smile.

"Hi, Jackie, Halle said with a dazzling smile.

"You remembered," I said with great delight.

"How could I have ever forgotten my twin sister," Halle said.

"It's good to see you again, Halle," I said. "Halle, I don't believe you've met Mr. Tarantino.

We both can't help ourselves and have a great laugh as Tarantino looks over at me and up at Halle several times. His eyebrows shoot up into his forehead, his jaw levitates several inches above the table, and he's unable to speak a single word—hard to believe, I know.

Quentin jumps up and shakes Halle's hand. A moment later and looking puzzled, he stares at me.

I extend my hand...

"I'm Jackie O'."

I stood up and gestured Halle to slide in first.

Tarantino takes the cue and scoots back into the booth. A moment later, like Muhammad Ali, Quentin delivers a flurry of apologies like punches to Sonny Listen's head.

And then, unexpectedly, there is silence. Curious, I gaze over at Quentin and see him looking over my shoulder with sparkling eyes and a shit-eating grin. That could only mean one thing—Brooks has arrived—at six foot one; she is a drop-dead gorgeous blonde surfer.

I cranked my neck around for a glimpse of my friend, then moved out of the both to give her a hug and kiss...

"Woodie, this is Halle Berry and Quentin Tarantino. Guy's, this is Brooks, my longtime friend.

As Brooks slips in next to Quentin, the attraction becomes most apparent. Halle and I sit back and look at each other with a grin while Quentin takes a silent look at Brooks...

"Woodie? Did I hear your friend call you ... Woodie?"

"Yes, that's my surfing handle," Brooks said, with a giggle, looking into Quentin's eyes.

"Your ... surfing handle?"

With both eyebrows fully cocked, he turns an eye toward me with a devilish smile creeping out at the corner of his mouth with one eye narrowed more than the other.

Quentin is grasping for an answer, I give him a shrug and then give it a try...

"I'm not sure if it's because of her restored Ford woody station wagon or a mystical name the surfer dudes gave her."

"It's obvious that the surfer dudes got it right—mystical she is."

With excitement showing like a glow stick—Quentin settles his eyes on Brooks.

She responds by giving him her sizzling, sensuous look. Leaning closer, her back-lit green eyes grow wide, and with her seductive smile, she places her hand on his forearm, and then delivered her sexy Marlin Monroe impression...

"I'll bet you've had a lot of girlfriends ... big guy."

Quentin doesn't know it yet, but she's captured him—as he reacts nervously licking his lips.

"Yeah ... you got that right," Quentin said. "The only problem is... They won't ever give me a chance for a second date."

What a guy—everyone has a great laugh.

ACT II - SCENE 13
ENHANCING THE LEARNING PROCESS

Question 1
What questions should one ask before considering the idea of moving an assembly or component for outsourcing?
Give an example.

Question 2
Why doesn't *ABC* accounting meet the acid test?

Question 3
What are the two major things that make *Throughput Accounting* (*TA*) a problem with GAAP rules? Explain.

Question 4
How does *Lean Accounting* resemble both *ABC* and *TA* in its design?

Question 5
What is the most significant aspect of *Target Costing*?

Question 6
You may not of learned much from Lunching with the Stars, but hopefully, you had a few good laughs to lighten the load while advancing your knowledge in new business theory...
However, if you're wondering why they call Brooks Woodie, it's because...
Well, give it a shot...

ACT II SCENE 14
The Application of Product Overhead

WEEK 7 – THURSDAY, JACKIE, DISCUSSES PRODUCT THROUGHPUT COSTING = VALUE

AWESOME BURGERS AND BEAVER PELTS

By ten-thirty, I had finished up at the University giving me time for an early lunch before heading to my one o'clock meeting at ATC.

Taking the coast highway toward Santa Monica, I pull off Lincoln Boulevard into a small parking lot next to Mother Chucker's little community restaurant that serves awesome burgers. One shouldn't ever tire of a good burger.

When entering the restaurant, *Mellow Yellow* is playing in the background. Donovan recorded the record in 66'. As a kid, we used to say *if it's yellow, it's mellow; if it's brown, flush it down*. This ideation brings with it a titter while scanning the room. The place reminds me of a sixties commune with quilted blankets on the wall, colored beads hanging from the doorways, potted plants, and purple tablecloths—made from bedsheets, perhaps.

A pleasant, elderly, free-thinking hippie lady with stringy gray hair down to her waist seats me at a table near the window and a large tomato plant. Her saggy, banana-like boobs show through her psychedelic sleeveless-tee-shirt, worn thin over time. A faded stenciling on the back reads *A WOMEN'S PLACE IS IN THE HOUSE... AND SENATE*, which perhaps makes her an early feminist. Her eyes seemed to match the various colors of her tee-shirt—well, they do. She has long thick, dark hair under her arms pits that matches the hair on her legs. Hmmm... I do believe this must be the same hairy-legged waitress Johnny mentioned, but he assumed she must've been wearing beaver pelts on her legs.

Ms. Pleasant Lady smiles at me with her mellow-yellow stained teeth glistening in the sunlight waiting for me to take my order. While going through the menu, I am like a little girl deciding which Christmas gift to open first. I'm salivating as I point to the menu and order a huge ninety percent fat-free juicy burger and a Caesar salad. Oh, I mustn't forget my hippy-hippy *organic* banana shake—probably sprinkled with organic hashish…

Some would say I eat like the *Tasmanian devil*, a cartoon character in Loony Tunes—what a silly thought…

Nonetheless, I'm out of Burger Heaven in short order. While walking to my car, I rub my taut belly with a satisfying smile which always occurs during and after eating. Feeling a high after my organic shake, I corralled my ponies and head them south on the freeway.

THE TRAINING ROOM

I'm the first one to arrive in the training room, even after a stop in the restroom—just checking my eyeliner, of course, what little I use. As the folks filter in, I'm saying my hellos and sipping my coffee as we jaw about what we eat for lunch. Most of the women were bugged-eyed or rolled their eyes at me when hearing about my lunch at Mother Chuckers for a quick burger…

At the lectern, I review my notes in silence while waiting for the audience to settle in, then say my good afternoon spiel and receive a nice response…

"Yesterday, we covered such topics as Standard Cost… Activity-Based Costing… Throughput Accounting… Lean-Accounting, and to a degree, Target Costing… Now, with me being an educator, I must ask you, what did we discover about these accounting terms?

Yes, Nancy?"

"Thanks, Jackie. I believe it was our first clue that these different applications had no relevance when it came to the idea that throughput time influenced the overhead contribution—which affects product costing and profit margin."

"That was excellent, Nancy, thank you."

She responds unconsciously with a gleeful open mouth mumbled titter.

"That leaves us with a need for an enabler that will allow us to add the overhead in a way that meets the acid test. This means it's time to examine the Jake Jensen Group Accounting Theory, aptly named—*PRODUCT THROUGHPUT COSTING*…

Hmm… You know, Nelson Mandela once said…

I believe where you stand, depends upon where you sit."

I wait a moment as I watch the audience absorb that thought…

"So, when I say *PRODUCT THROUGHPUT COSTING = VALUE* is aptly named, I'm wondering where Eli Goldratt would've of sat had he heard the word *costing* being associated with *Product Throughput?*"

With a lazy grin, I notice a few who understood the association has a gleeful chuckle.

"For those who of you didn't catch my meaning, Doctor Goldratt may have felt more comfortable if the word *COST*, were disassociated from the business community and shot into outer space."

The audience nods understandingly and smiles along with a few chuckles.

THROUGHPUT COSTING MEETS THE ACID TEST

"Not unlike Throughput Accounting and Lean Accounting, the aim is to focus on the fastest possible product throughput or elapsed time. Unlike Throughput and Lean Accounting practices, THROUGHPUT COSTING considers the system processes a value-added part of the total cost of businesses...

Because we live in a GAAP world, we must continue to move manufacturing overhead into inventory, enabling profitability outcome by product.

The great thing about PRODUCT THROUGHPUT COSTING = VALUE is the ability to focuses on throughput as Throughput Accounting, and Lean Accounting does...

THROUGHPUT COSTING'S additional upside is there's little change in the Standard Accounting process—that and no change in the cost roll-up for product costing. I would also note there is a short learning curve in the changeover process...

THROUGHPUT COSTING is the best of both worlds, with cost still measured, but differently... If I may, I would like to take a sidebar here for a moment to discuss engineered labor standards...

DEVELOPING PRODUCT LABOR STANDARDS USING PROCESS CAPABILITY

"What's important to remember about engineered labor standards is that when measuring them, the method has no real relevance in product-process output-performance...

When product labor standards need evaluation, Control charts provide us with their ability to *measure process capability* by product or part number.

When the process is producing both *stability* and *capability* is the best time to measure labor cost, resulting in a computed average unit output over time. Because of unseen variables, the use of engineering labor standards has little relationship to the actual process time."

a fluttering hand begins to rise in the audience.

"It looks as though, I've raised a question headed my way...

David, what a surprise... For a guy who heads up marketing and sales, you have certainly been a wallflower."

"Thanks, Jackie—I think," David said. "I try to keep a low profile, so I don't show my ignorance in these new areas of business theory. Anyhow, how do you measure the *stability* and... What was it?"

"*Capability*," I said.

"Oh, that's right ... capability."

"David, to help answer that question, I'll need to draw a simple control chart up on the whiteboard. And for our purpose, an *attribute control chart* would be the chart of choice. It's the simplest form of control charts. It measures quality as either *good* or *bad*... Please excuse my back while I work up the drawing."

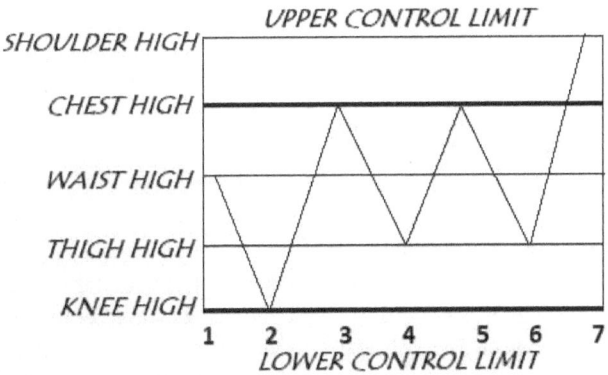

After finishing, I turn around and take a deep breath...

"David, have you ever played catch as a kid? Or for that matter, do you play catch now with your kids or a bud?"

"Yes, on both counts."

"Good. For our example, I'm using a good or bad measurement in a baseball strike zone chart. Anything in the strike zone as noted in my drawing you can consider *good*. This idea will help you understand what I'm about to discuss. It's also an oversimplification of how to use the chart, but it should get my point across. Variable control charts used for most of our process measurements could complicate matters for this discussion. Well, David, I'm going to assume that you're an accomplished player where most of your throws and those of your partner will be inclined to hit in the strike zone."

"Not if David is throwing them," David's friend, Ed points out.

Ed's mischievous expression allowed everybody a good boff.

"Well, before we give in to Ed's *pitch* about his friend, David—no pun intended—"

A few chuckles drift through the audience.

"I was about to say, the ball should stay in the strike zone when throwing it in a relaxed pitch environment between friends. Well, at least until you tire of fatigue... In Act One of our make-believe world, both David and his partner do a good job of throwing the ball within their *capability*—with capability, being the key word here. However, no two throws will be alike. There will be an inherent variation as you increase or lower the speed of the ball but within predictable limits or *stability* of the throwing process..."

Up to this point, there is no outside influence as you throw the ball to one another. This condition would reflect numbers one through six on the control chart... In Act Two, however, let's say as a kid, you're throwing a ball around with your father trying to stay in the strike zone. Unexpectedly, your mom opens the kitchen door and calls you and your father in for dinner. When hearing her call, you turn your head as you throw the ball. The ball goes flying over your father's head. We call this an *outside influence*. That's number seven on the chart."

"No... This is where David cries," Ed said, looking at his friend with a grin.

Maybe it was Ed's look, but the audience and I crack up. Even David chortled.

"You're too much, Ed."

"Sorry. That's it; you'll hear no more from me the rest of the day."

The audience has a slaphappy time with Ed's response turning Ed's face beet red.

I take a moment for the dust to settle before continuing...

"You can measure production processes in this same manner using control charts over any specific period of time. When using trained employees with the appropriate tooling, and no outside influence, the parts or assemblies become producible within an acceptable margin of elapsed time and quality...

This process results in accurate labor hours for costing products and evaluating direct labor, which puts the emphasis on controlling the process during the operational steps in the workflow...

But when we keep track of engineered labor variance reports after the fact using a standard cost system, this helps you how?" I said with a devilish grin...

"Yes, Ed. I'm sure you'll give us a colorful answer."

"You bet, Jackie. The variance reports help you by *sucking* up lots of time chasing your tail to find out what caused the variance—which, of course, you can do nothing about after the fact. Even if you could determine what the hell caused the problem, how does that help improve the system performance?"

"Okay, Ed, evidently, you've had trouble with this process for much of your career in manufacturing, and you in all likelihood knew that something was amiss in this time-consuming task?"

"You got that right, Jackie."

"No surprise here, knowing of your experience... Products using engineered standards will no longer need variance reports measuring manufacturing product process performance. Why? ... Because our only concern now is *process capability*—meaning it's the total process that needs measuring—not the product...

Moreover, measuring manufacturing processes is not an accounting function—implicating labor variance reports have no relevance, as Ed so colorfully pointed out...

Well, that's not altogether true. There is a need for tracking total labor variance at the macro level, but I'll cover that later...

For now, we are moving on to another subject—one where I've set up three different scenario tables to show you. The purpose is to display how product throughput hours enable the distribution of overhead contribution and the resulting profits."

PRODUCT THROUGHPUT COSTING = VALUE

"I'll begin with a reminder about *Activity-Based Costing* due to its popularity in the manufacturing world where I noted General Motors interest earlier. ABC uses the product's assigned cost for each step during manufacturing, resulting in the total cost build-up.

PRODUCT THROUGHPUT COSTING = VALUE looks at only one resource, and that's the total system, not individual events or theoretical constraints within the system that need dealing with individually—and those are separate issues...

The *truth* about product costing is how long the product is in the system—and time is critical, the longer a product is in the system, the more it ties up the system resources... Now, with that rationalization in mind, show me the hands who would like to give us comparisons of service industry companies concerned with time in the system?

Nancy, you appear as though you're hankering for a stab at it?"

"Yes. A hankering I do," she said, creating chuckles. "It seems to be akin to staying in a hotel or hospital—the longer you tie up a room, the more you pay."

"That's great, Nancy, thank you...

Let's tag other types of services that require a price tag to be based on time in the system. I'm raising this question because it's essential to understand manufacturing's fixation with their old ways of applying overhead... So, what other service industry charges time in their system...? Yes, Keith."

"Yes, thanks, Jackie. Gee that would include the various types of transportation such as trucking, railroads, buses, and the airlines...

Take the airline industry for instance. You pay the price based on flight duration or time in the system. Then, of course, knowing it's not that simple having so many variables in their pricing structure, but they sure as hell don't charge you less for being in their system longer. Their pricing system has to use throughput as its base for calculations. Nothing else makes sense. So, your point seems to be, why do we manufacturing folks need to do things differently—true?"

"Wow... You said that with such conviction. That was dynamite, Keith. And as Keith said, for airline pricing, it's not that simple. Each airline has its own throughput cost; therefore, throughput influences the price of another airline when competing for passengers... On the surface, these price fluctuations appear to be all helter-skelter—reminding me of columnist Dave Barry's joke...

Rudy the Airfare Chicken pecks at a keyboard sprinkled with corn to determine ticket prices. If Rudy is sick, he added, *Conrad the Airfare Hamster takes over."*

Laughter barnstorms through the audience.

PRODUCT THROUGHPUT COSTING = VALUE

"I'll begin with a reminder about *Activity-Based Costing* due to its popularity in the manufacturing world where I noted General Motors interest earlier. ABC uses the product's assigned cost for each step during manufacturing, resulting in the total cost build-up.

PRODUCT THROUGHPUT COSTING = VALUE looks at only one resource, and that's the total system, not individual events or theoretical constraints within the system that need dealing with individually—and those are separate issues...

The *truth* about product costing is how long the product is in the system—and time is critical, the longer a product is in the system, the more it ties up the system resources... Now, with that rationalization in mind, show me the hands who would like to give us comparisons of service industry companies concerned with time in the system?

Nancy, you appear as though you're hankering for a stab at it?"

"Yes. A hankering I do," she said, creating chuckles. "It seems to be akin to staying in a hotel or hospital—the longer you tie up a room, the more you pay."

"That's great, Nancy, thank you...

Let's tag other types of services that require a price tag to be based on time in the system. I'm raising this question because it's essential to understand manufacturing's fixation with their old ways of applying overhead... So, what other service industry charges time in their system...? Yes, Keith."

"Yes, thanks, Jackie. Gee that would include the various types of transportation such as trucking, railroads, buses, and the airlines...

Take the airline industry for instance. You pay the price based on flight duration or time in the system. Then, of course, knowing it's not that simple having so many variables in their pricing structure, but they sure as hell don't charge you less for being in their system longer. Their pricing system has to use throughput as its base for calculations. Nothing else makes sense. So, your point seems to be, why do we manufacturing folks need to do things differently—true?"

"Wow... You said that with such conviction. That was dynamite, Keith. And as Keith said, for airline pricing, it's not that simple. Each airline has its own throughput cost; therefore, throughput influences the price of another airline when competing for passengers... On the surface, these price fluctuations appear to be all helter-skelter—reminding me of columnist Dave Barry's joke...

Rudy the Airfare Chicken pecks at a keyboard sprinkled with corn to determine ticket prices. If Rudy is sick, he added, *Conrad the Airfare Hamster takes over.*"

Laughter barnstorms through the audience.

PRODUCT THROUGHPUT COSTING = VALUE, THE PROCESS

"**O**kay, it's time we get back to business..."

I'm looking for another answer from the audience about my next question...

"Why do manufacturing companies continue to act as though they need to burden the products in discrete ways?"

I see a sea of shrugs rolling through the audience.

"And the answer is?" Ed said, waiting for a reply.

"Well, Ed, I was kind of hoping a few of you folks might have the answer, because, I have no friggin idea."

The audience has a good time with my response.

"But, I do know this—the Jake Jensen group would like to change the old ways. So, pay close attention now, while we go over the five different tables that I'll display for you.

As we address each one during a hypothetical month, I'll present the appropriate table along with its CONTINUATION TABLE for tables one through four. The various levels of calculations require two tables to best illustrate the process and arrive at the profit return rates for each product...

Please remember that we are using TOTAL OVERHEAD for the pricing exercise, which includes *manufacturing* and the *total operating cost*—with *R&D, selling, general, and administrative overhead*... Why use total overhead? ...Because each process produces value for the business...

For discussion purposes in TABLE ONE using both tables, we will zero in on two of the shaded columns and one horizontal line item, product C.

	TP= Throughput			Table 1	Total O.H. = 7.5 M	
Product	Qty	Unit Selling Price	Unit TP Hours	Total TP Hours	% Total TP Hours	Total OH Contrib. Millions
A	180	51,200	75	13,500	61%	4.56
B	140	45,500	60	8,400	38%	2.84
C	10	33,300	30	300	1%	0.10
			165	22,200	100%	7.5

Continuation in Dollars - Table 1

Unit OH Contrib.	Unit Labor Std	Unit Material Std	Total Unit Cost	Total Cost Million	TP Revenue Million	Total Profit Million	Profit % Of Revenue
25,338	9,000	12,500	46,838	8.43	9.22	0.79	8.5%
20,270	6,000	12,100	38,370	5.37	6.37	1.00	15.7%
10,135	4,000	12,600	26,735	0.27	0.33	0.07	19.7%
				14.07	15.92	1.85	11.6%

In the upper table's Unit TP Hours in the first shaded column—shows the throughput hours calculated by work-in-process value. Remember, if you had a *hundred thousand* dollar WIP, and the input and output were *one thousand* dollars per hour, the throughput time would be *one hundred* hours.

However, in real life, we need to measure the specific steps in product processing as noted in the table below...

This table is representative of Product C in Table 1 showing the breakdown giving us the 30 hours of throughput time... It's here where we need to look in great depth how we can shorten throughput time...

The number of queue setback time looks excessive, so, one may want to start there...

But, be sure that the total product processing time is the same as the throughput hours calculated by work-in-process value before making any changes...

Product	Product Processing	Numer of Setbacks	Total Time in Hours
C	Manufacturing Process	8	19.2
	Inspection	5	1.3
	Queue Setbacks	8	8.5
	Constraint Time	1	1
		Total Hours	30

Listen up now—this is important...

Seeing how THROUGHPUT COSTING overhead contribution influences individual product profitability also illustrates the importance of focusing on the *total system processes* as opposed to just *Throughput Time* only...

In CONTINUATION TABLE ONE, product C, a new product, looks to have great potential because of its potential fast throughput, low price, and high profit of just under twenty percent.

TABLE TWO has a spanking new scenario having gone through each of their products to reduce the unit throughput hours, creating a vast change in their individual profit margins.

TP= Throughput				Table 2		Total O.H. = 7.5 M	
Product	Qty	Unit Selling Price	Unit TP Hours	Total TP Hours	% Total TP Hours	Total OH Contrib. Millions	
A	180	51,200	65	11,700	59.5%	4.47	
B	140	45,500	55	7,700	39.2%	2.94	
C	10	33,300	25	250	1.3%	0.09	
				19,650	100%	7.5	

New Continuation in Dollars - Table 2

Unit OH Contrib.	Unit Labor Std	Unit Material Std	Total Unit Cost	Total Cost Million	TP Revenue Million	** Total Profit Million	Profit % Of Revenue
24,809	7,799	12,500	45,108	8.12	9.22	1.31	14.2%
20,992	5,499	12,100	38,591	5.4	6.37	1.04	16.3%
9,542	3,332	12,600	25,474	0.26	0.33	0.09	25.5%
				13.78	15.92	2.44	15.3%

** Total Profit with Labor cost Reduction

With Table 1 showing a 1.85 million dollar profit, and now in Table 2, we have a decrease in throughput time reducing the labor content time needed to produce the products, resulting in an increase profit of 0.59 million dollars.

Yes, Rosie, you seem to be in possession of a question?"

"I do, thanks, Jackie... How would a *process-driven* manufacturer such as a foundry compute their overhead contribution and profitability?

"You must have clairvoyance, that's my next subject...

Here it is on the screen... TABLE THREE is not a foundry, but one showing an aluminum extrusion manufacturer processing its overhead contribution and computing profitability by product...

Table 3 — Total Fixed Cost: 3,760,100

TP= Throughput June production run for product:	Total pounds by product	Selling price per pound	TP net pounds per hour by product	TP hours – two shifts, five-day wk	Percent TP hours
A	950,000	2.54	8,000	119	34.25%
B	825,000	2.25	10,000	83	23.80%
C	800,000	3.12	5,500	145	41.95%
Total	2,575,000		23,500	347	100%

Billet cost per lb. $0.95

Continuation in Dollars - Table 3

Total fixed cost Overhead and direct	Total cost of billet aluminum	Total material and fixed cost	Total selling price	Total profit	Profit % of Revenue
1,287,874	902,500	2,190,374	2,413,000	222,626	9.2%
894,734	783,750	1,678,484	1,856,250	177,766	9.6%
1,577,492	760,000	2,337,492	2,496,000	158,508	6.4%
3,760,100	2,446,250	6,206,350	6,765,250	558,900	8.3%

The format and computation throughput would be the same for the foundry, industrial painting, rolling mill, glass producer, and so on... As you can see, the TABLE THREE layout and format for computing are different for those of TABLES ONE and TWO, but the throughput results work the same.

If you were computing an industrial painting facility, you would change from pounds to gallons and use square feet to measure throughput per hour...

The most obvious change is COMBINING both DIRECT and TOTAL OVERHEAD COST shown as the TOTAL FIXED COST of three-point seven six million. This is the brilliance of Eliyahu Goldratt's theory that comes into play with our approach to process manufacturers using Product Throughput Costing. The difference between his theory and our method is that Jake's theory other than labor cost also incorporates the material cost to show the individual product profit. True, I did mention this earlier, but I wanted to drive it home, it's a relevant distinction...

Well, Rosie, did that cover things for you?"

"Wow, did it ever. That is so cool, it's simple and clean."

PRODUCT THROUGHPUT COSTING = VALUE SUMMARY

"Are there questions up to this point...?

Yes, Vinnie, I see you have an inquisition coming my way."

With the audience knowing Vinnie, they had a few gleeful chuckles.

"Inquisition? Heavens no, it has to do with my parents always telling me to ask a question when in doubt," Vinnie said. "So, are there other benefits other than just profit improvement?"

"That's an interesting question, Vinnie...

Does anyone in the audience have an answer for Vinnie...?

After a few long seconds, I get a strike as Marty yells...

"Ahh... That would be an improvement in cash flow owing to a lower work-in-process."

A short silence...

"Greater capacity allows you to make simple *what-if* scenarios that help drive strategic plans to gain market share and improve profitability," Ed broadcast.

"Improved customer perception," Nancy yells out.

"It helps to identify the products that clog up the system while using up our resources for little profit margin. With this information, we can make strategic decisions whether we should discontinue the product or replace it with a product that can scream through the manufacturing process," Ed said.

"How about knowing what products in the market to focus on for the highest return," Gary said. "Oh, and another would be when product C increases in volume, the overall profit margins rise big time."

After a long second, Gary delivers an enthusiastic conclusion...

"Christ, after saying that and hearing what's been said, I would presume this fits into one of those, HOLY SHIT categories ... *that's incredible!*"

The audience is stunned by Gary's contribution as they gaze around at each other in astonishment.

Ed Blackburn jumps in...

"You folks never cease to amaze me. It becomes obvious when you envision these incredible ideas you've presented to us today, and how we were able to help articulate and summarize it so well," Ed said.

"It's evident you see the significance of its impact on the process and how helpful it is as a decision-maker when using such a simple, but powerful tool. However, it's much more—when you consider this..."

I watch the audience for a moment seeing them gloating in their newfound approach to throughput costing...

"As I've mentioned, the total overhead is the biggest contributor to product cost. Now, with your latest low overhead organizational architecture, and armed with knowing what products suck up the overhead due to time in the system, you've put yourself into a leadership position—a force to reckon with."

The response brings with it a grinning audience, then applauding followed by others as they giggle and high-five one another.

After a long minute, I speak out...

"Let's take a ten-minute break to let this settle in, then we'll finish up with how to use this process in adding overhead to inventory... See you in ten."

I'm still blown away by the power of Product Throughput Costing = Value and its ability to help in the transformation process.

Right after the break, everyone settles down eager to continue.

ADDING OVERHEAD VALUE TO INVENTORY

"Let's begin our discussing by showing you how to add a product's OVERHEAD VALUE to inventory. At this point, the overhead value requires *only manufacturing overhead*, NOT THE TOTAL OVERHEAD...

Your manufacturing overhead consists of indirect material and indirect labor related to materiel and manufacturing. Plus, equipment depreciation, utilities, its share of facility costs like repairs, maintenance, and insurance...

In TABLE 4, there is but one table, PRODUCT THROUGHPUT COSTING."

TABLE 4 PRODUCT THROUGHPUT COSTING						$4.0 M
1	2	3	4	5	6	7
Product C	Unit Assembly Throughput Hours for part # C	Total Product Assembly Hours	Unit Percent of Total Hours per product	Run Qty	See Table 2, row C column 6 - (1.3%) times Mfg overhead (4.0 M) Divided by run qty (10)	Unit Overhead Allocation For part C 10% times $5,200
C	25	250	10%	10	$5,200	$520

"I'm using *Four Million Dollars* as a manufacturing overhead to illustrate how *Product Throughput Costing = Value* adds manufacturing overhead to finished goods and work-in-process inventory... I should add; the idea is not to put finished goods into inventory, but build ready to ship to a customer. Spare parts for your product should be the only exception.

You also don't want to build subassemblies in large or small quantities for your current shippable products, and then put them into inventory to be used later in time. They should be built as part of the workflow intended for the current month's shipments.

With that said, there will always be exceptions, therefore a need to have your inventory to accept finished goods. So, please focus your attention on the table, and I'll explain the process.

The three key columns are numbers four, six, and seven. Column four's ten percent represents the percentage of C's 25 unit assembly hours relative to the total products assembly hours of 250.

The five thousand two hundred dollar result shown in column six begins the calculation by borrowing the one point three percent from TABLE THREE, row C. This one point three percent is C's share of the combined product's total throughput hours, times the four million dollars of manufacturing overhead, and then divided by ten—the unit run quantity.

For those of you who prefer a simple formula, I'll write it on the whiteboard...

UNIT O.H. ALLOCATION: $520.00 =
UNIT ASSY HRS X O.H. CONTRIBUTION / TOTAL PRODUCT HRS.
25 $5,200.00 520

To use the data, you must incorporate the formulas into the ERP software under the appropriate headings that need to be added.

This segment of our discussion is now complete...

Next, I'd like to spend a few minutes on labor standards and variance reports.

LABOR STANDARDS AND VARIANCE REPORTS

Now, I've been waving the flag to remind you there'll be no need for the labor standard cost variance report...

However, having said that you'll still need to contend with the TOTAL ACTUAL LABOR DOLLARS incurred by product, versus the STANDARD COST CLOSED, leaving a variance report. There would be no need to track down the noted variance as you would for a Standard Cost Accounting Variance report because it would have already been flagged at the appropriate process...

This would require a control chart that measures labor variances over a period, resulting in normal minimal fluctuation between the upper and lower line limits between periods...

If there is no indication that the processes are running out of control, then the variance fluctuation becomes acceptable for the manufacturing system...

There'll be a point; you'll need to have the average variance added to the pricing roll-up in the ERP system. Any variance below or above that figure is a separate line item expense in the manufacturing overhead.

Understanding that, you don't ever want to be surprised when there is a spike in the control chart... I say this because you've been forewarned when a process is running out of control, and make an immediate correction to cushion the variance...

That's it, folks. This end's our session on the application of overhead. We still have a few minutes for questions, assuming you have some?"

I wait for several heartbeats.

"No hands, I see. This was a serious journey we took today, and I must thank you for taking part in our discussions. Participation makes a huge difference in how you digest the information thrown at you.

Oh... One more thing... If I remember correctly, our next session on *Target pricing* will be on Tuesday morning..."

While turning off my computer, I notice Nina is about to say something.

"Jackie, I can't thank you enough for your presentation you gave us to today and told in your normal and understandable way... And, as Gary mentioned, this was a... HOLY SHIT, presentation... Pardon my French."

Not ever hearing Nina use a swear word, she giggled along with the laughing audience.

Nina wasted little time as she cut in with...

"I will prepare a plan for implementation and responsibilities this week."

"Thanks, Nina, that's a good move—the faster, the better."

I thanked everybody in the audience again and then waited for them to shuffle out the door while chatting with Nina, then headed home.

THE NEXT DAY – LUNCH WITH WOODIE

I received a call this morning from Nina on questions about our discussion yesterday, ones too complex to discuss over the phone; so, I jumped on the 405 and headed south.

After spending less than an hour with Nina, I drive north on the freeway to meet Brooks. We've scheduled a quick lunch at the fast-food Fish Taco for catch-up time due to our unexpected guests with Halle and Quentin.

Within twenty minutes of freeway driving, I'm knee-deep in sludge owing to stop and go traffic. Later, we're funneled into a one-lane caravan as we pass a multiple-vehicle pileup involving a milk tanker that jackknifed and spilled milk across six lines on the 405. Not long afterward, I'm on I-10 heading into Santa Monica and onto Palisades Beach Road, with a right turn on Wilshire Blvd.

While cruising down the Boulevard, a car weaves back and forth traveling at a snail's pace when all at once—I have a chance to pass by the crazy driver. Ahh... No wonder, it's a blue-haired old lady with a cigarette in her left hand and an inhaler in the other. She's alternating them back and forth while trying to see over the dash as I giggle and think only in Santa Monica.

Four blocks later, I'm in front of the Fish Taco restaurant looking for a place to park. It didn't take long when I spot an empty space further down the street waiting for me to nose my way in. While hoofing it back to the restaurant, I see colorful kids with tri-colored hairdos, painted faces, weird tattoos, and outlandish clothing—or lack thereof—saunter by. One girl looked as though a trinket grenade had detonated near her and then arranged artistic decorative pierced metal over her entire body. One would imagine no matter what direction she faced when sitting down, she would always end up facing magnetic north. Just like our little furry doggie friends taking a pee during their territorial marking always facing north or south—owing to an awareness of the Earth's magnetic field, it would seem.

Mixed in with the normal folk, are girls from the beach. They're wearing serious, teeny bikinis. Most have sand in their crotches, colorful flip-flops, beach hats, oversize sunglasses covering half their face, and towels were thrown over their shoulder—ah, to be young again.

Several doors down from the Fish Taco, two guys with tie-dye hair and matching tee-shirts skate toward me while the tall one watches his reflection in the store windows. All of a sudden, he runs into a young man wearing a suit and knocks him into a large palm tree landing him in a heap. The shorter of the two guys takes a look at his friend... "Not to worry, he's just a suit."

Both tie-dyes have a good laugh as they clicky-clack toward me on their skates when I close-lined the tall one—landing him on the sidewalk looking dazed as though he had spent a few too many rounds in the ring.

I then rattled off in a singsong voice...

"Not to worry, he's a just clumsy little skater."

When I opened the restaurant door, I spot Brooks sitting at a table with a bunch of guys hanging around trying to get her attention. She's looking extra sultry today with windblown hair and a well-tanned, gorgeous body.

Woodie looks my way and responds with an open smile, and then shoos the guys away like unwanted flies. We agreed to have lunch at this place because they'll have you in and out in thirty minutes owing to my heavy schedule today.

Taking a seat at the table, I explain my problem on the freeway...

"Sorry, I'm late, a few thousand gallons of milk spilled over the freeway."

"You need to keep your glove box full of Oreos for such occasions."

I cracked up with the visual idea of me getting out of my car and dunking Oreos in the spilled milk—it's a childish idea, but friendship has that effect.

We laugh together for a moment and then order our lunch. Strange, but Brooks tells me not to order the fish tacos at this place.

"So, babe ... what's with you and Quentin?"

Woodie gives me one of those looks with her eyebrows moving upward while blinking her eyes like a camera lens snapping multiple photos...

"Quentin?"

"Yeah, Quentin... So, what's going on—are you two going out or not?"

Brooks gives me a fake yawn...

"Well ... maybe."

"Did you know that you're a serious nut case...?

By the way, did I tell you Toni is coming over for dinner tonight?"

She shakes her head, then grins from ear to ear as she counters my jab about Quentin...

"So, tell me, Jackie, are you going to try out his oversize power tool?"

"Power tool? Well, if he had one, I wouldn't know what to do with it."

When hearing her snort, I look up to see her eyes roll upward to express her disbelief. Then just as she was about to say something, I interrupt her...

Don't tell me what you're thinking. Surely, it won't be as funny as what's going through my mind."

At this point, we have an outburst of the giggles.

"To ease your mind, Toni and I are just friends, and I'm fixing us a yummy south-of-the-border dinner. He may be a graduate of Annapolis, but he's still a down-home Creek Indian Okie."

"Yeah, but he's damn smart and a looker. If it were me, I'd be cozying up to him and saying in my best Mae West impersonation: *Hello big boy, why don't you come up and see me sometime?*"

We both have a good laugh.

Thirty-five minutes after my arrival, having caught up on essential stuff like men, surfing, handbags, shoes, clothes, and other unmentionables, I leave her to fight off the immature guys still buzzing around.

As I near my Shelby pony car, I use the Viper remote starting system to hear the wonderful sound of eight hundred fifty horse's whinny—anxious to take flight like their wild ancestors. Horses act this way when idle too long and need to burn off their pony gas into the atmosphere. Buckled in, we flitted into a gallop off toward Pepperdine.

After the administrative meeting, I drove to *Pacific Coast Greens*, a great market near me on the Pacific Coast Highway and picked out a fresh chicken for the grill and a few additional items for making tasty salsa.

As I head home driving along the sandy beach, I can hear the surf kicking spray into the air generating that aromatic smell of the Pacific Ocean. The seaside produces negative ions that increase the flow of oxygen to the brain resulting in an increase in alertness and mental energy. One in three of us feels like we're walking on air. It's the next best thing to feeling in love...

Hmm... Must have read that somewhere.

With a chuckle, I remember Johnny telling me where those wonderful ions come from that makes him feel so good. He thinks they come from the volumes of beautiful girls lying on the beach.

ACT II - SCENE 14
ENHANCING THE LEARNING PROCESS

Question 1
Why is the measurement of the manufacturing process capability superior to an engineered standard?

Question 2
What are other ideas that relate to organizations or industries that use throughput time as part of the equation for determining the cost of the service?

Question 3
Is the Jake Jensen application of applying overhead practical or a doable method?
Can this overhead application be implemented with ease in any manufacturing environment?
Can this application help influence our ability to grow the economy through improved throughput, and productivity gains?

Question 4
Why is it essential to measure the month-end labor variance?
Give us a few examples.

Question 5
What are your thoughts of Jackie close-lining the tall guy on skates landing him on the sidewalk looking dazed as though he had spent a few too many rounds in the ring?

ACT II SCENE 15
Target Pricing

WEEK 8 – TUESDAY MORNING – JACKIE, DISCUSSES TARGET PRICING

JACKIE AND TONI TAKE A HIKE IN THE WILDERNESS

At my place during dinner last night, Toni asked me if I've done any hiking in the mountains lately.

When hearing this, I contemplated how to answer him while taking my time chewing up a bite of chicken nestled inside my whole-wheat burrito. I wondered if climbing sand dunes at Pismo Beach and hiking the trails in Malibu hills qualified as an appropriate answer...

"A little," I said.

Evidently, Toni took my answer as one who has spent time in the wilderness. So, here I am Friday afternoon with us pulling into Independence for gas—a small town in the Sierras. It's the end of civilization, as I know it. This wide spot in the road has a flourishing population of about six hundred at the base of the Sierras. With that in mind, I take the last chance for a lady's room pit stop.

Later, after climbing into my seat, I tell Toni about the monster bug watching me and giving me the creeps.

Toni looks at me with narrowed eyes and snorts, and then silence.

By late afternoon, we were at the trailhead with no cars in sight, and a nervous hunger builds. It would have been nice if someone ran a burger stand up here...

"I could do with a chocolate malt about now."

Silence.

After slipping into our backpacks, we head into the unknown. The first thing I learned about backpacking is the advantage of wearing a long-sleeved tee-shirt. It's a great alternative to wipe your nose on during a hike.

We are now several hours into a region that my mother would have called the hinterland that others might call the boonies, the willowwacks, the tules, the puckerbrush, or the, willy-wags. A short time later, the sun slipped behind the mountain tops just as we found a nice secluded spot to spend the night in the willowwacks.

While Toni's putting up our Sierra backpacking tent, I'm getting frustrated trying to hang our bag of food on an overhanging limb. The line keeps running through my fingers and opened a cut. I expressed a few choice words while applying a bandage owing to my lack of woodsmanship. After licking my lips with determination, I try it again.

A short time later, Toni yells out...

"Did you make the tie fast, babe?"

"Fast? You mean fast like a three-legged chicken?"

"No," Toni yelled. "If bears happen to visit us tonight, you need to make the line fast, as in tighter than a bobcat's ass in the fly season."

"Bears?"

Later that night, Toni with his six foot five frame snuggles into our two-person tent like a giant light-footed grizzly bear. And later, as the night wore on, I whispered...

"Have you noticed a chorus singing in a minor scale coming through the trees?"

"It's the wind, babe... Or, perhaps, the nearby spirits of the old mill town saloon girls."

"What? ...Well, whatever it is, it gives me the heebie-jeebies..."

Silence.

Later into the night, still spooked, I take peek out into the night and see movement in the moonlight, a gigantic bush or a bear. With a little hysteria, I whisper in Toni's ear, but he just snorts and grunts a few times and turns over. Here I am with a carnivorous-eating animal ready to drag me away, and he snorts.

At first sign of morning light, I'm out and behind a tree. *No way* was I going to be making peepee in the dark behind moving bushes or with wild animals lurking about—even with a bursting bladder.

Toni soon follows me out of the tent, stretches his body like a cat with his long strapping arms grabbing for the sky.

With a big yawn, he looks in my direction...

"Don't you just love sleeping outdoors?"

"Ah... There's nothing like sleeping in the forest under the moonlight."

I can't let Toni find out the wilderness isn't my style, especially, with a crick in my back and little or no sleep.

While Toni gets a breakfast fire going, I'm selecting two packages of dried eggs with cheese, red and green bell peppers, onions, and seasoning for our breakfast—yummy. I'm starved. It must be the fresh mountain air and no sleep.

I found a bag of hash brown potatoes and pulled them out along with the instant coffee...

After breakfast, we clean up our campsite. So, with toilet paper in hand, I excuse myself and head toward the woods.

"Hold up, babe, I got something for you."

"Not now, Toni, I'm in a hurry."

He walks toward me with a twitch of his lower lip holding a black plastic bag.

"What's that for?" I said with urgency in my voice.

Laugh lines begin crinkling at the corners of his eyes...

"It's your poop bag, babe."

My nose wrinkles up along with my upper lip rising in disgust...

"MY WHAT?"

"What you bring in, you take out, babe."

"Yeah, right, I'll remember to put that on my bumper sticker."

"Well, if not a bag, don't use toilet paper—consider Mother Nature's way, such as stones, vegetation—or snow, if we had any."

"A FRIGGING STONE? I screamed.

I took an abrupt about-face and ran into the bush with toilet paper trailing behind me. When I returned, Toni shakes his head giving me a shameful look, as I feel my eyebrows narrow and my lips compress.

I'm thinking bears, woods, and poop bags, so I give Toni the squinty-eye...

"Does a bear shit in the woods and put the droppings in a plastic bag?"

He snorts and walks away.

"Oh... One other thing; I better not see any black plastic bags swinging in the breeze from your backpack, like a bunch of scalps."

He turned to say something with his mouth open and moving, but no words were coming out.

Later into our hike, I noticed the mountainous terrain had changed some.

So, with little having been said in our trek through the wilderness, I decided to liven' things up a bit...

"Our surroundings look different; did we just cross a border? What state are we in?"

I hear nothing but silence thinking Toni had no intention of responding to such a senseless question, and then...

"We just crossed over and into the Appalachian Mountains."

To some, his answer would seem to be repellent, but Jackie just smiles within knowing Toni responded with a full, playful sentence.

With that said Toni treks off toward a serene little lake in the distance.

Hopefully, the campsites are deserted and populated only with birds, rabbits, chipmunks, and a self-serve hamburger stand. Except for wildlife, we haven't seen a soul since yesterday afternoon.

As we begin our trudge down a mountain slope on what resembles a path toward *our* little lake, I admire the beautiful wildflowers protruding with their colorful floral above the rocks. Full of excitement, I point to a bird that's hanging upside down on a branch like a bat...

"Is that a bat-bird? It's so cute."

"Chickadee," Toni said.

"*Chickadee?*"

Having a little fun, I walk up next to Toni and give him my best WC Fields impersonation...

"*My Little Chickadee,*" I said, pretending to flick ashes off an imaginary cigar.

Toni responded as though he was exhibiting a wry smile.

"You're far and away one of a kind."

"That's a compliment, right?"

Silence fills the air...

"The chickadee, parrot, and falcon are related."

Who would have thunk—Toni Nakni, zoologist?

A moment later, I spot something moving about down the trail...

"What's that? Yikes... BEAR!"

Toni looks up and fixes his eyes on my bear...

"Marmot."

He's forever the unpretentious conversationalist.

"Marmot? What the hell kind of bear is that?"

"Damn good thing you noticed the varmint, babe."

"Hmmm... Jackie O', Pathfinder."

Toni gives me a bewildered look...

"Pathfinder?"

"Marmot, varmint—make up your mind, what is it?"

"Well, it's not a bear. It's a marmot, a vicious, dangerous, yellow-bellied, ground squirrel. Good eyes, Pathfinder...

Oh, and you may want to keep your eyes opened for any leporine running through the bush."

"What's a leporine?"

"It's best described as a large jackrabbit with antelope horns, often called a jackalope. It's considered far more dangerous than a marmot.

My lower lip protrudes while digesting what a marmot and a leporine are. Then feeling like Davie Crockett, I hike up my breeches and walk tall toward the lake in the distance.

Along the way, the sky turns dark as a robust rumbling wind strong-arms its way towards us bringing hostile black clouds.

"Those are storm clouds coming our way, we're going to need shelter," I said.

It wasn't long when the sky opens up and delivers a torrent of rain not unlike the night that Noah's Ark floated.

The sky illuminates with bolts of lightning that strikes nearby, startling me and bringing back my last terrifying altercation with lighting. It was then; I tried to sidestep a fast flowing rush of mud and stepped into a hole filled with mud and debris running down a slope. I lost my balance and tumble down the hill in a fast-moving current of mucky mud, not unlike Kathleen Turner in *Romancing the Stone*.

I try to ride it out like surfing a monster wave, but as one can imagine, the degree of difficulty and the aftermath is several notches higher with an ugly ending...

I finished my ride in a pool of sludgy muck on my back facing uphill with my legs spread like the wings of an eagle. I lift my shoulders and head out of the sludge feeling woozy. It was then, with blurred vision, I detect Desi Arnaz playing *Babalu Conga Bongo* on his bongo drums in my head, but more likely, the sound came from Toni scrambling down the slope.

With yukky-encrusted eyes, I look down and see large long creature wiggling toward my crotch—a hallucination, of course. But now, I'm considering the idea of screaming. Except, Toni arrived in the nick of time.

He leans down and grabs the wiggling thing from behind, rockets his arm straight up into the clouds, twirled the slimy monster above his head, and then snapped his arm down in front of him. This bull-whip trick left the slimy bulge at the other end static for a nanosecond. Then his ad hoc whip brought the hissing head traveling at Mach-one along a straight plane trying to catch up to its tail—and then passed it as you hear a crack, a miniature sonic boom. And then, like magic, the hissing pissed off head flies through the air and into the thicket and deluge—still trying to sink its poison fangs into anything around it, including the briar.

Unruffled, Toni held onto the squirming snake as he gazes down at me with what may have looked like actual concern...

"You okay, babe?"

My first response is with hysterical laughter...

"Oh yeah, I wouldn't have missed this outing for the world."

With a warm smile, he reaches down and pulls me out of the slime while holding the wiggling makeshift whip...

"Babe, this is a rattler. These babies make for a great dinner. Back home, we would prepare them like a fish fillet and serve it as prairie whitefish..."

Seeing my disdainful look, he flung the floundering remains up on a rock outcropping for the hawks and eagles to have a whitefish treat.

A moment later, he points to a shelter in the distance, a large overhang of rock—you have to love the man's resourcefulness.

I'm flat out, out of my element. I've surfed, the giant waves of Hawaii, driven fuel dragsters in a five-second quarter-mile, and fought the best in women's kickboxing, but this wilderness thing is like stepping into a whole new world, being a city girl.

My father once told me that a bond can form between individuals who share a common experience that can evolve into a strong friendship. After this little adventure, I sure hope so—not that I have any ideas about Toni and me.

With no use for the shelter, I stand out in the rain allowing the mucky mud to wash off, but like everything else around here, the rain left as fast as it came.

Toni sets up camp near the lake that evening next to a large bleached skeleton of a tree, he called a rampike. Me, I walk along the shoreline to find a place for a quick bath. In a secluded spot, I strip down and jump in the frigid water and splash around. Now, I'm one with perky boobs. Perky is good, right? I'm what they call a late bloomer. When I made out as a young teenager, my bra was so padded—I seldom knew when I was being felt up. With a bath and fresh clothes, I was *yearning* for a campfire and *grub*—a little mountain talk helps set my mood.

Toni asked me if I wanted to make the campfire tonight. So, not wanting to turn down a challenge, I accepted.

"Okay, babe, try shaving slivers from this branch."

Toni hands me his Spyderco military folding knife and a twig. After finishing with the shaving task, and not wanting to be asymmetrical, I bandage my finger on the other hand. With multiple tries and determination, I get a flame going.

Now that we have a roaring campfire, we both prepare fixins for us ridge runners. After dinner and all fat'n sassy with a full tummy and a warm fire, I begin to sing on into the night...

"Whoopee-ti-yi-yo, git along little doggies ... for you knows Wyoming will be your new home..."

Toni stares at me for the longest time, then shakes his head in a bewildered way, trying hard not to encourage me, but the corner of his mouth is forming the slightest of a smile.

Later, with a full bladder, I excuse myself and hike up the hill, squat behind a tree, and take a pee. When finished, I find my way down and enter the campsite where Toni is looking down at a puddle of water collected at the foot of the hill with a smirk on his face.

"I shall always remember you as LITTLE RUNNING RIVER."

At that moment, I sent Toni my best piercing glance as I ramble over to the fire and giggle. Later in the night, surrounded by darkness, an orange-red smear comes from the glowing coals of the campfire. You can well-nigh listen to the smoke rise into the quiet of the night.

We lay bundled up in the hard, cold thin air on the mountainside looking up at the stars so close you could taste them when Toni points out the many constellations and their Greek myths. Whoo... Maybe it's me, but he's talking in full sentences...

"Thoreau once wrote in his novel, Walden...

I have my own sun and moon and my own stars, and a little world all to myself...

That's us, here and now, babe."

I get a lump in my throat. Tears form in my eyes.

Silence fills the night as a slight breeze rustles the tree leaves...

"Ahh... Smell that wonderful mountain air."

"Mountain air?" I said with a sniff, "All I smell is pine trees."

"Don't you smell the hint of snow in the wind?"

I spike my eyebrows...

"SNOW? WIND?"

"Well, it's not so much the smell of snow as it is breathing in a heavier air—not wet like during and after a rainstorm, but heavy with frost crystals, a sharp cold. This gets me thinking that we might get an early summer snowstorm."

"Early? Just how early are we talking about?"

All at once, the DONNER PARTY in a raging blizzard came to mind.

"In this region, it could happen overnight—making it a three-dog night."

"A THREE-DOG NIGHT...?"

"It's a term the Indians use in the northern regions during a williwaw, a sudden and violent storm of rain, snow, or sleet."

Three-dog night leaves a bad taste in my mouth considering we don't have any dogs to keep us warm, and only have a few meals left...

Later into the night, the orange glow from our campfire sizzled and sputtered as a light drizzle of rain sent a signal for us to hit the sack. To be safe, Toni poured water on the coals. Me, I'm feeling a frosty breeze run up my back as I crawl into the tent. While snuggling up into my sleeping bag, the big guy climbs in taking up every square inch of space as he worms his way into his bag. I guess I needn't' worry about having three-dogs with Toni in the tent.

Now that we're settled into our warm but hard sleeping quarters, I'm thinking I need to come clean with Toni and tell him, I'm not a woodsy person...

"Oh, is that right?" He said as though shocked.

"Well, I thought that might surprise you...

And, I must confess, I'm one who has the need to grab a burger on the run, and to feel a flat sidewalk under my feet rather than tripping over rocks...

And, to see neon lights, not glowing amber. I need to find my way using street signs, not a notch in a tree... To hear the sound of civilization, not winds that hit a high note when the wind isn't blowing...

Oh yeah, most importantly, not having to worry I'll wake up in the morning and find myself making my last meal out in a blizzard."

To silence my whining, he put things into perspective by telling me about a pioneer lady by the name of Nancy Kelsey, who also had never traveled in the wilderness. The story took place in 1841. She's best known for being the first white woman to walk on Utah soil and to cross the Sierra Nevada Mountains. But get this, she did this with her baby girl on her hip—so anytime when you're having a tough day, consider what Nancy Kelsey had to go through. For me, though, Toni's story puts my bitching to a stop.

Later into the night, I dreamed of being Nancy Kelsey. At the crack of dawn, I gaze over at Toni...

"I'm reckoning we needs to get something straight betwixt us... I knows we've had a hog-killin' time, but I ain't gonna say this 'cept once, ya hear. Don't ya never minds or doubt Jackie will take care of her end," I said, slapping my ample butt with my open hand noticing the cold icy air funneling through an opening in the tent. "I ain't no bean master, but I'll take care of the morn'n fixins. So, we have a lot of things that gotta git did this morn' Toni... Now, let's get a move on."

After throwing back the tent's flap, I skedaddled out into the morning air.

"YIKES," I said in a panic.

My world has turned effin' white, and it's effin' freezin'.

"SHEEEIT..." Thinking it's colder than a basement toilet seat.

Snowflakes are dancing on an Arctic wind. I can feel the brittle cold air on my face while stumbling around in shock knowing we will die.

And then Toni arrives on the scene as he climbs out of the tent breathing out vapor into the frigid air...

"SPECTACULAR."

"We're both going to die, and you yell SPECTACULAR. Are you NUTS?"

He tromps over and leans in close...

"Not to worry, babe. Now, as you so eloquently pointed out this morning about how you would take care of *your* end," he said slapping my generous butt, "and fix us our morning grub."

Reluctantly, I begin our morning fixins fussing over my colossal size mouth...

Later, after finishing our morning vittles around a roaring campfire, we headed our separate ways to do our morning constitutionals—without Toni's dern black plastic bag, I might add...

Just as that thought crossed my mind, Toni shouted...

"Jackie, we have snow now, so use the nice white fluffy stuff instead of the toilet paper."

With that revolting thought, I continued onto the wilderness...

My theory is if you're in nature's wilderness, one must follow the custom of those animals that inhabit the region. In doing so, I too will leave my share of feces to feed the many organisms, bacteria, fungi, and insects in their ecosystem. You can cover the poop along with your biodegradable toilet paper with leaves, pine needles or brush, so I'm sure Nancy Kelsey would agree…

The snowflakes were now well-spaced suggesting that they were in no hurry to accumulate any snowpack as we have our final cup of hot coffee warming our bellies.

"Babe," Toni said as he stood letting me know it was time to break camp and make sure our site looks as pristine as when we arrived.

While hiking out of the wilderness, we soon reached an elevation without snow. Even so, the air has not lost its chill as we near an area of ankle-twisting rocks. I'm now finding out when coming down a mountain, the trek can often be more difficult than going up. After a long hike, we reach Toni's car.

Late Sunday night, Toni drops me off at my beach home. I hesitate for a moment, then kiss him on his cheek and tell him I've had a wonderful time— Well, it's true, even though I was out of my element, but being with Toni was fun. He responded with "Babe," telling me he also enjoyed himself. At least, I hope it was that kind of babe. Hmm … I wonder where this is going.

Monday morning, I'm on the phone with Nina to discuss our Tuesday session. In our conversation, I just *happen* to mention my trip to the mountains. Well… Not true—I blabbed out everything—that's what women do, we get more excited and more emotional than men.

TUESDAY MORNING IN THE TRAINING ROOM

Tuesday morning at seven thirty-five, I'm heading past the reception area on my way to Nina's office for a little natter, and then walk with her to the training room…

With coffee in hand, I have small talk with the folks. As eight o'clock rolled around—I'm fired up ready to deliver my session on target pricing…

I stood at the lectern for a moment having said my good mornings when Nina stands up.

"Excuse me, Jackie… You should take a moment and tell us about your adventurous weekend."

Mischievous smile forms as she covers her mouth from the giggles getting everybody's curiosity up. Her actions gave me no choice but to tell my story— that's what women call payback for blabbing.

In my storytelling, I may have exaggerated and stretched the truth here and there, but the audience seemed to enjoy my adventure with lots of interruptions and laughter.

"You're a great sport, Jackie, thanks for your weekend story."

I nodded with a playful smile toward Nina.

"It's time to get back to our morning session…

Last Wednesday, we discussed overhead applications for various costing alternatives. Today, we will cover a few of those subjects in more depth, but first, let's discuss—what is cost?"

WHAT IS COST?

"When pricing products and evaluating individual product profitability, it will require a complete understanding of product cost....

There are two basic components of product cost: PURCHASED MATERIAL and VALUE-ADDED PROCESSES—better known as direct labor and total manufacturing *and* operating cost.

PURCHASED MATERIAL by itself adds no value to the customer. The value comes when the value-added processes produce an assembled or fabricated product to the customer's specification or needs. Sorry, I repeat myself here because of new faces I see in the audience.

All purchasing and material stocking costs are included in the manufacturing overhead and not charged as a separate line item to purchased parts through a form of allocation as many companies do...

This new approach creates opportunities for working with the customer to leverage costs or make joint purchases from common suppliers to achieve economies of scale, therefore, reducing the customer's purchase price and improving customer perception.

A VALUE-ADDED PROCESS is a subject we've discussed in our many sessions. However, there are a few other points I'd like to make—traditionally, material and labor have been *direct* cost and overhead has been *indirect*" cost. These terms emphasize a *direct* cost reduction and ignore the overhead, *indirect* cost. We need to change our way in how to view *indirect* costs, namely, as an inseparable part of value-added processes...

Is this *costing* discussion making sense so far?"

The audience reacts with a positive response and nodding.

TARGET COST

"Our next subject is target cost...

Product cost decisions affect customer and stockholder value. Within that light, I would say most company pricing policies are fraught with the idea their quality of products or services is proportional to their price, when in fact, it's more likely, proportional to the manufacturing cost...

Now, let's talk target cost with customer value as part of the equation...

TARGET COST IS THE VALUE REMAINING after subtracting the required rate of return from the target price—a return rate that supports a positive EVA.

When assuming the target price is at the proper level, one must achieve the target cost—because altering the price to achieve either a higher value for the customer or stockholder would not end well...

If for instance, the selling price is to maximize stockholder return, then the customer value would suffer—and eventually, it would affect the stockholder's value. If the selling price is to maximize customer value, one must be careful it's not at the expense of stockholder value.

When pricing a product, one must begin with a defined target cost that sets goals for your business processes. You may require new processes that reduce total operating and product-specific costs at or below the target cost. When innovating a specific process within the business system, it may be necessary to bring down overhead cost...

Why does overhead cost play such a vital role in the costing of products? That question is for you bright folks in the audience?"

It didn't take long.

"Yes, Donald?"

"This is a test to see if we were paying attention last week, right?"

"This is true, but today, we have folks that weren't at our last meeting."

"Nonetheless, I would like to tackle your question...

If I recall correctly, you explained to us, overhead allocation plays a huge role in the outcome of the costing process owing to the burden's high ratio...

To better understand the burden rate, we use Product Throughput Costing = Value that applies the burden to the product by its time in the system...

If we are looking for a reduction in price after reviewing all the possible design scenarios, we must fall back on how to improve one of two alternatives: faster throughput or a reduction in the burden rate..."

Donald nodded and took his seat.

"Excellent answer, Donald," I said. "To verify the incoming data, it will be necessary to run a simulation to verify compatibility within the business processes, which I'll discuss shortly..."

PRELIMINARY PROCESS FOR TARGET PRICING

"Before setting your competitive product target price, we need to review a few important steps in the process... We'll begin by analyzing the various purchasing categories a customer uses in their procurement decisions. A discussion we had in several of our meetings.

For instance, using the one to ten scale, and the highest customer rating category is a *seven* for product *timeliness*, you would compare it to the customer's weighted *pricing* expectations that might be an *eight*.

So, when the CUSTOMER-WEIGHTED PRICE is equal to or greater than the other purchase criteria, the market is PRICE-SENSITIVE. However, the influence of price on purchase decisions may be different between market segments—so let's not forget this subtle difference in the final review.

Lastly, develop a business strategy for penetrating the market such as improving customer perception by increasing the performance level of the business processes specified by MPV.

The company's pricing decisions should also be an integral part of your internal business strategy which may include one or more of the following...

An increase in profitability and cash flow...

To maintain or expand market share...

Keep current capacity by lowering the product market demand.

Next, we need to check the system's capacity constraints using *isee system* model simulation and real-time scheduling simulation software such as nMetric. To confirm the results, you'll need to use financial modeling software...

Not to overstate the obvious, but all three modeling software results will require the same input data. Modeling financial software is of great importance, a subject we'll be discussing in a few weeks, but for now, let's review value price-curve charts...

But wait, it would seem Ed has a question..."

"Thanks, Jackie... I'm really curious to see if you might have an example of the critical nature for this type of change?"

"I didn't have anything a few days ago, but I just happened to develop some information for a meeting with Jake on our new project...

So, let me bring up Tesla's net income to loss chart. This should fill the bill as a great example...

As you can see, it's a real jaw-dropper showing their huge losses since inception in 2008..."

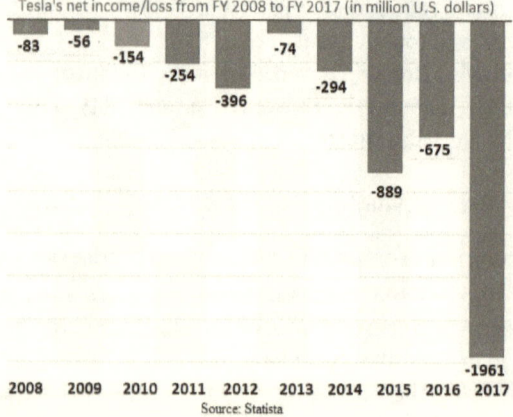

There was a fast response with gasps coming from the audience...

"Please, let me explain...

I'm sure many of you have heard about Tesla's Electric Vehicles lack of producing a profitable year since inception in 2008. Why is that? Because, they have focused on nothing but achieving a good gross margin for their three different models, with no concern for the huge Research and Development and Sales General and Administration cost. And, had they understood and used our new *Horizontal, Systemic Organizational Architecture,* along with the *Product Throughput Costing = Value* and *Target Costing,* they could have designed a profitable company from the get-go... But, Elon Musk, their CEO had no understanding of the importance of such thinking and built a company incapable of producing a profit to date as seen in this chart. I would note that the FIRST QUARTER IN 2018, they had the biggest net loss to date, seven hundred and ten million dollars…"

More gasps…

"I take it this answers your question, Ed?"

"It does indeed. Thanks, Jackie."

"Okay, let's move on now to target pricing, beginning with a survey table…"

TARGET PRICING

"Our, or *The Business* is highlighted in the MARKET-PERCEIVED VALUE SURVEY TABLE illustrating the MPV rating position and unit price relative to its three top competitors as you'll see in the next price-sensitive flowchart…

Market-perceived Value Survey – Table

Business	Total MPV Rating	Unit Price
Competitor 1	7.85	123.00
Competitor 2	7.1	124.00
Competitor 3	5.95	126.00
The Business	6.4	127.50

Notice, my value price-sensitive table shows the top three competitors with the lowest price at the top and lastly, THE BUSINESS information…

Next, is a PRICE-SENSITIVE MARKET FLOWCHART where customers want to receive maximum value for the minimum expense. The visual representation correlates minimum price with maximum value noted as zero through ten, and the most desirable positions are in the upper right-hand corner.

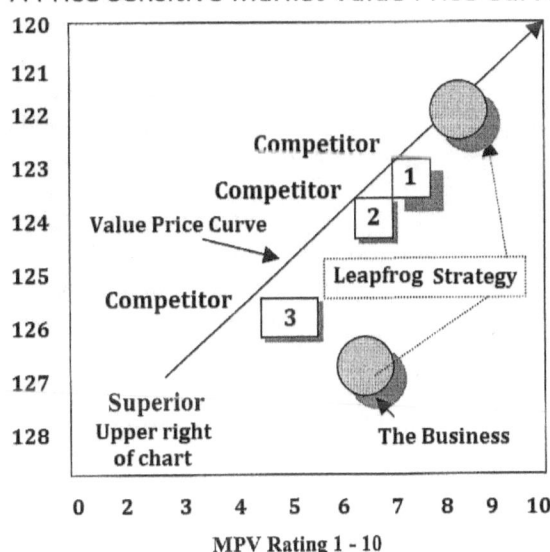

When the market price is non-sensitive as presented in the second flowchart, the business shows an opportunity to develop your strategic planning...

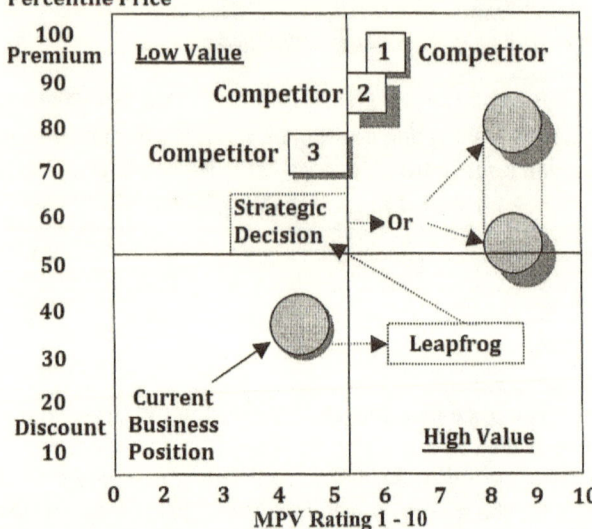

For instance, the *business* could develop a product that supports a fifty-five dollar price generating good profits at the lower discount rate noted in the chart—and then above it is the leapfrog position.

One would introduce the new product at the eighty dollar level with a nine MPV rating, getting the market's attention, and yet, give your company extraordinary profits. However, when the competition begins to improve their MPV ratings with lower prices, and market growth is affected, there would be room to drop the price just below the two top competitors and keep a strong profit margin. This strategy is not unlike Apple's iPhone starting out at extraordinarily high prices...

It's all straightforward at this level, but do we have questions."

With the audience showing no sign of inquiry, I moved on...

"Lastly, I would say, to confirm the strategy, you need to run the financial modeling software to see that the plan *IMPROVES THE VALUE-ADDED ECONOMIC INDICATOR* or EVA as we call it..."

With a need to summarize my presentation, I pause to review my notes.

"I'll finish up with a summary, and we'll call it a day..."

SUMMARY

"From either of these two target-pricing examples we just covered, you can evaluate your current position and determine the unit target price and MPV rating. This market strategy will allow you to surpass or leapfrog your competition...

Ah... Something you need to remember...

You mustn't ever try to leapfrog a market position by sacrificing the desired profit level. As I mentioned, the EVA needs to be reviewed when pricing is changed to ensure we have no infractions.

The leapfrog position is part of the design process that includes the targeted profit. Your current product may not meet your new strategy—and require a new product design.

Once you have the MPV rating in operation and have your new leapfrog designed product ready to market, you have positioned the company for a dramatic increase in business growth and market share.

I have one other point I'd like to make...

Companies continue to look at reducing their supplier base along with establishing long-term relationships that provide extraordinary service and excellent products. To accomplish this, suppliers must understand product cost to maintain long-term competitive pricing. When understanding the product pricing process by both supplier and customer helps build the trust necessary for long-term relationships...

Product Throughput Costing = Value is a great tool in helping you establish your target cost. It delivers you the needed flexibility in your strategic pricing decisions and allows the business to have a better understanding of its strengths and weakness in the manufacturing and marketing of their products.

Manufacturers' biggest struggle is their product total cost and profit compared to the value to their user.

In most markets, companies make a normal profit. When a company earns excess profits, it's evidence that the company enjoys a powerful growing market.

As a growing market share leader, the company has the potential for creating improved profitability for three reasons:

FIRST, growing market share leaders attract the premium employees who bring with them experience and creativity.

SECONDLY, strong name recognition is a safe bet for having your market segment purchase from a strong, growing market share of suppliers.

LASTLY, as I mentioned earlier in our discussion, the economy of scale enhances material procurement. When taking advantage of this option, you have a few choices to make with the savings. Lower the price to influence price sensitivity markets and improve market position, or keep the saving to improve near-term profit margins...

Okay, folks, I have one more question for you...

Why struggle to reduce a product's price to achieve greater market share, when your current pricing brings in a good profit...?

I see a new face, Theresa, is it?"

She's a nice-looking lady with blonde hair and ultra-light-blue eyes who's sitting in the front row.

With a sudden smile that looked nice on her, she answered...

"Well, Jackie, I'll give it a try. If the market wasn't price-sensitive, you wouldn't want to reduce the price. However, if the market is price sensitive, it's just a matter of time until a competitor comes along and eats your shorts," Theresa said with her delightful Spanish accent.

All of a sudden she begins to giggle, and then covers her mouth with both hands as color rises to her cheeks—bringing joyful chortles from the class.

I gave Theresa a wide smile...

"Not to worry, Theresa, we're laughing at your unexpected brilliant answer, *getting your shorts eaten*. It gets right to the point of what happens, well that, and your wonderful accent," I said. "Are you from Spain?

"Spain? No, Cuba. I'm Castilian, and much of my family live in Northern Spain, but my great-grandfather built a large plantation in Cuba and raised a family. I graduated from Havana University and left Cuba to come here about three years ago."

"Well, I'm sure there is an interesting story there, but I'm glad to see that you found a new home here in the United States—particularly here at ATC."

We applaud her, along with hoots and whistles from the audience.

"Thank you. Thank you. That is most kind of you."

With a blush, she stands there with hands held against her thighs while looking around the room. When taking her seat, she buries her face in her hands as tears form and runs down her cheeks.

I wait for a moment with a warm smile...

"Okay, for those of you who wish to expand their knowledge on market value, you should buy Bradley T. Gale's 1994 book, *Managing Customer Value*. There is no other book that covers this topic better. I'm sure you can find Bradley Gale's book on the Amazon book site."

All of a sudden, Nina stands and faces the audience...

"I would like the department heads to please let me know who would like a copy of the book, and I will have them ordered for you."

"Thanks, Nina that's a good move."

A few minutes later, I end the session.

While walking out through the front entrance, I added spring to my gait when I thought about how the combination of throughput overhead allocation and target pricing had its positive impact on a manufacturing business.

When heading out toward my herd of ponies, the wind picks up, so I gaze upward and see a pastel-blue sky poking out among the gathering clouds. The sun is trying to push through, but getting weaker by the moment as the wind brings in a mass of serious dark clouds forming off the coast. Surely, they will pass me by. And, of course, this kind of weather seems to be an everyday occurrence in Portland.

Why Portland? Well, when asking a fellow professor friend who moved to

Portland last year if he had a nice summer, he responded: *Yes indeed,* he said, *We had a wonderful picnic that one sunny afternoon.* With a giggle, I unlocked my car door and slid into the seat of *Little Miss Sunshine.*

JACKIE REMEMBERS BACK WHEN...

I've always named my cars—even for the dragster I once built—the FUBAR Special, a deserving name. At the tender age of sixteen, my buddy, Tom, and I built a B altered coupe. We designed, assembled, and welded a chrome-moly frame. Now, when I say design, we're talking a charcoal sketch with arrows and notes on butcher paper supplied by the local corner grocery store. With our design complete, we wallpapered the garage walls with it. The idea was to attach a gutted-out body from a 1946 Crosley.

In the end, however, we elected to leave off the body and convert our design into a D gas dragster. The configuration left us with an ill-designed dragster frame, but with a shrug, we continued. For power, we selected a Jimmy inline-six for our starter engine.

But later, we found a deal we couldn't refuse at the scrap yard—a small block 265 cubic inch 56' Chevy V8 engine. We rebuilt the engine, installed a Hilborn mechanical fuel injection, an Esky Polydyne Profile 505 Magnum' cam, and etcetera. Using an adapter plate, we coupled the engine to a 1939 Lincoln Zephyr transmission modified for two speeds. The Zephyr transferred the power to a 1939 Ford narrowed rear end with locked-spider gears that lit up the asphalt using hand-me-down M & H slicks.

While working at Barney's Automotive during the summer months, it gave us enough money to pay for the engine parts. Most of the other equipment came from junkyards and discount automotive houses. Barney let me drive his four-door washed-out, pea-green 41' Studebaker to pick up parts for his business. Later, he told me to drive the car as if it were my own while I worked for him.

Drag machines and their spinning smoking wheels can sometimes lose direction, even with the dual traction narrowed and locked spider gear rear-end. By having the driver near or behind the rear wheels of the machine, one has a better chance of making the necessary correction; therefore, the extra-long wheelbase of today's dragsters. Weight distribution also plays a part in the equation.

However, sitting right up front, as in our machine, it was easy to over-correct the steering, making for a nerve-wracking ride—especially, when compounded with our short wheelbase. The sensation was not unlike driving a go-cart at over a hundred forty miles per hour. At sixteen, what the hell did we know? It was a squirrelly machine, but fast enough to make the scary part short-lived and bring in a few trophies.

People in the stands always gave a loud cheer when the announcer called out that *The FUBAR Special* was coming up next. I've never been sure if it was the name, FUBAR, or to hear the crazy chick scream over the sound of the engine at is it shrieks its way down the strip. It's the same scream when riding a roller coaster—and yet, you keep going back for more. Then there was always the possibility for the crowd to go *nutso* at seeing poor ol' FUBAR disintegrate on the track.

About six months later, during the final elimination run for the night, I rolled up to the starting line after a wild burnout heating the tires into a nice sticky gum for good traction. With the engine percolating, I cranked it up to ear-shocking crackling thunder as I anticipated the Christmas tree green light down to a nanosecond and jumped ahead with my superior low-end torque. The other driver burned his tires filling the air with smoke before taking a good bite and sending him down the strip.

Unexpectedly, FUBAR drifted off course and having over-corrected, I find myself in wonderland before realizing what had happened. I'm now looking at the starting line as the other dragster blew past me as I almost tip over in a wild spin. My engine and the rest of the machine took a short trip gyrating out of control down the strip and burst out in a blaze of glory. Good ol' FUBAR had severed itself aft of my cockpit.

Evidently, a bad weld and weak point, and no cross braces. When metal flexes, it eventually breaks in a poorly designed chassis, especially, after receiving such high torque after six months of racing, thus, causing a catastrophic systemic reaction to the chassis. In other words—torque, one, welding and design, zero—but the fans loved it, and now they got what they'd come to see.

After climbing out of the machine unhurt, they gave me my first standing ovation, with lots of whistles, hoots, and applauding. I stood for a moment not knowing how to respond. So, I took off my helmet showing my long hair, grease pit face, and a colossal smile while giving them a bow. They seemed shocked to see a girl driver for a short silent moment, then with enhanced yelling and screaming, they showed their appreciation, they loved it—my first showgirl gig.

And with a glance at poor ol' FUBAR, I'm thinking, damn, our high school metal shop welding class was way overrated.

Today, I miss the sound of an eight thousand horsepower top-fuel dragster crackling to life. It has always been music to my ears. Oh, how I miss the ride. But it's no way as daunting as a hike in the wilderness—yikes; the idea makes me shiver at the thought...

Having given this wilderness dilemma some thought, it would be like finding a lost unknown tribe in the Amazon, and then transporting a tribesman out of his habitat and let him off at Times Square. He's now standing in front of the New York Times Tower, featuring all its electronic billboards, honking cabs, and four hundred thousand pedestrians streaming down the sidewalks every day...

Get my drift?

Now, back to my love...

I'm sure you consider this racing stuff overrated. However, as a kid, my mother gave me a record with nothing but the sound of fuel dragsters taking a run down the drag strip. Believe me, it's true. I told her the record was the greatest gift she ever gave me—and I meant it, but the gift was a serious error on her part.

When having friends over, we listened to my recording, but the smoking light was out. Sometimes, I'd spray a touch of *nitro-methane fuel* in the air using my grandmother's 1940's glass *perfume* atomizer and then crank up the sound. We would trade off sitting between the two speakers that would shake Dad's reclining chair and inhale the nitro fumes to experience the full simulation of driving down the drag strip. It must have driven my mother nuts with the speakers shaking our house down to the foundation—giggle.

With that thought and a twist of the wrist, I fire up my insignificant eight hundred fifty mustang ponies and head my *Little Miss Sunshine* home.

ACT II – SCENE 15
ENHANCING THE LEARNING PROCESS

Question 1
Have you ever experienced a few days in the mountains or woods anything close to what poor Jackie had gone through? If so, please tell us your story.

Question 2
In product costing, what is the unique idea about the way the author discusses material cost? What are your thoughts on that idea? Explain both.

Question 3
If the target price is too low, what are the repercussions?
And, if the price is too high, what will the results be?

Question 4
What are the customers' expectations when considering what they must pay?

Question 5
What are a few good strategies for pricing when the market is not price-sensitive?

Question 6
What are your thoughts about Jackie using her grandmother's 1940's glass perfume atomizer to spray *nitro-methane fuel* in the air?

ACT III
The Resolution

ACT III SCENE 1
Good Processes Equals Style

WEEK 8 – FRIDAY MORNING – JOHNNY SAYS THE BEST EXECUTIVES, POLITICIANS, ACTORS, ARTISTS, COURTROOM LAWYERS, WRITERS, AND DIRECTORS HAVE ONE THING IN COMMON...

PONDERING OVER OUR DIFFERENT HERITAGE

Sheri has been flying the Pacific Rim for a week now and due in around three tomorrow morning for a weekend stay.

Tonight, I enjoyed dinner with a few faculty friends and arrived home early. After placing the mail on the coffee table, I walk over to my CD and turn it on. In the kitchen, I pull out a Corona from the refrigerator and pop the top. While contemplating Sheri's letter in my stack of mail, I take a swig and head back into the living room to grab her letter and collapse on the sofa.

When opening the envelope, Frank Sinatra is singing *Love Me Tender*. The letter reads...

I love you, Sheri.

Frank's timing is perfect—that's why they called him Chairman of the Board.

When looking around the room, the last glitter of sunlight filters its way through the plantation shutters creating long shadows over the floor and walls. For the first time, I'm noticing and appreciating the things Sheri has given me that she made while at the Rocky Mountain College of Art: two beautiful abstract paintings, an incredible abstract ceramic multi-colored end table with a thick glass oval top, and a cute little sterling silver bear sitting in white coral, and of course, my funny pink poke a dot silly little elephant, I call Elli.

As Old Blue Eyes finishes *Love Me Tender*, I consider how he sounds a lot like me...

Well, maybe not—Sinatra once said *Good singers are connected between the throat and the heart*. For me, I guess, I'm missing the interconnect part of it.

On my bedroom dresser, I have a large framed color picture of Sheri and me squatting on the balcony looking into our room at the Coronado Hotel, San Diego. It's my favorite picture—we appear to have a good presence together—

happy. Damn, this kind of thinking scares the crap out of me. Hell, one day, Sheri asked me, why don't we get married? Well, being a typical wisenheimer, I told her that's a wonderful idea, but who would have us?

Toni once told me, if the Navy wanted you to have a wife, they'd have issued you one—my feelings exactly. One day, I asked my dad what is it about women us guys don't get. He told me we've been missing the understated subtitles when they were speaking.

Well, anyhow, having wondered how a middle-class girl with a father who owned a few gas stations gave me this feeling she came from aristocracy, and I soon discovered why. Sheri's father is one of the top five hundred wealthiest men in the world...

He owns a natural *gas* exploration company in Oklahoma. Hey, what do I know from gas? When one is surrounded by wealth their whole life and saying *my father is in gas*—well, that's just the truth—owning a gas station would never enter their minds.

Her great-great-grandfather was a general in the Confederate army, her great-grandfather a general in the Spanish-American War, and her grandfather the one-time mayor and a famous Oklahoma City judge. She gave me his autobiography to read—interesting guy.

Her ninety-year-old grandmother is president of a real estate firm in Beverly Hills, California. By American standards, Sheri is royalty and comes from strong stock.

For me, on the other hand, with my ignoble heritage is being related to Emiliano Zapata, the famous leader of the Mexican Revolution, and with family having lived in California for over two hundred years. We weren't rich, but have been a happy middle-class family—well, for at least the last hundred and fifty years...

When living at home with four brothers, each of us received a lot of phone calls. When a friend called, they would ask for Zapata. My mother's answer would always be the same... *There's a whole house full of 'em*, and hang up.

My great-great-great-grandfather once owned a California land grant given to him by Mexico's government in 1824, at the time, an independent nation of Mexico. He named his ranch, Rancho de la Angeles.

By the late 1840s, the American economic sphere of influence in California began to take hold. Nevertheless, the real change came during the gold rush period of the 1850s. In the words of author *J.S. Holliday, the world rushed in*.

After the American-Mexican WAR and the treaty of 1848, the Mexican landowners became United States citizens allowing a guarantee of their land under their constitutional property rights. Regrettably, the old American tradition of squatter's rights became a serious problem for the landowner. It's the idea that occupying vacant land entitled them to ownership, which soon became a serious problem for the rancho owners.

The legal battles with the squatters, along with their property taxes broke the back of the Mexican land-grant owners. Therefore, any wealth passed on from land ownership dissolved into the land itself. Now, if we still owned the land, our property would have been worth billions of dollars today.

My father taught aircraft maintenance at Los Angeles Technical Institute for over twenty-five years and retired last year. So how does a woman like Sheri fall for a guy like me?

I've done well financially—which is relative, of course. However, I'm in the farm club league when compared to the friends she grew up with—except, it feels more like the Princess and the Pauper...

As of late, I've not handled myself well with her. This division in our background has been at the root cause of my problem. So, wanting to move forward, I must get my act together and get this behind me. I pondered on this for a while watching a Netflix movie before turning in.

I've not yet fallen asleep as I descend into a state of reverie when Sheri gets in around two-thirty in the morning.

A half-hour later, she slips into bed and snuggles up with me like a small stack of spoons. Now, I ask you, why do woman take so long to ready themselves for bed? For me, it's always been a mystery.

When seven-thirty rolls around and less than four and a half hours sleep, it's time to get up. I wander around for a few minutes letting the blood circulate, splash water on my face, and then into the kitchen, where I fix myself scrambled eggs, toast, and coffee. After cleaning up my dishes, I head to my office to catch up on a few things. Later, I'll take Sheri down to the beach, and with any luck, take a run.

Finished with my work, I stroll back into the bedroom where Sheri has her blanket pulled over her head lying motionless with the sun splashing its golden light around the room

I shook her shoulder several times and got no response, so I whisper in her ear...

"Babe, if you don't show signs of life soon, I'll need to call the taxidermist."

Hearing this, she pokes her head out from under the covers with huge pink curlers in her hair. Ah ha—some of her pre-bed routines come to light.

I express my good morning with my best Lubbock, Texas accent...

"Well, howdy doody, little Ruby Jo, you must be hankern' to go to the dance tonight after the game. It's either that or you're wearing antennas for listening to old Hank Williams radio shows."

"Ruby Jo?" She said.

"Your curlers, babe—I've never seen you in curlers."

She rubs her eyes...

"Huh? What time is it?"

"It's nine-thirty."

"Yikes."

"Yikes?"

"Yes, yikes."

Excited, she jumps out of bed and runs over to give me a hug...

"We've got two seats on United 808, a twelve fifty-five to San Francisco to meet my parents today."

More accurately, that would be her father and stepmother. Her mother died when she was a child.

With the idea of meeting her parents, I'm sucking wind...

"Your PARENTS?"

"Yes. My dad reserved us a room at the Westin St. Francis."

"You want to introduce me to ... ah ... *your* parents?"

"Why yes, silly. Why not, I love you."

"You do? And here I thought you only enjoyed our sex."

"Well there is that," She said, "You also make a mean breakfast."

"Ah... Fantastic sex and a mean breakfast—that's an unbeatable combination—it's no wonder you love me."

"Ah... I don't believe I used the word *fantastic*."

"Well, I'm sure you meant to."

Sheri giggles as she walks' away shedding my pajama top and oscillates her cute little butt toward the shower.

"Would you like a little distraction before hitting the shower?"

Sheri turns with a flirtatious look...

"What kind of a little distraction are we talking about here?"

"I'm planning on poking a little fun at you."

She advances toward me with her alluring moves. She moved her hips to the left, she moved hips to the right, and then she gave me the hippy, hippy, shakes... With hips swaying, head down, and her blue eyes looking up at me in a seductive way, she grabs my hair and pulls me toward her moist lips.

After stepping out of the shower, Sheri sees me in my walk-in closet, sashays over and checks out my creative way of organization...

"So tell me, Johnny, did you just get burglarized?"

Wisenheimer broad...

Later, we're both dressed to the nines. Sheri's bringing her new purse—gigantic enough to serve as a steamer-trunk movie-prop.

"Are you bringing along your hairdresser so he can run around in that purse of yours keeping things tidy?"

"Silly you, one needs room for a can of Mace."

"I can appreciate that, babe, but *that* purse could hold a container ship full of Mace."

She ignored me.

Greeting me when walking from the living room into the entry hall is a stack of luggage dropped off by the L.A. Lakers basketball team.

"What the hell? Did you hire a moving van to drop this off when you arrived last night?"

"Oh, Johnny, it's only a few carry-on bags."

THE FLIGHT TO SAN FRANCISCO

Later, we're standing in line waiting to be screened for dangerous carry-on items, when one of the security guys came over and asked me to step out of line and move to the special security line.

"Why lovable me, do I appear suspicious to you?"

"We pick a number at random and select that person—sorry, sir."

"So... If I'd not been selected with a random number, even though I looked suspicious such as ahh... One passing through from Sand Land wearing a kufiya wrapped around my head, an ISIS flag armband, bandoliers strapped across my chest with an AK-Forty Seven assault rifle hanging on my shoulder, and camel dung squished up between my toes, you'd let me through, right?"

He looked at me long and hard before he began to laugh...

"Maybe not, but that is a funny image you've painted."

Having made it through TSA's security screening without further ado, we find ourselves sitting and people watching waiting to board our plane. At a nearby agent's desk of an overcrowded flight, we see an angry passenger push his way to the head of the line. After slapping down his ticket on the agent's counter, he shouts...

"I must be on this flight... Oh yeah, one other thing—it better be first class."

The agent looks up at him, then in a calm voice...

"I will be happy to take care of your needs as soon as I help these folks ahead of you."

Not happy with the agent's reply, he yelled loud enough for half the people in the terminal to hear him...

"DO YOU HAVE ANY *IDEA* ... WHO I AM, YOUNG LADY?"

The agent takes a moment to observe the man and smiles as she grabs her public address phone and announces...

"ATTENTION PLEASE, MAY I HAVE YOUR ATTENTION FOR THOSE OF YOU IN THE VICINITY OF GATE SEVEN?"

She takes in a deep breath and continues...

"THERE IS A MAN AT THE GATE WHO HAS NO KNOWLEDGE OF WHO HE IS—IF THERE IS ANYONE IN THE TERMINAL THAT CAN HELP IDENTIFY THE MAN, PLEASE COME FORWARD."

The crowd around the agent's desk goes into hysterical laughter.

Mr. Self-importance retreats to the back of the line to meet Mr. Humble.

When boarding the aircraft, I get this uncomfortable feeling of sitting in first class. It's not from air sickness or white knuckles—but being from the middle-class. Hey, now you're considering me to be a serious nut case. But hear me out. I've always had a problem with people paid to be nice to me such as flight attendants, waiters, and limo drivers—well, except for a good-looking waitress. Now you can see why I carry this problem around with me about Sheri and our different heritages.

When trying to get over this dilemma using my wisecracking, my humor didn't appear to go over well at high altitude. So, I tried looking around to check out the flight attendants, but that didn't work as I wondered how *hot* they must have looked when in their twenty's. Hey... You guys grasp what I mean. Right then, Sheri elbows me in the arm...

"Honey, I picked up a little surprise for you in Hong Kong."

I answer with a lackluster voice...

"What's that?"

Sheri opens her steamer-trunk and hands me a small red, felt-covered snap-open box.

Looking at the jewelry box, my body temperature rises eight degrees, which creates rivulets of sweat pouring off my brow. Good God, Sheri is going to propose to me—all at once, sharp tongue woman comes to mind. This is scary shit going through my mind as I open the box.

"What the hell?" I said, "An Omega watch."

"Isn't beautiful?"

"It is, but I'm sure it set you back a fortune."

"You're more than worthy of such a gift darling. It's a Seamaster James Bond limited edition."

"Come on now, you bought this from a schlockmeister with his inside coat lined with several hundred watches made from recycled plastic and tin cans, right?"

"You're such a silly. No... It's the real thing."

While grabbing my wrist, she removes my fifteen dollar Walmart Casio Men's Digital Sports Watch and slips on the Omega.

"Wow, I don't know what to say, I'm lost for words."

she leans over to kiss my cheek...

"Well, that tells me everything I need to know—you love it."

"Thanks, babe, but why did you spend so much money on me?"

"Because I love you and can afford it, and it'll impress dad to see you with such a fine watch."

Well, the good news is, it's a watch, not an engagement ring. It was, after all, very considerate on her part...

"Thanks, babe—I shall wear this wonderful gift until the day I die."

"Let's hope that isn't too soon, Johnny."

"Good point."

The flight was the worst ever. Severe turbulence followed us the whole time. When we approached the runway, Sheri gazes out her window seat...

"We seem to be a trifle high for a good landing."

I observe her with a puzzled expression...

"What are your thoughts on that?"

"Well, knowing where we should have touched down, the pilot ought to have aborted the landing."

I snickered with a tough-guy attitude...

"Should we be thumbing through our prayer beads?".

Just then, the plane powered up and then dropped like a rock and hit hard.

The wing spoilers whined as they increased the drag followed by the jet engine's thrust reversers kicking in along with severe breaking. Things began happening too fast as we skidded down the runway. The bumping begins to get worse. And then, we decelerated enough we didn't overshoot the runway while a few of us looked around to see if this was the *Big One*.

Sheri looks at me with a grin on her face. Me, I'm looking down hoping not to see I've pissed in my pants.

"That was fun," she said.

"Oh yeah, if you want to get your money's worth, I like all my flights to end with a flare like this one."

Sheri giggles.

The plane seemed to hold together as we began our taxi approach to the gate. The flight attendant told us to please remain seated until United's 808 flight parks—and thanks us for flying the friendly skies of United.

"Friendly?"

A few minutes later after docking, we deplane. The captain is standing at the door with a joyful smile when Sheri nudges my arm and reminds me of the captain's poor landing performance.

"No kidding," I said. "Well, you should say something to Flyboy. You're qualified to do so."

With that, she shouted... "CAPTAIN, DID WE JUST LAND? OR WERE WE SHOT DOWN?"

Gee, I wish I'd of thought of that, giving my babe a look of admiration, and crack up with the rest of the joyful passengers.

The captain joins in with the passengers, and then hollers...

"WE WERE SHOT DOWN, BUT BEING THE GOOD CAPTAIN I AM, I MADE A ROUGH BUT SAFE LANDING."

This, of course, brings out a burst of laughter and applauding from the cabin crew and passengers. You have to admire the guy, great comeback.

"It's an old joke among us pilots, but I've never heard such a great retort," She said. "I'm sure the captain will make a point to tell his wife about it tonight over dinner. Landings account for a third of general aviation accidents... Aircraft landing is an art form—lots of flying and training are required with the same type of aircraft. Even so, sometimes, you get it wrong."

ST. FRANCIS HOTEL

Soon after checking into the St. Francis hotel, we are escorted to our room on the thirty-second floor that overlooks Union Square in downtown San Francisco. Union Square acquired its name during the Civil War. Back then, construction in and around the square is where pro-Union folks held rallies to support the war effort. Hm... It would seem things seldom change—especially, in this town with its diversity of cultures...

The St. Francis has an old and a new tower with over a thousand rooms.

Fatty Arbuckle, a once-famous silent-film comedian, held a rowdy party where actress Virginia Rappe died. They accused Arbuckle of her murder and then acquitted him. However, it took a long time for the fascinated public to forgive him following the Hollywood scandal. Those were the days.

Leaning near the windowsill, I feel the warmth of the sun penetrating through the glass. When looking down on the street, I see a river of cars not unlike a salmon run during the spawning season. Most appear to be yellow, cabs I guess, racing around as though they needed a place to go.

"I'm going to *refresh* myself, but I'll only be a few minutes," Sheri said.

The bathroom door closes.

I'm sure when she comes out of the bathroom—she'll assume it was *only* for a few minutes. But having experienced the time it takes for that mystical and unknown process, I take a test nap on our mattress. Thirty minutes later, she comes out and wakes me from my special little place and tells me to tidy myself up while she calls her dad.

After taking a couple minutes to refresh we're headed down the hallway toward her parent's room. I'm getting uptight having this need to impress Sheri's parents in the worst way...

Hmmm... What would my friend Tom do? Maybe I should try assembling my good traits...

Ah... My fantastic winsome smile—that's always a good one...

Okay then, how about giving them the ol' sparkling eye routine? No...?

What about showing my best profile the whole time—Tom's good at that...

Um... If that doesn't impress them, I can always do my Gold's Gym, swagger...

Ahh... If I could just strut around like a banty rooster while sitting down—like my friend Tom... Ah... Well, maybe not.

A moment later, I'm knocking on her parent's hotel room door.

I'm in sheer panic...

"How do I look?"

"Shouldn't I be asking that question?" Sheri said with a frown.

"Why? They already see you as the cat's meow."

"You appear okay."

"Just okay? Not great?"

I'm not insecure, but I am a little nervous.

Before Sheri could answer me, the door opens. I stood aside waiting for my introduction as I go into a state of trepidation and hypertension. Meanwhile; they welcome Sheri with hugs and kisses. With Sheri grinning from ear to ear, she introduces me to her father—we shake hands, and then a nice hug from her stepmom, Candice. Whew, I didn't collapse on the floor.

Sean is a ruggedly handsome man in his early sixties with an athletic build. Her stepmom, Candice, is beautiful and maybe ten years older than Sheri.

We made ourselves comfortable as we share a bottle of chilled white wine while getting acquainted. Evidently, I passed the test because Sheri's folks began to warm up to me...

Now, I realize you were against the idea about me cozying up to her parent's using my sparkling-eye routine, but now, I'm sure you recognize that's what did it. The wine, of course, helped a little.

Later, after the wine bottle showed little sign of additional life, Sean glances over at Candice and Sheri with a smile, and then over to me while taking two cigars from his travel humidor and put them in his inside breast pocket...

"Johnny, why don't we go down and have a few drinks in the hotel bar, I'm sure the ladies would like to get caught up on whatever women get caught up on," Sean said with a grin,

"I'd like that."

Rising from the sofa, I glance at each of the two ladies with an amiable smile and a nod...

"Ladies"

They try not to laugh, but the moment got to them with a giggle as we head toward the door—women.

"Gentlemen, we'll be down to get you in an hour," Candice said.

Sean had made dinner reservations at six o'clock, giving us enough time to arrive at the nearby Marines Memorial Theater for opening night at eight o'clock. We were going to see the off-Broadway hit, *Men are from Mars, Women are from Venus*. A well-timed play for my state of mind.

Getting off the elevator, we head into the lounge with its high ceilings, elegant black marble top bar, and well-appointed furniture. They decorated and painted everything in off-white with splashes of gloss black. It's a nice elegant place to enjoy a drink.

We belly up to the bar and order ourselves a Bushmills whiskey.

When heading toward a vacant table, Sean looked at me...

"So, you're a Bushmills guy, hey?"

"Yeah, but I have a story that goes along with drinking Bushmills."

After we settle in, along with a moment of silence, I jump in...

"You know, the funny thing is, I started drinking Bushmills after reading a Jack Higgins novel. Sean Dillon, the main character always ordered Bushmills in the pub when planning out his next move," I said, and then take a quick sip of my drink... "So, thinking it would give me the edge I needed at the appropriate time, I tried it.

"And?" Sean said.

"No such luck, I do better with a clear mind. I did, however, acquire a liking for an occasional taste."

Sean acknowledges with a nod and smile.

"I took my first drink of Bushmills at the Woodstock festival while Jimi Hendrix played *The Star-Spangled Banner*."

"Wow, it doesn't get any better than that—a one of a kind event...

I once read that Elvis Presley said that Woodstock was an excuse to get naked, get high and roll around in the mud—"

Sean began to laugh...

"Elvis nailed that one right..."

"Perhaps, someday, when we get a chance, I'd love to hear more about Woodstock."

GOOD PROCESSES EQUAL STYLE—A DISCUSSION IN THE ST. FRANCIS BAR

"So, tell me, Johnny, what does a Professor of Organizational Theory and Marketing at Pepperdine University *address* during your discourse? *And*, perhaps, expound on your new consulting job."

Waiting on my response, Sean removes a cigar, offered me one, but I shook my head to a cigar slightly smaller than a Little League bat. He leaned back puffing on his cigar while rolling it from side to side as he toasted it over his lighter, then put the unusual lighter down on the table.

Casting my eyes upward, I watch the smoke bluing the air as it drifts upward pooling at the ceiling, and then zoom in on his lighter.

"Excuse me, Sean, but I must comment on your lighter. It's a beautiful piece of art. I may be wrong, but it resembles the 007 logo on my watch."

"Thanks, Johnny, and yes, it is. It's a James Bond Spectre 007 black lighter."

Ahh... Now, I see the significances of my 007 watch...

Um... Very impressive..."

Well, back to answering your question..."

With pressed lips, I focus on Sean and then told him my story...

After giving him a brief rundown of my tenure at the university and my recent experiences at ATC, he wanted to hear more about the system processes. He found the subject most interesting—big mistake.

"Did you ever wonder why there are businesses capable of expanding and more profitable than other businesses with a similar product?"

"No, but I'm listening."

"Well, the answer lies within the performance characteristics of the business processes influenced by the individuality and behavior of its management and employees, but most of all, by the CEO...

Let's say you have two identical companies both in size, location, and within the same market. Now, these two companies went through the transformation process by the same consulting group changing them over to a horizontal open-systemic organization. Each will show dramatic results, but one will be superior."

"Why is that?" Sean asked.

"I asked Jake Jensen the same question. He told me that businesses are organic and that no two organisms are ever identical. The human brain, without a doubt, is the most complex organ in the known universe. And with that in mind, each CEO has a unique way of looking at the world that influences his or her perception of their company's place in their market.

Let's say, the first company under the leadership of their CEO has focused his recruitment to those with advanced degrees in their profession, especially, those with MBA's. He felt this would enable him to build their business system to a rhythm of consistency in their processes and move to the forefront in their level of performance—good, but not great...

For the second company, its CEO has pulled together a bunch of serious *creative* talent—"

"Excuse me, Johnny. Why select creativity over advanced degrees?"

"That's a great question, Sean...

In the business transformation of the sort we consult to our customer's, we have learned that creativity goes beyond one's intelligence or knowledge, and advances to a higher level of knowledge creation...

We travel beyond those who have earned their MBA's, knowing they have no relationship with our new organizational values. If anything, those who were taught the MBA way of thinking, can at times, hinder the transformation process—"

"That's fascinating, Johnny. It sounds as if your consulting group has made a major breakthrough in the business transformation process."

"Thanks, Sean. That was my first impression after Jake gave an introduction to their new way of building a business of the future...

Well, to continue...

The CEO and his creative talent used their complex and unpredictable organs to challenge the key weighted processes for higher MPV benchmark performance output, staying synchronized, while improving the total system...

In developing competitive systems, you must have well trained, and creative employees or the results will be mediocre...

Art would be a good example such as drawing or painting a picture is a process. If one possesses a good teacher, most anyone can produce an acceptable result—well, that may not be true—my grandmother said she can't even draw flies."

"I'm with your grandmother on that one."

"However, the difference lies in the painter's *style*, a creative process that can produce artists like, Warhol, Miro, Picasso, Pollock, Serra, and so on.

Better yet, let's take a filmmaker as a model...

How many filmmakers can make movies time and again that you can recognize who made the film by the style of their work? Not many. A few cases might be directors such as Hitchcock, Tarantino, and Eastwood...

I would add, the best of the businessmen, politicians, actors, artists, courtroom lawyers, writers, and directors have one thing in common—they too have learned a specific process that gets results. These processes become a system that becomes their *style*, resulting in good consistent results.

For companies, process design shouldn't ever be taken lightly. Processes are the arteries that put life into a system, and how they choose to process or develop the design will change the output of the system. And the style will determine the consistency of strength, or lack of, within that system...

In short, that's the organic side of the business...

Sorry, that must have sounded like you were sitting in on a lecture."

"Not at all, Johnny, that was fascinating," He said with a chuckle, "I'm so project and task-oriented, I've never considered how important the system processes can be to a business. When I contemplate about it, though, drilling for gas falls into your theory of process, style, and results."

"Nonetheless, you've discovered your own style because of your success in gas exploration. You just didn't recognize it as a process, or style."

Silence hangs in the air for a moment...

"The drilling of deep wells has always intrigued me, but I possess little knowledge about the industry."

"It's a rough business, Johnny. You can make a lot of money or lose a lot. It cost millions to drill a well, and a dry hole doesn't help the cash flow. Drill too many dry ones, and you're out of business—as you said its process, style, and results...

Our success rate is exceptional at eighty percent over the last ten years with the majority of the wells below fifteen thousand feet. But, hell, in Oklahoma's, Anadarko Basin, my good friend Robert Hefner drilled one over five and a half miles down in ol' mother earth back in the 1970s."

"That must be a record hole."

"Yeah, it's still the deepest in the Western Hemisphere.

Often, when we drill these deep wells, the drill bit slows down to two to four feet per hour at an operating cost of tens of thousands of dollars per day. Not making things any easier is controlling the precise trajectory of a well when the drill bit is approaching three miles below the surface of the earth."

"What a fascinating business, I'd love to go aboard one of those rigs and see the process in action."

"You're welcome to come down anytime, Johnny."

"I'd love to. But, please, tell me more about the gas industry?"

"Well, the rate of production in our industry per well has been declining each year. With the demand going up, we've increased drilling. For instance, overall, most wells are less than three years old and account for sixty percent of the country's natural gas production.

The reason for lagging gas production in the past had to do with old gas fields still in operation causing diminishing returns each year. The lack of new public lands for exploration is more difficult due to federal restrictions.

With that said, as geologists, we've known shale rock holds substantial amounts of natural gas, but until recent times, the gas was considered unreachable. But in today's world, gas producers have expanded the use of *horizontal* drilling...

A mile below the surface, the drill operator steers the drill into a horizontal position running across the shale layer, therefore, accessing more of the shale than in a vertical well. When using water and sand in the process, it forces a fracture in the shale, opening millions of tiny cracks in the rock, and enabling additional gas to seep out.

Conservatively speaking, a shale formation stretching from New York to West Virginia may hold as much as five hundred trillion cubic feet of natural gas. There are also large gas basins in Texas, Wyoming, Arkansas, and Michigan.

During the past decade, U.S. natural gas production has increased over fifty percent, and enough natural gas to power our economy for decades or perhaps centuries.

Robert Hefner, whom I mentioned earlier, told me...

At one time, I said the nation is awash in natural gas. Now I say we're drowning in it."

There is a moment of silence as Sean drew on his cigar to enjoy the flavor and aroma, then blew the smoke upward... Looked at his cigar, and then flicked the perfect barrel-shaped ash into the ashtray.

"In Hefner's recent book, *The Grand Energy Transition*, he lays out a case that natural gas would lower greenhouse gas emissions and reduce the U.S. dependence on foreign oil. Much of the nation's electrical power using coal has now switched over to natural gas...

As for vehicles burning imported oil, we could convert half our nation's vehicles to using natural gas and reduce oil consumption by an equal amount. I'd also add that over ten million vehicles now on the road are using natural gas.

Hefner and I both agree that in the near future, we will begin moving into a hydrogen economy with the help of natural gas in the transition period. And by mid-century, we should have a stabilized environmental hydrogen energy program as our end game."

"You and Jake Jensen should get together. He's big on natural gas and hydrogen, mainly for use as a vehicle's power source. He gets something into his head, and he makes things happen."

"Interesting."

Sean and I have now gotten around to the subject of women as most men do. At this point, I confess to Sean, I have a psychological problem trying to deal with Sheri's wealthy family background as opposed to my humble life. I'm bumfuzzled, I told him because I see future problems that would impede a happy future together.

Sean smiles and tells me stories from his worldly experiences that have great meaning and uplifting advice on women and how to better understand them—however, *he prefaced his advice by swearing me to secrecy*—sorry about that, guys.

After listening to him, I realized, he must be the smartest man on earth.

A moment before the ladies arrived, he told me he'd be proud to have me as a son-in-law if that's what I've been worried about. I feel as though a ton of bricks fell off my shoulders having talked with Sheri's father. My relief coincided well with Sheri and Candice entering the bar.

When seeing Sheri, I stand up, walk over to her and hug her while whispering in her ear...

"I am so in love with you."

With her arms around my neck, she looks up at me as tears began to form...

"Oh, how I've longed to hear you say that—I shall always remember this moment my darling."

Guys, I am so sorry about this mushy stuff—but the ladies like it.

ATTACK OF THE MUNCHIES

As we walk back toward the hotel after a great time at the theater, we had an attack of the munchies. With that in mind, Sean had the idea of taking us to a late-night place called the Witchery to experience a wonderful post-theater menu.

I wasted little time in hailing us a taxi. Coming toward us is a battered, dirty-yellow Chevy cab. Its engine sounds like a washing machine on steroids. He sees us and pulls over near the curb with its loose dangling muffler shooting out its black exhaust. At the curb, the tailpipe stuttered and rattled.

The cabbie waited for us to alight before he let the old girl leap forward jerking and sputtering as if this was a one-way trip to the scrap heap. I sat up front and watched the driver's knuckles tightened around the steering wheel as the dirty yellow cab melted into the traffic leaving the Marines Memorial Theater in the rearview mirror. As we enter an incoming fog bank, the cabbie turns on his one working windshield wiper, but luckily, it matched up to the driver's side and his one working headlight that would guide us to our destination. A few blocks from the Witchery, the taxi takes its last gasping breath and dies near the curb.

I paid the cabbie and wished him well. Locked arm in arm, we walk the rest of the way in the cold, damp fog that comes in from Golden Gate Bay. Sheri told us that the heat from the central valley causes the air to rise, creating a strong wind that pulls moist air in from the ocean through the break in the hills. This movement of moist air causes a dense fog to find its way into the bay area—Sheri, meteorologist.

From the outside, the restaurant looks like most any pub you'd find in old foggy London town. We're soon escorted to a table near a large open fireplace where we laughed and discussed the fun menu of late-night munchies.

During dinner, Candice asked me how Sheri and I met.

"Well, Sheri was on the Internet looking up the translation for *hombre,* and what she found was a picture of me and my phone number.

Sheri snorted, and her face turned red.

"I did nothing of the sort."

She was, of course, drowned out by laughter.

Sunday, we met for brunch with Sheri's parents where we said our thanks and goodbyes. Two hours later, we boarded our plane and headed south.

That night in bed, I told Sheri I had a wonderful weekend and thanked her for the opportunity to meet her parents. For the first time in my life, I held a woman in my arms the entire night—domestic bliss. Anything is possible...

By the way, I hope I wasn't moving too fast for you guys to miss anything.

ACT III - SCENE 1
ENHANCING THE LEARNING PROCESS

Question: 1
With a better understanding of how the Mexican land grant owners lost their land to squatters and land taxes back in the mid-1800s, was it justifiable?

What would have been on your mind if you were a land grant owner facing this problem?

Question: 2
In your own words, what have you learned about how companies producing products or services for the same market, can have such different results?

Question: 3
What are your ideas on why Sean made Johnny swear to secrecy when telling him the secret of how best to understand a woman?

Moreover, what do you think Sean told Johnny?

ACT III SCENE 2
Revenue Recognition

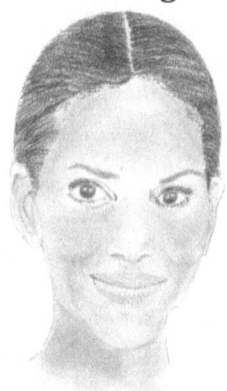

WEEK 9 – TUESDAY MORNING – JACKIE MEETS NINA IN HER OFFICE TO WRAP UP LOOSE ENDS, MOST NOTABLY, COST REVENUE RECOGNITION

A CABIN IN THE SKY

Monday evening I head toward Toni's place for a barbeque. Toni once told me he's light on fixing his own meals. Peanut butter and jelly sandwiches were about it for his time in the kitchen, but being an Okie saddle stiff, he knew how to cook over a campfire or do a mean outdoor barbeque.

Questioning Toni's culinary ability, I asked Jake if Toni was that bad about cooking for himself. Jake laughed...

"*Bad* you say, you bet. That boy has to count on the smoke detector to signal him when his dinner is ready."

When arriving at his condo at six o'clock, I engage in pleasantries with two elderly gentlemen sitting in the lobby and then check in with the security lady. She gives me a jolly wave of the hand acknowledging my expected arrival.

Waiting for the elevator is a hefty woman wearing an unusual dress of waving black and white stripes. We smile and say our good-evenings.

The door opens and we're confronted with a guy hanging onto the inside rail of the elevator. He has this perplexed appearance while staring at us with bloodshot eyes and his index finger jammed up his nose as his cigarette dangles from his lower lip. He reacted to the sight by delivering a shot-glass size shower of spittle mixed in with alcohol as he shouted...

"AIN'T ANY FRIGGIN ZEBRA GETTING ON THIS FRIGGIN ELEVATOR WITH ME."

I giggled to myself at the situation as I considered my options. The best way to handle a drunk is to be his best friend; anything else gets out of hand. With that thought, I motioned to the lady to hold up as I stepped into the elevator...

"Can you recommend a worthy place a lady can get a drink?"

This seemed to calm him down—Jackie O', method actor.

I put my arm around his shoulder and walked him out of the elevator and winked at Zebra Lady with a nod encouraging her to get on the elevator.

I wasted no time complimenting the guy on how big and strong he was, and asked him if he lifted weights. He mumbled something while stumbling along the corridor. The security guard hearing his yelling meets me halfway and takes over the situation and thanks me.

While riding the elevator to the sixteenth floor, I couldn't help but grin about the zebra remark. Halfway down the hallway, I stopped in front of a mirror to primp and touch-up my hair several times, then continue down to Toni's sanctuary.

I'm a scant nervous standing there looking at his door, so I take a deep breath and knock. A moment later in the still silence, my giant Indian friend suddenly fills the doorway like magic, but this is typical for Toni. No matter what he does, he emits no sound. He appears or disappears on an impulse. Jake once told me Toni could disappear while shaking your hand...

After reaching out and giving the big lug a hug, he moves aside as I step into a good-sized rectangular room. I'm immobilized by my mouth hung agape in an unnatural position. Blinking several times while glancing around, I have an awareness of the room's warmth with its beams and rough-cut wood ceiling. Indian rugs cover wide, wooden-plank floors. The rough-cut log walls, caulked with a form of off-white grout give you the feeling you've just stepped into the little house on the prairie.

"What the hell is a damned log cabin doing on the sixteenth floor of a condominium?" I mumble to myself.

Toni stands back with crinkles formed at the corner of his eyes.

As I gaze around the room, I'm fascinated with the old, worn and comfortable-looking furniture. There's the coffee table made from an ancient bellow mounted on three legs sitting in front of the leather sofa. Two chairs with beautiful throw pillows covered in Indian designs snuggled up on each, facing the sofa and adjacent to the bellows. The end tables and lamps are early twentieth-century rustic design, and placed about the room are several wicker chairs. My eyes then gravitate upwards...

"What the hell is that?" I mutter.

The added light in the room comes from a grand chandelier hanging from a chain. It's the most whimsical piece of art I've ever laid eyes on. The thing has five foxes sitting around on an ample size ring or hoop. They're dressed in old-fashioned western clothes holding a light in each paw with their eyes looking down at the floor.

With a heightened curiosity, I continue to observe this log cabin in the sky envisioning I may have walked into the twilight zone. Devoted to one wall are rough-cut shelves loaded with books and artifacts. On another wall, hangs a large painting by the prolific artist, Charles Russell depicting two riders roping cattle. Mounted on the wall on one side of the painting is an ancient pair of Indian handmade snowshoes, and on the other side are two medieval Norwegian skis. In the dining room are nineteenth-century American farmhouse table and chairs.

"Now that you've taken in this part of my little world like a cat eying its prey, would you like to check out the rest of the place?"

I nod with a wide-eyed look.

Toni grabs my hand and walks me to his bedroom.

"Oh... my... God," I uttered with a sotto voce...

"Did you say something?"

I ignore him. I'm in love with the masculine room, reminding me of the Ponderosa on the *Bonanza* series. On my left are two beautiful, black vintage wicker chairs with seats covered in leopard material. Between the chairs sits an English Victorian three-legged cast-iron side table with a round crystal glass top. Atop the table is an antiquated copper and mica lamp. Taking up one corner of the room is a sandstone fireplace. Above it is a beautiful watercolor painting of a desert scene at sunset. Next to the fireplace is a broad window that takes up the full length of the wall with a fantastic view of the ocean.

The bed sits before a grand cedar paneled wall with one side of the bed having an antler lamp and on the other an art nouveau, both placed on colonial handmade gloss black painted furniture with waxed natural mahogany tops.

Indian rugs placed handsomely about on the old used-plank wooden floors give softness to the room. Ralph Lauren linens cover the bed and pillows. My mouth continues to be in the slack jaw position.

"Are you all right?"

I'm in deep space. My mouth is still ajar.

"My grandmother would say you're going to attract and swallow a horsefly if you don't close your mouth."

"Horsefly ... you have horseflies, too?"

Now, this is a bit much, just to have timeworn cabin realism.

"You seem to be in a form of comatose shock, let me get you a beer and a bowl of nuts," Toni said.

"Not just yet, big boy."

My womanly instinct tells me there's more as I bit my lower lip, so I head for the master bath. When entering, I notice a huge floor to ceiling window overlooking the ocean to my left, and facing the entry is a wall-to-wall slate shower looking like a natural bathing grotto for a grizzly bear. The enclosed floor-to-ceiling glass wall and door reminds me of a wildlife exhibit—minus the grizzly bear—that keeps the water enclosed coming from two showerheads each the size of a trash can lid.

To my right is a light-colored wood, handmade rustic cabinet with a two-sink countertop covered in tumbled stone tile with the countertops several inches or more higher than the standard counter. And resting above the backsplash is a mirror running the length of the counter, expecting anytime for

Paul Bunyan and Babe the big blue ox to stare back at me from the mirror.

The floors are ample size sandstone tiles covered to some extent with a turn-of-the-twentieth-century Oriental rug running in front of the cabinet. Feeling a tug, Toni drags me into the hallway toward the living room like a puppy on her leash.

"Wait... What's behind that door?" I said, pointing to a suspicious door at the other end of the hallway.

"That's my garden-variety home office and attached half-bath."

"Can we see it?"

"If you haven't seen one before, be my guest."

Toni opens the door. I stood there scanning the room with cedar plank paneled walls, plush carpet, a nice spacious antique desk, two computers, fax machine, printer, copier, and a few military photos on the wall. Hmm... No green eyeshades, hand-crank adding machine or quill pens...

"Thanks."

I follow Toni heading toward the kitchen for beer and nuts.

"This tour isn't over yet, Davie Crockett," I said.

"Now what?"

"I want to check out your wood-fired stove with firewood storage, a wooden icebox filled with blocks of ice, and the leaky water pump over the sink," I said in my Ma Kettle voice.

Toni twitched his lower lip.

Entering, I observe a modern kitchen, except for the cabinets, they're dark green with well-worn areas showing shades of black and appear to be decrepit and well used.

"What's with the worn-out cabinets?"

"They're brand new, and yet, appear aged and timeworn."

"Hell, Toni, why didn't you just buy an old cabin instead?"

"Well, I would have, but I couldn't find any near the beach with a favorable view."

We have a pleasant laugh.

A few minutes later as I relax on the sofa, Toni brings out a tray holding two bottles of Sol beer, a bowl of nuts, and slices of lime and places the tray on the bellows coffee table.

"The wonderful thing about this furniture is the more abuse, the better it looks."

"Does that mean I can carve my name in this here end table?"

"My daddy would say you sure know how to make a mash on a man, sweet lady."

"A mash?" I said.

"Impress someone," Toni said.

"*Me* ... impress, *you*?"

"You're the smartest, funniest, most beautiful sweet thing I've ever laid my eyes on—and beauty can best be expressed as the sum of all parts, with nothing added or nothing subtracted."

"Are you sure that's me you're talking about?"

I looked at him with anticipation.

Toni reaches down, pulls me to my feet and kisses me...

A surfing parallel to this moment occurs as you pause before paddling like crazy to catch the downside of the forming wave, and at that point, you have a choice of a go or no-go. I seldom decided on a no-go, the fact is, I'm overcome by the waves seduction, and after that, the only true choice is to focus on the ride. Here I go...

An hour and a half later, I walk out of the bedroom in one of Toni's shirts and catch sight of Toni out on the balcony...

"What's cooking on the grill, big guy? No pun intended," I said with a titter.

He looks at me and tilts his head.

"I'm about ready to pull two tender two-inch steaks off the grill and our hot over-cooked potatoes. There are fixins in the kitchen for our vittles, would you mind getting them?"

"Fixins? Vittles?"

"Child ... haven't you been schooled?"

"Schooled? Hell, when looking around here darlin', I'd of thunk I must have just fallen off the turnip truck."

After finding the fixins, I take the Coleslaw and baked beans out to the balcony and place them on the table.

"Do you want my mom's hot sauce or my dad's 911?"

"I'm game for the 911."

My dad said this will put hair on your chest, so keep an eye out."

"Is that barbequed possum, Jethro."

"Jethro?"

"Yeah, this meal is like something the Clampett's would have cooked up on the *Beverly Hillbillies* TV show with Jethro at the grill."

"Oh yeah... Jethro... Wasn't he the big dumb guy?"

I'm fractured with laughter as I step up to give Toni a hug and a kiss.

With limited chitchatting during our meal, we did what we do best; shovel food down like a couple of timber wolves tearing into an elk.

"This Sol beer is superb. Its taste a lot like Corona," I said.

"Yeah... Sol competes with Corona. I've got more limes for your beer if you'd like."

"No thanks... But, I must say, I've never been in a log cabin, but your place is homey—and yet, beautiful. So, tell me, Toni, how the hell did you get the idea to change a modern condo into a cabin?"

"My neighbor on this floor is an interior designer. He invited me over for drinks one evening and asked how I liked my new home. I hesitated, and then told him that the view and convenience were commendable, but I missed the warm sensation of my folk's ranch house. He showed me pictures of a condo in New York City he transformed into a log cabin. I told him that's the one, and he was off and running over the next two months, drawing elevation views, showing me photos of different period furniture and swatches of material. Jake asked me to stay at his place during my renovation period. And that's it."

Finished with our cabin chitchat, we change the subject and spend the rest of the evening on the balcony, eating and drinking beer. At one point, I notice a Ziploc bag half-filled with water and a few pennies hanging above Toni's patio door.

"What the heck is the bag of water for?"

"It keeps out the flies."

"Get out of here; you're yanking my city girl chain."

"It's true. Never fly one in the house."

"How does it work?"

"No idea. Try it, and you'll see."

Later, sipping our beers, I notice Toni bathed in an orange-colored light coming from the living room, similar to the golden rays of the sun casting its engild as it blends into the darkness over the vast Pacific Ocean...

JACKIE MEETS DAKOTA ON THE FACTORY FLOOR

I had an appointment to see Nina at ten o'clock Tuesday morning to discuss cost revenue recognition. But, I arrived earlier than expected, so with time on my hands, I looked for and found Dakota on the factory floor. After our morning small talk, she walked me around the production area to take notice of the progress they're making on streamlining the Class C parts.

She tells me product throughput has made a dramatic leap in the right direction, with no line shortages for the last couple of weeks. And when this new arrangement is fully primed, they should be able to keep product lines flowing through the system.

My internal clock tells me I'm nearing my time to meet with Nina when we're politely interrupted by Jason, one of the purchasing agents. He introduces us to a salesman that may have the answer to a problematic purchase for a new servomotor needed in a prototype.

The young salesman throws his arm out like a connecting rod to the wheels of a steam engine running at full throttle ready to shake my hand. When taking hold, his handshake was one you'd get from a wannabe congressman on a campaign tour, a huckster, if you will. With a little interest, but to be polite, I stay long enough to listen to his spiel and then excuse myself.

As I head toward Nina's office, I mentally go through the various costs of revenue recognition steps during a project such as portions of the project results becoming billable when certain milestones are complete representing a specific percentage of the project is finished.

COST INCURRED AND REVENUE RECOGNITION

Nina's door was open as I stood there for a moment when she looked up from her desk.

"Come on in, Jackie. You look tremendous—so perky and healthy."

"Thanks, Nina. You're also looking beautiful as ever."

She stands and gestures for me to have a seat on the sofa, and then moves across the carpet to settle in the chair across from me. With my purse and briefcase next to me, I begin with small talk…

"I'm sure you remember Toni, right? He's the one I camped out with."

Nina nods with a lazy smile as she gets comfortable in her seat.

"Well, last night, he asked me over for dinner at his place."

Oh, here I go again, blabbing my way into trouble—it must be in our genes.

"That's wonderful, Jackie. I've met Toni; he's a quiet, tall and a good-looking man. You two make a nice couple."

"Thanks, Nina. That means a lot."

Luckily, Nina has trouble with small talk in a business environment, so moving on would be a good idea. Just then, Nina must have been thinking the same thing—

"Well, Jackie, if I remember correctly you wanted to talk about revenue recognition today."

"That's true. A few months ago you mentioned that you have a particular product line that is project-oriented. You build the product, write software code, and install or integrate the product at your customer's site over a set time period, with the cost incurred as a percent complete, making it a billable sale each month."

Nina is nodding her head in positive response as she settles into her chair.

"You also mentioned that you were having a terrible time with any kind of accuracy in cost-incurred revenue recognition—is that still true?"

"Yes, very much so—I find the process to be a serious problem not knowing with any degree of accuracy that the percent complete is correct when billing our customer. Just last month, our cost incurred ended up with additional time needed above our projected percent complete against the total estimated cost of the project during the month ending… And now, we're also faced with a late delivery and cost overrun based on the additional time needed to finish the project. So, your timing is good. I'm anxious to hear what you have to say."

"Well, Nina, let me begin by asking you how is the estimated cost of the project developed?"

"My understanding is mechanical, electrical, software engineers and project managers pull the estimated cost together and submit them to marketing," Nina said.

"Do you have a standard worksheet or software program that sets standards for the process steps involved in the design and installation?"

"I'm not sure; let me give Gary Eastwood a call."

A few minutes later, Nina gets off the phone.

"It seems we have no such thing as a standardized cost sheet for project designs. Gary doesn't believe it's possible to set standards for the design process."

"I must assume each of your projects has similarities, right?"

"True. Most products are the same, except for the software to run them using special options and commands, and the layouts of each project are different, requiring unique software code and installation tasks."

"As a rule, standardization is possible when projects are similar. Would you be interested in hearing an outline of the tasks involved in taking care of this cost revenue problem?"

"I'm ready. Carry on," Nina said.

With anticipation, she leaned forward a little.

"The hardware or the components you manufacture are not part of the project problem because they are part of the new costing procedures. However, software design and installation are where the problem lies...

Software design and installation are nothing more than a process. Each of these processes will fall under the eighty-twenty rule. For instance, there are certain tasks the software is required to do, and are common about eighty percent of the time within like-type projects.

If you build a software library of these common tasks, you could eliminate writing code over and over again. This process, in of itself, would reduce the throughput time and project cost, as well as improving your simulation and emulation time because of a library of standardization code. The balance of the twenty percent will require new coding, but a process one can now get your arms around—"

"Jackie, this sounds like the ticket, please continue..."

"I thought you'd like it. It's right up your alley...

Now, the process steps for site installation would be the same as the software with each installation task within the process being about eighty percent the same. Meaning you'll need a library of installation task standardization. But, the remainder of the configuration may be different allowing you to make good estimates.

The new standard cost-revenue-recognition procedure would develop its once-a-month sales incurred using the same procedure as your current cost-incurred revenue recognition...

Well, that is except using closed out standards or steps in the process as opposed to actual time worked against allowable quoted estimates. And when comparing the completed standardized task with that of the total standard cost of the project, your result will be a percent complete. The percent complete times the total sales convert into sales for the month, minus previously recorded sales. This same information will also result in a variance percent complete report of the scheduled delivery date.

Unlike your monthly work in process standard cost variance report, this is an ongoing event until the project is completed. And when you become aware that you're in negative territory, you have an opportunity to make course corrections before it's too late...

This new process also has another great benefit. It allows you to generate an accurate customer quotation from excel utilizing the database of standards.

For in-house, and on-site processing of the project, you would establish standards by using the average process control time as you now do in the manufacturing area...

Since none of the software development or site installation employees affects the total manufacturing system throughput, you need to develop a separate overhead allocation, or perhaps, develop it as a division. With that accomplished, you're ready to assign the new overhead rate and the expected rate of return for the proposed project quotation...

With this process, you would have a concrete, measurable result ending with an accurate financial statement. Also, you'd have a better chance of improved profits and on-time system delivery. The process is simple enough, but there is a lot of preliminary work to set up the procedures. What are your thoughts?"

"Gosh, Jackie, every time you or Johnny discusses solutions to improve our business, the subject is well-constructed and explained in good ol' fashioned logic, taking the mystery out of what looks like an overwhelming problem...

If you would, please inform Dakota the outcome of our discussion. Then perhaps, you can prepare a session on cost revenue and standards. And then when you're ready for a training session, give me a ring."

"I'll take care of it."

"I must say, Jackie, I've enjoyed our time together, so let's plan a dinner some evening. As you might guess, I don't get out much anymore, it would be fun."

"Better yet, why don't you come over to my humble home on the beach north of Santa Monica? I'll invite Dakota too, and I'll cook us some wonderful hot Thai food. Does Saturday afternoon work?"

"That would be nice, Jackie," We'll talk later about how to get to your place."

"Oh... If Dakota can make it, she can pick you up, it's on her way. I'll get out of your hair now, see you Saturday."

With our meeting over, I began looking for Dakota again and found her walking out of the engineering department. As we strolled down the hallway, I told her of my conversation with Nina. After a few questions and liking the idea, Dakota approved of the session and told me to schedule a date and time.

"Oh, I almost forgot, how about coming over for a Saturday afternoon dinner on the patio and stop by Nina's place to pick her up along the way? We'll have a pleasant time—I promise."

Dakota pauses...

"There is nothing that would make me happier; I'll call you later for a time—thanks, Jackie."

"That's great; I'll talk to you then."

JACKIE AND BROOKS GO SURFING

While driving home, I have Toni on my mind. He's flying with Jake today, and won't be back for a week. With no obligations this afternoon, I need to give Brooks a call after pulling off the highway.

"Surf's up at Malibu, babe."

"Hey, girl, I was about to call you having a need for speed. Yesterday, I repaired the dings and removed the old wax and re-waxed my longboard."

"Meet me at my house in an hour, and we'll have lunch and then head further up Malibu Beach."

Two hours later, with my ten-foot longboard, I saunter out of my garage and place the board alongside Brooks' board on the roof rack of her vintage modified four-wheel-drive 1946, Ford Woodie. This car turns heads. The metalwork is hand-rubbed high-gloss pale yellow lacquer. The sides and rear are pristine natural wood, finished with a clear varnish.

With my garage door locked, I climb into the passenger seat and buckle up. Brooks fires up the Woodie. The new police interceptor engine purrs at idle. Later, on the highway with our windows down, the only thing we hear is the wind, road noise, and the breaking surf.

After hanging a u-turn in the highway, Brooks pulls off to the side of the road. We lock up, remove our boards and hit the beach running. The day is warm but not hot, littered with a few locals and inexperienced surfers. Yikes, I just saw a few timeworn folks wearing Speedo briefs with their fat bellies hanging over. Why briefs? Ew... They must be Europeans on an American fast-food diet.

While paddling out, we feel the sets rolling in. The endless waves peel themselves with glassy faces and no one on them.

Note to the reader: *To be a seasoned surfer, one needs to know something about surf behavior.*
A swell will transition from a deep-ocean wave to a more shallow-water wave as the wavelength—measured from one wave to the other—transcends closer into shore causing its wavelength to contract, but owing to its mass, the wave height will increase until the wave breaks.

A longtime surfer will tell you that when a wave crest and troughs are in phase with each other, they produce a wave for maximum height—or the so-called seventh wave. The wavelength and the wave period determine the speed of the wave—in other words, the distance over time.

We're going to try for tube rides today on our longboards that are best used during a run down in the pocket or a curl. Getting a barrel ride with a longboard takes a substantial amount of skill—the longer the board, the less response time of getting into position for a successful ride. *Stoked* is what comes to mind when you can pull it off.

A worthy wave can only handle one surfer safely at a time. Knowing this, I pick paper, and Brooks picks rock allowing me to ride the first wave, while the norm is done with the inside surfer getting the wave. But we've been doing this our way from the time we were old enough to drag our boards into the surf. A massive wave is forming, and we agree this is the one.

I paddled hard with my long arms as they propel me through the water and I'm soon rewarded with a ride. On the face of the wave, I pop up on the board with a sense of exhilaration like the first hundred feet coming off the starting line in a top-fuel dragster.

The wave is forming a lip and then plunges downward as I grab a tube ride in my Quasimodo position. It's not a major-league tube, but a tube nonetheless. When coming out of the wave, I ax it and bail, falling into a cannonball and then hammered.

The wave turbulence continues to drag me deeper underwater when I get a break and fight my way to the surface for a gasp of air. After shaking the seawater out of my eyes, I squint upward just as a huge wave hovers over me and slams me again. This time, the surf pulls me deeper, tumbling me around like a dishcloth in a washing machine. This is bad.

You can't tell up from down when you're in a cloud of sand and foaming turbulent water, but one must pick a direction and go for it. The bad news is I picked wrong and hit bottom. The rare news is I'm able to kick off the bottom which sends me in the right direction. Moments later, light hovered above me while crawling to the surface when a terrible tug yanks on my leg, and then snaps as the board leaves its tether.

With my leash, free from the board, the loose end wraps around my leg when I breach the surface. While gasping for air, I gaze about, but no sign of my board. The swim back takes a while longer without a board during a double dipper. With an awareness of a kickboxer being TKO'd, I find a chunk of my board floating nearby allowing me to paddle the rest of the way in.

After dragging my sorry ass out of the surf, I take a look-see back at the incoming breakers trying to find Brooks.

Ah... There she is sitting on her board waving at me as I signal I'm all right. Seeing I'm okay, Woodie catches the next massive wave. Everyone nearby is watching her. She dazzles us with her style and confidence as Woodie rides the tube of a wave forming over her. A moment later after dropping out of the barrel, we applaud and whistle. Brooks is a regular here. She's a real icon of the California female surfers.

A local friend of Brooks loans me his board, but only if I promise to bring the board back in one piece. So, I took advantage of his offer and we both surf the day into exhaustion. Jake would say, we trekked up and down more waves than a whore's pair of drawers. After too many hours worked over by too many waves, we pack it in.

These locals live on a hot dog budget... With that in mind, I pay Brooks' local guy thirty bucks for the use of his board. We lay in the sun soaking up the rays for a while, but we got tired of the guys buzzing around trying to get our attention to rent their boards—the free market at work.

When arriving home, I opened the front door, and the first place I go in is the kitchen. We burned a lot of serious calories today, so I fixed us chocolate malts. We wolfed them down in a New York minute, then with a deserving laugh, I fixed two more.

After my shower and getting dressed, I'm in the kitchen fixing our evening meal while Brooks takes her turn in the shower. I'm preparing a high-protein Mexican dish tonight with Black Bean and Chicken Quesadillas covered with a ton of cheese—yummy.

Later, waiting for the cheese to melt over the Quesadillas in the broiler, I gaze over at Brooks on the sofa with a warm smile. The bottom half of her six-foot-one body looks like the unfolding of a damp bent straw as her long legs begin the process of stretching out.

After dinner and having had too many beers, it was late, so I asked Brooks if she wanted to do a sleepover. With a responsive saucy smile, she told me the idea sounds crackerjack to her. We walk upstairs to her room in the loft next to mine where I pull out my backup pink flannel pajamas covered with tiny yellow ducks from my dresser.

We both giggled when I handed my PJ's to her.

"Well, if you want an open window tonight and listen to the surf to put you to sleep, you'll be glad you had them on."

Back in my own room, I opened my window and pulled my bright yellow footie pajamas imprinted with red cars from my dresser. After washing my face and hands, I slid into my cozy bed under the soft glow of my bedside lamp.

I tried reading a novel by Agatha Christie, where Hercule Poirot, one of my favorite characters is gathering the possible suspects into the room and will soon, with enormous delight, point out the murderer. However, my peepers kept closing, so after reading one paragraph multiple times, I caved in, put the book on the nightstand and turned out the light.

When drifting off to sleep, I thought of Brooks. She has become a touch flaky of late. Her large inheritance leaves too much time on her hands. She is, however, my best friend. My father told me as a youngster, a foundation for true friendship can only begin and endure with loyalty and honor—we both have that in spades with each other.

ACT III - SCENE TWO
ENHANCING THE LEARNING PROCESS

Question: 1

Have you heard of or worked with cost revenue recognition? If not, you have now learned the basics of how the process works.

Using the book as a guide, explain how the new cost revenue recognition procedure works. Pick a simple subject matter as a project example.

Question: 2

As a reader, you have noticed the backdrop for the characters in the story has been the ocean. What are your thoughts on why the author gravitated toward the ocean as part of his storytelling?

For those non-surfers or sailors, do you have the same problem Johnny has for surfing? If so, tell us why.

For those of you who love to venture out into the sun, the open seas, and the roaring surf—tell us a frightening or funny experience with the ocean on either a boat/ship or surfing.

ACT III SCENE 3
Changing of the Guard

WEEK 9 – DAKOTA AND NINA AT JACKIE'S THAI DINNER SATURDAY AFTERNOON

PICKING UP NINA

Jackie's little Thai patio party will be fun not having been out with any lady friends in months. She called this morning asking if we could be there between four-thirty and five o'clock and if I wouldn't mind calling Nina to let her know what time I'd pick her up. As we talk, I mentioned that my CEO contract with ATC ends in a few months. We rationalized the dinner give us an opportunity to approach Nina about considering the need to take on the responsibility of CEO—the changing of the guard, so to speak.

I showered and primped for almost an hour. Refreshed, I gaze around my walk-in closet. Today has been a hot one, so I select a white flurry dress with multicolored flowers and adjustable straps. After stepping into it, I pick out my favorite pair of Giorgia Galassi light-gold sandals to titivate my dress and slip them on. I stood in front of my full-length mirror to check out my ensemble for today's outing. Satisfied with my selection, I fuss with my hair making those little female gestures that only a woman can make—knowing it makes little difference. In a good mood, I grab my new purse for the occasion and walk out to the car sitting in the shadow of the garage shading it from the hot sun having driven it to the car wash this morning. After pulling out of my drive, I head toward Nina's place in time to be there by three-thirty.

I'm looking forward to good conversation and feeling the cool sea breeze pushing inland replacing the rising warm air while enjoying ourselves on Jackie's patio. And adding to our delight will be the incoming surf providing a perfect setting for eating outdoors on such a hot day.

When arriving at Nina's, I park in her driveway where I'm greeted by a flat stone walkway interwoven with green moss that guides me through the lush landscaping to her front door. The architecture and pleasant aroma of the tropical plants, ferns, and flowers were like a well-groomed jungle. The lush landscape reminded me of homes in Indochina—or the Indochinese Peninsula as we often call it today.

At the door waiting for me is Li Pham, Nina's housekeeper dressed in traditional all-white cotton Ao Dai. She bows in her respectful way. I respond with a nod and follow her out to the patio where Nina is relaxing at a table in the shade of an umbrella, sipping a cold drink, and reading *House and Garden*.

Nina looks up, smiles, and graciously gets up from her chair and walks toward me while removing her Ray-Ban sunglasses. She's wearing all-white apparel: a cut blouse of fine Egyptian cotton worn over a pair of cotton pants. She's about as tall as I am with her Annadel leather sandals, sporting three-inch heels—looking as though she just left a photoshoot for *Vogue* magazine.

She bowed politely...

"Welcome Dakota, to my humble surroundings."

"Hi Nina," I said, looking around at her humble surroundings of beautiful floral colors.

"Wow... I love this place. You have a lot of unusual and beautiful flowers. Please, you must tell me about them"

"I'd love to. Although, I wish Thanh were here to tell you. This garden is his creation. Thanh brought in indigenous plants from Indochina, South Africa's Cape Peninsula, and Brazil," She said, taking a few steps toward a most unusual and beautiful flower near the patio. "This pink-colored flower is a protea from the southern area of the Western Cape. It was named after Proteus, a Greek god. Is it not one of the most beautiful flowers you have ever seen?"

"You called this plant a protea, but looks much like an artichoke exploded with color and surrounded with a large variety of its kind."

We admire the flowers for a moment.

"Well, Nina, I'm sure time will go by fast, and he'll be home with you. And when that happens, he'll be able to enjoy this beautiful garden again."

"That's kind of you to say, Dakota."

"Well... Are you ready for a little fun in the sun?"

MY NAME IS JACQUE

Due to limited parking alongside these coastal homes residing on the beach, I parallel parked in front of Jackie's garage. When heading back to her patio along the narrow sidewalk that runs on the south side of her house, we notice a strip of *overgrown green grass*. At the end of the walk is a gate that opens out to the beach and steps up to her deck with a wonderful view of the roaring surf.

Jackie sees us as we pass under her large kitchen window and waves.

"I'll be right out," she said.

As we step onto the deck, Jackie greets us with open arms. It's hard for me to get close to anybody, but Jackie is cutting through my armor.

She stops for a moment to give us a gracious bow and a welcoming smile. Jackie is in her bare feet wearing a beautiful dark-red sarong with printed large green leaves and white flowers. In her hair is a large matching flower.

"Greetings, welcome to the Royal Thai of Paris Café."

Having greeted us with a French accent, a hug and an air kiss on each cheek, we have a quick chat and giggles, then invited into her home...

"Dakota, would you mind showing Nina around? I'll fix you ladies a Blue Hawaii cocktail in the meantime."

"A Blue Hawaii... Now there's bribe I can't refuse."

I escorted Nina to the upstairs loft to show her the two bedrooms with an interconnecting bathroom that overlooks the living room. The pitched roof has huge skylights that open with an electrical switch letting in a sea breeze giving one a wondrous view of the ocean. Finished, we head back to the kitchen to check on our drinks and on into the living room, dining room, half-bath, and the den.

While we're in the den, Nina's looking at photos of dragsters and A-Altereds that Jackie drove in her younger years.

"Look, Dakota... Here is a picture of Jackie with smoke and flames pouring out from her car—she looks in trouble."

Jackie walked in at that moment...

"Jackie, were you burned in this picture where your car is on fire?"

Jackie stands there with drinks in her hand.

"On fire?" she said with a frown.

"This one," Nina said.

She pointed to the picture and then turns and reaches for her drink.

"Thanks, Jackie," Nina said.

She's acknowledged with a nod.

"Oh ... that one is a night photo where I'm doing what's called a *burn-in*. That means we apply a lot of power through the drivetrain. The tires spin at a high RPM which heats the tires that produce the smoke laying down molten rubber. The flames, of course, are from the engine exhaust pipes."

"Why do you do that?" Nina said.

"The hot sticky rubber allows the slicks... Ah, rear tires to have a better grip on the raceway helping in the acceleration and elapsed time."

Nina and I look at our friend and shake our heads in amazement.

Jackie shrugs with a warm smile...

"Why don't you ladies have a seat in the living room? I'm about ready to help the chef prepare our dinner."

"Can we be of any help?" Nina said.

"We of the Royal Thai are good, but thanks for asking."

Later, Jackie enters the room wearing a pair of black, heavy-framed horn-rimmed eyeglasses, a full black mustache, and a red beret slanted fashionably on her head...

"Mesdames... If you will, please be so kind as to follow me out to the terrace," she said in her phony French accent.

We stare at Jackie for a long moment and then eye each other as we become hysterical, staggering with laughter out onto the deck.

"Of the many choices on the veranda to eat, this is my favorite one. If this meets with your approval, I shall seat you."

After looking around, I give Jackie a joyful grin...

"But it's the only one."

"Correct, Madame... And duly noted," Jackie said with her nose in the air.

She pets her mustache as though it were a kitten needing attention. It would seem, the mustache acted more like a nervous black caterpillar.

Nina looks at Jackie and me and then giggles. She's trying to be modest and well-mannered by covering her mouth. It's considered rude to show an open mouth in Asian culture. My, what must they surmise of us loudmouth Americans?

Jackie seats us at her favorite and only table. As I survey the setting, my eyes wander over the beautiful white linen tablecloth with a full set service of silver alongside what looks like colorful hand-painted plates of tropical flowers. The elegant setting is highlighted with delicate crystal water glasses filled with ice water. In the center are three handpicked beautiful Cattleya orchids placed in a tall, slim, sparkling crystal vase.

After being seated, Jackie glances down at us...

"My name is Jacque, and I will be your waiter this afternoon. May I bring out your refreshment to enjoy before deciding on your meal? Or perhaps, you may wish to hear what the chef has prepared for the day before deciding on your drink?

"Please, tell us the chef's special," I said.

"It would be my pleasure, Madame. As your devoted server this afternoon, I would recommend our chicken satay served with two thin slices of chicken breast marinated in coconut milk with curry and grilled to perfection on our exclusive outdoor designed grill."

Jacque proudly points across the patio to a well-used crusty-rusted charcoal grill spewing out smoke.

Nina's eyes light up as we both have a good chortle.

"We serve it with a curry flavor sweet peanut sauce along with marinated cucumber and carrot salad.

For dinner, I am recommending our chef's special for tonight: stir-fried seafood combo of shrimp, scallop, and squid served with Thai chili peppers, fresh ginger, green beans, onion, and a bowl of rice.

For those of you who are faint of heart for the hot stuff, *difficile de merde*," Jacque said with a straight face as her mustache does a quick rendition of the hula.

Nina burst into giggles with tears streaming down her cheeks.

"I'm a little rusty on my French, but I believe she... Excuse me, *he* said, *tough shit* in referring to the hot stuff."

Nina responds with a nod and a giggle.

Jackie stands by with mischief in her eyes and a white linen towel draped over her arm with a pad and pencil at the ready...

"May I take your order now, Madame?"

I look at Nina dabbing her tears with a napkin as she glances over at me. I give her a nod. Nina takes a moment, then gazes up at Jacque...

"The chef's special, please."

"Good choice, Madame, and you, Madame?"

With a slight grin, I watch her mustache crawl down over her upper lip like a fuzzy black caterpillar taking a walk.

"I'll have the same," I said.

Jackie turns to adjust her mustache then returns her attention back to me...

"That's also, a good choice, Madame. Would you care for a refreshing Sam Miguel before your meal?" Jacque said gazing at me and then Nina."

We acknowledge Jacque with a nod.

"Very well, I will be right out with your drink. While you wait, you may want to enjoy our wonderful view of Pattaya Beach. It's the most famous and beautiful in Thailand."

"Pattaya Beach, Thailand?" Nina giggled,

With no response, she makes a hasty retreat into the house, still fidgeting with her mustache.

With dinner served, Jackie joins us as we chatter away while enjoying our incredible meal and the cool ocean breeze cutting through the hot late afternoon sun.

Finished eating, Jackie headed for the kitchen. It didn't take long when Jacque our waiter comes out to clean up the table. Satisfied, Jacque is back in the kitchen. A few moments later, he's headed our way with a linen towel over his left arm, pad, and pencil in hand.

"On this special occasion, we have for you, three dessert choices tonight. The first choice is grilled banana with French vanilla ice cream served with an animal cracker."

The two of us interrupted her with our giggling when she mentioned an animal cracker.

"Our next special is sweet rice prepared with sugar, coconut milk, and shreds of fresh coconut. Last but not least, we have fresh pineapple served with French vanilla ice cream, topped with an egg custard and covered in crushed peanuts... But, I'm told that the chef recommends the grilled banana with an animal cracker."

Jackie looked down at Nina...

"And your pleasure tonight would be?"

Nina gives Jackie a hopeful look...

"The sweet rice, please."

"Oh... I am *so* sorry Madame, we served up the last of our sweet rice a few minutes ago to the nice couple near the barbeque," Jackie said, looking toward an imaginary couple.

Nina and I crack up.

"The chef's recommendation tonight is grilled banana."

"Oh ... why of course, it sounds wonderful."

"And you, Madame?"

"It's a hard choice between the last two, but I'll take the fried banana."

"Not fried, but *grilled* banana, Madame, excellent choice. I'll be but a moment with your orders while the chef grills your bananas." Jacque said, then heads to the kitchen.

"Well, Nina... I believe our Jackie, or is it, Jacque...? Well, let's say our waiter is ready for the nut factory sooner than we thought."

"Nut factory?"

"You know ... the funny farm."

"Nut factory? Funny farm?" Nina said, with raised eyebrows.

"I'm sorry, the home for the insane."

Nina puts her hand over her mouth and blurts out a giggle.

Jacque walks out onto the patio and toward the grill with a plate of freshly peeled bananas. A few minutes later, she slides a grilled banana alongside each of the vanilla ice cream dishes and brings them to us.

"I'll be right back."

A moment later, Jacque arrives and pulls out the ladle from a copper pot and pours hot chocolate sauce over our desserts.

"We have here, *mesdames*, Telluride Truffle chocolate liquor—it's the best chocolate sauce in the world."

Jacque heads back to the kitchen. A moment later, Jackie is back with us. As we gabfest for a short while, Jackie picks up a partially eaten animal cracker from her dessert dish...

"Is this a hippo or an elephant?"

We both answer, "Elephant."

"Hmm... That's what I thought. But it tastes more like a hippo."

Nina looks at me... "You're right—funny farm," she said.

We can't help ourselves and break out with the giggles.

SOME SERIOUS TALK

Finished with our desserts, Jackie brings out a tray of freshly brewed coffee with a side of cream and sugar and takes a seat.

"Jackie, I have to ask you something... Where on earth did you find that mustache?"

"Well... Being desperate, I grabbed a handful of lint from my dryer, dampened and colored it with a dash of black liquid hair dye, shaped it, then sprayed it with hairspray to hold its shape."

"Ah-ha... That explains the black caterpillar look."

"Caterpillar? Why I never!" Jackie said all uppity.

A moment later, Jackie takes a few sips of her coffee, stares into her cup for a short moment while smelling the aroma along with a satisfying ahh. I waited for her to say *Good to the last drop* like Ricardo Montalban did back when during a coffee commercial. Instead, she raises her head and looks at Nina...

"Dakota tells me we have just a few months left until our contract is up with your company. That means we need to prepare for Dakota's departure as CEO. We've been told there are no guarantees, but I'm sure that Thanh will soon be out of his coma. However, his recovery will take time."

At that point, I jump in...

"Along with Jackie, Johnny, and Marty, we feel flat out you're the person to fill the CEO position."

There is silence as Nina looks out over the horizon with sadness...

"Well, I guess I've been hoping for a miracle to happen. I'm not sure I'm qualified for such a responsibility."

"Nina, everybody in this company looks to you for their future with ATC. They realize you're the obvious choice. You're as qualified as any person I can think of to fill Thanh's shoes until he's back on the job, and I'm sure Thanh would be of the same opinion."

Nina continues to stare in sorrow out toward the surf while resting her elbows on the table and nervously moves her water glass from side to side.

We decide to wait Nina out as a small flock of seagulls land on the patio railing squawking away at us.

Nina watches the seagulls in silence for a while as they strut about puffing out their chests and flapping their wings, threatening to take off. Instead of flying away, they continue to watch us with their curious beady little eyes making their strange little eeeek eeek sound. Then, of course, they slime up the railing with their runny poop. That slime comes from their little kidneys that mix the solid and water together with uric acid which forms a white paste. A minimal design when compared to us often constipated mammals...

Damn... I'm spending too much time around Johnny.

A few moments later, Nina's facial expression changes into a delicate smile and then turns her attention toward us...

"How can I refuse such kind words, especially, after counting the seven seagulls that parade up and down on the railing in front of me?"

"What about the seagulls?" Jackie said.

"In Cantonese, seven is a lucky number for good relationships reassuring I'd be doing the right thing for ATC," Nina said.

With a small smile, tears streamed down her cheeks.

Nina noticed we were about to say something and gestured for us to wait.

While wiping her tears away, she spots another seagull coming in for a landing on the railing—it is pure white. It ignores the other birds as it floats in and hovers for a moment before settling on the railing near Nina. The seagull focuses in on Nina with its pink-rimmed eyes, flapping its wings and squawking at her.

"Oh my goodness," Nina said in a startled voice.

"What?" We said all bug-eyed.

"Oh my, God," Nina said as she points her finger from one seagull to another. "There are now eight seagulls. That's another wonderful omen. In Cantonese, the word for eight sounds the same as the word for *making money, to prosper, or to create wealth*." Nina said with bubbling laughter.

The seagulls flap their wings and squawk as though they too were laughing. With a sigh of relief, we join Nina and the seagulls for a round of laughter…

What a nice ending for a day with the ladies.

ACT III - SCENE 3
ENHANCING THE LEARNING PROCESS

Question: 1
The author seems to have no comprehension of why women fuss with their hair making their little female gestures as though it made a difference.

What are your thoughts on why woman have this embedded in their DNA and believe it makes a difference?

Question: 2
Why was Jackie's grass running along the side of her house overgrown?

Question: 3
Was Nina the best choice for the next interim president of ATC?
If so, why?
If not, why?

Question: 4
With Nina knowing Cantonese, what would she have thought if only four seagulls had lined up on the railing?

ACT III SCENE 4
Financial Modeling

WEEK 10 – TUESDAY AFTERNOON - JACKIE'S FINANCIAL MODEL MEETING

PREDAWN PATROL

With salt in our veins, we thrive in the salinity of the sea from which our ancestors came—well, at least according to the aquatic ape theory, developed by Sir Alister Hardy. Now, when one considers such an idea, you can't deny that us humans like water: We spend lots of money for swimming pools, waterfront property, and go to the beach just to look at or swim in the sea...

There is something spiritual about surfing in the glimmer of the morning moonlight. You're outright alone as you float through the blackness of endless liquid space. Well, maybe not alone, owing to your occasional neighborhood sea creatures you bump into.

I'm at Little Point Dume east of Malibu doing predawn surfing. I glanced east to see the stars lose some of their shape and brilliance owing to a glimmer of light coming from a westerly sky that ran along a stretch of Santa Monica's horizon and the crest of the Santa Monic Mountains.

It wasn't long when the sun sent a brush-stroke of glowing promise and a subtle message that a new day is about to give birth. The pelicans are diving for their morning breakfast, shimmering sardines are skipping across the surface of the water, and a sea turtle raises its head above a swell to check me out.

Feeling a swell forming under my board tells me it's my get-go as I paddle like a Mississippi steamboat. With the peak forming, I slide onto the face of the wave cutting a line to the right and down into the tube. I reach out and touch the translucent wall, but before I'm locked in, I shoot out into the new day screaming in ecstasy.

I'm beginning to tire having surfed most of the good waves that came my way, so I paddle onto the beach. Damn... Only sex can compete with the feeling you get preceding the beginning of a new day when surfing—well, from a numerical point of view; of course, predawn surfing outscores the other by a large margin—well, at least in my world.

While sitting on my haunches and meditating, I faced west to watch the sun inch its way above the horizon and sensed the rhythm of the surf pound the beach. As my muscles relax, I lean over and pull out a crunchy chocolate protein bar from my beach bag, leave the wrapper in the bag, and the crunchy chocolate bar in my stomach.

Now that I'm energized from my crunchy bar, I'm ready to head out having finished wiping down my board. But as I gather up my belongings, I notice movement from the periphery of my eye. Turning toward the distraction, I gaze upon three local beach boys coming my way in the premature morning light. Until that moment, I was alone on the beach. With a nod, I acknowledge them.

As they walk toward me, I size up the leader of the group—sitting atop his head like a cocked beret is a clear disposable shower cap, obviously, making a declaration of his independence. He has bedraggled black hair sticking out from under the cap and pulled back into a ponytail. His shaggy eyebrows overhang narrow-set black eyes, a long thin nose, and a slit for a mouth embedded in an elongated chin.

He's wearing faded red boardshorts and a dirty white tank top allowing his long sinewy tattooed arms to hang out and swing at his side.

He stops short of running into me while engulfing me in a cloud of bad breath that is an insult to the freshness of the morning salt air. When looking into his eyes, I would have you picture two black beetles lying on their back in the sand, kicking their little legs and squinting into the blazing sun.

"Hey, Sweet Buns, you resemble that Halle Berry chick."

"I'm not her. Nor am I your sweet buns, but thank you."

I take a moment to assess his friends. They're both grinning at me, and as ugly as two bullfrogs each chewing on an unwanted wasp. At best, they have four front teeth between the two of them. Their total IQ's must be south of a plus sign, or from one with a more optimistic view, a trained poodle. Toni would say, if these boys were any dumber, someone would need to water 'em.

"What are you doing on *our* beach?" Bedraggled Hair said.

When moving closer, Bedraggled's breathe overwhelmed me with what seemed like the venting of a sewage treatment plant—either that or a dinosaur crapped in his mouth—which didn't soften his malignant presence.

"What are you talking about? And *back off*."

"You damn well grasp what I'm talking about," he said.

And then he pushed me.

"You back off bitch."

"See here, Moondoggie, I've no idea what your problem is—but it's best you don't *try* that again."

The three local bullfrogs enjoy a good laugh sounding like a sack full of starving kittens. Bedraggled hair looks at me as though a hawk was eying a rodent. He rocks his head forth and back as though he were a prizefighter relaxing in his corner waiting for the bell to ring. Bedraggled is now ready to make his move as he puts himself in a position to push me again and springs into action like a rosy boa…

Ahh… Sadly, his lower sternum has an *accident* as it slams into a sharp, precise jab—well, that surprised the heck out of me. His eyes crossed from the shock and awe as he collapses flat on his back. But with a little movement, he prepares for his next attack. To counter this and sending a strong message, I raise my right leg high in the air and drove an ax-kick down into his groin. The force of the kick shoved his balls deep into the sand, causing him to scream and then pass out—what a little baby. Well, I guess that's easy for me to say.

"May I gather up my things now and leave peacefully?"

The two bullfrogs are now looking like they need shock therapy seeing their alpha dog lying on the beach passed out from the pain. They submissively put their hands in the air and take several steps back. I hope my message takes root because fighting over surf turf is like rats competing for a single piece of cheese. This bad behavior needs to stop.

As I head out to my car, it occurs to me that if this were a novel, we'd meet later on, however, in real life—I won't ever see him again. Oh well, I need to put this nasty incident behind me.

When approaching *Little Miss Sunshine*, I signal her to unlock the doors. At her side, I lift my board up on the roof rack and secure it. With the trunk lid open, I grab my multi-colored sarong, fasten it around my waist, slip into my dark blue sweatshirt, and tie a colorful bandana around my head. I used a towel to beat the sand off my feet and slip into my new Diego di Lucca slingback sandals.

After opening my door, I slide my ample butt in behind the wheel. With my engine cranked up enough to allow my stable of ponies grazing time, I prepare myself for re-entry into civilization while gazing into my mirror and apply a little moisturizing lipstick.

Having secured my door, I buckle up, point the nose east and bring to bear a generous dose of G-force pushing me down the Pacific coast highway toward Gladstones, the best little breakfast in Malibu. As you may remember that's where I met Quentin Tarantino.

After pulling into Gladstone's parking lot, and before entering the restaurant, I find myself chewing on the corner of my lower lip wondering if my message to Bedraggled Hair was too strong. Oh well, I'm sure he'll survive.

Darwin knew as we do today, there are many ways one can avoid contributing to the future gene pool—which, I may have just acquired a say in by leaving him with undescended testicles.

These three troublemakers combined possess something less than room-temperature intellect. The only reason they are still alive is that it's illegal to hunt them in or out of season. Therefore, I may have lucked out and helped society by removing a supplier to the *stupid* gene pool. Hmmm… Well, that should make Bedraggled Hair eligible for the Darwin Award.

With that thought behind me, I walk into Gladstone's.

I see Kate and wave a hello. She's a sweet young girl working her way through Pepperdine. She's short, carrying a little extra weight, has long dark hair in a ponytail covered with a Giants baseball cap, and carries around a heart of gold. She eyed me from across the room and then heads toward me in the empty setting of the restaurant...

"Hi there, Jackie, it looks like you just came in from your predawn patrol?"

"Do I appear that bad? I tried to dress up a little before coming in."

"You look great, babe. The wet sarong and the time of morning gave you away," Kate said, handing me a menu.

An hour later, I finish my second mug of hot coffee, having put away a breakfast of ten-egg-whites, black beans smothered in Jack and Cheddar cheese, a swordfish fillet, O'Brien potatoes, and fresh fruit. While reading the newspaper and working on my third mug, I cast an eye up and see two Highway Patrolmen come in and take a seat near me.

"Hi, Timmy, hi, Earnest, got the hungries, do you?"

I met them both through Toni. He told me these two guys were friends in the military police before joining up with the California Highway Patrol. They seemed to bear a rough exterior, but can be as gentle and sweet as a mother with her newborn—but I'd never tell them that to their faces.

"Hi, Jackie," they both rang out.

"Yeah, we used the last of our energy hauling a beach local to the emergency room. Seems that someone kicked the eggs out of Surfer Boy's henhouse," Timmy said.

"Yeah, and then tried to bury the henhouse in the sand," Earnest said, with his southern drawl.

"Eggs? Henhouse?" I said with a frown.

"Yeah... He was delirious, though. The poor guy said a crazy surfer chick that looked like Halle Berry attacked him."

"REALLY?" I said with a hangdog stare.

"You wouldn't know anybody like that ... would you, Jackie?"

"Me, have knowledge of a crazy woman?" I said with a shake of my head and sweaty palms.

Kate hears what's going on and heads our way.

"I waited on a person who fills that description that walked in for a fast coffee. She slugs it down, leaves a few dollars, and runs out the door... Not long afterward, Jackie walked in," Kate said.

"That's okay, Kate, we won't follow up on her. I'm sure the guy deserved it," Earnest said, with a lopsided smile.

"Well then... What are you guys' ordering this fine morning?"

Later, having finished my coffee, I get up, walk over to Timmy, lean down, and kiss him on the cheek, and then Earnest—with a pleasant smile for both, I head toward the door.

"Say hi to Toni when you see him," Timmy yelled.

He looks over at Earnest and chuckles...

"I bet that that poor sap wished he hadn't ever opened that giant-sized can of whoop-ass by antagonizing that lady. She's tougher than a box full of roofing nails when pushed too far."

"You know... Jackie is a good match for Toni. As I understand it, he flosses with a crowbar," Earnest said.

"Yeah... I hear that too. Toni's tougher than Richard Simmons trying to take off his spandex," Timmy said.

Earnest lets out a guffaw...

"Now ... that is tough. Back to Jackie though, if she doesn't stop working out those glutes of hers, she'll need to get them licensed."

With both laughing at that thought, they high-five each other and continue eating their breakfast.

Arriving home, I take a shower and spend a little relaxing time in my little casa on the beach. Later, I prepare for work and slip into a new pinstriped suit and a white blouse, and then head toward ATC. I will miss my weekly sessions with such nice people, even though I'll be doing follow-up work and consulting with them over the next six months.

Pulling into the parking lot fifteen minutes ahead of time, I deliberate about this being my last engagement with less than a dozen people.

THE CONFERENCE ROOM: JACKIE AND FRESH PASTRIES

When walking into the conference room, I see that everybody has already arrived and busy chattering while having coffee and fresh pastries.

"Hi everybody," I said.

"Hi, Jackie," they responded.

"I hope you saved me a raspberry tart for an al desko snack."

Nina springs from her seat and dashed over to the pastry table, grabs a napkin and wraps up a pastry. Heading toward me with her gleeful smile, she gives me a polite bow and hands me a yummy.

"What's this sweet little thing?" I said with anticipation.

Ed Blackburn hollers...

"It's the best li'l thing you'll ever sink your teeth into."

"It's a *pain au chocolat*, a French puff pastry," Nina said.

After taking a bite, I'm captivated with a mouthful of yummy-yummy while looking toward Nina...

"I hope you have a whole lot more, Nina."

The select few at the table can't help but laugh...

After grabbing a paper cup, I pour myself a cup of coffee from the carafe and take a seat at the table. While finishing my pastry, we jabber about Nina's skill as a pastry chef. Nina, of course, keeps bowing with a subtle smile the whole time. You have to love the lady.

After wiping my hands and mouth with a napkin, I'm ready...

FINANCIAL MODELING

"As you know, we're about to discuss financial modeling today...

Due to the small number of you who need this session, and the short duration of the meeting, I thought the conference room would fill the bill. I would add, to your delight, however, there will be no overhead projections, but I have a booklet with today's discussion."

I took the booklets from my briefcase, passed them out and waited for them to thumb through it as I eye the *pain au chocolat pastries,* and entertain the idea, but then think better of it.

"Financial modeling or forecasting is more than a finance responsibility—it requires inputs from all the company officers. The financial people will model and test, but the officers must approve the process and results. As officers, your obligation to the company and its stockholders is to ask questions about anything you don't understand.

Our discussion centers on an underlying logic that encompasses the model—this is critical. Many of the terms and discussions we've studied in past sessions will be applicable in this session...

When most businesses design their financial modeling, their projections are more than likely two-dimensional by design. Meaning, it has no depth. Why is that? Well, as a rule, when establishing the inputs, it's done in various organizational departments by people who *contemplate* what they should be from their calculations and point of view.

This process possesses little relevance to the business strategy and its dynamic effect on stockholders, the market, policy, and the system processes. This is why organizational departmentalization does not belong in systemic thinking.

For instance, marketing will input what they consider the sales should be over a period with little regard for the capabilities of the internal or external constraints of the system. This is because current business experience encourages people to view activities by *function*, creating two-dimensional static output as opposed to dynamic output influenced by inputs and outputs of the system.

These two-dimensional models can bring disastrous results. The sale orders brought into the system processes can contribute to system failure due to either system capability or cash flow, and, there go future orders because of a bad financial model and poor input."

BUILDING THE FINANCIAL MODEL

"To build a dynamic and systemic model, you must begin with the basic strategy of system thinking... FIRST, the standard financial model must project a balance sheet, income statement, and cash flow...

Then, settle on an *economic value-added* return rate that's applicable in supporting a positive result—a discussion covered at the *Global Sharing of the Wealth* meeting Dakota scheduled for this coming Saturday.

To see if the EVA benchmark is possible, the productivity, market growth, and profit must be able to pass the demands put on them. However, these demands may not be possible. This is where the systemic effects of financial planning need consideration. As you remember, we delved into some in-depth discussions on this subject during our session, *A New Set of Measurement Tools,* a little over a month ago..."

BUILDING THE PROJECTED SALES MODEL

"When projecting sales, you must define how to increase market share, as opposed to inputting the projected sales. You need to conceive how the system can deliver a performance that meets the following *two requirements*:

The FIRST REQUIREMENT on the list is the New Potential Market with its internal policies and processes able to retain the ability to define its place in the market. Hmm... to be more specific, for one to open the door to increased market demand, the company needs to comprehend that their system can meet three import requirements:

NUMBER ONE... Is your customer perception equal to or greater than that of the three top competitors?

NUMBER TWO... Is the awareness level adequate to capture the forecasted market share, influenced by cash flow?

NUMBER THREE... The target-pricing policy must be in place for each product, and as you know, this influences market share and profitability.

The SECOND AND LAST *requirement* is the PROJECTED GROWTH RATE. After establishing the size of the new market potential, you'll need to include a growth rate limitation in the model. With that in mind, I have three questions to ask pertaining to the three internal constraints that can influence the company's growth rate:

The NUMBER ONE question on the list—is the system capacity capable of delivering on the forecast?

NUMBER TWO. Is the system constrained by cash flow?

NUMBER THREE. Are we developing new products, and has the customer helped influenced these new products in the design process?

When introducing the FIRST and SECOND *requirement* to the standard financial model, it improves your ability to project the impact of the company's strategy regarding both customer and stockholder satisfaction."

MODEL SIMULATION

"Using the FlexSim system or nMetric throughput simulator, calculate the output of the total system through scenario modeling, and it will confirm if there is a need for specific investments in technology, equipment, product development, and system processes... Computer-based modeling techniques are also useful for examining the current behavior of the business and exploring the impact of process change on its financial performance.

It's critical that both the system simulation modeling and the financial modeling are using the same inputs to show the system can meet the potential market and market growth rate. The two different types of modeling programs must support the strategy, but keep in mind that projections can only be as good as the execution.

By considering the effects of process changes before implementing them, you may learn of hidden constraints and wasted resources. Another advantage of business modeling is that it enforces systemic thinking among people who have traditionally ignored each other. As always, the usefulness of financial modeling depends on understanding their limitations and capabilities..."

I pause for a moment and sip my cold coffee—desperation.

DEVELOPING A PLAN

"Let me ask you this... How do you forecast financial projections now?"

Nina speaks up...

"We use spreadsheets to forecasts and develop cash flow and budgets. We develop income by marketing forecasts—which, of course, equals a two-dimensional process," She said with a grin.

"Don't consider yourself alone, the lion's share of businesses does the same thing. However, remember this...

FORECASTING IS ABOUT READING THE FUTURE, AND NO MATTER WHAT APPROACH ONE TAKES IT'S ONLY A BIT MORE SCIENTIFIC THAN ONE WHO CAST CHICKEN BONES ABOUT TO SEE THE FUTURE... TO DO SO, WOULD REQUIRE A COMPUTER WITH SPEED YET TO BE INVENTED.

Hearing this come from Jackie brought about a slaphappy response from everyone in the room.

"Now, I say that in jest, because your new MPV and response system is NOT READING THE FUTURE, it's responding to a known quantity of how the customer perceives their suppliers. As time moves on and the system is producing results, you will see how your guidance system is not unlike a ship navigating its way across the ocean. You are no longer reading the future—you now have some control over your future..."

Jackie's little gathering sat in their seats for a nanosecond with their slack jaws, and then they began to stand and applaud when Ed suddenly spoke up...

"Jackie, you sure knocked the ball out of the park on this subject. I'm thrilled at the thought, having been involved in wish-casting sales forecast while contemplating the only thing worse would be a root canal."

This brought about gleeful chuckles from everyone.

Well, let me get back to Nina's two-dimensional spreadsheet forecasting process... Maybe not everyone uses the spreadsheet, but the results are the same when using the numerous, financial projection software available when applying them to organizational departmentalization structured companies.

This gets to my next subject, the modeling software...

Now, as far as a software supplier, I have none to recommend. Nina, I would suggest starting with the Internet and browse for financial modeling software. Make up a specification sheet utilizing what I've suggested in this session and your demands and format you would consider comfortable to work with. My guess is the software provider will need to customize up to a degree.

You could do it on your own, but you have enough on your plate. Ed may want to discuss this with the president of nMetric, Chris Koski, to see if she may want to develop a real-time financial model."

"I'm on it," Ed said.

Okay then, as you know, this is my last scheduled session with you folks. I'm glad it was with those whom I've spent so much time with over the last couple of months. You've made tremendous strides in the transformation process, and I look forward to having Jake Jensen take a tour of your company sometime within the next four to six months. I'm sure, he'll be proud of the new organization you have built. I shall be on call for the next six months and will stop by each month during that time. This, of course, means I'll still take the time to bend your ear."

Everybody applauds with joyful smiles and then thanked me for my help and contribution to their new company. After everyone files out, Nina and I enjoy our small talk which has become much easier for her. As we near the end of our little chat, I asked her how Thanh, her husband is doing.

"Thanh is still in a coma, but I'm sure he will pull through. We Vietnamese don't go down easy," Nina said with a faded smile. "Well, Jackie, liven it up a little and tell me what you and Toni are up to?"

"Well, nothing lively, but Toni has been out of town this last week and gets back tonight—and tomorrow, we're having dinner at my parents' house."

"Wow, now that's a giant step. What's up?"

"Well, Nina, I believe I found a real man—a man I can trust and love for the rest of my life. In the past, neither Toni nor I ever considered marriage, until now. We're not getting any younger, and we've reached a point in our life where we're ready to have a long loving relationship with each other."

"Oh, Jackie, I'm so happy for you."

"Thanks, Nina, your friendship means a lot."

"Has he made a marriage proposal yet?"

"Not yet, but it could come at any time, well, at least, I hope so."

I ended with a titter, and then unable to take it any longer, I grab a *pain au chocolate* pastry to satisfy my nerves as Nina smiles with delight.

I'm helpless in trying to control my yummy session, so I take one more and chant in yummy tongue. Realizing that Nina has work to do, I give her a hug, and we say our goodbyes. Then grab one more yummy for the road...

ACT III - SCENE 4
ENHANCING THE LEARNING PROCESS

Question: 1

Was Jackie's response to her assailant by Bedraggled Hair justifiable? How would you have handled the threatening situation?

Question: 2

What is a financial dynamic modeling program capable of doing that a spreadsheet will not do when defining an *economic value-added* value, or for that matter, any leading indicator value? Explain.

Question: 3

When using model simulation, what can you learn about throughput capability? Try giving a few examples.

ACT III SCENE 5
Global Sharing the Wealth

WEEK 10 – SATURDAY MORNING, THE CATALINA ROOM, LA CASA CAMINO HOTEL IN LAGUNA BEACH

DAKOTA HEADS TO HER SATURDAY MORNING MEETING

It's a beautiful, dazzling, bright Saturday morning. A light warm breeze fills the air with a fresh scent of the sea. My recent purchase of a 1951 two-door W136 Mercedes-Benz 170S Cabriolet convertible is sitting in the driveway. The waxed surface sparkles in the sun showing off its midnight-green color accented with a tan soft top in the down position.

When opening the suicide door (now don't you have to love the slang term) I take notice of the beautiful leather seat as I reminisce back a few weeks when Jake took me to a car auction where I got lucky. Well... Lucky is relative—considering what I paid for it.

After pulling out of my driveway, I head south toward the La Casa Camino Hotel, several miles from my home in the heart of Laguna Beach...

The mild temperature and the wind blowing through my hair entered my mind when determining a favorable reason to buy the Cabriolet—being resultant in my mind when standing on the deck of an aircraft carrier. With my hair cut short, nothing beats the hair-meets-air, windblown look that falls back into place after a turbulent ride in an open convertible. Well, I may fuss with it a little, but only because we females carry a gene that won't allow otherwise.

I've not driven a manual shift transmission since I was a teenager making me a cautious driver. My main worry is driving back home—hoping I'm not stopped on a hill tormenting the clutch and gearbox while rolling back into the car behind me. But it shan't be long, and I'll have the hang of it.

The La Casa Camino Hotel is an elegant Mediterranean style landmark built in 1927. We're using Catalina's rooftop meeting room where we'll be discussing our employee sharing of the wealth program. Attending will be Nina, her director of human resources, and the company officers.

As I approach the hotel beachfront property, I hang a right and point my little Cabriolet into their private parking lot. After finding an isolated place to park, I back in without grinding any gears. Happy with that thought, I bounce out of my car and glance around for the applause—but the only sound comes from a single squawking seagull performing mid-air acrobatics.

THE CATALINA ROOM

During breakfast, we chatted about the normal things that influence our lives—family, vacation trips, our spectacular view, and the great meal we're enjoying this morning. With the table becoming quiet for a moment, I studied the inside of my coffee cup, then glance up and around at the small gathering...

"As you know, we're here today in a relaxed environment absorbing the fresh air and wonderful view while stimulating our brain cells discussing a new global sharing of the wealth program...

It's a program that will define a policy that benefits the employees, stockholders, and our company—the company of the future ... here today."

"It's a good thing you picked this place—my brain cells are falling out faster than my hair," Ed Blackburn said.

Everybody has a good laugh, as Gary Eastwood cuts in...

"But Ed, you've already lost most of your hair."

"Exactly, now you understand my disadvantage," Ed said

Additional chortles went around the table.

WHY INCENTIVE PROGRAMS DON'T WORK

We waited for a moment as our waiters cleared the table and then bring in several new carafes of coffee...

"I see you all have today's outline with you. So, I'll begin with a particular conversation I had with Jake...

It was about incentive programs, and most of what I'm about to say will surprise you. While a few others will see that incentive programs can cause problems and not accomplish what they are designed to do."

I paused while looking around the table.

"Employee-of-the-Year designations, competing prize contests, and reward programs supported with lots of hoopla and pizzazz—is management's rationalization it's a great incentive for the workers.

It's sincere I'm sure, but in reality, it's most often for managers to show their *employee-sensitivity*—a feel good for the managers, which is a natural element for them to be in...

If I sound rude, please excuse me. I've been there as a manager and took part in this type of program."

Seeing they took no displeasure in my remark, I continued...

"And yet, after the wonderment is over, they treat employees as objects of utility the rest of the year, with each measured on finite degrees of productivity which produce anxiety, depression, and hopelessness.

When offering rewards to employees with a desire to learn and a commitment to produce high-value results could be ineffective and counterproductive. Studies show that rewarding those doing something well, will eventually lead to a lower quality of work such as short-term thinking, the use of shortcuts and unethical behavior..."

What companies should consider is clearing away the disincentives and barriers that impede their employee's work, and allow them to be proud of what they're accomplishing. Have them know you need them by giving feedback about what customers and stockholders perceive of their services or products provided by your company, and a summary of the company's health.

SHARING OF THE WEALTH

"Now that I've expressed many of the problems with today's incentives and alternatives, I would like to define the best of both worlds for our employees and the business so you may consider its worth...

As policymakers for our company, we face the trade-off between sharing and keeping the company's profits. Now, keeping that in mind let me reveal what *Janet Yellen* had to say...

When the former *Federal Reserve Board Chairwoman, Janet Yellen* was CEO of the Federal Reserve Bank of San Francisco, she indicated during her lecture at the University of Irvine that there are signs of rising inequality...

Let me comment on an interesting point she made that is, on the whole, true today...

This inequality has been intensifying resistance to globalization, impairing social cohesion, and could, ultimately, undermine American democracy..."

I let a moment go by for Janet Yellen's words to sink in while pouring myself a fresh coffee.

"These are damn serious words... In the urban towns, the most frequent topic of conversation is economic inequality—which many blame on corporate CEOs. They're taking in historic profits driving the richest while losing the middle class. THE LACK OF INEQUALITY INTENSIFIES AS OUR PRODUCTIVITY DIMINISHES OUR QUALITY OF LIFE THAT WILL SOMEDAY BRING OUR ECONOMY TO ITS KNEES...

As responsible officers of your company, we should begin the process of sharing the company's wealth for more of our people. Only a change in our current business architecture will drive improved productivity and for others to take notice...

Let your company be the spearhead that will allow more money to flow into the economy and charge up the system that makes this economy run—the buying public. Only through your new architecture can other companies learn how to increase their employees' wealth and keep people employed.

PRODUCTIVITY AND PROPERLY PAID EMPLOYEES are the driving force of our economy – AND DON'T THINK FOR A MOMENT WE CAN GROW WITHOUT IT—AS OFTEN ADVERTISED. Well, at least not with an annual average GDP of ONE POINT EIGHT PERCENT from 2002 through the first quarter of 2017."

CURRENT BONUS PRACTICE

"Now, I'd like to begin by mentioning that there are few companies today that have implemented a similar program of what we call global sharing of the wealth. But their similarity ends with the *INABILITY* to show the employees how they contributed to market growth or increased company value.

Normally, the company uses an accounting performance measurement like a labor and expense budget margin compared to their forecast. Theoretically, it shows how an employee has worked hard to keep *productivity* high and controlled expenses. Then, of course, this accounting method has no relevance in system throughput improvement, therefore, meaningless...

It is, however, a momentary feel-good policy by management when passing out the money, well that and another version of cost accounting living in the Dark Ages.

Even if they use the EVA format, to be discussed in a moment for developing the available shared amount, it too is meaningless to the employees unless they know how *he* or *she* influenced the momentary gain.

These bonuses programs try to produce an incentive for one to do better. Then, of course, you must ask yourself the question—better at what? Unfortunately, no one has the answer to that question—except; the monetary part is momentarily great...

But where is the sense of self-satisfaction and fulfillment for performing their jobs well? Such as making a positive difference in the way the customer and stockholder perceive their company...

Is there anyone who would like to elaborate on what I said...?

Yes, Gary?"

"I get it. The bonus is great. But, what did I do to justify the money, well, other than I just happened to be at the right place at the right time? I'm happy for the moment, but over the long haul, I will have forgotten about it. Then, of course, when you don't get the bonus—perhaps due to owing to a fabricated reason, or it's just eliminated—you become unhappy with your management—meaning it's a two-edged sword."

"Excellent. Well stated, Gary," I said.

"Okay, now on to companies with incentive programs targeting but a select few for a generous increase. What's wrong with this kind of policy...?

Yes, Ed."

"First off, will this be on our midterm exam?" Ed said with a titter.

"Well, I guess I come off lecturing at times, don't I. Sorry," I said with a polite smile.

"No mid-term, Ed."

"Whoops..."

Give me a moment while removing my foot from my mouth," Ed said. "You have to know, I didn't mean it that way, but when you do lecture, you're the greatest...

Wait, a minute...

I'm not sure that came out right, either... Oh, shut my mouth."

Everybody has a good chuckle. Ed's face turns beet red.

"You can always count on Ed to bring spice to our meetings," I said.

"Okay, Ed, I'll repeat it again: Why do most companies with incentive programs target just a few with a sizable increase? And why is that a problem?"

"Hmm, they would say it's a good way to attract and keep good people. Now, speed and volume are good, but as we have learned, there is no substitute for quality. The result of their good people's action ends up with them displaying a lower quality of work than those offered no reward."

"Ed, for a guy with no hair and fewer brain cells, you've hit the nail right on the head."

With stimulated gleeful chuckles, I sip my fresh brew.

APPRAISAL POLICIES

"Appraisal or review policies are the norms for most companies...

For us, the problem with these subjective appraisal systems evaluating individual performance distract from our new organizational structure.

How any one manager perceives your capabilities will govern the outcome of the review. Appraisal policies try to manipulate behavior with their reward and punishment system. Management calls this type of action—motivation.

But an employee's behavior seldom changes, especially, with an uninteresting job. Unfortunately, for some, this practice leaves open disparity of wages between people of color and gender.

Employees need a position that can engage them in their day-to-day responsibilities. Finding ways to captivate an employee's interest in their work would be better spent—rather than treating them as if they were pet dogs by trying to change their behavior. Please take no offense," I said with a grin.

"Pet dogs?" Ed said with a titter. "I must say, you get right to the point at times, Dakota."

"I try, Ed," I said with a chortle, along with the rest of the folks.

"If you consider me as one being rough on performance reviews, let me read to you notes I have taken on the subject by Jake Jensen...

Jake's knowledge is broad in this area especially, with Wayne's background on the subject of performance reviews. The following is a highlighted summary and interpretation, that Jake has mixed in with what he's learned from Wayne...

It's well documented the purpose of a performance review. Its purpose is to let employees know what their managers expect of them in their job and any changes to their pay. The manager will present the employee's good aspects and shortcomings, followed by discussing the path to improvement and any changes to pay or possible promotions.

Jake feels this is as much about showing the manager's authority while the employee, on the other hand, has one thing on their mind, what is my pay raise, or the chance for advancement. The outcome, in the long haul, has only had little or no influence on improving performance.

Jake picked up on this idea from Wayne who had a clear understanding of this problem back in the late seventies when he stopped the performance review for his company. With no prior knowledge or books on the subject, he began to experiment with measuring quality output linked to dependability. This had its problems, until half-dozen years later, he settled on key indicators, a forerunner of our new system.

The perception of an employee comes from the manager, but the pay increase is defined by the company's financial position, the economy, and the company's budget. The manager's perception is where the problem lies. No two people view an employee's performance in the same light—SO CLAIMING THE EVALUATION IS OBJECTIVE—IS FLATLY RIDICULOUS.

To give you an idea of how people's perception can be so diverse, visit Netflix and select a favorite movie you've seen and then scroll down to the reviews. You'll find four and five stars that might reflect your own thoughts... Now, read the one and two stars, and you'll wonder if these people were looking at the same movie."

Everyone around the table shows their sympathetic nods and smiles.

"I can see that a few of you have already experienced the phenomenon. Okay, let us continue...

Each employee comes with a varying degree of strong suits and imperfections. They try to do their best with the endowment they were gifted with, but thanks to the performance review, the boss is the last person an employee would turn to for help.

This is because people resist help from those who they believe can't get them in proper focus, especially, when they have tried to tell them what their issues are. When the manager's responsibility is to train the employees and then fires one because of poor performance, I believe the manager has failed in their assigned task.

And yet, the manager receives their pay increase or promotions. And then, of course, not unlike cost accounting, employee reviews talk about the past and then expect performance to improve knowing where they had to show progress...

"Now, shouldn't one consider it unworkable to maintain the idea that annual pay and performance reviews lead to corporate improvement?

Our new policy, on the other hand, will enhance system performance for the best interest of both the employees and the company...

Are there questions or point of view on this subject...?"

"Yes, Ed."

"Well, if one is honest with themselves, everything you said is true. We like to fancy ourselves as being objective, but as you say, no two people will issue the same outcome for an employee review. I'm sure at one time or another, the problem has been given some thought...

However, considering the necessary change to replace this process, it's more than one could cope with—when we already have so much on our plate to deal with in our own environment." Ed said.

Just as Ed finished, Melinda Lockhart the human resources director jumps in...

"If we discard the appraisal policy, what will replace it, a sharing of the wealth?"

"Well, Melinda, that's true, but this program we'll be discussing is a true motivation system within our new organizational architecture..."

Melinda put her coffee down and then looked at me for a moment...

"Please forgive me, but old policies and procedures are well engrained. So, an outstanding individual performer gets the same share of wealth as a known slacker through this new system...

Now, with all due respect, how will that make things better?"

"Who would like to answer Melinda's question?

Gary, go ahead."

"I'll give it a try. I'd say, if you're meeting the benchmarks, eliminating the bottlenecks and unnecessary steps in the process, there should be no slackers—otherwise; one of these three areas would have suffered. Furthermore, the community within the system would not tolerate it. Am I close?" Gary said.

"Thanks, Gary, you're on the right track, but I might add a few other things: A slacker is relative to one's perception. There are those employees who may or may not stack up against those who excel, but they support the system output.

We do not measure individual productivity here because it has no relative meaning in the *system* performance. It's the system processes that count. If a person is creating a bottleneck, they disrupt the system flow which then brings up the question—did the person receive the proper training? Is the responsibility of that person or job too complicated? Is there a system processing problem? Does the process need to be redesigned? Does the process become less engaging? Or in Melinda's words is that person a real slacker? Whatever the case, during a bottleneck, a red flag arises.

Now, for those who excel in performance, they have the opportunity to advance in their pay grade. Sorry, I'm getting a little ahead of myself. We'll be discussing that momentarily...

Well, Melinda, is this new policy a little more digestible now?" I said.

"Oh my, that took the wind out of my sails, what a refreshing idea. Nina mentioned we would hear things contrary to our way of doing things, and hearing the logic behind the theory, I would see the world differently, thanks, Dakota."

"There is one other vital point. Not unlike the Pareto principle, only a small percentage of employees rise to the surface of excellence. So what happens to a system community when these same few keep getting the prize?" I said, glancing around the table. "Yes, Melinda?"

"Gee... Put in that light, I'd say the others will lose interest which could erect barriers to creative ideas and the possibility of improving the system processes or their quality of work."

"You got it. Does that make sense to everybody?"

With nodding, eager faces, I moved on...

WEALTH SHARING: THE WHAT AND HOW PROCESS

"The degree of a company's health for wealth sharing is proportional to the employees having specific goals and the authority to achieve them. The goals must be supportive to the customer and the stockholder—measured by MPV system drivers and leading indicators.

Businesses create products or services to fulfill the customers' needs and yield an adequate stockholder return—and this is, the *what* and *how* of sharing the wealth...

By this, I mean the term *what* relates to customer and stockholder fulfillment. And, *How* defines the cycle of transformation and degree of change for customer and stockholder satisfaction..."

AN INCREASED BUSINESS VALUE PLATFORM

"If improved performance increases market share, then the employees have *increased the business value*—and from this platform, we build the justification for a global sharing of the wealth...

You might say the improved value of the business is the catalyst for the sharing of the wealth. With measurable objectives, employees can observe the improved performance that allows the business and employees to reap the wealth or penalties for their efforts.

The compensation plan promotes cooperation among the employees to achieve the overall goal of improving the business value. When the business prospers, the employees receive compensation relative to achieving the business goals. The company officers *and* the employees share in equal percentages of their respective income, which is linked to their responsibility."

JOB DESCRIPTIONS

"Job descriptions will also be covered in my outline for today's discussions... Employees in structured vertical organizations require specific job descriptions. The idea is to ensure fairness through industry pay standards.

In our new organizational structure, individuals will use their new knowledge to elevate their pay grade when taking a formal test.

To open their career path, the written test will measure the employee's competencies depth of knowledge and communication skills. This process allows an employee to gain greater responsibility and assure the company we have the skill set to grow the company—"

"Dakota, I have the obvious question, how do we, accomplish that?"

"Ah... There lies the challenge, Gary...

We'll need to begin by defining the different levels of competencies and appropriate pay grades. And then we have the employee absorption rate into these different levels of pay grades to evaluate. Perhaps, we could use a sales-to-employee ratio as a start. But this is something we'll need to discuss along with the new platform for developing our new policy coming up...

The wealth creation system is just one of the necessary steps of an ongoing transformation strategy for improving the business performance which leads to increased sales and expanded market share...

This step in the process leads to employee sharing of the wealth that leads to new process improvement—and brings us back full circle in what we call the circle of influence..."

With everyone grasping the idea, I continue...

DEVELOPING POLICY

"Let's discuss policy. This new compensation idea may change most packaged programs. If businesses of the future wish to change for the right reason, such changes will be necessary."

Nina chimes in...

"Sounds like our final piece of the puzzle."

"That's right, Nina. If everyone buys in on the change, our task today is going over my outline and turn it into an acceptable rough draft that everyone can approve. We will ratify the completed document after a final draft.

Melinda, I understand you'll be composing our policy today."

"You bet, along with my laptop, this is what I do...

By the way, with your permission, I would like to submit this subject as a presentation at the Society of Resource Management conference and expo coming up in a few months."

"Your presentation at such a gathering is a great idea, Melinda. I would like to help you with it when and if you need it, and authorize the final paper owing to its great importance...

The outline I'm about to pass out gives us a base to operate from and develop our new policy. If I were to have the same meeting with another business tomorrow, the two policies would have subtle differences due to the views and personalities involved, but the basic concept would remain the same.

Well, there's a lot to cover by the end of the day...

Nina, take a folder and pass the others on around the table. I'd like for us to finish up no later than three o'clock...

ECONOMIC VALUE-ADDED PLATFORM

"We'll build our new policy platform centered on the *Economic Value-added indicator*. Nothing new with this idea, so let me explain what our proposed system and other EVA programs have in common...

EVA sets a performance target linking the distribution of money to the employees. It also establishes a single goal target for both the shareholder and the employees—as opposed to different goals with inconsistent outcomes. This allows employees to behave like owners.

Remember, a company's earnings should be equal to or greater than its cost of capital to satisfy the stockholders return...

When the earnings are higher, employees should get an appropriate share of the positive EVA results. But depending on the type of company, the handling of distribution could be dissimilar.

The EVA wealth-sharing system is one of the few ways employees can see how they contribute to the process to make more money for themselves in the sharing process, and create greater value for their shareholders and customers.

In this type of relationship, there is no limit to the upside. The greater the wealth and the company's value, the more content the shareholders—"

"Dakota, why are the shareholders so delighted that the employees are taking a chunk of their investment?"

"Who would like to answer Melinda's question?"

"I'll take a stab at it, Dakota," Ed said. "My guess would be that the shareholders know the company is producing money equal to or greater than their expected rate of return. And with the employees sharing the benefits greater than the expected return, they know they will continue to strive and build the stock value for a strong company... It's the increase in valuation through growth and profits, with the excess EVA invested back into the employee's income based on the performance outcome, and this inspires investors. More on that coming up..."

I look toward Melinda and see her nodding to Ed's response.

"Well said, Ed."

"Thanks, Ed, I get it now," Melinda said.

"Now, this is where our program and others differ...

I'll begin with the wealth-sharing allocation of a positive EVA...

EVA is inadequate as a single-source measurement for the wealth-sharing system decision-making.

To counter such inadequacy, benchmarks will need to be set at the appropriate level for our system processes to govern MARKET PERCEPTION CRITERIA as an EXTERNAL FACTOR. And INTERNAL FACTORS would be CASH FLOW FROM OPERATIONS, CURRENT LIABILITY RATIO, PRODUCTIVITY, NEW PRODUCT DEVELOPMENT LEAD-TIME, PRODUCT THROUGHPUT TIME, AND REWORK AND SCRAP RATE. EVA is the *perfect* marriage of a wealth-sharing system coupled with our new architecture...

The biggest difference from our EVA reward system and others is we share the wealth with all employees as opposed to companies defining their managers as the only worthy choice for a bonus.

Most companies using an EVA reward program payout at the end of a three-year period. Theoretically, this leads to long-term shareholder value. Not a bad idea when you are working with their legacy architecture.

But with our ability to make a quick response to benchmarks affecting the EVA, we can maintain long-term shareholder value—indicating it was not by *happenstance* that the company had a good year."

SHARING OF THE WEALTH OUTLINE

"Before establishing the degree of global sharing of the wealth, the EVA benchmark needs defining, along with shareholder value...

We'll begin by reviewing the following tables of illustrations...

STEP ONE – *MPV* Purchase Criteria
STEP TWO - Productivity,
STEP THREE – Operating Attributes resulting in an improved *Cash* position
STEP FOUR – Resulting Benchmark Improvement.
STEP FIVE – EVA result
STEP SIX – The Distribution of Wealth

For expeditious reasons, I used the following figures from a previous company turnaround for the following outline...

I'll *read the outline* as we go through it, keeping everyone in step...

Now, we'll begin by opening your folder to STEP ONE in the outline..."

THE OUTLINE

"**STEP ONE** – IS THE MPV PURCHASE CRITERIA TABLE...

The market-Perception target improvement table uses the MPV survey information feedback. In this scenario, the targeted improvement level has improved by 80%, WHEN COMPARING THE ACTUAL TO REQUIRED OR TARGET.

The shaded areas show the resulting formulation for the percent change in ROW ONE LAST COLUMN—TIMELINESS EQUALS 67%, computed by dividing CHANGE IN PERCEPTION (2)—BY REQUIRED IMPROVEMENT (3).

STEP 1 – MPV PURCHASE CRITERIA - TARGET IMPROVEMENT TABLE 1

Purchase Criteria	Current Perception	Projected Benchmark	Required Improvement	Actual Perception	Change in Perception	Percent Improvement
Timeliness	6	9	3	8	2	67%
Flexibility	7	9.5	2.5	8.5	1.5	60%
Acceptance	6	8	2	8.5	2.5	125%
Service	7	10	3	9	2.4	80%
Total			10.5		8.4	80%

"For your financial modeling during the fiscal year ending, finance must work with the other officers to define our internal and external benchmarks for the best possible EVA results...

Now, on to STEP TWO...

STEP TWO is our PRODUCTIVITY BENCHMARK illustrated in TABLE 2. THE PRODUCTIVITY TARGET calculations for PERCENT IMPROVEMENT HAPPENS WHEN COMPARING ACTUAL OF FOUR PERCENT TO TARGET IMPROVEMENT OF FIVE PERCENT EQUATING TO A WORKFLOW IMPROVEMENT OF 80% OR FOUR PERCENT DIVIDE BY FIVE PERCENT.

(Reference the TOTAL FACTOR PRODUCTIVITY TABLE we discussed in A NEW SET OF MEASUREMENT TOOLS, PART I.)

STEP 2 - PRODUCTIVITY TARGET IMPROVEMENT TABLE 2

Improvement	Productivity Contribution	Target Improvement	Actual	Percent Improvement
Workflow	70%	5%	4%	80%
Inform. Tech.	30%	10%	6.5%	65%
Total	100%	15%	10.5%	70%

STEP THREE is our Operating Attributes illustrated in TABLE THREE. These measurements influence the outcome of growth, profitability, and of course, the EVA. The table is self-explanatory.

STEP 3 – OPERATING ATTRIBUTES TABLE 3

Operating Attributes	Previous Year End	Projected Benchmark	Required Improve.	Actual Result	Improve. Change	Improve. Percent
CASH						
Ratio: Cash from Operations./ Current Liability	.75	1.25	0.5	1.0	.25	50%
THROUGHPUT TIME						
Product Development — Months	14.5	12	2.5	11.8	2.7	108%
Products—Days	15	10	5	11.5	3.5	70%
Total			8		6.45	81%
QUALITY						
Re-work Rate	1.5%	0.75%	0.75%	0.89%	0.61%	81%
Scrape Rate	2.00%	1.50%	0.50%	1.50%	0.50%	100%
Total			1.25%		1.11%	89%

STEP FOUR table four shows the summary of how the various results from TABLES ONE, TWO, and THREE govern the EVA outcome.

STEP 4 *RESULTING BENCHMARK IMPROVEMENT TABLE 4*

Reference Step #	Description	Percent Change	Weight	Weighted Result
1	Purchase Criteria	80%		
2	Productivity	70%		
3	Cash	50%		
3	Throughput Time	81%		
3	Internal Quality	89%		
	Total Average	74%		

It also illustrates the areas that need performance improvement. In a few cases, the criteria may require weighting. For our purpose, I left them blank. Coming up next is step five...

STEP FIVE is our EVA Result. THE COMPANY'S TOTAL NET EVA IS SIX POINT FIVE SEVEN MILLION ($6.57 MILLION). This value times the average benchmark performance OF SEVENTY-FOUR PERCENT *(74%) IMPROVEMENT* shown IN STEP FOUR gives us the final result: a positive FOUR POINT EIGHT SIX Million Dollars ($4.86 Million) for employee distribution shown in step six...

STEP SIX COVERS THE Distribution of the Employee's Share of FOUR-POINT EIGHT SIX million dollars ($4.86 Million). Here, let me write the formula...

$4.86 MILLION / $31.5 MILLION ANNUAL PAYROLL =
15.43% GAIN FOR EACH EMPLOYEE

Therefore, employees with a forty thousand dollar ($40,000) income times the percent gain per employee equals six point one seven one thousand dollars ($6,171) gain in the SHARING OF THE WEALTH... I'll give you a moment to digest this portion of our policy..."

While taking a sip of my coffee, I gaze out the window observing the never-ending reach of the Pacific Ocean...

"Okay, back at it... Ah... I see a look of concern coming from Ed."

"Concern, possibly. I'm thinking after a few years after we've supplied our customers with MPV rating of a 9 and 10 on all the various measurement, just assuming that was possible, we won't have any more room for improvement...

Meaning there is no gain to measure. This would also apply to productivity and operating improvements getting to a point we have reached our final goal...

Well, then what?"

"Ah... Great question, Ed, and, fortunately, I have a simple answer. When a company's MPV improvements for the various categories are hitting on a nine or ten, we would consider the results at ninety-plus percent...

And, when the productivity and operating events have reached their limitation determined by all the company's officers, the particular event would also be considered at ninety-plus percent... In other words, ninety percent times the EVA, and that's the long and short of it, Ed..."

"You were right, Dakota, a simple solution it is. I guess, at times, we just forget to remove our blinders when the answer is staring us in the face..."

"True, but that only makes us human... Are there any other questions before moving on to our next subject? ...No? ...Okay then, let's jump into the cost of living increase process..."

COST OF LIVING INCREASE

"Qualified members in the business system will also receive an annual cost-of-living increase.

INDIVIDUAL MERIT INCREASES *are biased and an unreliable view of an individual's contribution to a company's performance due to different managers reviews having dissimilar outcomes. And... And, any increase is governed by finance and their projected annual budget, with employee increases taking a backseat to most everything else, except for the cost of living expense...*

Up next is promotion reviews and career path..."

COMPETENCY PROMOTION REVIEWS FOR THE EMPLOYEE CAREER PATH

"FOR PROMOTIONS, there need to be levels of competencies for our employees within their professional career path...

With only two levels of management and a need for improved productivity, our workforce must have exceptional knowledge of their occupation, leadership capability, authority, and understand the organizational system processes. Not unlike the SEALs and Army's Special Forces—dedicated and well-trained.

COMPETENCIES can relate to our armed services' level of pay grades. To elevate in a pay grade or be promoted in your new company policy, one must take examinations that include three areas of knowledge: OCCUPATION/PROFESSION, SYSTEM PROCESSES, AND LEADERSHIP...

OUR POLICY MANUAL will need to identify the different levels of pay grades and test requirements. To get things started, you will need to reference unique books for reading and perhaps courses that can help further develop one's knowledge.

Next, I would encourage you to buy BUSINESS WIKI SOFTWARE and set up a special COLLABORATIVE INTRANET WEBSITE whose content is developed and edited by the employees—not unlike the WIKIPEDIA WEBSITE.

This will allow for a fast and useful base of knowledge, and a far better way to get the employees involved in the transformation process.

IT MUST BE A SELF-HELP PROGRAM, except for in-house training on process mapping, and the functional use of the system modeling simulation software.

THE TEST WILL BE SEMI-ANNUAL for the various levels of pay grades. They should be both multiple-choice and written answers. Each increase in the level of a pay grade becomes more difficult...

Is everyone following okay?"

Seeing smiling faces, I continue as we worked through the morning hours with diligence and with little change needed in the *Sharing the Wealth* outline, other than to be further developed into a policy format that included the *Cost of Living Increase* and *Reviews for Career Path*...

The COMPETENCY PAY-GRADE POLICY, however, is another matter we needed to cover after lunch...

LUNCHTIME

"We've accomplished a great deal this morning, and I'm sure our appetites tell us we're near lunchtime. Out on the deck, waiting for us are two tables under the shade of umbrellas overlooking the ocean and the recipient of a wonderful sea breeze..."

Later, with our lunch behind us, we felt re-energized and began the final stage of our policy...

"Each of the different pay grades will use the following structure in our discussion beginning with COMPETENCY PAY-GRADE POLICY. The rate of pay and occupational test questions may differ for the different occupations such as the direct and indirect competency pay-grade policy..."

COMPETENCY PAY-GRADE POLICY

"P1 – THIS IS AN ENTRY-LEVEL for employees out of college ready to work in a professional capacity - or for new employees without work experience in clerical or manufacturing jobs. There is a three-month probationary period, but the employee will not be eligible to move to the next pay grade until after one year of employment.

P2 - MUST HAVE A MINIMUM OF ONE-YEAR RELATED ON-THE-JOB EXPERIENCE able to perform the basic skills necessary for his or her assigned responsibility.

P3 - MUST HAVE A MINIMUM OF TWO-YEAR RELATED ON-THE-JOB EXPERIENCE able to perform the basic skills necessary for his or her assigned responsibility, and after a three-month probationary period, one must pass the P3 advancement tests.

P4 - GROUP LEADER – THE EMPLOYEE MUST HAVE BEEN A P3 FOR A MINIMUM OF SIX MONTHS and passed the P4 advancement and leadership tests. The employee must possess the knowledge, degrees of skill, and authority to improve the system and employee performance level while carrying out their normal hands-on duties.

P5 - SENIOR GROUP LEADER – THE EMPLOYEE MUST HAVE BEEN A P4 FOR A MINIMUM OF TWO YEARS and passed the P5 advancement and leadership tests. The new pay grade carries with it a higher responsibility and authority.

P6 – HEAD GROUP LEADER—THE EMPLOYEE MUST HAVE BEEN A P5 FOR A MINIMUM OF TWO YEARS and passed the P6 advancement and leadership tests. This pay grade manages a subsystem community and reports to the department head/director. After two or more years in this capacity, the employee is eligible for advancement into department head or director responsibility when an opening is available within the scope of his or her responsibilities.

The final selection is by review board officers."

QUALIFICATIONS FOR ADVANCEMENT TEST – PAY GRADES P3 THROUGH P6

"Employees who have demonstrated their accomplishments noted in the two following requirements shall be eligible to take the next pay grade test pay grades P3 through P6:

ONE - When the employee has established that they have studied the appropriate courses for the next higher pay grade.

TWO - When the department head signs off for the advancement examination."

COMPETENCY IMPROVEMENT TEST - P3 THROUGH P6

"No matter the profession, direct or indirect, the Organizational System Processing (OSP) portion of the test will be the same for every employee, the degree of difficulty increases with the level of pay grade.

The exam will consist of 200 multiple-choice questions based on Occupation and Organizational System Processing (OSP). Study groups are enhanced when the OSP test is the same for each occupation.

TABLE 1 shows the ratio of the two types of questions: Occupation and OSP and their Ratio of Questions.

Pay Grade	Occupation	OSP
P3	175	25
P4	100	100
P5	75	125
P6	50	150

Preparation will be the test's biggest hurdle, so, having good course material is essential in developing the knowledge to pass the test. THE COMPANY'S INTRANET WIKI WEBSITE WILL BE MOST HELPFUL...

Questions?"

"You seem to be doing just fine, Dakota. It's well laid out for us to understand your intent," Nina said.

"Good to hear. Okay then, let's move on..."

LEADERSHIP TEST - P4 THROUGH P6

"THE LEADERSHIP EXAM is for candidates moving up to P4 through P6. The exam will consist of 100 questions, both written and multiple-choice."

QUALIFICATION FOR ADVANCEMENT – P4 THROUGH P6

"The semi-annual examination will include the competency and leadership tests for every occupation P4 through P6.

When an opening is available, the employee with the highest score in knowledge and the oldest test date will get the first opportunity for an interview. The department head/director will conduct the interviews.

If there are openings at other facilities, and the candidate accepts the location, the company will pay moving expenses.

When chosen for the new position, the candidate must demonstrate his or her proficiently by taking on the responsibility of that pay grade during a three-month probationary period...

Well, as you can see, we made good progress having completed a rough draft of a new *Competency Pay Grade Policy* by our three o'clock afternoon deadline...

Melinda, if you would please, use your portable printer and print copies of the final draft and hand them out..."

Melinda nods with a smile...

"I have but one more comment about our policy, the stress during a test..."

STRESS DURING A TEST

"Most notably, the *Competency Improvement Test* for career path advancement... For me, *I have a reluctance to use a test as a way for our employees to advance.*"

The group gives me a bewildered look.

"However, it's either a test or someone's perception of one's capability whether an employee should advance as the *only* road for career advancement. *Clearly*... Clearly, that's not acceptable.

To continue with that thought, I'd say there are people *gifted* for taking tests. However, much of the time, these same employees are reluctant to take risks, lack flexibility, are poor listeners, prefer to work in solitude, and are quick to jump to conclusions.

Then we have those deemed academically slow, but often found to be insightful, venturesome, humorous, wondrous and exploratory. Labels, genetics, test scores, or the numbers of right answers cannot define intelligence. What's essential is being in the habit of applying skillful conjecture to perplexing problem situations that matter.

Therefore, we must allow any employee taking the test the necessary tutoring if needed. Moreover, the test should be taken in solitude with no peer pressure or time limit, other than within reason. For a normal two-hour test, you'd want to add in a factor of two—making four hours the limit..."

I take a moment for a response...

"Beautifully put, Dakota. What you say is thoughtful and insightful of those who contribute so much to a company and then held back because they don't do well during a *stressful* test. Such action would be a loss to our company, so it's to our benefit they do well, and we must make our best effort to help them along the way," Nina said.

We applaud her observation.

"Thank you, Nina—well-stated. Well, folks, I believe we have ourselves a final draft for our new Competency Pay Grade Policy. But let's not forget, we still have a good deal of work to do—the coursework material, *wiki* software, and the exams. Nina, you'll want to delegate this work to the appropriate officers."

After a nod, Nina hesitated for a moment...

"I have a question about preparing the OSP portion of the coursework and exam. I'd assume you'd like us to use the information we received from our sessions with Jackie and Johnny?"

"Sure, that would be a good start. However, if you'd like to expand on any subject, feel free to gather new information and apply it as you see fit. But let's not forget our ideas must conform to horizontal open-system organization architecture."

Nina gives me an understanding nod.

"Melinda, you should handle the pay grade policy for the different occupations and make sure to include the pay rate structure. After completion, submit the policy for review by the officers and department heads...

Oh... One other thing... In the policy review process, let's not forget that once we have trained our people, and the organization is performing properly, we should consider the different paygrades beginning at the high-end of an equivalent position for our competitors. We have invested a considerable amount of unique training for our employees resulting in a high-sales ratio per employee—head-and-shoulders-above the competitors..."

Looking around the table I see an attentive audience nodding their heads.

Melinda gives a nod and a smile...

"Good point, Jackie. I'll make sure I have accurate data that will help in our decision making,"

END OF MEETING

After a few more comments from the others, I called an end to our meeting.

"Well, Dakota, you expanded on what's left of my limited brain cells in this exercise. But, we did a hell of a job here today, and our work will make a sizable impact on our ability to grow this company, making it a breakthrough event...

I feel as though we are the legendary champions of knights in attendance with Charlemagne, being the paladins of this new policy," Ed Blackburn said.

Ed's response is applauding and smiling faces, soon followed by Nina's response...

"Well put, Ed. When I take into account what our company will be in the future, I get goosebumps. By raising our employees' level of competency through a pay grade system incorporated with the sharing of the wealth policy, we will have a group of employees equaled by none."

"There's no doubt, Nina, with a two-level management system, our employees must have exceptional knowledge of their occupation, good leadership capability, authority, and the understanding of our organizational system processes...

Let me add what the president of the Council on Competitiveness, Deborah

L. Wince-Smith said... *Talent would be the oil of the twenty-first century."*

"That being the case, we'll be like an oil gusher," Ed said, receiving another round of happy applauding and smiling faces from everyone.

"I'd like to give you our special thanks, Dakota, for hanging with us through this difficult process," Nina said.

"Thanks, Nina, but it's all of you who jumped in and made this happen today ... for me, I just showed you the way. From here on out, Nina, you will need to head up and finalize the program. Soon after that, you'll want to roll the new policy out to the employees...

Oh, by the way, I'm going to Jake's home this evening for dinner, and I'm sure he will be happy to hear of our progress we've made today. Well, that's a wrap, let's call it a day."

JAKE'S PLACE

I stopped at my place to change into khaki shorts, a red silk blouse, and my open-toed leather sandals. After stuffing my weekend bag with swimsuit and essentials, I'm out of the house.

Having thrown my bag in the Cabriolet's cramped back seat, I settled in and awaken my new baby into purr mode, then shift her into reverse with care, back out of my driveway and head north.

An hour and forty-five minutes later, I'm driving up Serra Road in the Malibu hills when I notice a hawk with sharp talons swooping down and picking up an afternoon snack. Later, up the road, I shift down into second gear when I'm distracted by a flash of late afternoon sun reflecting off the uppermost top of Jake's pyramid covered with hammered copper sheeting peaking above a hilltop. The copper peak rests atop the pyramid's glass construction as though floating in midair—it's breathtaking.

Jake tells me the pyramid, essentially, represents enlightenment or the spread of knowledge. I'm not into symbolism, and I'm sure Jake isn't either, but his mother's dad was a Freemason. Anyhow, I love going to his place, it is such a treat. Wait until we get there, and I'll take you on tour.

A little further up Serra Road, I take a left and then another left on Jake's private drive—*Camino del estiércol del burro,* which translates into Donkey Dung road. Jake told me the name added a little *whimsical charm* to the neighborhood.

After phoning Jake to tell him I was nearing his compound, the gate swung open at the top of his steep drive. I made a quick stop at the foot of the hill, shift into first gear and gun the motor up the hill where it levels out allowing me to let off on the gas. While idling down the driveway and onto a large circular drive, the tires crunch over crushed, white-and-pink-packed seashells where I park near the entrance under a tall palm tree. The palm is but one of many that add an artistic appeal that follows the periphery of the circular drive allowing one to feel as though you have entered Canon Drive in Beverly Hills.

After stepping out of my car, I grab my bag and sling it over my shoulder and shut the door. With wonderment, I glance up toward the high berm of earth half the length of a football field running north to south and covered in beautiful six-inch tall green Mondo grass. The grass is sculptured with California native groundcover displaying an array of beautiful colors. Off-center to the berm is a sandstone stairway that begins with wide steps and narrows at the top when running up the side of the steep slope. Parked under the palm on the opposite side of the stairway is a restored beautiful 1980 450 SEL not unlike Jake's Mercedes.

And there on the last step of the stairway is Wayne Coker, Jake's long-time friend. Wayne and Jake are two of a kind—tall, lean, and fit, still looking like surfer dudes with their long blonde hair. Jake met Wayne while surfing the waves at Playa Del Rey as kids during the mid and late fifties. They soon became good friends sharing their limited knowledge for board building and racing gear back in the days of low-budget quarter-mile drag strip racing.

"Wayne, long time no see."

"Dakota, you're looking swell."

"Swell," I said with a chuckle.

"Clearly, I watch too many old black and white movies, well, ancient to you."

"Well, speaking of those ancient movies," I said, "Everyone has a cigarette in one hand and drink in the other."

"Funny you should say that having just watched a 1934 movie *The Thin Man*, the other night with William Powell. If I'm not mistaken, I seldom saw a scene where he wasn't walking around with a Martini and puffing on a cigarette... Yeah, those were the days. In our teens, everyone smoked and drank a few beers during a party. Hell, I smoked until the early or mid-1970s."

"Why did you quit?"

"One evening, I ran out of cigs, so I borrowed a pack of Camels from a buddy. After a few of those, I became light-headed, and my whole body felt tingly causing me to sit down. While sitting there, I concluded I'm doing nothing more than digging my own grave. So, at work the next day, I took my pack of menthol Newport's off my desk, crushed them, and dropped them in the wastebasket—and that's the long and short of it."

"Wow, cold turkey. Why is it so hard for most to quit the so-called addictive habit?"

"I have no idea. For me, I don't like the idea of not being in control of myself. That's why I don't drink, except, for a glass of wine or a beer now and then."

"Hm... You're not alone there. So, what brings you to Jake's humble little shack?"

"Well, as you know, Jake and I have been sharing ideas with each other since we were tadpoles. Jake wanted to discuss a new theory I've been carrying around with me on how to manufacture ultralight composite vehicles in small facilities, satellites if you will—in large dense populations, not unlike islands. The island size is like dropping a pebble in a pond and seeing how far the rings expand. We'll need to determine how population density, culture, and other attributes will determine the boundaries and production volume. We may want Tony Gray of Dynamic Systems to build us a dynamic model to verify our results."

"Why not just manufacture them in one location?" I said.

"Well, due to massive startup cost being capital intensive—meaning huge fixed asset cost, while shackled with an additional thirty percent of your cost going to distribution sending cars around the country...

I would add that it's not those who first contemplate a particular innovation, but those who can put the right pieces of innovation together and change the market's reaction for the good."

"Damn, I've not thought of it that way before. Well, Wayne, I'm here for the weekend to discuss our plan of attack on this project—the timing couldn't be better."

"Sounds good, Dakota, please contact me if I can be of help. Seeing and talking to you has been a pleasure, but I need to dash out of here if I'm to make my flight."

"Good luck, Wayne."

I watched him get into his Mercedes; drive off, waited for the automatic gate to open, and then observed the SEL disappear down the hill.

While taking in the impressive view, I see traces of feathery clouds in a vivid blue sky hovering over the Pacific Ocean adding to the splendor of the day.

When walking up the sunny stairway, you'll notice the native bees courting the indigenous flowers doing their little pollinating ritual. They're attracted to the warm-colored flowers as they bound from one flower to the other as they dance to a rhythm that tries to keep them from encountering one another's wingtip. But when they do collide, one will emit tiny, whoops, the same way a stranger would say whoa when jostling you in a crowded room. They will at times, however, have a head-on crash, lacking the necessary information one might get from the LAX control tower. Among the plentiful bees is an array of colorful butterflies.

When nearing the top of the stairs, I feel a little vibration at my feet and hear the roar of a waterfall. All at once, a Golden Hairstreak butterfly appears before me fluttering in place while computing the wind speed and the rate of descent to land with ease on my nose. Feeling good about its landing and putting up with my giggling, it rides up the stairs with me to the top. As we take the last step, we're greeted with a spectacular sight of architecture, unlike anything you'll ever see in a lifetime. We stand there drinking in the majesty of such a noble sight.

One more step puts us perched on a large slab of sandstone, the gateway to the bridge that takes you over a narrow channel of water running the length of the berm that feeds the waterfall. Golden Hairstreak takes flight and waves goodbye as the beautiful little creature flies off to another adventure as it rises above the mist created by water cascading down into the pool of water.

Hovering above the waterline is a concrete base that anchors the large diameter sandstone-colored concrete pillars equally spaced around the eighty-foot square shape. Between the pillars are large sliding glass doors. Above the pillars, rises the pyramid at a slope equal to that of the ancient Egyptian Khufu pyramid—fifty-one and a half degrees.

And serving as a bridge between the front entrance and the berm is an exotic brown-oxidized, 2-inch thick plate of steel cut to resemble a swimming serpent spanning the water. The snake's tail tucks into the slab of sandstone on the berm. The head is flush with the upper base of the pyramid and wiggling out of the serpent's mouth is a blood-red ceramic tongue wedged into the teak mezzanine. Positioned in the pool below are two miniature islands ringed in concrete that straddle the bridge allowing two tall, slender palm trees to guard the entrance.

While crossing the bridge, I'm safeguarded by the heavy curved tinted-glass railing that conforms to the snake's moving shape. Jake is waiting for me at the massive, slightly concave hammered blood-red titanium double-door entrance, framed by two palm plants in colored sandstone pots. Behind Jake is an eight-foot-high four-dimensional piece of steel sculpture.

"Christ, Jake… I'm forever blown away by this entrance."

"Yeah, the crossing kind of grows on you," he said with a warm smile. "Come on in, Dakota, and make yourself homely."

"Damn, Jake, it's no wonder you're not surrounded by babes."

"Good Point. Did you run into Wayne before coming up?"

"Yes, we enjoyed a short but interesting conversation that we need to discuss in our meeting."

"That's good, I'm glad you caught him in time. He had an urgent flight out to Chicago and needed to hurry off."

Acknowledging Jake with a nod, we walked into the glass pyramid and onto a large suspended circular mezzanine. The deck had been laid down with dark well-worn Brazilian teak resting on steel girders bolted at four points of the pyramid. The builder acquired the wood from a San Francisco hotel renovation. In the center, you'll see a large free-form opening to allow light down to the lower floor and the placement of the escalator.

The mezzanine is where Jake's guests gather to relax and enjoy the breathtaking view, night or day. For safety, there is a glass railing running around the periphery of the mezzanine with glass shelves at the appropriate locations displaying a scattering of books and colorful ceramic and glass sculptures. There are comfortable chairs bordered by handmade area rugs with hints of Picasso, Dali, and Miro.

It appears that it's not just the architecture, but the interior design displaying the many unusual colors, textures, and materials used in the construction and furnishing.

Getting off the escalator and hobbling toward me is Li'l Kitty. After picking her up, we meow with each other for a little kitty chat, and then I lay my eyes on Jake...

"So, did you put in the escalator for you, or Li'l Kitty?"

No answer, other than a quirky smile and a shrug.

"You're such a softy."

I handed him my weekend bag and walked toward the escalator with Li'l Kitty in my arms.

During the ride down, Jake looked my way...

"I saw that butterfly on your nose."

"Wasn't it cute?" I said. "It remained on my nose while climbing the upper portion of the stairs."

"You know, I had a thing with a butterfly once and asked the beautiful little lady to the ball, but she couldn't come."

With a grin, I asked him why not?

"It was a mothball," Jake said with that stupid grin he gets.

I tried not to laugh, but unable to hold it back, I giggled until we reached what resembles the lobby floor of a luxury hotel.

"Shall I ring for the bell captain?"

With a shake of my head, we walk around an island of white sand with three tall palm trees and assorted ferns.

Polished sandstone covers the floor softened with colorful artsy-scattered area rugs and furnished with eclectic Asian furniture influenced by tropical design and flowering plants in large ceramic pots. The various angles of light and color create an overwhelming beauty.

With Jake still carrying my bag, we head toward the kitchen. He sets the bag down next to a comfortable chair...

"Why don't you and Li'l Kitty take a seat and you can canoodle her, while I grab us a beer."

"For Li'l Kitty, too?"

No response.

While Jake heads toward the kitchen, the most westerly room on the south side, Li'l Kitty and I waited for our beer and passed the time observing our surroundings. To my left are three large rooms that open out on an outside patio that runs the length of the south wall. There's the kitchen as I mentioned, the center room is the dining room with its twelve-seat glass table. Next, is the entertainment room surrounded by electronically controlled vertical glass panels that are adjustable from clear to any shade of darkness, and can open and close.

When looking straight ahead to the rear westwardly side glass wall of opened sliding doors, you'll see the deck and a large pool with a tropical garden making for a seamless relationship of indoors and outdoors. Along the northern end of the glass as you exit the living area is an extra-wide hallway running west beyond the pyramid base that leads you to two guest bedrooms and the master suite

Li'l Kitty and I glance up at Jake with an eye on our beer.

"Thanks, good buddy."

Jake sets Li'l Kitty's small bowl of beer down near me.

I put Kitty down next to her bowl so she could lap up her beer.

"She must have Irish blood in her," I said.

Jake looks down at me with a warm smile and hands me my beer...

"Most women sitting in that chair are asleep by now."

"Did I spoil your evening?"

"You've no idea, do you?" He said, with a quizzical smile tugging at the corners of his mouth.

"Shit, Jake. You're as harmless as my old pet turtle."

"That's not what my girlfriends say."

"Yeah... Thirty years ago."

"Damn, has it been that long? Well, after too many birthdays, I stopped counting."

You shouldn't look at it that way, the more birthdays you have, the longer you live...

It was quiet for a moment as he considered that thought, then a flat smile played over his lips...

"Ah, the journey of life—it can be hard for those who travel alone."

"How sad," I said. "Unfortunately, I understand ever so much... So, tell me, whatever happened to that girl you mentioned over the phone a few days ago that you planned to ask out?

"Huh?"

"Come now, you remember the one I'm talking about."

"Oh. You must mean the psychic."

"Yeah, that's the one."

"Well, she left me before we actually met."

"What? Oh... You wiseass. You and Johnny are two of a kind, it's no wonder he worships you."

We both go off into la-la land for a moment sipping our beer.

"Tell me Jake is that beautiful black grand piano over there just to collect dust or have you learned to play anything yet?"

"As you may remember my mother played the piano, and her dad played in his own band—there was no musical instrument he couldn't play. I've been taking lessons off and on for over two years and have now realized my place in a family of music."

Jake glides over to the piano and lifts the fallboard covering the keyboard. Satisfied, he throws out his make-believe coattails before sitting down. He then pretends to slide his make-believe coat sleeves up his arms, rotates his neck for relaxation, locks his fingers together for a good stretch, relaxes his wrists for a moment and adjusts his seat. And then with good posture, he looks over at me with a most serious face...

"I shall now play for you a well-known waltz written in 1877 by the British composer, Euphemia Allan."
Jake lowers his head and gazes over the keyboard, places his fingers on the ivories, then allows the sound of the keys to come to life playing a familiar waltz...

After listening for a moment, I giggle and clap my hands. Jake's playing a bad recital of Chopsticks.

He takes my action as a clue to stop playing, then gets up and takes a bow.
"Would you like to hear me sing too?" He said.
"No thank you," I said gleefully.
"Dyslexia has its drawbacks," Jake said with a grin. "That and my lessons were more off than on."
"Oh, Jake... Your family would've been proud," I said. "Can you play anything else?"
"Oh yeah, I can play *Tati-Tati*."
"Tati-Tati? ... I'm not familiar with that piece of classical music unless you're talking about Tatti, the Talking Tom Cat for kids."
"No, no, no, it's the Russian version of *Chopsticks*," Jake said.
With me giggling, Jake heads my way.
"So, tell me, Jake, how many years have passed since your first piano lesson?"
"Hmmm... I believe I was nine."
"Hey, I asked you how many years. Remember now, I don't do math—I'm a girl."
"Well yeah, and we're all the better for it, too."
"I'm sure we are."
There is a quiet moment when I observe a few books on the coffee table.
"I've noticed you're reading the novels I've been telling you about."
"*Yeah*, thanks to the recent housekeeper I hired."
"What does a housekeeper have to do with your reading?"
"She helps me with the big words."
I can't help but snicker...
"You can't help yourself can you."
He shrugs.
Li'l Kitty then jumped up on my lap spewing out a couple of meows while taking a few swipes with her tongue around her mouth, not wanting to waste the good beer. Next, she licks her paw and then does the face-washing ritual. Satisfied, she kneads my legs with her little paws, curls up, then goes into a deep sleep.

"I wish I could go to sleep that fast."

Jake looks over at Li'l Kitty and me...

"Well, that's Li'l Miss Kitty for you—the damn cat can't hold her booze. It's disgraceful...

I shake my head with a smile acknowledging his hopelessness.

"Hey... I'm getting the hungries, so when you finish your beer, pick out a guest room and put your stuff away. I'll meet you outside, and we'll sit down for dinner in short order."

"Sounds good," I said, "I'll be out shortly."

With my overnight things put away, I walk out onto the patio through a large glass door from the bedroom hallway. Off to my right at a right angle to the hallway, you'll take in the gym and the adjacent office facing toward the house—both wrapped in green-tinted glass. Then, unexpectedly, I'm distracted when seeing a Great Blue Heron hover and then settle on the roof for a better look-see at the blue metal corrugated roof partially covered with solar cells. Then as the wind picked up with Great Blue's curiosity satisfied, the Heron flew off looking for that prize of the day, a nice fat toad or mouse in the hills of Malibu.

I turned my attention to the south end of the pool to catch Jake from the waist up standing next to his grill in a large pit that's close to the kitchen. Blue anodized corrugated aluminum covers the grill area supported by four large sandstone columns.

"Grab a beer and take a seat," Jake shouted across the pool. "I need to stay with the fish—they grill up fast."

"Thanks, but the beer can wait until dinner," I said.

I just wanted to wander around and enjoy the backyard, so I head toward the long narrow eating area next to the pool with the semblance of the Art Deco period. When stepping down the five steps, you enjoy a view of the pool through the thick glass plate wall topped off with dark blue tile that runs the full length of the pool. When sitting at a table, you can watch the swimmers glide through the water.

Facing toward the office on the far side of the pool raises a spillway a few feet above the deck and shoots multiple streams of water into the pool. Beyond that is a long narrow tropical garden of colorful flowers and ferns with crushed seashell walkways running along the pool. Palm trees line the southern perimeter, protected with an appealing low profile fence where the property drops off to the lower level for the garage and staff housing.

A few minutes later, Jake headed toward the table with a large plate trailing steam off the edge and then placed it in the center of the table.

"Senorita, we now possess the makings of a fine Mexican recipe of red snapper fillets steamed in olives, tomatoes, onions, garlic, and jalapenos."

After feasting on this wonderful spread, we clean up the table, put everything in the dishwasher, and then head toward his office to begin our planning for a new company...

ACT III - SCENE FIVE
ENHANCING THE LEARNING PROCESS

This scene is complex and a controversial discussion on the sharing of the wealth, but one of the most significant in the book, requiring a higher degree of questions.

Question: 1
Can you give examples of why employee incentive programs don't work? Try using something from your own experience, or be creative with the idea.

Question: 2
What makes it so difficult for companies to begin a sharing of the wealth program?
How would the program influence you and the country?

Question: 3
Did the author nail it on his thoughts for appraisal policies and reviews?
If so, why? If not, why?
What has been your personal experience with appraisal reviews that you'd like to share?

Question: 4
In your own words, how would you explain the sharing of the wealth business platform?
Does this make sense to you? If not, why? If so, why?

Question: 5
What are your thoughts on eliminating rigid job descriptions?

Question: 6
Would you choose the author's idea of using EVA in the policy platform or another form of measurement? Explain.

Question: 7
In *The Sharing of the Wealth Outline,* the new *competency pay grade policy* is a lengthy process. Therefore, can you summarize in your own words what the author is trying to share with the reader?

ACT III SCENE 6
Hospital Transformation

WEEK 20 – FRIDAY LATE AFTERNOON
JAKE AND TONI'S DISCUSSION ON HEALTH CARE ISSUES

AURORA, ILLINOIS

Thursday morning, we landed at the Aurora Municipal Airport. An overnight stay at the Hampton Inn was mainly due to the prevailing winds blowing across North America prolonging our flight back to Orange County, California.

Toni and I were saddled with different agendas. Toni intended to hook up with a friend he knew during his stint in Naval Intelligence. My stretch was devoted to a business meeting at the American Purchasing Society.

REFRESHED FOR THEIR FRIDAY MORNING FLIGHT

"So, tell me, Toni, did you and your buddy have a lot to talk about?"

"Yeah, it was good to see him again—he talks less than I do."

I burst out in a fit of laughter...

"Well, that must have made for an interesting evening."

Toni ignored me...

"Let's get this Gooney bird in the air," Toni said with eagerness... "I'm ready to grab a little sky."

"Okay, little brother, let's turn over number two, the radio is off and firing switch on."

"Boost pump on," Toni said.

"Give me eight blades, Toni."

"One, two, three, four, five, six, seven, eight," Toni counted out.

"Switch on," I said.

One by one, the huge pistons chug and cough when a sudden huge belch of smoke and thunder come roaring out of the exhaust. With the props turning under the radial engine's power, the sound was that of a fuel dragster at the starting line.

"Check the oil pressure," I said.

"Roger that."

"Remember, it's slow coming up."

"Okay, let's turn over number one."

"The firing switch is ready," Toni said.

I looked out the window to count out eight blades for Toni. He turns the switch on, and the number one engine roars to life.

I glanced at Toni and see a minuscule of excitement...

"Listen and smell, little brother, the wonderment of those bad-boy radial engines."

Even though the DC-3 is a taildragger, there is excellent over-the-nose visibility from the cockpit as we taxi out to the runway. Our aircraft is driven by three-blade variable-pitch propellers transmitting their power by converting rotational motion into thrust from the two twelve-hundred horsepower Pratt and Whitney radial engines. She seemed to moan and groan along the way with its creaking and squeaking as though it were an industrialized, fire-breathing primeval monster.

"Here we go mate, off into the wild blue yonder as Captain Midnight used to say, or was it, Sky King?"

Hmm... No response, so I spoke up a little louder...

"I once treasured a Jack Armstrong glow-in-the-dark plastic ring from my Wheaties box."

Toni was in another place and continued to ignore me—nothing new.

After swinging the nose of the plane around, I pointed her down the runway. With the breaks locked, we go to full power transmitting the noise and vibration into the cockpit. When releasing the brakes, we move forward lumbering down the runway with forty-eight inches of manifold pressure, and then at twenty-seven hundred RPM, the aircraft leaves the runway. With our cowl flaps set in the trail position, we climb at seven hundred feet per minute.

After reaching our cruising altitude of ten thousand feet, and flying as gracefully as an eagle, I reduce the manifold pressure down to twenty-five inches and set the RPM to seventeen hundred fifty. Fifteen minutes out, we're on our flight plan back to Orange County.

With the nice weather and a low-pressure zone outside my window created by the shape of the windshield, I slide it open and rest my arm on the window sill, just like driving my restored 37' Chevy pickup truck. The noise level is not a problem, because the engines assault the ears whether open or closed.

"You know Toni, the thing I love about these babies is that they are rugged, reliable aircraft and fun to fly—especially, when the aircraft is in mint condition. Charlie told me they flew this aircraft in the D-day invasion."

"Ah... So, our aircraft became a C-47 at birth.

"Yep... She's one of the twenty-one C-47's converted to a DC-3 by Douglas and assigned a new serial number."

"Yeah, just sitting here, you can absorb the history," Toni said... And as you know, this Gooney Bird was designed to carry only twenty-one passengers. And yet, I read that Continental Air Services, an airlift operation in South-East Asia during the Vietnam War, holds the record for the number of people it evacuated in a flight out of Ku Lat, Vietnam. Get this ... that pilot took off with hundred-six people on board that included ninety-eight children, five flight attendants, and three crew members."

"That's an incredible story, Toni... Past and present waring nations bring with it evil and fantastic unending stories of civilian and military heroics by those with a love for mankind. And that flight crew certainly falls in the category of heroics during war-torn Vietnam...

Toni makes a slight nod agreeing with Jake... And there is silence for some time...

"Whoa..." I said. "We just dropped ten feet in the blink of an eye."

"We're getting a lot of wind-swirl in front of us," Toni said.

They both knew they were in for a wild ride as the thermals pushed them upwards and then down bobbing up and down in increments of one hundred feet or more. This, of course, required aggressive manipulation of all the primary flight controls.

A little later, the turbulence diminished...

"Have you noticed when making a thirty-degree bank turn at the yoke, how the plane responds? First, you wait for a reaction. Then you wait for the indicator calculations of the turn hoping it's thirty degrees, not unlike making a turn at the helm on a World War II Navy destroyer."

"What? I knew you were ancient, but World War II destroyers?"

"Stow it mate. Those babies were still going strong in the early sixties, and you know it."

"True."

Seven and half hours later, we approach the John Wayne airfield with our wings slicing through the moist, cool air as I align the nose of the aircraft with the runway...

"Here we go, Toni, actuate the landing gear."

"Roger that."

The electric motors wine as the landing wheels dropped from the fuselage followed by the thump of the landing gear as they lock in place. With the wheels down, we sense the aeronautical drag on the aircraft.

As our airspeed dropped, I show Toni one finger indicating a desire for one-quarter landing flap extension.

"Roger that, one-quarter."

A moment later, I show two fingers.

"Roger, half flaps."

Hearing this, I give Toni a three-finger sign.

"Roger, three-quarter flaps."

When hearing his response, I make a slight reduction to the throttles.

"Ninety knots... Eighty-five... Eighty..." Toni sounded out.

As our bird dropped gracefully out of the sky, we glide above the concrete surface at sixty-four knots. With the aircraft centered above the runway, there is a slight chirp-chirp, and a wisp of blue smoke appears as the tires kiss the hot fifteen-inch concrete runway.

It's three forty-six, Friday afternoon as we taxi up to a small commercial hanger at the southern end of the airport dedicated to private and charter aircraft and small cargo planes. A single-handed ground crewman met us on the apron and guided us into a position where he chocked the wheels of our DC-3. After waving to the ground crewman, we deplane and head toward the office.

After checking the plane in, we head toward the parking lot near the hangar where my restored 37' Chevy pickup truck is waiting for us. When rounding the corner of the hanger, I can see the ol' girl. The sun is reflecting off the hand-rubbed lacquer of the car's dark green body and black fenders.

The late afternoon is warm with a light ocean breeze coming in off the ocean as I haul my ass into the front seat, lean over and unlock the passenger door for Toni. We crank down the windows to let the heat out and the ocean breeze in. I slid the ignition key in, twisted it a few degrees, pressed the starter button, and fired up my small block fuel injected 57' Corvette engine. You can ingest the power of the engine coming up through the floorboards as I touch the gas pedal while letting out the heavy-duty clutch. A moment later, we are pulling out of the parking area headed toward the San Diego Freeway—northbound to Santa Monica.

The traffic is heavy, but we're able to purr along down the little-used carpool lane making good time. The other lanes are poking along like Conestoga wagon trains moving down the Oregon Trail. This is a throughput constraint at its ugliest. Unlike the Conestoga wagons, these four-wheeled fuel-burning monsters issue a low carbon haze of obnoxious fumes.

DISCUSSING BUSINESS DURING THE RIDE HOME

The traffic is moving until we crested a hill. Appearing before us as far as the eye can see is a ribbon of flashing red tail lights and the occasional honking horn by impatient drivers informing us of their importance in society. Evidently, there's an accident. I glance at the gas gauge. We're okay, but it wasn't long when our carpool lane begins to move. Five minutes later, we're back up to cruising speed.

Thinking about healthcare issues, I bounce my ideas around with Toni.

"Little brother, I have a few ideas Dakota has brought to my attention I'd like to discuss with you. It is a new healthcare business plan Dakota and I are working on, but first, let's roll up the windows so we can hear each other a little better."

After closing my window, I reach under the dash and adjust the 1936 *air-conditioning* system in the cowling by popping the air vent open.

"When do we eat? I feel as weak as that elderly feline of yours that hobbles around the house on crutches."

"Elderly? Crutches? I said. "I'll be sure to let her know about your feelings toward her. By the way, your eating habits are also about the same. I'm surprised you haven't meowed me to death by now. It's no wonder you and Jackie get along so well...

Let me take a stab at a place to eat... Um... How about sushi?

When looking over expecting a response, I see a slight facial change...

"Well, seeing such a colossal smile, I have just the place, a nice little Sushi restaurant about a five-minute drive from here. It would also be a more appropriate place to discuss the new business plan."

After taking the next exit, we drove down Harbor Boulevard toward Costa Mesa, and before long, we pull into the parking lot next to *I love Sushi*—catchy little name.

"Jackie would say sushi sounds, yummy," Toni said.

"Yeah, yummy is the operative word here. I'm considering taking a bag of sushi home for my *elderly* cat."

"You realize, of course, your friends have bets on who will outlast whom," Toni said.

"How's that?" I said.

"Most have bets on your cat, with you taking a dirt nap in the bone orchard."

"Smart move," I said. "Ah... Something you should know, if I go first, my will has you as the beneficiary of Little Miss Kitty.

"Wonderful," Toni said mockingly. "If Little Kitty goes first, who gets you?"

"Hilarious... Li'l Kitty is a great little buddy; we talk to each other all the time."

"You talk to one another?" Toni said with an eye roll.

"WHAT? You, an Indian and a onetime cowboy don't talk to animals?" I said. "I was sure you whispered to horses."

"Dude, I can hardly talk to humans much less an animal...

Are you going to sit in this heap the rest of the day or are we going in for chow?"

"HEAP?" I said. Toni shuts his door on me.

With Toni's urgency for food, we're soon sitting at a table across from the sushi bar. We place our orders and people-watch for a while.

HEALTHCARE ISSUES

"**W**ell, so far, we've discussed everything *but* health care," Toni said. "Get a wiggle on."

"Excellent point," I said. "Well, one of the major overhead costs that most companies face is health care, and Dakota has given this a lot of theorization. One of our core beliefs is controlling the throughput cost of business. It allows us to apply these throughput variables for costing a service or product. As you well know, these discussions are nothing new to you—"

For the moment, were interrupted as our meals are placed on the table. It would seem we've ordered almost everything on the menu with the idea of sharing. I jumped in taking a bite of sushi; take in the pleasure, then follow up with a sip of my Japanese Suntory beer. After eying Toni slam a slug of his beer down, I continue...

"You can't accuse Dakota of not thinking big. She hit me up with the idea to build a new kind of hospital."

I needed to keep a fast pace when eating with Toni, so I grabbed a California crab and avocado with my Hashi—*chopsticks*.

"WHAT?" ...You're going to build a new type of hospital, run your consulting group, and try to build an automotive company at the same time?" Toni said.

"You don't miss a thing, little brother."

Toni gives me a gimlet-eyed glance...

"Interrogation is my game."

"Yeah, I hear that, well, anyhow, Dakota and I have thought this through, and have a plan. Within our consulting crew—both Jackie and Johnny have shown that their leadership skills are far above the others. With that in mind, we're going to invite them in as junior partners in the firm..."

Jackie would take on two responsibilities. She'd head up the consulting firm and consult for Dakota on the healthcare project owing to her shrewdness in business systems and finance. Johnny has shown his skill in his field of knowledge and the ability to motivate people. But still a little wet behind the ears, he'll need Jackie's knowledge to help run the consulting group."

"Do they have a clue about this plan of yours?"

"No. Not yet, but you've been through the drill."

Toni responds with a snicker...

"You bet. Loose-lips-sink-ships... So tell me, what do you mean, by a *new* kind of hospital."

"Well, to begin with, we'd build a thirty-bed community medical center, funded separately, providing help to the local community and our facility...

The new medical organization and its operations are what I'd like to discuss.

Since I'm doing most of the talking, I need to stuff my belly full with a little of everything on the table. If you'd ever eaten with Toni or Jackie, you'd realize what I mean. Finished with this round, I wash it down with a couple of slugs of Suntory.

"I'm impressed with the way you came in for the kill," Toni said.

"Hey... I've heard you take no prisoners, so I decided I better scoop up what I can before you've leveled the table of anything eatable."

"It's hard to break good training."

"Hey... How about you finish what's left of the killing field, but first, if you will, please grab my briefcase and open it up."

Toni, yawns, stretches his huge arms, then reaches down for the briefcase.

HOSPITALS' INEFFICIENCIES

"Inside, you will find my working papers on our subject in a blue folder. Pull it out and turn to the divider that has quotes..."

A moment later, Toni shows me the papers.

"Yeah," I said. "If you would, read the one by Henry Aaron."

"You mean Hank Aaron, the famous baseball player?"

"Huh? No. This guy is an economist with the Brookings Institute."

"Sorry, I never heard of the guy. Ah... Here it is... Henry Aaron... He had this to say...

Like many other observers, I look at the U.S. health care system and see an administrative monstrosity, a truly bizarre mélange of thousands of players with payment systems that differ for no socially beneficial reason. As well as a staggeringly complex public system with mind-boggling administered prices and other rules expressing distinctions that can only be regarded as weird...

Now here is a man who pulls no punches."

"No kidding," I said. "For anyone who's been misfortunate to have been hospitalized in one's life, you have to love that quote.

However, I would add that hospital efficiency regarding systemic process controls is a design problem. They don't contemplate in those terms as Henry Aaron so vividly pointed out. Doctors have one thing on their mind—the patient—which, of course, is a good thing...

However, that does not mean you can't design hospitals as a well processed minimal step organization."

Finished with that thought, I drank what's left of my beer. Seeing our waitress heading our way, I decided to order us green tea.

"Explain something, Jake."

"What's that?"

"Are electronic medical records replacing the paper shuffling process, or is there more to it than that?"

"Hmm... Naval Intelligence taught you well," I said.

No response.

"Well, the answer to your question is yes, but much more. Today, many hospitals have a good comprehensive system allowing physicians to make their rounds toting wireless devices to check lab results, view X-rays, update electronic charts, and order prescriptions. Nurses might have wireless devices on wheels to record progress notes and check doctors' orders. If they administer medicine, they can track and update the patient's EMR record. It's clean and simple."

"If that's the case, what is different from your hospital and our current hospital systems?"

"Good question Toni."

ELECTRONIC MEDICAL RECORD COST

"Let me begin with the cost of electronic medical records...

Hospitals are and have been paying between twenty and hundred million dollars depending on hospital size and complexity of the system."

"That's a hell of a bill."

"It is."

"What are those computer systems you've used in your company turnarounds, and what did they cost you?"

"You've hit the nail on the head...

With that thought, let's switch gears for the moment and talk about Enterprise Resource Planning systems for manufacturing...

ERP systems perform the operational processing tasks for the entire manufacturing and financial system. This sophisticated software consolidates and communicates with all the different functions of the system. The software is expandable by the flexible use of plug-in modules.

The implementation cost includes conforming to the business processes, actual restructuring, and training. Other costs include changing and transferring data and systems from the old form to the new form.

These software systems are as complex as any hospital might have. Ah, maybe more so, and the price range is about two thousand dollars per user...

Uh... So, for six hundred users in a manufacturing environment, we're talking about one point two million dollars purchase price...

Annual support cost at twenty-two percent of the purchase price would be about two hundred sixty-four thousand...

And then we have the implementation cost running between six hundred thousand to four million dollars. So, let's call it two million dollars...

Now, we're talking about an outlay of three-point two million, not including the annual support cost. That's but a fraction of a hospital installation—"

"Tell me, Jake, why so much money for hospital IT systems," Toni said.

"The problem lies with each hospital thinking they are unique and want the software to conform to their way of conducting business.

The Electronic Medical Record software provider without plug-in modules for various applications, for essence, have to stitch together a framework of software to match the hospital's request—therefore, the extraordinarily high cost of their software system...

E. F. Schumacher would have told them...

Any intelligent fool can make things bigger and more complex. It takes a touch of genius and a lot of courage to move in the opposite direction...

With that thought, we begin the process of whittling down a hospital's fixed cost that drives up the never-ending rise in the hospital's operating cost..."

"You've done a bit of serious consideration on this, haven't you?"

"Dakota is the brains. I've just added my two cents in here and there."

I pause for a moment waiting for a smart remark from Toni.

"Gee, no response, after I gave you such an opening?"

"Why waste words on something, I know you already know what I was thinking," Toni said.

"Ah, good point..."

CHANGING PATIENT BILLING

"The next step is changing the patient billing statement...

The idea is to eliminate their current billing statement resembling the financial statement from a multi-national corporation to one sheet. The statement would show the medical procedure's hours in the system, hourly rate, plus a list of medications at cost, and the total. That's it.

It's my understanding there is a universal standard for the process time of the various procedures for a patient's hospital stay starting from entry to discharge. The standard is like a barometer of sorts so that hospitals don't take advantage of increasing revenue by having the patient stay any longer than necessary..."

I waved to our waitress to get her attention.

"Toni, do you care for a cup of green tea?"

Toni moves his head in what appears to be a resemblance of a nod.

I gazed up at the waitress...

"Two cups of green tea, please."

She bows and then scoots off.

PATIENT HOSPITALIZATION COST

"Now, to change the billing process, we would begin our next step by calculating the annual total operating cost plus a margin.

For the various time spent in a hospital, one is likely to have a procedural medical care in services such as outpatient, oncology, birthing center, intensive care, and so on, but you get my drift...

These MEDICAL CARE SERVICES have one thing in common—support services that include PHARMACEUTICAL, RADIOLOGY, PATHOLOGY, AND MICROBIOLOGY. They fall into the category of operating cost, not unlike engineering in a manufacturing environment.

As far as software capability, one could say each type of MEDICAL CARE SERVICE is COMPARABLE to VARIOUS MANUFACTURING PRODUCTS...

To compute a specific procedural event's gross margin, you'd average the hourly *billable* patient rate figure for a patient's unique procedure. *Let's call the billing two thousand dollars*...

Divided by the total annual average DIRECT AND INDIRECT cost. Hmm... We'll call it *fourteen hundred dollars*.

DIRECT being doctor's, and INDIRECT cost would include medical staff, their benefits, and any fixed costs associated with any unique procedure. This procedure or event would represent a mirror image of products and their manufacturing overhead.

Here, let me write it out on the napkin... There we go, the margin is forty-two point nine percent.

$$42.9\% = (\$2000 / \$1400) - 1$$

Profit before tax computation is the hourly rate for general and administrative, operating expenses if you will, of *three hundred dollars* for the hour-long procedure, plus the procedural *fourteen hundred dollar rate*... I've made this example an outpatient procedure to simplify the breakdown without adding in additional expenses for recovery time...

$$17.7\% = (\$2000 / (1400+300)) - 1$$

This is not unlike throughput overhead contribution for products in a manufacturing environment.

This hourly hospital rate is two thousand dollars an hour based on their need for a forty-three percent gross margin.

Now, the next step is to compare the hospital's standard against the universal standard. In our case for this procedure, the standard is one point one hours. This would result in a *twenty-two hundred dollar hourly rate*.

In this case a big plus in profit. However, if the hospital wants to attract a greater share of the market, they would consider lowering the rate to two thousand dollars, and whatever the total, the patient would pay for medication at hospital's cost.

This new standard of a medical procedure throughput, if you will, during the month measures the actual time incurred to the standard billing hours. When large favorable or unfavorable variances occur, a flag would appear to reevaluate the processes and the standard billing hours..."

Now, having served our steaming hot green tea, we take a moment of enjoyment.

"This is slick, Jake, You've got my interest."

"Thanks, Toni."

I take a sip of tea and set the cup down.

"Well, let's move on with patient billing...

Most hospitals have a partial facsimile of patient billing I just described, except the billing *only* covers the cost of the stay, not unlike a hotel...

As far as the rest of the billing for encounters with clinicians and capital assets, many hospitals use a cost accounting coding system. This system is about coders interpreting the encounters leaving open the possibility for errors in two simultaneous procedures getting double-billed, or choosing a code that maximizes reimbursement, and can be error-prone due to an improper entry.

And let's not forget, these cost in the new system are already carried in the throughput cost, making the coding process a double entry."

I took another sip of tea and continued...

The coding process is time-consuming, not unlike activity-based costing. By eliminating the coding process, you remove the additional burden of the operating cost of our hospitals and society.

The result is a one-page billing statement for the patient and easy payment processing by insurance companies..."

REDUCING THE COST OF HOSPITAL MEDICATION

"Reducing the high cost of medication is the next step...

I'll not go into the complex variable of pricing from one hospital to another due to its nature of being a disgraceful practice.

But I am going to highlight another problem...

Many hospital contracts with pharmaceuticals habitually provide a discount in return for an agreement not to disclose the acquisition cost of the drug. Then to add insult to injury, the hospitals tack on a price increase costing patients outrageous prices, even for generic medication.

The overall result is Americans pay the highest pharmaceutical cost of any advanced nation..."

"Sounds like hospitals are like women, you can't live with 'em, and you can't live without 'em," Toni said.

We chuckle, but I'm sure Dakota and Jackie would have something to say about that...

"Since the procurement of medication is part of the operational overhead and the medication goes into inventory as an asset at their discount rate, this is what the patient should be charged on their billing. Any markup would be redundant and uncalled for... Again, this is the same practice that goes into our new manufacturing system organization."

I looked down at my cold tea and finished it.

"Miscellaneous material like tape, gauze, and etcetera under the new process would issue boxes, containers, or bulk substances from the main inventory to the appropriate unique MEDICAL CARE SERVICE and expensed—after that, there is no need to monitor these type of cost for treating a patient. Currently, they spend more money tracking these items for each patient than the cost of material. Cost accounting at its finest—thinking they are doing the right thing."

HOSPITAL TRANSFORMATION SUMMARY

"To sum this up, I'd say if we're a leader in hospital transformation using these new ideas, there'd be others soon following this kind of drastic reduction in the overhead burden, reducing hospital care costs.

Insurance companies will also benefit from the one-page billing making for faster throughput and payments. Patients for the first time can scan a statement and have a clear understanding of what they are paying for and value received.

Another important ingredient of knowledge for the patient is that a procedure cost encounter, more or less, is the same from one hospital to another, but the overhead value will be the main difference between hospitals.

WHEN BUYING A BIG-TICKET ITEM LIKE A CAR OR HOUSE, YOU DON'T GET A BREAKDOWN OF THE LABOR AND MATERIAL ITEMS INVOLVED IN PRODUCING THE PURCHASE. YOU GET A PRICE AND THEN SHOP AROUND FOR THE BEST VALUE, SO, WHY SHOULD A HUGE MEDICAL BILL BE ANY DIFFERENT?"

Toni mumbled something...

"Another tool is now available for those needing medical care, a website that ranks hospital's quality of care using the *Centers for Medicare and Medicaid Services—CMS, website Hospital Compare...*

When using the CMS website and a price quote similar to the new billing for a procedure from a selected hospital spells out *value* allowing one an informed decision on their hospital of choice.

Until this point, hospitals needn't worry about rising costs, because there is no competition for *value* to keep prices in check.

All it will take is for a few hospitals to make these kinds of changes I've been discussing and have them take market share from the dinosaurs. With these market forces at work, the other hospitals will begin the need to improve process performance to bring down their overhead costs and make them more competitive."

"Damn, Jake, I'm at sea with that kind of thinking.

"Yeah, right, but thanks for listening."

I paid the bill and left a tip for both the chef and waitress. After that, it was quiet during our drive home.

NEARING HOME

"Little brother, that sense of humor you've kept buried down inside you for so many years has been surfacing a lot lately. And, it would seem, you have lost your ability to relate to your normal economy of words. What gives?"

"Economy?" Toni said with a slight twitch of his mouth.

"Ahh... You're smitten with Jackie aren't you?"

"SMITTEN?"

"That's it, isn't."

"Maybe."

"Well, answer me this...

Knowing you, I bet you've given Jackie an Indian name... So tell me."

"Little Running River," Toni mumbled.

"What was that? I said with a quizzical look.

When pulling up in front of Toni's place, there is silence in the air.

"Lucky for you I ran out of time for a captive conversation," I said, glancing over at Toni. "I did, however, enjoy our flight and time together, little brother. I'm glad you came along."

Toni looks at me with a tilt of his head and a minuscule lopsided smile, then we both knuckle up for a shake...

"Smack."

After waiting for Toni to grab his gear from the truck bed, I lock eyes with him when he takes a look-see through the window, then with a slight nod, he vanishes.

Eager to get home, I shift into low gear and head on down the road. Thirty minutes later, I'm cruising up into the Malibu hills on Serra Road where single-lane private drives shoot off the main thruway. While motoring past homes of assorted architecture crammed into the darkening crevices of the hillside, I take a moment to gaze at the beautiful sight of the Pacific Ocean. A moment later, I see a couple of coyotes loping along passing through several shades of shadows foraging for food. They kept a good eye on me during my entry into one of many hairpins going up the hillside.

Later, I break for a fat little groundhog that's on the coyote menu running across the road. The critter was so fat you could slip a feeler gauge between the underbelly and the ground and get a reading.

The groundhog's vast tummy bounced on the uneven roadside keeping the little paws paddling air trying to get a foothold while the critter's little tail wagged in excitement trying to move it along.

You just have to love the little critters.

A few minutes later, I gun my little Chevy effortlessly up the driveway. The grade is so steep that on a clear night my headlamps send their light beam up to do a losing duel with the bright stars illuminating their light over the vast Pacific. The driveway levels off as I approach and activate the gate. When entering the compound, I exhale a shallow breath and then watch the gate close behind me.

While scooting down my driveway toward the garage, I took a moment to stop for a last look at the sunset. The sun was about to plunge into the vast Pacific in a blaze of glory coloring the undersides of the gauzy clouds with tinted orange and red. The surrounding sky is turning into a navy blue watercolor wash that bleeds into a final *darkness*—always the vanquisher at the end of the day.

ACT III - SCENE 6
ENHANCING THE LEARNING PROCESS

Question: 1

You've read the author's reasoning for the current high cost of electronic medical records, so, what are your thoughts on why the medical industry pays such an astronomical premium for software equivalent to an ERP system complexity?

Question: 2

The author's idea of arriving at a billing statement for hospitals is a huge step in cutting our hospital bills.

What force is able to stand in the way of stopping this idea dead in its tracks?

And what ideas might you have to bring it to reality?

Question: 3

Inflated medication is a significant component of hospital cost. What would you consider doing to make the appropriate changes in bringing down the cost? Think big and be creative.

ACT III - SCENE 7
Epilogue: A Reason to Celebrate

WEEK 20 – THURSDAY EVENING – NINA'S CELEBRATION DINNER PARTY AT HOME WITH JACKIE, JOHNNY, DAKOTA, AND MARTY

ON THE WAY TO NINA'S HOME

I pulled out of my driveway onto the Pacific Coast Highway at six o'clock in the evening and headed south toward Johnny's condo. This time of day during the workweek, the warm beaches look friendless waiting for nightfall to withdraw the warmth of the sand and to disperse it into the moist and salty, cool night air blowing across the surface.

We're due at the Nguyen's place for dinner between seven and seven-thirty. Not wanting to be late, I arrive in front of Johnny's condominium to see him leaning against a tall palm tree. He has a shit-eating grin on his face looking as though he scored a major league goal as he climbs into the car.

"What's with you?" I said. "You look as though you enjoyed a night out with that celebrity who works out at out our gym and had fancied your way with her, Ah... You know, what's her name?"

"Thanks for that nice thought, but no challenge there, given I'm on so many other glamorous celebrity ladies to-do list."

I glance at Johnny with raised eyebrows...

"To-do list?"

"Oh yeah, do you want to listen to a few more celebrity to-do lists I'm on?"

"Good heavens, no..."

"Okay then, let me explain what I was smiling about. When watching extreme sports, my mind can wander. So, I conjure up extreme sports for mice before you arrived."

I gave him a quick glance.

"Mice?"

"Why not mice?" Johnny said defensively. "I envisioned a mouse standing in front of a mousetrap that held a chocolate-filled truffle. My mouse is wearing a yellow football helmet and sporting a blue jersey with red S and M letters stenciled on it and salivating at the mouth. He has determination written over his devilish little face as he springs into action."

"You're a sick man, Johnny. But I must ask, what do the S and M stand for, Super Mouse?"

He looked at me as though I'd asked him the stupidest thing he ever heard.

"No... Of course not. It's for *Sadist* and *Masochist*."

This binges out a giggle.

"You're a double-sick man."

As I pull away from the curb, Johnny turns around in the seat and picks up the flowers in the back seat. After reading the message attached to the flowers, he glances my way...

"You put my name on the card?"

"Of course, I did... Where's your gift?"

"Ahh... I didn't bring one."

"Didn't your mother tell you good manners don't stop at the doorway? Bringing an appropriate gift is de rigueur... And knowing you, I took the liberty to put your name on the card."

"Oh... Sorry, I mean thank you, growing up is a bitch."

"Why is growing up so hard for you, Johnny?"

"Well, there is no quick answer, but I'd be happy to tell you my story if you're interested..."

I took a moment before answering while crossing over to the fast lane from the freeway on-ramp...

"Please—we have a long drive ahead of us," I said.

"Okay... Well, it all began with what my father told me as a child, and I've never forgotten when he said most kids don't know when their childhood ends. So enjoy it while you can, because as you get older, it just fades, little by little, until one day— you realize your youth has been gone for years...

But what has continued to drive me in my sometimes childish ways is due to the important things learned from a delightful lady I befriended in college. Her name was Lois..."

Johnny paused for the longest time staring out the window.

"What about Lois?"

"Yeah, I'm still with you. I was gathering my thoughts...

Well, I met this eighty-five-year-old woman named Lois during our senior year in an organizational behavior class, and we became friends. We would often meet for a bite to eat and a cold drink or coffee at D' Amores pizza down the hill from the campus.

Lois would mesmerize me as I listened to her wisdom. It was like hearing things found and read from a time capsule. It wasn't long before I invited a few of my friends along to listen to her. She'd always dressed in a flattering young way and soon became our most beloved student on campus due to her vast knowledge of world travel and her cordial way with people.

On graduation day, the faculty had invited her to speak to the students and guests, being she was an honor student and voted the most congenial and respected of our student body—and I must say this was an unforgettable event...

After being introduced to the audience by the chief academic officer, she steps up to the lectern to deliver her message. Lois begins by fumbling with her prepared speech, and then all of a sudden, she purposely dropped the few sheets of paper at her feet...

Lois appeared a little frustrated and perhaps embarrassed being put into this unexpected position as she spoke into the microphone...

Sorry about that—I'm a little stressed out.

After taking a short pause, her gaze swept the audience and then continues with what's on her mind...

I guess my real problem lies in what my doctor recently told me. He said I needed to stop smoking, so I switched to chewing rum-soaked cigars and drinkin' whiskey."

Laughter rolls through the audience like a tidal wave while she clears her throat.

Lois possessed a natural stage presence and delivery. And then as the audience settles down, she tells us about the notes she dropped...

I should mention that my prepared speech, now lying at my feet, stays where it belongs—they were simply words, and perhaps, have little meaning on what was on my mind today.

With you gazing up at me behind this lectern, she said, *you can see that I have a lot to say about growing old.*

Again, she generated a rousing boffola throughout the audience then continues...

We only grow old when we stop thinking we are no longer having fun. We may not be mortal, but we also don't need to accept growing old means setting back in a rocker thinking we reached the inevitable point in our life.

We need to see the funny side of life and continue to acquire knowledge that can send waves of euphoria throughout our soul renewing our positive aspects of life and love...

Anything less than that, you will grow old and die not having lived a full life.

Unfortunately, this is true for most of us, and doing so, and not yet realizing it, you have already died...

The audience is quiet, hanging onto every word she has to say.

There is a vast difference between those who grow old and those who grow up. Each year, every living organism becomes a year older. Someone once said to grow old is the only thing that takes no special gift or skill.

This, of course, brings a loud roar of laughter from the addressees.

After waiting for the audience to quiet down, she said...

As you mature one should step forward when opportunities occur for change, grasp hold and have no regrets.

When we elders look back on our lives, we don't linger on those things we wished we hadn't done. The fear we carry with us about death the most, are those things we wished we would have done, but didn't. It's the regrets that we carry with us to our grave...

The audience is now stone-cold quiet...

Lois looks around at the audience while waiting and weighing the correct moment, and then with a clear voice...

I would like to end my little message today with a few of my favorite lyrics from a song made popular by Bette Midler, THE ROSE...

Bette Midler has always been a true inspiration in my adult life, and I'll try to sing a few lines, but please remember, I may not sound exactly like her. But fortunately, Bette Midler is famous for her belter voice which I'll try to mimic... I believe the lyrics of the song go something like this...

When she finished, I must say, she did an excellent representation of Bette Midler. And, evidently, the rest of the audience reflected much the same. There wasn't a dry eye in the audience. We give her a long-standing ovation. She humbly waits us out and then challenges each of us to study the lyrics and embrace them in our day-to-day lives.

Several weeks later, having received her MBA degree with honors, Lois passed away. At her funeral were thousands of students and their families along with the entire faculty who came to pay their respect and tribute to this wonderful woman. A woman who taught us by example, as one put on Earth to live, not to exist, and to be all that you can be.

Johnny paused looking my way...

"I must say, Jackie, when considering what a whizzo speaker she was, Lois could've been a real force to reckon with in this world if she'd taken her advice earlier in life...

Therefore, I must say that's why growing up is a bitch... That's it, babe."

Tears were streaming down my cheeks like an impressionable young teenager.

"Oh, my, oh my, what a beautiful story, Johnny."

"Sorry, girlfriend, I didn't mean to do the Oprah soap-star thingy on you."

Johnny has this way of making light of things and gets me to laugh at myself with my tears and a runny nose, so I let out a strange laugh mixed in with sobbing.

Johnny reaches into his jacket for a nice, folded white handkerchief and hands it to me—always the perfect gentlemen.

"Please, whatever you do, don't hand the soggy thing back when you're done."

With that, I give him a short jab to his arm.

"What?" he said.

As we ride along in silence, I compose myself, and then break the quietness...

"Johnny, you've grown up on the beach like I did as a kid, and yet, as far as I know, you've never tried surfing. Why is that?"

"There are lots of bad sea creatures that roam near the surf."

"Like what for example?"

"Well, for starters: there are the kelp beds that can grab you and pull you down into the depths of the sea. Then there is the spooky jellyfish with their toxic stings that can be fatal. Oh, and we can't forget the great white shark's need for our protein. But, if they don't get you, the monster wave will swallow you whole, slam you down into the seabed, and hold you there until you drown.

For me, babe, I'm the ankle-deep surfing dude on a skimboard."

"Johnny, you've no adventure in you."

Johnny responds with his Stan Laurel impersonation smile while scratching his head...

"Oh? You mean like your love for adventure in the wilderness."

"That's different."

"With you woman, it's *always* different."

"Hey. At least I tried it."

"Yeah, and if you had any idea what you were getting into, you would've behaved like Tweety bird let out of its cage and chased by Toni the cat. Oh... And screaming, I wegwet dat I have but one life to give to my countwy."

"That's not true," I giggled.

It's a bad time to be driving anywhere in Southern California as we continue to fight traffic on our way to Newport Beach. An hour later, after testing my patience with California drivers and a break in traffic, I go into NASCAR mode and pull up close to a truck in front of me to draft behind.

Now, with the advantage of pressure reduction, I down-shift, mash the gas, and rocket past the truck, delivering eight hundred fifty horsepower to the rear wheels, accelerating us like an F/A-18 Hornet jet fighter catapulting off an aircraft carrier.

And then, much like Butch Cassidy and the Sundance Kid jumping off the cliff, Johnny sings out... "Sheeeeeeeit."

A moment later...

"Are we there yet?"

ARRIVING AT NINA'S

After using a little g-force to scare the hell out of Johnny, I swing the wheel toward the off-ramp taking us to Nina's place. When turning onto Brighton Road I see Marty car and Dakota's car parked in the Nguyen's driveway, so after pulling in next to Marty's car—my herd of Mustangs takes a rest.

"Before getting out of the car, I need to change my shorts," Johnny said.
I giggle.

He starts to open his door, and then turns toward me with a hard look...

"You know, I will be working hard to get even with you crazy lady."

I'm thinking, crazy lady. Hmm... When did I get wind of that remark before?

As he walks around the car, I lean toward him and kiss him on the cheek.

"Are you all better now," I said.

"It appears to help, now that you mention it. A few more of those couldn't hurt."

"S & M," I muttered, walking away from the car with a giggle.

As we lightfoot it up the walkway with a rhythm, Johnny speaks up...

"Girl, you're radiating super glam in that outfit? It looks Eurasian. What do you call this hot getup?"

"Thanks. You're such a dear boy."

I stopped for a moment to model my outfit.

"Hey, I didn't ask you for a fashion gig—I just wanted to get an idea what the heck you call it."

"Don't get excited now. Nina introduced me to this wonderful apparel. It's a Vietnamese design, called, Ao Dai, or tunic dress, with a touch of Ralph Lauren thrown in, but it's not a Ralph Lauren."

"Somewhere along the way, I must've missed a link in that chain of logic. Women... You're always talking in circles."

"You didn't let me finish. I was about to say, Ralph Lauren no longer sells the garment, requiring my outfit to be made special for this occasion."

Johnny shakes his head with a blank stare on his face...

"Well, superstud, I must say, you've also dressed to the nines tonight."

This perks him up.

"Thanks, Jackie," Johnny said. "My tailor made this suit special for tonight's occasion, and my understated silk tie is one that Gucci would have sold his soul to Lucifer for."

It didn't end there, he did a quick pose with a tilted head, and a hand on his hip then emulates a model walking down the runway.

As he strolls past me on his make-believe runway, I snap out a punch and hit him with a solid right to the arm.

With a startled look on his face, he grabs his arm...

"Ouch... You forget you don't hit like any normal lady."

And then with a titter, he punctuates his open smile with two little dimples formed on each side of his pearly white teeth.

When seeing his response, I lift my arm again as though ready to strike, and then giggle the rest of the way up to the front door.

Before Johnny reaches to ring the doorbell, he looks at me...

"Now, I need a kiss on this cheek."

Without hesitation, I narrow my eyes at him.

"Babe, you need to make my arm better."

Not waiting for Johnny to announce us, I quickly switch my attention to ring the doorbell. Pushing the button, we hear the high-tone chime sound in the house. The bell saves me, so to speak when Li Pham, Nina's housekeeper answers the door and invites us in with a bow. We both acknowledge her with a polite nod and then hand her the flowers. She graciously takes them as we capture the elegant and tasteful surroundings of the entry hall with the beautiful hand-woven rug and eclectic Asian furnishing.

"What a beautiful Persian rug," I said.

"Well, not being worldly like myself, the rug is now referred to as an *Iranian* rug."

"Please," I said.

"What about an Oriental rug?" Johnny said.

"Can we discuss this later?"

Li Pham escorts us into the living room where I see Nina dressed in the traditional Ao Dai. It's a light-pink silk tunic worn over white pants and white sandals.

She sees me in my Ao Dai outfit, and her eyes sparkle along with a warm smile. I'm wearing a Hawaiian floral silk tunic, slit from the waist down and worn over wide white pants with natural-color leather sandals.

With a bow in the traditional Vietnamese way, I press my hands together in front of my chest. I glance up to see Nina delighted with pleasure and bows in return. Everybody stands in silence enjoying the moment followed by clapping and laughter. Everyone knew that Nina and I became good friends.

Dressed in a beautiful Vietnamese robe and blood-red silk pajamas, Thanh shuffles forward with tears in his eyes. He bows and then gives me a hug. He turns to Johnny and shakes his hand in his informal way, using both hands and then with his traditional bow. Johnny returns the bow and then turns and gives everybody his flashy white tooth little-boy grin with a twinkle in his eyes. We all love Johnny and enjoy his friendship.

Nina tells us Thanh needs to retire now for he is still weak from his ordeal. When Thanh bows to everybody, we respond with an appropriate bow to show our respect. Nina then escorts Thanh back to their master bedroom.

While having cocktails, Nina tells us how Thanh is progressing.

"Well, I soon learned the word coma comes from the Greek word, koma, spelled with a K, meaning deep sleep. It's like a twilight zone between life and death. Fortunately, it's a place few of us ever explore.

Thanh came out of his coma six weeks ago, and his physical recovery has been slow, but good. Mentally, he tells me it's like someone planted him in someone else's body. He's experiencing fatigue and memory loss, but it's making a slow comeback. Physical and occupational therapists are helping with his motor skills. Thanh is also getting strength training, but he's afraid he will soon resemble a young Arnold Schwarzenegger if he keeps this training up," Nina said, with a cute smile.

With that image conjured up in our minds, we enjoy a good laugh.

"The doctors expect a good recovery, but perhaps a year or two for Thanh to be mentally and physically able to come back to work.

I'm told his recovery is exceptional and not often found among coma patients. With so many others who never make a full recovery, I feel blessed that my Thanh is back with me."

Each of us asked a few questions, and when finished, Nina changed the subject...

"I'm told Jackie and Johnny are teeming with their matrimonial news that may interest us all. Jackie, please take the lead."

Yikes, I wasn't expecting this...

"Well, most of you carried around the idea of me getting serious with Toni—but Johnny, he's a total surprise?" I pointed to Johnny... "You first, I got to get this straight from the horse's mouth."

Everybody laughs and chants, "Johnny... Johnny..."

"Okay... Okay... So, I'm getting married. No biggie."

"No biggie," we shout with glee.

With a red face, Johnny begins his story...

"Okay, I understand you and other friends consider lovable me a self-centered bachelor, who wouldn't ever get married...

But then, Toni, who has always been my mentor and bachelor friend ups and tells me that he's fallen for Jackie. Ah... Well, those weren't his exact words, but that's how I interpreted it...

As you know, he's pretty tight with his words. And who couldn't fall for Jackie—she's smart, athletic, caring, and beautiful. But I regarded Toni as one too tough to fall for anybody."

Almost everybody reacts with an understandable nod as I sit tall and proud with my eyelashes fluttering a bit like a southern bell.

"My world soon fell down around me requiring rethinking on how old I was. I soon realized I needed to take on more personal responsibility if I ever expected to move ahead. So, I bought a few goldfish..."

Gleeful chuckles spread throughout the room.

"Just kidding...

So, having talked to a few bartender friends to get counseling, they told me, I must possess severe problems if I rationalized they'd be able to give out any serious advice of this nature."

Johnny finished with a lopsided grin.

"No kidding" Everybody sings out.

"Okay. Okay. Well, anyhow, this girl Sheri utterly loves me for whatever reason. Why I don't know with me being born in East L.A. and her father one of Forbes wealthiest men in the world, well, it felt like a class thing.

With that still on my mind, we flew to San Francisco to meet her family. The funny thing is, I ended up enjoying myself. Her father and I got along well. He gave me worldly advice on women, especially—on things I needed to take into account if I planned on a long happy marriage.

After my talk with Sheri's father, I felt different about my feelings toward Sheri, and a more worldly view of life. Ever since our trip to San Francisco, we've gotten along better than ever. She doesn't complain about me, and she doesn't mind me complaining about her."

We enjoyed a good chuckle knowing Johnny's wisenheimer ways.

"Well, I soon realized that I can love someone... And then one day, when things seemed right, I asked Sheri to marry me. She said yes, and then I passed out."

This gave us cause for a round of chortles.

"Sorry, I'm still having trouble getting serious about this recent state of affairs. Anyhow, we're getting married next year—that's it."

We all applaud and tell him how proud of him we are, and then us ladies give him a hug and kiss.

Marty then perks up with a hint of a smile...

"So, tell me, Johnny... Who's going to be the boss?"

"Well, as Woody Allen once said, I'm the boss. But she makes all the decisions."

The room fills with gleeful chuckles...

"Okay, enough about me, let my good friend Jackie, tell her love story."

I pause while giving thought as what to say...

"Well, my story is pretty short and not anywhere near as entertaining. I've known Toni now over four years and fell in love with him when I first set eyes on the man—if asked, I would have denied it. Everyone knew Toni to be a devoted bachelor, so my game plan spelled out for me to lie low—but it wasn't long until we started to spend more time together. Then one day out of the blue, Toni became romantic. So, I did a performance like in the movie *The Big Sleep*, where Martha Vickers leans back and falls into Bogart's arms. That's it, end of story..."

Everyone responds with smiling faces and applauding. Nina walks over, gives me a hug, and whispers a sweet thing in my ear as the rest all offer their best wishes, and then Marty raises a toast to both Johnny and me.

After the toast and kind words, we settle into small talk for the moment...

At that point, Marty gives Johnny a serious look...

"Johnny, I'd like for you to remember *two keywords* when finishing any discussions with your future wife..."

This gets everybody's attention...

Johnny glances at Marty with cocked eyebrows...

"And those two words would be?"

Marty replied with a high-pitched voice, "Yes, dear!"

The whole room burst out in laughter.

"That's a half-century of bad experiences talking, Johnny. So trust me."

There's a moment of cheerful silence.

"You know, men are such simple creatures," Dakota said.

"What makes you say that?" Johnny said.

"Dakota, let me answer that, okay?" I said.

"He's all yours, Jackie."

"Johnny... Who takes care of the wedding plans?"

"The lady and her family. Why?"

"You'll see soon enough where I'm going with this. How much will your rented tuxedo run you?"

"I'm not sure—not having ever rented one, maybe a hundred bucks."

"Well, my wedding dress will set me back five grand."

"So?"

"When you have a kid, who gets pregnant?"

"That's an idiotic question."

"Johnny, don't you see that you're digging yourself a hole?" Marty said with a grin.

"Huh?"

"Does your last name change after getting married?"

"Well, of course, not."

"Well, a woman's name can change, if desired. If so, she is required to obtain a new driver's license, apply for a new Social Security card, contact her company's human resources, and replace or renew her passport. Get on the Web to make changes to credit cards, bank and brokerage accounts, and any number of other accounts..."

Johnny looks dumbfound, then just shrugs...

"When you go on your honeymoon, how many bags will you pack?"

"One. Why's that?"

"Okay, Mister Slow-on-the-Draw, do people ever stare at your chest when you're talking to them?"

Johnny does a double-take...

"WHAT?"

That gets a giggle from Nina, with her hand covering her mouth.

"I'll bet you spend more time traveling to a mall than you do shopping for your relatives on Christmas. And I'll bet you spend less time on the phone—sixty seconds or less on the norm. Right?"

"Well, first off, I don't shop for my relatives, my mom does..."

This, of course, sets off a round of laughter.

Johnny looks puzzled for a moment...

"Let me finish and counter Jackie's phone thing. Young women can spend an hour talking on the phone spewing out words simultaneously, mind you, faster than us mortal men can talk—and yet, never say anything useful."

"May I finish this off, Jackie," Dakota, said. "I'll say it again—you men are plain, unassuming creatures. Your underwear is ten bucks for a three-pack. Your hairstyle stays the same for years if not your whole life. Take a glance at Marty—his haircut hasn't changed since he was a kid. Now, he has wrinkles on his face, which for men, add character."

Marty laughs...

"That's true, Johnny. They've got us in their crosshairs. It would appear that you already forgot what I told you."

"What's that, Marty?" Johnny said, uncomfortably.

"'Yes, dear,'" Marty said.

Everyone in the room cracks up.

"Women. Will I ever learn? Johnny said shaking his head.

His actions brought about more laughter.

After everyone settles down, Nina changed the subject in her gentle way...

"A few months ago, you recommended that I should take over the responsibilities of CEO, and I accepted the proposal. Well, on Tuesday, Marty made a formal request, and I accepted.

Tonight, I wanted you all here so I could personally thank the three of you for such a wonderful job you have done in making our company the company of the future, something I truly believe in."

We glanced at her and started to tell her our appreciation for the kind words when she holds up her hand—gesturing she has more to say.

"Our employees bought in on this new open-systemic architecture with open hearts. Our MPV feedback has revolutionized our ability to make the right changes for the right reason and rewarded us with increased growth...

Each employee feels they're able to make a difference in our ability to satisfy our customers and allowing us to grow. We are now the proud owners of an efficient horizontal, open-systemic organization.

We have been adding sales without additional indirect employees, giving us a real boost in productivity and profits. There are still a lot of system improvements ahead of us, and yet, we see no new indirect employees in our immediate future..."

We seldom hear her talk this much, so when she goes into a quiet moment, we all thought Nina had finished, and then...

"I've often wished we would have made a documentary to show the marvelous transformation our company has gone through resulting in high-performance growth and profitability...

Your causal presentations allowed the employees to digest your enlightenment with little effort, and then used their own intellect to carry out the changes that stimulated new ideas along the way."

DINING AT THE DINNER TABLE

Just then, Kim Phan, Nina's friend who owns the Pho Ho restaurant comes out of the kitchen and walks up to Nina, bows and then whispers in her ear. As Kim walks back into the kitchen, Nina stands and tells us Kim and Li are ready to serve dinner.

Never having a chance to thank her for praising our work, I watched Nina head toward the dining room. With everyone comfortably seated around the table, we chatted a little as Kim pours a milky liquid out of what looks like a wine bottle with Vietnamese writing.

"Marty, does this bottle of liquor look familiar to you?" Nina said.

"It sure does. But let me take a taste."

He pauses for a moment after a few sips...

"Oh my, does that bring back a flood of memories and conjuring up images of spiritual and cultural festivities. We used to drink this liquor through bamboo shoots stuck out of a large pot sitting around a bonfire in the central highlands.

As I remember, this was a deceptively strong drink and brought on serious hangovers. The drink is more like a wine whiskey due to its alcohol content, so when drinking from a glass, only take sips."

Everybody's eyes focused on the war hero realizing that's a first for Marty, never mentioning a word about being in Vietnam, other than knowing he served there.

"For those of you who are unfamiliar with Vietnamese liquor," Nina said, "There are three regions where they produce the liquor. One is in the Red River Delta, the other is in the Central Highlands that Marty spoke of, and the third one is the Mekong River Delta. This particular liquor comes from the Central Highlands, by Tay Nguyen.

It's a spiritual drink called *ruou can* (zuh-ooh can). Its origin comes from a period when man visited the god of the Porcupine and received a milky-white drink that made a man feel as if he were walking on air. Then the God taught man how to make it, as well as, how to drink it. Our people offer *ruou can* up to heaven and the God of the Porcupine before drinking it. So, if you would, please raise your glasses to heaven and enjoy the drink."

Everybody raised their glasses...

"To heaven and the God of the Porcupine..."

"What a wonderful story, Nina," Dakota said.

Others chimed in with a nice word.

"Thank you. You are much too kind."

Soon after the toast, Kim walks in, Nina nods, and a moment later, Kim and Li exit the kitchen and serve us spring rolls as an appetizer, along with a sour fish soup...

"This is a wonderful Vietnamese soup combining a little sour from sour bamboo and a little sweet from the catfish—highlighted with a salty taste from fish sauce. Please enjoy," Nina said.

Having finished our soup, Johnny is about to signal for more when I kicked him in the shins, giving him a scolding smile. He responds with a frown and protruding lower lip, but keeps quiet. He has learned, for the most part, that keeping quiet seldom leads to anything bad.

Nina looks around the table...

"Our next course will be pho, a Vietnamese favorite. It's both healthy and delicious. Jackie will vouch for that."

As Kim and Li bring out the pho, Nina looks at me with a saucy smile...

"Jackie, Kim told me she could not get your favorite meat selection for our pho meal and needed to substitute with rare beef, I hope you don't mind."

When looking up at Kim, I see she has her hand over her mouth holding back a mischievous smile.

"My, my, Kim, what a good memory you have."

Kim wasted not a moment as she runs in chaotic haste out of the room on her tiptoes, giggling her way into the kitchen.

"What's that all about?" Dakota said with a chuckle.

I looked at Dakota...

"We still on for lunch tomorrow?"

Dakota nods with a frown...

"Yes."

"I'll tell you then."

Johnny glances over at Marty...

"It's got to be woman-stuff, which means leave it alone."

"Yeah, I heed that, ol' worldly one."

Marty's slight dig sets off gleeful chuckles around the table, leaving Johnny somewhat embarrassed.

As we enjoy our pho, I'm of the idea I could eat this every night of the week. When everyone finished their meal, the table is cleared away as Nina excuses herself and heads into the kitchen. She didn't take long to return with a silver platter full of strawberry tarts.

"As you know, one of my passions is preparing French pastries. Tonight, I give you fresh, plump strawberries resting in a vanilla pastry cream, which is nesting in a flaky tart pastry shell and covered with a red apricot glaze."

We looked in astonishment at the culinary delight as Nina serves the dessert with the fresh smell of French pastries pleasantly permeating our surroundings.

"You shouldn't have," Dakota said.

"Yeah, right... When is the next platter coming out?" Johnny said.

Everyone laughed along with Johnny as we helped ourselves to the tarts. It wasn't long when Kim and Li brought out strange-looking coffee cups with metal hats.

"I thought you might enjoy traditional hot Vietnamese coffee with your tarts. We've partially filled your coffee cup with sweetened condensed milk and hot water. The little metal cup sitting on top is a Vietnamese coffee press. The bottom of the metal cup had perforated tiny holes and filled with a few teaspoons of roasted coffee and chicory. Hot water pours over the blend, and after four minutes you remove the metal cup. Then presto—you're ready to mix the coffee with the condensed milk and enjoy the best cup of coffee you ever tasted."

Everyone focuses on Nina as Marty tells her of our profound thanks for this magical meal and wonderful evening and proud that she has considered us as family and friends.

Nina sits with her head bowed in the silent room as we wait for her response. Watching her, we see tears forming that trickle down her cheek, and at that point, we too become misty-eyed.

Nina looks up with a gracious smile and tells us with her choked voice…

"The coffee is ready, so let's remove the metal cup and enjoy the hot brew with your strawberry tarts."

A moment later, one can only detect the many variations of "yummy" coming from our little gathering.

ACT III - SCENE 7
ENHANCING THE LEARNING PROCESS

Question: 1
For those of you who still qualify as young, did Lois's delivery to the students and guests allow you to take growing up in a different light? Explain.

For those of you, let us say, who are a bit long in the tooth, did Lois give you any insight into her secrets of staying young? Explain.

Question: 2
"Men are such simple creatures," Dakota said.
Well, ladies, can you expand on that idea?

For you guys out there, do you agree or disagree? Explain.

Question: 3
Stories can end heading off in limitless directions. Did this one work for you?
If so, why?
If not, why?
Furthermore, in a short summary, how would you end the story?

APPENDIX

GOOD MORNING LI'L KITTY, what is your favorite quote today?

Hmmm... It would have to be... Ah... A quote by Winston Churchill...

Success is not final, *failure is not fatal: it is the courage to continue that counts.*

RISK

*ULYSSES LASHED TO THE MAST SO THAT HE CANNOT SUCCUMB
TO TEMPTATION BY SIRENS*

Odyssey, by Homer in 800 B.C. knew that in the soul of man there is a foundation that drives him to firsthand discovery. Although this aspect is present in all humans, it is developed in only a few. In times of trouble, those few lead themselves and others to safety.

Change *for* the Right *Reason* represents innovation and a certain amount of risk. Taking the risk, of course, is relative. For some, it's a new journey to test their ability to be creative and challenge a wide range of knowledge. For others, it represents a personal risk that we're unable to deal with on an emotional level. Our feelings of the past have little meaning. They contribute naught; one must focus on the *now*. If there was ever a time to take the risk, it is now. Now, is the right time, for the right reason, and done the right way.

Every time we choose safety, we reinforce fear
Cheri Huber

Sometimes, we must have faith in ourselves to provide a future for our loved ones and our country. Risk, love, loyalty, and honor take many forms. Much of the time in life we look for as many obstacles as we can find to hide behind to avoid taking the risk. Fortunately, ever so often, people like you come along with a gift of free will and push down all these obstacles.

However, this gift of free will does not come free—you must fight for it. For those who have the slightest aversion toward risk, I would ask, please read Jeff Shaara's book *The American Revolution, The Glorious Cause*.

My hope is that after reading *Change for The Right Reason* and *The American Revolution, The Glorious Cause,* you will want to take the necessary risk to keep the American dream going and not let down the founders of our glorious country.

You need not wait until the universe lines up all the pins. Conditions are never going to be perfect. If you think you have an opportunity for change, take it, and have no regrets. Remember, those who fear death the most are those with regrets.

Yoda said...
There is no try. Only do.

THE TEACHER'S GUIDE
A Creative Opportunity

LET'S TRY AND AVOID THIS TYPE OF TEACHING IN SCHOOL AND BUSINESS

As a business theory novel, the teacher and the students have a wonderful opportunity to be creative in the learning process. The following guide is to prepare the teacher and students the basic idea of how to apply this new way of learning, gaining experience working as a community, and developing leadership skills.

FORMING THE TWO COMMUNITIES

The idea is to set up two communities within the class. While the **COMMUNITY ACTORS GUILD** teaches the class, the other, community, the **AUDIENCE**, enjoys watching their fellow classmates act out their role in the novel in each of their own creative ways. At the end of the scene, if there is time, the audience should be prepared to ask a few important questions that could spark interesting discussions.

So that each community gets an opportunity to play in the Actors Guild, communities would alternate responsibilities with one other from one scene to another. This allows the Community Actors Guild the opportunity to act out each of the scenes described in the book—less the vignettes. However, if the class wishes to insert a favorite vignette for fun, do so.

COMMUNITY ACTORS GUILD RESPONSIBILITIES

Each of the students will have an opportunity to play one of the characters in the book. It's not unlike a professional actor getting to know their character, getting inside their head, and picking up the necessary knowledge to teach the class.

Communities need leadership; therefore, each community needs to elect a leader. The community itself should define the process.

As a community, they must work together and assign responsibilities to each other. This process is to allow the students to dive deep down into the subject matter and express what they have learned. Before the student teaches a class, he or she must convince the community they are ready.

LEARNING TOGETHER

The teaching, of course, embeds the knowledge into the student that can result in a lifetime of planting the seeds of creativity.

Each community should look at itself as a system. For a system to work as it should, the parts must work together to produce the expected results. This is the beginning of putting the ideas of this book into a real-life business within a community.

Before marching ahead, there needs to be organizational planning. Set aside meeting times, define the objective, assign responsibilities, and expected standards from all—and ensure that all the crucial timelines of the deliverables are set.

Make sure no one is left out so that all are involved in producing the objective. If a given community member has special skills or knowledge to achieve their objective, let it be known.

The purpose, of course, is for all the students to learn the knowledge in this book, and then some.

During research on a given topic, can the student expand on the subject? By all means, add in the dialog to the story, using those misbehaving creative juices seeping from the brain. Nevertheless, keep it to a minimum because it will add to the overall time unless of course, you delete what the community thinks is non-essential dialog. Nevertheless, make sure that this is approved by the community.

The idea is to look at their responsibility as a community and then look at all the pieces evolved to see how best to make the deliverable effective.

DIFFERENT VIEWS WITHIN THE COMMUNITY

The learning process should include time for each participant to voice an opinion on all topics.

Remember, before moving forward after a discussion on a given topic, there must be a consensus.

GRADING THE STUDENTS

There is no wrong way or right way for grading the community or the student. The following are ideas that should help:

The teacher, in most cases, will not be involved with behind the scenes of community meetings, unless invited or getting them started. Nevertheless, when the deliverables are put forth in the class, the teacher is like a fly on the wall watching with great intensity. At this point, there is ample opportunity for grading in delivery, knowledge, participation, and leadership.

The teacher may want to consider the idea of each student within a community to grade each other on shared participation and the ability to work together in producing their deliverable.

ENTREPRENEURSHIP

Most people *think* they have a perception of what an entrepreneur is but few take the time to understand what makes them tick.

Entrepreneurs think differently from most other people. As economic, technology, political, and industry make unfavorable changes; most people complain or go to the trouble to make a public protest. The entrepreneur, however, comes up with a solution, why, because these problems represent an opportunity.

As an entrepreneur, I too see things in a different way due to my professional history, education, personality, and the way I perceive the world around me, being one with dyslexia. This allows me to see products or services designed to change the way a business is run, and possibly change the industry, or influence the economy. It's has nothing to do with an ego; one must be a builder and have the fortitude to make things happen.

One of the most important tasks at the beginning of a new start-up is the ability to find the key people that can participate as an equal and make the difference whether or not the business can grow and prosper.

When discussing new ideas with those qualified for key positions in managing the business sometimes end up responding with reasons it won't work, or standing on *principle* rather than asking *good questions* to understand the problems they foresee. This person creates a negative atmosphere that discourages creativity, and the process to find the answers and move forward. Most people don't think of themselves in this way, and yet most are.

The big question is, do they have a fear of failure? Regina Dugan, director of DARPA once said...

What would you do if you knew you could not fail? And then goes on to say, *when you remove the fear of failure, impossible things suddenly become possible.*

Now consider this, we were all born fearless and with creativity, but as we grow older our upbringing at times, education and business system negate these wonderful genes embedded in our mind. When we enter the first grade through our last years in college, we are well trained not to ask what may appear to be a silly question, or perhaps look stupid by society's approval rating. Then as adults in the workplace, we have become self-conscious of saying or doing something out of the norm. We don't want to look stupid in the eyes of others—thus, the roadblock of creativity and fearlessness.

Some of the candidates you talk to about the fear of failure, will cozy up to the challenge and have an immediate positive response, while others will want to think about the answer.

Now, we all know that there will be failure along the way, as progress tests us in our pursuit of the goal. Nevertheless, even if the goal is a failure, we can be proud that we at least tried to do what some would call impossible, and learn from it. This is how progress is made. Just ponder for a moment on all the failures we've had in thinking flight was a possibility in the early twentieth-century, and where we are today. In the process, there were thousands of failures of every conceivable type. Had we all had a fear of failure, where would we be today? That's right, living in caves and gathering acorns.

One can build all the models of design, manufacturing models, and financial models, but until you form a company and produce the product in the marketplace, it's just an idea that cannot go forward due to fear at any given level. First, fear is the biggest roadblock to one's own creativity. Secondly, fear is of those who would stop your creative dream of progress, and to change the world.

But once you have blown through all the roadblocks of fear along the way, you are now a real company that must perform. If you have chosen the right group of people, the following would be a normal course of events if a roadblock did in fact exist. The chosen few, who look forward to the challenges ahead, will want to think creatively, fearlessly, and objectively, by weighing each step of the process for the negative and positive attributes, by asking the right questions. If the findings are a real problem, responsibility can be assigned to solve the issue in the most economical and fastest way, making sure that all will contribute in helping where their background can be of assistance.

EXAMPLE OF NAYSAYER FEEDBACK

In late 1995, I had the idea of building low-cost PC's and selling them via the Internet. At the time, Gateway and Dell were already in the marketplace, but not yet on the internet, and I felt the market was still wide open and had potential. And I had the experience to pull it off. So, I discussed the idea with two good friends in the computer and peripheral industry, one an electrical engineer, the other a high-tech executive. Both found everything in the world why it would be a bad decision. The discussion was held at a dinner meeting, where both supported each other to convince me, it's a bad idea. Everyone else I discussed the idea with, just stared back in disbelief. With little support, I moved ahead and engineered an inexpensive PC prototype, but soon caved in with so many negative feedback responses from those who thought it was too late.

I've always regretted not moving ahead with the idea. I had planned to take my idea to Vietnam, along with two Vietnamese electrical engineers friends to set up a low-cost assembly facility. Now, this really had the naysayers coming out in full force. Well, you get my drift.

The naysayers are those who you share your ideas with will always tell you why your ideas will not work. Much of the time, it's because it puts them in a position of feeling smarter and less shameful of not coming up with a good solution to the idea you shared with them. On the other hand, they may have a good point. If you can, ask the naysayer to get involved in possible solutions to their reasons why it won't work, this will bring them around to feel they are part of a solution to what they perceive as a serious problem – why would you do that? Because they may have inevitably made a good point that could be helpful in moving forward.

In the end, however, you must have people in the new organization who are not naysayers and do not have a fear of failure, but those with the entrepreneurial spirit that may see a problem, but understand the necessity to help solve the problem with a healthy dose of questions that lead to a conclusion. This brings out the creative side of people moving things forward in a way that may seem impossible and yet become a breakthrough in thinking that can evolve into a promising company. Most of all, you must be the leader to move the overall dream forward as you perceive it.

Not taking the opportunity when it raises its head, the chances are 100 percent you won't make it. For those who think you are living in dreamland, ignore them and make your dream come true...

I would add, however, if you do strike a final dose of failure on a given quest, pull up your britches fast because you don't have time to feel failure, creativity, and progress only move forward with a few failures...

ACKNOWLEDGMENTS

Writing a book is like any process—going through the steps that start with a beginning, a middle, and an ending. It's not just the author that shapes the end result, but feedback from those folks who have taken their valuable time reading the book to contribute their input. But, before I discuss those who read the book and provided feedback, I must acknowledge Nina Nguyen for her inspiration to write her in as a main character in the novel and use her real name. She plays the role of VP of finance. Most of what I tell is about her secretly leaving Vietnam under cover of darkness on a boat, her education in finance and intelligence is true. Except In real life, the pirates cruising the Gulf of Thailand interrupted their escape from Vietnam on the high seas—a life-threating experience with many losing all their valuables. In the novel, they eluded the pirates. She is truly a remarkable and beautiful lady.

Until you have authored a book, it's difficult to appreciate the importance of the people who contribute to the result of a book's success. Without their help, we would all be the poorer for the lack of reading a more desirable book. Thus the importance of the following acknowledgments:

Daniel Keys, a scriptwriter, read my humble beginnings of the book, encouraging me in those areas of good writing, along with subtle hints of improvement – most notably in the dialog. Soon after finishing the early stages of the book, *Debra Nichols* and *Chuck Mallon* read the draft and played a role in setting me off in the right direction.

And to my sister, Rita Stringfellow for her encouragement thinking my writing reminds her of Robert B. Parker's humor and type of dialogue that might be used in the Spencer series novel. I can only hope that others can take to such a wonderful compliment.

Then, of course, Dr. Joanne Preston, previous Doctoral Dean of Management at Colorado Technological University, who worked with me in producing the final version that lends itself as a must-read for university students in business and engineering, business executives, and educators.

LI'L MISS KITTY

Li'l Miss Kitty was an integral and important part of writing this book. Hard to believe, I know. She took her responsibility very seriously. Li'l Kitty's job was to *meow* me to death to get me up early and feed her, and then when finished, playfully push me out the door for my morning sprints. The sprinting, of course, created those little endorphins that gave me the strength to enter my messy little world of solitude where I did research, wrote, and re-wrote a hundred different times over—trying to get the hang of writing a novel. Without her, I fear, most of these pages would have remained void of words, not unlike the lack of hair on a baboon's colorful butt.

IF YOU WERE WONDERING ABOUT HOW LI'L MISS KITTY WAS DOING...

Well, at twenty plus years old, she died in late fall 2009, after five years of meowing me to get with my run and work on the book. It became obvious one night that she was not going to see the rising sun. I watched her head towards her sandbox and then saw her hind legs collapse from under her. She turned her head to see if I saw her mishap. I will never forget the look on her face. It was so human-like. It was a face of despair. Cats have an ingrained displeasure of losing dignity.

Later that night while reading a book, she died next to me, with what looked like a smile on her furry little face. I buried her at first light in a beautiful spot with lots of small fuzzy little wildlife running around for companionship.

LATEST NOVEL

RECEIVED A 5-STAR FAVORITE READERS' BOOK REVIEW -

IF YOU ARE LOOKING FOR AN EXCEPTIONAL READ, you found it in this explosive military spy thriller. The story will captivate and absorb you into the actual events during the most desperate of times as you're transported back into the forgotten WWII Indochina war. General Donovan's OSS agents under orders from President Roosevelt sends them on a covert mission to link up with General Giap and Ho Chi Minh to decide their own future with the ability of self-determination and training in Jungle warfare while fighting Japanese occupation.

This extraordinary new adventure is a non-stop action thriller—with OSS WWII military intelligence agents fighting Nazis in the ice and snow of the Austrian Alps to the blistering heat as the OSS agents jump into the torrential rain of Indochina's jungles doing their part in helping Vietnam fight along with the allies against Japan.

The characters are of those men who dealt with death and destruction, and then light up your read with laughter as they exchange wit, wiseass remarks, and retorts, not unlike the brave men of our military.

The story centers on the idea that we humans, when in positions of high responsibility or power carry with it our pride, and ultimately, our denial.

ABOUT THE AUTHOR

Wayne Coker came into this world as a born polymath designing a breakthrough in high-tech manufacturing throughput, expanding the horizon for contract manufacturing in the high tech world, developing the idea of standardization in project engineering allowing a new way to measure *cost-revenue recognition*. And, developing a constraint theory scheduling software program. Creating the architectural design, engineering, and building two creative homes, the authoring of a historic breakthrough business theory novel, followed by an extraordinary Novel of the WWII OSS in Vietnam, and finally, a new journey, a long sought after quest, the Hydra Project...

Back when high-tech dinosaurs hobnobbed with each other on planet Earth during the late 1960s—Wayne Coker was one of the youngest executives in the early stages of this industry. As the Director of Manufacturing for Data Product, a major publicly held high-speed line-printer and disc-drive manufacturing company, he developed a revolutionary manufacturing process in high-tech products that produced throughput time of unheard inventory turns—now called *Just-in-Time Manufacturing, and years before the Japanese took credit for it in the 1970s...*

In parallel, he built in statistical process control enhancing quality and eliminated quality control line-inspectors—another major innovation during this period. The company shared these innovative ideas with visiting companies from around the globe. This innovation soon found its way into our high-tech world of manufacturing, and then over time, most other industries.

Wayne later became founder and CEO of CMI, an innovative and new type of contract manufacturing company in the early years. The company supplied products to the high-tech industry, ranging from electronic assembly, metal fabrication, industrial painting, machining, plastic injection molding, design and engineering work produced in a modern hundred-thousand square foot facility. This successful effort culminated in a sale to a robotics company.

Later, Wayne offered his services as the Director of Software and Project Engineering for an Automated Guided Vehicle (AGV) division of a close friend and Group Vice-President of Por-tec, a major corporation. This division had yet, turned a profitable year. After reviewing the project workflow, one could see the duplication of software coding for each new customer. With some key questions answered, Wayne, encouraged the development of a library with standardized software modules eliminating eighty percent of software coding.

With this innovative process, Wayne convinced finance to measure *cost-revenue recognition* using the STANDARDIZATION OF PROCESSED EVENTS—an accurate and revolutionary idea as opposed to ESTIMATING percent complete. These changes resulted in a drastic cut in project throughput time, the birth of actual

About the Author, continued

completion of projects, accurate quotes, and Income Statements...

For more on this subject, read Wayne's Book: Change *for* the Right Reason: *Act III - Scene Two - Revenue Recognition.*

Wayne now finds himself as COO at Data Power, a high tech turnaround, and publicly held company. He and the President, another friend did all the right things to improve the business processes. But, the company's original debt was so deep, and with the king demanding cash, it became a hopeless struggle.

Therefore, from success, we learn little—but from failure; we learn a great deal. In 1990, Wayne became a student of business theory and authored a business book in 1995.

Soon after the book's publication, he designed the architecture of a *bold new idea*, a CONSTRAINT SCHEDULING SOFTWARE PROGRAM that *Eli Goldratt* would have been proud of for an Oklahoma foundry with another long-time friend who wrote the code.

As a stimulating outlet, Wayne designed, engineered, and transformed two creative homes—with one featured in the Sunday "Home" section of the *Denver Post.*

In 2004, Wayne knew there was only one successful business novel ever written, THE GOAL by Eli Goldratt, a story about system, constraints. *So, he* turned his attention to re-writing his previous business book as a novel based on *system thinking*: CHANGE FOR THE RIGHT REASON – A NEW BEGINNING - A BUSINESS NOVEL. *It's* a novel about changing organizational structures, a story with such depth; it rises above any business book ever published.

In August 2014, Wayne began writing *Pride and Denial*—a *Captain Toni Nakni* novel about *The OSS and Viet Minh – Unexpected Allies in the War against Japan* and finished in mid-July 2018. In early 2019, Wayne published *Pride and Denial* along with a new updated *Change for the Right Reason*.

The author also left open for another *Toni Nakni* novel taking off where a *Pride and Denial* ends forming the Red Hawk Corporation, an intelligence, and special operations Company. *In today's world, our rules are that there are no rules. The bad guys don't play fair, so playing dirty is our game.*

The author has no regrets and feels happy in life, but for now, there's more to follow—*the end is nowhere in sight, for the old horse in the stable still yearns to run five hundred meters.*

We invite you to share your thoughts and reaction
Social Media
Amazon Books

www.ingramcontent.com/pod-product-compliance
Lightning Source LLC
Chambersburg PA
CBHW030604220526
45463CB00004B/1165